APPROACHES TO QUALITATIVE RESEARCH

A Reader on Theory and Practice

Edited by

SHARLENE NAGY HESSE-BIBER

Boston College

PATRICIA LEAVY

Stonehill College

New York   Oxford
OXFORD UNIVERSITY PRESS
2004

Oxford University Press

Oxford   New York
Auckland   Bangkok   Buenos Aires   Cape Town   Chennai
Dar es Salaam   Delhi   Hong Kong   Istanbul   Karachi   Kolkata
Kuala Lumpur   Madrid   Melbourne   Mexico City   Mumbai
Nairobi   São Paulo   Shanghai   Taipei   Tokyo   Toronto

Published by Oxford University Press, Inc.
198 Madison Avenue, New York, New York, 10016
http://www.oup-usa.org

Oxford is a registered trademark of Oxford University Press

Library of Congress Cataloging-in-Publication Data
Approaches to qualitative research : a reader on theory and practice / edited by Sharlene
Hesse-Biber, Patricia Leavy.
    p. cm.
    Includes bibliographical references.
    ISBN 0-19-515774-5 (alk. paper) — ISBN 0-19-515775-3 (pbk. : alk. paper)
    1. Social sciences—Research. 2. Qualitative research. I. Hesse-Biber, Sharlene Janice.
II. Leavy, Patricia, 1975-
H62 .A627 2004
001.4'2—dc21   2002042511

9 8 7 6 5 4 3 2 1

Printed in the United States of America
on acid-free paper

Contents

Acknowledgments vi

Contributors vii

Credits xiv

I DISTINGUISHING QUALITATIVE RESEARCH 1

1 Egon G. Guba and Yvonna S. Lincoln
Competing Paradigms in Qualitative Research: Theories
and Issues 17

2 Joey Sprague and Mary Zimmerman
Overcoming Dualisms: A Feminist Agenda for
Sociological Methodology 39

3 Sandra Harding
How Standpoint Methodology Informs Philosophy of
Social Science 62

4 Mark R. Rank
The Blending of Qualitative and Quantitative Methods
in Understanding Childbearing among Welfare
Recipients 81

5 Deborah L. Tolman and Laura Szalacha
Dimensions of Desire: Bridging Qualitative and
Quantitative Methods in a Study of Female
Adolescent Sexuality 97

II INTERACTION AND POSITIONALITY WITHIN QUALITATIVE RESEARCH 131

6 bell hooks
Culture to Culture: Ethnography and Cultural Studies
as Critical Intervention 149

7 Barrie Thorne
"You Still Takin' Notes?" Fieldwork and Problems
of Informed Consent 159

8 Kath Weston
   Fieldwork in Lesbian and Gay Communities   177

9 William L. Miller and Benjamin F. Crabtree
   Depth Interviewing   185

10 Charles A. Gallagher
    "White Like Me?" Methods, Meaning, and
    Manipulation in the Field of White Studies   203

11 Kathryn Anderson, Susan Armitage, Dana Jack,
    Judith Wittner
    Beginning Where We Are: Feminist Methodology in Oral
    History   224

12 Ingrid Botting
    Understanding Domestic Service through Oral
    History and the Census: The Case of Grand Falls,
    Newfoundland   243

13 David L. Morgan
    Focus Groups   263

14 Peter McDermott and Julia Rothenberg
    Why Urban Parents Resist Involvement in Their
    Children's Elementary Education   286

III UNOBTRUSIVE METHODS, VISUAL RESEARCH,
     AND CULTURAL STUDIES   303

15 Lindsay Prior
    Following in Foucault's Footsteps: Text and Context
    in Qualitative Research   317

16 Jon Prosser and Dona Schwartz
    Photographs within the Sociological Research
    Process   334

17 Diana Rose
    Analyses of Moving Images   350

18 Chris Mann and Fiona Stewart
    Introducing Online Methods   367

19 Denna Harmon and Scot B. Boeringer
    A Content Analysis of Internet-Accessible Written
    Pornographic Depictions   402

IV ANALYSIS, INTERPRETATION, AND THE WRITING
OF QUALITATIVE DATA   409

20 **John Van Maanen**
An End to Innocence: The Ethnography of
Ethnography   427

21 **Norman K. Denzin**
The Art and Politics of Interpretation   447

22 **Laural Richardson**
Writing: A Method of Inquiry   473

23 **Kathy Charmaz**
Grounded Theory   496

24 **Katherine Borland**
"That's Not What I Said": Interpretive Conflict in
Oral Narrative Research   522

25 **Sharlene Nagy Hesse-Biber**
Unleashing Frankenstein's Monster? The Use of
Computers in Qualitative Research   535

Acknowledgments

In the work toward this book, we appreciate the help of a number of people who supported the endeavor. We are also grateful to all our students who inspired us to think and teach from an interdisciplinary perspective. Sharlene Nagy Hesse-Biber wants to especially thank the students in her graduate Qualitative Methods course for their inspiration and careful comments on the articles for the volume. For their careful reading and comments on a preliminary draft of the introductions we are grateful to Dr. David Karp and Dr. Eve Spangler. We want to acknowledge especially the editorial assistance of Stacy Baron, who helped to edit Part IV of the introductions. Thanks to Boston College undergraduates Mary Fawcett, Melissa Farrell, Ann Batchelder, Wes Colgan, and Joanna Kels and Stonehill undergraduates Laura MacFee, Paul Sacco, and Lauren Sardie for their proofreading work for the manuscript. A special heartfelt thanks to Mary Fawcett for tending to the fine details of the preparation of the manuscript for production. We would particularly like to express our gratitude to Caroline Ruttner for her unfailing support and research assistance with the day-to-day operations of putting together an edited volume, especially her assistance with obtaining permissions. Sharlene Nagy Hesse-Biber is especially grateful to her family for their patience, love, and understanding during all phases of the preparation of this volume. Sharlene dedicates this work to her exceptional daughters, Sarah Alexandra and Julia Ariel. Patricia Leavy gives a heartfelt thanks to her parents for their help and support during this lengthy project, especially to her mother for assisting so much with childcare. Patricia lovingly dedicates her work on this volume to her amazing and magical daughter Madeline Claire. We want to acknowledge the enthusiastic support we received from the editorial staff at Oxford University Press. In particular, we extend a spirited thank you to Peter Labella, Sean Mahoney, Lisa Grzan, and Carey Schwaber.

Contributors

Kathryn Anderson is a professor at Fairhaven College, an interdisciplinary cluster college of Western Washington University, where she teaches courses in women studies, social history, oral history, and communications. She directed Western Washington University's women's studies program for fifteen years and was principal investigator for the Washington Women's Heritage Project. She has published several articles on women and politics.

Sue Armitage is Professor of History at Washington State University, where she edits *Frontiers: A Journal of Women Studies*.

Scot B. Boeringer is currently Visiting Assistant Professor of Sociology at the University of Central Florida. His primary research areas are the study of sexual violence, and the effects of sexually explicit media on behaviors and attitudes. His teaching areas are criminology, deviance, and gender studies. He lives in Orlando, Florida.

Katherine Borland is Assistant Professor of Comparative Studies in the Humanities at Ohio State University-Newark, where she has taught world literature and folklore since 1999. She received her doctoral degree in Folklore from Indiana University in 1994. Subsequently, she became founding director of Delaware Futures, a small educational nonprofit organization in Wilmington, Delaware where she works with inner-city youth. In 1999 she began collecting life stories of poultry plant workers; this project culminated in the nonacademic book *Creating Community: Hispanic Migration to Rural Delaware*, which was published in 2001. Currently, she is working on a book-length study of Nicaraguan festival enactments.

Ingrid Botting recently completed a Ph.D. in Women's History at Memorial University of Newfoundland. From 2002 to 2004 she will be doing postdoctoral research on the impact of social and economic restructuring on women's and children's health in resource-dependent communities through the Department of Sociology at Memorial University and the Newfoundland and Labrador Centre for Applied Health Research.

Kathy Charmaz is Professor of Sociology and Coordinator of the Faculty Writing Program at Sonoma State University. She assists faculty in writing for publication and teaches in the areas of sociological theory, social psychology qualitative methods, health and illness, and aging and dying. Her books include two recent coedited volumes, *The Unknown Country: Death in Australia, Britain and the USA* and *Health, Illness, and Healing: Society, Social Context, and Self* as well as *Good Days, Bad Days: The Self in Chronic Illness and Time.* Dr. Charmaz currently serves as editor of *Symbolic Interaction.*

Benjamin F. Crabtree is Professor and Director of Research in the Department of Family Medicine at the University of Nebraska Medical Center, where he is also a medical anthropologist. He has published extensively in the area of research methods, both qualitative and quantitative. He is coeditor of *Exploring Collaborative Research in Primary Care.*

Norman Denzin is Distinguished Professor of Communications, College of Communications Scholar, and Professor of Sociology and Humanities at the University of Illinois, Urbana-Champaign. He is a widely published scholar, and in 1997 he won the George Herbert Mead Award from the Society for the Study of Symbolic Interaction which recognizes lifetime contributions to the study of human behavior.

Charles A. Gallagher is Assistant Professor in the Department of Sociology at Georgia State University in Atlanta. His book, *Beyond Invisibility: The Meaning of Whiteness in Multiracial America* is under contract with New York University Press. He is the editor of *Rethinking the Color Line: Readings in Race and Ethnicity,* Mayfield Press (second edition, 2003). His recent publications include "Playing the Ethnic Card: Using Ethnic Identity to Negate Contemporary Racism" in *Deconstructing Whiteness, Deconstructing White Supremacy* edited by Ashley Doane and Eduardo Bonilla-Silva (Routledge Publishers, forthcoming 2002); "Colorblind Pleasures: The Social and Political Functions of Erasing the Color Line in Post Race America" in *The Power of Pleasure,* edited by Laurie Essig and Sarah Chinn (Duke University Press, forthcoming 2002); "Race, Romance and Reality: Youth Culture and Interracial Marriage" in *The Quality and Quantity of Contact between African Americans and Whites on College Campuses,* edited by Robert Moore (University Press of America, 2002); "Coming into the White: How the Dominant Group Expands its Borders and the Implications for Race Relations" in *The Multiracial Movement: The Politics of Color* edited by Heather Dalmage (State University of New York Press, forthcoming 2002).

Egon G. Guba is Professor Emeritus, Indiana University, Bloomington. He has written widely in the field of qualitative inquiry with emphasis on the constructivist paradigmatic undergirding of such work. Relevant books include *Effective Evaluation* (Jossey-Bass, 1980), *Naturalistic Inquiry* (Sage, 1985), *Fourth Generation Evaluation* (Sage,1989), and *The Paradigm Dialog* (Sage, 1990). The former three were written with his spouse and colleague, Yvonna S. Lincoln, with whom he resides in College Station, Texas.

Sandra Harding is a Philosopher of Science, and was Professor of Philosophy and Director of Women's Studies at the University of Delaware before joining the faculty at the University of California, Los Angeles, in 1996, where she is

Professor of Education and Women's Studies and is the Director of the Center for the Study of Women. She is the author or editor of ten books and special journal issues, including: *The Science Question in Feminism* (1986) and *Feminism and Methodology, Is Science Multicultural? Postcolonialisms, Feminisms and Epistemologies* (1998). She has lectured at over 200 universities and conferences in North America, Europe, South America Africa, South Korea, Australia, New Zealand, and Central America. She has also been a consultant to several United Nations organizations, including UNESCO's World Science Report, the Pan American Health Organization, and the United Nations Commission on Science and Technology for Development.

Denna Harmon is a graduate of Appalachian State University.

bell hooks is a widely published scholar/writer and is considered a leading public intellectual. She is a Distinguished Professor Emeritus at City College in New York. Her speaking presentations focus on issues of race, class, gender, and interconnectedness. Her books include *Ain't I a Woman, Feminist Theory, Talking Back, Yearning, Outlaw Culture: Resisting Representations, Black Looks: Race and Representation,* and *Teaching to Transgress: Education as the Practice of Freedom.*

Dana Jack teaches at Fairhaven University, an interdisciplinary college of Western Washington University. She is the author of *Behind the Mask* and *Silencing the Self.*

Yvonna S. Lincoln is the Ruth Harrington Chair of Educational Leadership and University Distinguished Professor of Higher Education at Texas A&M University. She is the coauthor of *Effective Evaluation* (1981), *Naturalistic Inquiry* (1985), and *Fourth Generation Evaluation* (1989); the editor of *Organizational Theory and Inquiry* (1985); and the coeditor of several other books, including the *Handbook of Qualitative Research* (1st and 2nd editions) (1994; 2000), and the four-volume set, *The American Tradition in Qualitative Research* (2001). She is also the author of more than 200 journal articles, book chapters, and conference papers. Her major interests lie in program evaluation in higher education and in qualitative research methods. She is the current coeditor of the bimonthly journal *Qualitative Inquiry*. She has pioneered work in constructivist evaluation models and qualitative research and evaluation work that promotes more democratic forms of stakeholder participation, wider social inclusion, and utilization-oriented evaluation practices.

Chris Mann is based at the Faculty of Social and Political Sciences, University of Cambridge, where she researches equity issues in education. She has published widely on the theoretical, methodological, and practical aspects of Internet use in qualitative research. See: Mann, C., and Stewart, F. (2000) *Using the Internet in Qualitative Research: A Handbook for Researching Online.* New Technologies for Social Research Series. (London: Sage); Mann, C., and Stewart, F. (2001) 'Internet Interviewing' in Gubrium, J., and Holstein, J. (Eds.), *Handbook of Interview Research* (Thousand Oaks, CA: Sage). In 2002 she was a Visiting Fellow at the Oxford Internet Institute (*www.oii.ox.ac.uk*), a multidisciplinary center of excellence in academic research on the impact of the Internet on society. There she focused on the ethical aspects of Internet research and designed stand-alone teaching modules to help incorporate Internet research into graduate training programs.

Peter McDermott is an associate professor at The Sage Colleges in Troy, New York. He is a former secondary and adult literacy teacher. He now specializes in literacy education at the graduate and undergraduate levels. His doctoral thesis was a qualitative study of the social contexts of adult literacy instruction. He regularly contributes to the Ethnography and Urban Education Research Forum that is held each year at the University of Pennsylvania. For the past five years he has been a volunteer for the Reading and Writing for Critical Thinking Project in Kazakhstan, Central Asia which is sponsored by the International Reading Association and the Open Society Institute.

William Miller, M.D., M.A., is Chair and Program Director at the Department of Family Medicine, Lehigh Valley Hospital, Allentown, PA. He is also a family physician anthropologist. He works at making qualitative research more accessible to health care researchers. His publications include step-by-step examples of qualitative research methods. His research interests focus on the role of the patient-physician relationship, on physician and patient understandings of pain and pain management, and on hypertension.

David L. Morgan received his Ph.D. in Sociology from the University of Michigan and is currently a professor in the School of Community Health at Portland State University. In addition to this work on focus groups, he also has done work on broad social science research methods. He is currently working on a book that describes practical approaches to combining qualitative and quantitative methods.

Lindsay Prior is a Reader in Sociology at the University of Wales, Cardiff. He recently served as Director of the Research Programme in Risk and Health at the University of Wales College of Medicine (1999–2002). His forthcoming book is titled *Documents in Social Research: Production, Consumption and Exchange* (Sage, 2002). Previous publications include *The Social Organisation of Death* (Macmillan/St Martin's Press, 1989), and *The Social Organisation of Mental Illness* (Sage, 1993). He is currently working on a number of projects relating to health issues. The latter include studies of risk assessment in genetics, the prescription of antidepressants in primary care, lay attitudes to flu vaccination, lay assessments of traumatic brain injury, lay perspectives on chronic fatigue syndrome, and how careers recognize symptoms of Alzheimer's in people with Down's syndrome.

Jon Prosser is Director of International Educational Management at the School of Education, University of Leeds, UK. His current research interests include image-based research methodology and the visual representational of institutional culture. His latest book is *School Culture* (1999), an edited volume published by Paul Chapman Publishing.

Mark R. Rank is a professor in the George Warren Brown School of Social Work at Washington University in St. Louis, Missouri. His recent work has focused upon estimating the lifetime patterns and probabilities of poverty and welfare use in the United States. He is currently completing a book that provides a new framework for understanding American poverty.

Laurel Richardson is Professor Emerita of Sociology, Professor of Cultural Studies in the College of Education, and Graduate Professor of Women's Studies at the Ohio State University. She has published extensively on qualitative research methods, ethics, and representation. She is author of *Fields of Play: Constructing an Academic Life* (1997), which received the C. H. Cooley Award for the 1998 Best Book in Symbolic Interaction.

Diana Rose is senior researcher at the User-Focused Monitoring team at The Sainsbury Centre for Mental Health in London. She received her Ph.D. from London University and has written extensively on qualitative research methods, sociolinguistics, television, and mental health.

Julia Johnson Rothenberg, Ph.D., is Professor of Education at The Sage Colleges in the United States. Her primary areas of teaching and research are the study and practice of teacher preparation, particularly for multicultural education, inclusion practices, and diverse student populations. In addition to her work in the United States, Dr. Rothenberg has taught at the University of Capetown, South Africa, and the University of Lesotho in the Kingdom of Lesotho, and she has been a guest of the Netherlands Institute for Advanced Study in the Netherlands, where she worked with faculty at the Rijksuniversiteit Leiden on issues in multicultural education.

Dona Schwartz is an associate professor at the School of Journalism and Mass Communication at the University of Minnesota. Her research in visual communication concerns historical, social, and institutional influences shaping visual media forms and content. Her ethnographic field research in visual sociology is represented in *Waucoma Twilight: Generations of the Farm* (Smithsonian Institution Press, 1992) and *Contesting the Super Bowl* (Routledge, 1997). Her most recent research focuses on the history and contemporary practice of photojournalism and documentary photography. Some of her work examining the emerging forms of multimedia documentary can be found at www.picturestories.umn.edu.

Joey Sprague is an associate professor of Sociology at the University of Kansas. Her research and writing center on the gendered dynamics of knowledge creation and the biases embedded in current forms of knowledge. Recent publications include: "Gender and Feminist Studies in Sociology," in *International Encyclopedia of the Social and Behavioral Sciences* (Pergamon, 2001); "Structured

Knowledges and Strategic Methodologies," in *Signs: Journal of Women in Culture and Society* (2001); and "Self-Determination and Empowerment: A Feminist Standpoint Analysis of How We Talk about Disability" (with Jeanne Hayes), in *The American Journal of Community Psychology* (2000). She is working on a book tentatively titled *Seeing Through Gender: A Feminist Methodology for Critical Social Research* (AltaMira Press).

Fiona Stewart is Director of Real World Research and Communications in Australia.

Laura A. Szalacha's methodological expertise lies in quantitative, qualitative, and mixed-methods research strategies and her substantive training is in adolescent psychology, with a particular focus on the development of sexual minority adolescents. Szalacha, who holds an Ed.D. research dimensions of adolescent lesbian sexual identity, the advancement of women and minorities in academic medicine, the safety of LGBT (lesbian, gay, bisexual, transgendered) students in schools, and the developmental trajectories of Puerto Rican children and adolescents. She is currently Assistant Professor at Brown University's School of Education and a methodologist at the Wellesley Center for Women.

Barrie Thorne is Professor of Sociology and Women's Studies at the University of California, Berkeley, where she has also directed the Center for Working Families. She previously taught at the University of Southern California and at Michigan State University. She is the author of *Gender Play: Girls and Boys in School* (1993) and co-editor of *Feminist Sociology: Life Histories of a Movement* (1997); *Rethinking the Family: Some Feminist Questions* (1992); and *Language, Gender and Society* (1983). She is currently working on an ethnography of childhoods in a mixed-income, ethnically diverse area of Oakland, California.

Deborah L. Tolman is currently Associate Director of the Center for Research on Women at Wellesley College. She is also Associate Editor of *Psychology of Women Quarterly* (2001–present), and Senior Research Scientist and Director of the Gender and Sexuality Project (formerly Adolescent Sexuality Project) at the aforementioned Center for Research on Women at Wellesley College (February 1995–present). Her recent book publications include *Dilemmas of Desire: Teenaged Girls Talk about Sexuality* (Harvard University Press, 2002); L. Brown, D. Tolman, & E. Debold, *Hearing Voices: Using the Listening Guide Method for Analyzing Narrative Data* (New York University Press, forthcoming); and D. Tolman and M. Brydon-Miller (Eds.), *From Subjects to Subjectivities: A Handbook of Interpretive and Participatory Action Research Methods* (New York University Press, 2000). She is also on the Board of Overseers, Planned Parenthood League of Massachusetts, 2001–present, and a Board Member, *Teen Voices*, Boston, MA, 1999–present.

John Van Maanen is the Erwin H. Schell Professor of Organization Studies at M.I.T. in Behavioral Policy Science. His general areas of expertise are organizational studies and occupational sociology.

Kath Weston is Professor of Anthropology at Arizona State University and is the author of *Long, Slow Burn: Sexuality and Social Science* (1998), *Render Me, Gender Me: Lesbians Talk Sex, Class, Color, Nation, Studmuffins . . .* (1996), and the acclaimed *Families We Choose: Lesbians, Gays, Kinship* (1991).

Judith Wittner is Professor of Sociology and Women's Studies at Loyola University Chicago. In 1979 she helped found the Women's Studies Program at Loyola, the first such program at a Jesuit university; she directed the program from 1987 to 1993. She has conducted ethnographic research on displaced women factory workers, state wards in the child welfare system, women's community organizations, and Chicago's domestic violence court. She is coeditor of *Gatherings in Diaspora: Religious Communities and the New Immigration* (Temple University Press, 1998), a collection of 12 ethnographies describing ethnic immigrant religious congregations in the United States.

Mary K. Zimmerman is Professor of Health Policy and Management in the School of Medicine and Professor of Sociology at the University of Kansas. She is the author of "Passage through Abortion" and many articles on topics related to health care and gender.

EDITORS

Sharlene Nagy Hesse-Biber is Professor of Sociology at Boston College. She cofounded the Women's Studies Program at Boston College. She also founded and is now director of the National Association of Women in Catholic Higher Education (NAWCHE). She is author of *Am I Thin Enough Yet? The Cult of Thinness and the Commercialization of Identity* (Oxford University Press, 1996) and coauthor of *Working Women in America: Split Dreams* (Oxford University Press, 2000). She is coeditor of: *Feminist Approaches to Theory and Methodology: An Interdisciplinary Reader* (Oxford University Press, 1999); *Women in Catholic Higher Education: Border Work, Lived Experience and Social Justice* (Lexington Books, 2003); *Feminist Perspectives on Social Research* (Oxford University Press, 2004). She has published widely on the impact of sociocultural factors on women's body image and is codeveloper of HyperRESEARCH™, a qualitative data analysis software package. She is recipient of the 2002 New England Sociologist of the Year Award from the New England Sociological Association.

Patricia Leavy is Assistant Professor of Sociology at Stonehill College. She received her Ph.D. in Sociology at Boston College in 2002, her masters in sociology from Boston College in 1999 and her B.A. from Boston University in 1997. She has published numerous articles in the fields of popular culture, research methods, social theory, and collective memory. She is currently completing a book-length manuscript, based on her dissertation research, tentatively titled *Representational Events: Titanic and Other Events as Case Studies in Collective Memory*.

Credits

Kathryn Anderson, Susan Armitage, Dana Jack and Judith Wittner, "Beginning Where We Are: Feminist Methodology in Oral History." From *Feminist Research Methods*. pp. 94–112. Reprinted with permission from Westview Press.

Katherine Borland, " 'That's Not What I Said': Interpretive Conflict in Oral Narrative Research." From *Women's Words: The Feminist Practice of Oral History*. Reprinted with permission from Routledge Press.

Ingrid Botting, "Understanding Domestic Service through Oral History and the Census: The Case of Grand Falls, Newfoundland" From *Feminist Qualitative Research*. Spring/Summer 2000, vol. 28, no. 1, 2.

Kathy Charmaz, "Grounded Theory." From *Rethinking Methods in Psychology*. Reprinted with permission from Sage Publications, London.

Norman K. Denzin, "The Art and Politics of Interpretation." From *Collecting and Interpreting Qualitative Materials*. pp. 313–334. Reprinted with permission from Sage Publications, Inc.

Charles A. Gallagher, "White Like Me? Methods, Meaning, and Manipulation in the Field of White Studies." From *Racing Research, Researching Race: Methodological Dilemmas in Critical Race Studies*. Reprinted with permission from New York University Press.

Egon G. Guba and Yvonna S. Lincoln, "Competing Paradigms in Qualitative Research: Theories and Issues." From *The Landscape of Qualitative Research: Theories and Issues*. pp 195–220. Reprinted with permission from Sage Publications, Inc.

Sandra Harding, "How Standpoint Methodology Informs Philosophy of Social Science". Reprinted with permission from author. Essay also appears in *Blackwell Guide to Philosophy of the Social Scienes*, Stephen Turner and Paul Roth (Eds.) Cambridge, MA, Blackwell Publishers: 2002. Blackwell Publishers retains copyright.

Denna Harmonn and Scot B. Boeringer, "A Content Analysis of Internet-Accessible Written Pornographic Depictions." From *Electronic Journal of Sociology*. September 1997, vol. 3, no. 1. Reprinted with permission from EJS.

Sharlene Hesse-Biber, "Unleashing Frankenstein's Monster? The Use of Computers in Qualitative Research." From *Qualitative Methodology*. 1995, vol. 5, pp. 25–41. Reprinted with permission from Elsevier Science.

bell hooks, "Culture to Culture: ethnography and cultural studies as critical intervention." From *Yearning: race, gender, and cultural practices*. Pp. 123–133. Reprinted by permission of South End Press.

Chris Mann and Fiona Stewart, "Introducing Online Methods." From *Internet Communication and Qualitative Research: A Handbook for Researching Online*. pp. 65–98. Reprinted with permission from Sage Publications, Inc.

Peter McDermott and Julia Rothenberg. "Why Urban Parents Resist Involvement in their Children's Elementary Education." From *The Qualitative Report*. October 2000, vol. 5, no. 3,4. Reprinted with permission from the authors and *The Qualitative Report*.

William L. Miller, and Benjamin F. Crabtree, "Depth Interviewing." From *Doing Qualitative Research 2nd* Edition. Reprinted with permission from Sage Publications, Inc.

David L. Morgan, "Focus Groups." From *Annual Review of Sociology*. 1996, no. 22. Reprinted with permission from *Annual Review of Sociology*.

Lindsay Prior, "Following in Foucault's Footsteps: Text and Context in Qualitative Research." From *Qualitative Research: Theory, Method, and Practice*. pp. 63–79. Reprinted with permission from Sage Publications, Inc.

Jon Prosser and Dona Schwartz, "Photographs Within the Sociological Research Process." From *Image-Based Research: A Sourcebook for Qualitative Researchers*. pp. 115–130. Reprinted with permission from Falmer Press.

Mark R. Rank, "The Blending of Qualitative and Quantitative Methods in Understanding Childbearing Among Welfare Recipients." From *Qualitative Methods in Family Research*. Reprinted with permission from Sage Publications, Inc.

Laurel Richardson, "Writing: A Method of Inquiry." From *Collecting and Interpreting Qualitative Materials*. pp. 345–371. Reprinted with permission from Sage Publications, Inc.

Diana Rose, "Analyses of Moving Images." From *Qualitative Researching with text, Images, and Sound: A Practical Handbook*. pp. 246–262. Reprinted with permission from Sage Publications, Inc.

Joey Sprague and Mark Zimmerman, "Overcoming Dualisms: A Feminist Agenda for Sociological Method." From *Theory on Gender/Feminism on Theory*. Reprinted with permission from Aldine DeGruyter Press.

Barrie Thorne, " 'You still takin' Notes?' Fieldwork and Problems of Informed Consent." From *Social Problems*. February 1980, vol. 27, no. 3, pp. 284–297. Reprinted with permission from the University of California Press.

Deborah L. Tolman and Laura A. Szalacha, "Dimensions of Desire: Bridging Qualitative and Quantitative Methods in a Study of Female Adolescent Sexuality." From *Psychology of Women Quarterly*. pp. 7–39. Reprinted with permission from Kluwer Academic/Plenum Publishers.

John Van Maanen, "An End to innocence: The Ethnography of Ethnography." In *Representation in Ethnography*. pp.1–35. Reprinted with permission from Sage Publications, Inc.

Kath Weston, "Fieldwork in Lesbian and Gay Communities." From *Through the Prism of Difference: Readings on Sex and Gender*. pp. 79–85. Reprinted with permission from Allyn and Bacon Press.

PART I

DISTINGUISHING QUALITATIVE RESEARCH

Qualitative research is a distinct field of inquiry that encompasses both micro- and macroanalyses drawing on historical, comparative, structural, observational, and interactional ways of knowing. Multiple epistemological positions, theoretical frameworks, and research methods are included in qualitative research. The interdisciplinary landscape of qualitative research is rich because it does not privilege one philosophical grounding or methodological approach to the research process. It is the array of epistemological, theoretical, and methodological choices made by qualitative researchers that sets qualitative research apart as a particular and fruitful way of understanding social phenomena. Accordingly, Part I of *Approaches to Qualitative Research: A Reader on Theory and Practice* presents articles that address epistemological and theoretical choices, the process of selecting methods of inquiry during research design, and multimethod approaches to research.

To better understand what is meant by the qualitative/quantitative division, it may be helpful to consider some real-world examples. For instance, quantitative researchers rely on numbers or percentages in a table or chart to convey meaning. They might approach the study of gender inequality in wages by displaying statistics of the pay gap between men and women over the past decades, taking into account such factors as job experience, work history, degree of labor force commitment, years of education, and so on. Quantitative researchers' interpretations hinge on identifying a set of factors that might account for the inequality in wages between men and women.

Qualitative researchers, on the other hand, might be interested in conducting intensive interviews with working women concerning their work situation. They may focus on such things as the meaning of the wage gap for women in terms of how women "experience" day-to-day living with lower wages and with what they believe to be the "hidden" structures within the workplace, such as the "glass ceiling" and "old boys' network," that might lead to a lack of mobility for women in certain occupations. Some of these barriers might appear invisible to a quantitative researcher using standard indicators of inequality because these forms of exclusion are the result of cultural practices and not written hiring and promotion guidelines (Hesse-Biber and Carter, 2000:60). In order to unravel the importance of "networking" and "mentoring" on the experience of working women, cultural practices within the workplace and the meanings assigned to them must be investigated through the eyes of those who experience it (Hesse-Biber and Carter, 60).

A qualitative researcher interested in studying how women actively resist and challenge gender inequality within their workplace, such as a critical scholar interested in complex relations of social power, might choose to conduct an ethnographic case study of female workers in a particular workplace. Greta Foff Paules conducted a participant observation of waitresses in a New Jersey restaurant in order to understand, from the perspective of the waitresses, how this group of service workers challenges common notions of "female passivity" and resists the varied forms of gender oppression its members encounter (1991:15). Paules's study exemplifies how qualitative researchers work from a variety of epistemological positions in order to address aspects of social life that would otherwise remain hidden. She describes the daily experience of power and resistance amongst this group of working women. She explains the necessity of a qualitative approach over a quantitative design to the success of her study as follows:

> In contrast to mainstream hypothesis-testing social science . . . the method participant observation, joined with the anthropological commitment to grasping the native's point of view (Malinowski 1922:25), allows those under study to contribute to the research—not only in providing answers to prefabricated questions, but in formulating the questions themselves. . . . The mutually participative character of the anthropological approach was critical to the outcome of this investigation, for as I took part in the work of the waitress, she took part in transforming this work from an examination of exploitation to an exploration of the many ways in which the oppressed may reject their oppression (1991:20).

As Paules's work about female service workers and social power illustrates, qualitative researchers are motivated to understand the world of the research subjects through the latter's "own eyes," opening up a range of possible subjects of inquiry.

This qualitative approach is infused with what is called epistemology, a theory of knowledge. Epistemologies ask questions about knowledge itself: How can we know what we know? This encompasses questions such as the following: Who can be a knower? What things can be known? How is knowledge created? The research process begins with conscious and unconscious questions and assumptions that serve as the foundation for an epistemological position. What researchers know or assume to be true about the wage gap and what they want to know as a result of the research process are the basis of an epistemology. Researchers' epistemological stances impact every phase of the research process, including subsequent theoretical and methodological decisions. Epistemology influences the choice of a research subject (which women we study), the goals of the research (what are we trying to explain), and consequently what and how we frame questions related to the real-life experience of the wage gap.

Theory can be broadly defined as an account of an aspect of the social world that goes beyond what is empirically known, such as the "old boys' network." To varying degrees, and with varying degrees of self-awareness, researchers apply theory during the research process. A primary goal of qualitative research is to generate or build theory. Generating theory helps researchers to explain and generalize the empirical data collected during their specific study to larger social phenomena. This is accordingly an important part of the qualitative endeavor. Building and using theory are dynamic processes and should be infused at all levels of the research.

Having said this, it should be noted that theory and methods are intimately linked in qualitative practice. Methods are the techniques or tools researchers use to collect and interpret data. In qualitative research there is a range of techniques available based on observation, interaction, interview, narrative and discourse analysis, and unobtrusive modes of gathering knowledge.

Robert Park, noted sociologist from the famed Chicago School of Sociology, told his students:

> You have been told to go grubbin in the library, thereby accumulating a mass of notes and a liberal coating of grim. You have been told to choose problems wherever you can find musty stacks of rottin records based on trivial schedules prepared by tired bureaucrats and filled out to be reluctant applicants for aid or fussy do-gooders or indifferent clerks. This is called 'getting your hands dirty in real research.' Those who counsel you are wise and honorable; the reasons they offer are of great value. But one more thing is needful; first-hand observation. Go and sit in the lounges of the luxury hotels and on the doorsteps of the flophouses; sit on the Gold Coast settees and on the slum shakedowns; sit in Orchestra Hall and in the Star and Garter Burlesk. In short, go get the seats of your pants dirty in real research (McKinney, 1966:71, as cited in Williamson et al., 1982:192).

Qualitative data is that which is nonnumerical, and it is usually obtained through any one of a variety of different research methods that range from unstructured to semistructured in their approach. These methods include interviews using all (unstructured) to a few (semistructured) open-ended questions, focus groups, intensive interviews, participant observations, the collection of oral histories, field notes derived from collecting respondent's letters and diaries, and public cultural/archival texts.

These texts may be preexisting in the form of magazines or Internet chat rooms or created by the researcher, such as photographs or web pages designed for the research project. Data can also take the form of audiotapes and disks, still and moving images, and computer-generated texts. Data does not have to be pure numbers or raw statistics analyzed formulaically and presented graphically. Qualitative data will be subjective, interpretative, process oriented, and holistic. If you are seeking to understand the meaning or worldview of a particular subject, if you want to listen to the subjective experiences of others and somehow make sense of them, or if you simply are not comfortable with the positivistic nature of "hard" science, then you may want to consider a qualitative methodology for your research project.

If we were to describe a list of words to distinguish qualitative from quantitative methods, we might find the following:

Quantitative	Qualitative
Hard	Soft
Objective	Subjective
Strong	Weak
Measurement	Meaning
Numbers	Words
Generalizability	Process
Positivistic	Interpretation
Significance Level	*Verstechen*
Tabulating	Writing
Representative	Representational
Value-Free	Political/Social Activism

This list, representative of the way quantitative and qualitative research is commonly characterized, is in need of analysis. How did it come to be that these words are used to describe the two traditions? What historical debates have shaped this list? What implicit assumptions about the nature of social inquiry and social meaning are embedded within the terminology we use to describe these two traditions? In short, how would a qualitative researcher analyze this list?

A qualitative researcher would analyze this list, looking for meaning, by observing the themes that emerge from the comparative words. The notion that quantitative research is "hard, objective, and strong," and that by comparison qualitative research is "soft, subjective, and weak" reveals assumptions about the nature of meaning. The overriding theme in quantitative research is that it is "real science" conducted by "rational researchers" and that qualitative research is interpretive and thereby less powerful. This assumes that social reality *can* be studied using the "scientific method" and that other methodologies are "less scientific." In other words, the themes embedded within this list represent how positivist assumptions about the nature of social reality are built into the very way that we characterize these two traditions. Therefore, the way we think about quantitative versus qualitative approaches to social scientific inquiry privilege positivist ways of conceptualizing meaning. The debate about the nature of social meaning, and what it means to study the social world, has a long history.

The interpretive tradition, also known as the hermeneutic tradition, has questioned the application of the scientific method to the study of social reality. The hermeneutic tradition is based on interpreting meaningful interactions. Under this tradition, social meaning is created during interaction, the techniques of observation typical within positivism do not reveal the meanings that social actors attach to their everyday experiences. By beginning with the epistemological position that social meaning is created during social interaction, interpretive researchers would argue that the themes embedded within how we characterize quantitative versus qualitative research are based on different understandings of social reality and social meaning. In other words, if meaning is created during interactions, then a methodology that focuses on interaction, meaning, and writing is not "soft" and "weak" but rather "scientific," at least when the starting point is the interpretive model. Schutz (1967) was a leader in developing the interpretive tradition. He explained that social meaning cannot be separated from human behaviors (Nielson, 1990). In other words, social scientific research must not only observe human actions, but also unravel the meanings that social actors assign to their actions.

Likewise, scholars of the Frankfurt School have argued against the application of the scientific method to the study of the social world (Nielson, 1990). Habermas (1970) has been a leader in developing this tradition, which aims at creating knowledge outside of the dominant discourse (Nielson, 1990). Epistemologically critical scholars believe that all knowledge is socially constructed and therefore reject the idea of a rational researcher conducting objective research in order to access preexisting data. A critical scholar might analyze the descriptive list by noting how it privileges the idea of objectivity over subjective and partial truths situated within a specific social context. In other words, a critical scholar would note that the way we conceptualize quantitative versus qualitative research is itself the product of hierarchical ways of thinking about knowledge building enmeshed within complex webs of historical power relations.

Moving away from the typical "list" used to describe the two major research traditions, which upon qualitative analysis seems to embody themes that we might not be comfortable with, let us move into a descriptive discussion of qualitative research.

What distinguishes the field of qualitative research is its diversity. It encompasses a wide range of epistemological positions and theoretical frameworks while offering many distinct research methods. Qualitative inquiry, then, allows researchers to ask different kinds of questions than its quantitative counterparts. Qualitative research allows for "thick descriptions" of social life (Geertz, 1973), detailed explanations of social processes, and the generation of theory on both micro and macro levels of analysis. Most quantitative analysis occurs from a positivist epistemological position because quantitative analysis is generally congruent with positivist assumptions about the nature of social reality and the relationship between the knower and the known. Qualitative research differs because it is conducted from a diverse category of epistemological positions including positivism, postpositivism, interpretive, feminist, postmodernist, phenomenology, ethnomethodology, critical, and standpoint. Because qualitative research is conducted from such diverse epistemological positions, qualitative researchers ask a broad range of social scientific questions. They are able to ask different kinds of questions than do quantitative researchers. Additionally, the use of varied methodologies allows for the study of a diverse subject matter. Qualitative inquiry is characterized by multiple research methods and multimethod approaches. The result is that a wide range of techniques of data gathering and analysis is available to researchers. This allows for not only a wide range of researchable topics, but also a wide range of approaches to the same topic. This lends a depth to qualitative research.

In order to better understand general questions or problems of epistemology, paradigm, and methodology, you will want to look at Egon G. Guba and Yvonna S. Lincoln's discussion of "Competing Paradigms in Qualitative Research." Here they define a paradigm as a "worldview that guides the investigator" in terms of epistemological and methodological questions. The notion that socially constructed worldviews might be referred to as paradigms was first advanced by Thomas Kuhn. He described paradigms as worldviews through which all knowledge is filtered (1970:175). Guba and Lincoln assert that paradigms supersede methods in distinguishing qualitative inquiry from quantitative approaches because the paradigm from which research flows impacts theory use and method selection and a paradigm might therefore determine whether a project will be qualitative by design. Their full definition of paradigms is as follows:

> A paradigm may be viewed as a set of *basic beliefs* (or metaphysics) that deals with ultimates or first principles. It represents a *worldview* that defines, for its holder, the nature of the 'world,' the individual's place in it, and the range of possible relationships to that world and its parts, as, for example, cosmologies and theologies do. . . . *Inquiry* paradigms define for *inquirers* what it is they are about, and what falls within and outside the limits of legitimate inquiry (Guba and Lincoln, 1998:200).

Under this conception the assumptions within a paradigm can be broken down into three components: (1) the ontological question; (2) the epistemological question; and (3) the methodological question (Guba and Lincoln, 198; 201).

Ontological questions ask, "What is the form and nature of reality and, therefore, what is there that can be known about it?" (Guba and Lincoln, 1998; 201). A researcher's ontological assumptions about the nature of the social world then act as a part of the filter, or paradigm, through which the research occurs. For example, a researcher's ontological position directly impacts the selection of a research topic, which itself derives from beliefs about what is researchable. If you decide to study the impact of the "old boys' network" on the wage gap, it is because you assume the relationship to be researchable. Epistemological questions refer to basic assumptions about the relationship between the knower, or researcher, and "what can be known" (Guba and Lincoln, 1998; 201). As the other articles in this section of the book will show, a researcher's epistemological stance is a central aspect of the selection of qualitative methods of inquiry and the overall practice of qualitative research. This is because different research methods presume and require different relationships between the researcher and researched. One then chooses a qualitative research method only if its application is congruent with ones epistemological position. Finally, methodological questions address how a researcher can ascertain the information believed to be knowable. In other words, what methods of inquiry will access the data a researcher is interested in? For example, how can one best study the experience of gendered wage inequality? This decision is based on the researcher's ontological and epistemological positions. In combination, the answers to these questions dictate the paradigm the researcher is working from and therefore the reasons for conducting qualitative research.

Joey Sprague and Mary K. Zimmerman's article "Overcoming Dualisms: A Feminist Agenda for Sociological Methodology" is written in response to one of the four major paradigms reviewed by Guba and Lincoln: positivism. Sprague and Zimmerman assert that the social sciences developed from a positivistic paradigm, or worldview. Using Guba and Lincoln's framework, let us answer the three fundamental questions that constitute a paradigm in relation to positivism. Ontologically, positivist science believes that, like the physical world, the social world is patterned and therefore predictable. This means that laws of causation apply to the study of social reality. A positivist might look for specific and measurable factors that cause the wage gap, such as years of education. As qualitative researchers hold a wide variety of ontological positions, their research topics can vary more than in positivist quantitative analyses. Epistemologically, positivists view the researcher as the knowing party and the social world, including its actors, as knowable. Therefore, the researcher and researched are on different planes within the research process. Qualitative researchers work from a wide range of epistemological vantage points, which include the traditional positivist conception, but also the relativist, standpoint, postmodern, poststructural, ethnomethodology, phenomenology, and interpretive positions. Under positivism, the social world can be known methodologically through the use of objective instruments of measurement operated by a rational and neutral researcher. Hypothesis testing is then appropriate because laws of causation and order constitute the social world. It then follows that the social world is patterned and therefore predictable. For example, a positivist might hypothesize that differential educational experience causes the gender wage gap. The researcher would then measure the relationship between years of education and wages earned and present this data in a table or chart divided between men and women. Qualitative science is characterized by multiple methodologies and therefore produces more diverse and elaborate knowledge than does quantitative.

At the heart of Sprague and Zimmerman's piece is a critique of these tenets of positivism on the basis that they create false dichotomies that bias the research process. They view positivism not as "Truth" but rather as a constructed worldview that distorts the knowledge it filters in ways that have historically perpetuated patriarchal modes of knowledge. In fact, under this paradigm the social sciences have constructed "a history of social domination" (1993:268). Positivist science has done little to question the patriarchal ordering of social life that perpetuates wage inequality. Critics of traditional positivist science might argue that it has produced knowledge about the wage gap that is infused with dominant patriarchal social power further subjugating working women.

Sprague and Zimmerman argue that the four dualisms within positivism must be integrated in order to develop a feminist qualitative methodology aimed at deconstructing dominant power-knowledge relations rather than perpetuating them. The first dualism they address is the subject-object split. This dichotomy within positivism asserts that the knower and knowable are on different planes. The researcher is thus privileged as the knowing party. Sprague and Zimmerman, like many feminists and critical scholars, explain that within the social sciences the knowable, or "object" of inquiry, is also a subject. Since the knowable are themselves subjects within the social world, they come from specific vantage points, or what many feminists refer to as "standpoints." Through process-rather than event-oriented research, qualitative researchers have the opportunity to develop knowledge *with* the subjects they study and accordingly access the experiential knowledge that different standpoints produce. The third dichotomy Sprague and Zimmerman address is intertwined with the subject-object split, and accordingly we will review it out of sequence. The third dualism is rational-emotional. They argue that assuming the researcher to be a neutral and solely rational practitioner has perpetuated traditional patriarchal science (Sprague and Zimmerman,1993: 270). Intellect and emotions must be integrated into social scientific practice because researchers are themselves subjects entering the research process with their own standpoints. For example, emotions often serve as the impetus for a research project (Jaggar, 1989; Sprague and Zimmerman, 1993). Additionally, many methods of qualitative inquiry rely on the development of relationships between the researcher and researched (such as in-depth interviewing and ethnography); these relationships may be emotional in nature and yield data that would not be obtainable in a neutral context.

Beyond the advantages of adopting a methodology that uses emotions and relies on reciprocity within the research relationship, many researchers warn against the dangers inherent in traditional positivist dichotomies. Zuleyma Tang Halpin (1989) explains that the subject-object split, in conjunction with the denial of emotions that characterizes traditional positivist science, has caused the "scientific oppression" of many groups along lines of race, class, and gender. This is because the "scientist" views the subject of inquiry as a detached object. The subject of research is relegated to the "other" category. This category entails all that is different than the "scientist" category. Historically, scientists were white males from the upper classes, so the "scientist" category developed to identify those characteristics as "self" and identify differences as "other." Combined with the denial of emotions, this dynamic process has led to scientific oppression.

The second dichotomy Sprague and Zimmerman address is the abstract-concrete dualism. While positivists divorce the generation of empirical data from theory, many feminists and other critical scholars argue for a methodology that integrates the abstract with the concrete, acknowledging that theory is generated from empirical or microsociological data. It is through the integration of abstract and concrete knowledge that social scientists are able to paint more inclusive pictures of the experience of social reality (which cannot be distilled down to "social reality" itself).

The last dualism Sprague and Zimmerman bring to our attention is the split between qualitative and quantitative methods. They advocate the integration of qualitative and quantitative methods as particular research projects necessitate because, as they explain, qualitative and quantitative methods are not in and of themselves exclusive of or better than one another, although their application often embodies epistemological divides. Charles Ragin concurs and explains the benefit of using multimethod designs by way of elucidating the fundamental difference between qualitative and quantitative research.

> Most quantitative data techniques are data condensers. They condense data in order to see the big picture. . . . Qualitative methods, by contrast, are best understood as data enhancers. When data are enhanced, it is possible to see key aspects of cases more clearly. (Ragin, 1994:92, as cited in Neuman, 1997:14–5).

The use of multimethod approaches can produce more comprehensive visions of the same social phenomenon. For this to occur, researchers need to embrace the notion of knowledge as deriving from different standpoints, or knowledge as contextually bound, and accordingly abandon the goal of discovering a "Truth" independent of the knower and knowable.

Sandra Harding's article "How Standpoint Methodology Informs Philosophy of Science" probes us to think further still about objectivity within the social sciences and the relationship between power, knowledge, and epistemology. Harding's piece complements the Sprague and Zimmerman article nicely while simultaneously challenging it, because Harding also advocates a feminist methodology, albeit one that differs from that of Sprague and Zimmerman.

Standpoint is a feminist critical methodology that challenges positivism. Harding begins by reviewing the origins of standpoint logic. Standpoint methodology represents the feminist transformation of Marxism. In essence, feminists noted the structural parallels between Marx's analysis of class relations and gender relations within patriarchal society. As knowledge and power are intimately linked, when social life is "hierarchically structured" different standpoints are produced. Feminist standpoint epistemology asserts that knowledge is always produced from a specific vantage point. Some scholars argue that the multiple perspective of the oppressed or marginalized in a hierarchical social order can yield greater (or at least very different) insights into a specific society (see: Collinis 1990, 1999; Harding, 1993; Hartsock, 1983; Smith, 1974; Sandoval, 2000). This is because those who are disadvantaged along lines of race, class, gender, and sexuality may be familiar with both the dominant discourse and their own position, resistive or counter, which is shaped by day-to-day experiential knowledge. Harding is quick to point out that standpoint is an achievement constituted by a struggle for vision and voice. In other words, standpoint is the result of lived experiences that occur within a web of material arrangements and relations of social power. For example, by studying the day-to-day lived experiences of working women, a researcher accesses the unique standpoint produced by women working under the "old boy's network" and the "glass ceiling." Ultimately, standpoint epistemology posits that all knowledge is situated and therefore cannot exist independently of the knower. This is in stark contrast to traditional positivist assumptions about objectivity within research.

Harding explains that the concept of "objectivity" in and of itself is not problematic. In fact, she calls upon feminists and other researchers to use objectivity within the research process. The defining component of her piece is her claim that historically the positivist notion of objectivity has not been applied to all aspects of the research process. Harding, drawing on the work of standpoint epistemologists and critical scholar Donna Haraway, explains that all knowledge is partial and situated. This means that knowledge is context dependent and that truth claims are misleading. Objectivity is a powerful tool within social scientific knowledge construction and should be applied to the entire research process. Positivist objectivity has typically been applied to the context of justification. This refers to how researchers justify their choices of research methods and data interpretation at the end of a research project. Harding urges researchers to apply "objectivity" to the context of discovery. This refers to why a researcher selects a particular project, how subjects are selected, what subjects are asked, and, how the biography of the researcher interacts with each phase of the research project. Harding (1993) urges researchers to use what she has called "strong objectivity," which involves a reflexive process whereby researchers disclose their own position within knowledge construction.

Standpoint methodology also challenges the traditional researcher-researched relationship proposed within positivistic science. Harding claims that the subject-object split is a form of colonialism that inherently disempowers the research subject. Ultimately, Harding asks how standpoint can transform the "inherently colonial relations of social research" and, furthermore, how the use of standpoint can help to raise new questions that might otherwise go unexamined.

Harding posits standpoint as a critical methodology that impacts each phase of research. First, it brings the context of discovery into methodological conversations. Second, standpoint produces "engaged" research. Third, standpoint calls on researchers to reconceptualize value-neutrality in order to *maximize* objectivity. This allows research to have a political component.

Finally, this methodology specifically allows subjugated voices to be heard, necessarily producing a more complex understanding of social reality. Standpoint is a way of producing new and transformed knowledge while simultaneously challenging dominant power-knowledge relations.

As discussed, the readings in the section "Distinguishing Qualitative Research" present some of the major epistemological and methodological choices researchers must consider. While the breadth of intellectual discourse regarding these choices is nearly impossible to cover, we hope these readings familiarize you with the range of considerations researchers face. Once these choices have been addressed, we are left with some of the nuts-and-bolts questions about how to proceed with conducting qualitative research.

It is during research design that researchers construct the form of their study, including what data gathering method or methods will be employed. In *Qualitative Research Methods for the Social Sciences* Bruce Berg explains how to design a qualitative research project and presents research design in an easy-to-follow step-by-step manner. Berg explains that a research project initially begins with an idea, such as the wage gap. He provides a general model of the steps a researcher can take in order to develop an idea into a research project. Berg advocates a model that incorporates theory at the beginning and middle of the research process, thereby distinguishing his model of research design from many others. Many authors of qualitative research argue for a "theory-before-research" or "research-before-theory" model of research design. Here a congruency between Berg's work and the Sprague and Zimmerman's piece is evident. Berg, like Sprague and Zimmerman, refuses to accept false dualisms in the research process. In his view, theory impacts research at multiple moments. For example, when researchers have an initial idea about what they wish to study, they may already have broad theoretical ideas about the topic or about how to proceed with investigation. These inclinations are theory driven.

Once researchers have an idea of what they wish to study, it is recommended that they conduct a literature review (Babbie, 1998; Berg, 1989; Neuman, 1997). This enables the researchers to see what other studies have been conducted on the same or similar topics. The literature review should be carried out prior to research design so that researchers can draw on the strengths and weaknesses of what research has already been performed. There is a wide body of knowledge on the wage gap, so researchers studying it need not reinvent the wheel. It is also important to make sure one's research fills a gap in current social scientific knowledge; to accomplish this requires a literature review early in the process.

Next it is time for research design. This is when researchers choose what methods of inquiry to use. The method selected should have as close a "fit" as possible to the research question and the researchers' ontological and epistemological positions, so at this point researchers must distill from their initial ideas a manageable research problem or research question. The way problems are framed will impact the selection of methods and will both influence and represent the theoretical framework of the project. Therefore we can say that the way researchers conceptualize their topics dictates their methodologies. For example, if you conceptualize the wage gap as the economic condition of a patriarchal society that produces different work experiences for men and women, then in-depth interviews or ethnography would be appropriate methods by which to access women's experiences. When considering other forms of hierarchically ordering social life, race and gender might be looked at together in order to examine the different work experiences of women of different races and ethnicities.

The selection of methods occurs during research design. At this point researchers have an opportunity to utilize a multimethod approach to inquiry as their project dictates. An advantage to multimethod designs is that they yield data in varied forms. Using different methods to study a given issue is often thought to increase the validity of our findings. As Neuman (1997) states: ". . . our confidence in measurement grows because getting identical measurements from highly diverse methods implies greater validity than if a single or singular method had been used." This should not be taken to mean that multimethod designs always *necessarily* result in a more accurate portrait of social reality. They may produce a more complex picture as well. There are many ways to combine methods, for instance, qualitative data can be used to help *explain* patterns within quantitative data. A qualitative study followed by a quantitative study can help researcher's clarify what are the important research questions they need to ask in their quantitative study (see Tashakkori and Teddlie, 2002).

Interpretive processes are unique within qualitative practice. Analysis and interpretation are not necessarily two distinct phases in the qualitative research process when working from a postpositivist, interpretive, feminist, or postmodernist position. The process is marked by constant fluidity, as the researchers often engage simultaneously in data collection, data analysis, and interpretation of research findings. Memo writing, which occurs with field methods and unobtrusive methods, is an important link from analysis to interpretation. With early observations in the field or with the first interviews conducted, early memo writing will help researchers to decide what ideas seem plausible and which ought to be revised. David Karp notes the following concerning early memo writing:

> Especially at the beginning you will hear people say things that you just hadn't thought about. Look carefully for major directions that had not occurred to you to take. The pace of shot memo writing ought to be especially great toward the beginning of your work. I would advocate the 'idea' or 'concept' memos that introduce an emerging idea. Such memos typically run 2 to 3 pages. Karp suggests that after pondering the ideas in the memos and coding the interviews, one may be able to 'grab onto a theme' (personal communication). It is at this time now that one should begin what he terms a 'data memo.' By this I mean a memo that integrates the theme with the data and any available literature that fits. By a data memo I mean something that begins to look like a paper. In a data memo always array more

data on a point than you would actually use in the research paper. If you make a broad point and feel that you have 10 good pieces of data that fit that point, lay them all out for inspection and later use. Also, make sure to lay out the words of people who do not fit the pattern (personal communication, April 2002).

Working with qualitative data, whether data is collected from fieldwork observations or intensive interviewing or unobtrusive methods, the task of the research is one of involvement with the data at an intimate level.

When we move from idea to data and then to interpretation during research design we are reminded of the important links between epistemology, theory, and method and how the choices made during research design both reflect and constitute a researcher's epistemological position, theoretical framework, and use of methods of inquiry. Accordingly, research design can be viewed as the practical manifestation of these philosophical and theoretical considerations.

The last piece in Part I is a practical research example of how to create and carry out a multiple-method approach to research that combines qualitative and quantitative levels of data collection and analysis. The goal of the study "Dimensions of Desire," by Tolman and Szalacha, was to explore the differences between the ways suburban and urban adolescent females experience sexual desire. Tolman and Szalacha used triangulation in its purest form by combining three methodologically varied phases of inquiry and analysis. The result was a combination of quantitative data in the form of statistics and narratives from in-depth qualitative interviews. This is an excellent article because it demonstrates step-by-step how researchers interested in a specific topic developed a complex research design in order to explain most fully patterns and the explanations of those patterns that in conjunction with one another can be used to generate social theory. Tolman and Szalacha conclude that their study would not have yielded such broad insights into this issue and thus could have been misleading had they not combined methodologies. Additionally, they were able to construct their project so that their research design was congruent with the feminist epistemological and theoretical underpinnings of the study. This is a real-world example of the theses of the Sprague and Zimmerman piece, in terms of breaking down false dichotomies between qualitative and quantitative research as a project necessitates while taking into account a range of ontological, epistemological, and theoretical positions.

Qualitative methods give researchers a broad range of choices, and they make clear that researchers bring to research assumptions that will eventually impact its process and results. Because of all of the ontological, epistemological, and methodological options available to researchers, qualitative research is an exciting terrain. The combination or triangulation of these research design options can also prove fruitful. Moreover, qualitative research allows us to ask and answer a wide range of socially relevant questions and develop theories with both descriptive and explanatory power.

BIBLIOGRAPHY

Babbie, Earl. 1998. *The practice of social research*. Wadsworth. Belmont, CA.

Berg, Bruce. 1989. *Qualitative research methods for the social sciences*. Allyn & Bacon. Boston, MA.

Collins, Patricia Hill. 1990. *Black feminist thought: Knowledge, consciousness, and the politics of empowerment*. Boston: Unwin Hyman.

Collins, Patricia Hill. 1999. Learning from the outsider within: The sociological significance of black feminist thought. In Sharlene Hesse-Biber, Christine Gilmartin, and Rubin Lydenberg, eds., *Feminist Approaches to Theory and Methodology* N.Y.: Oxford University Press, pp. 135–178.

Geertz, Clifford, 1973. *The interpretation of cultures*. New York: Basic Books.

Guba, Egon G., and Yvonna S. Lincoln. 1998. Competing paradigms in qualitative research: Theories and issues. In Norman K. Denzin and Yvonna S. Lincoln (Eds.), *The landscape of qualitative research: Theories and issues* (pp. 193–220). Thousand Oaks, CA: Sage.

Habermas, Jurgen. 1970. *Knowledge and human interest* (J. Shapiro, Trans.). London: Heinemann.

Halpin, Zuleyma Tang. 1989. Scientific objectivity and the concept of "The Other." *Women's Studies International Forum, 12*(3), 285–94.

Harding, Sandra. 1993. Rethinking standpoint epistemology: What is "strong objectivity?" In Linda Alcoff and Elizabeth Potter (Eds.), *Feminist epistemologies*. Routledge.

Harding, Sandra. 2002. How standpoint methodology informs philosophy of social science.

Hartsock, Nancy. 1983. "The Feminist Standpoint: Developing the Ground for a Specifically Feminist Historical Materialism." In Sandra Harding and Merrill Hintikka (Eds.), Discovering Reality: Feminist Perspectives on Epistemology, Metaphysics, Methodology, and Philosophy of Science. Dordrecht: Reidel, pp. 283–310.

Hesse-Biber, Sharlene, and Gregg Lee Carter. 2000. *Working women in America: Split dreams*. New York: Oxford University Press.

Jaggar, Alison. 1989. Love and knowledge: Emotion in feminist epistemology. *Inquiry, 32,* 151–72.

Khun, Thomas S. 1970. *The structure of scientific revolutions* (2nd ed). Chicago: University of Chicago Press.

McKinney, John. C. 1966. *Constructive typology and social theory*. Appleton-Century-Crofts. New York.

Neuman, W. Lawrence. 1997. *Social research methods: Qualitative and quantitative approaches* (3rd ed.). Allyn & Bacon: Boston, MA.

Nielson, Joyce McCarl (Ed.). 1990. Introduction. *Feminist research methods* (pp. 1–37). Westview Press. Boulder, Colorado.

Paules, Greta Foff. 1991. *Dishing it out: Power and resistance among waitresses in a New Jersey restaurant*. Temple University Press. Philadelphia, PA.

Ragin, Charles C. 1994. Constructing Social Research. Thousand Oaks, CA: Pine Forge Press.

Rank, Mark. R. 1992. The blending of qualitative and quantitative methods in understanding childbearing among welfare recipients. In Jane F. Gilgun, Kerry Daly, and Gerald Handel (Eds.), *Qualitative methods in family research*. Newbury Park, CA: Sage.

Sandoval, Chela. 2000. *Methodology of the oppressed*. Minneaplis, Minnesota: University of Minnesota Press.

Schutz, Alfred. 1967. *The phenomenology of the social world* (George Walsh and Frederick Lehnert, Trans.). Northwestern University Press.

Smith, Dorothy. 1974. "Women's Perspective as a Radical Critique of Sociology." *Sociological Inquiry* 44:7–13.

Sprague, Joey, and Mary Zimmerman. 1993. Overcoming dualisms: A feminist agenda for sociological method. In Paula England (Ed.), *Theory on gender/ feminism on theory* (pp. 00–00). New York: Aldine DeGruyter.

Tashakkori, Abbas and Charles Teddlie. 2002. *Handbook of Mixed Methods in Social and Behavioral Research*. Thousand Oaks, CA.: Sage.

Tolman, Deborah L., and Laura A. Szalacha. 1999. Dimensions of desire: Bridging qualitative and quantitative methods in a study of female adolescent sexuality. *Psychology of Women Quarterly*, 7–39.

Williamson, John B., David A. Karp, John R. Dalphin, and Paul S. Gray. 1982. *The research craft: An introduction to social research methods* (2nd ed.). Little, Brown.

CHAPTER 1

Competing Paradigms in Qualitative Research

Theories and Issues

EGON G. GUBA AND YVONNA S. LINCOLN

In this chapter we analyze four paradigms that currently are competing, or have until recently competed, for acceptance as the paradigm of choice in informing and guiding inquiry, especially qualitative inquiry: positivism, postpositivism, critical theory and related ideological positions, and constructivism. We acknowledge at once our own commitment to constructivism (which we earlier called "naturalistic inquiry"; Lincoln & Guba, 1985); the reader may wish to take that fact into account in judging the appropriateness and usefulness of our analysis.

Although the title of this volume, *Approaches to Qualitative Research*, implies that the term *qualitative* is an umbrella term superior to the term *paradigm* (and, indeed, that usage is not uncommon), it is our position that it is a term that ought to be reserved for a description of types of methods. From our perspective, both qualitative and quantitative methods may be used appropriately with any research paradigm. Questions of method are secondary to questions of paradigm, which we define as the basic belief system or worldview that guides the investigator, not only in choices of method but in ontologically and epistemologically fundamental ways.

It is certainly the case that interest in alternative paradigms has been stimulated by a growing dissatisfaction with the patent overemphasis on quantitative methods. But as efforts were made to build a case for a renewed interest in qualitative approaches, it became clear that the metaphysical assumptions undergirding the conventional paradigm (the "received view") must be seriously questioned. Thus the emphasis of this chapter is on paradigms, their assumptions, and the implications of those assumptions for a variety of research issues, not on the relative utility of qualitative versus quantitative methods. Nevertheless, as discussions of paradigms/methods over the past decade have often begun with a consideration of problems associated with overquantification, we will also begin there, shifting only later to our predominant interest.

THE QUANTITATIVE/QUALITATIVE DISTINCTION

Historically, there has been a heavy emphasis on quantification in science. Mathematics is often termed the "queen of sciences," and those sciences, such as physics and chemistry, that lend themselves especially well to quantification are generally known as "hard." Less quantifiable arenas, such as biology (although that is rapidly changing) and particularly the social sciences, are referred to as "soft," less with pejorative intent than to signal their (putative) imprecision and lack of dependability. Scientific maturity is commonly believed to emerge as the degree of quantification found within a given field increases.

That this is the case is hardly surprising. The "received view" of science (positivism, transformed over the course of this century into postpositivism; see below) focuses on efforts to verify (positivism) or falsify (postpositivism) a priori hypotheses, most usefully stated as mathematical (quantitative) propositions or propositions that can be easily converted into precise mathematical formulas expressing functional relationships. Formulaic precision has enormous utility when the aim of science is the prediction and control of natural phenomena. Further, there is already available a powerful array of statistical and mathematical models. Finally, there exists a widespread conviction that only quantitative data are ultimately valid, or of high quality (Sechrest, 1992).

John Stuart Mill (1843/1906) is said to have been the first to urge social scientists to emulate their older, "harder" cousins, promising that if his advice were followed, rapid maturation of these fields, as well as their emancipation from the philosophical and theological strictures that limited them, would follow. Social scientists took this counsel to heart (probably to a degree that would greatly surprise Mill if he were alive today) for other reasons as well. They were the "new kids on the block"; if quantification could lead to the fulfillment of Mill's promise, status and political leverage would accrue that would enormously profit the new practitioners. Imitation might thus lead both to greater acceptance and to more valid knowledge.

CRITIQUES OF THE RECEIVED VIEW

In recent years, however, strong counterpressures against quantification have emerged. Two critiques, one internal to the conventional paradigm (that is, in terms of those metaphysical assumptions that define the nature of positivist inquiry) and one external to it (that is, in terms of those assumptions defining alternative paradigms), have been mounted that seem not only to warrant a reconsideration of the utility of qualitative data but to question the very assumptions on which the putative superiority of quantification has been based.

Internal (Intraparadigm) Critiques

A variety of implicit problems have surfaced to challenge conventional wisdom; several of these are described below.

CONTEXT STRIPPING. Precise quantitative approaches that focus on selected subsets of variables necessarily "strip" from consideration, through appropriate controls or randomization, other variables that exist in the context that might, if allowed to exert their effects, greatly alter findings. Further, such exclusionary designs, while increasing the theoretical rigor of a study, detract from its *relevance*, that is, its applicability or generalizability, because their outcomes can be properly applied only in other similarly truncated or contextually stripped situations (another laboratory, for example). Qualitative data, it is argued, can redress that imbalance by providing contextual information.

EXCLUSION OF MEANING AND PURPOSE. Human behavior, unlike that of physical objects, cannot be understood without reference to the meanings and purposes attached by human actors to their activities. Qualitative data, it is asserted, can provide rich insight into human behavior.

DISJUNCTION OF GRAND THEORIES WITH LOCAL CONTEXTS: *THE ETIC/EMIC DILEMMA.* The etic (outsider) theory brought to bear on an inquiry by an investigator (or the hypotheses proposed to be tested) may have little or no meaning within the emic (insider) view of studied individuals, groups, societies, or cultures. Qualitative data, it is affirmed, are useful for uncovering emic views; theories, to be valid, should be qualitatively grounded (Glaser & Strauss, 1967; Strauss & Corbin, 1990). Such grounding is particularly crucial in view of the mounting criticism of social science as failing to provide adequate accounts of nonmainstream lives (the "other") or to provide the material for a criticism of our own Western culture (Marcus & Fischer, 1986).

INAPPLICABILITY OF GENERAL DATA TO INDIVIDUAL CASES. This problem is sometimes described as the nomothetic/idiographic disjunction. Generalizations, although perhaps statistically meaningful, have no applicability in the individual case (the fact, say, that 80% of individuals presenting given symptoms have lung cancer is at best incomplete evidence that a particular patient presenting with such symptoms has lung cancer). Qualitative data, it is held, can help to avoid such ambiguities.

EXCLUSION OF THE DISCOVERY DIMENSION IN INQUIRY. Conventional emphasis on the verification of specific, a priori hypotheses glosses over the source of those hypotheses, usually arrived at by what is commonly termed the discovery process. In the received view only empirical inquiry deserves to be called "science." Quantitative normative methodology is thus privileged over the insights of creative and divergent thinkers. The call for qualitative inputs is expected to redress this imbalance.

External (Extraparadigm) Critiques

The intraparadigm problems noted above offer a weighty challenge to conventional methodology, but could be eliminated, or at least ameliorated, by greater use of qualitative data. Many critics of the received view are content to stop at that point; hence many of the calls for more qualitative inputs have been limited to this methods-level accommodation. But an even weightier challenge has been mounted by critics who have proposed *alternative paradigms* that involve not only qualification of approaches but fundamental adjustments in the basic assumptions that guide inquiry altogether. Their rejection of the received view can be justified on a number of grounds (Bernstein, 1988; Guba, 1990; Hesse, 1980; Lincoln & Guba, 1985; Reason & Rowan, 1981), but chief among them are the following.[1]

THE THEORY-LADENNESS OF FACTS.   Conventional approaches to research involving the verification or falsification of hypotheses assume the independence of theoretical and observational languages. If an inquiry is to be objective, hypotheses must be stated in ways that are independent of the way in which the facts needed to test them are collected. But it now seems established beyond objection that theories and facts are quite *interdependent*—that is, that facts are facts only within some theoretical framework. Thus a fundamental assumption of the received view is exposed as dubious. If hypotheses and observations are not independent, "facts" can be viewed only through a theoretical "window" and objectivity is undermined.

THE UNDERDETERMINATION OF THEORY.   This problem is also known as the problem of induction. Not only are facts determined by the theory window through which one looks for them, but different theory windows might be equally well supported by the same set of "facts." Although it may be possible, given a coherent theory, to derive by deduction what facts ought to exist, it is never possible, given a coherent set of facts, to arrive by *induction* at a single, ineluctable theory. Indeed, it is this difficulty that led philosophers such as Popper (1968) to reject the notion of theory *verification* in favor of the notion of theory *falsification*. Whereas a million white swans can never establish, with complete confidence, the proposition that all swans are white, one black swan can completely falsify it. The historical position of science that it can, by its methods, ultimately converge on the "real" truth is thus brought sharply into question.

THE VALUE-LADENNESS OF FACTS.   Just as theories and facts are not independent, neither are values and facts. Indeed, it can be argued that theories are themselves value statements. Thus putative "facts" are viewed not only through a theory window but through a value window as well. The value-free posture of the received view is compromised.

THE INTERACTIVE NATURE OF THE INQUIRER-INQUIRED INTO DYAD.   The received view of science pictures the inquirer as standing behind a one-way mirror, viewing natural phenomena as they happen and recording them objectively. The inquirer (when using proper methodology) does not influence the phenomena or vice versa. But evidence such as the

Heisenberg uncertainty principle and the Bohr complementarity principle have shattered that ideal in the hard sciences (Lincoln & Guba, 1985); even greater skepticism must exist for the social sciences. Indeed, the notion that findings are created through the interaction of inquirer and phenomenon (which, in the social sciences, is usually people) is often a more plausible description of the inquiry process than is the notion that findings are discovered through objective observation "as they *really* are, and as they *really* work."

The intraparadigm critiques, although exposing many inherent problems in the received view and, indeed, proposing some useful responses to them, are nevertheless of much less interest—or weight—than the extraparadigm critiques, which raise problems of such consequence that the received view is being widely questioned. Several alternative paradigms have been proposed, some of which rest on quite unconventional assumptions. It is useful, therefore, to inquire about the nature of paradigms and what it is that distinguishes one inquiry paradigm from another.

THE NATURE OF PARADIGMS

Paradigms as Basic Belief Systems Based on Ontological, Epistemological, and Methodological Assumptions

A paradigm may be viewed as a set of *basic beliefs* (or metaphysics) that deals with ultimates or first principles. It represents a *worldview* that defines, for its holder, the nature of the "world," the individual's place in it, and the range of possible relationships to that world and its parts, as, for example, cosmologies and theologies do.[2] The beliefs are basic in the sense that they must be accepted simply on faith (however well argued); there is no way to establish their ultimate truthfulness. If there were, the philosophical debates reflected in these pages would have been resolved millennia ago.

Inquiry paradigms define for *inquirers* what it is they are about, and what falls within and outside the limits of legitimate inquiry. The basic beliefs that define inquiry paradigms can be summarized by the responses given by proponents of any given paradigm to three fundamental questions, which are interconnected in such a way that the answer given to any one question, taken in any order, constrains how the others may be answered. We have selected an order that we believe reflects a logical (if not necessary) primacy:

1. *The ontological question.* What is the form and nature of reality and, therefore, what is there that can be known about it? For example, if a "real" world is assumed, then what can be known about it is "how things really are" and "how things really work." Then only those questions that relate to matters of "real" existence and "real" action are admissible; other questions, such as those concerning matters of aesthetic or moral significance, fall outside the realm of legitimate scientific inquiry.

2. *The epistemological question.* What is the nature of the relationship between the knower or would-be knower and what can be known? The answer that can be given to this question is constrained by the answer already given to the ontological question; that is, not just *any* relationship can now be postulated. So if, for example, a "real" reality is assumed, then the posture of the knower must be one of objective detachment or value freedom in order to be able to discover "how things really are" and "how things really work." (Conversely, assumption of an objectivist posture implies the existence of a "real" world to be objective about.)

3. *The methodological question.* How can the inquirer (would-be knower) go about finding out whatever he or she believes can be known? Again, the answer that can be given to this question is constrained by answers already given to the first two questions; that is, not just *any* methodology is appropriate. For example, a "real" reality pursued by an "objective" inquirer mandates control of possible confounding factors, whether the methods are qualitative (say, observational) or quantitative (say, analysis of covariance). (Conversely, selection of a manipulative methodology—the experiment, say—implies the ability to be objective and a real world to be objective about.) The methodological question cannot be reduced to a question of methods; methods must be fitted to a predetermined methodology.

These three questions serve as the major foci around which we will analyze each of the four paradigms to be considered.

Paradigms as Human Constructions

We have already noted that paradigms, as sets of basic beliefs, are not open to proof in any conventional sense; there is no way to elevate one over another on the basis of ultimate, foundational criteria. (We should note, however, that that state of affairs does not doom us to a radical relativist posture; see Guba, 1992.) In our opinion, any given paradigm represents simply the most informed and sophisticated view that its proponents have been able to devise, given the way they have chosen to respond to the three defining questions. And, we argue, the sets of answers given are in *all* cases *human constructions*; that is, they are all inventions of the human mind and hence subject to human error. No construction is or can be incontrovertibly right; advocates of any particular construction must rely on *persuasiveness* and *utility* rather than *proof* in arguing their position.

What is true of paradigms is true of our analyses as well. Everything that we shall say subsequently is also a human construction: ours. The reader cannot be compelled to accept our analyses, or our arguments, on the basis of incontestable logic or indisputable evidence; we can only hope to be persuasive and to demonstrate the utility of our position for, say, the public policy arena (Guba & Lincoln, 1989; House, 1977). We do ask the reader to suspend his or her disbelief until our argument is complete and can be judged as a whole.

THE BASIC BELIEFS OF RECEIVED AND ALTERNATIVE INQUIRY PARADIGMS

We begin our analysis with descriptions of the responses that we believe proponents of each paradigm would make to the three questions outlined above. These responses (as constructed by us) are displayed in Table 1.1, which consists of three rows corresponding to the ontological, epistemological, and methodological questions, and four columns corresponding to the four paradigms to be discussed. The term *positivism* denotes the "received view" that has dominated the formal discourse in the physical and social sciences for some 400 years, whereas *postpositivism* represents efforts of the past few decades to respond in a limited way (that is, while remaining within essentially the same set of basic beliefs) to the most problematic criticisms of positivism. The term *critical theory* is (for us) a blanket term denoting a set of several alternative paradigms, including additionally (but not limited to) neo-Marxism, feminism, materialism, and participatory inquiry. Indeed, critical theory may itself usefully be divided into three substrands: poststructuralism, postmodernism, and a blending of these two. Whatever their differences, the common breakaway assumption of all these variants is that of the value-determined nature of inquiry— an epistemological difference. Our grouping of these positions into a single category is a judgment call; we will not try to do justice to the individual points of view. The term *constructivism* denotes an alternative paradigm whose breakaway assumption is the move from ontological realism to ontological relativism. These positions will become clear in the subsequent exposition.

Two important caveats need to be mentioned. First, although we are inclined to believe that the paradigms we are about to describe can have meaning even in the realm of the physical sciences, we will not defend that belief here. Accordingly, our subsequent comments should be understood to be limited to the *social sciences* only. Second, we note that except for positivism, the paradigms discussed are all still in formative stages; no final agreements have been reached even among their proponents about their definitions, meanings, or implications. Thus our discussion should be considered tentative and subject to further revision and reformulation.

We will first look down the columns of Table 1.1 to illustrate the positions of each paradigm with respect to the three questions, following with a look across rows to compare and contrast the positions of the paradigms.[3] Limitations of space make it impossible for us to develop our assertions in any depth.

INTRAPARADIGM ANALYSES COLUMNS OF TABLE 1.1

Column 1: Positivism

ONTOLOGY: REALISM (COMMONLY CALLED "NAIVE REALISM"). An apprehendable reality is assumed to exist, driven by immutable natural laws

TABLE 1.1 Basic Beliefs (Metaphysics) of Alternative Inquiry Paradigms

Item	Positivism	Post positivism	Critical Theory et al.	Constructivism
Ontology	Naïve realism—"real" reality but apprehendable	Critical realism—"real" reality but only imperfectly and probabilistically	Historical realism—virtual reality shaped by social, political, cultural, economic, ethnic, and gender values; crystallized over time	Relativism—local and specific constructed realities
Epistemology	Dualist/objectivist; findings true	Modified dualist/objectivist; critical tradition/community; findings probably true	Transactional/subjectivist; value-mediated findings	Transactional/subjectivist; created finding
Methodology	Experimental/manipulative; verification of hypotheses; chiefly quantitative methods	Modified experimental/manipulative; critical multiplism; falsification of hypotheses; may include qualitative methods	Dialogic/dialectical	Hermeneutical/dialectical

and mechanisms. Knowledge of the "way things are" is conventionally summarized in the form of time- and context-free generalizations, some of which take the form of cause-effect laws. Research can, in principle, converge on the "true" state of affairs. The basic posture of the paradigm is argued to be both reductionist and deterministic (Hesse, 1980).

EPISTEMOLOGY: DUALIST AND OBJECTIVIST.   The investigator and the investigated "object" are assumed to be independent entities, and the investigator to be capable of studying the object without influencing it or being influenced by it. When influence in either direction (threats to validity) is recognized, or even suspected, various strategies are followed to reduce or eliminate it. Inquiry takes place as through a one-way mirror. Values and biases are prevented from influencing outcomes, so long as the prescribed procedures are rigorously followed. Replicable findings are, in fact, "true."

METHODOLOGY: EXPERIMENTAL AND MANIPULATIVE.   Questions and/or hypotheses are stated in propositional form and subjected to empirical test to verify them; possible confounding conditions must be carefully controlled (manipulated) to prevent outcomes from being improperly influenced.

Column 2: Postpositivism

ONTOLOGY: CRITICAL REALISM.   Reality is assumed to exist but to be only imperfectly apprehendable because of basically flawed human intellectual mechanisms and the fundamentally intractable nature of phenomena. The ontology is labeled as critical realism (Cook & Campbell, 1979) because of the posture of proponents that claims about reality must be subjected to the widest possible critical examination to facilitate apprehending reality as closely as possible (but never perfectly).

EPISTEMOLOGY: MODIFIED DUALIST/OBJECTIVIST.   Dualism is largely abandoned as not possible to maintain, but objectivity remains a "regulatory ideal"; special emphasis is placed on external "guardians" of objectivity such as critical traditions (Do the findings "fit" with preexisting knowledge?) and the critical community (such as editors, referees, and professional peers). Replicated findings are probably true (but always subject to falsification).

METHODOLOGY: MODIFIED EXPERIMENTAL/MANIPULATIVE.   Emphasis is placed on "critical multiplism" (a refurbished version of triangulation) as a way of falsifying (rather than verifying) hypotheses. The methodology aims to redress some of the problems noted above (intraparadigm critiques) by doing inquiry in more natural settings, collecting more situational information, and reintroducing discovery as an element in inquiry, and, in the social sciences particularly, soliciting emic viewpoints to assist in determining the meanings and purposes that people ascribe to their actions, as well as to contribute to "grounded theory" (Glaser & Strauss, 1967;

Strauss & Corbin, 1990). All these aims are accomplished largely through the increased utilization of qualitative techniques.

Column 3: Critical Theory and Related Ideological Positions

ONTOLOGY: HISTORICAL REALISM. A reality is assumed to be apprehendable that was once plastic, but that was, over time, shaped by a congeries of social, political, cultural, economic, ethnic, and gender factors, and then crystallized (reified) into a series of structures that are now (inappropriately) taken as "real," that is, natural and immutable. For all practical purposes the structures *are* "real," a virtual or historical reality.

EPISTEMOLOGY: TRANSACTIONAL AND SUBJECTIVIST. The investigator and the investigated object are assumed to be interactively linked, with the values of the investigator (and of situated "others") inevitably influencing the inquiry. Findings are therefore *value mediated*. Note that this posture effectively challenges the traditional distinction between ontology and epistemology; what can be known is inextricably intertwined with the interaction between a *particular* investigator and a *particular* object or group. The dashed line separating the ontological and epistemological rows of Table 1.1 is intended to reflect this fusion.

METHODOLOGY: DIALOGIC AND DIALECTICAL. The transactional nature of inquiry requires a dialogue between the investigator and the subjects of the inquiry; that dialogue must be dialectical in nature to transform ignorance and misapprehensions (accepting historically mediated structures as immutable) into more informed consciousness (seeing how the structures might be changed and comprehending the actions required to effect change), or, as Giroux (1988) puts it, "as transformative intellectuals, ... to uncover and excavate those forms of historical and subjugated knowledges that point to experiences of suffering, conflict, and collective struggle; . . . to link the notion of historical understanding to elements of critique and hope" (p. 213). Transformational inquirers demonstrate "transformational leadership" (Burns, 1978).

Column 4: Constructivism

ONTOLOGY: RELATIVIST. Realities are apprehendable in the form of multiple, intangible mental constructions, socially and experientially based, local and specific in nature (although elements are often shared among many individuals and even across cultures), and dependent for their form and content on the individual persons or groups holding the constructions. Constructions are not more or less "true," in any absolute sense, but simply more or less informed and/or sophisticated. Constructions are alterable, as are their associated "realities." This position should be distinguished from both nominalism and idealism (see Reese, 1980, for an explication of these several ideas).

EPISTEMOLOGY: TRANSACTIONAL AND SUBJECTIVIST. The investigator and the object of investigation are assumed to be interactively linked so that the "findings" are *literally created* as the investigation proceeds. The conventional distinction between ontology and epistemology disappears, as in the case of critical theory. Again, the dashed line of Table 1.1 reflects this fact.

METHODOLOGY: HERMENEUTICAL AND DIALECTICAL.   The variable and personal (intramental) nature of social constructions suggests that individual constructions can be elicited and refined only through interaction *between and among* investigator and respondents. These varying constructions are interpreted using conventional hermeneutical techniques, and are compared and contrasted through a dialectical interchange. The final aim is to distill a consensus construction that is more informed and sophisticated than any of the predecessor constructions (including, of course, the etic construction of the investigator).

CROSS-PARADIGM ANALYSES ROWS OF TABLE 1.1

Having noted briefly the positions that proponents of each paradigm might take with respect to the three paradigm-defining questions, it is useful to look across rows to compare and contrast those positions among the several paradigms.

Ontology

Moving from left to right across Table 1.1, we note the move from

1. positivism's position of naive realism, assuming an objective external reality upon which inquiry can converge; to

2. postpositivism's critical realism, which still assumes an objective reality but grants that it can be apprehended only imperfectly and probabilistically; to

3. critical theory's historical realism, which assumes an apprehendable reality consisting of historically situated structures that are, in the absence of insight, as limiting and confirming as if they were real; to

4. constructivism's relativism, which assumes multiple, apprehendable, and sometimes conflicting social realities that are the products of human intellects, but that may change as their constructors become more informed and sophisticated.

It is the ontological position that most differentiates constructivism from the other three paradigms.

Epistemology

We note the move from

1. positivism's dualist, objectivist assumption that enables the investigator to determine "how things really are" and "how things really work"; to

2. postpositivism's modified dualist/objective assumption that it is possible to approximate (but never fully know) reality; to

3. critical theory's trasactional/subjectivist assumption that knowledge is value mediated and hence value dependent; to

4. constructivism's somewhat similar but broader transactional/subjectivist assumption that sees knowledge as created in interaction among investigator and respondents.

It is their epistemological positions that most differentiate critical theory and constructivism from the other two paradigms.

Methodology

We note the move from

1. positivism's experimental/manipulative methodology that focuses on verification of hypotheses; to

2. postpositivism's modified experimental manipulative methodology invested in critical multiplism focusing on falsification of hypotheses; to

3. critical theory's *dialogic/dialectical* methodology aimed at the reconstruction of previously held constructions; to

4. constructivism's hermeneutic/dialectic methodology aimed at the reconstruction of previously held constructions.

IMPLICATIONS OF EACH PARADIGM'S POSITION ON SELECTED PRACTICAL ISSUES ROWS OF TABLE 1.2

Differences in paradigm assumptions cannot be dismissed as mere "philosophical" differences; implicitly or explicitly, these positions have important consequences for the practical conduct of inquiry, as well as for the interpretation of findings and policy choices. We have elected to discuss these consequences for ten salient issues.

The entries in Table 1.2, which consists of four columns corresponding to the four paradigms and ten rows corresponding to the ten issues, summarize our interpretation of the major implications. The reader will note that the first four issues (inquiry aim, nature of knowledge, knowledge accumulation, and quality criteria) are among those deemed especially important by positivists and postpositivists; they are therefore the issues on which alternative paradigms are most frequently attacked. The fifth and sixth (values and ethics) are issues taken seriously by all paradigms, although conventional and emergent responses are quite different. Finally, the last four issues (voice, training, accommodation, and hegemony) are those deemed especially important by alternative proponents; they represent areas on which the received view is considered particularly vulnerable. The entries in the table are based only in part on public positions, given that not all is-

TABLE 1.2 Paradigm Positions on Selected Practical Issues

Item	Positivism	Post Positivism	Critical Theory et al.	Constructivism
Inquiry aim	explanation: prediction and control		critique and transformation; restitution and emancipation	understanding; reconstruction
Nature of knowledge	verified hypotheses established as facts of laws	nonfalsified hypotheses that are probably facts of law	structural/historical insights	Individual reconstructions coalescing around consensus
Knowledge accumulation	accretion—"building blocks" adding to "edifice of knowledge"; generalizations and cause-effect linkages		historical revisionism; generalization by similarity reconstructions;	more informed and sophisticated vicarious experience
Goodness or quality criteria	conventional benchmark of "rigor": internal and external validity, reliability, and objectivity		historically situatedness; erosion of ignorance and misapprenhension; action stiumulus	trustworthiness and authenticity
Values	excluded—influence denied		included—formative	
Ethics	extrinsic; tilt toward deception		intrinsic; moral tilt toward revelation	intrinsic; process tilt toward revelation; special problems
Voice	"disinterested scientist" as informer of decision maker, policy makers, and change agents		"transformative intellectual" as advocate and activist	"passionate participant" as facilitator of multi voice reconstruction
Training	technical and quantitative; substantive theories	technical; quantitative and qualitative; substantive theories	resocialization; qualitative and quantitative; history; values of altruism and empowerment	
Accommodation	commensurable		incommensurable	
Hegemony	in control of publication, funding, promotion, and tenure		seeking recognition and input	

sues have been addressed by all paradigms' proponents. In some cases, therefore, we have supplied entries that we believe follow logically from the basic metaphysical (ontological, epistemological, and methodological) postures of the paradigms. To take one example, the issue of voice is rarely addressed directly by positivists or postpositivists, but we believe the entry "disinterested scientist" is one that would be given by those proponents were they to be challenged on this matter.

An immediately apparent difference between Table 1.1 and Table 1.2 is that whereas in the former case it was possible to make a distinct entry for every cell, in the case of Table 1.2 there is considerable overlap within rows, particularly for the positivist and postpositivist columns. Indeed, even for those issues in which the entries in those two columns are different, the differences appear to be minor. In contrast, one may note the major differences found between these two paradigms and the critical theory and constructivist paradigms, which tend also to differ among themselves.

We have formulated the issues as questions, which follow.

Row 1: What is the aim or purpose of inquiry?

POSITIVISM AND POSTPOSITIVISM.   For both these paradigms the aim of inquiry is *explanation* (von Wright, 1971), ultimately enabling the *prediction and control* of phenomena, whether physical or human. As Hesse (1980) has suggested, the ultimate criterion for progress in these paradigms is that the capability of "scientists" to predict and control should improve over time. The reductionism and determinism implied by this position should be noted. The inquirer is cast in the role of "expert," a situation that seems to award special, perhaps even unmerited, privilege to the investigator.

CRITICAL THEORY.   The aim of inquiry is the *critique and transformation* of the social, political, cultural, economic, ethnic, and gender structures that constrain and exploit humankind, by engagement in confrontation, even conflict. The criterion for progress is that over time, restitution and emancipation should occur and persist. Advocacy and activism are key concepts. The inquirer is cast in the role of instigator and facilitator, implying that the inquirer understands a priori what transformations are needed. But we should note that some of the more radical stances in the criticalist camp hold that judgment about needed transformations should be reserved to those whose lives are most affected by transformations: the inquiry participants themselves (Lincoln, 1993).

CONSTRUCTIVISM.   The aim of inquiry is *understanding and reconstruction* of the constructions that people (including the inquirer) initially hold, aiming toward consensus but still open to new interpretations as information and sophistication improve. The criterion for progress is that over time, everyone formulates more informed and sophisticated constructions and becomes more aware of the content and meaning of competing constructions. Advocacy and activism are also key concepts in this view. The inquirer is cast in the role of participant and facilitator in this process, a position that some critics have faulted on the grounds that it expands the inquirer's role beyond reasonable expectations of expertise and competence (Carr & Kemmis, 1986).

Row 2: What is the nature of knowledge?

POSITIVISM.   Knowledge consists of verified hypotheses that can be accepted as facts or laws.

POSTPOSITIVISM.   Knowledge consists of nonfalsified hypotheses that can be regarded as probable facts or laws.

CRITICAL THEORY.   Knowledge consists of a series of structural/historical insights that will be transformed as time passes. Transformations occur when ignorance and misapprehensions give way to more informed insights by means of a dialectical interaction.

CONSTRUCTIVISM.   Knowledge consists of those constructions about which there is relative consensus (or at least some movement toward consensus) among those competent (and, in the case of more arcane material, trusted) to interpret the substance of the construction. Multiple "knowledges" can coexist when equally competent (or trusted) interpreters disagree, and/or depending on social, political, cultural, economic, ethnic, and gender factors that differentiate the interpreters. These constructions are subject to continuous revision, with changes most likely to occur when relatively different constructions are brought into juxtaposition in a dialectical context.

Row 3: How does knowledge accumulate?

POSITIVISM AND POSTPOSITIVISM.   Knowledge accumulates by a process of accretion, with each fact (or probable fact) serving as a kind of building block that, when placed into its proper niche, adds to the growing "edifice of knowledge." When the facts take the form of generalizations or cause-effect linkages, they may be used most efficiently for prediction and control. Generalizations may then be made, with predictable confidence, to a population of settings.

CRITICAL THEORY.   Knowledge does not accumulate in an absolute sense; rather, it grows and changes through a dialectical process of historical revision that continuously erodes ignorance and misapprehensions and enlarges more informed insights. Generalization can occur when the mix of social, political, cultural, economic, ethnic, and gender circumstances and values is similar across settings.

CONSTRUCTIVISM.   Knowledge accumulates only in a relative sense through the formation of ever more informed and sophisticated constructions via the hermeneutical/dialectical process, as varying constructions are brought into juxtaposition. One important mechanism for transfer of knowledge from one setting to another is the provision of vicarious experience, often supplied by case study reports.

Row 4: What criteria are appropriate for judging the goodness or quality of an inquiry?

POSITIVISM AND POSTPOSITIVISM. The appropriate criteria are the conventional benchmarks of "rigor": internal validity (isomorphism of findings with reality), external validity (generalizability), reliability (in the sense of stability), and objectivity (distanced and neutral observer). These criteria depend on the realist ontological position; without the assumption, isomorphism of findings with reality can have no meaning, strict generalizability to a parent population is impossible, stability cannot be assessed for inquiry into a phenomenon if the phenomenon itself can change, and objectivity cannot be achieved because there is nothing from which one can be "distant."

CRITICAL THEORY. The appropriate criteria are historical situatedness of the inquiry (i.e., that it takes account of the social, political, cultural, economic, ethnic, and gender antecedents of the studied situation), the extent to which the inquiry acts to erode ignorance and misapprehensions, and the extent to which it provides a stimulus to action, that is, to the transformation of the existing structure.

CONSTRUCTIVISM. Two sets of criteria have been proposed: the *trustworthiness* criteria of credibility (paralleling internal validity), transferability (paralleling external validity), dependability (paralleling reliability), and confirmability (paralleling objectivity) (Guba, 1981; Lincoln & Guba, 1985); and the *authenticity* criteria of fairness, ontological authenticity (enlarges personal constructions), educative authenticity (leads to improved understanding of constructions of others), catalytic authenticity (stimulates to action), and tactical authenticity (empowers action) (Guba & Lincoln, 1989). The former set represents an early effort to resolve the quality issue for constructivism; although these criteria have been well received, their parallelism to positivist criteria makes them suspect. The latter set overlaps to some extent those of critical theory but goes beyond them, particularly the two of ontological authenticity and educative authenticity. The issue of quality criteria in constructivism is nevertheless not well resolved, and further critique is needed.

Row 5: What is the role of values in inquiry?

POSITIVISM AND POSTPOSITIVISM. In both these paradigms values are specifically excluded; indeed, the paradigm is claimed to be "value free" by virtue of its epistemological posture. Values are seen as confounding variables that cannot be allowed a role in a putatively objective inquiry (even when objectivity is, in the case of postpositivism, but a regulatory ideal).

CRITICAL THEORY AND CONSTRUCTIVISM.   In both these paradigms values have pride of place; they are seen as ineluctable in shaping (in the case of constructivism, creating) inquiry outcomes. Furthermore, even if it were possible, excluding values would not be countenanced. To do so would be inimical to the interests of the powerless and of "at-risk" audiences, whose original (emic) constructions deserve equal consideration with those of other, more powerful audiences and of the inquirer (etic). Constructivism, which sees the inquirer as orchestrator and facilitator of the inquiry process, is more likely to stress this point than is critical theory, which tends to cast the inquirer in a more authoritative role.

Row 6: What is the place of ethics in inquiry?

POSITIVISM AND POSTPOSITIVISM.   In both these paradigms ethics is an important consideration, and it is taken very seriously by inquirers, but it is *extrinsic* to the inquiry process itself. Hence ethical behavior is formally policed by *external* mechanisms, such as professional codes of conduct and human subjects committees. Further, the realist ontology undergirding these paradigms provides a tilt toward the use of deception, which, it is argued in certain cases, is warranted to determine how "things *really* are and work" or for the sake of some "higher social good" or some "clearer truth" (Bok, 1978, 1982; Diener & Crandall, 1978).

CRITICAL THEORY.   Ethics is more nearly *intrinsic* to this paradigm, as implied by the intent to erode ignorance and misapprehensions, and to take full account of values and historical situatedness in the inquiry process. Thus there is a moral tilt that the inquirer be revelatory (in the rigorous meaning of "fully informed consent") rather than deceptive. Of course, these considerations do not *prevent* unethical behavior, but they do provide some process barriers that make it more difficult.

CONSTRUCTIVISM.   Ethics is *intrinsic* to this paradigm also because of the inclusion of participant values in the inquiry (starting with respondents' existing constructions and working toward increased information and sophistication in their constructions as well as in the inquirer's construction). There is an incentive—a *process tilt*—for revelation; hiding the inquirer's intent is destructive of the aim of uncovering and improving constructions. In addition, the hermeneutical/dialectical methodology itself provides a strong but not infallible safeguard against deception. However, the close personal interactions required by the methodology may produce special and often sticky problems of confidentiality and anonymity, as well as other interpersonal difficulties (Guba & Lincoln, 1989).

Row 7: What "voice" is mirrored in the inquirer's activities, especially those directed at change?

POSITIVISM AND POSTPOSITIVISM.   The inquirer's voice is that of the "disinterested scientist" informing decision makers, policy makers, and change agents, who independently use this scientific information, at least in part, to form, explain, and justify actions, policies, and change proposals.

CRITICAL THEORY.   The inquirer's voice is that of the "transformative intellectual" (Giroux, 1988) who has expanded consciousness and so is in a position to confront ignorance and misapprehensions. Change is facilitated as individuals develop greater insight into the existing state of affairs (the nature and extent of their exploitation) and are stimulated to act on it.

CONSTRUCTIVISM.   The inquirer's voice is that of the "passionate participant" (Lincoln, 1991) actively engaged in facilitating the "multivoice" reconstruction of his or her own construction as well as those of all other participants. Change is facilitated as reconstructions are formed and individuals are stimulated to act on them.

> Row 8: What are the implications of each paradigm for the training of novice inquirers?

POSITIVISM.   Novices are trained primarily in technical knowledge about measurement, design, and quantitative methods, with less but substantial emphasis on formal theories of the phenomena in their substantive specialties.

POSTPOSITIVISM.   Novices are trained in ways paralleling the positivist mode, but with the addition of qualitative methods, often for the purpose of ameliorating the problems noted in the opening paragraphs of this chapter.

CRITICAL THEORY AND CONSTRUCTIVISM.   Novices must first be resocialized from their early and usually intense exposure to the received view of science. That resocialization cannot be accomplished without thorough schooling in the postures and techniques of positivism and postpositivism. Students must come to appreciate paradigm differences (summarized in Table 1.1) and, in that context, to master both qualitative and quantitative methods. The former are essential because of their role in carrying out the dialogic/dialectical or hermeneutical/dialectical methodologies; the latter because they can play a useful informational role in all paradigms. They must also be helped to understand the social, political, cultural, economic, ethnic, and gender history and structure that serve as the surround for their inquiries, and to incorporate the values of altruism and empowerment in their work.

> Row 9: Are these paradigms necessarily in conflict? Is it possible to accommodate these several views within a single conceptual framework?

POSITIVISM AND POSTPOSITIVISM.   Proponents of these two paradigms, given their foundational orientation, take the position that all paradigms can be accommodated—that is, that there exists, or will be found to exist, some common rational structure to which all questions of difference can be referred for resolution. The posture is reductionist and assumes the possibility of point-by-point comparisons (commensurability), an issue about which there continues to be a great deal of disagreement.

CRITICAL THEORY AND CONSTRUCTIVISM.   Proponents of these two paradigms join in affirming the basic incommensurability of the paradigms (although they would agree that positivism and postpositivism are commensurable, and would probably agree that critical theory and constructivism are commensurable). The basic beliefs of the paradigms are believed to be essentially contradictory. For constructivists, either there is a "real" reality or there is not (although one might wish to resolve this problem differently in considering the physical versus the human realms), and thus constructivism and positivism/postpositivism cannot be logically accommodated anymore than, say, the ideas of flat versus round earth can be logically accommodated. For critical theorists and constructivists, inquiry is either value free or it is not; again, logical accommodation seems impossible. Realism and relativism, value freedom and value boundedness, cannot coexist in any internally consistent metaphysical system, which condition of consistency, it is stipulated, is essentially met by each of the candidate paradigms. Resolution of this dilemma will necessarily await the emergence of a metaparadigm that renders the older, accommodated paradigms not less true, but simply irrelevant.

> Row 10: Which of the paradigms exercises hegemony over the others? That is, which is predominantly influential?

POSITIVISM AND POSTPOSITIVISM.   Proponents of positivism gained hegemony over the past several centuries as earlier Aristotelian and theological paradigms were abandoned. But the mantle of hegemony has in recent decades gradually fallen on the shoulders of the postpositivists, the "natural" heirs of positivism. Postpositivists (and indeed many residual positivists) tend to control publication outlets, funding sources, promotion and tenure mechanisms, dissertation committees, and other sources of power and influence. They were, at least until about 1980, the "in" group, and continue to represent the strongest voice in professional decision making.

CRITICAL THEORY AND CONSTRUCTIVISM.   Proponents of critical theory and constructivism are still seeking recognition and avenues for input. Over the past decade, it has become more and more possible for them to achieve acceptance, as attested by increasing inclusion of relevant papers in journals and professional meetings, the development of new journal outlets, the growing acceptability of "qualitative" dissertations, the inclusion of "qualitative" guidelines by some funding agencies and programs, and the like. But in all likelihood, critical theory and constructivism will continue to play secondary, although important and progressively more influential, roles in the near future.

CONCLUSION

The metaphor of the "paradigm wars" described by Gage (1989) is undoubtedly overdrawn. Describing the discussions and altercations of the past decade or two as wars paints the matter as more confrontational than necessary. A resolution of paradigm differences can occur only when a new paradigm emerges that is more informed and sophisticated than any existing one. That is most likely to occur if and when proponents of these several points of view come together to discuss their differences, not to argue the sanctity of their views. Continuing dialogue among paradigm proponents of all stripes will afford the best avenue for moving toward a responsive and congenial relationship.

We hope that in this chapter we have illustrated the need for such a discussion by clearly delineating the differences that currently exist, and by showing that those differences have significant implications at the practical level. Paradigm issues are crucial; no inquirer, we maintain, ought to go about the business of inquiry without being clear about just what paradigm informs and guides his or her approach.

REFERENCES

Bernstein, R. 1988. *Beyond objectivism and relativism.* Philadelphia: University of Pennsylvania Press.

Bok, S. 1978. *Lies: Moral choice in public and private life.* New York: Random House.

Bok, S. 1982. *Secrets: On the ethics of concealment and revelation.* New York: Pantheon.

Burns, J. 1978. *Leadership.* New York: Harper.

Carr, W., and S. Kemmis. 1986. *Becoming critical: Education, knowledge and action research.* London: Falmer.

Cook, T., and D.T. Campbell. 1979. *Quasi-experimentation: Design and analysis issues for field settings.* Chicago: Rand McNally.

Diener, E., and R. Crandall. 1978. *Ethics in social and behavioral research.* Chicago: University of Chicago Press.

Gage, N. 1989. The paradigm wars and their aftermath: A "historical" sketch of research and teaching since 1989. *Educational Research* 18: 4–10.

Giroux, H. 1988. *Schooling and the struggle for public life: Critical pedagogy in the modern age.* Minneapolis: University of Minnesota Press.

Glaser, B. G., and A.L. Strauss. 1967. *The discovery of grounded theory: Strategies for qualitative research.* Chicago: Aldine.

Guba, E. G. 1981. Criteria for assessing the trustworthiness of naturalistic inquiries. *Educational Communication and Technology Journal* 29: 75–92.

Guba, E. G., ed. 1990. *The paradigm dialog.* Newbury Park, CA: Sage.

Guba, E. G. 1992. Relativism. *Curriculum Inquiry* 22: 17–24.

Guba, E. G., and Y.S. Lincoln. 1989. *Fourth generation evaluation.* Newbury Park, CA: Sage.

Hesse, E. 1980. *Revolutions and reconstructions in the philosophy of science.* Bloomington: Indiana University Press.

House, E. 1977. *The logic of evaluative argument.* Los Angeles: University of California, Center for the Study of Evaluation.

Kuhn, T. S. 1962. *The structure of scientific revolutions.* Chicago: University of Chicago Press.

Kuhn, T. S. 1970. *The structure of scientific revolutions,* 2nd ed. Chicago: University of Chicago Press.

Lincoln, Y. S. 1991. *The detached observer and the passionate participant: Discourses in inquiry and science.* Paper presented at the annual meeting of the American Educational Research Association, Chicago.

Lincoln, Y. S. 1993. I and thou: Method and voice in research with the silenced. In *Naming silenced hues: Personal narratives and the process of educational change,* edited by D. McLaughlin and W. G. Tierney. New York: Routledge.

Lincoln, Y. S., and E.G. Guba. 1985. *Naturalistic inquiry.* Beverly Hills, CA: Sage.

Marcus, G., and Fischer, M. 1986. *Anthropology as cultural critique: An experimental moment in the human sciences.* Chicago: University of Chicago Press.

Mill, J. S. 1906. *A system of logic.* London: Longmans Green. (Original work published 1843)

Phillips, D. C. 1987. *Philosophy, science, and social inquiry.* Oxford: Pergamon.

Phillips, D. C. 1990a. Postpositivistic science: Myths and realities. In *The paradigm dialog* (pp. 31–45), edited by E. G. Guba. Newbury Park, CA: Sage.

Phillips, D. C. 1990b. Subjectivity and objectivity: An objective inquiry. In *Qualitative inquiry in education* (pp. 19–37), edited by E. Eisner & A. Peshkin. New York: Teachers College Press.

Popper, K. 1968. *Conjectures and refutations.* New York: Harper & Row.

Reason, P., and J. Rowan. 1981. *Human inquiry.* New York: John Wiley.

Reese, W. 1980. *Dictionary of philosophy and religion.* Atlantic Highlands, NJ: Humanities Press.

Sechrest, L. 1992. Roots: Back to our first generations. *Evaluation Practice* 13: 1–8.

Strauss, A. L., and J. Corbin. 1990. *Basics of qualitative research: Grounded theory procedures and techniques.* Newbury Park, CA: Sage.

von Wright, G. 1971. *Explanation and understanding.* London: Routledge & Kegan Paul.

NOTES

1. Many of the objections listed here were first enunciated by positivists themselves; indeed, we might argue that the postpositivist position represents an attempt to transform positivism in ways that take account of these same objections. The naive positivist position of the sixteenth through the nineteenth centuries is no longer held by anyone even casually acquainted with these problems. Although we would concede that the postpositivist position, as enunciated, for example, by Denis Phillips (1987, 1990a, 1990b), represents a considerable improvement over classic positivism, it fails to make a clean break. It represents a kind of "damage control" rather than a reformulation of basic principles. The notion that these problems required a paradigm shift was poorly recognized until the publication of Thomas Kuhn's landmark work, *The Structure of Scientific Revolutions* (1962, 1970), and even then proceeded but slowly. Nevertheless, the contributions of pre-Kuhnian critics should be recognized and applauded.

2. We are reminded by Robert Stake (personal communication, 1993) that the view of paradigms that we present here should not "exclude a belief that there are

worlds within worlds, unending, each with its own paradigms. Infinitesimals have their own cosmologies."

3. It is unlikely that a practitioner of any paradigm would agree that our summaries closely describe what he or she thinks or does. Workaday scientists rarely have either the time or the inclination to assess what they do in philosophical terms. We do contend, however, that these descriptions are apt as broad brush strokes, if not always at the individual level.

CHAPTER 2

Overcoming Dualisms

A Feminist Agenda for Sociological Methodology

JOEY SPRAGUE AND MARY K. ZIMMERMAN

Positivism has been the ruling epistemology in sociology since its inception; however, critical epistemologies, most recently feminist, have made it clear that positivism holds little promise for sociology's future. The goal of this paper is to assist the birth of an inclusive feminist methodology—one that can accommodate a range of research strategies and will guide the research of all sociologists. To begin, we summarize the major contours of the critique of positivism and the common feminist methodological responses to this critique. We argue that too often the methodological alternatives offered by feminists have been simply a mirror image of positivism. Feminist alternatives, we maintain, must overcome the problems imposed by dualistic thinking: Otherwise, they are equally as limiting as positivism for the development of social understanding. We suggest that both positivistic and common feminist approaches are organized around four dualisms—object/subject, rational/emotional, abstract/concrete, and quantitative/qualitative—but that the two approaches differ in which half of each dualism is emphasized and normatively valued. Positivism claims an objective reality, perceivable independently of subjective experience, and values the rational, abstract, and quantitative. Feminists, in contrast, give priority to actors' own subjective experience and emphasize the emotional aspects of social life grounded in concrete, daily experiences. For them, data must be qualitative in order to reveal these aspects.

We take the position that rather than representing absolute dichotomies, these four oppositions express tensions that we should strive to integrate in doing research. We propose an inclusive feminist methodology based on the premise that social research is both collective and processual. Accordingly, we develop specific strategies for implementing a nondualist feminist methodology. We suggest working toward the integration of these dualisms at three points of the research process: the development of an agenda, the conduct of specific projects, and participation in discourse. We conclude with the observation that pursuing such a feminist methodology is in the best interests of developing the entire discipline of sociology.

THE FEMINIST CRITIQUE OF POSITIVISM

Positivism was linked with sociology at the beginning by its major founders, August Comte, the mathematician credited with founding the discipline, as well as Emile Durkheim, who played a major role in establishing the new discipline's credibility. Comte argued we could only be "positive" about knowledge obtained by dispassionately observing empirical data to uncover hidden laws. Disciplined observation could be facilitated through quantifying observations and using statistical principles to detect patterns. Empirical observations were facts; the adoption of specific routines assured the objectivity of the process; the ability to predict was the measure of a model's adequacy (Barzun and Graff 1970, pp. 222–29). Positivistic epistemology has enjoyed hegemony in sociological research up to the present, though not without challenge.

There has been a strong tradition within sociology of contesting positivistic assumptions. The sociology of knowledge has focused on demonstrating the degree to which knowledge is socially constructed (e.g., Berger and Luckmann 1966; Habermas 1979; Mannheim 1936). The Frankfurt school has criticized positivists for (1) a lack of awareness that positivism itself is rooted in a specific social order, (2) emphasis on the reporting of empirical findings isolated from the social processes underlying them, (3) a view of knowledge as inherently neutral, and (4) a blindness to the biases embedded in the observer's point of view (Farganis 1986).

In addition, Habermas (1971) challenges the positivistic notion that predictive power is the fundamental criterion of a theory's adequacy. He argues that simply being able to predict behavior does not enhance our ability to see that behavior from the point of view of the actors or to enable their emancipation from oppressive social relations. Under what circumstances is prediction an adequate criterion of knowing? Habermas suggests predictability is adequate when the goal is to be able to thwart undesirable behaviors or encourage desirable ones. For example, being able to predict what categories of people are most likely to use cocaine is more useful for allocating resources for social control than it is for revealing how drug abusers see themselves and the world or how to create a society in which people are not self-destructive.

Phenomenology and the interactionist school, with roots in the social behaviorism of George Herbert Mead and philosophical pragmatism (Stone and Farberman 1981), have also provided related, though by no means politically self-conscious, challenges to positivism within sociology. The interactionist tradition has placed major emphasis on the extent to which reality is constructed, interpreted, and reinterpreted as an ongoing and emergent process. Interactionism denies a single, objective reality independent of actors' meanings and instead recognizes the likelihood of multiple realities, each subject to renegotiation. Research methods within this tradition have focused on human actors' subjective accounts of experience and therefore have consisted largely of qualitative techniques.

Radical feminist critiques of positivistic notions of science have perhaps provided the most serious and pervasive challenge (Cook and Fonow 1986; Farganis 1986; Harding 1987; Harding and Hintikka 1983; Jaggar 1983; Keller 1982; MacKinnon 1982; Smith 1979, 1987). This work tends to cluster around two interrelated themes: (1) an expanded critique of the notion of scientific objectivity; (2) an analysis of the power relations embedded in the social organization of research.

The Feminist Critique of Objectivity

While other critics have debated the attainability of objectivity, feminists have added the issue of its desirability. Positivistic claims of objectivity are built on the idea that the scientist must be detached from the subject of her/his research. Thus, typically in the social and behavioral sciences, research subjects are treated as objects and the detached or "objective" researcher is privileged as the "knowing" party. In essence, the subjectivity of the researcher as well as that of the "object" of research are ignored. This has raised fundamental problems for feminists—both in terms of biases in the construction of knowledge and in terms of issues of political exploitation and subjugation. First, we consider the problem of bias.

A central argument in feminist epistemology has been that the separation of subject and object has negative consequences for validity (Cook and Fonow 1986; MacKinnon 1982; Ring 1987). The positivist researcher employing quantitative methods often "interacts" with the object of study only through the medium of a questionnaire or some other documentary evidence. In order to quantify, measures are constructed with a fixed set of categorical responses. In the interest of standardization, measures developed in one situation are frequently applied to another. The resultant data are fragments of decontextualized human experience. These fragments are recombined using analytic categories and interpretive frameworks drawn from previous work within the literature, itself built on the unexamined assumptions of a white male perspective (MacKinnon 1982; Smith 1979, 1987). Thus, in employing quantitative techniques the researcher widens the gap between her/him and those s/he is studying to such a degree that in-depth understanding is severely compromised and distortion can easily occur. It follows that research in this tradition is likely to be an expression of patriarchal ideology, useless for understanding and counterproductive for feminist goals.

In response to this epistemological critique, some feminists have advocated that all research and particularly studies of women should reject a priori constructs in favor of privileging the subjectivity of women (Farganis 1986). One argument to support such an approach is that oppressed group women have had to develop a dual perspective: the perspective to understand the point of view of their dominators as well as the perspective developed through their own experience. In struggling to overcome their oppression, they are sensitized to the social and psychological mechanisms of dominance (Mies 1983). As people assigned the daily work of meeting people's physical, emotional, and social needs, women have a clearer understanding of their connections with nature and with each other (Hartsock 1985; Smith 1987). Thus, like Hegel's slave, they have the potential to understand more completely and less perversely than their oppressors (Harding 1986).

In fact, a major contribution of feminist sociology has been to uncover and examine domestic life, revealing the intricate and often subtle ways that women's own domestic orientation and the expectations of others for their nurturing role maintain the conditions of gender inequality on a daily basis. Making the personal—and, in male terms, often the mundane—visible as an important part of the social system has been possible because of the development of a feminist standpoint. A way of understanding the world that is grounded in the practical experience common to women (Hartsock 1983) casts light on the connections between social structure and the microdynamics of daily experience (cf. Risman and Schwartz 1989).

This "standpoint" argument has been expanded to assert that gender intersects with class and ethnicity to create unique sets of experiences, giving rise to the development of distinctive perspectives (Collins 1986, 1989; Dill 1979, 1983; King 1988). The standpoints of those who have historically been intellectual outsiders are particularly valuable in revealing the distortions of mainstream white upper-class male frameworks (Collins 1986; King 1988).

Feminists also have insisted on the legitimacy of alternative ways of knowing, including intuition and emotionality (Cook and Fonow 1986). Such sources of knowledge defy conventional notions of rational thought, rooted as they are in the narrow assumptions of positivist science. Mistakenly dismissed as irrational, these alternative paths to knowledge can, in fact, further understanding. Even apart from the feminist critique, successful scientists have voiced understandings achieved through nonrational paths but have failed to recognize or acknowledge them as acceptable sources (Keller 1982).

The contribution of alternative ways of knowing to scholarly research has been hidden in part because positivistic science distinguishes between the *context of discovery* and the *context of justification* (Reichenbach 1938). The context of discovery refers to the origin of research questions. The context of justification refers to the set of processes through which research questions are tested. The context of justification is subject to rationalization and control through the procedural rules of the scientific method. Positivistic assumptions cannot, however, rationalize or account for the context of discovery, the seemingly idiosyncratic and mysterious process through which research questions and creative, novel hypotheses emerge (Harding 1987). Because it lies outside positivistic explanation, the context of discovery and the role of intuition and emotionality in generating insight and creativity are ignored.

If alternative ways of knowing were recognized as valid sources of information, women would be recognized as privileged observers partly because they have developed abilities to understand phenomena through intuition and emotionality (cf. Cook and Fonow 1986). In fact, the subjectivities of researchers would not be the only source for research questions and insightful understandings. Thus, feminists, particularly black feminists, have emphasized that the concepts and explanations of ordinary people can also be valid bases on which to develop our social analyses (Collins 1989; Dill 1983).

The Connection between Science and Domination

The other dominant theme in feminist critiques of conventional methodology is a recognition of the politics embedded in the social organization of science. Positivist ideology represents science as value neutral both as a set of processes and in its relationship to society. The procedures of the scientific method are assumed to guarantee against the infiltration of politics. The pursuit of knowledge is seen as independent of any political interests that knowledge may serve. Ethics is distinct from epistemology. Feminists have taken issue with these elements of positivist ideology, arguing that traditional science reproduces domination both in power inequities in the research process, and in the way it contributes to the reproduction of broader social inequality. More than that, the very form science takes in our culture equates it with power and domination.

Feminist epistemologists have specifically connected the practice of positivistic sociology with the imposition of social dominance at two levels: First, the conduct of research is carried out through social relationships of differential power with the attendant risks of exploitation and abuse. The researcher typically has more control over the situation—its definition and its outcomes—than does the subject of research. The research group—principal investigator, research assistants, clerical workers—is also organized hierarchically both in terms of decision-making and in the allocation of accrued benefits. Second, research is inherently political in facilitating particular structures of power within the larger society, either those already in existence or those through which the currently oppressed are empowered. The questions asked, the conceptualizations used, the research design, and the criteria for adequate answers all express a specific worldview (Smith 1987). Research expressing a specific worldview and resulting in knowledge claims that reflect this view is inherently value laden and therefore, raises issues of morality and ethics (cf. Reinhartz 1983). To avoid serving dominant interests, researchers must be self-consciously oriented toward the interests and struggles of the dominated. Specifically, research would have to address the dismantling of patriarchy and the empowerment of women (Cook and Fonow 1986; Mies 1983; Smith 1987).

The very orientation of positivistic science makes the subject under study an object of scientific dominance. Keller (1982) sees this as the outcome of a masculine perspective, which includes a high degree of individuation, of separation from the other (cf. Chodorow 1978). This masculine sense of self as cut off from other people and from the natural world is the basis for positivists' preference for a strict separation between subject and object. As Stacey and Thorne put it, "rationality divorced from feelings, and sharp separation between the knower and the known . . . [constitute] an objectifying stance basic to Positivist social science" (1985, p. 309). They ask, quoting Keller: "To what extent does the disjunction of subject and object carry an intrinsic implication of control and power?" (p. 309). It is failing to see ourselves as intimately connected with, as part of the physical as well as social world that allows us to see the world as something for us to use and control rather than to seek to understand how we can improve our harmony with it. It is depersonalizing others, shunning empathy, that makes it possible to ignore the question of the likely impact of our work on their potential for self-determination (cf. Hartsock 1985 for an extended argument).

A PROBLEMATIC FEMINIST RESPONSE

Feminists have criticized mainstream positivistic science for ordering its world into dichotomies—object/subject, rational/emotional, abstract/ concrete, quantitative/qualitative. In each, positivism places value on only one side of the duality, the first of each pair as given here. In contrast, as we have pointed out previously (Sprague and Zimmerman 1989), many feminist scholars have argued for just the opposite—research centered on the subjectivity of those studied, relying on emotional and intuitive evidence and staying close to the concrete, everyday world. Frequently, this has meant that only qualitative methods have been fully accepted as legitimate for feminist research.

Grant, Ward, and Rong (1987) cite three reasons why qualitative methods are arguably more appropriate for feminist research on gender: First, the topic of gender introduces issues that are not easily quantifiable, like emotions and context-specific events. Second, qualitative techniques allow the "use of emotion and self-reflection as data" (1987, p. 857). Third, they maintain that qualitative methods have more potential for correcting "androcentric bias" embedded in traditional questions, concepts, and theories than do quantitative strategies (1987 pp. 856-58). Grant, Ward, and Rong explicitly allow for the application of quantitative approaches after qualitative groundwork has been done.

Other feminist researchers are less sanguine about the feminist promise in quantitative methods. Reinharz (1983) presents an elaborate framework for a new method for feminist social science, which she calls "experiential analysis." She presents an extensive dichotomous inventory contrasting "conventional/patriarchal" with "alternative/feminist" methods. Her dualistic approach rejects quantification in favor of "nonlinear patterning." It considers survey and archival data as patriarchal as opposed to experienced or witnessed feelings and behavior, which are considered feminist.

The common feminist tendency to idealize qualitative research is not shared by all. Recently, qualitative research itself has been intensely examined, particularly the degree to which it actually achieves the feminist aim of privileging the perspective of women. Proponents of the "new," critical, or postmodern ethnography (Clifford and Marcus 1986; Marcus and Fischer 1986) point out that where the researcher interprets or reinterprets the views or behavior of women, it is the subjectivity of the researcher that is privileged and not the subjectivity of the women. Warren (1988), for example, reviewed recent work in anthropology that calls into question field notes, viewing them not as representations of facts or objective reality, but rather as texts, themselves data subject to study and analysis.

The question from this perspective becomes one of how women's lives and perspectives can accurately be revealed when the researcher studying them is in any way involved in the interpretation of data. In order to avoid privileging the researcher and to ensure that social scientists' interpretations do not muddy or distort the so-called pure data provided by women talking about themselves, some feminist researchers have advocated what essentially is the simple act of holding the microphone. They call for research that eschews interpretation, or the selective process inherent in the gathering and reporting of qualitative data (cf. McCall and Wittner 1989). The researcher's role is to interview by simply recording the subjects' words and to report results by distributing transcripts or extensive quotations. Advocates of this method fail to acknowledge that the researcher still interprets or edits through the choice of subjects, subject matter, and even decisions such as when to start recording and when to stop. What these strategies can do, though, is to encourage the illusion of an unmediated representation of the world, which is to hide the problem of the researcher's standpoint from view.

This "postmodernist turn" in social science has not gone without critical feminist examination (Harding 1987; Mascia-Lees, Sharpe, and Cohen 1989); and neither has the more basic feminist idealization of qualitative methods (Stacey 1988). We, however, are convinced that even more careful examination of feminist methodological alternatives is required. We argue that any kind of strict reliance on qualitative methods as a response to the problems posed by positivism is of limited value because it is fundamentally inconsistent with three basic principles of feminist theory and epistemology: a skepticism about dualisms, a recognition of the social construction of worldviews, and a commitment to the empowerment of women.

Skepticism about Dualisms

A recurrent theme in the feminist literature is that dichotomies should be viewed with a great deal of skepticism. A key feminist discovery has been the patriarchal character of many dichotomies. Jay (1981) identifies the specific form of dichotomy in question, which she calls a logical dichotomy. The logical dichotomy comprises two categories that are not merely distinguishable from one another but are defined in mutually exclusive and exhaustive terms: everything is in either one or the other category and there is no middle ground between them. Jay argues that the conception of logical dichotomy does not exist in nature and could not have been empirically derived. Rather, it is a social construction motivated by a basic requirement of patriarchal societies: the perception of a clear opposition between men and women. Jaggar illustrates the general feminist skepticism about logical dichotomies by quoting Robin Morgan: "The either/or dichotomy is inherently, classically patriarchal" (Jaggar 1983, p. 367).

O'Brien (1981) describes the structure of Western European thought as dominated by dichotomies like city of God/city of man, master/servant, capitalist/worker. She suggests that these are expressions of the degree to which "male-stream thought" is the result of men as an aggregate mediating their alienation from biological reproduction by opposing themselves to it and constructing social structures to control it. Rosser (1988) reviews feminist critiques of research in animal behavior, neuroscience, and endocrinology and argues that these critiques have all targeted the same underlying assumption: that biological processes can be isolated from contextual effects. She says this assumption is based on conceptualizing a (logical) dichotomy between nature and nurture that is unsubstantiated by the data (see also Tuana 1983).

Others have stressed that dichotomies bias and distort social life because they artificially channel us into thinking that less of one pole implies more of another (England 1989). The well-known criticisms of the masculinity-femininity dichotomy and the polar scales used to "measure" it provide a particularly compelling case in point. Being characterized as strong and assertive, for example, should not automatically indicate that one is not sensitive and nurturing at the same time.

It is instructive to consider these criticisms of dualistic thinking in light of the strong contrast between quantitative and qualitative methodologies and the accompanying polemical ways they are discussed in much feminist discourse. We have argued elsewhere (Sprague and Zimmerman 1989) that feminist critics tend to see quantitative research as it has been historically practiced but advocate qualitative research as it might ideally be practiced. Stacey (1988) observes that we tend to visualize the quantitative researcher as male and antifeminist and the qualitative researcher as female and feminist. In addition, much feminist work communicates the notion that separation (as between subject and object) is bad and connection is good (Sprague and Zimmerman 1989). Our point here is that it is possible to see this form of feminist epistemology as organized in terms of: quantitative/historical/separate/antifeminist/male versus qualitative/ideal/connected/feminist/female. Clearly, this itself is dualistic thinking; feminists who adopt such a view are in effect reproducing the logical dichotomy organized around the opposition male vs. female. We suggest that to be consistent with established feminist principles, another answer must be found to the problems posed by positivistic science.

Worldviews Are Socially Constructed

Another basic principle emphasized in the feminist literature is that the worldviews of individuals are constructed socially within a particular context. Furthermore, reflecting the social order, the standpoint of white upper-class males has dominated the discourse. This phenomenon has occurred within the scientific community as well as outside, and it is instructive to note the degree to which it characterizes the social sciences.

This bias within social science has been demonstrable partly because of the explicitness of quantitative methods. By rationalizing techniques of measurement, codification of resulting data, and processes of evaluation, quantitative strategies provide visible research standards and offer at least the potential for critical discourse within the community of scholars. For example, Bourque and Grossholtz (1974) reexamined the reported data in Campbell, Converse, Miller, and Stokes's classic study of voter turnout and preference, *The American Voter* (1960). They found evidence that lower female participation was not inevitable as the authors concluded but rather could be remedied if males took more responsibility for childrearing. Shabad and Andersen (1979) criticized masculine bias in the coding of reasons for candidate preference used in the same study and on reanalyzing the data found that the original claim that women are more personality oriented than men was an artifact of coding. Analysis of research on the negative psychological effects of abortion shows that studies prior to the late 1960s agreed that abortion caused women psychological harm; however, subsequent studies employing more precise, quantitative methods led uniformly to entirely the opposite results (Zimmerman 1981).

Earlier we argued that proposed qualitative strategies like simply holding the microphone cannot escape the interpretive influence of the researcher's subjectivity in selecting where to point the microphone and when to turn it on or off. The problem with the goal of these strategies is not just that it is not attainable, but also that it is based on the assumption that the unmediated worldviews of subjects constitute the best way to understand the world in which we live. Even if it were possible to gather such pure data, this position is inconsistent with the feminist critique of positivism and contradicts the arguments in feminist analyses of cultural domination.

Feminist and other critics of positivism have pointed out that by representing findings as a simple revelation of "what is," positivists obscure (and therefore help reproduce) the social processes behind the facts. Like positivists, our subjects are also viewing a world in which apparent facts are the outcome of the operation of social relations of domination. Like positivists, our subjects interpret their experience using frameworks provided by their culture.

Feminists and other students of culture have made us acutely aware of the degree to which our culture is dominated and the worldviews available to us to interpret our lives are distorted. Gramsci (1971) argued that "common sense" was the vehicle for hegemonic ideology. Many feminists have pointed out the ways in which the dominant culture gives legitimacy to a patriarchal worldview (Cantor 1987; Dorenkamp, McClymer, Moynihan, and Vadum 1985; Gledhill 1978; MacKinnon 1982). We cannot assume that the views of those we study, including those of women, are undistorted. For example, Bellah and colleagues (1985) have argued that in an individualistic culture we would never get a picture of social structures through interviewing people. Many housewives will testify, among other things that feminists don't necessarily agree with, that the place for women is in the home. To accept this as the only perspective on the situation of women is naive. Sociologists have long cited the example of the slave who claims to be happy and the ridiculousness of accepting such a self-report as an indication that there is no oppression involved in slavery.

The experiences of people who are in the front lines, doing the work of keeping our social institutions, both public and private, going on a daily basis, are an important point of access to the workings of this society (Hartsock 1985; Smith 1987). We cannot afford to disregard their perspectives. Taking a standpoint requires interpretation of these perspectives (Harding 1987), interpretation of the logics they reveal, logics of domination and of struggle against it. Sociological views of violence against women, for example, have been radically changed as a result of such feminist research. While many women report they have never experienced rape, studies asking women about the behavior of their partners show that their partners have, indeed, behaved violently in ways that conform to the definition of rape. Naively relying on women's reports of rape would lead to very inaccurate conclusions about the nature and prevalence of rape (Holmstrom and Burgess 1983). Jaggar contrasts the standpoint of women to the worldviews of specific women:

> [T]he standpoint of women is not something that can be discovered through a survey of women's existing beliefs and attitudes. . . . Instead, the standpoint of women is discovered through a collective process of political and scientific struggle. The distinctive social experience of women generates insights that are incompatible with men's interpretations of reality and these insights provide clues to how reality might be interpreted from the standpoint of women. (1983, p. 371)

The concept of a standpoint of women recognizes certain commonalities in experiences of women in a patriarchal society (cf. Smith 1987, pp. 12). It is not meant to contradict the reality that women occupy a diversity of social positions, including varying intersections of class and ethnicity, each of which can give rise to the development of distinct insights.

Commitment to Empowering Women

A third basic principle of the feminist project is that it is more than an intellectual stance: it is a commitment to the empowerment of women and other oppressed people. Thus, feminist research is connected in principle to feminist struggle. Making social change possible first requires evidence of what is necessary, specifically, the documentation of oppression in its various forms. For example, we need to demonstrate that recognized social values like equality of opportunity, personal security, and healthy families are not being realized under current arrangements. Arguments for broad change must demonstrate the pervasiveness as well as the seriousness of a problem. Convincing policy proposals are based on an identifiable analysis, an explanation of causes and consequences, and often on comparative research. Quantification can play a valuable role in such work.

Quantitative research has provided statistical data clearly revealing oppression not previously recognized. Diana Russell's epidemiology of sexual assault (1984) makes the extent and seriousness of violence against women difficult to deny. Research by Treiman and Hartmann (1981) and England, Farkas, Kilbourne, and Don (1988) on occupational sex segregation and its impact on wage discrimination and by Lenore Weitzman (1985) on the way in which the implementation of "no fault" divorce legislation has radically reduced the standard of living of women and children provide examples of the kind of information we need to be able to have a clearer sense of how to make conditions more equal across genders.

In fact, it is difficult to see how women can empower themselves without access to quantified information. Further, it is difficult to imagine empowerment without the analytic understanding and dismantling of patriarchal knowledge that comes from feminist analysis and theorizing. To be consistent with the feminist principle of empowerment, one cannot discard the interpretive work of the sociological researcher.

The wholesale rejection of quantitative methods and unqualified acceptance of qualitative ones is a violation of the feminist skepticism of dualisms and would deprive women of an important informational and persuasive resource in their struggles for empowerment. The discrediting of the project to develop general feminist social analysis flies in the face of our awareness that the worldviews of our subjects are also socially constructed and ignores the need for such an analysis to guide feminist political struggle.

A few feminist epistemologists have called attention to the irony in the postmodern position that all truth is rhetorical, a narrative, a text, an act of faith. Haraway says this position subjects feminism to the "epistemological electroshock therapy" of peeling away layer after layer of social construction, a practice that instead of getting women into "the high stakes tables of the game of contesting public truths, lays us out on the table with self-induced multiple personality disorder" (1988, pp. 577-78). Mascia-Lees and co-authors (1989) cite Sara Lennox's observation that just when Western white males realize they can no longer define the truth, they decide there is no truth to be discovered. Just as feminists have begun to challenge traditional patriarchal knowledge with their own quantitative tools, these tools are declared useless. Just as feminists have broken out of the constricting framework and conceptual language of patriarchal sociology to forge their own, such theoretical work is devalued.

Harding's distinctions among method, methodology, and epistemology can further clarify the nature of the mistake being made. A *method*, she notes, is a way of gathering data, including listening to respondents in interviews or through written answers to questions, observing behavior, and examining documents. A *methodology* is "a theory and analysis of how research does or should proceed" (1987, p. 3), including how a theory should be applied in a specific research area. An *epistemology* is a "a theory of knowledge," a set of beliefs about what can be known, who can be a knower, and what are legitimate ways of knowing.

Harding (1987) observes that positivist philosophy of science has collapsed epistemology and method, made beliefs about what is knowable identical with a specific set of techniques. This elision is expressed in the term *the scientific method*. It allows positivist researchers to avoid critically evaluating their methodological assumptions by narrowing their debates to technical issues. Feminists reintroduced the issues of methodology and epistemology but, we submit, have too often reproduced the positivist equation of method and epistemology in the process. They have linked their denial of the possibility of objective outcomes, in Harding's terms an epistemological argument, with a denial of the desirability of quantitative techniques, a stance on method.

INTEGRATING THE DUALISMS

We argue that a more careful reading of feminist theory and epistemology would recognize that the apparent duality of subject/object, abstract/concrete, and rational/emotional is the product of a history of social domination. Thus, rather than dichotomies between which we must choose, they identify tensions that we must struggle to integrate. For sociologists, this integration will require new ways of thinking about qualitative and quantitative methods. Rather than dualistic thinking that forces us into valuing one over the other—or viewing one as always a preliminary step to the other—we must recognize that both present a different yet equally fundamental view of what is ultimately the same social phenomenon.

Integrating Subject with Object

An important feminist contribution to integrating subject and object in social research has been an insistence on awareness that the objects of our research are themselves subjects. Whether we are studying individual consciousness, small-group interaction, social organizations, or world systems, the empirical bottom line is people acting in concert with others, responding to real or imagined others, making sense out of their lives (Smith 1987). Further, these are not interchangeable instances of some abstract universal subject; they—and we—are actual, embodied subjects, struggling with the constraints of a specific gender/class/ethnic intersection and developing perspectives out of that struggle (Collins 1989; Dill 1983). This means that we must anticipate the likelihood that categories and relationships developed in one intersection are not directly applicable in another. For example, the conceptualizations of middle-class, professional, white, female researchers—for example, their notions of work or leisure or community or even reproductive rights—are not likely to match those of the people they study in other social contexts.

Many have argued that the standpoints of those at the bottom of various social hierarchies have more potential for revealing the social world than do the standpoints of the dominant (e.g., Collins 1989; Hartsock 1983, 1985; King 1988; Lukacs 1971; Smith 1987). For one thing, those at the bottom of social hierarchies are more engaged in the day-to-day workings of society, know what needs to get done and how it is accomplished. Also, the survival of those who are in vulnerable social positions depends in part on an ability to anticipate the reactions of those able to exercise power over them. There are many examples of ways in which our thinking has been changed through analyses taking the standpoint of the dominated. Feminists have revealed the way masculine notions of work were blind to domestic labor (cf. Hartsock 1985; Molyneux 1979), volunteer work (Daniels 1987), and emotional labor (Hochschild 1983) and that the traditional distinction between work and leisure is irrelevant for those who do not work outside the home (Oakley 1974). Black feminists have shown the degree to which our understanding of slavery was based in male experience (Davis 1981; hooks 1981); have noted that white feminist identification of employment as an emancipator is not true for all women (King 1988) and that the distinction between work and family is not applicable to the experience of most black women (Collins 1986); and have demonstrated that additive models of oppression hide the experience and interests of black women (Dill 1983; King 1988).

To take a standpoint is not the same as to reproduce the subjectivity of those who occupy it, however. A standpoint is "achieved rather than obvious, a mediated rather than immediate understanding" (Hartsock 1985, p. 132). Haraway argues that to see clearly from any position requires a kind of dual orientation, not being fully identified with that position, but rather being partially connected and at the same time maintaining some distance. "Splitting, not being, is the privileged image for feminist epistemologies of scientific knowledge" (1988, p. 586).

Integrating Abstract with Concrete

Abstraction is important for feminist analysis because it reveals the underlying patterns in social life, allowing the dynamics of social relations to be examined across contextual differences. Developing a feminist standpoint itself raises questions about integrating the concrete or idiosyncratic with the abstract. As we pointed out earlier, concrete worldviews of specific women are essential for a feminist standpoint, but such a standpoint is developed out of a collective process—a level of abstraction that is grounded in daily experience but that does not invalidate the unique experiences of different groups of women.

The integration of abstract and concrete is suggested by considering the meaning of the Latin root of the verb *abstract*: to draw from. The theoretical and/or quantitative abstraction that engages feminist criticism is abstraction that is severed from the concrete phenomena, existing in its own plane. The abstraction that is informed by feminism would retain the marks of its embeddedness in the concrete circumstances from which it has been drawn.

Haraway (1988) uses human vision as fact and as metaphor to describe this integration at the level of theory. We see the world through concrete instruments—biological and technological—each from our own concrete position, point of view. This concreteness is, in fact, what gives material reality, objectivity, to our knowledge. The idea that any subject is free of a specific context, can see everything, can have totalized knowledge, is the illusion. If we own our vision as embodied, we will understand our knowledge as situated, meaning both partial and associated with a particular location. Theory is formed through "webs of connections" and "shared conversations" among people translating across local knowledges (Harraway 1988, pp. 587–89).

Integrating Rational with Emotional

Emotions and feelings are an integral facet of human social life, an expression of relationship and the means of human connectedness. The separation of rational and emotional is itself an artificial construct, an abstraction that is not grounded in everyday experience, but that has been useful in maintaining traditional, patriarchal science. Integration of rational and emotional can occur through recognizing their interplay in the motivation behind research, in the generation of specific hypotheses, and in the evaluation of evidence. This is not in itself a new idea, but to challenge the gloss imposed by positivism and to acknowledge the emotionality and mystery of this process is new.

Harrison (1985) argues that to distrust emotions shows disregard for the very way we connect to the world. She specifically urges us not to be afraid of anger, which expresses both connection and indignation. Anger is a signal that something is wrong in a relationship; as such, it can empower us to improve the relationship. This suggests a strategy for generating research questions: Being sensitive to what angers us about the social world will not just provide the emotional fuel for our work, it might point to an important gateway to understanding the crux of a social problem.

In the evaluation of evidence, procedures that integrate established scientific protocols with emotionality would embrace "nonrational" information, including folk understandings, intuition, and emotionally based logic. This is possible because there is no universal rationality independent of goals or values. We evaluate rationality either explicitly or implicitly with regard to a specific set of values or goals. Ruddick's (1980) account of "maternal thinking," for example, is the identification of a rationality emerging out of the goal of fostering the growth and development of children. Her analysis demonstrates the disparity between these values and those underlying dominant conceptions of scientific rationality.

A key to the feminist integration of rational and emotional lies in Smith's (1987) argument that we take everyday life as our problematic, our puzzle to be solved. Daily life appears episodic, unconnected, because it is organized by social relations external to people's direct experience. Smith discusses the extralocal relations of monopoly or even global capitalism; we certainly could add relations of patriarchy and racism. We begin, she says, by taking the standpoint of women and other frontline actors, those directly involved with the work of production and reproduction. We make the apparent irrationality in their lives understandable by uncovering the ways their actions are structured and constrained by relations of subordination to others outside their own immediate experience. In terms of this discussion, the process Smith is advocating could be described as uncovering the goals underlying the dominant rationality and developing alternative rationalities oriented toward feminist goals. These alternative rationalities would be based on the practical knowledge of frontline actors.

Integrating Quantitative with Qualitative Methods

The dichotomy between quantitative and qualitative methods overstates the degree to which these two methods are independent of each other. Often both methods present valid perspectives on an area of sociological inquiry. Each method informs the other and there are frequent occasions when quantitative research moves to qualitative concerns and vice versa.

Integrating quantitative with qualitative methods can be pursued both within and among specific research projects. In implementing quantitative methods we can draw our measures, analytic categories, and hypotheses by comparing previous quantitative and qualitative findings. At the same time we are quantifying and segmenting experience we can examine ways to generate data presenting actors' own views using themes and meanings drawn from their own words and conceptualizations. We can discuss our findings by going beyond speaking in coefficients to talking about the real human social processes inferred from them. In doing qualitative work we can strive to be explicit about the rationale behind our analytic categories and even deduce the implications of our findings for future quantitative work. We should not be afraid to present quantifiable data in quantitative terms within an otherwise qualitative study.

Substantive questions can be addressed by intentionally and carefully triangulating quantitative with qualitative projects. When we encounter apparently different findings from each method, we need not immediately assume that one should be refuted and the other accepted. We can entertain the possibility that, given that each involves selection and interpretation, the outcomes are each "partial truths," which need to be woven together for a more complete representation.

WORKING TOWARD A FEMINIST METHODOLOGY

In this section, we move out of the critique mode and into a practical framework by using the above arguments to make concrete suggestions for social researchers. In what follows we suggest ways of working toward the integrations of subject with object, of abstract with concrete, of rational with emotional, and of quantitative with qualitative methods in three phases of the research process: (1) the development of an agenda, (2) the conduct of a specific investigation, and (3) participation in discourse about the research.

Development of an Agenda

There are two aspects to a research agenda: the selection of a question and the development of a strategy for pursuing it empirically. Standard methodological discussions devote a great deal of attention to the latter—the *context of justification* or how hypotheses are tested—and none to the former—the *context of discovery* or where our questions come from (Harding 1987, pp. 6–7). If the source of questions is defined as a nonquestion, if there is no logic applied, then the choice appears to be exempt from criticism. The idea that research questions emerge "from the literature," as though knowledge pursued its own teleology, denies not only the subjectivity of the researcher but also the degree to which gatekeeping—preferences of funders, reviewers, editors, senior colleagues, etc.—has been a factor in the generation of literatures. Attributions of unbiasedness or even nonrationality in the process of selecting questions do not make sense given the regularity of the outcome: We end up asking specific kinds of questions, those of the managers not the workers, of the professionals not their clients, those of the ruling elites not ordinary people (Hartsock 1983; Smith 1987).

Integrating subject with object in the development of our research agendas seems more likely if we keep in mind that "there is no such thing as a problem without a person (or groups of them) who have this problem: a problem is always a problem *for* someone or other" (Harding 1987, p. 6). Harding suggests that our research agendas would look very different if we pursued the questions of the dominated, who are likely to be interested primarily in how to improve the conditions of their daily lives. We choose the standpoint or standpoints we want to operate from and generate questions from there.

This ties into the integration of rational with emotional. Agendas are about goals and goals imply values. We do not simply choose a standpoint— we make a commitment to a group of people, we own a relationship with them. We let our anger and theirs lead us toward our priorities. We may not ask the same questions they are asking. In fact, if we who are in relatively privileged social positions take the standpoints of those who are at the bottoms of social hierarchies, it is unlikely that our questions will be the same as theirs. Smith's suggestion that we take everyday life as our problematic is an important gateway, but not everything is knowable from even the standpoint of frontline actors. If we want to claim to be doing feminist research, however, we should be able to see how addressing our questions will facilitate their answers.

The integration of abstract and concrete will require reinterpreting our existing understandings, "the literature," as embodied knowledge, the local knowledge developed out of specific standpoints, often those of dominant groups. This is not to say we can afford to disregard existing knowledge; it is to insist that the value of that work can only be realized though seeing it contextually. We can critically assess the research questions posed, conceptualizations used, and the interpretation of findings, on the basis of their relation to lived experience. Gaps or questions of fit to the lived experience of a range of people can produce new research questions that better integrate concrete experience with the abstractions of the research process.

Integrating abstract with concrete and subject with object means we will have to broaden our notions of the existing literature. We will need to integrate understandings developed through quantitative with qualitative methods. We will also have to be prepared to learn from those who have been denied an academic voice and are speaking instead through the channels to which they have had access: literature, music, folk wisdom, ritual, and so on. Finally, the biases inherent both in quantitative and in qualitative methods mean that our research agendas should incorporate techniques of each.

As described here, implementing a feminist research agenda appears a daunting, if not impossible, task. That is probably the case if we maintain the ideology of research as individual enterprise. If, instead, we consciously build on what we know to be the case—that any piece of completed work is the product of many hands and minds—by constructing collaborative research agendas, these goals are achievable. We can form research teams consciously constructed of people from diverse social backgrounds (e.g., gender, ethnic, class, disability) and competent in a range of quantitative and qualitative methods, and develop team agendas. To be truly collaborative, communication and integration of efforts would have to be democratic, consensus based, and ongoing. For that to be practical we must train a diversity of scholars in our graduate programs and require training in both quantitative and qualitative methods.

Conducting Specific Projects

In working toward the integration of subject with object in a specific project, we can learn from an insight offered by Jean Baker Miller (1976). Miller observes that all hierarchical relationships are not the same. Some are organized in such a way that the relationship of inequality is maintained or exacerbated. These are the ones that usually come to mind when we discuss inequality. However, Miller notes, we have close at hand several models of a very different hierarchical relationship, one that is organized to reduce the degree of inequality between the members, or even to erase it. The relationships between a parent and a young child or between a teacher and a student are ideally constructed along this logic. If researchers, those working for them, and those whom they study cannot begin as equals, we can certainly organize the research process so that the skills of subordinates are developed and the dignity of those we study is affirmed.

One way to do the latter is through working toward integrating abstract and concrete. We should be careful to make sure that our quantitative measures, as well as our qualitative categories, are indeed drawn from concrete experience. Since the structure of domination means that the dominated are assigned the tasks of implementing the decisions of the dominators, the best sources of concrete categories are those at the bottom of hierarchies of power (Hartsock 1985; Smith 1987). This suggests the importance of quantitative practices like developing closed-ended items from an analysis of open-ended responses from a diversity of women and/or ethnic minorities of both sexes and a range of classes. Open-ended information could be obtained either from previous work or pretests. At the point of analysis, reliabilities of constructed scales could be compared across gender/class/ethnic groups within a sample. Stratified sampling strategies could assure adequate representation of minority segments. These recommendations also raise the question of how readily we can use scales and indices developed in previous research. We should be extremely cautious about the validity claims of these measures, and their grounding in the everyday experience of an adequate range of subjects.

Integrating rational with emotional in each research project means never being blind to the reality of emotional life and labor and the importance of subjective, intuitive, emotional evidence. As we look for relationships among variables or linkages between categories of meaning, we must remain open to discovering affective logics. Gilligan's (1982) work on the patterns of moral development in women and men and Keller's (1983) study of the work of an unconventional biologist are excellent examples of the benefits obtained from maintaining an openness to a different logic, the logic of connectedness.

Participating in Discourse

Working against these dualisms in our discourse requires attention to the form and content of our communication as well as the forums in which we participate. First, we must pay particular attention to our use of language. Discussions that, because of the predominance of technical, statistical, or esoteric theoretical jargon, operate at such a level of abstraction that even the highly trained specialist in a neighboring tradition cannot comfortably follow them are exacerbating the split between subject and object rather than facilitating a constructive reconnection. The feminist goal should be that a concerned, thinking individual totally outside the literature (e.g., a feminist activist) should be able to comprehend and make use of the information. A reasonable first step would be to write so that practicing feminist sociologists are empowered to do their/our work in more feminist ways. To do otherwise amounts to textual domination. We can all help not just by working on our own discursive style, but also by refusing to perpetuate the stereotype that the more obscure a text is, the more we should be in awe of it.

In addition to avoiding free-floating abstractions in our texts, we need to make our own concreteness visible. We should own our personal standpoints and be explicitly self-critical about the limits on our view. Similarly we need to remind ourselves and our readers of the standpoints of those we study. Specifically, we can alter the format of reporting results. We can spend time acknowledging the context of discovery by discussing the origins of the research and acknowledging the alternative ways of knowing involved. We can also address a specific section of our articles to the question of the real-world significance of the research, linking it to the broader aims of the feminist project.

We should review the journals in which we communicate in light of integrating these oppositions. We should make sure that evaluations of the significance of a manuscript are not made merely on the basis of standards like "cutting edge," which, given the history of our discourse, may signal the remoteness of its topic from the daily fives of most people. Rather we should weigh significance by the degree to which it helps us understand those lives. We should question the degree to which our journals are segregated by method, whether it be primarily quantitative or qualitative or even abstractly theoretical.

One way of integrating rational and emotional in our discourse is by expressing our advocacy. If we have connected with a group, we identify with them; we care about their outcomes. Commitment to a group implies a duty to facilitate their development. In academic discourse, the least we can do is express the implications of our work for their lives and life choices, to bring their humanity to the fore. Full commitment implies moving outside academic discourse, at least periodically, into conversations in the mainstream, by participating in popular discourse. The group to whom we have committed will determine the venue: We need to speak where they can hear in language they will hear. We must make this communication a dialogue by creating an atmosphere of collegiality and openness so that questions will be asked, answered and discussed. And, ideally, so that the agenda for future research will be a product of the mutual participation of researchers and subjects.

CONCLUSION

It may be true, as Rosser (1988) has argued, that a feminist science is impossible to achieve in a social context that is sexist. But we do have choices; some ways of doing science are more feminist than others. Feminist methodology along the lines developed here promises to be in the best interests of our profession. At a time when funding for social research is strained, public support should increase as we focus on problems that are meaningful outside narrow subdisciplines and communicate findings in ways that benefit ordinary people. At a time when universities have begun to question the importance of sociology, feminist sociology can provide the answer: scholarship that is passionate, committed, and engaged in the kinds of questions people care about, using strategies that carefully build on a diversity of skills and standpoints.

ACKNOWLEDGMENTS

We would like to thank Sandra Albrecht, Shirley Harkess, Mary Elizabeth Kelly, Joane Nagel, William Staples, and Carol Warren for their comments on earlier drafts of this paper and Cindy Wallis for a wide range of clerical help. We would particularly like to thank Paula England for her combination of contagious enthusiasm and incisive critique.

REFERENCES

Barzun, Jacques, and Henry Graff. 1970. *The modern researcher*, rev. ed. New York: Harcourt, Brace & World.

Bellah, Robert N., Richard Madsen, William M. Sulllivan, Ann Swidler, and Steven M. Tipton. 1985. *Habits of the heart: Individualism and commitment in American life*. Berkeley: University of California Press.

Berger, Peter L., and Thomas Luckmann. 1966. *The social construction of reality: A treatise in the sociology of knowledge*. New York: Doubleday.

Bourque, Susan, and Jean Grossholtz. 1974. Policy and unnatural practice: Political Science looks at female participation. *Politics and Society* 4:225–66.

Campbell, Angus, Philip E. Converse, Warren E. Miller, and Donald E. Stokes, 1960. *The American voter*. New York: Wiley.

Cantor, Muriel G. 1987. Popular culture and the portrayal of women: Content and control, pp. 190–214 in *Analyzing Gender: A Handbook of Social Science Research*, ed. Beth B. Hess and Myra Marx Ferree. Newberry Park, CA: Sage.

Chodorow, Nancy. 1978. *The reproduction of mothering: Psychoanalysis and the sociology of gender*. Berkeley: University of California Press.

Clifford, James, and George Marcus (eds.). 1986. *Writing culture: The poetics and politics of ethnography*. Berkeley: University of California Press.

Collins, Patricia Hill. 1986. Learning from the outside within: The sociological significance of black feminist thought. *Social Problems* 33:514–30.

_____. 1989. The social construction of black feminist thought. *Signs: Journal of Women in Culture and Society* 14(4):745–73.

Cook, Judith A., and Mary Margaret Fonow. 1986. Knowledge and women's interests: Issues of epistemology and methodology in feminist sociological research. *Sociological Inquiry* 56:2–29.

Daniels, Arlene Kaplan. 1987. Invisible work. *Social Problems* 34(5):403–15.

Davis, Angela Y. 1981. *Women, race, and class*. New York: Random House.

Dill, Bonnie. 1979. The dialectics of black womanhood. *Signs: Journal of Women in Culture and Society* 4:545–55.

_____. 1983. Race, class, and gender: Prospects for an all-inclusive sisterhood. *Feminist Studies* 9:131–48.

Dorenkamp, Angela G., John F. McClymer, Mary M. Moynihan, and Arlene C. Vadum. 1985. *Images of women in American popular culture*. San Diego: Harcourt Brace Jovanovich.

England, Paula. 1989. A feminist critique of rational-choice theories: Implications for sociology. *American Sociologist* 20(l):14–28.

England, Paula, George Farkas, Barbara Kilbourne, and Thomas Dou. 1988. Sex segregation and wages. *American Sociological Review* 53(4):544–58.

Farganis, Sondra. 1986. Social theory and feminist theory: The need for dialogue. *Sociological Inquiry* 56:50–68.

Gilligan, Carol. 1982. *In a different voice: Psychological theory and women's development*. Cambridge, MA: Harvard University Press.

Gledhill, Christine. 1978. Recent development in feminist criticism. *Quarterly Review of Film Studies* 3:457–93.

Gramsci, Antonio. 1971. *Selections from "The Prison Notebooks,"* Quintin Hoare and Geoffrey Nowell Smith, ed. New York: International Publishers.

Grant, Linda, Kathryn B. Ward, and Xue Lan Rong. 1987. Is there an association between gender and methods in sociological research? *American Sociological Review* 52:856–62.

Habermas, Jurgen. 1971. *Knowledge and human interests*. Boston: Beacon Press.

_____. 1979. *Communication and the evolution of society*. Boston: Beacon Press.

Harding, Sandra. 1987. Introduction: Is there a feminist method? pp. 1–14 in *Feminism and Methodology*, ed. Sandra Harding. Bloomington: University of Indiana Press.

Harding, Sandra, and Merrill B. Hintikka (eds.) 1983. *Discovering reality: Feminist perspectives on epistemology, metaphysics, methodology and philosophy of science*. Boston: D. Reidel.

Haraway, Donna. 1988. Situated knowledges: The science question in feminism and the privilege of partial perspective. *Feminist Studies* 14:575–99.

Harrison, Beverly Wildung. 1985. The power of anger in the work of love: Christian ethics of women and other strangers, pp. 3–21 in *Making the Connections: Essays in Feminist Social Ethics*. Boston: Beacon Press.

Hartsock, Nancy C. M. 1983. The feminist standpoint: Developing the ground for a specifically feminist historical materialism, pp. 283–310 in *Discovering Reality: Feminist Perspectives on Epistemology, Metaphysics, Methodology and Philosophy of Science*, ed. S. Harding and M. B. Hintikka. Boston: D. Reidel.

_____. 1985. *Money, sex and power*. Boston: Northeastern University Press.

Hochschild, Arlie R. 1983. *The managed heart: Commercialization of human feeling*. Berkeley: University of California Press.

Holmstrom, Lynda Lytle, and Ann Wolbert Burgess. 1983. Rape and everyday life. *Society* (July/August):33–40.

hooks, bell. 1981. *Ain't I a woman? Black women and feminism*. Boston: South End Press.

Jaggar, Alison M. 1983. *Feminist politics and human nature*. Totowa, NJ: Rowman and Alanheld.

Jay, Nancy. 1981. Gender and dichotomy. *Feminist Studies* 7(l):38–56.

Keller, Evelyn Fox. 1982. Feminism and science. *Signs: Journal of Women in Culture and Society* 7:588–602.

_____. 1983. *A feeling for the organism: The life and work of Barbara McClintock*. New York: Freeman.

King, Deborah K. 1988. Multiple jeopardy, multiple consciousness: The context of black feminist ideology. *Signs: Journal of Women in Culture and Society* 14(l):42–72.

Lukacs, George. 1971. *History and class consciousness*. Cambridge, MA: MIT Press.

MacKinnon, Catharine. 1982. Feminism, Marxism, method and the state: An agenda for theory. *Signs: Journal of Women in Culture and Society* 7:515–44.

Mannheim, Karl. 1936. *Ideology and utopia*. New York: Harcourt, Brace & World.

Marcus, George, and Michael Fischer. 1986. *Anthropology as cultural critique: An experimental moment in human sciences*. Chicago: University of Chicago Press.

Mascia-Lees, Francis E., Patricia Sharpe, and Colleen Ballerino Cohen. 1989. The postmodernist turn in anthropology: Cautions from a feminist perspective. *Signs: Journal of Women in Culture* 15:7–33.

McCall, Michal, and Judith Wittner. 1989. The good news about life histories." pp. 46–89 in *Cultural Studies and Symbolic Interaction*, ed. Howard Becker and Michal McCall. Chicago: University of Chicago Press.

Mies, Maria. 1983. Towards a methodology for feminist research, pp. 117–39 in *Theories of Women's Studies*, ed. G. Bowles and R. Klein. Boston: Routledge and Kegan Paul.

Miller, Jean Baker. 1976. *Toward a new psychology of women*. Boston: Beacon Press.

Molyneux, Maxine. 1979. Beyond the domestic labor debate. *New Left Review* 116:3–27.

Oakley, Ann. 1974. *The sociology of housework*. New York: Pantheon.

O'Brien, Mary. 1981. *The politics of reproduction*. Boston: Routledge and Kegan Paul.

Reichenback, Hans. 1938. *Experience and prediction*. Chicago: University of Chicago Press.

Reinharz, Shulamit. 1983. Experiential analysis: A contribution to feminist research, pp. 162–91 in *Theories of Women's Studies*, ed. Gloria Bowles and Renate Duelli-Klein. Boston: Routledge and Kegan Paul.

Ring, Jennifer. 1987. Toward a feminist epistemology. *American Journal of Political Science* 31:753–72.

Risman, Barbara J., and Pepper Schwartz. 1989. *Gender in intimate relationships: A microstructural approach*. Belmont, CA: Wadsworth.

Rosser, Sue V. 1988. Good science: Can it ever be gender free? *Women's Studies International Forum* 11:13–19.

Ruddick, Sara. 1980. Maternal thinking. *Feminist Studies* 6(2):342–67.

Russell, Diana E. H. 1984. *Sexual exploitation*. Newbury Park, CA: Sage.

Shabad, Goldie, and Kristi Andersen. 1979. Candidate evaluations by men and women. *Public Opinion Quarterly* 43:18–35.

Smith, Dorothy E. 1979. A sociology for women, pp. 135–187 in *The Prism of Sex: Essays in the Sociology of Knowledge*, ed. Julia A. Sherman and Evelyn Torton Beck. Madison: University of Wisconsin Press.

_____. 1987. *The everyday world as problematic: A feminist sociology*. Boston: Northeastern University Press.

Sprague, Joey, and Mary K. Zimmerman. 1989. Quality and quantity: Reconstructing feminist methodology. *American Sociologist* 20(l):71–86.

Stacey, Judith. 1988. Can there be a feminist ethnography? *Women's Studies International Forum* 11:21–27.

Stacey, Judith, and Barrie Thorne. 1985. The missing feminist revolution in sociology. *Social Problems* 32:301–16.

Stone, Gregory P., and Harvey A. Farberman (eds). 1981. *Social psychology through symbolic interaction*. New York: Wiley.

Treiman, Donald J., and Heidi I. Hartmann (eds). 1981. *Women, work, and wages: Equal pay for jobs of equal value.* Washington, DC: National Academy Press.

Tuana, Nancy. 1983. Re-fusing nature/nurture. *Women's Studies International Forum* 6(6):621–32.

Warren, Carol A. B. 1988. *Gender issues in field research. Qualitative research methods series #9.* Newbury Park, CA: Sage.

Weitzman, Lenore. 1985. *The divorce revolution: The unexpected social and economic consequences for women and children in America.* New York: Free Press.

Zimmerman, Mary K. 1981. Psychosocial and emotional consequences of elective abortion: A literature review, pp. 65–75 in *Abortion: Readings and Research,* ed. Paul Sachdev. Toronto: Buttersworth Press.

CHAPTER 3

How Standpoint Methodology Informs Philosophy of Social Science

SANDRA HARDING

Standpoint theory emerged anew in the 1970s and 80s as a feminist critical theory of the relations between knowledge and power and also as a guide to improving actual research projects—as a methodology. These authors argued that existing relations between politics and the production of knowledge were far from the scientifically and socially progressive ones claimed by economic, governmental and legal, medical, health, education, welfare, scientific and other dominant institutions and the research disciplines that serviced them. When it came to understanding and accounting for gender relations, the prevailing philosophies of science and the research projects they legitimated were politically regressive, philosophically weak, and scientifically less than maximally effective.

Evidence for such claims appeared in the increasing documentation of sexist and androcentric results of research in biology and the social sciences. Standpoint theorists analyzed causes of the gaps between actual and ideal relations between knowledge and power, and reflected on causes of the successes of feminist research in the social sciences and biology. Such work led to prescriptions in some of these writings for how to produce empirically and theoretically more successful research. Even though such research was guided by feminist political goals, such epistemic and scientific successes were possible because certain kinds of "good politics" in themselves had the potential to advance the growth of scientific knowledge: some kinds of politics could be productive of knowledge.[1]

Such arguments insured that the subsequent history of standpoint theory would be a tumultuous one. In the fast-moving world of feminist theory, where few analyses have been unchallenged within the field let alone outside it, one observer notes that standpoint theory has nevertheless managed to achieve a certain distinction.

Standpoint theory may rank as one of the most contentious theories to have been proposed and debated in the 25–30 year history of second wave feminist thinking about knowledge and science. Its advocates as much as its critics disagree vehemently about its parentage, its status as a theory and, crucially, its relevance to current feminist thinking about knowledge. (Wylie forthcoming: 1)

Some reasons for its contentiousness are immediately apparent: it challenges or, worse, undermines still widely-held dogmas of rationalism, empiricism, and positivism. Some of these, such as the commitment to the exclusion of politics from and selection of value-neutral methods of research, have been retained in some forms of postpositivism.[2] Moreover, critics persist in attributing to standpoint writings three positions that standpoint theorists mostly never held or perpetrated, and have subsequently again and again denied and countered. These are essentialist assumptions about women (and men), assumptions that claims to knowledge by the oppressed are always automatically privileged, and commitment to or unintended perpetration of a damaging epistemological relativism.[3]

Yet other sources of its contentiousness may be less obvious. For example, the histories of standpoint theory's independent development and subsequent debate within several distinct disciplinary contexts, with their different histories and preoccupations, have produced emphases on different aspects of it. This is clear if one examines the concerns of theorists and researchers working in the sociology of knowledge, political philosophy, and the philosophy of science and epistemology, to mention three central sites of standpoint development. Moreover, the theory has served as a site for debate about more general intriguing or troubling contemporary intellectual and political issues that are only partially about rethinking the positivist legacy. Is it postmodernist or anti-postmodernist, stuck in modernity or creatively updating modernity's problematics? Is its goal to recover the (epistemically privileged) "ways of knowing" of the (essentialized) oppressed, to produce "situated knowledge," "ethnoscience," or "identity epistemologies," or instead to engage in ideology critique? Is it a kind of ethnography or a critical theory? . . . an epistemology, a sociology, a methodology, or a social theory? What are its uses for anti-Eurocentric and postcolonial projects? . . . for the natural sciences and post-Kuhnian science and technology studies?

After all this controversy, what is surprising is that standpoint theory appears to have survived and even to be flourishing anew after more than two decades of contention. In the last few years a flurry of reappraisals have begun to chart its recent history and its still promising potential (Campbell and Manicom 1995, Garcia Selgas forthcoming, Harding forthcoming, Hekman et al 1997, Kenney and Kinsella 1997, Pels 1997, Wylie forthcoming). Moreover, other authors continue to do it the honor of claiming it to be a serious threat to feminism, science, and civilization more generally (Gross and Levitt 1994, Walby 2001). Disturbing though virtually everyone may find some or other of its claims and projects, standpoint theory apparently is destined to persist at least for a while as a seductively volatile site for reflection and debate about persistent contemporary dilemmas.

This essay focuses on just one part of these debates and discussions: the methodology issues and the challenges they raise to conventional epistemology and philosophy of natural and social sciences. Philosophers of science and political philosophers have tended to focus on standpoint theory as an epistemology. Yet Dorothy Smith, Patricia Hill Collins, and other empirical social science researchers have always understood it as a prescription for research practices. Some explicitly see it as a particular kind of participatory action research. Standpoint approaches have been widely taught and used nationally and globally as a research methodology in social science departments, professional schools, and independent research institutes and projects. They have been used as a theory of how to improve the scientific quality and political effects of research projects. In such contexts, standpoint theory enters debates about how to counter the inherently "colonial" politics and scientific/epistemic challenges of social research projects, and thereby highlights one kind of threat standpoint theory raises for even postpositivist epistemologies and philosophies of science.[4] Thus methodological considerations provide resources for epistemological and philosophy of social science arguments. And they also suggest one important reason why this theory can persist in spite of widespread unease about it: it does tend to produce, as well as to "rationally reconstruct," empirically and theoretically more robust research results.

The next section briefly outlines the origins of standpoint theory and some major themes that have appeared in the diverse histories of its development. These origins and themes shape central strengths of its development as a research methodology, which are identified in the second section.

1. *Standpoint Logic: Origins.* Frederic Jameson points out that it was not until the work of feminist theorists of the 1970s and 80s that Lukacs' abandoned arguments about the logic of the Marxian "standpoint of the proletariat" were again pursued (Jameson 1988, Lukacs 1971).[5] Yet this "logic of inquiry" has other sources in which such a legacy is not directly visible. Moreover, echoes of its themes appear in other writings. The sociologists cite also powerful themes in Mannheim (1954), Merton (1972), and Simmel (1921) about the resources provided by the "stranger's" social position. Collins develops this into the "outsider within" position of trained researchers' from marginalized social groups—a position which is capable of detecting aspects of social relations not accessible by those who are only outsiders or only insiders (Collins 1986, 1991).[6] The writings of Paulo Freire (1970) and the participatory action researchers also echo standpoint themes[7] (McTaggart 1997, Maguire 1987, Petras and Porpora 1993). Other feminist writers at least partially independently developed standpoint arguments. For example, Catharine MacKinnon's (1983) influential essay on jurisprudence advanced standpoint arguments on how we can see that "the state is male" in its insistence on standards for the purportedly objective understanding of violence against women which coincide with the way men but not women understand and evaluate the existence and nature of such vio-

lence.[8] From a perspective in post-Kuhnian science and technology studies and the history of primatology, Donna Haraway (1981, 1991) engaged with standpoint authors on their ambivalence toward their own insistence on the situatedness of knowledge—a notion which she influentially articulated. Kuhn's project "to display the historical integrity of . . . science in its own time," as Kuhn famously put the point (1970: 1) opened the way for thinking about the "historical integrity" of social and natural science conceptual frameworks, methods and practices with the gender relations of their day.[9] Meanwhile, a standpoint logic can now be seen to structure much recent work in the multicultural and postcolonial science and technology studies movements: Western natural sciences and technologies, no less than those from other cultures, are "local knowledge systems." Western sciences have an "historical integrity" with the global social relations of their eras that they in turn helped to constitute and maintain.[10]

The "logic of inquiry." What was this abandoned "logic of inquiry" that the feminist standpoint theorists took up?

In the Marxian accounts, bourgeois understandings of class relations were articulated not only in specific claims about such matters as the inferiority of workers and superiority of educated classes, but also in the abstract conceptual frameworks within which research was organized and conducted on such topics as human evolution, reproductive practices, the distinguishing features and distribution of intelligence, social deviance, the appropriate organization of work and of the economy, and the thought and behavior of "masses" (Sohn-Rethel 1978). Feminist theorists made a similar claim about the way sexist and androcentric understandings of gender relations appeared in the most abstract conceptual practices. They noted, as had Marx himself, that the social relations between women and men in significant respects resembled those between workers and their bosses: gender and class relations had parallel social structures. Men, in their double capacity as the largely exclusive designers and managers of social institutions and as heads of households, intentionally or not exploited women's reproductive and productive labor. They benefited as men, as well as in the capacity of some of them as managers, administrators, and capitalists, from male control of women's bodies, their unpaid domestic labor, and discrimination against and exploitation of their work in wage labor. The exploitation of women in the spheres of domestic and wage-labor were causally linked, for each undermined women's power in the other domain.[11]

Feminist sociologists, political scientists, legal theorists, anthropologists, psychologists, economists, and biologists, often actively participatory in the public politics of the then emerging women's movements, began to provide accounts of how gender relations were articulated not just in explicit claims about women and men and their appropriate social roles, but also in the apparently value-neutral abstract conceptual frameworks of the dominant institutions and of the disciplines that serviced them. They began to look at the "conceptual practices of power," in Dorothy Smith's phrase (D. Smith 1990a). They did so, the theorists argued, by starting off research from women's concerns and practices in everyday life rather than from the concerns of those institutions and disciplines. For example, Carol Gilligan's analyses (1982) started off thinking about the gap between the distinctive kinds of moral decisions women faced as mothers and caretakers, on the one hand, and on the other hand, moral theory. The latter elevated to the highest ethical categories only the kinds of decisions that tended to arise in the kinds of social relations outside the household where men made moral decisions as managers, administrators, lawyers, and the like—decision-making from which women had long been excluded. Why was it that the most influential authors on morality and moral development (such as Kant, Freud, Piaget, Rawls, and Kohlberg) could not perceive women's moral decisions as exemplifying the highest categories of moral thought? Similarly, MacKinnon identified how what counted as rape and what counted as objectivity had a distressingly close fit with only men's conceptions of such matters—conceptions that reasonably arose from their distinctive kinds of social experiences with women and in courts of law.[12]

Natural and social science disciplines lacked both the will and effective mechanisms to examine critically how their own conceptual frameworks served hierarchical power relations in the larger society. Traditional philosophy of science held that the "context of discovery" should be left free of methodological controls. Yet this stance blocked from critical scrutiny a major route for the entrance of social values and interests into parts of the research process that were thus relatively immune to the kinds of controls of which even the most rigorous of scientific methods were capable. Scientific method could come into play only in the "context of justification," after researchers (and their funders) had selected the social or natural phenomena to be examined, what they identified as problematic about them, the hypotheses and concepts they favored to examine such problems, and had designed a research process. It was only in the research design that the methods of research were specified; obviously these could not exercise any control over the processes that led up to their very designation.[13]

In starting off inquiry from women's lives, feminist research projects appeared to violate the norms of good research in the disciplines in several ways. They failed to respect the autonomy of the "context of discovery" from methodological controls. They were importing into research feminist political agendas. Since most of these researchers were women, they thereby failed to respect the importance of impartiality, separation, distance in the researcher's relation to the researched. Moreover, they proposed something that appeared outrageous to conventional philosophies of science, namely that the purportedly culturally-neutral conceptual frameworks of research disciplines, including standards for objectivity and good method, were not in fact culturally neutral. Yet it was hard to deny that substantive feminist research in the social sciences and biology that did start off from women's lives often produced empirically more accurate and theoretically more comprehensive accounts of nature and social life. Indeed, the achievements of such substantive research tended to be systematically ignored by critics of standpoint epistemology and philosophy of science. Appreciation of a standpoint approach as methodology provide another kind of evidence for its value as an epistemology and philosophy of science.

How was this kind of apparently illicit feminist research practice to be understood? The abandoned standpoint epistemology seemed to provide resources that traditional epistemologies lacked for responding thoughtfully to such a question. Several central themes in the standpoint accounts provide a fuller picture of such resources.[14]

First, how societies are structured has epistemological consequences. Knowledge and power are internally linked; they co-constitute and co-maintain each other. What people do—what kinds of interactions they have in social relations and relations to the natural world—both enables and limits what they can know.[15] Yet what people typically can "do" depends in part upon their locations in social structures—whether or not they are assigned the work of taking care of children, and of people's bodies and the spaces they inhabit, or of administering large agencies, corporations, or research institutes. Material life both enables and limits what people can come to know about themselves and the worlds around them. So the social structures of societies provide a kind of laboratory within which we can explore how different kinds of assigned or chosen activities enable some insights and block others.

Second, when material life is hierarchically organized, as in societies structured by class, gender, race, ethnic, religious, or other forms of oppression and discrimination, the understandings of such hierarchical relations that are available to "rulers" and "ruled" will tend to be diametrically opposed in certain respects, and the understandings available to the dominant group tend to be perverse (Hartsock 287). The slave-owner can see his slaves' actions only as (unwilled) "behavior" caused by slaves' inferior nature or obedience to the master's will: he commands and they obey. Slaves don't appear to be fully human to their masters. However, following around the slaves in their everyday life, one could see their purportedly natural laziness as the only kind of political protest they reasonably think that they can get away with, or their smiling at the master as a subterfuge to obscure that they are secretly planning to run away or perhaps even to kill him. One can see them struggling to make their own human history in conditions not of their choosing. Similarly, the women's movement of the 1970s revealed how women's work was both socially necessary and exploited labor, not just an expression of their natural inclinations or only a "labor of love," as men and public institutions saw it. Feminists revealed many more inversions, perverse understandings, of social relations in the conceptual frameworks of dominant institutions. To take another example, women never "asked for" or "deserved" rape or physical violence, contrary to the view of their abusers and the legal system; rather "the state is male" in its insistence on regarding as objective and rational a perception of violence against women that could look reasonable only from the perspective of men's position in hierarchical gender structures (MacKinnon 1982).

Thus, third, the oppressors' false and perverse perceptions are nevertheless made "real" and operative, for all are forced to live in social structures and institutions designed to serve the oppressors' understandings of self and society. These hierarchical structures and institutions engage in conceptual practices, in ideologies, that solidify and disseminate as natural, inevitable, and desirable their continued power. Social and natural sciences play an important role in developing and maintaining such ideologies, involuntarily or not.[16]

Fourth, consequently, it takes both science and politics to see the world "behind," "beneath," or "from outside" the oppressors' institutionalized vision.[17] Thus a standpoint is an achievement, not an ascription. It must be struggled for against the apparent realities made "natural" and "obvious" by dominant institutions, and against the ongoing political disempowerment of oppressed groups. Dominant groups do not want revealed either the falsity or the unjust political consequences of their material and conceptual practices. They usually do not know that their assumptions are false (that slaves are fully human, that men are not the only model of the ideal human), and do not want to confront the claim that unjust political conditions are the consequence of their views. It takes "strong objectivity" methods to locate the practices of power that appear only in the apparently abstract, value-neutral conceptual frameworks favored by dominant social institutions and the disciplines that service them (Harding 1992, 1998). Importantly, the standpoint claim is that these political struggles that are necessary to reveal such institutional and disciplinary practices are themselves systematically knowledge producing.[18]

Thus such liberatory research "starts off" from the everyday lives of oppressed groups, rather than from the conceptual frameworks of the dominant social institutions and the disciplines that provide them with the resources they need for administration and management of the oppressed. However, such research doesn't stop there, in the lives of oppressed groups, as do conventional hermeneutic and ethnographic approaches. Rather it "studies up" to identify the "conceptual practices of power," in the words of Dorothy Smith (1990a). Standpoint theory is part of post-Marxian critical theories that regard ideology critique as crucial to the growth of knowledge and to liberation. The causes of the conditions of the lives of the oppressed cannot be detected by only observing those lives. Instead, one must critically examine how the Supreme Court, Pentagon, transnational corporations, and welfare, health, and educational systems "think" in order to understand why women, racial minorities, and the poor in the United States have only the limited life choices that are available to them. Because the maintenance and legitimacy of these institutions depend on the services of research disciplines, one must critically examine the conceptual frameworks of sociology, economics, and other social (and natural) sciences to understand the thinking of dominant institutions.

Fifth, the achievement of a standpoint brings the possibility of liberation.[19] An oppressed group must become a group "for itself," not just "in itself" in order for it to see the importance of engaging in political and scientific struggles to see the world from the perspective of its own lives. Women have always been an identifiable category for social thought—an object conceptualized from outside the group. But it took women's movements for women to recognize their shared interests and transform themselves into groups "for women"—defining themselves, their lives, their needs and desires for themselves. They learned together to recognize that it was not just "their man" (father, husband, boss) who was mean or misbehaving; rather cultural meanings and institutional practices encouraged and legitimated men's treatment of women in such ways at home, in workplaces, and in public life. Women's movements created a group consciousness in those that participated in them (and many who only watched) that enabled feminist struggles and then further feminist perceptions. Similarly, it took civil rights struggles and Black nationalist movements of the 1960s to mobilize African Americans into collective political actions that could, it was hoped, end racial inequities. The Chicano/a movement developed to mobilize Mexican Americans to a group consciousness capable of advancing an end to the injustices visited upon them. The Lesbian and Gay Pride movement had a similar goal and effect. New group consciousnesses were created through these processes, consciousnesses that could produce new understandings of social relations, past and present.

It should be noted that while standpoint theorists were originally concerned to distance their projects from positivist ones, they have recently had to articulate their distance also from relativist excesses of postmodernisms or poststructuralisms and of some ethnographic and cultural studies approaches to research. Early articulations of standpoint approaches, from Marx through feminist writings of the 1970s and early 1980s, retained without critical examination problematic Enlightenment concepts and goals that have for the most part now been jettisoned or revised by the original feminist standpoint theorists and by later thinkers. Thus, some standpoint theorists explicitly have brought poststructuralist insights to bear on scientific epistemologies.[20] Others de facto do so. After all, Marxism provides a powerful theory of how knowledge is socially situated; this insight was not invented only recently. Rather than completely reject the Enlightenment legacy, one can find in these writings, as well as in the work of others working in postcolonial and science studies especially, new and often stronger standards for and recodings of objectivity, rationality, good method, "real science" and other such central notions for philosophies of the natural and social sciences.[21]

It is not difficult to see how these themes embed methodological prescriptions that violate the conventional norms of good research and its "objectivism". Such prescriptions thus bring into even sharper focus important breaks between standard epistemologies and philosophies of science, including self-proclaimed postpositivist ones, and those of standpoint theory. Standpoint theory provides both epistemological and philosophy of natural and social science insights and methodological directives.[22]

Moreover, three sources of criticism of standpoint approaches as epistemologies and philosophies of science are more easily countered if one looks at the recommended research practices of standpoint approaches. As indicated in the opening section, these are the charges that standpoint theories either embrace or inevitably commit essentialism, relativism, and the assumption of automatic epistemic privilege for the understandings of oppressed groups. While such charges have repeatedly been countered by standpoint theorists, their persistence is likely since the successful avoidance of such positions, without the crutch of positivist assumptions, deeply threatens prevailing epistemic and philosophic assumptions, even among those who otherwise distance themselves from positivist excesses.[23] Perhaps approaching such anxieties from the perspective of standpoint-recommended research practices can give courage to a least a few skeptics of standpoint possibilities.

2. *A Philosophy of Method.* Let us enter this topic by way of criticisms of the colonial structure of the conventional model of good social research (Blauner and Wellman 1973, L.T. Smith 1999, Wolf 1996). Feminists are certainly not the only critics to argue that the conventionally-recommended relation between the researcher and the researched is intrinsically politically unequal, even a "colonial" relation. Conventionally it is the researcher, influenced by the assumptions of her discipline and her culture—not to mention of her potential funders—who decides on what social conditions, peoples, events or processes the research project will focus, how it will be organized, conducted, interpreted, and, to a large extent, disseminated. She decides which social situations to study, what is problematic about them, which hypothesis to pursue, upon which concepts and background literatures to rely, what constitutes an appropriate research design including the choice of methods, how to interpret, sort, analyze and write up data into evidence, and how and to whom the results of research will be disseminated. Conventionally, the researched are allotted little say in this process. Through self-discipline plus rigorous attention to disciplinary methodological rules, the researcher is to secure her own disinterest, impartiality, and distance from the concerns of those she studies—control of the research process is to belong entirely to her, the researcher. If this were not the case, according to conventional thinking the project would not be sufficiently objective and scientific.

Yet emancipatory movements have two kinds of reasons to criticize this level of researchers' control of research. One is political. The researched have usually belonged to social groups already less powerful than the researchers and their sponsors. It is the behaviors of the less-powerful—workers, union activists, militaries, prisoners, students, potential consumers, women, welfare users, already economically and politically disadvantaged races and classes, plus actual or soon-to-be colonized groups—that the institutions funding social research have wanted to discover how better to manage. Yet the researched are disempowered—further disempowered in the case of already disadvantaged groups—by such research processes. Such disempowerment illuminates also reasons for the resistance dominant groups have to becoming the object of study of social scientists. "Studying up" is politically offensive to those studied.

However, the other reason is scientific: the disempowerment of the researched in the research process (as well as outside it) tends to nourish distorted accounts of their beliefs and behaviors. Left to their own devices, researchers, like the rest of us, will tend to impose on what they observe and how they interpret it the conceptual frameworks valued in their cultures and disciplines, which all too often are those valued by the already powerful groups in the larger society. Moreover, as is well-known, such a colonial situation simultaneously nourishes distorted accounts of the researchers and the social groups to which they belong and that their work services. The dominant groups' perverse understandings of themselves, too, are reinforced by research that further disempowers the groups likely to be most critical of their dominance.

This is not to imply that researchers do not seek to block such conceptual imposition; they often do so for both reasons. The history of ethnography, sociology and other disciplines shows constant attempts to control the cultural impulses of inquirers—attempts that have been successful in many respects. Nor is it to imply that all such imposed conceptual frameworks are unreliable; many are valuable since "the stranger" often can detect patterns and causes of behavior that are difficult for "the natives" to see. Rather the issue is that even the most well-intentioned researchers lack some of the resources that the researched possess—resources that can be used to critically evaluate researchers' own taken-for-granted conceptual frameworks. This is the case regardless of the relative social status of researcher and researched. However, the chances that the researchers' conceptual frameworks are unreliable increase the greater the difference in social power between the observers and the observed. So the disempowerment of already politically disadvantaged research subjects not only tends to further disempower them; it also tends to produce "bad science" (L.T. Smith 1999, Wolf 1996).

How can the kind of disempowering and distorting power of the researcher, apparently inherent in the research process, be blocked to prevent such colonialization of research? How can this be accomplished without losing the valuable "powers of the stranger"? First of all, the futility of several widely practiced strategies requires recognition. For example, it should be recognized that the social statuses that the researcher and researched bring to research processes are for the most part permanent. No amount of empathy, careful listening, or "going native," valuable as such strategies may be for various reasons, will erase the fact that the Western, white, masculine, university-educated, or international-agency-funded researcher is going to leave the research process with (for the most part) no less than the economic, political, and cultural resources with which he or she arrived. And the researched will leave with largely whatever such resources they brought to the research process. Of course research processes frequently do enlarge the vision, invite self-reflection, and in other ways contribute to ongoing personal growth in both researcher and researched. Perhaps each becomes inspired to experience more of the resources available in the other's lifeworld. Yet the fundamental economic, political, and social structural inequalities that positioned the researcher and the researched in their social relation initially will not be changed by the research process alone (Blauner and Wellman 1973).

Another inevitably unsuccessful strategy for equalizing the power between researcher and researched—a strategy that young (and, alas, not so young) researchers attempt—is for the researcher to try to disempower herself personally by "confessing" to the reader her particular social location: "I, the author, am a woman of European descent, a middle-class academic, trained as a philosopher, who has lived all her life in the U.S." Some such information can be useful to the reader, but for the researcher to stop her analysis of her social location here, with just the confession, is to leave all the work up to the reader. It is she, the reader, who must figure out just how such a location has shaped the disciplinary and other conceptual frameworks used, the questions asked, how they are pursued, and so forth. Moreover, such a strategy makes the familiar Liberal assumption that individuals are capable of voluntarily identifying all of the relevant cultural assumptions that shape their research practices; Marx, Freud, and historians have taught us how self-deluding that assumption is.

Yet another futile strategy researchers attempt, or at least think their methods courses have directed them to pursue, is to try to forego any theoretical or conceptual input into the research process itself. Researchers sometimes think the most useful procedure they can undertake is simply to "record the voices" of their subjects. Critics (and even misguided defenders) of standpoint approaches have often thought that this was the standpoint project. To be sure, there are good reasons to want to record the voices of all kinds of subjects. Moreover it is valuable to recommend that researchers try to set aside their own assumptions when approaching a research situation, whether or not it is familiar. Yet to restrict research in such ways would be to reduce the researcher to a kind of (inevitably inaccurate) transcription machine. This strategy has the effect of discarding some of the most valuable political and scientific resources of the researcher. These include precisely the often higher social status carried by the researcher that instead of enacting a colonial destiny can be deployed on behalf of the researched. It includes the expertise and resources to conceptualize and articulate social relations in, paradoxically, the kinds of disciplinary and institutional languages that can be heard by public policy-makers and the disciplines and institutions upon which they depend.

So what contributions can standpoint approaches make to blocking the inherently colonial relations of social research? And how do they raise new philosophic and scientific questions that conventional philosophies of science ignored or disallowed? The research process can be divided into four sites where such "colonial" relations between the observer and the observed can flourish. The first is the selection of the research problematic and the design of the research project": the "context of discovery." The second is the conduct of the research—the field or archive work. The third is the writing up of the research findings—the interpretation and theorization of the data. The last is the dissemination procedures, intended or not by the researcher. Standpoint methodology can be valuable in the last three parts of the process; yet it has unique value in the first stage.

Standpoint approaches innovatively recommend that the "context of discovery" be brought under methodological controls. The dominant group's values and interests perhaps powerfully shape research projects at this stage of inquiry in ways identified earlier. Yet it is only the "context of justification" that is regarded as legitimately controllable by method. The so-called "logic of scientific inquiry" does indeed begin with bold conjectures, yet the sciences have designed their methods to focus only on the process of seeking the severe refutations of primarily those hypotheses that manage to get thought up by people who can get research funded. Indeed, in fields where research is expensive, it is only such hypotheses that reach the starting line to face the trials of attempted refutation. Thus a new question arises: which are the politically and scientifically valuable and which the not-to-be-valued ways to bring the context of discovery under methodological controls? Pursuing such a question deploys a stronger kind of reflexivity: a robust attempt critically to evaluate the selection of research problems and their conceptual frameworks and methods.[24]

Second, contrary to conventional methodological prescriptions, standpoint methods are engaged. They are not dispassionate, disinterested, distanced, value-free. It takes politics as well as science to see beneath, behind, or through the institutional rules and practices that have been designed to serve primarily the already most economically and politically advantaged groups. Standpoint methods recognize that some kinds of passions, interests, values, and politics advance the growth of knowledge and that other kinds block or limit it. Politics can be productive of the growth of knowledge as well as an obstacle to it, as it often is. Here, too, a form of the first new question arises: which such political engagements promote and which limit the growth of knowledge? The hypothesis standpoint analyses make plausible is that vigorous commitments to democratic inclusiveness, fairness, and accountability to the "worst off" can also advance the growth of knowledge. Such commitments do not automatically do so, but neither should they automatically be excluded from playing a possibly productive role in research processes.

Thus such considerations require reevaluation of the conventional requirement of value-neutrality in order to maximize objectivity. The standpoint argument is that such a requirement blocks the deployment of politics that increase the inclusiveness, fairness, and accountability of research. If research is to be accountable only to disciplinary conceptual frameworks and methodological requirements that in fact often service ruling institutions but not the "ruled," more research will succeed in further entrenching such ruling conceptual frameworks and increasing the gap between the "haves" and the "have nots." The solution here is not to abandon the project of maximizing objectivity, but rather to cease to require the maximization of complete social neutrality in order to achieve it (Harding 1992a, 1998 Ch. 8).

Finally, economic, social, psychological, and cultural heterogeneity is to be exploited rather than suppressed in standpoint methods. The dominant assumptions are abstractly encoded in the conceptual frameworks of a society's institutions and research disciplines. Yet these represent only one distinctive cultural point of view, and an especially suspiciously unreliable one at that—the point of view of the ruling group. Bringing into focus accounts of nature and social relations as these emerge from the lives of many different subjugated groups creates a broader horizon of understanding of how nature and social relations work. It is not that these subjugated understandings are automatically the best ones on sound empirical and theoretical grounds, but rather that they can lead to the identification of additional problematic or just interesting natural and social phenomena, suggest different hypotheses and conceptual frameworks for investigating them, suggest different lines of evidence and challenges to favored evidence practices, uncover unnoticed cultural tendencies in the writing up of data, and make strong arguments for dissemination practices that differ from those favored by contemporary research property rights systems.

The ideal conditions for exploiting heterogeneity require genuinely democratic societies in which inequality has already disappeared and no group is or can legitimately be silenced through formal or informal means. All would be equally articulate in the selection of problems to research, the specification of what is problematic about them, the selection of a conceptual framework and methods of research and so on. Of course we do not have such a situation. My point—and the argument of standpoint theorists—is that standpoint epistemologies, philosophies of science, and methodologies can help move toward such a goal. There is no easy formula for insuring that subjugated groups will become empowered in research processes. Yet there is plenty of reflection on this topic now available (Collins 1986, McTaggart 1997, Maguire 1987, Petras and Porpora 1993, D. Smith 1987, 1990a, 1990b, 1999, L.T. Smith 1999, Wolf 1996).

I have hoped that an examination of the methodological prescriptions of standpoint theory can help to dispel widely articulated anxieties about some of the ways this philosophy of science and epistemology differs from its conventional predecessors. However, it is valuable also to focus on two facts that discourage such a hope. On the one hand, critics of standpoint approaches persist in charges of essentialism, relativism, and conferring automatic epistemological privilege on the assumptions and perceptions of the oppressed in the face of decades of argument against such positions by standpoint theorists themselves as well as by others. On the other hand, standpoint approaches continue to develop and proliferate in ever more research contexts here and around the world in the face of the persistence of such criticisms. These facts suggest that more is at stake in standpoint approaches than the direct discussions of these charges confront. Often it takes changes in social relations themselves for new ways of thinking about knowledge and its production to become widely plausible. We may just have to live through the ongoing contentiousness of standpoint theory as some sort of such changes are underway around us. Articulation of just what sort of changes these are can make a project for another time.[25]

NOTES

1. The earliest of such accounts were Dorothy Smith's, from the late 1970s and early 1980s, subsequently collected in her 1987 and 1990a. (See also her 1990b and 1999.) Shortly thereafter appeared Hartsock 1983, Rose 1983, Jaggar 1983, Collins 1986 (and 1991) and Harding 1986.

2. Some of these projects are shared with feminist science studies more generally. See Rouse's (1996) account of the way feminist science studies, in contrast to contemporary (postpositivist) sociologies of science and traditional philosophies of science, takes what Rouse calls a "post epistemological" stance toward the production of scientific knowledge.

3. All three of these attributed positions are excessive versions, or perhaps the only imaginable alternatives in the eyes of critics, of standpoint rejections of conventional positions. Thus critics assume that someone who claims that women are a political group, rather than only the individuals of Liberal political philosophy, must have an essentialist understanding of women. They suppose that if a standpoint theorist thinks that women's claims about their own or others' lives have any authority at all, standpoint theory must be giving women automatic epistemic privilege. If someone claims that women or feminists can have a distinctively different epistemic position than that held by dominant institutions, standpoint theory must be committing epistemic relativism, they say. See Hartsock (1998) and Wylie (forthcoming) for two reviews of responses to such charges.

4. Especially, but not exclusively, social science research. (See Harding 1986, 1991, 1998, Sismondo 1995, Weasel 2000 for discussions of its usefulness in the natural sciences.) As the post-Kuhnian science studies have again and again revealed, the objects of natural science scrutiny are always already objects-of-knowledge, identified and characterized by prior scientific discourses and contemporary social concerns. Hence starting off projects about nature's order from the lives of subjugated groups can reveal yet additional patterns and causal relations to those detected by pursuit of the concerns of dominant institutions. Postcolonial, multicultural, and feminist science studies have all made this point in their own ways. (See Harding 1998, Hess 1995 for overviews of postcolonial natural science issues.)

5. Hartsock 1983, Jaggar 1983, and Pels 1997 also review the Marxian history of this approach. The feminist theorists have generally avoided Lukacs' Hegelian machinery. What caused standpoint theory to languish between Lukacs' writings and the Second Wave of the U.S./European women's movement? Of course Lukacs' work was controversial within marxism from the beginning. However, U.S. marxian social scientists in the 60s, 70s and later tended to prefer the Popperian form of a positivist philosophy of science to justify their research strategies (Popper 1972). Given the prevailing political climate of McCarthyism and the Cold War, it is

understandable that researchers and philosophers distanced their work from an epistemology/methodology that wore both its political engagement and its specifically marxian origins on its sleeve, so to speak.

6. Representations of similar researcher positions appear in Anzaldua's (1981) "borderlands" consciousness, hooks' (1983) "theory from margin to center," and D. Smith's (1987) "bifurcated consciousness" of the woman sociology graduate student. W.E.B. DuBois' "double consciousness" of African Americans is one precursor of this kind of representation.

7. As Alison Wylie (forthcoming) notes.

8. Hartsock 1998, Hirschmann 1997, and Pels 1997 review some of these analogous accounts.

9. In philosophy, W.V.O. Quine's work on how scientific "networks of belief" seamlessly link everyday and scientific thought, and other aspects of his criticisms of logical positivism, directly influenced at least some standpoint theorists. (Quine 1953, Harding 1976)

10. For perspectives on different aspects of this literature see Harding 1998, Hess 1995, and Selin 1997. Figueroa and Harding (forthcoming) is part of the dissemination project of a National Science Foundation grant to the American Philosophical Association.

11. Such an analysis did not usually illuminate the lives of women domestic workers, as feminist scholars of color and standpoint theorists themselves subsequently noted. (Collins 1991)

12. Note that standpoint approaches start off from the lives of the oppressed, but that they refuse to end there. Standpoint approaches are not ethnographies. Rather they are a form of critical theory that "studies up." This point is explored further below.

13. I have discussed this problem in a number of papers on "strong objectivity." See, for example, Harding 1992, 1998 Chapter 8.

14. As indicated earlier, such theories were developed within a number of different disciplines with diverse histories and preoccupations, and by theorists with commitments of varying strength to Marxian and to Enlightenment projects. Consequently, it is risky to try to summarize this approach in any way that attributes to it a unified set of claims. Nevertheless, theorists from these different disciplines do share important assumptions and projects that differ from conventional understandings of what makes good science, including, I propose, the following. (I articulate them in a form which stays close to Hartsock's account [1983].) Of course not every theorist equally prioritizes or emphasizes each of these, since what is perceived to be important in the context of sociology may be less important to political philosophers or philosphers of science and vice versa. Nor are disciplinary concerns, themselves heterogeneous, the only ones that lead to divergence in how standpoint approaches have been developed.

15. Note that this theme echoes standard beliefs about the effectiveness of scientific methods: which interactions with, or kinds of observations of, natural and social worlds are pursued both enables and limits what one can know.

16. I use the term "ideology" here to mean systems of false interested beliefs, not just of any interested beliefs.

17. Of course one's understanding can never completely escape its historical moment—that was the positivist dream that standpoint approaches deny. All understanding is socially located or situated. The success of standpoint research requires only a degree of freedom from the dominant understanding, not complete

freedom from it. It is the structural position of the oppressed that provides the possibility of often small but nevertheless important degrees of freedom from prevailing discourses, including institutions, their practices and cultures.

18. A motto of the early days of the women's movements of the 1970's said, "The degree of his resistance is the measure of your oppression." If this point is lost, and even some standpoint defenders sometimes lose it, "standpoint" seems like just another term for a perspective or viewpoint. Yet the standpoint claim about the epistemic value of some kinds of political struggle—the epistemic value of the engagement of the researcher—is thereby made obscure when its technical use, which I retain here, is abandoned. This point is related to the disagreement over whether the theory is best articulated as about a feminist or a women's standpoint. Hartsock has opted for the former, and D. Smith for the latter for reasons which I suspect have to do with concerns about their respective disciplines—a topic for another place.

19. I shall refer to standpoint approaches as inherently progressive since that is the way they have been understood today through the marxian legacy inherited by leading movements for social justice. Yet it is useful to recall that Nazi ideology also (ambivalently) opposed modern science on standpoint grounds and, indeed, conceptualized its murderous program as one of advancing social justice. See Pels 1997. Religious fundamentalist, geographically-based ethnic, and patriot or neo-Nazi social movements usually are not reasonably characterized as dominant groups. Nevertheless, they too are threatened by modernity's political values and interests. They often make something close to politically-regressive standpoint arguments. So theories about which kinds of social movements are liberatory, and for whom, must be articulated to justify research projects in the natural and social sciences. See Castells 1997 for interesting discussion of the different political potentialities of various identity-based social movements around the world today, and his 2000 for an overview of the project within which this discussion is set. See also Harding (forthcoming a) for a discussion of epistemological issues in such a context.

Of course there is nothing new about natural and social science research *assuming* such political theories; conventional philosophies of natural and social science always assumed—consciously or not—Liberal political philosophies and their understandings of relations between knowledge, politics, and social emancipation. Sciences and their philosophies are always at least partially integrated into their larger economic, political, social formation, to put Kuhn's point another way. Thus it is not standpoint theory that introduces the conjunction of social theory and epistemology, let alone their "integrity" with actual historical features of a society.

20. This is true of Haraway 1991 and Harding 1991, 1998. Garcia Selgas (forthcoming) discusses standpoint theory's resources for resolving problems that postmodernist insights create for critical theory. See also Hirschmann 1997.

21. For a sampling of such epistemological recodings, see Galison and Stump 1996, Haraway 1991, Harding 1991, 1998, Forthcoming, Hess 1995, Jaggar 1989, Latour 1988, Rouse 1987, Schuster and Yeo 1986, Selin 1997, Shapin 1994, Shapin and Shaffer 1985, D. Smith 1987, 1990a, 1990b, 1998.

22. As Joe Rouse (1996) pointed out, this is one of the places where feminist science studies parts ways with post-Kuhnian sociology of science. The sociologists, like conventional philosophers of science, left up to scientists final authority about what should count as "good method" and good results of research. Standpoint and other feminist (and other social movement) approaches do not.

23. For example, see Harding's 1992b, Hartsock's 1998, and Wylie's (forthcoming) review of such responses by standpoint theorists.

24. Of course research proposals face peer review. But the problem standpoint approaches address is the common situation in which the entire "peer group" shares the widespread ethnocentric assumptions that the proposed researchers also make: assumptions that are androcentric, Eurocentric, white supremacist, class based, heterosexist, etc.

25. I thank Stephen Turner and Alison Wylie for helpful comments on an earlier draft of this essay.

BIBLIOGRAPHY

Anzaldua, Gloria. 1981. *Borderlands/La Frontera*. San Francisco: Spinsters/Aunt Lute.

Blauner, Robert, and David Wellman. 1973. Toward the decolonization of social research, pp. 310–330 in *The Death of White Sociology*, ed. Joyce A. Ladner. New York: Random House.

Campbell, Marie, and Ann Manicom, eds. 1995. *Knowledge, experience, and ruling relations: Studies in the social organization of knowledge*. Toronto: University of Toronto Press.

Castells, Manuel. 1997. The power of identity. *The Information Age: Economy, Society & Culture*, Vol. 2. Oxford: Blackwell.

____. 2000. Materials for an exploratory theory of the network society. *British Journal of Sociology* 51(1): 5–24.

Collins, Patricia Hill. 1986. Learning from the outsider within: The sociological significance of black feminist thought. *Social Problems* 33 (6): S14–S32.

____. 1991. *Black feminist thought: Knowledge, consciousness, and the politics of empowerment*. New York: Routledge.

Figueroa, Robert, and Sandra Harding, eds. Forthcoming. *How does diversity matter to philosophy of science?* New York: Routledge.

Freire, Paulo. 1970. *Pedagogy of the oppressed*. New York: Herder & Herder.

Galison, Peter, and David J. Stump, eds. 1996. *The disunity of science*. Stanford: Stanford University Press.

Garcia Selgas, Fernando J. Forthcoming. Feminist epistemologies for critical social theory: From standpoint theory to situated knowledge. *The Standpoint Reader*, ed. Sandra Harding.

Gilligan, Carol. 1982. *In a different voice: Psychological theory and women's development*. Cambridge, Mass.: Harvard University Press.

Gross, Paul R., and Norman Levitt. 1994. *Higher superstition: The academic left and its quarrels with science*. Batimore: Johns Hopkins University Press.

Haraway, Donna. 1981. In the beginning was the word: The genesis of biological theory. *Signs* 6:3.

____.1991. Situated knowledges: The science question in feminism and the privilege of partial perspectives. *Simians, Cyborgs, and Women*. New York: Routledge.

Harding, Sandra. 1986. *The science question in feminism*. Ithaca, N.Y.: Cornell University Press.

____. 1991. *Whose science? Whose knowledge? Thinking from women's lives*. Ithaca, N.Y.: Cornell University Press.

____. 1992a. After the neutrality ideal: Politics, science, and "strong objectivity". In *The Politics of Western Science: 1640–1990*, ed. Margaret Jacob. Atlantic Highlands: Humanities Press.

_____. 1992b. Rethinking standpoint epistemology. In *Feminist Epistemologies*, ed. L. Alcoff and E. Potter. New York: Routledge.

_____. 1998. *Is science multicultural? Postcolonialisms, feminisms, and epistemologies.* Bloomington, Ind.: Indiana University Press.

_____. Forthcoming a. Identity and social transformation in the net society: Epistemological resources. In *The Future of Minority Studies: Redefining Identity Politics*, ed. Linda Alcoff, Satya P. Mohanty, Paula Moya, and Michael Hames-Garcia.

_____, ed. Forthcoming b. *The standpoint reader.*

Hartsock, Nancy. 1983. The feminist standpoint: Developing the ground for a specifically feminist historical materialism. In *Discovering Reality*, ed. Sandra Harding and Merrill Hintikka. Dordrecht: Reidel/Kluwer.

_____. 1998. The feminist standpoint revisited. In *The Feminist Standpoint Revisited and Other Essays*. Boulder, Colorado: Westview Press.

Hekman, Susan. 1997. Truth and method: Feminist standpoint theory revisited. *Signs: Journal of Women in Culture and Society* 22 (2): 341–65. See also: responses in the same issue by Patricia Hill Collins, Sandra Harding, Nancy Hartsock, and Dorothy Smith, and Hekman's reply, pp. 367–402.

Hess, David J. 1995. *Science and technology in a multicultural world: The cultural politics of facts and artifacts.* New York: Columbia University Press.

Hirschmann, Nancy. 1997. Feminist standpoint as postmodern strategy. In *Politics and Feminist Standpoint Theories*, ed. Sally J. Kenney and Helen Kinsella. New York: The Haworth Press, Inc.

hooks, bell. 1983. *Feminist theory: From margin to center.* Boston: South End Press.

Jaggar, Alison. 1983. Chapter 11. *Feminist Politics and Human Nature.* Totowa, N.J.: Rowman and Allenheld.

_____. 1989. Love and knowledge: Emotion in feminist epistemology. In *Gender/Body/Knowledge; Feminist Reconstructions of Being and Knowing*, ed. Alison Jaggar and Susan Bordo. New Brunswick: Rutgers University Press.

Jameson, Frederic. 1988. "History and class consciousness" as an unfinished project. *Rethinking Marxism* 1: 49–72.

Kenney, Sally J., and Helen Kinsella, eds. 1997. *Politics and feminist standpoint theories*, The Haworth Press, Inc. Published simultaneously as a special issue of *Women and Politics* 18 (3).

Kuhn, Thomas S. (1962) 1970. *The structure of scientific revolutions*, 2nd ed. Chicago: University of Chicago Press.

Latour, Bruno. 1988. *The pasteurization of France.* Cambridge: Harvard University Press.

Lukacs, Georg. (1923) 1971. *History and class consciousness*, trans. Rodney Livingstone. Cambridge: MIT Press.

MacKinnon, 1982–83. Feminism, Marxism, method, and the state. Parts I and II in *Signs: Journal of Women in Culture and Society* 7 (3): 515–44; 8 (4).

McTaggart, Robin, ed. 1997. *Participatory action research: International contexts and consequences.* Albany, N.Y.: State University of New York Press.

Maguire, Patricia. 1987. *Doing participatory research: A feminist approach.* Amherst, Mass.: The Center for International Education, University of Massachusetts.

Mannheim, Karl. (1936) 1954. *Ideology and utopia: An introduction to the sociology of knowledge.* New York: Harcourt, Brace & Co.

Merton, Robert. 1972. Insiders and outsiders: A chapter in the sociology of knowledge. *American Journal of Sociology* 78 (1): 9–47.

Pels, Dick. 1997. Strange standpoints. *Telos.*

Petras, E.M., and D.V. Porpora. 1993. Participatory research: Three models and an analysis. *The American Sociologist* 23 (1): 107–26.

Popper, Karl. 1972. *Conjectures and refutations: The Growth of scientific knowledge.* 4th ed. rev. London: Routledge and Kegan Paul.

Quine, W.V.O. 1953. Two dogmas of empiricism. In his *From a Logical Point of View.* Cambridge: Harvard University Press.

Rose, Hilary. 1983. Hand, brain, and heart: A feminist epistemolgy for the natural sciences. *Signs: Journal of Women in Culture and Society* 9 (1).

Ross, Andrew, ed. 1996. *Science wars.* Durham, N.C.: Duke University Press.

Rouse, Joseph. 1987. *Knowledge and power: Toward a political philosophy of science.* Ithaca, N.Y.: Cornell University Press.

____. 1996. Feminism and the social construction of scientific knowledge. In *Feminism, Science, and The Philosophy of Science,* ed. Lynn Hankinson Nelson and Jack Nelson. Dordrecht: Kluwer Academic Publishers.

Schuster, John A., and Richard R. Yeo, eds. 1986. *The politics and rhetoric of scientific method: Historical studies.* Dordrecht: Reidel.

Selin, Helaine, ed. 1997. *Encyclopedia of the history of science, technology, and medicine in non-western cultures.* Dordrecht: Kluwer.

Shapin, Steven 1994. *A social history of truth.* Chicago: University of Chicago Press.

Shapin, Steven, and Simon Shaffer. 1985. *Leviathan and the air pump.* Princeton: Princeton University Press.

Sismondo, Sergio. 1995. The scientific domains of feminist standpoints. *Perspectives on Science* 3 (1): 49–65.

Simmel, Georg. 1921. The sociological significance of the "Stranger". In *Introduction to the Science of Sociology,* ed. Robert E. Park and Ernest W. Burgess. Chicago: University of Chicago Press.

Smith, Dorothy E. 1987. *The everyday world as problematic: A sociology for women.* Boston: Northwestern University Press.

____. 1990a. *The conceptual practices of power: A feminist sociology of knowledge.* Boston: Northeastern University Press.

____. 1990b. *Texts, facts, and femininity: Exploring the relations of ruling.* New York: Routledge.

____. 1999. *Writing the social: Critique, theory, and investigations.* Toronto: University of Toronto Press.

Smith, Linda Tuhiwahi. 1999. *Decolonizing methodologies: Research and indigenous peoples.* Atlantic Highlands: Zed Press.

Sohn-Rethel, Alfred. 1978. *Intellectual and manual labor.* London: Macmillan.

Walby, Sylvia. 2001. Against epistemological chasms: The science question in feminism revisited. *Signs: Journal of Women in Culture and Society* 26 (2): 485–510. See also: responses in the same issue by Joey Sprague and Sandra Harding, and Walby's reply, pp. 511–540.

Weasel, Lisa. 2000. Laboratories without walls: The science shop as a model for feminist community science in action. In *Feminist Science Studies,* ed. Maralee Mayberry, Banu Subramaniam, and Lisa Weasel. New York: Routledge.

Wolf, Diane L., ed. *Feminist dilemmas in fieldwork.* Boulder, Colorado: Westview Press.

Wylie, Alison. Forthcoming. Why standpoint matters. In *How Diversity Matters to Philosophy of Science.*

CHAPTER 4

The Blending of Qualitative and Quantitative Methods in Understanding Childbearing among Welfare Recipients

MARK R. RANK

Perhaps the place to begin is with a personal story. Some time ago I was revising a manuscript on families receiving welfare. The article combined qualitative and quantitative data. One reviewer had been positive about the blending of methods. The other suggested eliminating the qualitative material altogether. While I was attempting to resolve these differences, a colleague of mine stopped by, and I quickly sought his advice to the problem. His solution was simple—write two different papers. One paper could present the qualitative data, the other the quantitative data. I tried to explain how one of the main contributions of my work, as I saw it, was bringing several methods to bear in the same analysis. I argued for the insights to be gained, the greater validity of the findings, and so on. My arguments were to no avail. With a shrug, he wished me good luck and said I would need it for the reviewers who lay ahead.

This chapter expands upon the arguments presented to my colleague that summer afternoon. The purpose is to demonstrate the use of a multiple method approach to address family research questions—specifically the blending of qualitative with quantitative data. My research on families receiving welfare is used to demonstrate the processes and types of analysis that can result from applying this technique to family research questions. The arguments and examples in this chapter are an extension and illustration of more general work advocating triangulation in constructing research designs (e.g., Brewer & Hunter, 1989; Bryman, 1988a; Denzin, 1978). The arguments are applied here, however, to family researchers interested in combining qualitative and quantitative approaches.

A scanning of family journals and books reveals an exceedingly low number of studies relying on both qualitative and quantitative data. Yet, such an approach has the potential for improvements in the construction, execution, and analysis of family research designs. Interestingly, a number of early studies dealing with family issues combined qualitative and quantitative data in their research designs and analyses. As Cavan (1983) and LaRossa and Wolfe (1985) noted, much of the family research that came out of the University of Chicago during the 1920s and 1930s employed both quantitative and qualitative data analyses. The work of Burgess, Cavan, Frazier, and others were reflective of this. There was a concern with "how qualitative methods and quantitative methods could complement each other" (LaRossa & Wolf, 1985, p. 534). Likewise, the Lynds' (1929, 1937) Middletown studies were characterized by a blending of methodologies: Surveys, interviews, and ethnographic data were used in conjunction with each other to portray a picture of life in Middletown and its families.

Beginning in the later 1930s, family researchers increasingly, turned to the survey as their method of choice (e.g., Burgess & Cottrell, 1939; Terman, 1938). Although survey research had been used prior to this time, it quickly became the dominant and sole method for many family researchers. This trend characterized not only family research, but the social sciences as a whole (Kalton, 1983). With a greater use of survey methods, data analysis began to rely heavily upon quantitative and statistical techniques. Reviews of family research methods note that the past 30 years have seen a trend toward greater quantification and more elaborate statistical methods (Galligan, 1982; Hodgson & Lewis, 1979; Miller, 1986; Nye, 1988). Both LaRossa and Wolfe (1985) and Nye (1988) documented that most articles published by family researchers became exclusively quantitative. Certainly, qualitative family studies were conducted during this time as well (e.g., Komarovsky, 1962; LeMasters, 1975; Ostrander, 1984; Stack, 1974). Yet these studies constituted a small percentage of the total research output. Research projects employing both qualitative and quantitative data were rarer still.

What might account for the avoidance of combining qualitative and quantitative data in family research over the past 30 years? First, some, like Filstead (1979) and Rist (1977), argue that quantitative and qualitative research are based upon fundamentally incompatible epistemological positions. Thus, many researchers view them as mutually exclusive research models (Bryman 1988a). Second, the tendency to follow the natural scientific paradigm often precludes the use of qualitative methods for anything other than exploratory research (Miller, 1986). Third, cost may be an obstacle. Bringing several methods to bear upon a specific issue can be expensive (Bryman 1988b). A fourth potential obstacle is the perceived difficulty in publishing such research. Researchers may feel they are leaving themselves open to unnecessary criticisms from reviewers who take either a quantitative or qualitative approach. Finally, the training of family researchers has been heavily weighted towards quantitative methods. Such training may result in a reluctance to combine various methodologies (Reiss, 1968).

Although these obstacles are real, there are significant advantages for family researchers in integrating qualitative and quantitative methods into their research designs. To illustrate this, I first will describe a research project blending qualitative and quantitative data. Next, I will discuss several specific findings of this study to illustrate the types of analysis possible from blending qualitative and quantitative data. Finally, I will examine at length the advantages of executing such a design and analysis.

STUDY DESIGN

Various research designs could be constructed for integrating qualitative and quantitative data. Elsewhere I have discussed the techniques of embedding in-depth interviews within random sample surveys, adding survey research to fieldwork, and using targeted small-scale research with available records (Rank 1988a). In this chapter, I describe a study of families receiving public assistance in which both qualitative and quantitative data were gathered. I used three separate yet complementary sources of data in this project. All three sources deal with a similar population. The emphases in each data set, however, clearly differ. The quantitative analysis of case record data was longitudinal and designed for statistical modeling of various events, with in-depth interviews and fieldwork providing greater insight into these and other events. Each is described below.

Data Gathering from Case Records

In 1980, administration of the Aid to Families With Dependent Children (AFDC), Food Stamp, and Medicaid programs in the state of Wisconsin was computerized. Those applying for one or more of the three programs are required to fill out a combined application form. The information is entered into a mainframe computer, stored, and updated with periodic reviews.

As the universe of welfare recipients is contained in this data base, it was relatively easy and inexpensive to draw a large, random sample of households on public assistance. I drew a 2% random sample of all cases that were participating in one or more of these three welfare programs as of September 1980. This resulted in a sample of 2,796 households. There was no refusal rate, as case records rather than actual individuals were sampled.

The cases were then followed at 6-month intervals for 3 years, through September 1983. The variables available in these files were primarily economic and demographic, including information on heads of household as well as all other household members. In addition, as family, economic, and welfare status changes occurred, such information was updated in the case records, allowing for a detailed analysis of specific events occurring to families while on welfare. Such events included length of welfare recipiency, changes in household structure, and shifts in employment status.

In-Depth Qualitative Interviews

During June and July 1986, I gathered qualitative data through in-depth interviews of welfare recipients. In drawing this sample, I used procedures similar to those used in drawing the longitudinal case record sample. The sample was stratified by household type and welfare eligibility status. Of interest were families both on and recently off welfare. Because the interviews were face to face, it was impractical to take a random sample of the entire state, given the cost and time constraints involved. I chose a representative county with characteristics reflecting the overall state population on such factors as urban and rural areas, occupational diversity, race, and socioeconomics.

The response rate was 76%. This represents the number of interviews conducted, divided by all households we attempted to locate, whether contact was made or not. For those we were able to contact, the refusal rate was 5%. Individuals without telephones were tracked down. We conducted several interviews in Spanish with the aid of an interpreter. In short, I used a variety of ways to contact potential subjects. Participating respondents were paid $15.

A research assistant and I interviewed 50 families along with five families in the pretest. By design, the demographic composition of the sample approximately mirrored that of the longitudinal data set. We conducted the interviews in respondents' homes. Length of interviews was between 1-$\frac{1}{2}$ and 3 hours. All interviews were tape-recorded. For female-headed families and single welfare recipients, the heads of households were interviewed. For married couples, we attempted to interview both the husband and wife together. In several cases, however, we were only able to interview the wife.

At the outset of each interview, we informed respondents there were no right or wrong answers to the questions being asked. Our concern was in understanding their honest appraisals of their feelings, experiences, and behaviors. In addition, we stated that our affiliation was university based, and that we were not a part of the welfare system or administration. We also stated verbally and in writing that all responses would be confidential.

Most respondents appeared open and frank about their feelings and behaviors. For example, respondents would often volunteer information about sensitive subjects (e.g., incest, violence in the family, painful childhoods). They often expressed genuine emotion. Overall, rapport between interviewers and interviewees was excellent. This was assessed in two ways. First, after each interview, my assistant and I recorded our evaluations of the rapport during the interview. Second, I also assessed rapport by listening to each interview several times.

The interviews were open ended and semistructured around such major topics as attitudes regarding welfare, family dynamics (such as marriage, divorce, pregnancy, and raising children), employment, and the experience of getting on and off public assistance. Based on my prior research and knowledge of the field, the interview schedule was constructed to cover what I felt were the most critical areas in understanding a family's situation of being on public assistance. As a reliability check on the answers given during the interviews, information from respondents' case records, which the state had made available to me, was compared to information given during the interviews. The match was high, thus lending confidence in the interview data.

In addition to the interviews, I kept notes describing the settings in which the interviews took place, the recipient's dwelling, the surrounding neighborhoods, the rapport during the interview, the physical appearance of the recipient, and any other information that might provide greater understanding of respondents' situations. Photographs were taken of recipients who gave their consent. The interviews were transcribed verbatim into files on a mainframe computing system. Each transcript was triple checked with the original tape for accuracy.

Fieldwork

A third source of data was through fieldwork in which I explored observable aspects of welfare systems. The fieldwork took place between 1986 and 1988. It occurred almost entirely in the same county as the in-depth qualitative interviews. I took extensive field notes, which served as a third source of data. I observed several aspects of the welfare system, beginning with visiting various social service offices and sitting in on the process of applying for public assistance. Offices were located in both urban and rural locations and served a wide range of individuals and families. I then attended several job-training programs that were mandatory for welfare recipients. The programs were designed to increase the likelihood of locating and landing employment. I also observed the daily routines and activities in low-income housing projects and neighborhoods and a wide variety of food pantries. Toward the end of the month, welfare recipients often rely on emergency food from food pantries.

I relied on other sources of data as well. Throughout the fieldwork, I spoke with dozens of individuals associated with the welfare system. These included both welfare recipients and those dealing directly with welfare recipients, such as case workers, state employees, and volunteers. To keep a visual record of various aspects of welfare systems, I also took photographs.

CHILDBEARING DYNAMICS AMONG WELFARE RECIPIENTS

The issue of family dynamics among welfare recipients has been debated long and hard among policymakers. Within these debates is an underlying fear that welfare contributes to the breakdown of families and, more specifically, encourages families to become dependent upon public assistance, women to have more children, and marriages to dissolve (Gilder, 1981; Murray, 1984; Working Group on the Family, 1986). I have addressed these issues in a number of studies, examining patterns of welfare recipiency by household structure (Rank, 1985, 1986), probabilities of marriage and dissolution (Rank, 1987), and differences in exiting from welfare for black and white female-headed families (Rank, 1988b).

The Fertility of Women on Welfare

The fertility among women on welfare has been the subject of controversy for many years. How often do women receiving welfare give birth? Is their fertility rate higher or lower than that of the general population? What factors are related to childbearing for women on welfare? Although such questions have been frequently asked, no single study has provided a satisfactory answer. As a result, I became interested in exploring these issues. (See Rank, 1989.) The analysis described here illustrates how qualitative and quantitative data can be brought to bear upon such questions. The analysis also demonstrates how the research process moves between qualitative and quantitative data. As described below, I began with qualitative insights from the fieldwork, shifted to a quantitative analysis of the caseload sample, and then returned to qualitative interviews for further investigation.

Preliminary Insights through Fieldwork

Fieldwork began the research process. The interviews I conducted with persons working in the welfare system provided opportunities to begin an examination of fertility and welfare. Through informal discussions, I was able to explore the perceptions of those in daily contact with welfare recipients as well as with recipients themselves. During these discussions, I began to view critically the stereotype of women on welfare bearing more children to get larger public assistance payments. That is, although caseworkers and recipients could point to individual examples fitting such a stereotype, they believed most women on welfare did not wish to have more children but rather wanted to get off public assistance. These observations provided me with preliminary insights that pushed me to delve further. I wondered whether these perceptions reflected the reality of the situation or perhaps something else. If they were correct assessments, why did the stereotype not hold up?

Incidence and Rates

As a result of the fieldwork, I decided to address several questions using the longitudinal quantitative data. Among these questions were, first: What was the likelihood of childbearing among women on welfare? And, second: How did these rates compare with those of the general population?

THE LIKELIHOOD OF CHILDBEARING.   Table 4.1 presents a life table analysis of childbearing among women on welfare aged 18 to 44. The life table allows us to calculate the proportion of women giving birth during a specified period of time.[1] The table lists the six observed half-year intervals during which women could enter into the analysis. The 0–6 month Interval represents September 1980 to March 1981, the 6–12 month interval represents March 1981 to September 1981, and so on. Column 1 shows the number of women of childbearing age. I allowed women who had not been on welfare for 9 months prior to September 1980 to enter the analysis during the 6–12 or 12–18 month intervals. Column 2 presents the number of births occurring during intervals. Column 3 shows the proportion of births among women (Column 2 divided by Column 1), and Column 4 represents the cumulative proportion of births that occur across intervals.

**TABLE 4.1 Life Table Analysis of Births Among Women
Aged 18–44 on Welfare**

Monthly Interval	Number at Risk	Number of Births	Proportion of Births	Cumulative Proportion of Births
0–6	795	15	.0189	.0189
6–12	950	26	.0274	.0458
12–18	910	22	.0242	.0689
18–24	717	12	.0167	.0844
24–30	624	13	.0208	.1035
30–36	553	7	.0127	.1149

During the first observed 6-month interval, 1.89% of women on welfare gave birth (Column 3). During the 6- to 12-month interval, 2.74% gave birth. The percentage giving birth during any 6-month interval is relatively stable at approximately 2%. In Column 4, it is estimated that 4.58% of women will give birth during a 1-year interval. The overall fertility rate for women on welfare, therefore, is 45.8 per 1,000 women on welfare. In addition, 11.49% of women will bear children during a 3-year period on welfare.[2]

COMPARISONS WITH THE GENERAL POPULATION.   How do these estimates compare with the overall population? One-year fertility rates among women on welfare occurred from 1980 to 1981. Based on data from the Wisconsin Department of Health and Social Services (1981) and the U.S. Bureau of the Census (1981), the fertility rates in Wisconsin and the national population in 1980 per 1,000 women aged 18–44 were 75.3 (Wisconsin) and 71.1 (national population). These rates are considerably higher than the 1-year fertility rate of 45.8 for women on welfare. Consequently, women on welfare have a substantially lower fertility rate than women in the general population.

Yet, to what extent are these differences the result of differences across populations? For example, perhaps the demographic structure of the welfare population lends itself to a lower overall fertility rate. The key demographic differences between women on welfare and women in the general population (which can be controlled for) are race, marital status, parity, education, and age. Women on welfare are more likely to be black, unmarried, have at least one child, possess less education, and be in their 20s compared to women in the general population.

To account for these population differences, I standardized welfare fertility rates for the national and Wisconsin populations on the above characteristics.[3] In other words, if the welfare population had the same demographic makeup as the general population (in age, race, parity, marital status, and education), what would the fertility rate for women on welfare be? Table 4.2 in-

TABLE 4.2 Welfare Fertility Rates Standardized for Population Characteristics

Characteristics	Standardized for National Population Characteristics	Percentage Difference from National Rate	Standardized for Wisconsin Population Characteristics	Percentage Difference from Wisconsin Rate
Age	45.8	−35.6	48.3	−35.9
Children	50.2	−29.4	50.6	−32.8
Marital Status	53.1	−25.3	53.3	−29.2
Race	37.1	−47.8	34.3	−54.4
Education	37.7	−47.0	36.3	−51.8
	71.1—National Rate		75.3—Wisconsin Rate	

dicates that when I standardized for age, children, marital status, race, or education, the fertility rates of women on welfare were still considerably below those of the national and Wisconsin populations. The lower overall fertility rate among women receiving public assistance programs is therefore not an artifact of a more favorable demographic structure. Rather, it clearly is lower even when major demographic factors are taken into account.

Finding Reasons through In-Depth Interviews

The two tables indicate welfare recipients have a relatively low fertility rate, a rate considerably below that of women in the general population, and is not an artifact of a more favorable demographic structure. I then asked: Why is the rate of fertility among women on welfare relatively low? What accounts for these findings? At this point, I turned to the in-depth interviews, which were well suited for exploring the potential reasons behind the overall demographic patterns found in Tables 4.1 and 4.2. The interviews enabled women on welfare to construct their experiences and attitudes regarding pregnancy and childbirth. These experiences and attitudes shed considerable light on why fertility behavior appears to be suppressed. Twenty-nine of the 50 interviews were with female household heads or wives aged 18–44. Ages ranged from 18 to 43, with most women in their 20s or 30s. Two women were pregnant at the time of the Interview. Most of the women had one or two children.

None of the 27 nonpregnant women wanted a child in the near future, and only a handful were considering having more children in the long term. Consistent with findings from the quantitative analysis and the fieldwork, women clearly wished to avoid childbearing. Several examples illustrate these attitudes and, more important, the reasons behind the attitudes. A 25-year-old separated woman was asked: "Do you think you'll ever want to have any more children?"

> No. No. I don't think that I ever [with emphasis] want to have another child.
> I think that will stop me from doing things that I want to do. And it won't

be fair to me. It won't be fair for the new child. And it won't be fair at all for the two that I have.

A never-married woman in her early 30s with one child commented:

Try to avoid the accidents now. I figure, well, it's bad enough . . . it's not bad enough . . . it's hardest to get by with one, let alone have another one just me by myself, you know. Trying to raise two.

Another example of not wanting more children was the following exchange that took place with a married couple aged 29 and 31:

INTERVIEWER: Have you ever thought about having any more children?

WIFE: [answers very quickly] No!

HUSBAND: No! Not at all. . . . Never crossed our minds.

INTERVIEWER: Could you say why?

HUSBAND: Why? Nowadays you can't afford it. And three of them are enough. Yeah. Three of them. It's just right. Just the way it is.

When a 19-year-old woman with one child was asked if she had considered having any more children, she said:

Not quite yet. [laughs] I kinda thought about, you know, the age difference. I don't want it to be real far, but I'm not quite ready for another kid, financially or mentally. I don't think I could handle two kids. [laughs]

These examples illustrate several of the predominant feelings and attitudes of families who were interviewed. They provide a potential explanation for why the fertility rate of women on public assistance is relatively low. That is, the economic, social, and psychological situations in which women on welfare find themselves simply are not conducive to wanting more children. The women and their families perceived becoming pregnant and having a child as making the situation worse, not better.

Virtually all of the interviewed women also expressed the desire to get off public assistance. They saw another child as severely limiting the likelihood of escaping welfare dependence. A married woman in her late 20s was asked why she was planning not to have a third child. She said:

I suppose mostly, it has to do with me. Depression is a factor. I just don't know that I can handle more than this. And also, I want to get on preparing for my own career. And I don't want to have to go back to square one and raise a child, and stay home with it again.

In the interviews, we directly addressed the issue of whether having additional children was motivated by wanting more money from welfare. The question was: "Did knowing that the welfare payments were there have anything to do with having another child?" Recipients overwhelming rejected this as an option. As one woman put it:

Well, for one thing, with aid you don't get enough money to live on. I don't see how someone can do it. I know they keep having babies so they get more money. But then you got to take care of those babies. There's just no way for that to happen. Even if there was, I don't think I could do that. I'd have to be doing something.

A female head of household with two children said:

> I know a person says you get more money the more children you have, but then again they backfire because it doesn't work like that. You had more money, but you need more than what you got, because you're going to spend it.

Finally, a woman in her 30s responded quickly to the question of how much the additional money from welfare was a factor in her having children:

> Nothing. I've read a lot of studies about that, and they're not true. No. It had nothing to do with it. You know . . . having a child is very traumatic. It's a very beautiful experience, but it's also very traumatic. And I suppose there are some women that just might have additional children to get an increase in money, but I would say that that's less than a very small percentage. Because you're committing yourself to anywhere from 15 to 20 years of your life to that individual. You're taking 9 months from the very beginning and doing all kinds of traumatic things to your body. So, no. That [more money from welfare] was not a consideration in having additional children.

A question about qualitative findings is the representativeness of quotes. In this study, 26 of the 27 nonpregnant women responded in a manner consistent with the attitudes reported here. The one exception was a married woman who stated that although she was not planning on having any more children (she was in her 40s), when she was in her early 20s and on welfare, she had had several children in order to collect greater welfare benefits.

Women often described their pregnancies as accidental. Several examples are typical of this pattern. A never-married woman in her mid-20s was questioned about her previous three pregnancies, all of which ended in abortion, and whether she had wanted to have a child.

> Never. After that first time [her first pregnancy], my mom kept drilling into me about school and the importance of education and all. So that stuck with me all those years. And I always got pregnant through carelessness, you know. I kept saying, Well, when I get married one day and settle down and make sure my life is secure, then I'll have the children.

Another woman who had recently had a child was asked:

INTERVIEWER: Was she planned? I mean, did you plan to get pregnant, or was it pretty much an accident?

WOMAN: It was an accident, because Tom and I had been only going out for like 3 months. And then I got pregnant.

A never-married women, aged 33, was asked about her only child:

INTERVIEWER: Can you say, is there a reason why you got pregnant?

WOMAN: It was an accident [small laughter]. Put it that way [more laughter]. That was the only thing that happened. It was just one accident that happened. But, I don't regret it.

The two women who were pregnant at the time of the interviews stated that their pregnancies were accidental. When asked about becoming a parent, a 19-year-old, pregnant, never-married woman replied:

> I was a little nervous, and kind of scared because we didn't have the funds. We don't really have the money for it but. . . . We have a lot of people supporting us, like his family and his aunts and uncles and everybody. And my parents are kind of supportive about it.

She was then asked about her boyfriend's reaction to the pregnancy. She answered:

> Well, he's pretty scared because he doesn't have a job. And he's . . . he's been looking for quite awhile now, and he can't seem to find a job.

To summarize, the in-depth interviews suggested that the financial and social situations in which women on public assistance find themselves are not conducive to having additional children. These women appeared to be motivated by cost-benefit considerations. But it was the costs that outweighed the benefits, not vice versa. The economic, social, and psychological costs of becoming pregnant and having a child on public assistance are perceived as clearly outweighing the benefits. The economic and psychological stress that virtually all welfare recipients experienced exerted a powerful effect on women's fertility behavior. That effect was to lower the overall fertility rate.

From the point of view of public policy, these findings are significant. They indicate that receiving public assistance suppresses the likelihood of childbearing. Yet, policy analysts often implicitly accept the assumption that public assistance encourages women to have more children. For example, President Reagan's Working Group on the Family (1986) noted,

> Does the welfare system, particularly AFDC, give some women incentives to bear children? Statistical evidence does not prove those suppositions; and yet, even the most casual observer of public assistance programs understands that there is indeed some relationship between the availability of welfare and the inclination of many young women to bear fatherless children. (p. 35)

For women on public assistance, such beliefs simply are not supported by the analyses presented here.

DISCUSSION: ADVANTAGES OF COMBINING METHODS

Complementary Nature

The term complementary is defined by Webster as "mutually supporting each other's lack." The integration of qualitative and quantitative data fits such a description in that their strengths and weaknesses are largely opposite of each other. Methodologically speaking, a strong argument can be made for such an integration.

The strength of qualitative data lies in its richness and depth, as the chapters in this volume demonstrate. Field notes, verbatim transcripts from in-depth interviews, document analysis, and other qualitative data can provide a wealth of information. Furthermore, these approaches allow participants to structure the world as they see it, rather than as the analyst sees it. As a result, researchers are able to come to a deep understanding of a particular research topic.

However, if research goals include generalizing to a population with a probable estimated error, quantitative data derived from large random sampling is the more appropriate approach. Qualitative approaches do not lend themselves to studies of incidence and prevalence. Data gathered through random sampling of large populations obviously can describe the characteristics of a population as well as model statistically events and processes occurring within the population. When questionnaires and instruments are standardized, researchers can argue for reliability.

Nevertheless, quantitative data from such studies reduce social or family processes to numbers. The results of these studies may suffer from superficiality to explain complex issues. Second, quantitative analyses seldom capture the overall context and underlying mechanisms behind predicted events—for example, why women on welfare have a relatively low fertility rate. Again, such outcomes often result from the reduction of social patterns into quantifiable categories. Third, biases may exist in how individuals respond to standardized questions as well as how they behave in an experimental situation, which consequently affects the quality of the data. Again, the issue is one of validity. In short, quantitative data tend to be strong in relation to reliability and generalizability, yet the validity surrounding such data may be questionable.

Depending upon the research question, therefore, qualitative and quantitative analyses can be complementary. In my study, by combining quantitative data from a large longitudinal sample with qualitative data from in-depth interviews and fieldwork, I was able to answer my research questions in ways that built upon the strengths of both approaches.

Additional Insights

A second advantage of blending qualitative and quantitative data in research design and analysis are the additional insights attained as result of such an integration. Like theoretical perspectives, specific methodological approaches are various ways of viewing and interpreting the world. They are not necessarily correct or incorrect, but rather they often grasp at different aspects of reality. Family researchers should be interested in understanding such multiple dimensions of reality. By bringing together both qualitative and quantitative data in an analysis, insights are gained that may have been unattainable without such an integration. As Denzin (1978) stated:

> Each method implies a different line of action toward reality—and hence each will reveal different aspects of it, much as a kaleidoscope, depending on how they are approached, held, and acted toward, different observations will be revealed. This is not to imply that reality has the shifting qualities of the colored prism, but that it too is an object that moves and that will not permit one interpretation to be stamped upon it. (pp. 292–293)

Bryman (1988a) discussed how combinations of methods can work together: "Quantitative research can establish regularities in social life while qualitative evidence can allow the processes which link the variables identified to be revealed" (p. 142). This is precisely the type of analysis I utilized in my own research study. The longitudinal quantitative data were ideal for describing and modeling specific events occurring to families on welfare (here, fertility rates). At the same time, the qualitative data acquired from in-depth interviews then provided insight and understanding into the mechanisms driving these events. By bringing together these disparate analyses, I was left with a richer understanding and insight into my research topic.

Increased Validity

A third advantage of combining quantitative and qualitative data is the potential increment in the validity of the study's findings. Assuming researchers discover consistent results across the qualitative and quantitative methods, such findings acquire a greater validity. As Webb, Campbell, Schwartz, and Sechrest (1966) stated, "When a hypothesis can survive the confrontation of a series of complementary methods of testing, it contains a degree of validity unattainable by one tested within the more constricted framework of a single method" (p. 174). Consistent findings across methods increase our confidence in the results. Assuming that the findings are consistent, the validity of the results acquired from integrating qualitative and quantitative data is enhanced.

In the analysis here, fieldwork generated serious doubts about the idea of women on welfare bearing large numbers of children. In the analysis of case records, I found women on welfare to have a relatively low fertility rate in comparison to other women. In the interviews, women emphasized they did not want to have more children. The data from these three approaches reinforced each other and enhanced the validity of the findings.

Pushing the Research Further

Surely, though, qualitative and quantitative results will not always be consistent with each other. Rather than a disadvantage, this can be seen as a fourth advantage or reason to combine such data. Researchers are faced with a dilemma when the qualitative and quantitative results appear at odds with each other. Which is the correct interpretation? Some may choose one over the other. Analysis who confront discrepancies head on, however, are likely to push their research one step further. By probing into the reasons behind such discrepancies, they may redirect the research process. Thus, as Bryman (1988a) stated, researchers could:

> Use the incongruent findings as a springboard for the investigation of the reasons for such contrasting findings. After all, since quantitative and qualitative research undertaken in the same investigation may provide mutually reinforcing results . . . the possibility of discrepant findings also exists. When there is evidence of a clash, further exploration of the issue would seem warranted. (p. 133)

Such exploration furthers research processes by redirecting both the hypotheses and the research design intended to test those hypotheses.

These, then, are several of the major advantages of gathering and integrating qualitative and quantitative methods. They include a strengthening of the research design and analysis through their complementary nature, greater acquired insight, enhanced validity, and the potential for redirecting the inquiry in positive and fruitful directions. When brought together, the blending of qualitative and quantitative methods provide a powerful tool for understanding the processes and dynamics behind family life.

NOTES

1. Analysis is confined to women aged 18 to 44, which is one of the two standard age brackets used for estimating fertility rates. This age bracket is used rather than 15 to 44 because there are very few women aged 15 to 17 who are heading households on welfare. Using either age bracket allows for a comparison of welfare fertility rates with the overall national and state rates.

The analysis pools married and unmarried women. This is standard procedure for calculating and reporting overall fertility rates of women. Marital status is taken into account in the aggregate comparison, however.

The event being modeled in the life table analyses is the first observed spell of childbearing. Once a birth has occurred, women are no longer included in later time intervals. The numbers of women experiencing a birth are extremely small, which prevents a detailed analysis of the occurrence and determinants of a second observed birth.

Once women exit from the welfare rolls they are no longer included in the analysis even if they subsequently reenter the welfare system. Including such women distorts the representativeness of the sample. Separate analyses were also conducted including such women, however. No significant differences were found from the results presented here.

Finally, I included in the analysis all women who have been on welfare for at least 9 months. The reason for this is obvious. Some women may have entered the welfare system as the result of an upcoming birth. In these cases, cause and effect are reversed—forthcoming birth leading to welfare use, rather than welfare use leading to birth. By including only women who have been receiving welfare for at least 9 months, this bias is eliminated.

2. Thus the average fertility rate over this period was 38.3. The 1-year rate of 45.8 is used for comparison purposes instead, however. To use a 3-year average distorts the representativeness of the sampled welfare population (e.g., longer-term cases are overrepresented).

3. These characteristics were categorized as follows: age (18–24, 25–29, 30–34, 35–39, 40–44); children (no children, one or more children); marital status (married-spouse present, not married); race (white, black); and education (less than 12 years, 12 or more years). The fertility rates for each of these categories were calculated for women on welfare. The rates were then multiplied by the proportion of women in each category for the Wisconsin and national populations. This technique results in a direct standardization using the general population as the standard. (See Shyrock & Siegel, 1976.) The population proportions for the nation were based upon information from the U.S. Bureau of the Census (1981); the Wisconsin proportions were derived from the Wisconsin Department of Health and Human Services (1981) and the U.S. Bureau of the Census.

REFERENCES

Brewer, J., and A. Hunter, 1989. *Multimethod research*. Newbury Park, California: Sage Publications.

Bryman, A. 1988a. *Quantity and quality in social research*. London: Unwin Hyman.

Bryman, A. 1988b. Introduction: "Inside accounts" and social research in organizations, pp. 1–20 in A. Bryman, ed., *Doing research in organizations*. London: Routledge & Kegan Paul.

Burgess, E. W., and L.S. Cottrell. 1939. *Predicting success or failure in marriage*. Englewood Cliffs, NJ: Prentice-Hall.

Cavan, R. S. 1983. The Chicago school of sociology, 1918–1937. *Urban Life* 11: 407–420.

Denzin, N. K. 1978. *The research act*. New York: Aldine.

Filstead, W. J. 1979. Qualitative methods: A needed perspective in evaluation research, pp. 33–48 in *Qualitative and quantitative methods in evaluation research*, eds. T.D. Cook and C.S. Reichardt. Beverly Hills, California: Sage Publications.

Galligan, R. J. 1982. Innovative techniques: Siren or rose. *Journal of Marriage and the Family* 44: 875–886.

Gilder, G. 1981. *Wealth and poverty*. New York: Basic Books.

Hodgson, J. W., and R.A. Lewis. 1979. Pilgrim's Progress III: A trend analysis of family theory and methodology. *Family Process* 18: 163–173.

Kalton, G. 1983. *Introduction to survey sampling*. Beverly Hills, California: Sage Publications.

Komarovsky, M. 1962. *Blue-collar marriage*. New York: Random House.

LaRossa, R., & Wolf, J. H. 1985. On qualitative family research. *Journal of Marriage and the Family* 47: 531–542.

LeMasters, E. E. 1975. *Blue-collar aristocrats*. Madison: University of Wisconsin Press.

Lynd, R. S., and H. M. Lynd. 1929. *Middletown: A study in American culture*. New York: Harcourt Brace.

Lynd, R. S., and H.M. Lynd. 1937. *Middletown in transition: A study in cultural conflicts*. New York: Harcourt & Brace.

Miller, B. C. 1986. *Family research methods*. Beverly Hills, CA: Sage.

Murray, C. 1984. *Losing ground*. New York: Basic Books.

Nye, F. I. 1988. Fifty years of family research, 1937–1987. *Journal of Marriage and the Family* 50: 569–584.

Ostrander, S. A. 1984. *Women of the upper class.* Philadelphia: Temple University Press.

Rank, M. R. 1985. Exiting from welfare: A life table analysis. *Social Service Review* 59: 358–376.

Rank, M. R. 1986. Family structure and the process of exiting from welfare. *Journal of Marriage and the Family* 48: 607–618.

Rank, M. R. 1987. The formation and dissolution of marriages in the welfare population. *Journal of Marriage and the Family* 49:15–20.

Rank, M. R. 1988a. *The blending of quantitative and qualitative data in family research.* Paper presented at the preconference workshop on Theory Construction and Research Methodology, November 11–13, at the National Council on Family Relation in Philadelphia.

Rank, M. R. 1988b. Racial differences in length of welfare use. *Social Forces* 66: 1080–1101.

Rank, M. R. 1989. Fertility among women on welfare: Incidence and determinants, *American Sociological Review* 54: 296–304.

Reiss, A. J. (1968). Stuff and nonsense about social surveys and participant observation, pp. 351–367 in *Institutions and the Person*: Papers presented to Everett C. Hughes, eds. H.S. Becker, B. Geer, D. Reisman, and R.S. Weiss. Chicago: Aldine.

Rist, R. C. 1977. On the relations among educational research paradigms: From disdain to detente. *Anthropology and Education Quarterly* 8: 42–49.

Shyrock, H. S., and J.S. Siegel. 1976. *The methods and materials of demography.* New York: Academic Press.

Stack, C. B. 1974. *All our kin.* New York: Harper & Row.

Terman, L. M. 1938. *Psychological factors in marital happiness.* New York: McGraw-Hill.

U.S. Bureau of the Census. 1981. *Fertility of American women: June 1980* (Current Population Reports, Series P-20, No. 364). Washington, DC: U.S. Government Printing Office.

Webb, E., D. T., Campbell, R.D. Schwartz, and L. Sechrest. 1966. *Unobtrusive measures: Nonreactive research in the social sciences.* Chicago: Rand McNally.

Wisconsin Department of Health and Social Services. 1981. *Public health statistics: 1980.* Division of Health, Bureau of Health Statistics, Madison, WI.

Working Group on the Family. 1986. *The family: Preserving America's future.* Washington, DC: United States Department of Education, Office of the Under Secretary.

CHAPTER 5

Dimensions of Desire

Bridging Qualitative and Quantitative Methods in a Study of Female Adolescent Sexuality

DEBORAH L. TOLMAN AND LAURA SZALACHA

The meaning and importance of women's sexuality and its systematic suppression (Rich, 1980) has been central in second-wave feminist research, theory, and politics (e.g., Snitow, Stansell, and Thompson, 1983; Vance, 1984). This study is a response to an acute absence of acknowledgment in psychological research of sexual desire as a normative aspect of female adolescent development (Tolman, 1994a). The work of several feminist scholars has suggested that girls' experiences of sexuality and sexual desire in particular are a significant, albeit neglected, force in girls' development (e.g., Cowie and Lees, 1987; Nava, 1987; Thompson, 1984, 1995) and as such are potentially crucial in girls' developing a sense of entitlement and empowerment (Fine, 1988; Tolman, 1994b). Feminist social psychologist Michelle Fine identified a "missing discourse of desire" in adults' discussions of girls' sexuality (Fine, 1988). Her research suggested that girls do know and speak of desire, despite anxious or even well-meaning denial of female adolescent sexual desire on the part of the adults in their lives. Fine's research raised the question of how girls speak about and experience their own sexual feelings. The goal of this study was to begin to understand the dimensions of the experience of sexual desire for adolescent girls.

There are several intertwining reasons that psychology, even feminist psychology, has not made significant inroads into the question of adolescent girls' sexual feelings. Feminist scholars have theorized how patriarchal suppression of female sexuality is a key aspect of women's oppression (i.e., Rich, 1980; Vance, 1984). Despite extensive inquiry into female adolescent sexual *behavior* (e.g., Delameter and Mae-Corquodale, 1979; Lees, 1986; Levinson, 1986; Scott-Jones and Turner, 1988) and a history of theorizing sexuality development (e.g., Benjamin, 1988; Freud, 1905; Jordan, 1987), there have been no studies that include the question of girls' sexual desire (Thompson, 1984; Tolman, 1994a). Buried within all ostensibly objective stances is the historical denial and denigration of female adolescent sexuality (Tolman, 1996). These studies also belie the politics of adolescent pregnancy as they trickle down into the research world. Conducted primarily by sociologists and demographers, such studies offer a limited conception of girls' sexuality. They focus on whether or not and when girls have had sexual intercourse and whether or not they have used effective measures of contraception and seek to identify trends in the outcomes of girls' choices about heterosexual intercourse. The agenda of such studies has not been to understand or support the development of healthy sexuality among girls (Tolman, in press). To achieve the goals of marking behavioral trends and distinguishing between "good" and "bad" groups of girls, these studies almost exclusively rely on survey method. This methodology has framed and limited for girls what the pertinent questions and possible answers are about what is important in the development of their sexuality.[1]

The current study represents a different research agenda by locating a question about girls' sexuality development within a query about girls' healthy psychological development. Moving away from a focus on sexual intercourse, sexual behavior, sexual attitudes, or even sexual outcomes, our research question is phenomenological: How do girls describe their sexual experiences and sexual feelings and in what ways do they speak about their own bodies in telling their stories of desire? This theoretical shift ushers in a movement away from survey methods toward methods that provide research participants with opportunities to convey the meanings they make of their experiences. It also requires the explicit use of a feminist methodological approach.

Qualitative, phenomenological methods that enable understanding of people's experiences (Denzin and Lincoln, 1994; Packer and Addison, 1989) and the feminist perspective necessary to inform inquiry into an aspect of female experience that is systematically denigrated and denied in a patriarchal society (Irigaray, 1981; Omolade, 1983; Rich, 1980) do not yet enjoy wide respect within psychology (Morowski, 1994). Even within feminist psychology, the question of what constitutes feminist methods continues to be intensely debated and unresolved (Crawford and Maracek, 1989; Fine, 1992; Maracek, 1989; Riger, 1992). This debate has often revolved around two approaches to understanding feminist methodology and the role of methods in feminist transformation of psychology. One approach to feminist methods is to work within psychology's methodological traditions, using conventional quantitative methods to answer research questions driven by feminist theory. Such research is more easily accepted by the discipline and thus has been thought by some to have more potential to transform it (Lykes and Stewart, 1986). The second approach holds that feminist methods are subject centered and therefore necessarily qualitative, disruptive of the tradition of objective experimental and survey methods in the field (Fine and Gordon, 1989). Such methods are aimed at generating knowledge about women's lives previously not produced by psychologists, thus transforming the information as well as the practices that constitute psychological knowledge and its production.

These two approaches have consistently been positioned in opposition to one another and framed as a choice in practice for feminist researchers.

These very different perspectives on feminist methodology have contributed to the debate about the very concept of feminist methods itself. By demonstrating how both qualitative and quantitative methods can be used synergistically in a way that balances and integrates the concerns and demands of both feminist perspectives on methods, we hope that the methodological approach to learning about adolescent girls' experiences of sexual desire described in this article may serve as a contribution to defusing and reconfiguring this often divisive debate within feminist psychology.

The disagreements about methodology within feminist psychology reflect larger concerns within psychology and within the social sciences as a whole about what constitutes good research in the wake of poststructuralism and the ensuing postmodern debates about research paradigms (e.g., Cook and Reichardt, 1979; Sechrest and Sidani, 1995; Shadish, 1995; Weedon, 1987). In offering an approach that integrates qualitative and quantitative methods in a feminist research project, we begin by contextualizing the feminist debates within these larger issues. The debate on the relative value, appropriateness, and possible integration of quantitative and qualitative research paradigms has been a part of research in psychology's landscape for almost two decades (Cook and Reichardt, 1979; Healy and Sewart, 1991; Jayaratne and Stewart, 1991). Quantitative and qualitative approaches are often understood as separate paradigms of research, with radically differing assumptions, requirements, and procedures that are rooted in completely different epistemologies. One position of the philosophical debate contends that the integration of quantitative and qualitative paradigms is impossible, as they represent irreconcilable worldviews (e.g., Cuba and Lincoln, 1989; Mishler, 1986). The opposite position, maintained on both philosophic and pragmatic grounds, is that not only can the two paradigms be combined at the hands-on level of research practice, at the sociological level of methodological assumptions, and at the metaphysical level of metatheoretical assumptions, they should be so combined, because these concerns are superseded in importance by political goals about how research findings should be used (Firestone, 1993; Tashakkori and Teddlie, 1998).

Finally, there are those who maintain that the point is not to accommodate or reconcile distinct paradigms but to recognize each as unique, historically situated forms of insight.[2] Lee Schulman (1986) argued that each research paradigm is bound by the programs and departments that teach them. Each research paradigm has grown "out of a particular perspective, a bias of either convention or discipline, necessarily illuminating some part of the field of teaching while ignoring the rest" and that "the danger for any field of social science or educational research lies in its potential corruption (or worse, trivialization) by a single paradigmatic view" (pp. 2–3). Rather than force a dichotomous choice, Kidder and Fine (1987) have suggested that researchers both avoid "homogenizing research methods and cultures," and strive to be "bicultural" (p. 57). Sktric (1990) suggested that the goal of researchers should be to understand both quantitative and qualitative paradigms, to learn to speak to them and through them, and to recognize that each are ways of seeing that simultaneously reveal and conceal.[3]

Unfortunately, the ongoing philosophical debate and discussion, although alive at conferences, on faculties, and in some journals, are rarely incorporated explicitly into actual research. At the same time, the substantive combination of qualitative and quantitative methods has gone forward, despite or in lieu of this epistemological unrest (Shadish, 1995). Guided mostly by pragmatic perspectives such as those of Patton (1990a) and Greene (1994), the qualitative/quantitative "joint venture" has become a feature in many disciplines, most notably in public health (e.g., Carlson, 1996; Keenan, 1996), program evaluation (e.g., House, 1994; Patton, 1990a, 19901); Reichardt and Rallis, 1994), education (e.g., Goldfarb, 1995) and, to some extent, in psychology (e.g., Debats, 1995; Gladue, 1991; Hines, 1993; Way, Stauber, and Nakkula, 1994). Indeed, some have claimed that "methodological pluralism is an absolutely necessary strategy in the face of overwhelming cognitive limitations and biases inherent in human mental processing and responding" (Sechrest and Sidani, 1995, p. 80). The challenge of grappling with increasingly complex social problems, particularly those that confront activist and applied psychologies like feminist psychology, demands that we investigate further the hidden potential in combining quantitative and qualitative research methods.

The combination of methods has appeared in several recognizable forms. A "pseudo-combination" is a study conducted wholly under one rubric, with the other type of method serving simply as a support or illustration. The "logic-in-use" (Kaplan, 1964) of the study largely ignores one of the two approaches. Quantitative studies of this sort often have some illuminating portraits to "liven up the numbers" or to add richness. Qualitative studies may provide some "quasi-statistics" (Becker, 1986), which serve to add the legitimacy that numbers have traditionally commanded.

There are, however, studies in which both approaches are genuinely and equitably used. One possibility is a concurrent approach (Whitbourne and Powers, 1994). In this type of study, there is a peaceful coexistence or parallel process wherein two studies are conducted simultaneously, though each is whole and separate from the other. The chief difficulty lies in the integration of the findings of two very different, almost separate studies. Kidder and Fine (1987) cautioned that different methods within different paradigms are not simply addressing the same questions differently. Instead, they are addressing different questions, revealing different levels of activity, and leading to different knowledge, interpretations, and explanations. Such differences raise thorny questions of how to square or interpret contradictory findings.

A second possibility for an integrated design is a sequential approach, in which a study is conducted in phases, using one method for one part of the study and then another method for another part. Most often this has taken the form of an exploratory qualitative study, which gives rise to the formulation of an instrument and then a confirmatory quantitative study. It can also be, however, that one would conduct a quantitative survey in order to provide profiles to frame questions and sampling for a qualitative phase. It is important to note that in this approach, neither the qualitative nor the quantitative method is superior and neither sequence is preferred (Maxwell, 1996). A third possibility is what Patton (1990b) suggested as "methodological mixes," in which one combines various methods simultaneously. This "technical eclecticism" requires a pragmatic point of view; methods, regardless of whether they originate in a qualitative or quantitative paradigm, are irrelevant to the question of what makes research viable. Finally, there is also the possibility of a wholly "integrated approach," wherein one combines both quantitative and qualitative approaches throughout the entire process from the formation of research questions, to decisions about sampling, to data collection and analyses. A real advantage in this option is the possibility of a methodological dialogue—an ongoing, dialectically informative interaction at each point of the research.

The study we report here does not fit neatly into any of these specific strategies for combining qualitative and quantitative methods; rather, the blend of qualitative and quantitative methods at which we have arrived is a kind of sequential integration. What distinguishes this approach is that it is explicitly feminist in nature; what drove our decisions was a feminist organizing principle of listening to and taking women's voices seriously (Andersen, Armitage, Jack, and Wittner, 1990; Belenky, Clinchy, Goldberger, and Tarule, 1986; Gilligan, 1982; Oakley, 1981), particularly in data collection and data reduction, as well as in data analysis and interpretation. Working with a single database, a set of intensive, semi-structured interviews with 30 adolescent girls attending public schools in urban and suburban settings, we posed and answered a series of questions grounded in feminist theory and research on female adolescent sexuality. Our method of data collection is anchored in a qualitative epistemology and methodology, and we use multiple methods of data analysis, including careful interpretations of narrative data and also more reductive, statistical methods of analysis, to answer an array of related feminist questions about female adolescent experiences of sexual desire. By choosing the method of data analysis that enabled us to answer each emerging question, the result has been an eclectic merging of both approaches to feminist methodology, producing a kind of feminist eclecticism that has at its heart the perspectives and experiences of these young women.

METHOD

Participants

The design of this study was grounded in the possibility that both qualitative and quantitative analyses would be performed. Tolman chose a random sample size of 30,[4] balancing concerns that the sample be large enough to conduct statistical analyses, while at the same time producing a manageable amount of rich narrative data.[5] Tolman collected data from eleventh grade girls, who ranged in age from 15–19, at an urban public high school ($n = 15$) and a suburban public high school ($n = 15$).[6] The sample thus represents an age group in which sexual activity is part of the social landscape and includes girls who are subject to various sexual stereotypes: Urban girls (often girls of color) are considered to be overly sexual, whereas suburban girls are thought of as asexual (Tolman, 1996). The design was meant to enable a challenge of such stereotypes of girls and to open the question of what normal sexuality is for all adolescent girls. In the urban school sample there were seven Black, three Latina, and five White girls.[7] In the suburban school, we spoke with 14 White girls and 1 Latina girl. The suburban girls are from Protestant, Catholic, and Jewish families, whereas the urban girls are from Protestant and Catholic backgrounds. One of the girls is a self-described lesbian, and two describe desire for both boys and girls.

In this analysis, we focus on the differences between and similarities among girls who live in an urban and a suburban social location. Tolman did not collect specific data on socioeconomic status (SES) for several reasons. As we will discuss in the text that follows, because Tolman was asking girls to speak about something that is essentially unspeakable, she made careful choices about what she did and did not ask so as to enhance the development of trust. Rather than collect conventional socioeconomic data on participants' parental, educational, and occupational background, which in the context of these interviews could have been experienced by the girls as alienating, she asked them to tell her in their own words about their families and social contexts. Based on their descriptions of their parents' work lives and their daily experiences with crime, housing, and need for social services in their neighborhoods and communities, Tolman concluded that although there was some variation within each group, the urban girls were all from poor and working-class families, and the suburban girls were all living in middle- and upper-middle-class families. In addition to girls' descriptions, differences such as levels in obvious poverty, explicit violence, community and educational resources, neighborhood stability and general well-being were discernable from observation, substantiating the girls' reports of their environments. We conclude that the urban/suburban difference in this case is a reasonable reflection of gross class differences in terms of the experiences and meanings associated with these girls' daily lives. Because these class designations are not precise, we understand and interpret our data in terms of differences in social locations rather than class per se, with these two distinct social locations offering it meaningful interpretive context for understanding how girls speak about, make meaning of, and experience their sexuality. In other analyses from this study, Tolman has integrated cultural characteristics in interpreting these data (e.g., Tolman, 1994a, 1996).

Procedure

A key component of this feminist inquiry is the method of data collection. Grounded in an explicitly feminist method of data collection (Brown and

Gilligan, 1992, Taylor, Gilligan, and Sullivan, 1996; Way, 1995), Tolman invited in-depth narrative and descriptive data from girls on their thoughts about and subjective experiences of sexuality, including sexual desire, sexual pleasure, feeling sexy, and sexual fantasies, during private, one-on-one, semi-structured clinical interviews that lasted from 45 minutes to 2 hours. One of the primary tools of oppression of women is the maintenance of silence about their experiences and perspectives (Lorde, 1984; Rich, 1980). Acknowledging the possibility of female adolescent sexual agency, desire, pleasure, and fantasies through the act of asking about these realms of experience renders this approach a feminist research method. This method departs from a survey design by creating an opportunity for girls to put into words and to name their experience in and questions about a realm of their lives that remains unspoken in the larger culture. Thus, as a form of data collection, it enables us to learn from girls what might otherwise remain an unknown perspective on this part of their lives.

Each interview included a standard set of questions; follow-up questions guided by a feminist relational approach to psychological inquiry were asked in direct response to the specific contours of each interviewee's particular experiences (Brown and Gilligan, 1992; Way, 1995). The consent of participants and their parents (for girls who were under 18) was obtained prior to the interview. All interviews were tape-recorded and transcribed. Confidentiality and anonymity in reporting were ensured. No girl disclosed an experience of current sexual abuse or violence. The girls who disclosed past sexual abuse and dating violence were referred, with their permission, into appropriate therapeutic situations when they so wished.

This study as a whole has three iterations that are organized by three separate and synergistically related research questions, which emerged sequentially in response to the findings generated by pursuing the previous research question. These three questions demanded three different methods of analysis of our interview data. Together, the results emerging from these three analyses shed a multilayered light on adolescent girls' experiences of sexual desire.

DATA ANALYSIS AND RESULTS: QUESTION 1

Question 1: How do girls describe their experiences of sexual desire?

The aim of this component of the study was to understand how the girls in this sample experience and describe their own sexual desire and to learn about the place of their bodies in this experience. The focus on the embodied nature of sexual desire was grounded in a view that psychological health and vitality, self-knowledge, and lived relationships are anchored in the body (Gilligan, Brown, and Rogers, 1989; Young, 1992) and that the meanings we make of our bodily experiences are socially constructed (Rubin, 1985). The findings from this component have been previously reported (Debold, Tolman, and Brown, 1996; Tolman, 1994a, 1994b, 1996; Tolman and Higgins, 1996), but in order to present the interlocking quality of the evolving methodological choices we made in this study, we will describe the methods and results of this analysis.

Data Analysis

The data were analyzed by combining two methods of qualitative analysis. This approach to data analysis was also used in part in answering Question 3 of this study, so we provide a complete description of our approach at this juncture. Tolman identified one narrative in which the girls told a story about all experience of sexual desire to analyze in depth using a method of narrative analysis called The Listening Guide, a feminist interpretive method (Brown, Debold, Gilligan, and Tappan, 1991; Brown, Tappan, Gilligan, Miller, and Argyris, 1989; Gilligan et al., 1989; Rogers and Gilligan, 1988). Acknowledging the multilayered nature of narratives and of the psyche, the "polyphonic and complex" nature of voice and experience (Brown and Gilligan, 1992, p. 15) highlights how there is no single way to understand any given narrative. Therefore, each narrative is read or "listened to" several distinct times; for each listening, the researcher focuses on or "listens for" a given aspect of the experience under study, underlining with a colored pencil the parts of the narrative in which the identified "voice" is expressed. A voice is a way of speaking that has an identifiable set of coherent features. Throughout this process, the researcher continuously checks and records her own thoughts, emotional and embodied feelings, and reactions as part of the data analysis. This method is grounded in a feminist standpoint (Nielsen, 1990), acknowledging that patriarchal culture silences and obscures women's experiences by providing the listener with in organized way to respond to the coded or indirect language of girls and women, especially for topics such as sexuality about which girls and women are not supposed to speak. This psychological approach to data analysis is accomplished in part because this method is explicitly relational, in that the researcher brings her self-knowledge into the process of listening by using clinical methods of empathy to contribute to her understanding of what a girl is saying. This relational practice increases the listener's ability to avoid bias or "voicing over" a girl's story with her own reactions, much like a skilled therapist can use countertransference to inform rather than overwhelm psychotherapy (Tolman, 1992).

In this analysis, Tolman listened for four voices associated with girls' experience of sexual desire: A voice of the self, an erotic voice, a voice of the body, and a voice of response to one's own desire. In listening for self, a standard voice of The Listening Guide, the reader attends to the interviewee as the narrator of the story by following the verbal markers for self, such as "I" or "me." Listening for the self is an efficient way of laying bare in what relationship the narrator places herself to her experience. The listening for self reveals agency and absence of agency, as well as the narrator's experience of herself as a subject and as an object, in the narrative context. Tolman then identified two desire voices, an erotic voice and a voice of responses to one's own desire, which are specific to analyzing what girls say about sexuality, using a grounded-theory approach (Strauss, 1987). Listening for all erotic voice tracks the ways in which girls speak about how sexual desire felt and what it was like for them, such as the intensity or specific quality of their sexual feelings. Listening for a voice of response to their sexual desire tracks how girls describe their thoughts and behavior in reaction to feeling their own sexual desire. Finally, listening for the voice of the body tracks how girls describe the explicitly embodied character of their desire and sexuality experiences.

The result of these sequential listenings and underlinings is a visual map of the different layers of a given experience in a narrative. The way that each voice maps in relation to the other voices is observed and recorded. Then the underlined parts of the narrative are transferred onto worksheets, so that interpretations can be made for what the narrator is saying in close proximity to her actual words. This tracking system enables the researcher to create a trail of evidence (Brown et al., 1989) for the interpretation that is developed. The result is a voice-centered interpretation of girls' narratives of sexual desire, which presents one way to understand these stories, a way that privileges feminist questions of agency, body, and relationship. By providing ample text in reporting results of such analyses (e.g., Brown and Gilligan, 1992; Tolman, 1994a, 1994b), the researcher enables others to develop alternative interpretations informed by different theoretical perspectives.

The second form of data analysis used was the construction of a conceptually clustered matrix for identifying patterns within and between groups (Miles and Huberman, 1984). Using the voice of self, the voice of the body, the erotic voice, and the voice of response as the frame for organizing the interpretations of these narrative data, Tolman incorporated the difference of urban and suburban social locations into the construction of this matrix. This way of organizing the qualitative data revealed how these two groups of girls voiced similar experiences of sexual desire and how their experiences had different qualities. This method also highlights individual variation within each group of girls, so that exceptions to patterns can be examined and understood as part of the diversity of experience for each group of girls.

Results

As Tolman has reported, about two thirds of the entire sample said they felt desire; the remainder said they were confused about whether or not they felt desire, or that they did not feel desire. There were several patterns in the data that were the same for both urban and suburban girls. In the stories of all of the girls who said they felt desire, an erotic voice was audible and characterized by the power, intensity, and urgency of their feeling. All of these girls described their experience of sexual desire in physical terms, defying the common conception of girls' desire as relational rather than embodied by expressing an audible "voice of the body." At the same time, there was an overall pattern for both the urban and suburban girls who voiced desire in these ways to question their entitlement to their own sexual feelings and to express doubt about the possibility of acting directly on their own desire and then being considered good or normal.

Although an erotic voice and a voice of the body sounded similar for urban and suburban girls, differences emerged in how they described their responses to their sexual desire—a kind of "main effect" of social location. One way to characterize this difference is that urban girls describe an agency in the service of protection, whereas suburban girls tell of an agency in the service of pleasure. In this analysis, Tolman heard the urban girls voice self-control and caution and conflict between the voices of their bodies and what they know and say about the reality of their vulnerabilities to AIDS, pregnancy, and getting a bad reputation. Most of these girls make a conscious choice to sacrifice pleasure to protect themselves from danger, at the cost of a severed connection with themselves and little real safety. For instance, Inez describes how her body says "yes" and her mind says "no," which she understands as her "mind lookin' towards my body," protecting her from the relational and physical dangers that can result from her own strong feelings.

In contrast, the suburban girls who said they felt desire all speak of a sexual curiosity that is hardly audible among the comparable group of urban girls. This curiosity is tempered by their wish to control themselves when they feel desire. Rather than speaking directly about the problems of physical or social vulnerability like the urban girls did, these suburban girls voice a more internal conflict in relation to their sexual desire, a discrepancy between what they describe feeling in their bodies and the cultural messages about female sexuality and appropriate female sexual behavior that they had internalized. For instance, while Emily offers a detailed description of what desire feels like to her, she also explains that "I don't like to think of myself as feeling really sexual . . . I don't like to think of myself as being like someone who needs to have their desires fulfilled . . . I mean I understand that it's wrong and that everybody has needs, but I just feel like self-conscious when I think about it, and I don't feel self-conscious when I say that we do these things, but I feel self-conscious about saying I need this kind of a thing."

This qualitative difference between the urban and suburban girls was a striking one. Drawing on the realities of their distinct social locations, we interpreted these differences as reflecting and relating to differentials in girls' sense of safety and violence, and the meanings and implications of girls knowing and exploring their sexuality in urban and suburban contexts. The urban girls live in overtly dangerous neighborhoods, where the consequences of their responses to their own sexuality can have enormous negative social, educational, and economic consequences, whereas the suburban girls live in a relatively safe environment, where the consequences of their sexuality are more psychological and internal and less threatening to their material futures. This analysis suggests the crucial importance of young women's social locations in how they experience their own bodies. Two constructions of how these girls understand their own sexual desire emerged: as perceived vulnerability and as possible pleasure.

Although the qualitative significance of this difference was apparent in the distinct voices of these two groups of girls, we wanted to know more about this difference: What is the magnitude of the difference between how urban and suburban girls experience sexual desire? Can this difference be understood quantitatively as well as qualitatively? The content of the difference, focusing on the interplay between pleasure and vulnerability associated with sexuality for girls, contributes new questions as well: Might personal experience with sexual violence play a role in girls' associations of their own desire with pleasure or vulnerability—or a balance between the two?

Is such an association different depending oil girls' social location? These questions called for a quantitative analysis.

DATA ANALYSIS AND RESULTS: QUESTIONS 2A AND 2B

Question 2a: What is the size and significance of the difference between urban and suburban girls' experiences of their own sexual desire?

Question 2b: Is there an interaction between social location and reported experience of sexual abuse or violence in whether urban and suburban girls associate their own desire with pleasure, vulnerability, or both?

The goal of this component of the study was to explore the difference we had identified between the urban and suburban girls' descriptions of desire. We wanted to understand how pleasure and vulnerability were associated differently for these two groups of girls. Evaluating whether there was an interactive effect of sexual abuse or violence through a quantitative analysis would provide useful insights into these dimensions of desire.

Data Analysis

Our challenge was to choose or develop a feminist approach to data reduction so that our interview data could be analyzed statistically. In the qualitative analysis, we had listened intensively to the nuances in a single narrative told by each of these girls, learning about the complexity of their experiences. In order to develop a broader understanding of the patterns in their experiences that could tell us more about what sexual desire is like for girls, we wanted to include more data in this next level of analysis. We shifted from intensive listening to reductive thematic coding as a strategy for including many more narratives in the analysis.

Because we had engaged in a feminist process of listening to girls voice their selves, desire, and bodies, we were able to code their narratives based on the emic themes and categories that we had learned *from them* were significant aspects of their experiences of sexual desire. One of the challenges for us was to continue to represent the complexity we noted in girls' voiced experience. The qualitative analysis had suggested two broad dimensions of girls' experience of desire: pleasure and vulnerability. Individual girls were not easily categorized simply as those who associated desire with pleasure and those who associated desire with vulnerability. In fact, no girl told desire narratives only about pleasure or desire narratives only about vulnerability. Therefore, we shifted our unit of analysis from girl ($N = 30$) to narrative ($N = 128$). We thus avoided collapsing data from multiple narratives told by each girl into a single "pleasure" or "vulnerability" score for her by identifying predominant themes of pleasure, vulnerability, or an equal presence of pleasure and vulnerability for all narratives about desire told by each girl. Increasing the database for each girl by including all of her desire narratives for this analysis met the feminist challenge to preserve the contradictory, complex quality of these girls' lived experiences while reducing our data.

This shift in level of analysis poses two possible problems. The first is whether differences in numbers of narratives told by urban and suburban girls could account for any differences we might find in the expression of pleasure and vulnerability in the narratives told by these two groups. As Table 5.1 illustrates, there were no significant differences in numbers of desire narratives told by urban versus suburban girls. The second problem is whether using multiple narratives from each girl as the basis of our analysis violates the assumption of independence of observations for linear modeling.[8] We have accounted for the clustering of multiple measurements for each girl in later analyses by estimating a series of fixed-effects logistic regression models. This analytic approach allows us to control for the number of narratives told by each girl and thereby reject the possibility that the differences among groups of girls that we have identified can be attributable to differences in how many narratives each girl or each group of girls told.

We coded the 128 narratives for themes of vulnerability and pleasure that girls associated with their experiences of sexual desire. To recognize the complex nature of both vulnerability and pleasure and to preserve the com-

TABLE 5.1 General Characteristics of the Participants ($N = 28$) and Their Narratives ($N = 128$)

Characteristics	Total Number of Girls[a]	Total Number of Narratives	Mean Number of Narratives per Girl	SD	t
Urban	14	53	3.78	2.00	
Suburban	14	75	5.35	2.87	1.67[b]
Reported sexual violence	13	56	4.53	2.53	
Did not report sexual violence	15	72	4.60	2.66	.062[c]

[a]Although the total number of participants was 30 girls, 2 of the girls did not tell any desire narratives at all.
[b]$p = .105$
[c]$p = .95$

plexity of the girls' experiences, we included six different types or domains of pleasure and vulnerability within each theme, derived from examining their narratives: personal identity, interpersonal relationships, social relationships, physical, psychological, and other. For example, the theme of vulnerability can represent the physical danger of sexually transmitted disease, the interpersonal risk of loss of friends, or the psychological danger of being emotionally hurt or disappointed. Each narrative was then coded for its predominant overall theme: vulnerability, pleasure, or equal presence of both vulnerability and pleasure. The narratives were double-blind coded; interrater reliability was high (Cohen's Kappa = .87).

To identify whether a girl had experienced sexual violation, we relied on how she answered the question, "Has anything bad ever happened to you that has to do with sex that you would like to tell me about?"[9] The girls in this study reported various experiences of sexual abuse and sexual violence, including acquaintance rape and attempted rape, and molestation and rape by adult male family members and by teenage male baby-sitters, as well as by strangers. Because of the small number of reports of sexual harm within each category, we coded all instances as "reported sexual violation" for purposes of this analysis. Of the urban girls, seven did not report sexual violation, whereas eight did, and among the suburban girls eight did not report sexual violation, whereas seven did. Notably, whether a girl lived in an urban or a suburban social location was not significantly related to whether she had reported an experience of sexual violation (Likelihood Ratio chi-square statistic [LR_X^2] .114, df 1, $p = .705$), nor was there any difference in numbers of desire narratives told by girls who did versus did not report sexual abuse or violence (see Table 5.1).

Results

In order to explore the differences in urban and suburban girls' associations of pleasure and vulnerability with their own sexual desire, we began examining the frequencies with which the girls told desire narratives that were predominantly about pleasure or vulnerability or in which both pleasure and vulnerability were equally present. Of these 128 narratives, 60 (46.9%) were predominantly about vulnerability, 37 (28.9%) were about pleasure, and 31 (24.2%) included both pleasure and vulnerability themes equally. The proportions of the urban and suburban girls' narratives that had vulnerability as their predominant theme were somewhat different, with 54.7% of urban girls' narratives focusing on vulnerability, whereas 41% of suburban girls' narratives did so. The difference between percentage of narratives in which vulnerability and pleasure were equally present was also small, with 28% of urban girls' narratives versus 21% of suburban girls' narratives falling in this category (see Figure 5.1).

A striking difference emerged between these two groups of girls, however, when we examined the frequency of a predominant theme of pleasure in their narratives. Suburban girls told many more narratives about pleas-

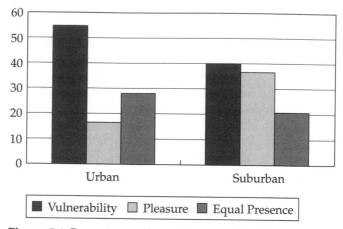

Figure 5.1 Percentages of narratives stratified by predominant theme and social location ($N = 128$).

ure than did urban girls. 37.3% of suburban girls' narratives were about pleasure as compared to 17% of urban girls' narratives (see Figure 5.1). Contingency table analyses support this observed difference (Likelihood Ratio chi-square statistic [LR_{X^2}] 6.54, df 2, $p < .04$). Specifically, suburban girls tell equal numbers of narratives expressing pleasure and vulnerability, whereas urban girls tell 3.2 times more narratives about vulnerability than about pleasure. These patterns suggest that although urban and suburban girls all associate their experiences of sexual desire with vulnerability and, to a lesser extent, a mix of vulnerability and pleasure in comparable proportions, the place of pleasure in their experiences differs.

In examining what kind of narratives were told by urban and suburban girls who had and had not reported sexual violation, we expanded our understanding of how pleasure and vulnerability figure in the desire experiences of these girls. Figures 5.2A and 5.2B display the number and percentages of desire narratives told by the girls, stratified by social location, report of sexual violation, and predominant theme. Three groups of girls—one of the suburban girls who reported sexual violation and two of urban girls (those who did and did not report sexual violation)—display a similar pattern in predominant themes: They all tell many more vulnerability narratives than narratives about pleasure or narratives in which vulnerability and pleasure figure equally. There is almost no difference in the numbers or proportions of narratives about pleasure versus vulnerability told by urban girls who had and had not reported sexual violation. The group that stands out is the suburban girls who did not report sexual violation. They tell more narratives about pleasure and fewer narratives in which vulnerability and pleasure were balanced than did the other three groups of girls. In addition, a higher percentage of their narratives had a predominant theme of pleasure than narratives that included vul-

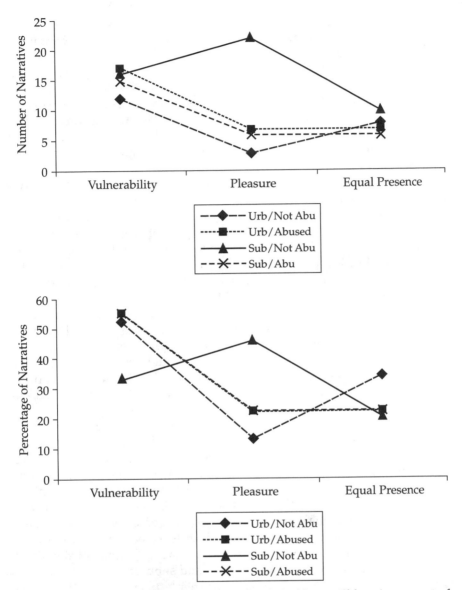

Figure 5.2 Top: The number of narratives stratified by social location, report of sexual violence and predominant theme ($N = 128$). Bottom: The percentage of narratives stratified by social location, report of sexual violence, and predominant theme ($N = 128$).

nerability. These findings suggest a further elucidation of the relationship between social location and experience of sexual desire—that, for suburban girls, sexual violation is related to an increased association of vulnerability and diminished association of pleasure with their experiences of sexual desire.

Contingency table analyses support these observations. We found that there was a relationship between a suburban girl's location, her exposure to sexual violence, and the predominant theme of her narratives (LR_X^2 statistic 6.41, df 2, $p < .04$). Specifically, suburban girls who *had* reported sexual violation told 4.3 times more narratives that expressed vulnerability versus pleasure than those told by suburban girls who *had not* reported sexual violation. Furthermore, the narratives told by the girls in the other three groups expressed vulnerability versus pleasure or both pleasure and vulnerability nearly three times (2.8) more than those of suburban girls who had not reported sexual violation.

In order to determine whether these relationships were statistically significant, we fit three fixed-effects logistic regression models: for narratives with a predominance of pleasure, narratives with a predominance of vulnerability, and narratives with an equal balance between vulnerability and pleasure. By including dummy variables to estimate each girl's effect, we were able to address the potential problems associated with the lack of independence of each narrative and not overestimate the independent degrees of freedom (Green, 1993; Hanushek, 1990).

The regression models confirmed our earlier findings associating an interaction between a suburban social location and absence of sexual violation with telling more pleasure narratives. The estimated odds[10] that a suburban girl who had not reported sexual violation would relate a narrative expressing pleasure was 5.89 times that of urban girls who had not reported sexual violation (Wald chi-square = 6.7679, $p < .0093$). Furthermore, suburban girls who did report sexual violation told narratives with a predominant theme of pleasure only a quarter of the time (.269), as compared with suburban girls who had not reported such abuses.[11] A girl's social location, report of sexual violation, or an interaction between the two were not significant indicators of narratives with a predominant theme of vulnerability or of narratives with equally expressed themes of vulnerability and pleasure (Wald chi-squares = 5.21, $p = .390$ and = 4.45, $p = .485$, respectively).

This quantitative analysis enables us to elucidate further our understanding of how these urban and suburban girls experience their own sexual desire. We are able to describe specifically the magnitude of the difference we noted qualitatively between urban and suburban girls' experiences of desire. We are also able to highlight that an interplay between these girls' social locations and personal histories of sexual violation figures significantly in how they experience and give meaning to their own desire, specifically pinpointing how they are limited and supported in the possibility of associating their own sexual desire with pleasure. This analysis allows us to retain and extend the complexity of our understanding that vulnerability is a key aspect of sexual desire for all of these girls.

DATA ANALYSIS AND RESULTS: QUESTION 3

Question 3: How do descriptions and narratives of sexual desire offered by suburban girls who have not reported sexual violence or abuse compare with the descriptions and narratives offered by urban girls who have and have not reported sexual violence and abuse and suburban girls who have reported sexual violence and abuse?

Our statistical analysis suggested that sexual violation can be a dimension of desire. The quantitative approach indicated that there were differences in how sexual violation shaped urban and suburban girls' experiences of desire. Our finding of a significant interactive effect between social location and report of sexual violation for suburban but not urban girls suggests the need to understand more about the comparative quality of their experiences of sexual desire. To pursue this lead, we chose to focus on how the girls spoke about their bodies in a second qualitative analysis, because, as the site of both vulnerability and pleasure (Vance, 1984), the specific context of bodily experience offers a theoretically compelling focal point for deepening our understanding of this dimension of desire.

Data Analysis

To explore this question, we returned to the original transcripts of the interviews and examined the complete text of each interview, an expansion on the original in-depth analysis of a single desire narrative. Using the same analytic method as described for answering Question 1, we tracked how the girls talked about their bodies and also tracked specific descriptions of how they related their bodies to their minds and their emotions (often referred to by the girls as their "selves"). Using The Listening Guide method, we marked all parts of each transcript where the girls mentioned their bodies for a voice of the body. We then listened for the self voice in each of these transcripts. This second time through the transcripts enabled us to determine how each girl related her experience of her body in her experiences of sexual desire and pleasure with her self, that is, how she related or integrated her mind and her emotions with her bodily experience. After completing a worksheet reflecting our interpretations of the girls' words, we organized these interpretations into a conceptually clustered matrix that would allow us to explore further and characterize the differences we had identified in the previous statistical analyses between the suburban girls who had not been sexually violated or abused and the other three groups of girls. We provide a section of this matrix to illustrate how this method makes it possible to identify similarities and differences within and between categories (see Table 5.2).

Results

In returning to the voices of urban and suburban girls who did and did not report experiences of sexual abuse or violence, we were able to investigate further the relative predominance of pleasure narratives spoken by suburban girls who have not experienced sexual abuse or violence as compared to the other groups of girls. We observed marked differences in how suburban girls who did not report sexual violation voice their bodies and speak about the relationship between their bodies and their psyches as compared with the other three groups.

TABLE 5.2 Partial Conceptually Clustered Matrix of the Voice of the Body, Relationship between Body and Self, and Girl Stratified by Social Location and Report of Sexual Violence

Suburban Girls—No Report of Sexual Violation

Girl	Voice of the Body	Relationship between Body and Self
Zoe (White)	Sexual desire and pleasure described in specific physical terms: "tingling," "shivering" Specific knowledge of pleasure: varying intensity and depth of feeling observed: "sometimes I kinda feel it's more deeper" Desire identified through embodied feeling	Desire as interplay between mind and body: interplay between "mental" and physical" feelings Linking physical feelings with mental feelings through relationship: "I don't know if you can feel it (desire) if you did it with someone who you didn't really love"
Eugenia (White)	Sexual desire and pleasure described in specific physical terms: "strong," "wet," "between my legs," "throbbing," "burn," "waves," "your body's excited" Specific knowledge of pleasure: orgasm as loss of "control" that is positive and pleasurable, linked to "comfort" in a relationship; explicit detailed knowledge of how body does and does not respond Desire identified through embodied feeling; strength of physical pleasure as motivation to continue behavior	Desire as interplay between mind and body Chooses to act on physical feelings only if they occur in the context of a relationship Enjoyment in experiencing embodied pleasure and quiet body when required; specific pathway relating emotional and physical feelings (mind and then body); link between focus of mind and experience of body; interplay of expressing self in relationship and increasing sexual feelings: "when there's emotions behind it, it makes it like that much more exciting" Exploration of her relationship to own body: question about lack of sense of entitlement to self-pleasure through masturbation Knowledge of benefits of knowing own sexual, physical responses and bringing information into relationships Link of self-confidence to self-pleasure through masturbation
Jane (White)	Embodied feeling described in nonspecific terms: "good," "expectant," "demanding," a "need," "jumpy," "excited" Link of physical pleasure to feeling of "happiness" and "being intimate"	Sense of entitlement to own body and its pleasures yet masturbation not sexually exciting or "natural" Link of pleasure and intensity of feeling to emotional anticipation

(continued)

TABLE 5.2 (*continued*)

Girl	Voice of the Body	Relationship between Body and Self
Suburban Girls—No Report of Sexual Violation		
	Desire linked to being touched physically: mouth, neck, skin, hair, "everywhere" Intimate knowledge of sexual pleasure as interplay of intensity and physical stimulation	
Urban Girls—No Report of Sexual Violation		
Beverly (African American)	Specific body parts associated with vulnerability to pleasure: "weak spot" on neck Descriptions of pleasure and desire suggest dissociation: "numb" Different descriptions of sexual pleasure and desire: as both numbness of body and body "saying yes"	Prohibition of action if absence of own embodied feeling: "If you want to do it, do it. If you don't want to, don't do it. Mind acts as vigilant guardian of responsive body: mind censors body "My body was saying yes, but my mouth was saying no" Body difficult to control, body as rogue: "my whole body is just going"
Charlene (White)	Sexual desire and pleasure described in specific physical terms: "having the shakes," "butterflies," "getting wet" Disembodied descriptions of desire: "felt like Jell-O," "in a daze," "I go to sleep" Specific knowledge of presence and absence of sexual satisfaction: "I think I get satisfied just by like hugs and kisses"; "sometimes he stops before like, you know, I am done" Specific knowledge of pleasure: "We have like different spots, you know, he touches you, that just makes you go in a daze or whatever"	Sense of entitlement to satisfaction Mind acts as vigilant guardian of responsive body: mind censors and silences body: "the more I like feel myself getting wet or something, it's like, just change my mind and think about something else" Experience of desire associated with mistrust of self and fear of pregnancy
Rochelle (African American)	Specific knowledge of pleasure: enjoys sex intermittently ("once in a while" vs. "all the time") Specific knowledge of desire: moderate sex associated with more desire Desire expressed in terms of specific physical terms: a "tingle," "like a fever or drugs"	Distanced from own body: intimidated by idea of masturbation Fear of pregnancy interferes with embodied feeling: "I don't really think I have any type of sexual pleasure . . . cause like I always have in the back of my mind, I'm gonna get pregnant . . . it's like, when I'm having sex, I just think about that"

(*continued*)

115

TABLE 5.2 Partial Conceptually Clustered Matrix of the Voice of the Body, Relationship between Body and Self, and Girl Stratified by Social Location and Report of Sexual Violence (*continued*)

	Suburban Girls—No Report of Sexual Violation	
Girl	**Voice of the Body**	**Relationship between Body and Self**
	Embodied feeling described in nonspecific language: "this feeling, to get rid of"	Fear of voicing own desire: "I just find it hard to come out and say . . . I would sort of like him to do it (cunnilingus)"
	Desire experienced more when alone than being touched	Mind quiets body: "I just, you know, just be quiet and just go away by myself, I just be calm, and like they'll (sexual feelings) go away"
	Connection between desire for thinness and desire to explore sexuality (discomfort with body, and with "being looked at")	Internalized cultural norms of femininity short-circuit sexual curiosity: "I just sorta have in mind that a woman's not supposed to be like aggressive doing stuff like that (being "on top")"
	Suburban Girls—Reported Sexual Violation	
Alexandra (White, bisexual, raped by boyfriend)	Distinction between physical arousal and pleasure	Response to desire and pleasure is to close body down, "refuse to let myself go"
	Pleasure and desire described in specific physical terms: "makes me tingle," "feel giddy and tingly," "physically turned on"	Resists cultural norms of femininity about female sexuality
	Specific knowledge of pleasure: soft things vs. "classically sexual acts, such as feeling up"; on top of the vagina, not inside	Equal importance of "physical, mental, social and emotional parts" of desire, although no clear relationship between them identified
	Sexual stimulation associated with pain and discomfort as it intensifies: "a very sore sensation, a sort of nauseous feeling in my stomach" (associated with experiences with males)	Mind as consultant for body: body as censor for self when mind is not vigilant enough
	Describes having physical needs (in association with her girlfriend)	Specific pathway relating emotional and physical feelings (mind and then body): "You meet a guy, you like him, you want to have sex with him, it's all in your mind . . . and then when he touches you, you get pleasure from it"
Nikki (White, hit repeatedly by boyfriend)	Absence of embodied feeling or desire: "I don't really feel anything"	Sexual pleasure and desire associated primarily with the mind, in thoughts
	Disembodied desire for sex associated with wish to get it over with and avoid pain when drunk	Specific pathway relating ideas and physical feelings (mind and then body)

(continued)

116

TABLE 5.2 (*continued*)

	Suburban Girls—Reported Sexual Violation	
Girl	**Voice of the Body**	**Relationship between Body and Self**
Liz (White, molested by adult male, rape averted by circumstances, single occurrence)	Embodied feeling described in nonspecific language: "satisfaction," "tiring," "exhausted," "really tense and then I rest, it melts" Physical pleasure associated with specific behavior Absence of knowledge of body-part names yet knowledge of bodily response and pleasure Specific knowledge of what is pleasurable and not pleasurable Desire described in specific physical terms: "hot," "a burning sensation," "feeling sweaty" Distinguish between feelings of love and lust	Mind as eraser: "If you think about it long enough, you just forget" Dissociation of mind and body: "I know I want him but it doesn't make me feel anything" Sexual desire includes desire for physical closeness in a relationship Discomfort with own body (self-conscious about weight) Desire emerges out of interactions that are not specific "sexual" behaviors Mind as a distraction to embodied response: concern about being found out doing something taboo Idea of a behavior can be pleasurable even when physical experience itself is not: "it makes me feel good, I think, just thinking about it being there (boy's erect penis), it just seemed so like sexual, so neat, it wasn't like I was getting excited, I was just doing it (fellatio) for him"

	Urban Girls—Reported Sexual Violation	
Laura (African American, repeatedly molested and raped by male babysitter in childhood)	"Not sure" about having experienced sexual pleasure or desire Embodied feeling described in nonspecific language: "jumpy," "like taking drugs," "hyper," "strange," "feel it all over," "want to do something"	Desire is something that happens to her: desire is an "unwanted visitor" Pleasure located in mind rather than in body Pleasure begins in the mind, leads to desire (not clear if that is associated with the body) and behavior, though sometimes it "just happens" Lack of clarity about whether desire occurs in mind and/or body; I just felt different" Relationship of mind and body is one of control; mind as a controllable part of self vs. body, which eludes control, things "just happen"

(*continued*)

TABLE 5.2 Partial Conceptually Clustered Matrix of the Voice of the Body, Relationship between Body and Self, and Girl Stratified by Social Location and Report of Sexual Violence (*continued*)

	Urban Girls—Reported Sexual Violation	
Girl	Voice of the Body	Relationship between Body and Self
Barbara (White, molested regularly between ages of 5 and 9 by adult male)	Sexual pleasure described in physical terms: body is "sensitive," "whole body can feel good," "gets your whole body turned on," "pressure in (chest)" Specific knowledge of pleasure and desire: "they (boys) can manipulate the clitoris and that drives any girl crazy"; "overwhelming"; "good if you can get it fulfilled," if not, an annoyance; orgasm "totally blew my mind" Specific knowledge of what she wants: "not just backrubs, do the whole body"	Interplay between mind and body: "when you concentrate, it brings more pleasure" Tries to avert mind's tendency to function as censor Desire needs to be communicated to other person to have pleasure Pleasure is physical and can be associated with emotional feelings too; physical desire is associated with emotional and mental knowledge Mind acts as guardian and censor of responsive body (refers to body and mind as "we"); mind speaks to body Express wish to feel pleasure and sexual desire led to "working upon [feeling desire] myself a lot"
Lily (Latina, attempted rape averted)	Intense sexual pleasure experienced when drunk and asleep: "best, funniest, most incredible time" Sexual pleasure is not experienced in her body (with the above exception) but described as emotional, being touched sexually is associated with disembodied "happiness" Disembodied perspective on pleasure of sex (pits relationship against physical experience) Disembodied experience of desire: feels it "in heart not body"; "tickling your heart"; "just a feeling inside, not a physical feeling at all" Experienced orgasms but not very important to her vs. emotional aspects of physical intimacy First experience of sex: no desire, "didn't know what was going on," "never thought about it"	Emotional rather than physical pleasure "counts" and is "fun" Physical pleasure outside of emotionally meaningful context is "disgusting" When physical pleasure is experienced, it is because of what boyfriend does—not responsible for physical pleasure and "do[es] not care" if it occurs Logic of emotions and desire: could only feel desire in a relationship, so has not felt desire for someone she hasn't loved

These suburban girls speak about their desire as an embodied experience that they associate with intense feelings of pleasure and also with self-knowledge. Both sexual desire and sexual pleasure are known to them as profoundly physical experiences—as feelings that they perceive in their own bodies. They are able to describe these experiences in specific terms, reflecting their clear acquaintance with these feelings: Zoe called it a "tingling or a shivering," Eugenia explained that it is "a burn, a throbbing down there, in between my legs . . . sometimes I get wet . . . it was just like my body wanted to just be like touched and explored." They describe sexual feelings in the way that a naturalist might make observations, noting the specifics of how their pleasure and desire occur and unfold, as Jane reported:

> I want to be with him and touch him and have him touch me, in your fingers, in your mouth, like your neck and like everywhere, just on your skin . . . when you are finally alone, then it is like that much better, because you've waited so long that it's like the feelings are so strong inside you that they're just like ready to burst, and it's sort of like you've both been waiting so that when you're finally together, it's that much more exciting or special.

Jane, like the other suburban girls who did not report sexual violation, voiced a sense of entitlement to her own desire and pleasure, as well as an intimate knowledge of how her desire "works" (see Table 5.2).

There is a consistency in how these girls describe the relationship between their bodies and their selves when they talk about their desire.[12] They all explain that both emotional and physical feelings contribute to their overall experience of sexual desire. That is, they describe an equitable interplay of mind and body, working in collaboration to generate what they call sexual desire. For instance, Eugenia explicated the difference that she understood between having "really strong emotions towards him" and "hav[ing] sex" with someone who is attractive:

> I think I would enjoy it so much more than having a one-night stand, even if it was something really like you just like saw each other and just wanted to get together and so it was kinda sexy, but I just feel like when there's like emotions behind it, it makes it like that much more exciting.

She continued to elaborate her experience of having feelings in her mind and in her body engaged in an interplay of pleasure:

> I think part of it was in my mind and then part of it was just that physical thing, just knowing you're doing something that you want to physically want somebody like that, sexual pleasure's something that's like so intensely emotional and so intensely physical.

These girls appear to be taking on and succeeding in working out the unarticulated and ostensibly insurmountable task that society has set up for young women, to figure out how to unite their sexual feelings with their emotional feelings in a cultural context that generally splits emotions from embodied experience along the lines of gender, distributing emotions to girls and sexual desire to boys.

This integration of emotions and body in voicing desire is unique to the suburban girls who did not report sexual violation and serves as an explication of our observation in the quantitative analysis that this group of girls told relatively more desire narratives about pleasure than did the other three groups. This description of desire suggests a connection between mind and body that is present for the group of girls who have relatively little violence to negotiate in their lives, in their general sociocultural situation, their relational landscapes, or in their personal histories. These girls speak about having feeling bodies and about knowing that their bodies and sexuality can be a source of physical, emotional, and relational pleasure and even strength. The multiple privileges of a safer suburban community and the absence of oppressive violence means that these girls have the freedom to associate their own desire more with pleasure than with vulnerability.

This qualitative analysis also enables further understanding of the findings of the quantitative analysis that the remaining three groups of girls—suburban girls who reported sexual violation, urban girls who did and did not report sexual violation—told more narratives about vulnerability than about pleasure. Distinct from the embodied and integrated voices of body and desire that are audible among the suburban girls who did not report sexual violation, the other three groups of girls are similar to each other in how they talk about their bodies and how they articulate the relationship between their bodies and their selves. We discern a general pattern of dissociation and disconnection in how these girls voice their bodies, ranging from reports of dissociation in specific situations to consistent absence of physical feelings. For instance, although Rochelle, an urban girl who does not report sexual violation, says that "I don't really have no pleasure," she also reports that "just like certain times I really really enjoy it [sex] but not a majority of the time, it's only sometimes, once in a while." Ellen, another urban girl who did not report sexual violation, said of desire, "I don't feel it very much in my body." Alexandra, a suburban girl who was raped, explains, "I can enjoy it, but I'm always you know just sorta like looking at it." And Lily, an urban girl who reported narrowly escaping a rape, said, "Nothing really happens with my body." In addition, some of these girls associate the experience of desire with physical discomfort, nausea, or tension.

There are also interesting differences between and within these groups that this analysis makes visible. The suburban girls who had experienced sexual abuse or violence are in fact the most different from the suburban girls who have not reported these experiences. When they talked about their desire, their descriptions reflect the *idea* of desire and pleasure more than or as often as the actual embodied experience of it. Nikki said that "if you like someone, then you know that's sexual pleasure but you have to think about it." And Liz explained the pleasure she associates with fellatio, "It wasn't so much that it makes me feel good, I think that just thinking about it being there, it just seemed so sexual, like so neat." They described an out-of-sync relationship between their selves and their bodies, such as Alexandra's recollection that "when you're in a situation and your body's saying one thing, you don't really consult your mind all the time. And that's another reason that I think I get tense." For Nikki, her mind and her body sound like separate entities, "It's all in my head, I think about it, but my body has nothing to do with it. You know, sure my body feels desire if someone touches me or feels pleasure, but pretty much it's in what you're thinking about." In describing having sex with a boy who was more inexperienced than she, Liz said, "It wasn't even like pleasurable, I don't think" but went on to explain that she enjoyed the feeling of power she experienced "in my mind."

The two groups of urban girls sound quite similar, more so than the two groups of suburban girls, and very similar to the suburban girls who reported abuse or violence. This qualitative similarity explains the weakness of the interaction effect from our quantitative analysis, which distinguishes suburban but not urban girls who have and have not been abused or sexually violated. All of the urban girls are subjected to daily doses of frightening violence that appear to contribute to a kind of dissociation from one's own body and a conflictual relationship between the mind and the body when it comes to sexuality. Among the urban girls, there was a distinct split between their minds and bodies reflected in their narratives and descriptions. They described how their minds offer a type of control over their responsive bodies, associated with fear of trouble and negative consequences. Laura, an urban girl who described years of molestation at the hands of a male baby-sitter, said, "But, I mean your body doesn't always listen to your mind, so sometimes, you might not want your body to react that way but it might anyway," whereas Ellen, who did not report sexual violation, said, "Your mind might say 'no' and your body will say 'yes.' Like if you see a guy and you think he's cute or something, your body might send out different signals but, you know, your mind might say, 'well no, not really.'" She went on to explain why her mind and body may "send out different signals": "Once I'm in that mood, I know like I don't know, I don't really trust myself. I always think I'm gonna end up pregnant."

The urban girls who reported sexual violence or abuse includes a subset of girls who sound quite distinct from the other girls in these three groups and somewhat similar to the suburban girls who did not report sexual violation. They are girls who voice a clear resilience and a conscious articulated resistance to being dissociated from their own bodies in the wake of their experiences with abuse and violence. Exemplified by Barbara, their voices echo the suburban girls who did not report sexual violation in the kind of vitality, integrity, and sense of entitlement to their own bodies inscribed in their desire narratives. Barbara explained that, although she had been repeatedly molested as a young child, she "wanted to be able to feel pleasure . . . cause in the back of my mind, I knew that I couldn't just go on being this way, cause if I got married, I was never going to enjoy it. And I wanted to be able to enjoy it. And so I worked upon it myself a lot." They are, girls who described sexual pleasure in specific physical terms and demonstrated a detailed knowledge of their own pleasure and desire. Barbara offered these descriptions of her experience and embodied knowledge of desire: "Most of my friends and me, our bodies are very sensitive, you're making out and your whole body can feel good . . . [boys] have this thing they can do with their hands, they can manipulate the clitoris and that drives any girl crazy, I know it does, it comes somewhere between being pleasure and pain, it's very overwhelming . . . your whole body gets turned on." There is an important complexity in how they voice the relationship between their selves, voicing a split yet also some sense of mind and body working together in the experience of desire and pleasure. Barbara explained that when "you're just concentrating on the pleasure, then it brings more pleasure than when you're thinking about something else." She also described her mind as a kind of chaperone for her body in risky situations, "I'll just tell myself, 'no, not today, we can wait, no need to rush it.' . . . I'm telling my body that I can wait." This small group of urban girls who reported sexual violation weave in and work for pleasure from within social locations and personal histories that highlight vulnerability—living in selves and bodies that have been harmed. This qualitative analysis reveals an important caveat to the general quantitative group finding that urban girls who had reported sexual violation associated their own desire more with vulnerability than with pleasure.

DISCUSSION

Together, the results of these three analyses contour a multidimensional understanding of adolescent girls' experiences of sexual desire. Grounded in a method of data collection that gave girls an opportunity to interrupt the usual silence about their sexuality and using qualitative and quantitative methods to analyze these data, we learned far more about this aspect of female adolescent development than forcing a choice between qualitative and quantitative methods would have afforded. This triangulation of analyses reinforces the basic finding that the dimensions of pleasure and vulnerability scaffold some pointed differences between urban and suburban girls in their experiences of desire.

In the first analysis, we found that urban and suburban girls described their experiences of sexual desire in both similar and distinct ways. They described the feeling of desire in comparable terms and spoke of desire as an embodied experience. There were discernable differences, however, in how they interpreted or understood their desire and in how they dealt with and managed their own sexual feelings. We interpreted these differences to be associated with the social locations in which their development and desire experiences occurred. We know that urban girls are subject to overt, constant violence and heightened chances of sexual experiences resulting in devastating consequences in a resource-constrained environment, whereas suburban girls live in a safer environment, at least in terms of the palpability of violence in their community, in which they have access to social and financial safety nets that can soften the blow of negative consequences of sexual exploration.

We expanded our understanding of this difference first by determining its magnitude, which was substantively and statistically significant. We refined our knowledge of pleasure and vulnerability as dimensions of desire by examining the effect of reported sexual violation. Our discovery that suburban girls who had not reported sexual violation told relatively more narratives about pleasure than the other three groups of girls offers insight into both urban and suburban girls' experiences of their sexual desire. Entering this dimension into our inquiry enabled us to fine-tune our understanding of how exposure to violence, sexual as well as environmental, is a significant factor in these girls' ability to know their own sexual desire as pleasurable.

Returning to our data with a third question and a new qualitative analysis refined and complicated this understanding further. We learned that suburban girls who had not reported sexual violation experienced their own desire as deeply grounded in their bodies and told narratives in which their desire integrated their emotional and physical feelings. The girls who had experienced sexual violence or were exposed to general violence in the community in which they lived sounded more dissociated from their own bodily feelings, an important source of self and relational knowledge (Debold, Wilson, and Malave, 1994) and voiced a split between their selves and their bodies. Suburban location brings the impact of sexual violation into high relief. Here, the blighting effects of sexual violence emphasize the vulnerability and eradicate the pleasure that girls can associate with their own sexuality. We also learned that within the group of urban girls who had experienced sexual violation, some had engaged in an active practice of resistance to being cut off from the pleasure and power that their bodies and sexuality could afford them. Despite having been sexually violated, they were still able to express pleasure in some of their narratives.

This study inscribes key shortcomings and suggests new challenges in expanding what we know about female adolescent sexuality. Although the urban sample was racially and ethnically diverse, it was too small to examine these crucial differences in female experiences of sexuality (Collins, 1991; Espin, 1984; Tolman, 1996), and the suburban sample lacked this variation. The same shortcoming applies to differences in religious backgrounds and religiosity. In addition, the small numbers of bisexual and lesbian girls did not allow us to examine how sexual orientation may be incorporated into this analysis of how vulnerability and pleasure figure in girls' experiences of sexual desire. Collecting and analyzing more desire narratives from these girls' perspectives is an important next step in learning about female adolescent sexual desire.

The findings of this study support and extend feminist theory that has asserted that sexual violence is a form of patriarchal oppression, disabling women by dividing them from the pleasure and power of their own bodies and of their erotic connections with other people (Lorde, 1984). The reality that female sexuality incorporates both pleasure and vulnerability for all women living in a society under the constraints of patriarchy suggests an important caveat in response to these findings. All of these girls demonstrated some capacity to balance both vulnerability and pleasure in their desire narratives. These two contradictory aspects are associated with female sexual desire in a world of AIDS, vibrators, insufficient access to any development of contraception, mass-mediated representations of sex, and powerful emotional and physical connections with other people. Knowing about and developing such a balance may be a crucial element of the healthy development of women's sexuality at this moment in history.

CONCLUSIONS

This study offers an illustration of one way to combine qualitative and quantitative methods to develop a comprehensive understanding of adolescent girls' experiences of sexual desire. Asking a series of questions informed by feminist theory, analysis, and methods, this study fills a research gap in girls' development left by conventional developmental psychology. We wish to emphasize that this study represents a feminist approach to bridging qualitative and quantitative methods of data analysis. A key component of our study was to begin with the voices of girls. As feminist psychologists, our central goals are to ask and answer questions that illuminate and challenge patriarchal assumptions about and negative effects on the lives of women and girls and to identify complexities in women's and girls' experiences and potential that have been difficult to know within the traditional practice of psychology. The use of a feminist eclectic approach to methods of data analysis in this study provides one way around the split that has tended to exist among feminist psychologists along epistemological and political lines, a split that may serve to diminish the impact that feminist psychologists can and need to have on the discipline.

NOTES

1. In more recent years, the use of focus groups has increased. This approach has been used to identify barriers to contraceptive and condom use (i.e., Kisker, 1985; Stanton, Aronson, Borgatti, and Galbraith, 1993)—to fulfill the agenda of preventing pregnancy and disease among adolescents—than as part of an inquiry into their experiences and the meanings they make of sexuality.

2. Maxwell (in Maxwell and Lincoln, 1990) contends that the debate rests, by and large, on in invalid assumption of paradigmatic unity; that is, that each paradigm constitutes a uniquely integrated and consistent whole that cannot be disaggregated and recombined with parts of other paradigms without creating philosophical and practical contradictions. This uniformity, according to Maxwell, is largely illusory and there are not, therefore, any generic qualitative or quantitative research paradigms. If we abandon the notion that the components of each paradigm are inseparable parts of larger methodological and epistemological wholes, we have removed any objection to the integration of approaches as pursued by Patton (1990a, 1990b).

3. Reinharz (1990) suggested that the dominance of one method over the other—primarily of quantitative methods over qualitative ones, with some excep-

tions (e.g., see Fine, 1992)—is a not-accidental reflection of larger patterns of dominance and powerlessness in our society.

4. Tolman performed a clustered random sampling based on membership in White, Black, Latina, Asian and "other" racial/ethnic groupings for each social location. The proportions of girls in each group in the sample from each site represent the proportion they represent of the school population, with the exception of Asian girls (see note 7). There was a 45% refusal rate in the urban school and a 33% refusal rate in the suburban school.

5. This sampling approach represents an important compromise in the overall study design. One argument would have been to select a purposive sample of girls who had sexual experience or who could say definitively that sexual desire was something they had experienced. Part of the inquiry of the study, though, was to develop a sense of whether sexual desire was something that girls said they knew about or experienced. Balancing this open question with the power of a random sample for exploring differences quantitatively led to the decision to take this approach.

6. In addition, Tolman approached a gay and lesbian youth group to include self-identified lesbian and bisexual girls in this sample. Two girls were included in the sample from this group; based on their description of their social environments, one was added to the suburban sample and one was added to the urban sample.

7. No Asian girls from either school chose to participate. Asian colleagues explained that it was countercultural for Asian girls to talk about sexuality with a White woman in school. This study in some ways thus leaves open the question of how race is incorporated into girls' experiences of sexual desire. Feminist and cultural studies scholarship suggests that race may be crucial and further research in this direction is warranted.

8. Both the *t*-test statistics and the X^2 statistics need to be interpreted cautiously as there is a violation of independence of the narratives. Note, however, that our purposes here are exploratory, and we address this in further analyses.

9. This question was suggested to the first author by Mary Belenky.

10. The reported estimated odds ratios are the antilogs of the estimated slope coefficients from the fitted fixed-effects logistic regression models.

11. This pattern arises in the group of girls who tell far fewer pleasure versus vulnerability narratives than do suburban girls who did not report sexual abuse or violence, but more pleasure narratives than the two groups of girls who did report abuse.

12. See Tolman (1994a) for a qualitative analysis of how a heterosexual, bisexual, and lesbian girl described their experiences of sexual desire in this study.

REFERENCES

Andersen, K., S. Armitage, D. Jack, and J. WittNer. 1990. Beginning where we are: Feminist methodology in oral history, pp. 94–114 in *Feminist research methods*, ed. J. Neilson. Boulder, CO: Westview Press.

Becker, H. 1986. *Writing for social scientists: How to start and finish your thesis, book, or article*. Chicago: University of Chicago Press.

Belenky, M., B. Clinchy, N. Goldberger, and J. Tarule. 1986. *Women's ways of knowing*. New York: Basic Books.

Benjamin, J. 1988. *The bonds of love*. New York: Pantheon.

Brown, L., E. Debold, C. Gilligan, and M. Tappan, 1991. Reading narratives of conflict for self and moral voice: A relational method. In *Handbook of moral behavior and development: Theory, research and application*, eds. W. Kurtines and J. Gewirtz. Hillsdale, NJ: Lawrence Erlbaum.

Brown, L., and C. Gilligan. 1992. *Meeting at the crossroads*. Cambridge: Harvard University Press.

Brown, L., M. Tappan, C. Gilligan, B. Miller, and P. Argyris. 1989. Reading for self and moral voice: A method for interpreting narratives of real-life, moral conflict and choice, pp. 141–164 in *Entering the circle: Hermeneutic investigation in psychology*, ed. M. Packer and R. Addison. Albany: State University of New York Press.

Carlson, R. 1996. Attitudes toward needle "sharing" among injection drug users: Combining qualitative and quantitative research methods. *Human Organization* 55: 361–370.

Collins, P. H. 1991. *Black feminist thought*. New York: Routledge.

Cook, T., and C. Reichardt , eds. 1979. *Qualitative and quantitative methods in evaluation research*. Beverly Hills, CA: Sage Publications.

Cowie, L., and S. Lee. 1987. Slags or drags? In Feminist Review, pp. 105–122 in *Sexuality: A reader*. London: Virago Press.

Crawford, M., and J. Maracek. 1989. Feminist theory, feminist psychology. *Psychology of Women Quarterly* 13: 477–491.

Debats, D. 1995. Experiences of meaning in life: A combined qualitative and quantitative approach. *British Journal of Psychology* 86: 359–376.

Debold, E., D. Tolman, and L. Brown. 1996. Embodying knowledge, knowing desire: Authority and split subjectivities in girls, epistemological development. In *Knowledge, difference and power: Essays inspired by women's ways of knowing*, ed. N. Goldberger, J. Tarule, B. Clinchy, and M. Belenky. New York: Basic Books.

Debold, E., M. Wilson, and I. Malave. 1994. *Mother-daughter revolution*. Boston: Addison-Wesley.

Delameter, J., and M. MacCorquodale. 1979. *Premarital sexuality: Attitudes, relationships, behaviors*. Madison, WI: University of Wisconsin Press.

Denzin, N., and Y. Lincoln. 1994. *Handbook of qualitative methods*. Thousand Oaks, CA: Sage Publications.

Espin, O. 1984. Cultural and historical influences on sexuality in Hispanic/Latin women: Implications for psychotherapy, pp. 149–164 in *Pleasure and danger: Exploring female sexuality*, ed. C. Vance. Boston: Routledge and Kegan Paul.

Fine, M. 1988. Sexuality, schooling and adolescent girls: The missing discourse of desire. *Harvard Educational Review* 58: 33–53.

Fine, M. 1992. *Disruptive voices: The possibilities of feminist research*. Ann Arbor, MI: University of Michigan Press.

Fine, M., and S. Gordon. 1989. Feminist transformation of/despite psychology, pp. 45–65 in *Gender and thought: Psychological perspectives*, ed. M. Crawford and M. Gentry. New York: Springer-Verlag.

Firestone, W. 1993. Accommodation: Toward a paradigm-praxis dialectic, pp. 105–124 in *The paradigm dialog*, ed. E. Guba. Newbury Park, CA: Sage Publications.

Freud, S. 1905. The transformations of puberty, pp. 73–96 in *Three essays on the theory of sexuality*, ed. S. Freud. New York: Basic Books.

Gilligan, C. 1982. *In a different voice*. Cambridge: Harvard University Press.

Gilligan, C., L. Brown, and A. Rogers. 1989. Soundings into development, pp. 55–58 in *Making connections: The relational worlds of adolescent girls at Emma Willard School*, eds. C. Gilligan, N. Lyons, and T. Hanmer. Cambridge: Harvard University Press.

Gladue, B. 1991. Qualitative and quantitative sex differences in self-reported aggressive behavioral characteristics. *Psychological Reports* 68: 675–685.

Goldfarb, E. 1995. Gender and race in the sexuality education classroom: Learning from the experiences of students and teachers. *SIECUS Report* 24(1): 2–6.

Green, W. 1993. *Econometric analyses* (2nd ed.). Englewood Cliffs, NJ: Prentice-Hall.

Greene, J. 1994. Qualitative program evaluation: Practice and promise, pp. 530–544 in *Handbook of qualitative methods*, N. Penzin and Y. Lincoln (Eds.) Thousand Oaks, CA: Sage Publications.

Guba, E., and Y. Lincoln. 1989. *Fourth generation evaluation*. Thousand Oaks, CA: Sage Publications.

Hanushek, A. 1990. *Diversity and complexity in feminist therapy*. New York: Haworth.

Healy, J., Jr., and A. Stewart. 1991. On the compatibility of quantitative and qualitative methods for studying individual lives. Vol. 3 in *Perspectives on personality: Theory, research and interpersonal dynamics*, ed. A. Sewart, J. Healy Jr., and D. Ozer. Greenwich, CT: JAI Press.

Hines, A. 1993. Linking qualitative and quantitative methods in cross-cultural survey research: Techniques from cognitive science. *American Journal of Community Psychology* 21: 729–746.

House, E. 1994. Integrating the qualitative and quantitative. Speech to the American Evaluation Association, Seattle, WA, pp. 13–22 in *The quantitative-qualitative debate: New perspectives, new directions in program evaluation*, ed. C. Reichardt and S. Rallis. San Francisco: Jossey-Bass.

Irigaray, L. 1981. This sex which is not one, pp. 3–37 in *New French feminisms*, ed. E. Marks and I. De Courtivron. New York: Schocken.

Jayaratne, T., and Stewart, A. 1991. Qualitative and quantitative methods in the social sciences: Current feminist issues and practical strategies, pp. 85–106 in *Beyond methodology: Feminist scholarship as lived research*, ed. M. Fonow & J. Cook . Bloomington, IN: Indiana University Press.

Jordan, J. 1987. Clarity in connection: Empathic knowing, desire and sexuality. *Work in progress/ Stone Center for Developmental Services and Studies* 29. Wellesley, MA: Stone Center for Developmental Services and Studies, Wellesley College.

Kaplan, A. 1964. *The conduct of inquiry*. San Francisco: Chandler.

Keenan, D. 1996. Use of qualitative and quantitative methods to define behavioral fat-reduction strategies and their relationship to dietary fat reduction in the patterns of dietary change study. *Journal of the American Dietetic Association* 96:1245–1251.

Kidder, L., and Fine, M. 1987. Qualitative and quantitative methods: When stories converge, pp. 57–75 in *Multiple methods in program evaluation. New directions for program evaluation*, eds. M. M. Mark, and R. L. Shotland. San Francisco: Jossey-Bass.

Kisker, E. 1985. Teenagers talk about sex, pregnancy, and contraception. *Family Planning Perspectives* 17: 83–90.

Lees, S. 1986. *Losing out: Sexuality and adolescent girls*. London: Dover.

Levinson, R. 1986. Contraceptive self-efficacy: A perspective on teenage girls' contraceptive behavior. *Journal of Sex Research* 22: 347–369.

Lorde, A. 1984. Sister outsider: Essays and speeches. *The Crossing Press feminist series*. Trumansburg, NY: Crossing Press.

Lykes, B., and A. Stewart. 1986. Evaluating the feminist challenge to research in personality and social psychology: 1963–1983. *Psychology of Women Quarterly* 10: 393–412.

Maracek, J. 1989. Introduction [Special Issue on Feminist Research Methods], pp. 367–377 in *Psychology of Women Quarterly* 13.

Maxwell, J. 1996. *Qualitative research design: An interactive approach.* Thousand Oaks, CA: Sage Publications.

Maxwell, J., and Y. Lincoln. 1990. Methodology and epistemology: A dialogue. *Harvard Educational Review* 60: 497–512.

Miles, M., and A. Huberman. 1984. *Qualitative data analysis: A sourcebook of new methods.* Beverly Hills, CA: Sage Publications.

Mishler, E. 1986. *Research interviewing: Context and narrative.* Cambridge: Harvard University Press.

Morowski, J. 1994. *Practicing feminisms, restructuring psychology.* Ann Arbor, MI: University of Michigan Press.

Nava, M. 1987. "Everybody's views were just broadened"; A girls' project and some responses to lesbianism, pp. 245–276 in *Sexuality: A reader,* eds. *Feminist Review.* London: Virago Press.

Nielsen, J, ed. 1990. *Feminist research methods.* Boulder, CO: Westview Press.

Oakley, A. 1981. Interviewing women: A contradiction in terms, pp. 30–61 in *Doing feminist research,* ed. H. Roberts. Boston: Routledge & Kegan Paul.

Omolade, B. 1983. Hearts of darkness. In *Powers of desire: The politics of sexuality,* ed. A. Snitow, C. Stansell, and S. Thompson. New York: Monthly Review Press.

Packer, M., and A. Addison. 1989. *Entering the circle: Hermeneutic investigation in psychology.* Albany, NY: State University of New York Press.

Patton, M. 1990a. *Debates on evaluation.* Newbury Park, CA: Sage Publications.

Patton, M. 1990b. *Qualitative evaluation and research methods* (2nd ed.). Newbury Park, CA: Sage Publications.

Reichardt, C., and S. Rallis, eds. (1994). *The quantitative-qualitative debate: New perspectives, new directions in program evaluation.* San Francisco: Jossey-Bass.

Reinharz, S. 1990. So-called training in the so-called alternative paradigm, pp. 290–302 in *The paradigm dialog,* ed. E. Guba. Thousand Oaks, CA: Sage Publications.

Rich, A. 1980. Compulsory heterosexuality and lesbian existence. *Signs: Journal of Women in Culture and Society* 5: 31–62.

Riger, S. 1992. Epistemological debates, feminist voices: Science, social values and the study of women. *American Psychologist* 47: 730–740.

Rogers, A., and C. Gilligan. (1988). *Translating girls' voices: Two languages of development.* Unpublished Manuscript. Harvard University Graduate School of Education, Project on women's psychology and girls' development, Cambridge, MA.

Rubin, G. 1985. The traffic in women: Notes on the political economy of sex, pp. 157–210 in *Toward an anthropology of women,* ed. R. R. Reiter. New York: Monthly Review Press.

Schulman, L. 1986. Paradigms and programs, pp. 35–60 in *Handbook of research on teaching* (3rd ed.), M.C. Whitrock. Riverside, NJ: Macmillan Reference.

Scott-Jones, D., and S. L. Turner. 1988. Sex education, contraceptive and reproductive knowledge and contraceptive use among Black adolescent females. *Journal of Adolescent Research* 3: 171–187.

Sechrest, L., and S. Sidani. 1995. Quantitative and qualitative methods: Is there an alternative? *Evaluation and Program Planning* 18: 77–87.

Shadish, W. 1995. The quantitative-qualitative debate: "DeKuhnifying" the conceptual context. *Evaluation and Program Planning* 18: 47–49.

Sktric, T. (1990). Social accommodation: Toward a dialogical discourse in educational inquiry, pp. 125–135 in *The paradigm dialog,* ed. E. Guba. Newbury Park, CA: Sage Publications.

Snitow, A., C. Stansell, and S. Thompson, eds. 1983. *Powers of desire: The politics of sexuality*. New York: Monthly Review Press.

Stanton, B. F., R. Aronson, S. Borgatti, and J. Galbraith. 1993. Urban adolescent high-risk sexual behavior: Corroboration of focus group discussions through pile-sorting. *AIDS Education and Prevention* 5: 162–174.

Strauss, A. 1987. *Qualitative analysis for social scientists*. New York: Cambridge University Press.

Tashakkori, A., and C. Teddlie. 1998. *Mixed methodology: Combining qualitative and quantitative approaches*. Thousand Oaks, CA: Sage Publications.

Taylor, J., C. Gilligan, and A. Sullivan. 1996. *Between voice and silence*. Cambridge: Harvard University Press.

Thompson, S. 1984. Search for tomorrow: On feminism and the reconstruction of teen romance. In *Pleasure and danger: Exploring female sexuality*, ed. C.Vance. Boston: Routledge & Kegan Paul.

Thompson, S. 1995. *Going all the way: Teenage girls' tales of sex, romance and pregnancy*. New York: Hill and Wang.

Tolman, D. 1992. Listening for crises of connection: Some implications of research with adolescent girls for feminist psychotherapy. *Women and Therapy* 15: 85–100.

Tolman, D. 1994a. Doing desire: Adolescent girls' struggles for/with sexuality. *Gender and Society* 8: 324–342.

Tolman, D. 1994b. Daring to desire: Culture in the bodies of adolescent girls, pp. 250–284 in *Sexual cultures and the construction of adolescent identities*, ed. J. Irvine. Philadelphia: Temple University Press.

Tolman, D. 1996. Adolescent girls' sexuality: Debunking the myth of the urban girl, pp. 255– 271 in *Urban girls: Resisting stereotypes, creating identities*, ed. B. Leadbeater and N. Way. New York: New York University Press.

Tolman, D. (in press). Female adolescent sexuality in relational contexts: Beyond sexual decision making. In *Beyond appearances: A new look at adolescent girls*, ed. N. Johnson, M. Roberts, and J. Worrell. Washington, DC: American Psychological Association.

Tolman, D., & Higgins, T. (1996). How being a good girl can be bad for girls, pp. 205–225 in *Bad girls/good girls: Women, sex and power in the nineties*, ed. N. Maglin and D. Perry. New Brunswick, NJ: Rutgers University Press.

Vance, C. 1984. *Pleasure and danger: Exploring female sexuality*. Boston, MA: Routledge & Kegan Paul.

Way, N. 1995. Can't you hear the courage, the strength that I have: Listening to urban adolescents speak about their relationships. *Psychology of Women Quarterly* 19: 107–128.

Way, N., H. Stauber, and M. Nakkula. (1994). Depression and substance use in two divergent high school cultures: A quantitative and qualitative analysis. *Journal of Youth and Adolescence* 23: 331–358.

Weedon, C. 1987. Feminist practice and poststructuralist theory. Oxford: Blackwell.

Whitbourne, S., and C.B. Powers. 1994. Older women's constructs of their lives: A quantitative and qualitative exploration. *International Journal of Aging and Human Development* 38: 293–306.

Young, L. 1992. Sexual abuse and the problem of embodiment. *Child Abuse and Neglect* 16: 89–100.

INTERACTION AND POSITIONALITY WITHIN QUALITATIVE RESEARCH

The readings in Part II, "Interaction and Positionality within Qualitative Research," address a range of the methodological choices and concerns that qualitative researchers encounter when working with human respondents through either ethnographic research or interviewing. Four important methods of observation and interviewing available to qualitative researchers are (1) ethnography, (2) in-depth interviewing, (3) oral history, and (4) focus group interviewing. These interaction-based methods of social inquiry cannot be discussed as if they were distinct from the actual activity of performing them in the "real world" and the concerns and transformations that arise during research. Several crucial epistemological questions need to be addressed as researcher and researched " bump up against each other" in an effort to understand and create meaning during the research process: Who gets to be a knower? What are legitimate models for knowing? What research questions get raised and who raises them? How do differences in race, class, sexuality, and gender between the researcher and researched impact how research is gathered and interpreted?

The scientific model of research relies heavily on the tenets of "positivism." A positivist framework of knowledge building depends upon two basic beliefs: that the social world is knowable and that there is an "objective" patterned social reality waiting to be known if only the researchers can separate themselves from the researched in order to observe reality unfettered by their own values and other biases. It is only through the separation of the knower and the objective world (subject) that true knowledge of "objective" reality can be obtained. In addition, positivism holds that there is order to the social world and that social life is patterned in such a way that one can discern cause and effect (Neuman, 1997). This assumption has caused a history of objection from the interpretive, critical, and feminist traditions (Nielson, 1990).

Yet the Western scientific enterprise has become an arena where knowledge and power are closely interlinked. Kuhn (1970) explains that "paradigms," or dominant worldviews, act as "filters" through which knowledge is constructed in relation to power. Foucault (1976) has greatly enhanced this debate by explaining that knowledge and power are intimately linked, creating a complex web of power-knowledge relations. Early on, the methods of positivist science were critiqued for being inherently masculine, and there are numerous examples of the androcentric (male bias) and race bias practices of scientists. Zuleyma Tang Halpin (1989) has critiqued the positivist conception of "scientific objectivity" for placing women and people of color in the "other" category, thus perpetuating a form of scientific oppression wherein white males are privileged as the "knowers." Susan Bordo (1989) has likewise shown the "maleness" (and we would add "whiteness") of the positivist philosophical tradition. Emily Martin (1991) has explained how this bias has infiltrated even biological categorizations of reproductive processes through the use of "stereotypical" notions of gender roles.

A good example of this type of bias is in the study of work and occupations. The types of questions asked and research conducted in this area clearly reflects biased assumptions concerning gender roles. The study of work and occupations for the most part, up until the early 1970s, had been concentrated on the study of men at work. Studies of work and occupations centered on male groups, settings, and concerns. What literature there was on women in the workforce at that time was often characterized by a "social problems" model. Researchers asked: Why do women work? Studies generally focused on "unusual" factors that influenced women's participation—such as being single, child-free, divorced, or having a low family income (why else would women want to work?). Researchers (read: white male researchers) often asked: What effect will work activities have on her family? Will her children become delinquent? How will work affect her relationship to her husband? Is divorce prevalent among working women? No questions were asked about whether or not women were satisfied with their working lives or if housewives were unhappy. Placing all women into one category shows little recognition of the vast array of differences among women and their work and occupational lives by race, class, age, sexuality, and so on. Those researchers studying women and work tended to generalize their research from the perspective of the white middle-class, heterosexual woman worker. Women's experiences, however, are shaped not only by their gender, but also by their racial, ethnic, cultural, sexual preference, age cohort, and economic background. Beyond looking at these factors as isolated from each other researchers must look at the *interconnections* among these categories as well. Patricia Hill Collins refers to this as a "matrix of domination" in which status characteristics, including race, class, and gender, are overdetermined in relation to each other. As Evelyn Glenn, among others observes:

> It may be tempting to conclude that racial ethnic women differ from white women simply by the addition of a second axis of oppression, race. It would

be a mistake though, not to recognize the dialectical relations between white and racial ethnic women. Race and Gender interact in such a way that the histories of white and racial ethnic women are intertwined (Glenn, 1987:72).

For example, many white women have relied on the labor of women of color to themselves move forward economically, paying mostly minority women poor wages and few benefits. (See Hochschild, 2000; Rollins, 1985.)

Yet once the practice of reflexivity is under way, "other" angles of vision of the research process begin to emerge as our focus of attention begins to shift: We are made aware of how important differences in positionality between the researcher and researched impact all phases of the research process—from the questions asked to how data is interpreted and analyzed. For example, we can note that remaining objective during the research process does not necessarily eliminate our "values" from the research process since these "values" can crop up in the types of research questions we ask or do not ask. Researchers who have a particular bias against working mothers may in fact lean more toward a "social problems" orientation in their questions concerning working women. It does not matter how objective they attempt to be when carrying out the project because the questions have already determined the type of conclusion that will, more or less, emerge from the data.

What is also important to address is that "subjects " of research, who are often treated as "objects," have traditionally been excluded from knowledge building. These often have been women and other marginalized groups. It is clear that making a commitment to listening to the meanings assigned by "others," and being aware of their differing positions in terms of race, class, and gender, provides the researcher with what Sandra Harding has termed "stronger objectivity" (1993). This type of objectivity is more complete than that based on the perspectives of those in power. Sandra Harding encourages scientists to practice "strong reflexivity." Feminists are not alone in this vein, as postmodernists and other critical scholars share this concern. Critical scholar Donna Haraway (1991) encourages researchers to conduct "power-reflexive" research, whereas critical sociologist Stephen Pfohl (1994) uses the term "power-sensitive" to denote a similar style of research practice. An excellent definition of reflexivity comes from anthropologist Helen Callaway. She notes:

> " . . . reflexivity . . . can be seen as opening the way to a more radical consciousness of self in facing the political dimensions of fieldwork and constructing knowledge. Other factors intersecting with gender—such as nationality, race, ethnicity, class, and age—also affect the anthropologist's field interactions and textual strategies. Reflexivity becomes a continuing mode of self-analysis and political awareness" (1992:33).

Reflexivity is the recognition on the part of the researcher that research is a process that contains a variety of power dimensions. It is crucial for researchers to become aware of their positionality—that set of attributes and identities that they bring to the research setting, including their gender, their race/ethnicity, and their class position. These factors entail a certain power dynamic and may impact the research process—from the questions researchers ask to how they interact with those they research and how they interpret and write up their research findings.

One of Sandra Harding's goals is to move the sciences and social sciences toward "emancipation," she asks: "What can be done to enhance the democratic tendencies within the sciences and to inhibit their elitist, authoritian, and distinctively androcentric, bourgeois, Eurocentric agendas? (1991:217)." Accordingly, the readings in this section explain the research methods available to researchers wanting to conduct interactive research but also present the implications of positionality within the process as experienced by researchers gathering qualitative data. Researchers and the researched occupy different standpoints determined by their race, class, gender, sexuality, and so on. These spaces of difference are a part of the entire research process. Both the theoretical and practical articles selected for this section of the book address issues pertaining to difference within discussions of particular methods.

Scholars working from critical epistemological perspectives such as standpoint and feminism argue that in practice all research is impacted by researcher/researched standpoint. There is a unique way in which issues of difference impact the interactive methods reviewed in this section that is directly related to the broad goal of ethnography and interviewing. This category of qualitative methods contains methodological techniques aimed at understanding the point of view of the respondents. In other words, qualitative researchers using methods of observation, interviewing, and ethnography are interested in how the research participants interpret and give meaning to their own experiences. Researchers are interested in understanding social life, or some aspect of it, from the perspective of those being studied. Positionality, or what some sociologists call "status characteristics" (Bailey, 1996:20), impacts every aspect of social life and is thus an important factor in how people structure and give meaning to their social experience. As such, issues of difference permeate the qualitative research process.

The goal of this kind of qualitative research is to understand something about social reality from the viewpoint of those being studied. This means that the questions asked within the research process are crucial. For example, we might be interested in the challenges that working women face, and their strategies for dealing with those challenges. The questions we choose to ask will directly influence the emergent data. Consider three possible interview questions: (1) What struggles do you face trying to balance work and family responsibilities? (2) Describe barriers to advancement that you encounter in your work environment. (3) Explain the kinds of challenges you deal with as a working woman. The first question has a built-in assumption that women deal with challenges trying to balance work and family. The second question presupposes that all women struggle with advancement in the workplace and is aimed at generating data about such obstacles. The third question is the most "open-ended" and places the respondent in a position where she can choose what work-related issues to emphasize according to how *she* interprets her worklife challenges. All of these questions might be perfectly appropriate depending on the research goals in question but they will elicit different kinds of data. Questions are guides for the researcher and respondent.

The questions asked are linked to both method and epistemological approach. As we saw from the readings in Part One, qualitative research can be conducted using a highly diverse variety of approaches, ranging from positivism to feminism. The approach employed is likely to affect the method selected, the application of that method, and the questions being asked. These research methods can also be employed in formats ranging from semistructured to nonstructured designs. These formats impact the level to which a researcher guides and controls the research process. Consequently, the degree of structure impacts the questions asked.

A researcher working from a positivist epistemological position might be more likely to ask research questions best answered through in-depth interviewing or focus group interviewing. These methods allow the researcher to maintain, if desired, a moderate level of control within data collection by structuring the interview questions and process. A researcher interested in understanding a particular aspect of a person's life, or interested in capturing and recording how a group of individuals experiences some aspect of social life, might be inclined toward the method of oral history. Feminist researchers typically use this method as a way of giving voice to the silent experiences of women. Accordingly, feminists have used the oral history method to build knowledge about the varied struggles women encounter in both the public and private spheres. A researcher interested in understanding some aspect of social life as experienced by a specific group, might use an ethnographic approach that combines interviewing, observation, and even participation. Ethnography is often used by researchers working from the interpretive tradition with the intent of understanding social meaning as inseparable from its construction and application in the social world. These possibilities are meant to serve only as examples, as the methods can be employed in a variety of ways by researchers working from any number of epistemological positions. Ethnography differs from interviewing in that it occurs in a natural environment and involves high degrees of observational data. For example, in the Introduction to Part One we saw how Greta Foff Paules used ethnography in order to understand how New Jersey waitresses deal with, and resist, power relations within their workplace.

Each method lends itself to particular kinds of qualitative questions, as we see in the readings that follow. Qualitative questions tend to be open-ended, encouraging respondents to emphasize what they feel is important (within the confines constructed by the researcher). The epistemological position researchers begin from impacts the kinds of questions they ask and therefore the selection and application of an appropriate research method.

Qualitative methods of ethnography and interviewing allow researchers to ask a broad range of questions aimed at understanding social life as experienced by those who live it. While the readings show that these methods can be time consuming, exhausting, and ethically challenging, they allow social researchers to generate data and build knowledge that would not otherwise be attainable. The breadth of questions explored by these techniques is a distinguishing characteristic of qualitative research. While these methods can be challenging, they are also immensely rewarding, and at the end of the day qualitative researchers use these methods because, as we will see, they are intellectually and personally fulfilling.

ETHNOGRAPHY

Anthropologists originally practiced ethnography, also commonly referred to as "field research," as a method of studying and writing about different cultures (Silverman, 2001:45). Sociologists and other social investigators now conduct ethnographic work in order to study not only "exotic" cultures but also everyday life within their own culture. Ethnography involves studying a real social group within a natural setting. The setting is referred to as the "field" or "site." Data gathering occurs within a natural setting that exists independent of the research. The people within the setting—the research participants—are engaged in ongoing, naturally occurring social interaction. In other words, the research participants are engaged in their daily activities regardless of whether or not the study is being conducted. The waitresses Paules studied would have been working regardless of whether or not the research was occurring. Carol A. Bailey defines field research as follows:

> the systematic study, primarily through long-term interactions and observations, of everyday life. The goal of field research is to understand daily life from the perspectives of those in the setting or social group being studied. Field research is classified as a longitudinal design because data collection takes a long time—usually months or years (Bailey, 1996:2).

The extent to which researchers interact with research participants varies greatly. Observation (eyes and ears), interviewing, and participation are all techniques employed by ethnographers. While observation is a necessary component of ethnography, the extent to which researchers will interact with participants through formal or informal interviewing and/or participating in the activities the researched are engaged in is context dependent. "Participant observation" is a term frequently used to denote researcher involvement in the activities of those being researched. When Paules worked alongside the waitresses she was studying she was engaging in "participant observation." A combination of the specific research questions, research goals, epistemological framework, and, ultimately, researcher choice dictate the level of interaction engaged in. Participation and specific techniques of observation can be classified as methodological choices. It is thus important to remember that methods are always linked to research questions and the overall theoretical approach.

Ethics are an integral part of ethnographic research, and indeed of all interactive qualitative research. In this text we have primarily included discussions of ethics in our ethnographic selections; however, the same principles can be applied to methods of interview. Many of the methodological choices already discussed are informed by ethical considerations. The extent to which researchers disclose their true identities and purposes for being in the setting will impact the techniques of data gathering available to them. Formal interviewing is nearly impossible (minus direct deceit) unless researchers have disclosed their identities. Likewise, it may be difficult for researchers to gain access to the setting or group they are interested in if the research participants are made aware of the researcher's status and intentions. Furthermore, those at a higher level of authority may not want the research to be performed. Consider a study of structural barriers toward advancement that women or other minorities face in the workplace. Management may not allow a researcher access to conduct an ethnographic study if it is concerned that the research will be damaging to the business. Such human barriers to research or disclosure are called "gatekeepers." The presence of a researcher may also impact the behaviors of those being studied. Bailey posits that ethical field researchers have an obligation not to harm the research participants, research setting, relationships formed in the field, themselves, or the profession represented (1996:13). Informed consent, voluntary participation, and confidentiality are the main (broadly conceived) ethical considerations qualitative researchers must face and address. Again, these considerations are not limited to ethnography but also pertain to methods of interviewing.

Ethnography is one of the qualitative methods that has often been used to give voice to those historically excluded from processes of knowledge building along lines of race, class, gender, and sexuality. In this way, ethnography and other methods of qualitative research often maintain an activist component. In "Culture to Culture: Ethnography and Cultural Studies as Critical Intervention," bell hooks addresses several of the theoretical concerns scholars must consider when conducting and reviewing ethnographic research along planes of difference. Concerned with researching those frequently marginalized along racialized and gendered hierarchies, hooks urges scholars, particularly white scholars who already occupy a racialized position of privilege, to interrogate their work on "black people" or "black culture." This critical interrogation, a basic component of reflexive practice, is a proactive technique scholars can employ so as to avoid "reinscribing" Western traditions of oppression that perpetuate racist (and sexist) domination through power-imbued knowledge construction.

hooks asserts that researchers must reexamine the traditional practice of ethnography so as to effectively study difference in terms of race/ethnicity and gender in order to build knowledge removed from cultural oppression. Traditional applications of ethnography have colonized the researched by essentializing difference. Essentialism destroys the resistive possibilities (such as resistance to dominant power) in ethnographic work.

The rapidly growing field of interdisciplinary cultural studies opens up an academic space for such critical inquiry. The interdisciplinary nature of cultural studies allows for a global perspective and the abolishment of constraining disciplinary boundaries. Furthermore, interdisciplinary research allows researchers to ask questions they would not otherwise be able to. The surge of academic interest in cultural studies has also served to legitimize concerns about race and gender historically posited only by marginalized academics working from within feminist and multiculturalist epistemological frameworks. hooks's article is important because it prods scholars to conduct reflexive research. Attention to issues of difference is intimately linked to the ethical construction of social scientific knowledge within academia.

A direct discussion of ethics within ethnography is presented in Barrie Thorne's article "'You Still Takin Notes?' Fieldwork and Problems of Informed Consent." Thorne provides an in-depth review of informed consent, the main tenet of ethical research, within the practice of ethnography. Showing how some methodological techniques are easier in theory than in practice, Thorne reviews the difficulty with informed consent within the field. Beyond this practical discussion he also presents ethical issues scholars must consider and critique, making this an excellent overview of ethics and informed consent.

"Informed consent" means that research participants have made an "informed" decision to participate in the research project, which means that they understand the research goals. Confidentiality is considered a given in ethical research. The other two of the main tenets of informed consent are "voluntary choice" and "knowledge." Within the context of participant observation, Thorne reviews the practical problems with ensuring participants' consistent voluntary participation and knowledge. In a longitudinal study, does informed consent ever expire? Must the researcher ever reobtain consent from research participants? If so, how often must informed consent be renewed? How much information (presented by the researcher to the participants) constitutes "knowledge" of the research project? The amount researchers disclose about themselves and the research project is context dependent. A researcher must weigh the impact full disclosure will have on the research process against ethical obligations to obtain informed consent. There are different concerns about voluntary participation in ethnography than there are in interviewing. Research participants are necessarily asked to participate in the interview process, as it is a special activity. This means that the participants would not be engaged in the activity unless the researcher had asked them to be. Interviews are conducted in artificial settings, such as offices or labs, not the natural environment of the participants. Ethnography is conducted in natural settings where the participants would be present regardless of the research. This would be the case when conducting an ethnographic study of women in *their* work environment.

After reviewing the practical problems surrounding informed consent, Thorne posits that there are broad ethical issues pertaining to informed consent that show informed consent is not exhaustive in scope. The focus on the individual participant within applications of informed consent ignores larger questions about how the knowledge generated by the research project will be used. What are the purposes of this research in terms of knowledge building?

The issues of difference, disclosure, and ethics that permeate hooks's and Thorne's articles are all raised in our last ethnography piece, an excellent example of ethnography in practice. In "Fieldwork in Lesbian and Gay Communities" we are shown how Kath Weston made methodological choices while actually conducting an ethnographic study. Many of the topics covered in the first section of this book are revisited in this practical research example.

Weston was interested in studying the (recent and broad) term "gay families." She decided to conduct ethnographic research with "gay families" living in the San Francisco Bay area in order to give social meaning to that term. Here we can see how a general research idea, or researcher interest, develops into a research question which then informs methodological decision making. Weston explains that her "field" selection is somewhat of an anomaly but that despite problems of generalization it would be a fruitful area in which to conduct her study. This is an example of actively accounting for the context of discovery in a reflexive manner, as discussed by Sandra Harding.

Weston's methodology included a mix of semistructured in-depth interviews and ethnographic observation. Weston explains that her standpoint as a gay person aided her research in multiple ways. First, her lesbian identity helped her to gain access to the group she wished to study. She was able to use her positionality to create rapport and build trustful reciprocal relationships, which are an invaluable part of the ethnographic endeavor. Additionally, Weston was not studying something "exotic" to her but rather was systematically discovering the mundane everyday experiences of "gay families." This study is an example of how ethnography can be used to study the mundane from the viewpoint of the research participants. How do they interpret and give meaning to their own experiences? What does the term "gay family" mean to them and how do they experience their lives in relation to that term?

Finally, Weston's article addresses issues of difference in terms of race/ethnicity and social class. Not only does Weston account for and attempt to access diversity, but she also probes further by showing the very material aspect of language in carefully deciding what terminology she will use to gather and interpret her data. Her attention to the power of language is a part of her attempt at ethical research. From disclosing her own standpoint to practicing reflexivity throughout the research process, Weston's study shows the importance of process-oriented ethical considerations.

IN-DEPTH INTERVIEWING

In-depth interviewing is a frequently used qualitative method of data gathering. Intensive interviews can yield large quantities of descriptive qualitative data but are less time consuming than ethnography. They can typically be conducted within a one- to two-hour time frame. This makes in-depth interviewing a highly viable research option for many researchers who wish to gain descriptive information from the viewpoint of respondents but who might not have the resources (especially the time and money) to engage in a longitudinal ethnographic study. Depending on the nature of the research project, an interviewer may choose to conduct multiple interviews with one respondent or one interview per respondent. The number of respondents interviewed depends on the context of the research.

The subjects explored through in-depth interviews cover the gamut of social scientific interests. Unlike ethnography, the researcher and respondents arrange in-depth interviews in advance. A location is selected, typically an office, home, or lab, and a meeting time is specified. As with all research involving human subjects, informed consent agreements must be signed by the research participants and confidentiality must be assured. With respondent consent, a researcher may elect to tape an interview. While some researchers take written notes, typically tape recorders are used to fully capture the interview. Note taking can also be used in conjunction with a tape recording; however, eye contact is an important part of a successful qualitative interview, and note taking may impair a researcher's ability to maintain eye contact. Some researchers even elect to use video cameras. This is less common but would be appropriate in circumstances where the respondent's body language is an important part of the data. The best way to understand qualitative interviewing, aside from personal experience, is to read both theoretical discussions and practical examples of the process from the reflective vantage point of a researcher.

William L. Miller and Benjamin F. Crabtree focus on the details of conducting semi-structured in-depth interviews in "Depth Interviewing." The authors concentrate their attention on the field of clinical research and, more specifically, the area of primary care. Miller and Crabtree are interested in exploring how best to conceptualize the interview process so that both patient and care provider can be heard and understood. Moreover, asserting that pain is a physiosubjective experience, the authors contend that to understand pain is to ask questions and to participate in making in-depth interviewing an effective research method.

The authors used in-depth interviewing within a clinical setting, citing the sample interviews of six family physicians and six paired patients from a small suburban community in Connecticut. Miller and Crabtree are interested in how best to create an interview setting in which both patient and care provider can be heard and understood. Furthermore, the authors illustrate that both interviewer and interviewee have numerous social roles beyond the personification of interviewer/interviewee. In this way, the authors contend that the interview is better understood as a special type of "partnership" and "communicative performance." While the interview situation has traditionally been viewed as a type of "one-way" interaction, with the researcher providing a set of questions and the respondent giving a set of answers, within Miller and Crabtree's partnership model, the interview can be viewed as a "conversational research journey with its own rules." In this way the interview becomes interactive and intimate, allowing "depth, detail, vividness and nuance." Data to be interpreted include not only verbal communication but also gestures, facial expressions, and other nonverbal forms of expression. For example: How can we give voice to the patient's concerns and symptoms? How can a patient's problems best be understood by their care provider?

The authors provide a complete overview of the five steps necessary to depth interviews: (1) mapping, (2) designing, (3) preparing, (4) interviewing, and finally (5) transcribing. Miller and Crabtree conclude that the in-depth interview is intended to focus on "specific research questions and is characterized by open, direct verbal questions that elicit stories and case-oriented narratives." The authors advise researchers to balance intimacy with distance within the interview, and they provide ways for the researcher to overcome resistance during the interview process. Additionally, Miller and Crabtree provide useful guidelines for interviewing, such as " The interviewer should display desired enthusiasm; be non-judgmental; show interest in the information as it unfolds." Useful guidelines on transcribing the interview are also provided. Finally, Miller and Crabtree emphasize that a good in-depth interview serves to preserve the "multivocality and complexity of lived experience." Many of these issues are put in practice in our next selection.

In " 'White Like Me?' Methods, Meaning, and Manipulation in the Field of White Studies," Charles A. Gallagher shows the importance of researcher standpoint within qualitative practice. While this provocative piece contributes to the literature on in-depth interviewing and multimethod approaches as well as containing substantive content in the area of "white studies" as an explicitly "antiracist project," it is a distinct contribution to the insider/outsider phenomenon specific to interactive qualitative methods.

Gallagher is interested in contributing to the emergent field of "white studies" in order to create a better understanding of racial privilege and ultimately resistance to racialized hierarchical ways of knowing. Gallagher is a white male from a working-class background. As such he has had exposure to overt racism. In his life he moved among different social classes. He noticed that middle- and upper-class white people practiced a kind of "soft racism," expressing racist beliefs, but with careful attention to their language (which he calls "qualifying" language). His life experience has shown him that there are multiple white racisms. Drawing on his own personal experience and intellectual interests, he decided to systematically study white racisms through intensive interviewing.

As a part of reflexive practice Gallagher openly discloses that he thought he would have easy access to research participants because he was of their race. In this way, Gallagher saw himself as "unburdened" by his race. A female researcher conducting interviews with working women might make the same assumption. During the research process Gallagher realized that his status made him an insider and outsider at different times. For example, in a bar a white male freely disclosed what Gallagher refers to as a "white story," which is a racist narrative, because he and Gallagher shared the same race and (presumably) economic background. Gallagher's status within the context of the following interviews included his race, age, gender, and social class. His assumption that he would be an instant insider was thus false, as standpoint reflects a range of characteristics and experiences. Social class was also a significant factor in his ability to access data. The same would again be true for a female researcher studying working women, depending on differences and points of convergence in, for example, sexual preference, race, and economic background. The assumption of "insider" status on the basis on only one shared characteristic is thus problematic in practice, as standpoint is far more multifaceted.

ORAL HISTORY

Oral history is a method of in-depth biography interviewing in which a researcher spends an extended period interviewing one respondent about his or her life or about an aspect of it. Oral histories can be done in one or multiple sittings, and a particular research project can consist of one or multiple oral histories. It is important to allow the respondent to speak as much as possible and share his or her story. The goal of an oral history is to help the respondent give meaning to his or her own life experience through a detailed narrative. Feminist researchers interested in obtaining the oral histories of women have most frequently used this qualitative interview method, which traditionally has been marginalized within the social sciences. Feminists' attraction to the method of oral history arises from their commitment to including the previously unaccounted for experiences of women. Oral history data has been used to build feminist theory, give voice to those previously silenced, show the inadequacy in our current body of social scientific knowledge, and raise new topics as important potential subjects of inquiry. Oral history has been integral to the development of knowledge about working women and the varied struggles and rewards different kinds of women face in diverse workplaces. The articles in this section reflect the theoretical considerations that go into understanding oral history as well as the practical benefits of documenting previously silenced history.

In "Beginning Where We Are: Feminist Methodology in Oral History" Kathryn Anderson, Susan Armitage, Dana Jack, and Judith Wittner explain why oral history fits with feminist inquiry. They assert that oral history data builds theory and challenges old biased assumptions. Oral history is then a tool used by feminist researchers to incorporate previously excluded knowledge into our repository of knowledge. Child rearing, sexuality, reproduction, and, housework are topics that have been discovered and explored through the oral history method. Women are able to reveal their own experiences with these (and other) topics through storytelling. In order to understand and document the life experiences of women, scholars must recognize that women are experts on their own behavior. They are the primary source of this formerly unclaimed data. Oral history offers a methodology whereby women can be asked how they interpret and assign meaning to their life experiences.

Anderson et al. undertook this feminist exploration of oral history from an interdisciplinary standpoint, bringing in sociological, psychological, and historical viewpoints. This writing technique is congruent with their discussion of oral history, which is an interdisciplinary method of social inquiry used by researchers from multiple academic disciplines. They present a specific theoretical framework for looking at oral history. Drawing on standpoint epistemology they explain that in a hierarchical society, women, who are not in a position of gendered privilege, both conform to and oppose that which limits their freedom. As a result there may be a disjuncture between what women think and how they behave. Researchers can use the oral history method to help women tell their stories by beginning with everyday life material experiences (i.e., work, housework). In the end, the data collected are the result of both the researcher and research subject. Researchers must learn to be highly attentive listeners but also practice reflexivity and recognize that their own standpoint impacts how they hear and interpret the data. The importance of oral history as a method of writing otherwise excluded history is evidenced in our next selection.

In "Understanding Domestic Service through Oral History and the Census: The Case of Grand Falls, Newfoundland," Ingrid Botting explains how she used oral history to fill a gap in a current body of knowledge. Botting wanted to study domestic servants who in the 1920s and 1930s migrated from coastal communities to a mill town in Newfoundland in order to work. She wanted to contribute to our knowledge of the work and migration experiences of these women, who represented an extraordinarily high percentage of wage earners in that time and place. She decided to combine written census data and oral histories. There were some ethical considerations regarding the use of the census data because many of the documents in question were private sources; however, these documents made her research possible, and she ultimately felt ethically able to use the material. Botting perceptively explains the similarities in the census data and oral history data. As she puts it, both data sets were the products of complex relationships between researcher and subject. These relationships embody positions of power and privilege wherein the researcher is coming into the lives of these women. Botting discloses that despite her status as a woman, she was more different from her research participants than she was the same. This is similar to how Gallagher found that race alone did not make him an "insider" with his interviewees.

Botting's article is an excellent example of a multimethod approach suited to the specific goals of the study. Moreover, Botting illustrates the importance of reflexivity, she twice modified her project based on the availability of data and later on her early findings. This kind of adaptability is very important in the practical application of any qualitative research method. Botting initially had made two different question sheets for her oral histories, based on the way she had categorized respondents. However, Botting soon learned that the participants were not as different from each other as she had thought they would be. Through a process of reflexivity her project continually evolved and ultimately produced original data documenting the experience of women who would otherwise be written out of history.

FOCUS GROUP INTERVIEWING

Focus groups are a distinct method of qualitative interviewing in that multiple participants are interviewed in the context of a group. The researcher is thus both interviewer and moderator. Focus groups are used not only in a wide range of academic disciplines, including the social sciences, but they are also a routine method of data collection in marketing and advertising. Focus groups are often used in the context of evaluative research. For example, in marketing a researcher might be trying to increase the vendibility of a product, and in sociology a researcher may be trying to evaluate an educational program. Additionally, although focus groups can be the only method used within a particular study, they lend themselves to multimethod approaches and are frequently used in conjunction with surveys and/or in-depth interviews. Accordingly, focus groups are often used in multimethod qualitative research and in combined qualitative and quantitative designs. David L. Morgan discusses the use of focus groups as a part of multimethod designs and the overall advantages and disadvantages of qualitative focus group interviewing in his contribution, "Focus Groups."

As with other methods of qualitative interviewing, focus groups are often used to give voice to groups otherwise excluded from knowledge construction. The focus group format can be particularly empowering for participants because they largely determine their level of interaction. When differentiating focus group interviews from in-depth interviews and oral histories, the distinguishing feature is clearly that within the context of a focus group multiple respondents are simultaneously participating in the interview. But what does this actually mean in terms of the data collected and the role of the researcher? Morgan asserts that within focus groups the role of the group in producing interaction is crucial. The role of the researcher as guide or moderator is also a primary aspect of focus groups.

In terms of sociological uses, the topics explored using focus groups run the gamut of sociological subjects of inquiry. Focus groups are often used in multimethod designs where focus group data can confirm or amplify survey data. Morgan posits that while surveys are very useful in accessing breadth, focus groups add depth. As focus groups are less time consuming than in-depth interviews, since multiple respondents are interviewed at once, focus groups can be used in conjunction with in-depth interviews in order to increase the scope of the data. According to Morgan, the selection of focus group interviewing versus in-depth interviewing is context dependent. Both methods yield qualitative data from participants, and, as always, researchers should select the method that best suits their specific research goals. Morgan explains that an advantage of the focus group method is a product of "group effect." By using a group, consensus and diversity in responses emerge, adding a comparative dimension to the research.

The "group effect" is another weakness of this method. First, members of the group may influence each other, even if only by their presence. For example, if respondents are asked about their work lives in a mixed-gender group, women, conditioned not to show vulnerability if they are to succeed in the public sphere, may be reluctant to talk about structural barriers or personal challenges. Second, some topics are not appropriate for focus groups, as interviewing involves self-disclosure on the part of participants and some risqué subjects might be impossible in a group context. Another weakness of focus groups is the extent to which a researcher/moderator can influence the production of data; however, as Morgan is quick to point out, this is a concern with other methods as well (including surveys and in-depth interviews).

Once focus groups are chosen as the appropriate method there are multiple research designs that can be used. Morgan offers many of the possible examples. The decisions that guide research design concern standardization, sampling, and moderation. Standardization is the extent to which each research participant, and each focus group, will be asked the same questions. Sampling is the way in which research participants are selected. "Segmentation" is a technique often used in focus groups. It involves placing participants with "like" characteristics in groups together. For example, if the effect of gender on respondents' attitudes is relevant to the study, as in our working women example, the researcher might segment the sample into male groups and female groups. Morgan explains that this technique builds a comparative dimension into the research and facilitates discussion by allowing for commonality amongst group members. The level of moderation an interviewer provides can range from high moderation, commonly used in marketing, to almost no moderation. Moderation determines the structure of the interview (from semistructured to nonstructured). The amount of control a researcher chooses to maintain, as with all of the other considerations that go into research design, should be based on the specific goals of the study. It is also important to remember that one choice may impact another. For example, the size of the group impacts the level of control a moderator will likely be able to maintain. Some of these issues will be illuminated by the practical research example we have selected as our last article in Part II.

"Why Urban Parents Resist Involvement in Their Children's Elementary Education," by Peter McDermott and Julia Rothenberg, is an excellent example of how focus groups function as a part of a multimethod research design. McDermott and Rothenberg are interested in the different ways teachers and families perceive family involvement in lower economic urban schools. Initially the researchers constructed a survey completed by 25 teachers. Anomalies in the survey responses raised many questions. At this point McDermott and Rothenberg decided to use qualitative focus group interviewing to better understand the "contradictions and complexities" the surveys revealed. Focus group data thus served to clarify and add depth to survey data.

Their selection of focus groups as a research method was given the range of qualitative methods available, a result of both their particular research problem and their theoretical position. The former is self-evident, but the latter needs elaboration. McDermott and Rothenberg conducted a literature review and discovered that focus groups privilege communication from marginalized groups. Certainly the participants in the parent groups were marginalized based on social class and race/ethnicity, at least according to the data. Additionally, the researchers incorporated standpoint epistemology and a constructivist conception of knowledge into their theoretical position. Focus groups met both their methodological and epistemological needs.

Issues such as structure (based on moderator control) are explained as occurring in relation to the group interaction. In other words, the researchers altered their level of moderation based on what was happening in the group, again showing that flexibility is an important part of the qualitative endeavor. The practice of qualitative research is process oriented. The substantive contributions of this study are significant, exemplifying the importance of focus group analysis.

CONCLUDING THOUGHTS

We hope the readings in this section help elucidate the theoretical considerations that emerge when conducting interactive research, the range of methods and multimethod approaches available, and the diversity of topics that can be studied through methods of fieldwork and interviewing. Ultimately, each of the methods reviewed allows researchers to ask questions with a depth that is not possible in quantitative analysis. In this way qualitative research continues to distinguish itself as a distinct form of inquiry on the basis of the issues it raises, knowledge it produces, and research partnerships it forms.

BIBLIOGRAPHY

Anderson, Kathryn, Susan Armitage, Dana Jack and Judith Wittner. 1990. Beginning where we are: Feminist methodology in oral history. In Joyce McCarl Nielson (Ed.), *Feminist research methods* (pp. 94–112). Boulder, CO: Westview Press.

Bailey, Carol A. 1996. *A guide to field research.* Thousand Oaks, CA: Pine Forge Press.

Bordo, Susan. 1989. Feminism, postmodernism, and gender skepticism. In Linda Nicholson (Ed.), *Feminism/Postmodernism.* New York: Routledge.

Botting, Ingrid. 2000. Understanding domestic service through oral history and the census: The case of Grand Falls, Newfoundland. *Feminist Qualitative Research, 28*(1, 2).

Callaway, Helen. 1992. Ethnography and experience: Gender implication in field-work and texts. In J. Okely and H. Callaway (eds.), *Anthropology and autobiography*. Routledge, Chapman & Hall.

Hill Collins, Patricia. 1991. Toward an Afrocentric feminist epistemology. In *Black feminist thought: Knowledge, consciousness, and the politics of empowerment* (pp. 201–19). New York: Routledge.

Foucault, Michel. 1990. *The history of sexuality, volume one: An introduction*. Vintage Books.

Gallagher, Charles A. 2000. "White like me?" Methods, meaning, and manipulation in the field of white studies. In France Winddance Twine and Jonathan W.War-ren (Eds.), *Racing research, researching race: Methodological dilemmas in critical race studies*. New York: New York University.

Glenn, Evelyn Nakano. 1987. Racial ethnic women's labor: The intersection of race, gender, and class oppression. In Christine Bose, Roslyn Feldberg, and Natalie Sokoloff (Eds.), *Hidden aspects of women's work*. Praeger.

Halpin, Zuleyma Tang. 1989. Scientific objectivity and the concept of the "Other." *Women's Studies International Forum, 12*(3), 285–94.

Haraway, Donna J. 1991. *Simians, cyborgs, and women: The reinvention of nature*. New York: Routledge.

Harding, Sandra. 1991. Whose Science? Whose Knowledge? Thinking from Women's Lives. Ithaca, N.Y.: Cornell University Press.

Harding, Sandra. 1993. Rethinking standpoint epistemology: What is "strong objectivity?" In Linda Alcoff and Elizabeth Potter (Eds.), *Feminist epistemologies*. Routledge.

Hochschild, Arlie. 2000. The nanny chain. *The American Prospect, 11*(4).

hooks, bell. Culture to culture: Ethnography and cultural studies as critical intervention. In *Yearning: Race, gender, and cultural practices* (pp. 123–33). Boston, MA: South End Press.

Kuhn, Thomas S. 1970. *The structure of scientific revolutions*. (2nd ed.) Chicago: University of Chicago Press.

Martin, Emily. 1991. The egg and the sperm: How science has constructed a romance based on stereotypical male-female roles. *Signs: Journal of Women in Culture and Society, 16*(31)485–501.

McDermott, Peter, and Julia Rothenberg. 2000. Why urban parents resist involvement in their children's elementary education. *The Qualitative Report, 5*(3, 4, October).

Miller, William L., and Crabtree, Benjamin F. 1999. Depth interviewing. In Benjamin F. Crabtree and William L. Miller (Eds.), *Doing qualitative Research* (2nd ed.) pp. 89–107. Thousand Oaks, CA: Sage.

Morgan, David L. 1996. Focus groups. *Annual Review of Sociology* (22), 129–52.

Neuman, W. Lawrence. 1997. *Social research methods: Qualitative and quantitative approaches* (3rd ed.). Boston: Allyn and Bacon.

Nielson, Joyce McCarl. 1990. Introduction. Joyce McCarl Nelson, ed. *Feminist research methods* (pp. 1–37). Boulder, CO: Westveiw Press.

Paules, Greta Foff. 1991. *Dishing it out: Power and resistance among waitresses in a New Jersey restaurant*. Philadelphia, PA: Temple University Press.

Pfohl, Stephen J. 1994. *Images of deviance and social control: A sociological history* (2nd ed.). New York: McGraw-Hill.

Rollins, Judith. 1985. *Between women: Domestics and their employers*. Philadelphia, PA: Temple University Press.

Silverman, David. 2001. *Interpreting qualitative data: Methods for analysing talk, text and interaction*. Thousand Oaks, CA: Sage.

Thorne, Barrie. 1980. "You still takin' notes?" Fieldwork and problems of informed consent. *Social Problems, 27*(3, February), 284–97.

Weston, Kath. 1998. Fieldwork in lesbian and gay communities. In Maxine Baca Zinn, Pierrette Hondagneu-Sotelo and Michael A. Messner (Eds.), *Through the prism of difference: Readings on sex and gender* (pp. 79–85). Boston: Allyn and Bacon.

CHAPTER 6

Culture to Culture

Ethnography and Cultural Studies as Critical Intervention

BELL HOOKS

Through the "talk story" and the telling of aphorisms, Sarah Oldham, my mother's mother, communicated her philosophy of being and living. One of her favorite sayings was "play with a puppy he'll lick you in the mouth." Usually this pronouncement prefaced a long lecture that began with declarations like "I ain't no puppy, I'm a big dog, that don't like mess." These lectures were intended to emphasize the importance of distance, of not allowing folks to get close enough "to get up in your face." It was also about the danger of falsely assuming familiarity, about presuming to have knowledge of matters that had not been revealed. Sometimes the lectures were about putting yourself on the same level as someone who was different and then being surprised that they took certain liberties, even, say, that they treated you with contempt. Often these lectures focused on the notion of "difference" and "otherness."

If it happened that white folks were the subject and the talk was about the feasibility of bonding with them across racial boundaries, they were the puppy. I remember these talks often happened after white folks came to visit (usually they wanted something). You have to understand that in the racially segregated South it was unusual for white folks to visit black folks. Most of the white visitors called my grandmama Aunt Sarah, a more dignified version of the word "auntie" used by whites to address black women in slavery, reconstruction, and the apartheid period known as Jim Crow. Baba never called these visitors by their first names irrespective of the number of years that they had been dropping by. Anyhow these white folks would sit in her living room and talk for hours. Some of these conversations led to the making of ties which lasted lifetimes. Though this contact appeared intimate, Baba never forgot slavery, white supremacy, and the experience of Jim Crow. There was never any bond between her and a white person strong enough to counter that memory. In her mind, to be safe one had to "keep a distance."

I remember these lectures as I read new work in literary and cultural studies focusing on race, noting how often contemporary white scholars writing about black people assume positions of familiarity, as though their work were not coming into being in a cultural context of white supremacy, as though it were in no way shaped and informed by that context. And therefore as though no need exists for them to overtly articulate a response to this political reality as part of their critical enterprise. White scholars can write about black culture or black people without fully interrogating their work to see if it employs white western intellectual traditions to re-inscribe white supremacy, to perpetuate racist domination. Within academic and intellectual climates that are striving to respond to the reality of cultural pluralism, there should be room for discussions of racism that promote and encourage critical interrogation. It should be possible for scholars, especially those who are members of groups who dominate, exploit, and oppress others, to explore the political implications of their work without fear or guilt.

Cultural studies has emerged as that contemporary location in the academy that most invites and encourages such analysis. This seems appropriate since much of the new critical work by white scholars and non-white people focusing on issues of "otherness" and "difference" is informed by the recent emphasis on culture and by academic concern with the question of race and post-colonial discourse. Feminist movement played a major role in generating academic focus on these concerns. Significantly, feminist academic and/or intellectual focus on race began with critical contestation about racism, thereby bringing to the academic context a revitalized focus on race as a political issue, assertively linking anti-racist radical politics with scholarly work. This only happened within feminist studies because of the powerful critical intervention of black women/women of color. It must be remembered that black studies programs have explored issues of race and culture from the moment of their inception. To black scholars who are exploring these subjects in programs that are not shrouded in contemporary radical "chic," programs that are definitely not administered by white men, it can be disheartening when new programs focusing on similar issues receive a prestige and acclaim denied black studies. Cultural studies programs are definitely in this category. They are most always administered by white men and are quickly gaining a legitimacy long denied African-American and Third World studies. At some campuses cultural studies programs are seen as potential replacements for black studies and women's studies. By making this observation I in no way want to denigrate cultural studies. It is exciting to have a new arena for the validation and proliferation of interdisciplinary work. Working and writing, as I do, across disciplines, with English, women's studies, and black studies as starting points for work that is focused on contemporary culture, I am as at "home" in cultural studies as I am in these more familiar locations where issues of difference and otherness have long been a part of the discourse.

Cultural studies is an exciting and compelling addition, as it makes a space for dialogue between intellectuals, critical thinkers, etc. who may in the past have stayed within narrow disciplinary concerns. It calls attention to race and similar issues and gives them renewed academic legitimacy. And it is rapidly becoming one of the few locations in the academy where there is the possibility of inter-racial and cross-cultural discussion. Usually scholars in the academy resist engagement in dialogues with diverse groups where there may be critical contestation, interrogation, and confrontation. Cultural studies can serve as an intervention, making a space for forms of intellectual discourse to emerge that have not been traditionally welcomed in the academy. It cannot achieve this end if it remains solely a privileged "chic" domain where, as Cornel West writes in his essay "Black Culture and Postmodernism," scholars engage in debates which "highlight notions of difference, marginality, and otherness in such a way that it further marginalizes actual people of difference and otherness." When this happens, cultural studies re-inscribes patterns of colonial domination, where the "Other" is always made object, appropriated, interpreted, taken over by those in power, by those who dominate.

Participants in contemporary discussions of culture highlighting difference and otherness who have not interrogated their perspectives, the location from which they write in a culture of domination, can easily make of this potentially radical discipline a new ethnographic terrain, a field of study where old practices are simultaneously critiqued, re-enacted and sustained. In their introduction to the collection of essays *Writing Culture: The Poetics and Politics of Ethnography* editors James Clifford and George Marcus present a critical background against which we can consider work that breaks with the past, to some extent work that redefines ethnography:

> Ethnography is actively situated between powerful systems of meaning. It poses its questions at the boundaries of civilizations, cultures, classes, races, and genders. Ethnography decodes and recodes, telling the grounds of collective order and diversity, inclusion and exclusion. It describes processes of innovation and structuration, and is itself part of these processes. Ethnography is an emergent interdisciplinary phenomenon. Its authority and rhetoric have spread to many fields where "culture" is a newly problematic object of description and critique . . .

This book includes many compelling essays which break new ground in the field of ethnography. I was particularly excited by the essay by Michael M.J. Fischer, "Ethnicity and the Post-Modern Arts of Memory."

Despite the new and different directions charted in this collection, it was disappointing that black people were still being "talked about," that we remain an absent presence without voice. The editors state at the end of their introduction that "the book gives relatively little attention to new ethnographic possibilities emerging from non-Western experience and from feminist theory and politics." They also give no attention, no "play" as we would say in black vernacular speech, to the anthropologists/ethnographers in the United States who are black, who have either been "indigenous ethnographers" or who entered cultures where they resemble the people they are studying and writing about. Can we believe that no one has considered and/or explored the possibility that the experiences of these non-white scholars may have always been radically different in ways from their white counterparts and that they possibly had experiences which deconstructed much old-school ethnographic practice, perhaps reaching conclusions similar to those being "discovered" by contemporary white scholars writing on the new ethnography? Their voices cannot be heard in this collection. It in no way challenges the assumption that the image/identity of the ethnographer is white and male. The gap that is explained and apologized for in this text is the lack of feminist input.

The construction of the anthology, its presentation, compelled me to think about race, gender, and ethnography. I was drawn again and again to the cover of this book. It is the reproduction of a photograph (Stephen Tyler doing fieldwork in India). One sees in this image a white male sitting at a distance from darker-skinned people, located behind him; he is writing. Initially fascinated by the entire picture, I begin to focus my attention on specific details. Ultimately I fix my attention on the piece of cloth that is attached to the writer's glasses, presumably to block out the sun; it also blocks out a particular field of vision. This "blindspot," artificially created, is a powerful visual metaphor for the ethnographic enterprise as it has been in the past and as it is being rewritten. As a script, this cover does not present any radical challenge to past constructions. It blatantly calls attention to two ideas that are quite fresh in the racist imagination: the notion of the white male as writer/authority, presented in the photograph actively producing, and the idea of the passive brown/black man who is doing nothing, merely looking on.

After I completed this essay I read a similar critique of this photograph by Deborah Gordon in her essay "Writing Culture, Writing Feminism: The Poetics and Politics of Experimental Ethnography." Gordon writes that, "The authority of the white male is present but not unambiguous—it is now watched, and we watch it being watched." Unlike Gordon, I see nothing active or critical about the watcher; if anything he is curiously fascinated, possibly admiring. To simply be an "observer" does not imply the displacement or subversion of the white "authorial presence." The brown male gaze can be read as consensual look of homoerotic bonding and longing, particularly since he is visually separated from family, kin, community, his gaze turned away from them. The photo implies however subtly that this brown man may indeed desire the authorial, "phallocentric power" of the white man. Significantly, we cannot discuss the brown female gaze because her look is veiled by the graphics of the cover; a black line drawn across her face. Why does this cover doubly annihilate the value of brown female gaze, first by the choice of picture where the dark woman is in the shadows, and secondly by a demarcating line? In *Writing Culture* Paul Rabinow's essay "Representations are Social Fact: Modernity and Postmodernity in Anthropology" suggest that the politics of culture, and here he draws on the work of Pierre Bourdieu, "Has taught us to ask in what field of power, and from what position in that field, any given author writes." Added to that might be the question of what politics of representation are enacted by images. Is it possible that an image, a cover can undermine radical writing—can reinscribe the colonizing anthropology/ethnography that is vigilantly critiqued in *Writing Culture*? Describing this image in his introduction, James Clifford writes, "The ethnographer hovers at the edge of the frame—faceless, almost extraterrestrial, a hand that writes." As an onlooker, conscious of the politics of race and imperialism, looking at this frontispiece I am most conscious of the concrete whiteness and maleness. To my gaze it is anything but extraterrestrial.

Another aspect of this cover strikes me as powerful commentary. The face of the brown/black woman is covered up, written over by the graphics which tell readers the title of the book and its authors. Anyone who glances at this cover notes that the most visible body and face, the one that does not have to be searched for, is the white male image. Perhaps to the observer trained in ethnography and anthropology this cover documents a very different history and vision from the one I see. I look at it and I see visual metaphors of colonialism, of domination, of racism. Surely it is important as we attempt to rethink cultural practice, to re-examine and remake ethnography, to create ways to look at and talk about or study diverse cultures and peoples in ways that do not perpetuate exploitation and domination. Starting from such a perspective one would have to consider intentionality and visual impact when choosing a cover like the one I have been discussing. One would need to consider the possibility that people who might never actually read this book might look at the cover and think that it illustrates something about the information inside. Surely the cover as representation has value and meaning that are not subverted when one reads the content. Inside, black/brown people remain in the shadows. When I look at this cover, I want to know who is the audience for this book.

Linking this question to the development of cultural studies, we must also ask: who are the subjects this discipline addresses its discourse and practice. To consider that we write about "culture," for only those of us who are intellectuals, critical thinkers, is a continuation of a hierarchical idea of knowledge that falsifies and maintains structures of domination. In the introduction to *Writing Culture*, the authors explain their exclusion of certain voices in this way, speaking here about feminism:

> Feminism clearly has contributed to anthropological theory. And various feminist ethnographers, like Annette Weimer (1976), are actively rewriting the masculinist canon. But feminist ethnography has focused either on setting the record straight about women or on revising anthropological categories (for example the nature/culture opposition). It has not produced either unconventional forms of writing or a developed reflection on ethnographic textuality as such.

Similar assumptions have been stated about scholarship by black academics of both genders. After making this statement, the authors of *Writing Culture* emphasize the relevance of exploring "the exclusion and inclusion of different experiences in the anthropological archives, the rewriting of established traditions," declaring, "This is where feminist and non-Western writing have made their greatest impact." To many feminists, especially women of color, the current scholarly trend of encouraging radical rethinking of the idea of "difference" has its roots in anti-racist black liberation efforts and resistance struggles globally. Many new trends in cultural studies and ethnography seem to be piggybacking on these efforts.

It is particularly disturbing to read work that is informed and shaped by the intellectual labor of women of color, particularly black women, which erases or de-emphasizes the importance of that contribution. Often this work is subtly devalued by the evocation of conventional academic standards of judgment that deem work that is not written in a particular manner less important. Clifford writes in a footnote to the statement quoted in the last paragraph:

> It may be generally true that groups long excluded from positions of institutional power, like women or people of color, have less concrete freedom to indulge in textual experimentation. To write in an unorthodox way, Paul Rabinow suggests in this volume, one must first have tenure. In specific contexts a preoccupation with self-reflexivity and style may be an index of privileged estheticism. For if one does not have to worry about the exclusion or true representation of one's experience, one is freer to undermine ways of telling, to focus on form over content. But I am uneasy with a general notion that privileged discourse indulges in esthetic or epistemological subtleties whereas marginal discourse "tells it like it is." The reverse is too often the case.

Like Clifford, I am suspicious of any suggestion that marginalized groups lack the freedom and opportunity to engage in textual experimentation.

Marginalized groups may lack the inclination to engage in certain ways of thinking and writing because we learn early that such work may not be recognized or valued. Many of us experiment only to find that such work receives absolutely no attention. Or we are told by gatekeepers, usually white, often male, that it will be better for us to write and think in a more conventional way. A distinction must be made between our freedom to think and write in multiple ways and the choice to write in accepted ways because we want particular rewards. My struggle over form, content, etc., has been informed by a desire to convey knowledge in ways that make it accessible to a wide range of readers. It is not a reflection of a longing to work in ways that will enable me to have institutional power or support. This is simply not the only form of power available to writers and thinkers. There is power in having a public audience for one's work that may not be particularly academic, power that comes from writing in ways that enable people to think critically about everyday life. When I do write in a manner that is experimental, abstract, etc., I find the most resistance to my choosing that style comes from white people who believe it is less "authentic." Their need to control how I and other black people write seems to be linked to the fear that black folks writing in ways that show a preoccupation with self-reflexivity and style is a sign that they no longer "possess" this form of power. Of course work exists by black folks/people of color which indicates a preoccupation with textuality and style. Here the work of academic and writer Nathaniel Mackey comes to mind. Such work may be an index of privileged aestheticism and a reflection of a concrete need to rethink and rewrite the conventional ways of exploring black experience, as well as the desire to re-vision the nature of our resistance struggle. It may very well be that certain efforts at black liberation failed because they were strategies that did not include space for different forms of self-reflexive critique.

One exciting dimension to cultural studies is the critique of essentialist notions of difference. Yet this critique should not become a means to dismiss differences or an excuse for ignoring the authority of experience. It is often evoked in a manner which suggests that all the ways black people think of ourselves as "different" from whites are really essentialist, and therefore without concrete grounding. This way of thinking threatens the very foundations that make resistance to domination possible. It is precisely the power to represent and make certain knowledge available that is revealed in the collection *Writing Culture*. Despite much that is radically new and intellectually engaging in this work, it is disappointing that the authors did not work to have a more inclusive perspective or make a space for including other voices (even if that meant reconceptualizing the work). Their partial explanations for exclusions are inadequate. Progressive scholars in cultural studies are eager to have work that does not simply suggest new theoretical directions but that implements change. Surely those in power are best positioned to take certain risks. What would have happened had the editors and/or authors in *Writing Culture*, or those among us who are in similar positions, taken the necessary steps to include perspectives, voices, etc. that they tell us are missing, even as they tell us they consider this a lack? Many of us are suspicious of explanations that justify exclusions, especially as this seems to be "the" historical moment when shifting certain paradigms is possible. If white male scholars support, encourage, and even initiate theoretical interventions without opening the space of interrogation so that it is inclusive, their gestures of change appear to be ways of holding onto positions of power and authority in a manner that maintains structures of domination based on race, gender, and class.

The recent academic focus on "culture," epitomized by the formation of cultural studies, has led many white students to explore subjects where they must grapple with issues of race and domination. The courses I teach on black women writers and Third World literature are overcrowded, with large waiting lists. Enthusiasm for these courses is ongoing. To some extent student interest in areas of study that allow for discussion of otherness and difference is changing faculty preoccupations. Professors who were never drawn to these subjects in the past are exploring them, using material in classrooms that they might have considered unsuitable at another time. These shifts in direction transform the academy only if they are informed by non-racist perspective, only if these subjects are approached from a standpoint that interrogates issues of domination and power. A white woman professor teaching a novel by a black woman writer (Toni Morrison's *Sula*) who never acknowledges the "race" of the characters is not including works by "different" writers in a manner that challenges ways we have been traditionally taught as English majors to look at literature. The political standpoint of any professor engaged with the development of cultural studies will determine whether issues of difference and otherness will be discussed in new ways or in ways that reinforce domination.

Those cultural studies programs emphasizing post-colonial discourse bring a global perspective that is often sorely lacking in many traditional disciplines. Within the academy, concern with global perspectives and global issues has been a re-vitalizing response to the crisis in western civilization and western thought. It is both ironic and tragic when conservative academic politics lead to the co-optation of these concerns, pitting Third World scholars and African-American scholars against one another. We not only compete for jobs, we compete for recognition. Anyone who has attended a conference on African-American studies recently knows that there are growing numbers of Third World nationals who are, for diverse reasons, engaged in scholarship on African-American culture. They may be non-white, but they may not necessarily have a radical politic or be at all concerned about challenging racial hierarchies. They may choose instead to exploit the privileged location already allotted them in the existing structure. In such situations all the necessary elements exist for the re-enactment of a paradigm of colonial domination where non-western brown/black-skinned folks are placed in positions where they act as intermediaries between the white power structure and indigenous people of color, usually black folks.

These negative dimensions are countered only by the radical political actions of individual professors and their allies. When conservative forces combine to privilege only certain kinds of discourse and particular areas of study, the expansive invitation to engage in multiple discourses from diverse perspectives that is a core concept of cultural studies is threatened. These days when I enter classrooms to teach about people of color and the students present are nearly all white, I recognize this to be a risky situation. I may be serving as a collaborator with a racist structure that is gradually making it much more difficult for students of color, particularly black students, from impoverished and in some cases privileged backgrounds to participate in undergraduate or graduate study. Their absence can be easily ignored when the subjects studied focus on non-whites, just as their absence in the professorial role can be ignored when white professors are addressing issues of difference. In such circumstances I must interrogate my role as educator. Am I teaching white students to become contemporary "interpreters" of black experience? Am I educating the colonizer/oppressor class so that they can better exert control? An East Indian colleague of mine, Anu Needham, says that we can only respond to this circumstance by assuming a radical standpoint and radicalizing these students so that they learn to think critically, so that they do not perpetuate domination, so that they do not support colonialism and imperialism, but do understand the meaning of resistance. This challenge then confronts everyone who participates in cultural studies and in other inter-disciplinary programs like women's studies, black studies, anthropology, etc. If we do not interrogate our motives, the direction of our work, continually, we risk furthering a discourse on difference and otherness that not only marginalizes people of color but actively eliminates the need for our presence.

Similarly, unless progressive scholars actively pushing for further institutionalization of cultural studies remain ever mindful of the way discursive practices and the production of knowledge are easily appropriated by existing systems of domination, cultural studies cannot and will not serve as critical intervention disrupting the academic status quo. Concurrently, as individual critical thinkers, those of us whose work is marginalized, as well as those whose work successfully walks that elusive tightrope with one foot on the radical edge and one foot firmly rooted on acceptable academic ground, must be ever vigilant, guarding against the social technology of control that is ever ready to co-opt any transformative vision and practice.

If the recent international conference Cultural Studies Now and in the Future is any sign of the discipline's direction, it is evident that grave tensions exist between those who would have cultural studies be that discipline which radically questions and transforms the academy and those who would make it (as one concerned white male put it) "the latest hip racism," where every culture and everybody being talked about is "colored" but those doing the talking and writing are white, with few exceptions. Furthermore, it was noted by the same white male participant that "the most extended discussions of African-American culture and politics came from people outside the United States." When individual black scholars made similar public critiques, their words were dismissed as mad ravings. Given the context of white supremacy, we must always interrogate institutional structures which give voice to people of color from other countries while systematically suppressing and/or censoring the radical speech of indigenous folks of color. While black Americans have every political reason to recognize our place in the African diaspora, our solidarity and cultural connections with people of African descent globally, and while we do appreciate cross-cultural exchange, we must not abdicate intellectual responsibility for promoting a cultural studies that will enhance our ability to speak specifically about our culture and gain a hearing. As a radical critical intervention, cultural studies "now and in the future" can be a site of meaningful contestation and constructive confrontation. To achieve this end, it must be committed to a "politics of difference" that recognizes the importance of making space where critical dialogues can take place between individuals who have not traditionally been compelled by politicized intellectual practice to speak with one another. Of course, we must enter this new discursive field recognizing from the onset that our speech will be "troubled," that there exists no ready-made "common language." Drawing from a new ethnography, we are challenged to celebrate the polyphonic nature of critical discourse, to—as it happens in traditional African-American religious experience—hear one another "speak in tongues," bear witness, and patiently wait for revelation.

CHAPTER 7

"You Still Takin' Notes?"

Fieldwork and Problems of Informed Consent

BARRIE THORNE

It has long been acknowledged that the openings of field research—gaining access, entree and rapport, and developing a workable relationship with those one wants to study—involve serious ethical questions. Such questions enter into recurring debate over the ethics of disguised research (e.g., Davis, 1960; Roth, 1962; Erikson, 1967; Humphreys, 1970; von Hoffman *et al.* 1970) and over initial promises of confidentiality and eventual decisions about what to publish (e.g., Fichter and Kolb, 1953; Becker, 1971; Colvard, 1967; Rainwater and Pittman, 1967). Old debates have assumed new, more urgent form, and the question of *who* should make ethical determinations has become a heated topic in response to new federal regulations governing social research.[1]

Implemented by granting agencies and university review boards as a condition for funding or sponsoring research, HEW regulations for "Protection of Human Subjects" have begun to affect research practices and the terms of ethical discussions. According to the guidelines, review boards are initially to examine proposed research projects to decide if human subjects are at risk:

> If it is decided that risk is involved, the review must further determine whether the risks are outweighed by any benefit that might come to the subject or by the importance of the knowledge to be gained, that the rights and welfare of the subjects will be adequately protected, that legally effective informed consent will be obtained, and that research will be reviewed at timely intervals (Bond, 1978: 149)

This paper is focused on only one part of the regulations, the requirement that researchers must obtain "legally effective informed consent" from those they study. The federal regulations have highlighted the notion of informed consent and placed it in the center of ethical discussions about the opening phases of research and ongoing relationships of researchers and subjects. Using the federal regulations as a starting point, I will explore some of the practical difficulties involved in implementing informed consent within the contexts of participant-observation. I will then return to assumptions involved in the doctrine of informed consent—especially the premise of abstract individualism and the neglect of social stratification and the uses of knowledge—and I will argue that discussions of ethics and fieldwork should involve a critique, as well as serious consideration, of informed consent.

THE "PROTECTION OF HUMAN SUBJECTS" REGULATIONS AND THEIR APPLICABILITY TO FIELDWORK

The notion of informed consent, as spelled out in the federal regulations, was originally designed to protect patients from abuses by medical researchers. The language of the regulations reflects this context. According to the regulations, informed consent means "the knowing consent of an individual or his legally authorized representative, so situated as to be able to exercise free power of choice without undue inducement or any element of force, fraud, deceit, duress, or other forms of constraint or coercion" (Annas et al., 1977: 291). The regulations specify basic elements of information necessary to such consent: "fair explanation" of the purpose of the research and the procedures to be followed; a description of risks and benefits which might reasonably be expected; an offer to answer any inquiries concerning the procedures; and instruction that the person is free to withdraw consent and discontinue participation in the project at any time.

As Wax (1977) and Cassell (1978) have argued, the federal regulations are based on a biomedical, experimental model of research, and there is some question about their suitability as guidelines for ethnographic research. In fieldwork the risks are less dramatic than, say, in medical intervention; the benefits, too, are less striking than they might be in biomedical research—and both risks and benefits (especially long-term ones) are often difficult to assess, especially at the beginning of a field study. Fieldworkers have less control over the research setting than do experimentalists; in the immediate research situation, the gap of power between researcher and subject is less than in experiments, and the flow of interaction is broader and more reciprocal and open-ended. Finally, the new federal regulations, especially when they are translated into highly standardized activities, such as asking each member of a setting to sign a consent form before one even begins observing, seem overly legalistic, formalized, and intrusive in the more fluid context of field research.

Beyond the fact that the new government regulations are cut from a pattern which doesn't quite fit the practices of fieldwork, there are serious questions, which I will not pursue here, concerning the government's intrusion into the processes of social research.[2] The requirement that one obtain signed consent forms from everyone one studies may violate anonymity and actually create risks for some groups of subjects. In the end, the procedures may result in meaningless rituals rather than improving the ethics of field research.

However, the notion of informed consent is relevant to the ethics of fieldwork. Although it has important limitations, as I will later argue, the ethical perspective embodied in the notion of informed consent can help illuminate the array of research "bargains"—as Everett Hughes (1974) describes the often shifting connections between the observer and the observed—which have been struck in the course of field research.

THE COMPONENTS OF INFORMED CONSENT

The notion of informed consent helps put into focus specific strands in the relationships between fieldworkers and those they study. According to the regulations, informed consent is consent which is *knowledgeable*, exercised in a situation of *voluntary* choice, made by individuals who are *competent* or able to choose freely. As Freedman (1975) suggests, the legal requirement of informed consent embodies a "substantial requirement of morality," anchored in the Kantian categorical imperative, the belief that all individuals have a right to be treated as persons rather than objects, and to have their autonomy and dignity respected (also see Cassell, 1980).

The federal regulations mix both utilitarian and Kantian lines of reasoning. A utilitarian calculation of risks and benefits is required when review boards determine whether the regulations are applicable to a proposed research project, and when they determine if the subjects' rights seem adequately protected. Once granted approval, the researcher is required to inform the subjects of both risks and benefits entailed in the research. The principle of informed consent—based on Kantian assumptions—is included to protect individual rights against researchers' claims of broad social need or benefit (e.g., "the public's right to know"; "the development of science") which are often included in utilitarian calculations (Soble, 1978). (I will later return to the balancing of individual rights and broader social and moral claims.)

The three dimensions of informed consent—knowledgeability, voluntary and competent choice—are merely starting points, since it is unclear just how much information needs to be imparted or present for consent to be knowledgeable, or how to know exactly when a given choice is sufficiently voluntary and responsible (Kelman, 1972: 1002). Furthermore, as the guidelines suggest, as risks increase, so does the importance of informed consent, because the actions taken by the researcher thereby become more fateful and the abrogation of rights more serious.

As many have noted, to understand the meaning of informed consent in the context of fieldwork requires going beyond abstract formulations to explore particular situations—and the fieldwork literature contains a large array. I will discuss two of the components of informed consent—knowledgeable and voluntary choice[3]—with reference to some of the specific situations and vicissitudes which fieldworkers have encountered.

WHEN IS CONSENT INFORMED? HOW MUCH INFORMATION SHOULD BE GIVEN?

The new regulations imply that uninformed consent is "tantamount to no consent at all" (Freedman, 1975), that researchers are obligated to disclose whatever information potential subjects would need to make an intelligent decision about participating in a study. Such an obligation, even in minimal form, has by no means been acknowledged by all fieldworkers, as evidenced by the flurries of debate following the appearance of field studies based on total deception (e.g., Lofland and Lejeune, 1960; Davis, 1960; Humphreys, 1970; von Hoffman *et al.*, 1970).

Erikson (1967) and Kelman (1972) have summarized the ethical objections to studies which involve deliberate misrepresentation of identities: such deception is intentionally dishonest, violating the trust basic to all social relationships; it invades privacy, denying subjects a chance to weigh possible risks and to determine what they want to reveal; special harms (e.g., stress if the fraud is uncovered or even suspected) may follow from acts of total deception, which also diminish the general public climate of trust toward sociology. Erikson concludes with a rough set of guidelines:

> . . . it is unethical for a sociologist to deliberately misrepresent his (sic) identity for the purpose of entering a private domain to which he is not otherwise eligible; and . . . it is unethical for a sociologist to deliberately misrepresent the character of the research in which he is engaged (1967:373).

Erikson has identified a domain which many fieldworkers agree constitutes unethical conduct. As I will later elaborate, some kinds of disguised research may be defended on other ethical grounds, but from the Kantian perspective of informed consent, deliberate deception is unethical—and rests at a polar extreme from fully informed consent.

Although one can identify extremes, the actual dividing line between informed and uninformed remains unclear. Roth (1962: 283) has argued that "all social research is secret in some ways and to some degree—we never tell the subjects everything." One major reason for this, which Wax (1977) has emphasized, is that fieldworkers usually enter the field with an open-ended sense of purpose; they tend to work inductively and may shift interests and outlooks as the research proceeds; practical exigencies may force extensive change of plans. The very flexibility which is often cited as a major strength of field research poses obstacles for implementing a tight notion of informed consent, especially at the start of a research project.

And yet, do fieldworkers generally even *try* to fully share what they do know of their research goals, frameworks, methods, patterns of sponsorship, and expected reporting? I believe the answer is no; fieldworkers are rarely as honest and forthcoming with information as they could be. Barnes (1963) has noted that when they explain research to informants, ethnographers often stress the most innocuous aspects of their studies; for example, anthropologists say they are collecting legends or information on technology, rather than admit that their focus is on more controversial topics like land tenure and social control. Self-introductions are bound up with efforts to gain access, and that practical motive, weighted heavily by investments of time, money and career, tends to squeeze honesty to the side.

Reviewing ethnographies to examine modes of self-introduction (when they are mentioned at all), I have been struck by the widespread use of partial truths. Gathering data for *Asylums*, Goffman spent a year doing fieldwork in a large mental hospital. According to the book's preface he told the hospital administrators something of his purpose, but with the patients—whose daily experiences were the focus of his study—Goffman assumed the role of an assistant to the athletic director, "when pressed, avowing to be a student of recreation and community life" (1971:ix).

When he was a participant-observer in the West End of Boston, Gans (1962) told community residents that he was "doing a recent history of the area," mainly surveying the institutions, organizations and the redevelopment process in the neighborhood. Gans mentioned, but did not emphasize, his interest in observing the everyday life of residents, and he did not tell them that he attended social gatherings "in the dual role of guest and observer" (1962:344). Gans writes that with hindsight and additional fieldwork experience in another community, he came to believe he could have been more open about his research role. Lofland (1966) introduced himself to leaders of a religious cult as "a sociologist interested in social and religious movements"—true as far as it went, but the cult leader translated that role into "chronicler of the beginning of the New Age in America," an understanding which Lofland didn't try to correct. Gusfield (1955: 29, 32) told WCTU leaders that he was a "disinterested investigator of American social movements," but he acknowledges that "their conception of a sociological study was rather naive and at a highly formal level"; he felt, in the end, that he had used them.

The practical problem of gaining access to the groups they want to study has led investigators to provide vague and even misleading initial statements of identity and purpose. Another part of the problem—less within the control of fieldworkers—is that identities are a negotiated matter and even the most forthright observers cannot fully determine what they will be taken to be. When she studied the Thrashing Buffalo Indians, R. Wax (1971: 369) discovered that she was "variously taken for a teacher, an FBI investigator, a social worker, a professional cowgirl, a Wave recruiter and a communist agitator." This list is by no means unusual in the annals of ethnography, and since one may discover such misconceptions long after they have circulated, they may be difficult to correct. When I was a participant-observer in the draft resistance movement, I discovered (partly by piecing together silences and some conversations I heard about but never directly witnessed) that some movement members suspected I was a federal agent. Such a charge is difficult, if not impossible, to shake, especially if one's activities—in my case, taking notes, asking questions which extended beyond daily movement concerns, and trying to move freely among movement groups—are not so distant as one might hope from the other kind of special witnessing engaged in by political spies (see Thorne, 1979).[4]

When I did fieldwork among 4th and 5th grade school children, they sometimes took me to be a teacher's aide or a "yard duty" (playground supervisor). I tried to clarify that I had no formal role of authority in the school, partly because I wanted to get close to the children's world as it emerges when unconfined by adults. When I tried to explain to the children what I was up to with my constant roaming and busy scribbling, I often felt frustrated. For a while I explained that I was interested in "understanding the way children behave," until a boy said defensively "I didn't do nuthin'," and I realized the disciplinary connotations of the word "behavior." Sometimes I tried to explain what sociologists do, our interest in groups and in patterns of relationship, but when I finished my long-winded explanation, almost inevitably the child would utter a short and bored, "Oh," and run off. Gaps in understanding due to differential experiential worlds may hamper a researcher's ability to provide informed consent.

A More Complete Telling?

In developing relations in the field, how open can and should participant-observers be? The answer, of course, depends in large part upon context. One's ability to provide an informative and accurate form of self-identification varies with the group one is studying. As will later be argued (a line of argument not suggested by the notion of informed consent), the type of knowledge sought, and the nature of the group being studied (e.g., powerful, publicly accountable groups, vs. more vulnerable private ones) may also have ethical bearing on choices about how to identify oneself.

There is another consideration: what sorts of information will individuals need in order to make a meaningful decision about participating? The federal regulations offer a listing suited for experiments: a description of risks and benefits, an offer to answer questions about the procedure, and instruction that the person is free to discontinue participation at any time. The list seems less pertinent in the looser and lengthier "research designs" of ethnography.

Subjects may, with good reason, want to know one's analytic framework since starting assumptions may pose long-term risks for a group. As Cassell (1978) has suggested, frameworks which reaffirm a "blaming the victim" or a "deficiency" approach to oppressed segments of society may affect public policy and reinforce existing inequalities. When I proposed to study the draft resistance movement, one of the leaders questioned me to see if I regarded resisters as "deviants"; he considered sociological conceptualizations of deviance to be politically and intellectually objectionable and wanted (understandably, in my view) to protect the movement from that sort of definition.

Patterns of sponsorship are also of no small import when one has a larger political understanding of the locations and potential uses of knowledge; Stephenson (1978) provides frightening documentation of secret CIA sponsorship of his study of Hungarian refugees, who, he notes, would probably "not have been so candid in the interviews," had they known the funding source. In some situations, researchers' naivete is small defense against the risk to which they may be putting the subjects. Especially in studying vulnerable groups, we have an obligation to try to understand, and to share with those we study, the political and social contexts of our projects.

These types of information bear on the long-range harms and benefits of social research. The day-to-day process of doing fieldwork may also entail felt harms. People aware of a fieldworker's general purpose and presence often do not realize what the methodology entails: making daily and detailed written records of ongoing behavior. I realize more fully now than I did at the time that my cumulative fieldnotes on the draft resistance movement were a potential source of jeopardy for participants who acted on the margins of the law and were the target of government surveillance. My fieldnotes could easily have been stolen and used to document group and individual activities (although I changed names in my notes, the contexts would have facilitated identification). The notes, of course, were subject to subpoena, and although I vowed to burn them, were I subpoenaed, that intent didn't vitiate the fact that my daily research acts created risks for others— and risks not under *their* control.

In some settings the special kind of witnessing which is the essence of most fieldwork—the detached and analytic perspective, the gathering and recording of concrete detail to be sifted into analytic reports which will circulate to outsiders—may feel like a particular violation (Hughes, 1971: 505). Groups demanding extreme commitment and partisanship may not want the presence of an avowed neutral; parties and other sociable occasions presume expressiveness, unseriousness, and suspension of consequentiality— tacit rules which conflict with the instrumental attitudes and tasks involved in doing a field study. Those wishing to do research in such settings are probably less likely to reveal their purposes and methods than, for example, fieldworkers in a school or a hospital.[5] The opportunity to exercise informed consent seems to vary by *setting*, which may not be defensible on any ethical grounds. (Although disguised research may be more justifiable in fleeting encounters and public settings—where the stakes are low and people are already on guard—than in intensive, private sorts of settings.)

How and When Should One Inform?

The new HEW regulations have the effect of standardizing the initial phases of social research; getting a signed consent form has become an opening ritual. Some institutional review committees require ethnographers as well as experimentalists to obtain signed consent forms as a condition for obtaining funds or using the university's name.[6] Bortner (1979) documents such a case in a field study of a juvenile court. The review committee in her university stipulated that she had to obtain written informed consent from all those she observed. She asked court officials to sign consent forms, and then asked the presiding officer to read a statement as each juvenile came for a hearing. The statement identified her as a researcher, promised that she would not record or disclose individual identities, requested permission for her to remain, and appraised them of their right to order her departure at any point in the proceedings. Bortner not only experienced this procedure as a great nuisance (as, she reports, did the court officials), but also had doubts about whether the resulting consent was fully informed and voluntary.

The setting Bortner studied—a courtroom—is more in the spirit of the HEW legalistic opening ritual than are most fieldwork situations. Mann's (1976) description of how she gained access to observe in a bar is at another extreme. She was already a waitress before she decided to study the setting; the mode of interaction between bartenders and waitresses was one of joking and constant banter, with a tacit rule to avoid serious discourse. Mann informed the other employees (but not, apparently, bar patrons) of her research identity after she had been gathering data for some time; and she did so not by speaking to each person individually, providing them detailed information and a chance to refuse to participate (which is another dimension involved in the new regulations about informing), but by letting word about her activities get through the grapevine. She used a more direct explanation only near the end of her research, when she had developed good rapport with the other employees in the bar, and even then, she found her low status as a female prevented serious discussion of the topic. A great deal—the nature of the setting, the sequence of her research involvement, the way she was regarded—sets this fieldwork endeavor apart from the model for informing and asking consent which is embodied in the federal regulations. It may be worthwhile to ask if she *could* have come closer to the ideal of informed consent.

Mann's approach to gaining access is more typical of field studies than is Bortner's. Ethnographers do not tend to give extensive information to each person they observe, nor do they usually offer them an explicit moment of choice, telling them they have a right to decline participation or to withdraw from being studied at any time. Fieldworkers tend to assume that if their presence is tolerated, if they aren't told to leave, consent has been granted. I will return to this practice when I discuss the question of whether the consent is voluntary, but I want to call attention to the gap—partly anchored in the practical exigencies of research in natural settings—between customary fieldwork practice and the model embodied in the federal regulations.

Should Informed Consent Be Renewed?

Experiments and interviews are bounded events of short duration. Fieldwork, however, is a longer-term venture, sometimes extending to several years. Ethnographers try to become a part of ongoing daily worlds, and their lives intertwine with the lives of those they study much more fully and complexly than is the case with other types of research. Relationships between observer and observed emerge and change over time, and there may also be changes in the setting, organization or group being studied. Such changes may warrant a new, explicit effort to communicate one's purpose and one's methods as a researcher, and to ask for a renewed granting of consent. Cohen (1976) was sensitive to this situation when she did fieldwork with the

American Indian Movement. As the movement shifted from a local to a national context and as its participants changed, she reassessed her relationship to the group, believing (although the leaders apparently didn't feel this way) that the consent the original group had given extended only to that original situation. She assessed the risks and dangers at the new stage of movement activity, and decided not to continue her research, partly for ethical reasons.

To meet the ethical requirement that consent should be informed, researchers may need to reassess their activity and provide fresh communications along the way. Informed consent may need renewing through another kind of effort: reminding those one is studying about the research purpose, if it seems to have slipped from awareness. This problem is not as acute in experiments or formal interviews, where the relationship of researcher and subject is highly segmentalized and limited, and where the situation—presence in a laboratory, or a short-term encounter defined as an interview—provides a steady reminder that research is in progress.

In contrast, fieldworkers often have what Chrisman (1976) calls "multiple identities." In addition to being observers, they may have a work role (Mann was a waitress; Goffman, a recreation director); they may be a committed member of a group (as I was in the draft resistance movement); they may share ethnic identity where that is a salient quality of participants (as Chrisman did with the Danish Americans he observed); they may—to return to an earlier point—*be taken to be* any number of things. And—most complicated and painful of all—fieldworkers may become good friends with those they are observing. Having other connections and modes of relating can be a source of access, acceptance and trust, and may provide ways of giving something back to those one has studied (e.g., my doing draft counseling and other movement work was a form of reciprocity, and of tacit warrant for their putting up with my research role).

But many-stranded relationships also pose ambiguities. They make it easier for one's subjects to forget they are subjects, to think of the researcher *only* as a friend, movement member or co-worker. This is especially true if one's social categories—age, sex, culture, ethnicity—don't visibly mark one as an outsider, as open note-taking or tape-recording tend to do. Fieldworkers often do not try to prevent this forgetting of the research purpose; the trust and acceptance feel good; information is more readily forthcoming. It is not a case of total deception because they indeed may be what they are taken to be—but they are also more. If the observed forget about the research activity—for example, if they give information with the understanding they are talking *only* to a friend or co-worker and the information then goes into fieldnotes—is that ethical behavior? Many fieldworkers apparently feel it is not. Davis (1960) calls this problem the "sociologist's original sin"; fieldworkers often report experiencing guilt when they deliberately befriended someone, or manipulated a preexisting friendship in order to get data (e.g., Harrell-Bond, 1976; Glazer, 1972: 88–95).

Part of the difficulty in these many-stranded relationships is that pressure against informed consent may come from subjects as well as from the fieldworker. Millman (1975: 619) has observed that it may be easier for everyone concerned if the researcher acts like part of the group; flaunting "mental outsidership" is interpersonally disruptive.

The Kantian idea that people should not be treated as objects suggests they should know they are being studied, and should be able to withhold information they don't want made into grist for the researcher's mill. A utilitarian calculus of harms and benefits also suggests people should be told when they are being studied, for the research role changes the horizon of consequences for the information conveyed. The information would not otherwise be systematically recorded, nor find its way to outside audiences.

IS THE CONSENT VOLUNTARY?

The notion of informed consent contains an image of a moment of individual, free choice—an occasion when a potential subject decides if she or he wishes to participate, understanding what participation would entail (especially possible risks), and without "intervention of any overt or indirect element of force, fraud, deceit, duress, overreaching, or other ulterior form of constraint or coercion" (Annas et al., 1971: 291). This is the ideal, but given the complex conditions of the real world, we are left with the usual sort of sticky question: at what point is the consent sufficiently voluntary?

If one is recruiting subjects for an experiment, a survey or an interview, one must ask them to do something special: to come to one's lab and follow instructions, to fill out a questionnaire, to answer questions. The methods themselves provide points of choice, and asking subjects to sign a consent form can be fitted fairly easily into the opening phases of research. In contrast, participant-observers don't recruit individual subjects. They go to natural settings and tend to work their way in slowly, developing contacts, building trust, carving out a workable social position. The beginnings, as R. Wax (1971) has beautifully illustrated, are often fraught with false starts and difficulties, especially if the fieldwork is in a different culture. Participant-observers hope their subjects will continue their usual activities as if the observer weren't there; nothing special is typically required of the subjects except putting up with the observer's presence and perhaps answering questions that wouldn't arise in the course of normal interaction. Hence, the method of participant-observation does not in itself lead to moments of announcement and choice, unless one must formally request access to a setting, is asked to justify one's presence, or asks subjects for interviews.

In some situations there is such rapid turnover of participants (as in the draft resistance office, where new people continually came in for information) that it would be impossible to gain consent from every individual one might observe. In addition, the nature of the situation may be at odds with the action of providing formal choice points, as in the bar setting which Mann (1976) describes.

There is an added obstacle to realizing the ideal of informed consent (that each individual should have adequate information about the research and a chance to voluntarily choose to participate). Ethnographers seek access to natural groupings—communities, institutions, work groups, associations, social movements—and the organization of these groupings may have a strong and unavoidable effect on how much information each individual receives about the study, on whether or not consent is specifically requested, and on how truly voluntary an individual's consent might be.

Gatekeepers or potential sponsors are more likely to be told about the research project and to realize they have a right to say no, than are group members not in these positions. To gain access to a prison, one must get formal consent from prison authorities, but not necessarily from prisoners; to study a hospital, the administrators, but not every patient, must officially agree. To be sure, gaining acceptance from captive populations (prisoners, patients, students) requires additional effort, and fieldworkers often take great care to try to separate themselves from the official lines of authority, especially if they want to study the subordinated groups (Becker, 1970). But there is still stratification of ability and opportunity to extract information about the study, to negotiate conditions, and to formally deny consent.

When I wanted to observe in an elementary school, I first approached the principal who asked knowledgeable questions about my background, purpose and method, and who set conditions: I was not to disrupt the classroom activities and take up their time, and I was to share my findings. I had similar entry discussions with the classroom teacher. The teacher introduced me to the children simply by name, and—I confess a bit ruefully now that I've been persuaded of the ethical importance of a fuller sense of informed consent, especially when one is studying relatively powerless groups—it never occurred to me to provide an initial explanation of my presence to the children, nor to ask them if they would consent to being observed. As the fieldwork proceeded, I often tried to explain my research to the children. These moments of explaining often followed inquiries related to my continual note-taking ("What are you writing?" "You still takin' notes?" "Are you gonna be a writer?"). But my explanations did not include a reminder that they could decline being part of my study. Were they told they had such a right, I think a few of them might have exercised it. One child, in particular, tended to avoid me, ceased conversing when I came near, and occasionally warned others, "She's writing a book on us." Other children were full of questions and eager to participate, volunteering information, and demonstrating routines on the jungle gym when I said I was interested in children's play and games. Still others seemed uninterested in the fact of my research.

Patterns of sponsorship and introduction affect the voluntary quality of individual choices to participate in field research. A powerful sponsor who vouches for a fieldworker may, in effect, abrogate the rights of other individuals in a setting to decide if the research should go on. Whyte (1955) gained access to a streetcorner gang through the sponsorship of Doc, who turned out to be the gang leader. If the gang members' bowling scores tended to be lower than Doc's (with game performance following social status— one of Whyte's findings), isn't it also possible that the other gang members felt constrained to accept Whyte's presence because Doc had agreed to it? Liebow describes the slow and often unpredictable route he took towards acceptance in a male streetcorner world in an urban black community. After he had hung out for four months, accepted and vouched for by a number of the men, he reports that "at least two men did not trust me or like me, but by then I was too strongly entrenched for them to challenge successfully my right to be there, even had they chosen to do so" (1967: 269). Did the situation deny those two men the right of voluntary consent? And what if some members of the gang wanted to be studied, while others did not—whose choice should prevail?

Even when consent forms are used, the organization of the immediate situation can diminish subjects' sense of choice. The juveniles and parents whom Bortner (1979) observed in a courtroom were each asked to sign a consent form, and told they had rights to refuse her presence, but their acceptance (in all but 2 of 250 hearings) was influenced, she believed, by their knowledge that court officials had already granted permission for her to observe. Situational rules—e.g., constraints to be polite and not to make the sort of scene which expelling a researcher might require[7]—may hamper the voluntary quality of a subject's participation. Furthermore, if a fieldworker was already present in the setting, as an employee, a group member or a resident, *before* undertaking the study (or at least revealing the research role), those observed may also feel less choice about letting the researcher stay on and observe.

THE ASSUMPTIONS OF INFORMED CONSENT:
WHAT ETHICAL ISSUES ARE NEGLECTED?

Thus far I have described the obstacles to informed consent as *practical* difficulties. The last general point—that the contours of the natural groups and settings of field research run against the individual model of informed consent—leads to broader ethical questions. I have emphasized (as I believe the doctrine of informed consent tends to do) the right of individuals to say, "No," to being researched. But is there also a right to say, "Yes?"[8] What if a group of prisoners or mental patients want their situation studied and made public, but the wardens or the hospital administrators, fearful of exposure, refuse a researcher's request for access to the institution? If it made unjust conditions known so they might be remedied, such a study could be justified on ethical grounds, but if researchers had to disguise their purpose to conduct the study, they would violate the ethical principle of informed consent. The abstract, universal and individualistic assumptions of informed consent limit its ability to help resolve this sort of ethical dilemma. The doctrine of informed consent does not take account of ethical dimensions of the knowledge a researcher may seek. Informed consent applies to individuals, each of whom is to be treated the same, and ignores social structure and deep-seated differences of power.

Is Everyone Equally Deserving of Informed Consent?

Informed consent is asserted as a universal right, and the federal regulations apply to all potential subjects. But the regulations were instituted because some groups of subjects lack power relative to researchers and hence have less capacity to freely choose to participate. (Note that movements for advocacy research, and the organizing of groups to demand a say in the research process are also efforts to empower disadvantaged subjects *vis-à-vis* researchers.) As Kelman persuasively argues, ethical problems arise "because of the fact that, and to the extent that, the individuals, groups, and communities that provide data for social research are deficient in power relative to the other participants in the research process" (1972: 989) Patients, who are dependent upon doctors, may not feel able to say, "No," to medical research; other vulnerable groups, like children and mental patients, and subordinated populations (deviants, ethnic minorities, prisoners, students) may need special protection against possible exploitation by researchers. The requirement of informed consent is most easily justified with reference to relatively powerless groups, as a way of giving them a sense of countervailing power in research situations where they may feel coerced.

In itself, the universal principle of informed consent does not distinguish between the powerful and the powerless, but it offers some protection to the powerless simply by extending a right to be left alone which the powerful have always claimed for themselves.[9] It has often been observed that to be powerful is to be able to guard one's interests, to protect one's self from unwanted intrusions. The literature of the social sciences bears out this fact: the bulk of research has been on the less powerful, to whom researchers have greater access; only recently have ethnographers begun to urge the importance of studying up.

Elite groups are less in need of the protection granted by the principle of informed consent. They may also *warrant* less protection. In a much cited essay, Rainwater and Pittman argue that when the powerful are publicly accountable figures—government officials, police officers, physicians, college teachers—the public has a right to know what they are up to. Social scientists, they argue, have an obligation to generate information which will help further public accountability "in a society whose complexity makes it easier for people to avoid responsibilities" (1967: 365). In a similar vein, Nader (1967) reasons that to be effective in a democracy, citizens need (and presumably may even have a right) to know something about the major institutions which affect their lives.

In trying to further public accountability, Rainwater and Pittman argue that researchers may need to avoid promising confidentiality. They do not discuss whether disguised research is ethical in such circumstances, but others (e.g., Galliher, 1973; Christie, 1976) have argued that it might be. Galliher argues that ethical principles like informed consent ostensibly protect individuals, but also serve to protect powerful groups; they neglect the organization as a unit of analysis, and fail "to hold actors accountable in their organizational and occupational roles (1973: 96). He calls for discussion of "whether only people in their roles as private citizens are to be protected, or if this protection also extends to actors filling roles in government and business."

The ethical dimensions of knowledge may qualify the principle of informed consent not only in situations of public accountability, but also in situations where behavior is so reprehensible or immoral that it warrants exposing. Fichter and Kolb suggest that if those studied have, in effect, renounced membership in a moral community by "choosing modes of action which violate . . . basic values of dignity and worth (1953:549), rights to privacy may not apply. They offer the example of individuals like Hitler or Stalin, and groups like "Murder Incorporated" and the Ku Klux Klan, whose activities deserve to be reported in full detail. Fichter and Kolb also emphasize the great responsibility entailed in judging people or groups to be outside the moral community, and they warn against making the decision lightly, especially when "unpopular" groups are involved.

This warning points to difficult ethical judgments. But the element of judgment, in a concrete situation, is always crucial to considerations of ethics. While the principle of informed consent in some ways seems appealing because it is absolute and hence apparently an ideal for all circumstances, that is precisely one of its limitations. In its abstract individualism, the vision is narrow; it ignores historical and social contexts and questions about the purposes of knowledge. By itself, the doctrine of informed consent does not do full justice to the complexity of the ethical judgments fieldworkers confront.

There is danger that contemporary discussions of the ethics of social research will follow primarily along the lines set forth in the new federal regulations. While the doctrine of informed consent is central, it is not exhaustive, and we should not let it blind us to important questions about the responsibilities of social scientists and the ethical uses of knowledge in contemporary society.

NOTES

1. The traditional autonomy which fieldworkers have claimed to study what they want in the ways they choose and to make their own judgments about ethics has also been challenged by groups of subjects who—like patients disenchanted with the medical profession—are less acquiescent than in the past to the conditions set by researchers. Groups of blacks, Native Americans, and other minorities, and mem-

bers of protest movements have begun to claim the right to review research proposals and to negotiate conditions; sometimes they have refused to be studied at all. Another challenge to the right fieldworkers claim to define the terms of their research has come from within the ranks of social scientists. Advocates of "action anthropology" (Lurie, 1973), "advocacy anthropology" (Schensul and Schensul, 1978), and "participatory research" (Cain, 1977) seek to develop more cooperative arrangements between researchers and the communities or groups to which they are attached, to work "with" or "for" rather than "on" a particular group (Jacobs, 1974). These movements have all emerged in research settings where the subjects are economically, socially and politically disadvantaged.

2. This paper deals only tangentially with emerging legal control of the relationship of researchers and subjects of research. It should be emphasized that many matters which used to be handled as more or less private ethical decisions are increasingly subject to official, including legal, sanctions and controls.

3. I will not deal with the third component of informed consent—the requirement that the consenting individual be competent, able to comprehend the information and to make a reasonable decision—partly because it has practical bearing only in fieldwork among children and the mentally ill. (Although, as John Kitsuse has pointed out to me, the more general question of how much subjects understand, of how they interpret and make sense of the researcher's presence, also bears on questions of whether consent is "competent.") It should be noted that for research involving children and institutionalized mental patients, government regulations specify that permission of parents or guardians must be obtained, as well as the assent of the child or the mental patient. In the case of children, such assent is required after the age of 7, although at any age the child's objection to nontherapeutic research is binding. In the case of mental patients, the individual's assent to participation must be secured if the consent committee judges that "he or she has sufficient mental capacity to understand what is proposed and to express an opinion as to his or her participation" (Annas *et al.*, 1977: 322).

4. Fieldworkers are often taken to be spies of one kind or another, an equation which Gans observes has some psychological truth. Even if the information isn't conveyed to enemies or potential exploiters and does no injury to those studies, the activity is "still, psychologically a form of espionage" (1968: 314) because the observer deceives people about her/his feelings and observes them when they don't know it. Gans argues that this has two personal consequences: "a pervasive feeling of guilt and partly in compensation, a tendency to over-identify with the people being studied."

5. Riesman and Watson (1967) and Mann (1976) describe the difficulties they encountered when subjects in sociable settings (parties and a bar) learned they were being studied. Festinger *et al.* (1956) resorted to totally disguised research, and Lofland (1966) to vague self-description to gain access to millenarian cults.

6. According to Cassell (1978), citing information from William C. Sturtevant of the American Anthropological Association, institutional review boards interpret the federal regulations in varying ways: prestigious private universities tend to exempt ethnographic research from institutional review, with some routinely finding that ethnography constitutes no risk (so informed consent is not made an issue). Smaller, less prestigious institutions tend to apply the regulations with great literalness to fieldwork.

7. See an anonymous note in *The American Sociologist* (vol. 13, Aug., 1978) from a sociologist who describes the situational constraints s/he felt to continue as a respondent in an interview which s/he found offensive.

8. 1 am grateful to Howard Becker for drawing this question to my attention.

9. As Richard Colvard (1967: 341) has suggested, informed consent is closely tied to the right to privacy, a broad right to be let alone and free from intrusion in one's personal life. Legal conflicts between the rights to privacy and free speech are pertinent to the ethical dilemmas bound up with informed consent.

REFERENCES

Annas, George J., Leonard H. Glantz and Barbara F. Katz. 1977. *Informed consent to human experimentation: The subject's dilemma.* Cambridge: Ballinger.

Barnes, J. A. 1963. Some ethical problems in field work. *British Journal of Sociology* 14:118–134.

Becker, Howard S. 1970. *Sociological work: Methods and substance.* Chicago: Aldine.

Becker, Howard S. 1971. Problems in the publication of field studies, pp. 267–284 in *Reflections on Community Studies*, ed. Arthur J. Vidich, Joseph Bensman, and Maurice R. Stein. New York: Harper Torch Book.

Bond, Kathleen. 1978. Confidentiality and the protection of human subjects in social science research: A report on recent developments. *The American Sociologist* 13:144–152.

Bortner, Peg. 1979. *The dilemma of human subjects regulations and research within the juvenile court.* Unpublished paper, Sociology Department, Washington University, St. Louis, Missouri.

Cain, Bonnie J. 1977. *Participatory research: Research with historic consciousness.* Participatory Research Project Working Paper No. 3 (24 Prince Albert, Toronto, Ontario, Canada M5 1B2).

Cassell, Joan. 1978. Risk and benefit to subjects of fieldwork. *American Sociologist* 13:134–143.

Cassell, Joan. 1980. Ethical principles for conducting fieldwork. *American Anthropologist* (in press).

Chrisman, Noel J. 1976. Secret societies: The ethics of urban fieldwork, pp. 135–147 in *Ethics and Anthropology: Dilemmas in Fieldwork*, ed. Michael A. Rynkiewich and James P. Spradley. New York: John Wiley and Sons.

Christie, Robert M. 1976. Comment on conflict methodology: A protagonist position. *Sociological Quarterly* 17:513–519.

Cohen, Fay. 1976. The American Indian movement and the anthropologist: Issues and implications of consent, pp. 81–94 in *Ethics and Anthropology: Dilemmas in Fieldwork*, ed. Michael A. Rynkiewich and James P. Spradley. New York: John Wiley and Sons.

Colvard, Richard. 1967. Interaction and identification in reporting field research: A critical reconsideration of protective procedures, pp. 319–358 in *Ethics, Politics and Social Research*, ed. Gideon Sjoberg. Cambridge: Schenkman.

Davis, Fred. 1960. Comment on 'Initial Interaction of Newcomers in Alcoholics Anonymous.' *Social Problems* 8:364–365.

Erikson, Kai T. 1967. A comment on disguised observation in sociology. *Social Problems* 14:366-373.

Festinger, Leon et al. 1956. *When prophecy fails.* New York: Harper and Row.

Fichter, Joseph H. and William L. Kolb. 1953. Ethical limitations on sociological reporting. *American Sociological Review* 18:455–550.

Freedman, Benjamin. 1975. A moral theory of informed consent. *Hastings Center Report* 5:32–39.

Galliher, John F. 1973. The protection of human subjects: a reexamination of the professional code of ethics. *The American Sociologist* 8:93–100.

Gans, Herbert J. 1962. *The urban villagers: Group and class in the life of Italian-Americans.* New York: Free Press.

Gans, Herbert J. 1968. The participant-observer as a human being: Observations on the personal aspects of fieldwork, pp. 300–317 in *Institutions and the Person,* ed. H.S. Becker et al. Chicago: Aldine.

Glazer, Myron. 1972. *The research adventure: Promise and problems of fieldwork.* New York: Random House.

Goffman, Erving. 1971. *Asylums.* New York: Anchor Books.

Gusfield, Joseph. 1955. Fieldwork reciprocities in studying a social movement. *Human Organization* 14:29–33.

Harrell-Bond, Barbara. 1976. Studying elites: Some special problems, pp. 123–134 in *Ethics and Anthropology: Dilemmas in Fieldwork,* ed. Michael A. Rynkiewich and James P. Spradley. New York: John Wiley and Sons.

Hughes, Everett C. 1971. *The sociological eye: Selected papers.* Chicago: Aldine.

Hughes, Everett C. 1974. Who studies whom? *Human Organization* 33:327–334.

Humphreys, Laud. 1970. *Tearoom trade: Impersonal sex in public places.* Chicago: Aldine.

Jacobs, Sue-Ellen. 1974. Action and advocacy anthropology. *Human Organization* 33:209–215.

Kelman, Herbert C. 1972. The rights of the subject in social research: An analysis in terms of relative power and legitimacy. *American Psychologist* 27:989–1016.

Liebow, Elliot. 1967. *Tally's corner.* Boston: Little Brown.

Lofland, John F. and Robert A. Lejeune. 1960. Initial interaction of newcomers in Alcoholics Anonymous: A field experiment in class symbols and socialization. *Social Problems* 8:102–111.

Lofland, John F. 1966. *Doomsday cult: A study of conversion, proselytization and maintenance of faith.* Englewood Cliffs, N.J.: Prentice-Hall.

Lurie, Nancy Osterich. 1973. Action anthropology and the American Indian, pp. 4–14 in *Anthropology and the American Indian: Report of a Symposium.* San Francisco: Indian Historian Press.

Mann, Brenda J. 1976. The ethics of fieldwork in an urban bar, pp. 55–109 in *Ethics and Anthropology: Dilemmas in Fieldwork,* eds. Michael A. Rynkiewich and James P. Spradley. New York: John Wiley and Sons.

Millman, Marcia. 1975. Review of R. Fox and J. P. Swazey "The Courage to Fail: A Social View of Organ Transplants and Dialysis." *Contemporary Sociology* 4:617–619.

Nader, Laura. 1969. Up the anthropologist—Perspectives gained from studying up, pp. 284–311 in *Reinventing Anthropology,* ed. Dell Hymes. New York: Random House.

Rainwater, Lee and David J. Pittman. 1967. Ethical problems in studying a politically sensitive and deviant community. *Social Problems* 14:357–366.

Riesman, David and Jeanne Watson. 1967. The sociability project: A chronicle of frustration and achievement, pp. 270–371 in *Sociologists at Work,* ed. P. E. Hammond. Garden City: Anchor Books.

Roth, Julius. 1962. Comments on "Secret Observation." *Social Problems* 9:283–284.

Roy, Donald F. 1965. The role of the researcher in the study of social conflict. *Human Organization* 24:262–271.

Schensul, Stephen L. and Jean J. Schensul. 1978. Advocacy and applied anthropology, pp. 121–165 in *Social Scientists as Advocates*, ed. George Weber and George McCall. Views from the Applied Disciplines. Beverly Hills: Sage.

Soble, Alan. 1978. Deception in social science research: Is informed consent possible? *Hastings Center Report* 8:40–46.

Stephenson, Richard M. 1978. The CIA and the professor: A personal account. *The American Sociologist* 13:128–133.

Thorne, Barrie. 1979. Political activist as participant observer: Conflicts of commitment in the study of the resistance movement of the 1960's. *Symbolic Interaction* 2:73–88.

Von Hoffman, Nicholas, Irving Louis Horowitz and Lee Rainwater. 1970. Comment—an exchange: Sociological snoopers and journalistic moralizers. *TransAction* (May 1970):4–8.

Wax, Rosalie. 1971. *Doing fieldwork: Warnings and advice*. Chicago: University of Chicago Press.

Wax, Murray L. 1977. On fieldworkers and those exposed to fieldwork: Federal regulations and moral issues. *Human organization* 36:321–328.

Whyte, William F. 1955. *Street corner society*. Chicago: University of Chicago Press.

CHAPTER 8

Fieldwork in Lesbian and Gay Communities

KATH WESTON

This study addresses a deceptively simple set of questions: What is all this talk about gay families? Where did those families come from, and why should they appear now? . . .

The fieldwork that provides the basis for my analysis was conducted in the San Francisco Bay Area during 1985–1986, with a follow-up visit in 1987. San Francisco is a port city with a large and extremely diverse population of lesbians and gay men, as well as a history of gay immigration that dates at least to World War II (D'Emilio 1989). A wave of lesbian and gay immigrants arrived in the Bay Area during the 1970s, when young people of all sexualities found themselves attracted by employment opportunities in the region's rapidly expanding service sector (FitzGerald 1986). Some came for the work, some for the climate, and some to be a part of "gay mecca." Others, of course, grew up in California.

Several San Francisco neighborhoods—Folsom, Polk Street, the Castro, Bernal Heights, parts of the Tenderloin, and increasingly the Mission—were recognized even by heterosexual residents as areas with high concentrations of gay men and/or lesbians.

> *The third tour bus in as many hours rolls through the Castro. I watch from behind the plate glass window of the donut shop, trying to imagine this neighborhood, so symbolic of "gay America," through tourist eyes. Every television reporter who covers AIDS seems to station herself somewhere on this block. The Castro used to be a place where gay men could come to cruise and enjoy one another, objects (if not always subjects) for themselves. Nowadays, says the man sitting next to me, when you see those buses coming around, you feel like you're in a museum or a zoo or something.*

With its unique history and reputation as a gay city, San Francisco hardly presents a "typical" lesbian and gay population for study. Yet the Bay Area proved to be a valuable field site because it brought together gay men and lesbians from very different colors and classes, identities and backgrounds. One estimate for 1980 put San Francisco's combined self-identified lesbian, gay, and bisexual population at 17 percent. Of those who placed themselves in one of these categories, 30 percent were women and 70 percent were men (DeLeon and Brown 1980). Lesbians were a visible presence on both sides of the bay. In contrast to many smaller cities, the region supported an abundance of specialized organizations aimed at particular sectors of the gay population, from groups for people over or under a certain age to associations of individuals who played music or enjoyed hiking. With its multicultural population, the Bay Area also hosted a variety of social organizations, political groups, and informal gathering places for gay people of color.

Among lesbians and gay men in the country at large, San Francisco is known as a place that allows people to be relatively open about their sexual identities. Carol Warren (1977) has emphasized the need to be especially protective of respondents' identities when working with gay people, in light of the social stigmatization of homosexuality. Although I follow anthropological tradition by using pseudonyms throughout this study, I feel it is important to note that the vast majority of participants expressed a willingness to have their real names appear in print. Fear of losing employment and a desire to protect children's identities were the reasons offered by the few who requested assurances of anonymity. Unlike many studies of gay men and lesbians, this one assigns surnames to participants. In a Western context, introducing strangers by given names alone paradoxically conveys a sense of intimacy while subtly withholding individuality, respect, and full adult status from research participants. Because the same qualities are routinely denied to lesbians and gay men in society at large, the use of only first names can have the unintended consequence of perpetuating heterosexist assumptions.

> While we sit at the bar watching women play pool, Sharon Vitrano is telling me about her experience walking home through the Tenderloin after one of the annual Gay Pride Parades. As she and a woman friend approached a group of men in front of a Mom-and-Pop grocery store, the two stopped walking arm in arm. On her mind, she says, were the tensions growing out of San Francisco's rapid gentrification, and escalating street violence linked to perceptions of gay people as wealthy real estate speculators. To Sharon's surprise and delight, one of the men shouted out, "Go ahead, hold hands! It's your day!"

In addition to the long hours of participant-observation so central to anthropological fieldwork, my analysis draws on 80 in-depth interviews conducted while in the field. Interview participants were divided evenly between women and men, with all but two identifying themselves as lesbian or gay. Random sampling is clearly an impossibility for a population that is not only partially hidden or "closeted," but also lacks consensus as to the criteria for membership (Morin 1977; NOGLSTP 1986). In general, I let self-identification be my guide for inclusion. Determined to avoid the race, class, and organizational bias that has characterized so many studies of gay men and lesbians, I made my initial connections through personal contacts developed over the six years I had lived in San Francisco previous to the time the project got underway. The alternative—gaining entree through agencies, college classes, and advertisements—tends to weight a sample for "joiners," professional interviewees, the highly educated, persons with an overtly political analysis, and individuals who see themselves as central (rather than marginal) to the population in question.

By asking each person interviewed for names of potential participants, I utilized techniques of friendship pyramiding and snowball sampling to arrive at a sample varied in race, ethnicity, class, and class background. While the Bay Area is perhaps more generally politicized than other regions of the nation, the majority of interview participants would not have portrayed themselves as political activists. Approximately 36 percent were people of color; of the 64 percent who were White, 11 (or 14 percent of the total) were Jewish. Slightly over 50 percent came from working-class backgrounds, with an overlapping 58 percent employed in working-class occupations at the time of the interview.

At the outset I had intended to arrange second interviews with a portion of the sample, but decided instead to seek informal contexts for follow-up that would allow me to interact with participants as part of a group. Most of the direct quotations in this study are drawn from interviews, but some arose during dinner table conversations, birthday parties, a night out at a bar, or asides during a ball game. I strove not to select interview participants on the basis of the kind of experiences they claimed to have had. Individuals' characterizations of their personal histories ran the gamut from "boring" to "incredible," but I found these assessments a completely unreliable index of interest from an anthropological point of view.

Out of 82 people contacted, only two turned down my request for an interview. A few individuals made an effort to find me after hearing about the study, but most were far from self-selecting. The vast majority demanded great persistence and flexibility in scheduling (and rescheduling) on my part to convince them to participate. I believe this persistence is one reason this study includes voices not customarily heard when lesbians and gay men appear in the pages of books and journals: people who had constructed exceedingly private lives and could scarcely get over their disbelief at allowing themselves to be interviewed, people convinced that their experiences were uneventful or unworthy of note, people fearful that a researcher would go away and write an account lacking in respect for their identities or their perceptions.

To offset the tendency of earlier studies to focus on the White and wealthier sectors of lesbian and gay populations, I also utilized theoretic sampling. From a growing pool of contacts I deliberately selected people of color, people from working-class backgrounds, and individuals employed in working-class occupations.

What a busy day for a Friday, I think to myself, sinking into a chair after three back-to-back interviews. At the first apartment, stacks of papers had covered every counter table, desk, and anything else approximating a flat surface. Before the interview began, Bernie Margolis, a Jewish man in his sixties, insisted on showing me his picture gallery. In one frame, a much younger Bernie stood next to Martin

Luther King, Jr.; others held snapshots of children from a previous marriage and distinguished service awards from a variety of community organizations. Before I left, he asked me to proofread a political leaflet. From his Mission district flat I traveled up to the Fillmore to meet Rose Ellis, an African-American woman in her thirties. Laid off from her construction job, she was cooking a batch of blackeyed peas and watching soap operas when I arrived. After the interview, Rose asked me to play back part of the tape through her roommate's stereo system—so that she could hear what her voice sounded like. A little later I hurried home to interview Annie Sorenson, a young white woman who described herself as a "lesbian virgin" with few gay or lesbian friends. From the vantage point of an easy chair reflecting back upon the day, my initial reaction is to wonder what these three people are doing in the same book.

In any sample this diverse, with so many different combinations of identities, theoretic sampling cannot hope to be "representative." To treat each individual as a representative of his or her race, for instance, would be a form of tokenism that glosses over the differences of gender, class, age, national origin, language, religion, and ability which crosscut race and ethnicity. At the same time, I am not interested in these categories as demographic variables, or as reified pigeonholes for people, but rather as identities meaningful to participants themselves. I concentrate here on the interpretive links participants made (or did not make) between sexual identity and other aspects of who they considered themselves to be, always with the awareness that identical symbols can carry very different meanings in different contexts.

Despite my efforts to incorporate differences, the sample remains weak in several areas, most notably the age range (which tends to cluster around the twenties and thirties), the inclusion of relatively few gay parents, and a bias toward fairly high levels of education. Given the age-, gender-, and race-segregated structure of gay institutions and social organization, these results may partially have been a function of my own situation and identities. I was in my late twenties at the time of the study, had no children, and usually ran out of boxes to check when asked to number my years of education on forms or surveys. But the sample's deficiencies also indicate my emphasis during fieldwork, since its composition does not reflect other aspects of identity as a White woman from a working-class background. I made the greatest effort to achieve breadth in the areas of present class, class background, and race/ethnicity.

In retrospect, I wish I had added age to this list of priorities. Judging from the gay men and lesbians in older age cohorts that I did interview, people who came out before the social movements of the 1950s-1970s may possess distinctive perspectives on the issue of disclosing their sexual identities to others, including relatives (cf. Hall 1978). Although those movements affected people of all ages who lived through that time period, older interview participants often cast their experiences in a comparative framework, distinguishing between what it meant to pursue same-sex erotic relations "then" and "now." Life experiences had made many acutely aware of the negative social and economic consequences that can follow from disclosure of a lesbian or gay identity. In her study of lesbians over 60, Monika Kehoe (1989) found that women who had married before they claimed a lesbian identity were likely to have maintained close ties with blood relatives (especially female kin) after coming out. Yet some of the same women had suffered ostracism at the hands of their heterosexual adult children.

To date there is conflicting evidence regarding the relationship between lesbian or gay identity and aging. Both the older gay men studied by Raymond Berger (1982b) and Kehoe's survey respondents reported loneliness and isolation, but their responses may have reflected the loneliness experienced by many people in the United States following retirement or the death of a partner. Further research needs to be conducted on the development of friendship networks among gay people over time, particularly given the high value historically placed on friendship by both lesbians and gay men. Do those networks expand, contract, or maintain their size as individuals grow older? Do gay people look more often to friendships, as opposed to other types of social relations, for support and assistance as they age? Are older gay men and lesbians participating in the discourse on gay families to the same extent as their younger counterparts? Since most existing studies compare lesbians to heterosexual women and gay men to heterosexual men within their respective age cohorts, there is also a need for research that contrasts the experiences of older lesbians and gay men.

> *"Are you a lesbian? Are you gay?" Every other day one of these questions greets my efforts to set up interviews over the telephone. Halfway through my fieldwork, I remark on this concern with the researcher's identity while addressing a course in anthropological field methods. "Do you think you could have done this study if you weren't a lesbian?" asks a student from the back of the classroom. "No doubt," I reply, "but then again, it wouldn't have been the same study."*

As late as 1982, Raymond Berger experienced difficulty locating lesbians of any class, color, or creed for a study of older gay people. Concluding that lesbians had little in the way of a visible public community, he gave up and confined his book to men. While gay male institutions may be more apparent to the eye, lesbians have their own (actually quite accessible) organizations and establishments, most well-documented in local community newspapers. My point here is that lesbians remained invisible *to Berger*; for me, as a woman, finding male participants proved more of a challenge. Recent work in cultural anthropology has stressed the importance of recognizing the researcher as a positioned subject (Mintz 1979; Rosaldo 1989). In my case, being a woman also influenced how I spent my time in the field: I passed more hours in lesbian clubs and women's groups than gay men's bars or male gyms.

Once I started to gain referrals, my lesbian identity clearly helped me lay claim to those bywords that anthropologists like to apply to relationships in the field when information is forthcoming: "trust" and "rapport." Many participants mentioned that they would not have talked to me had I been straight, and one or two cited "bad experiences" of having had their words misinterpreted by heterosexual researchers. In interviews with me people devoted relatively little time to addressing anti-gay stereotypes, and spoke freely about subjects such as butch/fem, gay marriage, sadomasochism (s/m), and drag queens—all topics controversial among gay men and lesbians themselves. Occasionally, of course, the larger context of eventual publication would intrude, and individuals would qualify their statements.

Presumptions of a common frame of reference and shared identity can also complicate the anthropologist's task by leaving cultural notions implicit, making her work to get people to state, explain, and situate the obvious. To study one's own culture involves a process of making the familiar strange, more the province of the poet or phenomenologist than of fieldworkers traveling abroad to unravel what seems puzzling about other societies. Early in the research my daily routine was structured by decisions about what to record. Everything around me seemed fair game for notes: one day I was living a social reality, the next day I was supposed to document it. Unlike anthropologists who have returned from the field to write ethnographies that contain accounts of reaching "their" island or village, I saw no possibility of framing an arrival scene to represent the inauguration of my fieldwork, except perhaps by drawing on the novelty of the first friend who asked (with a sidelong glance), "Are you taking notes on this?" My task could not even be characterized as an exploration of "strangeness inside the familiar," a phrase used by Frances FitzGerald (1986) to describe her investigation of the gay Castro district. For me, doing fieldwork among gay and lesbian San Franciscans did not entail uncovering some "exotic" corner of my native culture but rather discovering the stuff of everyday life.

> *After three rings I put aside the interview I've been transcribing and reluctantly head for the phone. It's my friend Mara calling for the first time in months. With a certain embarrassment, she tells me about the affair she's been having with a man. Everything is over now, she assures me, maintaining that the affair has no wider implications for her lesbian identity. "The reason I'm calling," she says half in jest, "is that I need an anthropologist. How would you like to ghostwrite a book about this whole thing? I'm going to call it* My Year Among the Savages.*"*

During interviews I used coming-out stories as a point of departure for investigating issues of identity and relationships with blood or adoptive relatives. Such narratives are customarily related to and for other lesbians and gay men rather than for the benefit of a heterosexual audience. Coming-out stories had the advantage of representing a category meaningful to participants themselves, a category so indigenous that one woman asked, "Do you want the 33 or the 45 rpm version?" Making new acquaintances was one type of occasion that often called for telling a coming-out story, and it seemed to me at times that my role as interviewer began to blend with the role of "lesbian friend of a friend."

> *In New York to do research at the Lesbian Her-story Archives, I notice that local news programs are dominated by coverage of the Statue of Liberty Restoration proj-*

ect. "Miss Liberty" and "Lady Liberty," the newscasters call her. To people in the
United States, "Mrs. Liberty" would sound like a joke.

A note on terminology is apropos here. I frequently refer to "lesbians and gay men" to remind readers of gendered differences and to undermine the all too common assumption that findings about gay men hold equally for lesbians. At times, however, I employ "gay" and "gay people" as generic terms that embrace both women and men. In the Bay Area, women themselves held different opinions regarding the application of these terms. Those who had come out in association with the women's movement were inclined to call themselves lesbians and reserve the word "gay" for men. Younger women, women who maintained social ties to gay men, and women with less connection to lesbian-feminism, were more apt to describe themselves as gay. In certain contexts a broad range of people employed "gay" as a contrasting parallel to the categories "straight" and "heterosexual."

Readers may also notice the conspicuous absence of the term "American" throughout the text. A Latino participant playfully suggested the modifier "United Statesian" as a substitute that would demonstrate respect for residents of Central and South America—as well as Canada, Mexico, and the Caribbean—who also reside in the Americas name. I have elected to avoid such summary terms altogether, not only in deference to the linguistic claims of other peoples, but also because the label "American" is so bound up with nationalist sentiment ("the American way") that it defies limitation to a descriptive reference.

I have interchanged "African-American" with "Black," "Native American" with "American Indian," and "Mexican-American" with "Chicano" and "Chicana." Preference for one or the other of these terms varied with regional origin, generation, political involvement, and personal likes or dislikes. In many contexts people referred to more specific racial and ethnic identities (Cuban-American rather than Hispanic, Chinese-American rather than Asian-American). Occasionally, however, they appealed to a collective racial identity defined vis-à-vis the socially dominant categories "White" or "Anglo." "Minorities" is clearly unsatisfactory for describing this collectivity, since White people represent the numerical minority in many parts of the Bay Area, not to mention the world as a whole. I employ "people of color" for lack of a better term, although the phrase remains problematic. Racial identity and skin tone do not always correspond to the color symbolism used to depict race in the United States. The term "people of color" can also reinforce racist perceptions of White as the unmarked, and so more generically human, category. White, of course, is also a color, and white people are as implicated in race relations as anyone else in this society.

Defining class is always a vexed issue, especially in the United States, where class consciousness is often absent or superseded by other identities (Jackman and Jackman 1983). Rayna Rapp (1982) has astutely observed that class is a process, not a position or a place. Class in this sense cannot be indexed by income or plotted along a sociological continuum from "upper" to "lower." Nevertheless, to convey the range of the interview sample, I have organized a rough classification of participants based on occupation (or parents' occupations, in the case of class background), following a Marxist interpretation of class as a relation to processes of production. Where the term "middle class" appears in the text, it is always in quotation marks to indicate its status as an indigenous term used by people I encountered during fieldwork, rather than an analytic category of my own choosing.

REFERENCES

Berger, Raymond M. 1982a. The unseen minority: Older gays and lesbians. *Social Work* 27(3):236–242.

_____. 1982b. *Gay and gray: The older homosexual Man*. Urbana: University of Illinois Press.

D'Emilio, John. 1989. Gay politics, gay community: San Francisco's experience, pp. 456–473 in *Hidden from History: Reclaiming the Gay and Lesbian Past*, ed. Martin Bauml Duberman, Martha Vicinus, and George Chauncey, Jr. New York: New American Library.

DeLeon, Richard and Courtney Brown. 1980. Preliminary estimates of size of gay/bisexual population in San Francisco based on combined data from January and June. *S.F. Charter Commission Surveys*. Mimeograph.

FitzGerald, Frances. 1986. *Cities on a hill: A journey through contemporary American cultures*. New York: Simon & Schuster.

Hall, Marny. 1978. Lesbian families: Cultural and clinical issues. *Social Work* 23(4): 380–385.

Kehoe, Monika. 1989. *Lesbians over 60 speak for themselves*. New York: Harrington Park Press.

Jackman, Mary R. and Robert W. Jackman. 1983. *Class awareness in the United States*. Berkeley: University of California Press.

Mintz. Sidney W. 1979. The anthropological interview and the life history. *Oral History Review* 17:18–26.

Morin, Stephen F. 1977. Heterosexual bias in psychological research on lesbianism and male homosexuality. *American Psychologist* 32:629–637.

National Organization of Gay & Lesbian Scientists & Technical Professionals (NOGLSTP). 1986. *Measuring the gay and lesbian population*. Pamphlet.

Rapp, Rayna. 1982. Family and class in contemporary America: notes toward an understanding of ideology, pp. 168–187 in *Rethinking the Family*, ed. Barrie Thorne with Marilyn Yalom. New York: Longman.

_____. 1987. Toward a nuclear freeze? The gender politics of Euro-American kinship analysis, pp. 119–131. *Gender and Kinship: Essays Toward a Unified Analysis*, ed. Jane Fishburne Collier and Sylvia Junko Yanagisako. Stanford: Stanford University Press.

Rosaldo, Michelle Z. 1983. The shame of headhunters and the autonomy of self. *Ethos* 11(3):135–151.

_____. 1984. Toward an anthropology of self and feeling, pp. 137–157. In *Culture Theory: Essays on Mind, Self, and Emotion*, ed. Richard Shweder and Robert Levine. New York: Cambridge University Press.

Warren, Carol A. B. 1974. *Identity and community in the gay world*. New York: Wiley.

_____. 1977. Fieldwork in the gay world: Issues in phenomenological research. *Journal of Social Issues* 33(4):93–107.

CHAPTER 9

Depth Interviewing

WILLIAM L. MILLER AND BENJAMIN F. CRABTREE

Seeing, listening, and touching are primary sources of information about the world. The interview is a research-gathering approach that seeks to create a listening space where meaning is constructed through an interexchange/cocreation of verbal viewpoints in the interest of scientific knowing. Traditionally, research interviewing in primary care represented an attempt to "standardize" listening in an effort to mine the gold of information stored in the respondents. This narrow and limiting understanding is appropriate only within the paradigm of materialistic inquiry. Research speaking and listening occurs in various forms and includes listening as an unobtrusive outsider; actively participating in everyday conversation or therapeutic conversation; sharing and hearing within a study-specific, confidential, open-ended discourse; or confronting respondents with forced-choice questions. These latter two situations have been the most common ones used in primary care research. This chapter explores the interview as a partnership on a conversational research journey and details the depth interview as an example of one qualitative, semistructured (focused) interview approach to the gathering process in primary care research.

It's flu season; the waiting room is packed; staff are out sick; the doctor has a headache; the nursing home keeps calling to report more fevers. Into this maelstrom strides Carmelita. She is 39, a single mother of two, and has recently moved into the area. She is working two jobs, attending school, and has unrelenting hand, hip, and lower back pain not relieved by maximal dose nonsteroidals. She wants relief so she can remain in control of her life. Carmelita and the doctor meet. The doctor can't quickly identify a pathologic diagnosis and is worried about the possibility of addiction if she gives Carmelita narcotics, so she recommends a new nonsteroidal. The doctor also wants relief and to remain in control of her day. Carmelita is angry, leaves the office, and never returns. Both remain in distress and not in control. What is going on? Who are these people? What is important here? What meanings and practices occurred in this lived experience? Why did this occur as it did? What does pain mean to these two individuals?

How shall we seek answers to these questions? How do we investigate the relations of individuals and context? How do doctors and patients think about pain? Our present knowledge about pain informs us that seeing (observation, pain drawings) and touching (examination, experimental stimulation) are inadequate sources of data (Fields, 1987; Frank, Moll, & Hurt, 1982; Melzack, 1975). Pain is a physiosubjective experience. Understanding pain requires participating with and asking patients and physicians about their experiences of pain. Thus, how are we to listen? We can position ourselves within social situations where people are in pain and eavesdrop on the conversations that spontaneously arise, or we can casually enter into these same conversations. When pain is mentioned within the discourse, we can even interrupt and informally explore the topic further. These approaches are informative and work best within a participant observation/key informant interview framework. An alternative is to formally develop a common set of questions, lists, or ratings about pain and expose selected respondents to these same sets of stimuli (Melzack, 1975). This structured approach runs the high risks of phrasing the researcher's own concerns into the mouths of the respondents and never giving voice to the interviewee's own perceptions and meaning making about pain. It also ignores the role of the interviewer in this meaning-making process. Qualitative depth interviews are an option that accounts for these risks.

We used depth interviews to hear six family physicians and six paired patients from a small suburban community in north-central Connecticut. The goal was to identify and compare their understandings and experiences of pain. The depth interview is a powerful qualitative research tool when the focus of inquiry is narrow, the respondents represent a clearly defined and homogeneous bounded unit with an already known context, the respondents are familiar and comfortable with the interview as a means of communication, and the goal is to generate themes and narratives.

In the remainder of this chapter, we will demonstrate the "doing" of depth interviews, illustrating each step with the pain research outlined above. To provide a context for depth interviews, we will first give a brief overview of the interview as a partnership, as a communicative performance, and as a conversational research journey.

PARTNERSHIP, COMMUNICATIVE PERFORMANCE, AND CONVERSATIONAL JOURNEY

The traditional understanding of the interview in clinical research is that it is primarily a behavioral event consisting of controlled verbal informational exchange from a repository of personal knowledge to a skilled listener/recorder. The interviewer supplies a stimulus and the interviewee responds; each question and answer is independently meaningful and isolatable and can be coded and counted accordingly. It is becoming increasingly clear that all of these assumptions are false. In every interview, there are also nonverbal and emotional interchanges and a continuous exchange of multilayered messages being differentially perceived (Mishler, 1986). The questions/transmissions are complex, ambiguous, and jointly constructed from within the context of the discourse. Both the interviewer and the respondent have multiple social roles beyond their roles as interviewer and interviewee. These different roles influence the many different motivations each has for engaging in the interview. Some of these interactional goals include requests, performance/expression, politeness, persuasion, attention, exerting authority, therapy, ritual, evaluation, and/or reference to specific knowledge. The interviewer's goal may be a particular type of knowledge, but this goal may not be shared by the respondent.

The interview is better conceptualized as a special type of partnership and communicative performance or event. It is not political oratory, storytelling, rap, a lecture, a small group seminar, or a clinical encounter. Rather, it is a conversational research journey with its own rules of the road. Figure 9.1 depicts a simplified contextual understanding of the interview as a communicative performance (derived from Briggs, 1986; Gottlieb, 1986; Gumperz & Hymes, 1972). Interview discourse occurs within a specific social situation consisting of a physical place, actors, and activities. A second context for any communication event is the communication or discourse itself (the arrow in Figure 9.1). This includes the form of the message (verbal, gesture, facial expression, etc.), the actual message or sign, and the "something else" represented by the sign. This "something else" can refer either to some person, object, event, or process in the world (referentiality) or to some other index feature of the discourse itself, such as the meaning of "I" in a conversation (indexicality).

Sociolinguistic studies of the "conventional" interview reveal many cultural assumptions and expectations. Hierarchical interviewer-respondent role relations are presumed, and rules for introducing new topics, taking

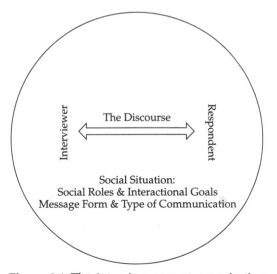

Figure 9.1 The interview as a communication event. source: Briggs (1986), Gottlieb (1986), and Gumperz and Hymes (1972).

turns, and judging the relevance of statements are included. There are also expectations for etiquette, linguistic forms, and an understanding that the major purpose of the interaction is to provide referential information. When communicating in the interview or other interaction, the respondent talks the most, turn order is fixed, the length of exchange is specified, topics are fixed, and turn allocation and interview rapport are controlled by the interviewer (Sacks, Schegloff, & Jefferson, 1974; Werner & Schoepfle, 1987b). The research interview as partnership, communicative performance, and conversational journey recognizes this knowledge but expands on it and alters its meaning. Partnership reminds us that there are two active participants involved in "meaning-making work." Both are participants in an interpersonal drama with a plot that develops around the area of inquiry (Holstein & Gubrium, 1995). The journey does begin with a hierarchical relationship, as the interviewer initiates the process and sets the opening scene with a question. And the "rules of interviewing" noted above are initially in effect because they are usually shared cultural knowledge, due to the pervasive public presence of television "interview" role models such as Oprah Winfrey, Barbara Walters, and Ted Koppel. The metaphor of journey, however, also helps us open to change in the process as the two (or more) partners develop their relationship and construct meaning. The hierarchy may shift; rules may change; improvisation emerges.

DEPTH INTERVIEWS

A profound implication of understanding the interview as a communication event is the clarification of when and which interview to use as a data collection tool. The interview is appropriate only if interviewing is a known communication routine of the respondent and if it is a culturally appropriate communication form for the topic of interest (Briggs, 1986). The type of interview depends on the interviewer's and the respondent's preexisting shared level of knowledge and the culturally appropriate form of questioning related to the topic of interest (Werner & Schoepfle, 1987b). As Briggs (1986) notes, learning how to ask requires that we first identify the different ways in which people communicate and then decide on the appropriate research methods.

The depth interview is a particular field research data-gathering process designed to generate narratives that focus on fairly specific research questions. As such, it is not the "holistic" ethnographic approach most often used by anthropologists in which the details of all aspects of a *culture* or *subculture* are investigated. The depth interview concentrates on the figure at the expense of the ground—it focuses on facilitating a coconstruction of the interviewer's and an informant's experience and understanding of the topic of interest and not necessarily on the context of that understanding. The depth interview is personal and intimate, with an emphasis on "depth, detail, vividness, and nuance" (Rubin & Rubin, 1995, p. 76).

Depth interviews primarily use open, direct, verbal questions that elicit stories and case-oriented narratives. We chose this data collection tool in our pain study because (a) we know our potential respondents are familiar and comfortable with the interview as a communicative performance and event; (b) discourse about pain in the study community often takes the form of stories (by patients) and of cases (by physicians); (c) the discourse about pain between doctors and patients usually occurs within an interview format using direct, verbal questions; (d) our study is exploratory; and (e) our goal is to discover and cocreate individual perceptions and narrative understandings about pain.

The complete interview-to-transcription process involves a series of carefully designed steps. It starts with mapping the research topic landscape through a cultural, literature, and self-review. This is followed by a designing phase, which includes developing a sampling strategy; constructing an interview guide; and planning informed consent, confidentiality, and protection strategies. The next step consists of preparing for the interview. This often-neglected phase consists of learning the language(s), gaining access to interview settings, practicing self-presentations, and conducting pilot interviews. Finally, the actual interviewing occurs, followed by the transcription and/or elaboration of field notes. Although interpretation and analysis are not discussed in this chapter, it is critically important to remember that all qualitative designs, including those using depth interviews, are flexible, iterative, and continuous. Interpretation and analysis are occurring during the interview itself, and interviews are analyzed, sampling strategies changed, and interview guides altered as the study proceeds. Even the analytic styles will change as the study evolves.

Mapping the Journey: Beyond the Literature

There are three separate aspects to mapping. Kvale refers to mapping as "thematizing" (1996). The first aspect is that of the literature review. Second is a cultural review or uncovering of the everyday, "commonsense" understandings of the research topic. The third aspect of mapping is a self-review; to hear another, one must first listen to and know oneself.

An initial *literature review* is used to identify the existing descriptive, theoretical, and analytic categories for the research topic. McCracken (1988) refers to this as the discovery of analytic categories. The review needs to be broad and not confined to citations found in *Index Medicus*. For most topics, many important studies are also reported in the social science, psychology, history, and philosophy literature. The initial goal is to search out the literature's assumptions and expectations and then to identify key conceptual domains around which an interview guide can be developed. A later goal, after the research is nearly done, will be to relate the specific research findings back to this theoretical literature.

In our review of the literature on pain, we discovered that most of the articles and other written material are broadly categorized into the domains of "socialization," "types of pain," "types of pain people," and "management of pain." Some articles, particularly in the medical literature, focus on physicians and their management of pain (e.g., pharmacotherapy, behavioral strategies, fear of addiction) and on issues of control in the doctor-patient relationship. Other material focuses on physician perspectives about types of pain (e.g., acute, chronic, terminal) and about types of pain patients (e.g., overusers, manipulators, crocks) (e.g., see Barnhouse, Kilodychuk, Pankratz, & Olinger, 1988; Diamond & Grauer,1986; Kotarba & Seidel, 1984; Williams & Wood, 1986). The social science literature, on the other hand, more often reports a patient-centered view. Issues raised from this frame of reference include "real versus nonreal pain," functional limitation, legitimizing pain, suffering, balancing priorities, and idioms of distress (e.g., see Engelhardt & Spicker, 1975; Fagerhaugh & Strauss, 1977; Hilbert, 1984; Kleinman & Good, 1985).

Both the researchers and the respondents have professional and everyday or "commonsense" understandings about the research topic and about the research methods. These are referred to as cultural categories (McCracken, 1988). We recommend a *cultural review* of the "ethnographic" reports on the culture or subculture of the respondents and some preliminary direct contact with individuals from the cultural group being studied. Newspapers, radio shows, and key informants are important sources of such information. Another approach to discovering the cultural categories of the respondents is to convene some focus groups. Finally, it is important to investigate any sociolinguistic studies of the respondents' cultural group(s) to learn the correct language and modes of presentation and to make sure the interview is an appropriate tool for investigating the research topic, particularly when the cultural group is not well acculturated into North American society (Briggs, 1986).

To "bring out" the researcher's preconceptions (some authors refer to these as "biases"), members of the research team must be willing to expose their inner thoughts and emotions both to themselves and to the other members of the team. Each person inventories her or his own past incidents, associations, and assumptions related to the research area. This is usually a very painful and discomforting process, especially when hidden personal feelings and value inconsistencies are uncovered. This cultural *self-review* is important for the analysis process when the revealed cultural categories influence interpretation of the collected data. The self-exploration helps tune the research instrument, the interviewer, for playing his or her part in the interview act, for being a better listener, for heightening intuition, and for knowing how to use self-disclosure wisely. It also prepares a reservoir of empathy for the researcher when the respondent shares similar thoughts and emotions.

The cultural self-exploration of our own pain experiences and understandings not only substantiated the four domains discovered in the literature review, it also introduced the interpretive concept that health care professionals have both personal and professional pain experiences that are often in conflict. We also exposed a negative bias against physicians on the part of one of the interviewers. Her anger resulted from a perceived undertreatment of a family member's cancer pain.

The next challenge for the research team is to select the actors and create an interview guide that facilitates the reproduction of this dramatic and intimate self-disclosure in the research interview.

Designing: Selecting the Actors, the Dramatic Outline, and Ethics

Designing a depth interview study begins with developing a sampling strategy. Once the sampling frame is known and combined with the mapping information, it is then possible to create an interview guide. The final step in the designing phase is accounting for core ethical considerations, including informed consent and issues of confidentiality.

For depth interviews, respondents should be selected so as to maximize the richness of information obtained pertinent to the research question. As such, the *sampling* strategy should be purposeful and not random. Patton (1987) and Kuzel discuss several types of purposeful sampling strategies, including extreme or deviant case, maximum variation, homogeneous, typical case, critical case, snowball or chain, criterion, confirmatory or disconfirming case, and sampling politically important cases. One or more of these can be used, depending on the particular research situation. Homogeneous sampling is particularly important in depth interviews because it is often important to account for cultural and contextual influences prior to the actual interview. Recall that depth interviews are usually not a good means for learning about cultural context; they focus on the relations of individuals to that context.

In our research on pain, we used a combination of homogeneous, criterion, and snowball sampling. We wanted folks from a homogeneous community with recent exposure to pain, and we wanted their family physicians. Therefore, we selected the first four family physicians from a small homogeneous community and asked them to provide the name of a patient over age 21 who had been discharged from the hospital within the previous 2 weeks. Two more pairs were identified later in the study to serve as disconfirming cases. When interpretation of those interviews revealed no new significant insights (data saturation), interviewing was stopped.

Depth interviews are organized around an *interview guide* consisting of some relatively closed identifying questions and a few (one to six) open-ended "grand tour" questions, with associated prompts/probes and follow-up questions. This guide outlines the dramatic format for the interview. The stage is set by rapport-building biographical questions, followed by the introduction of research themes through questions designed to elicit narratives detailing the informant's conception of the identified domains. Prompts and probes are used throughout to expand the rich context.

The first set of questions often consists of standard biographical ones that ask for short, structured, direct answers. These introductory questions serve the following seven functions: (a) establish interview style, (b) build rapport, (c) jog the respondents' memory, (d) build a bridge to intimacy, (e) "assign competence" to the interviewee (Holstein & Gubrium, 1995), (f) provide context data for analysis, and (g) weave a discourse context for the topical research questions. These 10 to 20 minutes spent talking about birthplace, family, religion, and occupation create a climate of trust, communication, and self-disclosure. The interviewing couple is prepared for the grand tour. Because the introductory questions "condition the interview" (Holstein & Gubrium, 1995), there may be times when these identifying questions aren't asked until the end of the interview. This is especially true when you want the interviewee to take the lead in the interview.

Grand tour or main questions are open, easily understood, descriptive questions that seek to elicit understandings, feelings, key terms, and major features or attributes about people, acts, time, goals, expectations, motivations, and experiences (Spradley, 1979; Werner & Schoepfle, 1987b). They open a space for discovering what others (and yourself) think and feel about some aspect of the research topic (Rubin & Rubin, 1995). A good grand tour question engages the respondent in the topic of interest. To succeed, the question must be broad, use clearly defined terms, provide necessary time and space perspectives, supply needed facts, stimulate memory, avoid jargon and emotionally loaded words, be easily and clearly understandable, delimit the scope of the question, avoid suggesting an answer, and arouse the respondent's interest and motivation (Gordon, 1975). The grand tour questions are based on the categories discovered during the literature reviews and cultural category explorations. They are designed to provide answers that ultimately relate to the theoretical literature and yet are open to new meanings being made.

In our pain study, the four broad categories found in the literature review were consistent with those discovered in the search for cultural categories. Thus, four grand tour questions were developed for the interview guide based on these domains (see Table 9.1). The final wording of each question followed lengthy group discussions. For example, the initial wording of question 3 was "Would you explain your management approach to pain?" Group analysis revealed that this question presumes the respondent has already described the management and is now to explain why, when we really wanted a description about what they do. The word *management* represents confusing jargon from medical, political, and economic perspectives. The question is also not clear as to whose pain is to be managed and for whom the description is intended—the interviewer or some other audience. In response to these issues, the final question form is, "Would you describe for me how you decide what to do when you have pain?"

Once launched on the grand tour, the interviewer must be prepared to keep the story flowing and maintain narrative competence. This is accomplished through the use of "floating prompts." Seven such prompts include *silence*, or the permissive pause that gives control to the respondent, enhances

TABLE 9.1 Grand Tour Questions from Interviews with Patients and Physicians in a Study of Pain

1. Would you take me through an experience that has influenced the way you deal with pain now?
2. From your experience, can you tell me about usual and typical kinds of pain?
3. Would you describe for me how you decide what to do when you have pain? (For patient interview: If a doctor has a patient with pain, would you describe for me how the doctor would decide what to do?)
4. From your experience, would you tell me about the usual or typical kinds of people with pain.

spontaneity, and creates a thoughtful mood; *the attentive lean*, where the interviewer leans toward the respondent with an affirmative head nod; the *eyebrow flash*; *affirmative noise*, such as "uh-huh"; the *echo prompt*, or repeating the last word spoken by the respondent in an interrogative style; the *reflective summary*, where the interviewer summarizes the respondent's last statement; and *recapitulation* or re-presenting in summary form something mentioned earlier in the interview (Bernard, 1988; Gordon, 1975; Schatzman & Strauss, 1973).

A successful grand tour facilitated by strategically placed floating prompts elicits key terms and features, but not all of these terms are fully detailed. The details, depth, vividness, and nuances characteristic of depth interviews are obtained from minitour questions and probes. The most commonly used minitour questions are *category questions*, which simply seek elaboration and/or clarification of all the parts, settings, relationships, activities, and relative worth or value of the domain being discussed. These include the "what else," "where," "when," "how," "why," and "why important" questions. Another common type of minitour is the *contrast question*, which seeks to clarify the similarities and differences between two key terms or features: "What is the difference between _____ and _____?" (Fetterman, 1989; Spradley, 1979).

There are steering probes, depth probes, and housekeeping probes. *Steering probes* refer to gentle comments that keep the interview flowing into the mainstream. It is important to allow both partners in the conversation to explore upstream along many tributaries, some of which may initially seem like dead ends or unrelated. Steering probes that link the conversation back to the research question can help relate these sidelights to the main narrative; they become part of the meaning-making work of the interview. *Depth probes* facilitate expanding and deepening understanding of the coevolving narrative and can include the *hypothetical question, devil's advocate questions, special incident probes,* and *posing the ideal probes* (Bernard, 1988, 1994; Schatzman & Strauss, 1973). Finally, there are *housekeeping probes*, which enhance the details and nuances. These include *elaboration probes, clarification probes, continuation probes,* and *completion probes*. Table 9.1 details the pain management grand tour question from our interview guide; however, the actual interview guide also includes associated probes that act as cues for the interviewer. Probes must be as carefully worded as the grand tour questions and must avoid "leading" the respondent. For example:

INTERVIEWER: Well, see if you can tell me. . . . Think of something that's. . . . And you can tell me as a story. I want you to start at the beginning and telling me like a tale, like, "I woke up in pain, etc.," or whatever the situation is.

RESPONDENT: Well, back then I'd be limited because there is nothing to tell there. I wake up and it's there. [story continues]

In this segment of the transcript, the interviewer is trying to get the respondent to recite a narrative about her experiences with pain; unfortunately, the respondent may have chosen this "wake up" story because the interviewer suggested it.

Once the initial sampling strategy is known and the first draft of the interview guide completed, one is ready to address three important *ethical considerations* in depth interviews. The first issue is informed consent, which is part of any institutional review board protocol. Depth interviews usually deal with personal, intimate material and stories. It is essential that potential interviewees clearly understand what type of relationship they are being asked to participate in and what the topics will be and how they can disengage from the relationship without risk. If tape recorders are being used, the respondent needs to be so informed and be able to turn them off if desired. It also means that the right to privacy, protection of identity, is assured and that all precautions are taken to protect the respondent from immediate or future harm.

Preparing: Staging the Scene

Once the dramatic outline is complete and the actors selected, final preparation for the interview begins. The dramaturgical metaphor is most applicable for this step because an interview is really a staged communication event; it is a purposefully situated process (Douglas, 1985). Each social situation or scene has its own culturally prescribed norms of nonverbal and verbal interaction that influence the interpretation of what is expressed (Briggs, 1986). Thus the components of this step include setting the scene, learning the part, equipment checking, and practicing or doing pilot interviews. Preparing starts with *setting the scene*. This includes initial preinterview contact to set up the interview. This contact is usually by telephone. The goal of depth interviews involves maximizing narrative competence, so most such interviews should occur in a "grass hut" setting. "Grass hut" refers to the usual, everyday location where the research topic is discussed, as opposed to a "white room," or sterile context site (Werner & Schoepfle, 1987b). Good lighting (to facilitate observation of nonverbal communication), a minimum of external disturbance (sound or activity), privacy, a face-to-face encounter with a six- to eight-foot separation, and well-mannered informality are also helpful staging parameters (Douglas, 1985).

In the pain study, we elected to conduct the family physician interviews at the physicians' offices, where they routinely engage in interviews about pain with their patients. The patient interviews took place in the privacy of the patients' homes.

Once on the scene, the interviewer has six goals for the preinterview contact. It should (a) introduce the interviewer (i.e., identify role and give name), (b) identify sponsorship, (c) explain purpose, (d) explain selection of respondent, (e) assure anonymity, and (f) obtain informed consent. The interviewer may also wish to discuss note taking, recording, and the anticipated length of the interview (Gordon, 1975). It is usually better to have done all of this at least a day before the actual interview; this prevents any possible ego threat at the time of the interview. The preinterview contact also involves a negotiation type of discourse that is quite different from the interview discourse. In the pain study, this preinterview contact took place by telephone, usually a week before the interview.

There are three major aspects to *learning the part*. It is important to know as much about the interview partner and the local setting as possible. Who is the partner? What are the partner's patterns of identification (Levy & Hollan, 1998)? What are the local norms for presentation and speech? Spending time in the neighborhoods of your future interview partners and gaining linguistic competence is time very well spent. The depth interview is an "organized occasion" for constructing knowledge (Holstein & Gubrium, 1995), thus its success and quality are contingent on the nitty-gritty preparation work at learning the language of the partner. Idiomatic expressions and nuances of meaning that are not recognized or understood in the conversation become lost opportunities for sensemaking. For example, learning the metalanguage of doctors and nurses greatly facilitates depth interviews with them. The second and third aspects to learning the part are learning how to dress and learning how to define, present, and negotiate your role in the interview. These are especially important when interviewing across genders, across ethnic groups, or across social cleavages (Rubin & Rubin, 1995). Again, these issues are optimally addressed by doing some brief participant observation and key informant interviewing.

Always remember to do *equipment checking*. Before arriving for an interview, the interviewer must thoroughly check and clean all equipment, including changing the batteries in the tape recorder (don't assume AC will be available). Interviewers must have extra batteries, a supply of blank tapes, informed consent forms, and note taking materials. Nothing is more embarrassing, undermining of professional status, or disruptive of the interview journey than having equipment that doesn't function properly.

The final step in preparation is to conduct one or more *pilot interviews*, initially with friends and then with partners culturally like the actual people to be interviewed (Douglas, 1985). This process will help in finalizing the sequence and wording of the grand tour questions and will suggest additional minitour questions and probes. The pilot interviews also serve as a training tool for the interviewers. Finally, we recommend that the researchers themselves transcribe the pilot interviews. This process will help them appreciate the need for good recordings and will aid in deciding what style of transcription they want.

Interviewing: Let the Play Begin

As we have presented it, the depth interview is a constructed dialogue focused on a creative search for mutual personal understanding of a research topic. It is situated communication requiring sincerity, cooperative mutual disclosure, and warmth (Douglas, 1985). The discourse must be open; no two interviews are the same. Only the grand tour questions are "standardized," and even they may change from interview to interview. The goal is to seek deeper collective interpersonal understanding. The validity or quality of the interview craft is seriously jeopardized with further standardization (Kvale, 1996). Thus, the interviewer needs to love to engage the pain and uncertainty of self-discovery and human existence. The interviewer, not the research guide, is the research instrument. The interviewer's role is to assume a low profile but encouraging stance, to put the informant at ease, to acknowledge the value of the information and assign competence to the interviewee, to take on the role of the respondent (Holstein & Gubrium, 1995; Schatzman & Strauss, 1973), and to reinforce the continuance of the conversation—to facilitate improvisational storytelling.

In the actual interview, the attitudes expressed by the interviewer should reinforce the interviewer's role. The interviewer should display desired enthusiasm; be nonjudgmental; show interest in the information as it unfolds; be empathic; and avoid forgetting previous answers, condescension, and rigidity (Gordon, 1975). The organization of the interview guide is designed to assist in these efforts by beginning with biographical information that grounds the interviewer into a brief life history of the interview partner and places later conversation in a context.

The interview is as paradoxical a tool as the human existence it seeks to probe. Having just pleaded for the interviewer to engage his or her travel partner with warmth and intimacy, we now argue for the interviewer to manufacture and maintain distance within the interviewer-respondent relationship (McCracken, 1988). Phenomenologists refer to this distancing as "bracketing"—putting the self aside so a phenomenon can be experienced as it is (Denzin, 1989b). This process requires the self-understanding undertaken earlier when discovering cultural categories. The interview is a dance of intimacy and distancing that creates a dramatic space where the interview partners disclose their inner thoughts and feelings and the interviewer knowingly hears and facilitates the story and recognizes, repairs, and clarifies any apparent communication missteps. Humor, gentle surprise, and the use of metaphor (such as our dramaturgical one) are a few helpful techniques for manufacturing distance in an intimate and respectful way (Mc-Cracken, 1988). For example:

R: I think losing a child must be, must be terrible, really terrible. I think a husband and wife always expect, some day you're going to lose each other. I would hope if I had to lose one of those four kids, I could handle that. They're nice kids, they really are. I sound like a mother! (laughs)

I: (laughs) What are mothers for? Let's talk a little bit. . . . You were telling me about the pain if you lost a child or pain for a death. Could you tell me, from your experience, what the usual or typical kinds of pain are?

A good interview has a steady, slow, progressive flow and should maximize the facilitators and minimize the inhibitors of this flow. Gordon (1975) describes four inhibitors that limit the willingness or motivation of the interview partner to provide information: (a) competing demands for time, (b) ego threats (evasion, denial, minimization, confession, and depersonalization), (c) etiquette, and (d) recollection of a traumatic event. He also mentions four inhibitors that limit the ability of the partner to provide information: (a) forgetting, (b) chronological confusion, (c) inferential confusion, and (d) unconscious behavior. Note that all of these factors also pertain to the interviewer. Facilitators discussed by Gordon (1975) to maximize the interview flow include (a) fulfilling expectations, (b) recognition, (c) altruistic appeals, (d) sympathetic understanding, (e) new experience, (f) catharsis, (g) need for meaning, and (h) extrinsic rewards.

Judicious use of prompts and probes as the grand tour stories evolve is essential to maintaining the progressive flow of conversation. Two general rules of thumb are to (a) avoid dominance-submission or parent-child games (Douglas, 1985) and (b) use the least direct probe necessary. Begin with silence and slowly progress to self-disclosure. Paddling in the flow of interview discourse is much like paddling a canoe. In slow, smooth water, paddle harder with more directness; in choppy water, just use the paddle gently to maintain course (Whyte, 1984).

Not all interviews proceed smoothly. The interviewer should have several strategies for dealing with the different types of resistance that occasionally emerge. If a fearful respondent wants to know, "Why are you taking notes?" just tell them. For the commonly encountered, "I don't remember," a permissive pause often brings results. If the interview partner becomes tongue tied, use a reflective probe (immediate elaboration). Steering runaways back on course often necessitates a gentle change of topic (Schatzman & Strauss, 1973; Gordon, 1975). Gordon (1975) suggests that when a reluctant interviewee says, "I don't know anything," the interviewer can use retrospective elaboration and encouragement. In the following example, the respondent is having difficulty with a question eliciting information about what doctors should think about when dealing with pain (question 3 in Table 9.1):

R: With a doctor relieving my pain?

I: Whatever occurs to you.

R: Um. Maybe I'm not getting the question right.

I: Could be. Let's start with. . . .

R: You mean if the doctor thought the patient might become addicted to a pain medicine, he might not give it to them? He'd have to know his patients pretty well. Still, I suppose he'd still have to give you something to relieve whatever you had. I don't know what to tell you on that one.

I: If you went to a doctor with pain, what would you hope that the doctor would do for you?

R: Well I would hope that if I went to him with pain, that he would give me something that would relieve it. And if it was something that was going to continue, that he'd tell me what he was going to do about it like an operation or something like that. I'd want it right away. I wouldn't want to stay on medication.

Here an encouraging reframe keeps the discourse flowing.

The alert interviewer also continuously evaluates the content of the ongoing conversation. The interviewer listens for key terms; watches for changes in the type of communication, such as switching from interview discourse to performative discourse; and listens for possible misunderstandings. It is also important to identify those times when the conversational partner is attempting to create an impression or self-presentational image. Similarly, it helps to recognize "positional shifts," such as when the interviewee shifts from speaking as a mother to speaking as an employee or as a daughter (Holstein & Gubrium, 1995). Every person has aspects of him- or herself that remain outside of self-awareness—what Douglas (1985) calls our personal "black holes." Sensitive interview partners will recognize the other's (and their own) black holes when they encounter persistent topic avoidance, exaggerated behavior/responses, or a culturally inappropriate lack of emotional display. These are signals to ease up and to go more slowly, to manufacture distance, and possibly to use self-disclosure, as in the following example:

R: Well I think (laughs) you've brought back a few memories I'd forgotten I even had! The first time I ever had real pain was when I had the first baby. And Joseph was very. . . . He was the second one. Sue was a tough one. She was the last one. She couldn't make up her mind if she wanted to come out or not. (laughs) Like I say, I've never really thought of pain until this week when you called and asked me if I would talk to you and I thought, what can I tell her about pain? I don't even have headaches. So I guess there's a lot to be said about it.

I: What's it like to think about it?

R: I don't know because I never think about it.

I: Now that you are thinking about it. (laughs)

R: Yes, right. Um, I think even as much compassion as I have for Charlie, for all this length of time, I would even have a little more for him, because I know he doesn't have any pain with the ah, you know, the stoma and all that sort of thing. But I often think when I change it for him, if there's pain there he's not telling me about it. And once you've had cancer I suppose you always hope that there isn't a little bit floating around in there because you hear. . . . [story continues uninterrupted for several minutes]

Here the black hole of denial is gently and slowly entered with a touch of distancing humor.

During the interview, the interviewer is taking brief notes, referred to as "field jottings" by Bernard (1988) and Bogdewic. These notes include observations about the respondent (i.e., nervous or evasive), about the surroundings (i.e., temperature, noise, distractions), and about the interview itself (i.e., the number of interruptions, changes in type of communication). Notes to facilitate the remembering of key terms and names are also kept. As soon as possible after the interview, the interviewer expands on these jottings and dictates extensive methodologic, descriptive, and analytic observations for his or her field notebook.

When the official interview is over and the tape recorder is turned off, it is important to linger for 5 to 15 minutes of postinterview contact. This is the time for closing small talk that sets a tone of empowerment and good relations. This is also an opportunity to elicit your interview partner's impressions of the interview and to be alert for the unexpected moment when new information is revealed (Gordon, 1975; Werner & Schoepfle, 1987b). Say thank you!

There is no one way of doing depth interviews. It is a craft. The above discussion purposely avoided naming a series of steps, as that presumes more control and direction from the interviewer than we believe is appropriate in a quality depth interview. Both participants are active in the exciting and unpredictable world of collaborative storytelling. Thus we provided some helpful guides for the journey. Nonetheless, there is a common, implicit map to the depth interview process that can help you know where you are and where you may still need to go (Holstein & Gubrium, 1995; Rubin & Rubin,1995). This path starts with *naturalizing*, creating a feeling of natural involvement for both participants, and often involves just chatting. The journey moves on to *assigning competence* and then to *activating narrative*, both of which are discussed above. Once the stories are flowing, you travel to *getting the details*. As comfort, trust, and intimacy increase, it becomes possible to ask the more difficult and sensitive questions; you have arrived at *getting deep*. Borrowing from the wisdom of the scuba diver, we recommend surfacing slowly from these depths. Thus the latter part of the interview process usually involves *toning down* the emotional level. The journey ends with *closing*. Just recognize that great adventures await those who journey afar and aren't afraid to leave the map. Have faith in your partner.

Transcribing: The Final Script

Before transcription, an interview needs to be evaluated for quality and then transcribed only if acceptable. This *evaluation process*, as discussed by Whyte

(1984) and Werner and Schoepfle (1987b), is to ensure the quality of the tape, the overall quality of the interview, and the assessment of ulterior motives, possible distortions, and surprises. This screening prevents unnecessary transcription expense and is the first step in indexing the interview. Schatzman and Strauss (1973) also recommend noting the following for each interview: (a) length; (b) rate of speech; (c) number and length of silences; (d) length of preliminary and closing interchanges; (e) relative amounts of talking by each participant; (f) percentage of remarks couched as questions, and who asks; (g) who controls the interview and when; (h) who signals termination; and (i) tone of the conversation. Kvale (1996, p. 145) suggests six criteria for assessing the quality of an interview: (a) extent of spontaneous, rich answers; (b) longer responses than questions; (c) degree to which interviewer follows up and clarifies; (d) interpretation goes on throughout interview; (e) each partner attempts to verify his or her interpretations; and (f) interview is story in itself, is self-communicating.

Transcription involves the complicated process of translating from oral discourse to written language. The interview is an oral, visual, and kinesthetic dance between two living, active bodies with multiple levels of communication (see Figure 5.1). The transcription of this performance will never capture that reality. This must be remembered when using the transcriptions for analysis; they are frozen interpretive constructs. Thus, it is important to be clear about the *style* of transcription, about how the transcription is made (Kvale, 1996). There are several choices. Do I transcribe word by word, verbatim (see examples above)? Do I "clean it up" and formalize it? Do I include pauses, emotional expressions, intonations? How much detail? Do I summarize and condense? The answers are mostly dependent on the original research question and the evolving interpretations. Thus, transcription style can change during the course of the research; keep your original tapes until the research is finished. Actual transcription takes approximately 4 to 6 hours for every 1 hour of interview.

CONCLUSION

The creative depth interview is an entranceway to narrative understanding. It is a situated, encapsulated discourse balancing intimacy and distance, which opens the way to understanding how particular individuals arrive at the cognitions, emotions, and values that emerge from the conversational journey. It is an adventure in sensemaking. The purpose is to construct a metanarrative of the many stories heard from the many interview partners. This interpretive process is on-going and informs each subsequent interview. The artificial separation of gathering and interpreting present in this chapter is unfortunate. In actual field research, both of these processes occur in circular iterative fashion. Interviews are analyzed as they are collected, and modifications in the guide or changes in the sampling strategy are made before the next series of interviews. The understanding of "truth" emerges within the research process and not in a significance level at the end. Qualitative "truth" gives voice to the hidden, to the silent, to the noisy, to the unspoken obvious, to the hurt, to the joy. Good depth interview research preserves the multivocality and complexity of lived experience.

It's flu season; Carmelita and her family physician have met. Both were separated in distress and feeling out of control. Through depth interview research on pain, on their pain, we can connect with their distress, and the pain becomes ours. We risk being changed. Carmelita and her physician begin seeing ways of turning themselves around to each other again. We see ways of changing physician socialization and physician-patient communication (Miller, Yanoshik, et al., 1994). A new journey begins!

BIBLIOGRAPHY

Barnhouse, A.H., Kilodychuck, G.R., Pankratz, C. & Olinger, D.A. 1988. Evaluation of Acute Pain: A Comparison of Patient and Nurse Perspectives. *Journal of Nursing Quality Assurance*, 2, 54–63.

Bernard, H.R. 1988. *Research Methods in Cultural Anthropology*. Newbury Park, CA: Sage.

Bernard, H.R. 1994. *Research Methods in Anthropology*. Newbury Park, CA: Sage.

Briggs, C. 1986. *Learning to Ask*. Cambridge, UK: Cambridge University Press.

Denzin, N.K. 1989. *Interpretive Interactionism*. Newbury Park, CA: Sage.

Diamond, E.L, & Grauer, K. 1986. The Physician's Reaction to Patients with Chronic Pain. *American Family Physician*. 34, 117–122.

Douglas, J.D. 1985. *Creative Interviewing*, Beverly Hills, CA: Sage.

Englehardt, H.T., & Spicker, S.F. (Eds.). 1975. *Evaluation and Explanation in the Biomedical Sciences: Proceedings of the First Time Trans-Disciplinary Symposium on Philosophy and Medicine Held at Galveston, May 9–11, 1974*. Boston: Reidel.

Fagerhaugh, S.Y., & Straus, A. 1977. *Politics of Pain Management: Staff-Patient Interaction*. Menlo Park, CA: Addison-Wesley.

Fetterman, D.M. 1989. *Ethnography: Step-by-Step*. Newbury Park, CA: Sage.

Fields, H.L. 1987. *Pain*. New York: McGraw Hill.

Frank, A.J.M., Moll, J.M.H., & Hurt, J.F. 1982. A Comparison of Three Ways of Measuring Pain. *Rheumatology and Rehabilitation*, 21, 211–217.

Gordon, R.L. 1975. *Interviewing: Strategy, Techniques and Tactics*. Homewood, IL: Dorsey.

Gottlieb, M. 1986. *Interview*. New York: Longman.

Gumperz, J.J., & Hymes, D. (Eds.). 1972. *Directions in Sociolinguistics: The Ethnography of Communication*. New York: Holt, Reinhart & Winston.

Hilbert, R.A. 1984. The Acultural Dimensions of Chronic Pain: Flawed Reality Construction and the Problem of Meaning. *Social Problems, 31*, 365–378.

Holstein, J., & Gubrium, J. 1995. *The Active Interview*. Newbury Park, CA: Sage.

Kleinman, A., & Good, B. (Eds.). 1985. *Culture and Depression: Studies in the Anthropology and Cross-Cultural Psychiatry on Affect and Disorder*. Berkeley: University of California Press.

Kotarba, J.A., & Seidel, J. 1984. Managing the Problem Pain Patient: Compliance or Social Control. *Social Science and Medicine, 19*, 1393–1400.

Kvale, S. 1996. *Interviews: An Introduction to Qualitative Research Interviewing*. Newbury Park, CA: Sage.

Levy, R.I., & Hollan, D.W. 1998. Person-Centered Interviewing and Observation. In N.R. Bernard (Ed.), *Handbook of Methods in Cultural Anthropology*. Walnut Creek, CA: Alta Mira.

McCracken, G. 1988. *The Long Interview*. Newbury Park, CA: Sage.

Melzack, R. 1975. The McGill Pain Questionnaire: Major Properties and Scoring Methods. *Pain, 1 (3)* 277–299.

Miller, W.L., Yanoshik, M.K., Crabtree, B.F., & Reymond, W.K. 1994. Patients, Family Physicians, and Pain: Vision from Interview and Narratives. *Family Medicine, 26 (3)*, 179–184.

Mishler, E.G. 1986. *Research Interviewing*. Cambridge, MA: Harvard University Press.

Patton, M.Q. 1987. *How to Use Qualitative Methods in Evaluation*. Beverly Hills, CA: Sage.

Rubin, H.J., & Rubin, I.S. 1995. *Qualitative Interviewing: The Art of Hearing Data*. Newbury Park, CA: Sage.

Sacks, H., Schelgloff, E.A., & Jefferson, G. 1974. A Systematics for Organization of Turntaking for Conversation. *Language, 50*, 696–735.

Schatzman, L. & Strauss, A.L. 1973. *Field Research: Strategies for a Natural Sociology*. Englewood Cliffs, NJ: Prentice Hall.

Spradley, J.P. 1979. *The Ethnographic Interview*. New York: Holt, Reinhart & Winston.

Werner, O., & Schoepfle, G.M. 1987. *Systematic Fieldwork: Ethnographic Analysis and Data Management*. Newbury Park, CA: Sage.

Werner, O., & Schoepfle, G.M. 1987. *Systematic Fieldwork: Foundations of Ethnography and Interviewing*. Newbury Park, CA: Sage.

Whyte, W.F. 1984. *Learning from the Field: A Guide from Experience*. Beverly Hills, CA: Sage.

Williams, G.H, & Wood, P.H.N. 1986. Common Sense Beliefs about Illness: A Mediating Role for the Doctor. *Lancet, 2* (8521–8522), 1435–1437.

White Like Me?

Methods, Meaning, and Manipulation in the Field of White Studies

CHARLES A. GALLAGHER

I came to my research project with the understanding that my racial background would be an asset. As a young white male from a working-class neighborhood I had been exposed to a raw, unadulterated, unapologetic kind of racism. The filtered and perfumed racism I encountered when I left my neighborhood and interacted with individuals from middle- and upper-middle-class backgrounds was made socially palatable by use of qualifiers, caveats, and appeals to meritocratic and individualistic principles. Being white and moving in different social circles has allowed me to sample (and at times be a part of) the way racism is expressed in different white communities. The "white stories" I heard growing up had, I was told, sensitized me to the ways of whites, which would inform and guide my research project. I thought I was uniquely positioned, a native son of white America, who could easily and readily chronicle the souls of white folks.

When I started my initial research on white identity construction by focusing on the way whites view themselves I did not need—or so I thought—to do much more than quickly gloss over how my social location might affect the interview process. I was trained to take into account the background characteristics of those we research and, to a lesser extent, the way the researcher's race, class, gender, and personal biography influence the research enterprise.

Reflecting on how personal biography influences the research process is a well-traveled road. But the development of the field of "white studies" has introduced new methodological terrain that has yet to be adequately mapped. If this line of research is to move from description to one concerned with rethinking and dismantling the way racial categories are constructed and made static, assumptions about access, rapport, and automatic insider status based on one's race need to be revisited and reconceptualized. In order for whiteness to be demystified and stripped to its political essence, our interviews must generate counternarratives of whiteness which give respondents the opportunity to rethink the white scripts, those "unquestioned assumptions" about race that are constantly being written, rewritten, and internalized.

I saw myself, at least in retrospect, as unburdened by my color because whiteness was the focus of my study, because I am white, and because I would be interviewing other whites about the meaning they attach to their race. In addition, the first phase of my research as an advanced graduate student involved interviewing white respondents from the metropolitan area in which I had been raised. I knew the stereotypes, economic profiles, and racial tensions which characterized my respondents' neighborhoods.[1]

There was a temptation to assume that I had access to respondents simply because of our skin color. Access to others because of one's race is often perceived as a methodological given. Describing how middleclass researchers use their own experiences as a template in which to bracket those they interview, Norman Denzin warns of the dangers of taking social location for granted in the interview: "They assume that all subjects will have a common perspective on such matters as annual income, patterns of sexual behavior, attitudes towards war, and so on: and they translate their stance on those issues into the interaction process, seldom questioning the legitimacy of their decision."[2]

It may be assumed that since the researcher and respondents are white and the interviews are about what whiteness means, the social biography and location of the researcher need not be scrutinized as critically as when, for example, a black researcher interviews Korean grocers in a black neighborhood or a self-identified Jewish researcher interviews members of Posse Comitatus. The legitimacy of one's role in the research process may be questioned, but because race and racial divisions are so central to the way we structure every aspect of our lives, the belief in a common perspective or narrative of whiteness may guide research assumptions and the interaction between respondent and researcher. One may be—as I initially was—lulled into the belief that the experiences of 200 million whites in the United States are linked by a common cultural thread because whites are the dominant racial group. However, while the majority of whites enjoy many privileges relative to other racial groups, one must nevertheless critically access where one's social location, political orientation, religious training, and attitudes on race fit into the research project.

Not only did I imagine myself having access to whites because I was white, but much of the literature on qualitative methods suggests that ascribed status should guide (at least in part) who one is able to study. John and Lyn Lofland, while cautioning researchers not to overemphasize the ascribed status of the interviewer, post this warning in their widely used qualitative methods textbook: "If you are black, studying Ku Klux Klan members and sympathizers will probably not be feasible. Nor are you likely to reach the desired 'intimate familiarity' if you are male and attempting to study a radical lesbian group."[3]

Providing an overview of how social location influences what researchers "see and do not see," John H. Stanfield II argues that "only those researchers emerging from the life worlds of their 'subjects' can be adequate interpreters of such experiences."[4] As a white researcher studying whites I saw myself situated squarely within the insider doctrine, which "holds that insiders have monopolistic or privileged access to knowledge of a group."[5] While inscribing myself within these interviews as a racial insider I was also able to maintain the role of the "objective" outsider. This methodological legerdemain could be maintained simply by embracing the neutral techniques of qualitative methods outlined in textbooks which define the field. I could embrace the role of detached dispassionate researcher-outsider with access to knowledge "accessible only to nonmembers of those groups" while simultaneously being an insider because of my color.[6]

However, being an insider because of one's race does not mute or erase other social locations which serve to deny access, create misunderstanding, or bias interviews with those from the same racial background. Nor does perceiving or defining oneself as an outsider allow one to claim that one's research is value-free. Skin color does not necessarily allow one to automatically pass into and have access to individuals or communities because of shared ascribed characteristics.

"Being white," like being a member of any social group, has a host of contradictory, symbolic, and situationally specific meanings. As a northerner raised in the working-class section of a big city who now lives in the South, being white will not provide me with automatic cultural access to the whites I will be interviewing in rural southeast Georgia. How will my whiteness smooth over differences based on my age, gender, or presumed ethnicity in my interviews? Will my Yankee dialect and status as professor with an urban university affiliation position me as a cultural outsider? Will the perception that I am Jewish, and the racial confusion many have concerning this category, make me a "racial" outsider? The argument could be made (and I have been told this already) that even though most people view me as white I will still be viewed as an outsider here in Georgia. In either scenario, as a cultural and/or racial outsider, I will have to consider how my perceived characteristics may shape the interview.

WHITE LIKE ME: WHO'S INSIDE, WHO'S OUTSIDE?

After my partner and I had settled into a somewhat integrated working-class neighborhood in Philadelphia we went to our corner bar and began talking with the proprietor about our new surroundings. His father had owned the eponymous Tony's before him and his extended family had lived within one block of the bar for over sixty years. In an almost boastful manner I explained to Tony that until the late 1950s my Italian grandparents had lived four blocks away. As a boy my mother frequently and figuratively traveled back to her old neighborhood to shop and expose me to "authentic" Italian-American culture. I intimated to Tony that moving into this neighborhood was a third-generation return to a community that had always had larger-than-life status in my family's history. The exchange with

Tony was pleasant, respectful, and even somewhat nostalgic. I then asked him how the neighborhood had changed since the 1950s. He looked at me for a moment and out poured a string of epithets and expletives about how blacks had destroyed what had once been a beautiful, cohesive community. The intensity and maliciousness of his comments caught me off-guard but did not surprise me. I have been privy to such language before. What was startling was his assumption that my partner and I would be responsive to such an ugly racist creed.

Upon further reflection, however, I realized that I had projected a kind of racial solidarity with this man. No doubt this connection was due in part to a shared ethnic affiliation, working-class roots, and family histories—but the common denominator that linked us was our whiteness. As this gray-ing middle-aged bartender saw me, I was a white man who would be sup-portive of or at least sympathetic to the emotional grief blacks had caused him. Within fifteen minutes of chatting our race had linked us in a perceived union of mutual hate.

During our conversation a neighborhood black man dressed in a city tran-sit worker's uniform entered the bar. Our conversation was suspended, Tony greeted this local warmly, and the man left with a sixpack. There was no an-imosity or disrespect toward him, nor was there any indication on Tony's part that this black man was part of the group that had "destroyed" his commu-nity. Tony smiled at this neighborhood resident and politely took his money.

On a different occasion, a young white male travel agent sitting next to me on a plane confided to me that when he could save enough money he was moving from New York City to Australia. Identity politics, multicul-turalism, gay rights, feminism, affirmative action, political correctness, and the influx of nonwhite immigrants had made the United States a perverse, hostile, almost foreign environment for straight white "American" men like himself. Going to Australia, he explained, would be like going back to the United States in the 1950s. Although this man was too young to have expe-rienced the white racial bliss of this imagined era nonetheless it represented for him a time when the cultural practices of straight white males had been the invisible and unchallenged norm.

More recently, a real estate agent in Atlanta, angry that she could not make a left turn because the oncoming black driver was going too slow, made the off-hand comment that "some groups of people just do not know how to drive." This college-educated, middle-class white woman was at ease using racial stereotypes in our company because our whiteness served as a common currency and language which presumably links all whites to an omnipresent antipathy toward blacks; it is a "white thing" that other whites understand.

WHITE STORIES: LINKED BY RACE AND RACISM

What I found most surprising when recounting these experiences with other whites was that almost everyone had similar "white stories." A white colleague was told by a white barber that white men needed to keep a watchful eye on "our white women" or they would be sexually abused by nonwhites. A white taxi driver explained to a white friend why he did not pick up black passengers. A white neighbor told me about the "open-minded" white coworker who told a racist joke when the setting became all-white.[7]

All these white stories have this in common: many whites are comfortable expressing their racism to white strangers because they believe their skin color makes them kindred spirits in racism, or at least sympathetic to the "white experience." White researchers examining the meaning whites attach to their race are cognizant of this, either explicitly capitalizing on their whiteness to gain access and rapport to respondents, or, more dangerously, tacitly believing that their whiteness makes it unnecessary for them to examine their own racial biography. One's whiteness becomes a form of methodological capital researchers can use to question whites about the meaning they attach to their race.

Perceiving oneself as a white insider and interrogating whiteness from the outside as a researcher creates a number of methodological and ethical questions. For example, did the kinds of comments made above by whites I did not know give me immediate or easy access to any of these people as potential respondents simply because I am white and my questions were about their racial identity? Am I automatically an insider because of my skin color? Is the potential for tension, misunderstanding, or lack of rapport minimized because race is so central to the way we structure our lives that the whiteness shared by researcher and respondent transcends other social markers? Is it possible to be manipulated into reproducing the racist stereotypes of whites, particularly working-class whites, by asking questions about race and race relations that use the language and ideology of white victimology constructed, circulated, and endorsed by neoconservatives, the media, and survey research?

To what extent does the "objective interviewer" stance taken by many researchers allow white respondents to validate and justify the existing racial hierarchy that privileges whites, while simultaneously allowing these respondents to claim they are now at a social and economic disadvantage because of their skin color? The ethical and moral implications for those working in white studies is clear. Asking questions which decontextualize and treat whiteness as normative or existing outside the established racial hierarchy makes the researcher complicit in valorizing and creating a narrative of whiteness which absolves researcher and informant of the responsibility of challenging white racism and white privilege.

In this section I want to explore some of these concerns and examine how my status as a white middle-class male affects various aspects of the research enterprise. I have conducted fourteen focus groups and forty in-depth interviews with white adults and college students in the Northeast and Rocky Mountain regions of the United States. I am currently interviewing whites in two working-class and poor communities in rural Georgia. One county is 99.7 percent white, while the second is almost 80 percent black. Both counties mirror each other on a number of socioeconomic measures, namely, median household income, levels of education, and the percentage of whites at or below the poverty line. I will contrast how whiteness is understood by whites in an all-white community to those whites who live in a community where they are the racial minority.

A number of overlapping and interrelated concerns emerged in my research which led me to question the extent to which I was engaged in antiracist scholarship or whether my questions were reproducing a variation on what Stuart Hall calls "inferential racism." Hall argues that the way we represent or frame the idea of race, "whether 'factual' or 'fictional' which have racist premises and propositions inscribed in them as a set of unquestioned assumptions . . . enable racist statements to be formulated without ever bringing into awareness the racist predicates on which the statements are grounded."[8] Hall's "inferential racism" is a critique of the way the media normalizes racist ideology through various representations of race. Hall's examination of the pernicious ways in which the media maintains and reproduces racial hierarchy could just as easily serve as a warning to researchers, prompting them to question how their research normalizes whiteness by relying on "unquestioned assumptions" about racial identity construction, racism, or the dominant belief that whites do not think of their whiteness or their race in relation to other racial groups.

Many of my white respondents would often frame their own racial identity based on information about race that was factually incorrect. Respondents routinely double- and triple-counted the black and Asian population in the United States, dismissed contemporary racism as a thing of the past, and saw the workforce as significantly biased against whites. As an academic committed to antiracist research, it became unclear to me whether I was conducting the "normal science" of a racist paradigm or was engaging in "inferential racism" by allowing my respondents beliefs to go unchecked. Since I did not explain to my respondents that whites make up about 75 percent of the U.S. population, was I confirming and lending academic legitimacy to their anxious and fearful version of U.S. race relations and white victimology? Was it possible that those I interviewed thought that whiteness was under attack or unfairly maligned, and therefore in need of academic attention? This concern was made clear to me when an older secretary to whom I explained that I was examining the meaning whites attached to their race retorted sharply, "Good, it's about time somebody studied us." Was I condoning racism or encouraging white supremacy by validating a view of race and power relations that was largely fictive? By not challenging these reactionary versions of white identity construction the chance to engage in direct antiracist action was lost. Furthermore, responses that might have generated counternarratives or created a crisis of whiteness could not emerge or be explored.

I also want to suggest that there is an inherent danger in claiming insider status because researcher and respondent are both white. Henry Giroux reminds us that "racial categories exist and shape the lives of people differently within existing inequalities of power and wealth."[9] These inequalities exist both within racial categories as well as between them. The recent scholarship on the cultural meaning of "white trash" is yet another way whites have been sorted along a socioeconomic continuum by academics.[10] When I first started asking questions in my focus groups and interviews, I had partially leveled the "within" group differences that existed among my respondents. The internal variation which exists in the way 200 million whites in the United States understand, mark, and articulate their race creates formidable research challenges. The "unquestioned assumption" of white invisibility, that whites view themselves as colorless or, as Richard Dyer agues, "having no content," or, as Alastair Bonnett puts it, "existing outside of the political and economic forces that seem to shape other racialized identities is a metanarrative which should be resisted."[11] In my interactions with whites throughout the country, there was enormous variation in the way individuals came to understand, ignore, or validate their whiteness depending on their spatial location in a city or suburb, as well as within a particular region of the United States. Class, geography, education, political ideology, sexuality, religion, age, gender, local culture—these qualify and shape the construction of whiteness for my respondents, just as they did for me as an interviewer.

The "social geography of race," to borrow Ruth Frankenberg's phrase, varies in real and idiosyncratic ways.[12] Researchers studying whiteness and the various meanings, expressions, and emotions whites attach to their racial position need to reexamine the insider/outsider dilemma which arises when studying something as slippery as racial identity construction. Being white may be a necessary condition to gain access and trust with some white respondents, but being white is not sufficient in and of itself. Access or rapport based on skin color may be negated by other aspects of one's social identity that pose a greater threat or suspicion among respondents.

I was reminded of my white-as-"outsider" status among whites when an elderly working-class Italian-American I had been building rapport with in Philadelphia was told by a neighbor that I was a graduate student. This seventy-year-old high school dropout and numbers runner no longer viewed me as just a "young white guy" from the neighborhood. Recently in Georgia I was talking with an older woman at a yard sale and she asked me, "What country are you from?' "Pennsylvania" did not appear to be a satisfactory answer. In the eyes of some southerners, my olive skin color, dark hair, and brown eyes had cast me as the generic, racially ambiguous, foreign "other." It was not clear if this woman thought I was white, but I was left pondering how her view of my racial identity might unfold, influence, and shape the outcome of an interview about her definition or understanding of her whiteness.

I also want to suggest that researchers examining whiteness can be unintentionally (or intentionally) manipulated into racism by embracing a set of "commonsense" assumptions about white racial attitudes which guide their research. Henry Giroux's work on how whiteness is reproduced and normalized is instructive. A counterhegemonic narrative which provides a cultural space for whiteness to be "renegotiated as a productive force in a politics of difference linked to a racial democratic project" should be as central to white studies as the inclination to demonstrate that white identity construction is based only on "what one isn't and on whom one can hold back," to quote David Roediger.[13]

Finally, I want to suggest that the whole enterprise of white studies and the rush to critique whiteness as a sociohistorical category results in an essentialized and ultimately racist discourse. While whiteness is understood as a socially constructed category, the internal variation within this category is often leveled. Without acknowledging how culture, politics, geography, ideology, and economics come together to produce numerous versions of whiteness, researchers will continue to frame and define whiteness monolithically. Just as we might cringe in a classroom when a student starts a conversation by stating that "all blacks do this . . . " or "gays always seem to . . . " we should be careful not to accept the political construction that whiteness is culturally or ideologically monolithic. Without critically examining how the questions we ask as researchers reshape the meaning of race, whiteness can be reconstituted and rearticulated, and the essentialist beliefs which undergird the idea of race go unchallenged.

LOCATING RESEARCHER AND RESPONDENT

Was I perceived to be an insider by the nineteen-year-old white woman from a Montana trailer park, the white thirty-seven-year-old single mom ex-junkie who despised black women on welfare, the right-wing white retired military colonel, or the gay white college professor? Does my status as a white interviewer erase other cleavages that typically divide individuals? How does the interview itself, as a socially and politically situated endeavor, level, fail to capture, or mute the various ways white identity is understood and expressed? How can the highly nuanced and ever-shifting social locations which position and reposition whiteness as a salient social identity be captured by an interview?

As a researcher in my mid-thirties, to what extent did my age influence the discussion I had with young respondents about the *contemporary* meaning of whiteness? In one focus group exchange John, a twenty-year-old white college student, asked the other white respondents to consider the idea that being raised in the post-civil rights era had allowed them to transcend the old fashioned racism which many thought characterized the racial beliefs and discriminatory actions of the generations that preceded them. Speaking for the focus group John used age to sort those older folks who possibly engaged in the vile, overt racism of yesterday from the more enlightened, innocent colorblind post–civil rights cohort. At least in the eyes of many whites born in the generation after 1975, the "old fashioned racism" had gone the way of the buggy whip and phrenology:

We are past it [old fashioned racism]. You know we are not our ancestors. We didn't do that stuff. We don't do it now—none of us. I don't know how old you are but nobody in this room was alive in 1965. . . . I don't think any of us in this room have gone out and tarred and feathered someone or done anything like that. . . . I haven't been around black people enough to really do anything really bad. . . . I've never done any prejudiced act. I don't think anybody else in here has either but still, you guys are white and you're the enemy.

John may have included me in the "enemy" category because we were both white, but since I was born before 1965 had I been marked as an outsider because of my age? Did this generational divide "race" these young whites in a way that was different from the way I came to understand my own racial identity? Mary, a nineteen-year-old, also used the civil rights movement as a way to distinguish between older whites who were responsible for overt forms of racism and her generation, which she viewed as being unfairly linked to the racist behaviors and attitudes of the older generation:

They say they have been oppressed. They have not. The students here at this university right now have not been oppressed. They have not experienced the Watts riot, they didn't experience being hosed down by the police. Granted, the white population was responsible for that but we are not. We are not responsible. Therefore, we should not be put out because of that. We didn't do it. We're not doing it now, therefore they have no right to say, well, we've been oppressed.

It was unclear whether Mary viewed me as being part of the generation that was responsible for black oppression, and I was left wondering what role my age played in the dynamics of the focus group interactions. Would the responses have differed if I had been a twenty-two-year-old or a sixty-two-year-old interviewer?

Being born before 1965 may have indirectly linked me to traditional Bull Connor forms of racism with the early twenty-something crowd, but it was also a source of pity among those a generation or two older than myself. Sarah, a fifty-three-year-old executive secretary born and raised in Atlanta, described how white privilege had changed from one generation to the next:

I think probably that in generations before me, as in my parents and my grandparents, I think that they probably were given preferential treatment because they were Caucasian. I do not know [whether] that was the case with the beginning of my generation. And I am glad because we should remove all prejudice. . . . I think that if anything there is a bit of reverse discrimination because particularly blacks are put in positions when more qualified whites are there, so I think it has gone just the reverse.

Did Sarah view me as being part of the generation that was now subject to reverse discrimination in the labor market? Was I viewed as both a researcher and a white male victim as we talked about the meaning of whiteness in the United States? Is it possible that I was viewed as doubly disadvantaged by my race and gender?

In a number of my interviews my class background and that of my respondent framed how whiteness was discussed. As I ran focus groups and individual interviews throughout the country I realized I was more in tune with the social and cultural background of lower-middle and working-class respondents. My questions were relatively consistent throughout my interviews but my own class position, or at least the one in which I was raised, allowed me to more throughly probe respondents who were from a similar class background. The economic anxieties of the working class and of lower-middle-class whites and the way those fears become racially grounded was something I understood viscerally and intellectually. However, I was not able to draw on the same cultural markers and reference points when I interviewed respondents from very wealthy backgrounds. We may have been white but the stark contrast in our class backgrounds created diffrent understandings and narratives of whiteness. Dan, a twenty-year-old from a self-described "rich" neighborhood in Phoenix, Arizona, commented that he did not use race to place people in categories. Within his social circles it was class, not color, that mattered. In a focus group with other well-off students attending an elite, expensive private school, Dan outlined how class overrode color:

> I don't ever think about being white or identifying with white. It's more of class. I came from a high school where everyone was like me, even if they were black, you know, people drive their own car, go to the club, and play golf. You know that kind of stuff, if I see someone who has a nice car and I see them hitting balls, I'll go and talk to them. It doesn't matter what race you are. But then I don't identify with people who don't have money to wear nice clothes and don't have the money to go to this school, or people on financial aid. I feel uncomfortable around them.

Based on his description I would not be one of those toward whom Dan would feel a sense of social solidarity. I grew up wearing my older brother's hand-me-downs and irregular clothing, and was on financial aid throughout college. Ironically, for three summers in elementary and early high school I had worked on a golf course selling hot dogs and Italian ices to the Philadelphia golfing clique, many of whom were from the social background Dan described. Perhaps divulging my class experiences to Dan might have provided him with the opportunity to reconsider the extent to which class triumphs over race as a social identity. Dan said he was not "trying to show off" or sound "conceited," but it was difficult for me to think otherwise. As Dan was describing his upper-middle-class country club white existence I thought to myself that while we were both male and white I had very little in common with the way he lived his life or constructed his worldview. However, upon further reflection perhaps my slightly condescending view of Dan's privileged bourgeois existence was driven in part by a deepseated, working-class resentment and jealousy of the leisure class.

Throughout my interviews, it was quite obvious that whiteness was spatially as well as socially located. The researcher and respondent are as sociably situated as the site of the interview. As a number of interviews and focus groups slowly revealed to me, respondents became conscious of their race as they moved from one setting to the next. Many respondents could ignore whiteness or be preoccupied with it in different ways throughout the day. For instance, a respondent may be racially unconscious while shopping in the early morning with his white friends at a suburban mall. His late morning layup shots are a deliberate, much rehearsed combination of Michael Jordan's and Dennis Rodman's best moves. He grooves to a TuPac Shakur song on his car radio as he weaves his way from his white neighborhood to the city for his afternoon class. Driving through the black northern part of the city to Urban University, however, makes him nervous. He thinks about what might happen to him if his car breaks down five blocks from campus. He feels a bit anxious parking near the projects or staying late on campus. He is reminded of his race and his outsider racial status when he sees recruitment posters of the Daughters of Kush, the Black PreLaw Society, and the Korean Cultural Club on campus kiosks. He walks quickly through the surrounding black neighborhood relieved his car is still there, gets in, and drives home through the black part of the city with locked doors, and slowly, as the racial terrain becomes familiar, his anxiety eases and his world becomes "normal" again. In the course of his day this respondent has thought about his whiteness in different ways in response to changing circumstances.

Taking into account the social location of a participant and the personal biography of the researcher, and approaching the interview knowing that the meaning whites attach to their race varies by region, class, gender, sexual orientation, and political philosophy allows for a more reflexive and nuanced understanding of the complex and contradictory ways whites understand their race and define who they are. Apart from benefits that accrue to whites because of their skin color no single metanarrative of whiteness exists. The "white stories" I defined earlier may link racist and nonracist, researcher and respondent together in a perceived or fleeting sense of racial understanding or solidarity. However, if whiteness is treated as a monolithic identity based on privilege or the assumption that all whites harbor certain negative (or positive) attitudes toward other racial groups, researchers will miss the opportunity to examine the social complexities and the social geography of how and where racial identities are constructed and the multiplicity of meanings that define whiteness. The difficulty mapping white racial identity construction is poignantly problematized by John Hartigan, Jr. in his research on race and whites in Detroit. He notes that it is not possible to "compile a more or less thorough aggregate of whites, abstract out from them a common condition or an intrinsic set of connections, and have neatly defined by these efforts a succinct, abiding identity—whiteness."[14]

MARKING OR MANIPULATING WHITENESS:
RESISTING THE RACIAL TEMPLATE

The field of inquiry now defined as "white studies" has grown enormously in the last decade. A number of "white scholars" are examining the ways in which white identity intersects with the issues of class, gender, law, economics, and popular culture. Influenced by postmodern theories of deconstructionism, this nascent field of inquiry has taken it upon itself to strip away the subjectivity of whiteness and expose the relational and situational nature of white identity. This intellectual scrutiny has moved whiteness from being merely a backdrop in the discourse on racial identity formation to becoming the subject of study.

When I started my project in 1992 little empirical work had been done on how whites define whiteness, on the social and political situations which push whiteness to the forefront as a social identity for whites, and on the way the construction of whiteness is linked to structural elements which shape those meanings. This is no longer the case. However, the systematic, empirically grounded gathering and telling of white people's narratives about their understanding of their race, as opposed to the way whites define the racial "other," is still relatively unexplored.

When I initially formulated the questions that would inform my data collection I was not aware just how much my research project was being manipulated by my own assumptions about whiteness. In an attempt to provide different measures of the same social phenomena I employed focus groups, in-depth interviews, and a survey. But using surveys to tap something as complex as how someone constructs their racial identity raised a number of thorny issues. Could I examine whiteness so as to capture the social complexities and varied cultural nuances which define racial categories by using a questionnaire? Could racial identity be conceptualized as a temporally static and discreet category, like height, weight, or income? Could I, as I was instructed at one point, create a "white index" using factor analysis which would rank on a single scale the "whiteness" of one respondent relative to another? If I did not produce data that could stand up to at least a test of Chi-square would I be left, as I was told, with "only stories" about whiteness based on my focus groups and interviews which could not, by themselves, stand up to peer review?

After much deliberation and pretesting, my position was that by their very design, surveys could neither tap nor measure how, why, or to what extent whites come to understand the complex, contradictory, and subtle ways whiteness is articulated. A mixed methodological approach allowed me to use the cultural expressions of whiteness voiced by respondents in my interviews to frame and complement the survey questions. This allowed me to examine the underlying ideological and structural influences that mediate the process of white racial identity formation.

My struggle to create a methodological approach that included both rich textured accounts of the *meanings* whites attached to their racial positions and surveys that allowed for some generalizability beyond my population masked the more pressing ethical and political concerns that became apparent in subsequent interviews. As is the common practice in survey research, my questions were drawn from existing studies that purported to tap the attitudes of whites. The final survey questions and semistructured interview guide were drawn from "commonsense" notions about whites derived from surveys, popular opinion polls, social science research, the input of my committee members, and what I perceived to be the issues that shape white identity construction.

The resulting white template I designed, and which guides much of the research on race relations, is based on a priori assumptions about how social scientists understand and define white attitudes, white fears, and white culture. These survey-generated beliefs become the white attitudinal baseline which influences how researchers in other fields structure their interview guides and data matrices, or redesigned their survey questions. If white identity is conceptualized only in oppositional terms, alternative narratives of whiteness cannot emerge in the interview.

A portion of my survey and interview schedule have been included in Appendix 1 and 2. The overwhelming majority of questions in Appendix 1 reflect an early and (in retrospect) rather simplistic understanding of how and why whites attach meaning to their race. My survey questions tap a narrow version of whiteness that frames racial identity construction only in opposition to racial minorities. However, the open-ended questions in the survey did sensitize me to issues of identity construction which had not been adequately addressed in the literature. Not all whites construct their racial identity in opposition to blacks, Asians, or Latinos, nor did whiteness serve as a proxy to a reactionary worldview. These expressions, which challenged the "commonsense" literature on whiteness, became the basis for questions I would later ask in my focus groups and interviews. While relatively unstructured, my interview schedule reflects an approach to whiteness that attempts to capture whiteness as being constructed in oppositional and cultural terms. I believe the field of white studies is moving to a more nuanced yet critical understanding of white identity construction. The view that "Whites' consciousness of whiteness is predominately unconsciousness of whiteness"[15] or that "Transparency, the tendency of Whites to remain blind to the racialized aspects of that identity, is omnipresent"[16] is no longer a sustainable narrative in the wake of racial identity politics. The view of whiteness as invisible will be supplanted by a theoretical approach to whiteness that will, as Henry Giroux argues, mark "whiteness as a form of identity and cultural practice" which "makes the distinction between 'whiteness' as a dominating ideology and white people who are positioned across multiple locations of privilege and subordination."[17] The idea of whiteness is being constructed, reinterpreted, and molded by whites for whites as a cultural product understood in ways other than being in opposition to nonwhites.[18]

RESEARCHING WHITENESS AS AN ANTIRACIST PROJECT

In almost all my focus groups I asked or respondents offered their views on affirmative action. Respondents who had been reticent throughout the focus group discussion suddenly came to life, arguing forcefully about the need for, or more often the inherent unfairness of, affirmative action. In many interviews this topic was a turning point. Many whites took the opportunity to articulate a narrative of their whiteness that was based on victimization.[19] This conversation often led to a discussion about welfare, multicultuarlism, and downward economic mobility because the labor marked now preferred blacks and Asians to whites. The laments, outrage, and pent-up guilt about this topic were fascinating, sociologically rich, and deeply troubling.

But what if, after these issues had been exhausted, I had asked my focus groups to consider another scenario? What if they had been provided with a number of social facts about the relative social standing of whites compared to other racial groups in the United States? How might whites define themselves if it was demonstrated that racial discrimination in the labor market is unquestionably still a sorting mechanism that privileges whites, that whites are twice as likely to graduate from college as blacks, that the face of welfare in the United States is white, that almost every socioeconomic measure—from infant mortality, to home ownership rates, to the accumulation of wealth—favors whites over blacks, Latinos, or many Asian groups?

If the belief that whites are losing out to blacks or Asians was refuted in the interview and whites had a chance to articulate an identity that could not be based on victimology, what would that white racial identity look like., Would there or could there be a white racial identity that was not merely "a politically constructed category parasitic on blackness"?[20] My experiences suggest that when white respondents are given counterarguments that demonstrate that racial inequality still exists they *modify* many of their positions.[21]

While critical of my own work for bracketing a narrative of whiteness within a reactionary and conservative framework, Henry Giroux asks how, as antiracist researchers and educators, we might provide: "the conditions for students to address not only how their 'whiteness' functions in society as a marker of privilege and power, but also how it can be used as a condition for expanding the ideological and material realities of democratic public life."[22]

The conditions required to think ourselves out of an oppositional understanding of whiteness means breaking the racial template which seduces researchers into asking questions which merely reproduce a "common-sense," neoconservative definition of whiteness and race relations based on whites' perceived marginalization. Those who wish to "abolish the white race" or define whiteness *only* as a source of power equally shared by all whites, level the social, political, and economic differences among whites while creating a simple racial dichotomy which is easily and routinely manipulated politically.[23]

Data does not "speak for itself" nor does it "emerge" in a vacuum. Who we are (and appear to be in a specific context) influences the questions we ask, the responses we get, and the scholarship we produce, which is reproduced by yet another cohort of graduate students. Some of this scholarship finds its way into *Newsweek*, the *Wall Street Journal*, or as a discussion topic on *The Oprah Winfrey Show* or *Montel*, where it becomes part of our collective understanding of race relations. I was reminded of this trickle-down understanding of race relations by a white male in a focus group. He insisted that Rodney King was a threat to the police officers who savagely beat him because he kept moving when he was on the ground. "If you want to know what is really going on," he told the group, "You gotta watch Rush [Limbaugh]."

Unfortunately, the counternarratives that might challenge the existing racial status quo go in large part unexplored. A colleague from a working-class background who was familiar with my work told me the purpose of my project was to demonstrate that working-class whites are racist. I would, as others had done before, paint a portrait of working-class whites as racists. This was not my intention, although his prediction was fairly accurate. I was steered toward a version of whiteness that had been framed by the narrow binary ways in which many researchers choose to explore racial identity construction and had accepted the script that had been provided to my respondents.

BEYOND WHITE ESSENTIALISM

An agitated white male in a focus group, typical of many I interviewed, complained that whites are the new minority group in the United States. Talking about the treatment of blacks, Mike explained to me: "It's not like they're discriminated against anymore, it's like the majority is now the minority because we are the ones being discriminated against because we are boxed in. We can't have anything for ourselves anymore that says exclusively white or anything like that. But everyone else can. You know what I mean."

Throughout my research white respondents generally embraced the belief that the U.S. class system was fair and equitable. Most respondents argued that those who delay gratification, work hard, and follow the rules will succeed, irrespective of color.[24] Many white respondents felt the leveled playing field argument has rendered affirmative action policies a form of reverse discrimination and source of resentment. Jennifer Hochschild calls this "whites' quandary." "Whites are more sure that discrimination is not a problem," that blacks can succeed, that self-reliance pays off, that blacks now "control their own fate" *and* whites feel that their life chances have eroded.[25] This was how my respondents were able to define themselves as victims. As the above quote by Mike explains, it is whites who are "now the minority." Like the white stories I outlined earlier, the whites-as-victim perspective can be added to the ever-growing list of those situations, attitudes, or injustices that make up the "white experience."

Like many other young whites from modest backgrounds, Mike defined himself as the racial "other." He viewed himself as lacking agency in a world where he was marginalized because of his race. This perception lends itself to the development of defensive strategies based on an essentialist understanding of whiteness. What, many of my respondents asked me, would blacks do if we wore a "It's a white thing. . . . You wouldn't understand" t-shirt? My point here is not to examine whether whites can be the subaltern, the racial outsider in a white society, or the other "other." My question concerns the shift from a racial identity that is invisible to one made explicit and the way this process may essentialize whiteness. Michael Omi and Howard Winant explain that "a racial project can be defined as racist if and only if it creates or reproduces structures of domination based on essentialist categories of race."[26] While ostensibly concerned with social justice and racial equality it is unclear to what extent white studies, as a racial project, can embrace an antiessentialist epistemology or methodology.

Much of the work being done in white studies embraces an essentialist standpoint in two ways. First, we have allowed a narrative of whiteness to emerge which has been molded by a reactionary political and cultural climate with a vested interest in defending the racial status quo. We might challenge the tendency for white respondents to validate and justify white privilege by inverting the questions we ask, so that respondents are forced to think of the structural advantages that accrue to them because of their skin color. How might a white informant respond to the question that requires him or her to consider how a fifty-year-old, white-collar black or Asian woman might view their whiteness? Do we ask questions which challenge our respondents to think about race as a political category, or do we reproduce, normalize, and continue to make whiteness invisible by uncritically validating the version of whiteness we expect to hear? White studies is in a position to explore counternarratives of racial identity construction which imply that whites have agency in the way they define themselves, and suggest that they might take responsibility for, or at least have a fuller understanding of, racial privilege in the United States.

This is of course a double-edged sword. To not talk about the ways in which whiteness retains its invisibility and hence its power is to "redouble its hegemony by naturalizing it."[27] However, to talk about whiteness as a visible, meaningful identity with definable particularizing qualities, is to treat this category as if it were real. It is unclear at the time of this writing whether "white studies" will embrace a critique of whiteness that challenges racial hierarchy through an explicit antiessentialist discourse, or whether it will become the vehicle through which a sophisticated, critical essentialism is articulated.

APPENDIX 1

Survey Given to 514 Students at a Large Urban University

The entire original survey was thirteen pages. For this publication I have only included those questions that explicitly address white identity construction. Questions on race and residence, standard background variables, social networks and race, interracial dating, social distance scales, and the strength of ethnic identity measures have been omitted.

For a complete copy of the survey please contact me at: The Department of Sociology, Georgia State University, Atlanta, GA 30303-3083, or cgallagher@gsu.edu.

1. What is your racial/ethnic background? _____

2. What percentage of the U.S. population is:

   White _____ %

   Black _____ %

   Asian _____ %

   American Indian _____ %

3. Think for a moment about the neighborhood or area were raised. When I am in the area where I was raised:

   (check one)

   _____ I sometimes think about my race

   _____ I often think about my race

   _____ I never think about my race

   If you answered "sometimes" or "often" what are the situations that make you think about your race?

   _____

   If you answered "I never think about my race" what kinds of events in your neighborhood would make you think about your race?

   _____

4. When I was in high school:

   (check one)

   _____ I sometimes thought about my race

   _____ I often thought about my race

   _____ I never thought about my race

   If you answered "sometimes" or "often" what were the situations that made you think about your race?

   _____

If you answered "never" why might that be the case?

_____

5. In the course of my school day at Urban University:

_____ I sometimes thought about my race

_____ I often thought about my race

_____ I never thought about my race

If you answered "sometimes" or "often" what were the situations that made you think about your race?

_____

6. In the course of your school day at Urban University in what situations are you likely to think about your race? (check all that apply)

_____ on public transit

_____ in the dorms

_____ in the classrooms

_____ in Student Activities Center

_____ in the library

_____ driving to Urban University

_____ dealing with the administration (bursar, financial aid)

_____ when I am a numerical minority in a class

_____ when I am interacting with students from different racial grounds than my own

_____ parking off campus

_____ when I interact with faculty

_____ at fraternity/sorority parties

_____ staying late on campus

_____ sporting events

_____ eating lunch on campus

_____ being approached by the homeless

7. What other Urban University situations or specific encounters on campus are likely to remind you of your race?

_____

8. Are there any situations on campus that you find threatening?

_____

9. What percentage of the Urban University population is:

White _____ %

Black _____ %

Asian _____ %

Other _____ %

10. Do you think more about your race since attending Urban University?

_____ yes _____ no _____ no opinion

APPENDIX 2

Focus Group and Individual Interview Schedule

1. General background questions: age, place of birth.
2. Where were you raised? What was your neighborhood like? Was it integrated?
3. How would you define your class background?
4. What was the class background of the family in which you were raised?
5. How do you define yourself ethnically?

   What is it—single, multiple, hybrid, symbolic?

   What meaning do you or does your family attach to your ethnicity?

   Are these things ethnically important: holidays, food, dating, neighborhood dynamics?
6. What does it mean to be white in the United States in 1999?
7. Are you conscious of being white? When?
8. In what situations do you think about being white?
9. What would you define as white culture?
10. Why do some whites feel threatened about the current state of race relations?
11. How is being white different from being black or Asian?
12. How is being white similar to being black or Asian?
13. What objects would you place in a museum of white history?
14. Define yourself politically.
15. What does that mean?
16. Once again, what does it mean to be white?

NOTES

I would like to thank France Winddance Twine for editorial guidance and comments on earlier versions of this chapter.

1. See Charles A. Gallagher, "White Reconstruction in the University," *Socialist Review* (1995) 94 (1/2): 165–88.

2. Norman Denzin, *The Research Act: A Theoretical Introduction to Sociological Methods* (Englewood Cliffs, N.J.: Prentice Hall, 1989).

3. John Lofland and Lyn H. Lofland, *A Guide to Qualitative Observations and Analysis*, 2d ed. (Belmont, Calif.: Wadsworth, 1984).

4. John H. Stanfield II, "Ethnic Modeling in Qualitative Research," in *Handbook of Qualitative Research*, edited by Norman Denzin and Yvonna Lincoln (Thousand Oaks, Calif.: Sage, 1994).

5. Maxine Baca Zinn, "Field Research in Minority Communities: Ethical, Methodological, and Political Observations by an Insider," *Social Problems* (1979) 27 (2): 209.

6. Ibid.

7. I am indebted to Kevin Delaney for helping me develop the idea of white stories.

8. Stuart Hall, "The Whites of Their Eyes: Racist Ideologies and the Media," in *Silver Linings: Some Strategies for the Eighties*, edited by G. Bridges and R. Brunt (London: Lawrence and Wishart, 1981).

9. Henry A. Giroux, "Racial Politics and the Pedagogy of Whiteness," in *Whiteness: A Critical Reader*, edited by Mike Hill (New York: New York University Press, 1997), p. 294.

10. See Matt Wray and Annalee Newitz, eds., *White Trash: Race and Class in America* (New York: Routledge, 1997).

11. Richard Dyer, *White* (New York: Routledge, 1997); Alastair Bonnett, "Constructions of Whiteness in European and American Anti-Racism," in *Debating Cultural Hybridity: Multi-Cultural Identities and the Politics of AntiRacism*, edited by Pnina Werbner and Tariq Modood (London: Zed Books, 1997), pp. 173–92.

12. Ruth Frankenberg, *White Women, Race Matters: The Social Construction of Whiteness* (Minneapolis: University of Minnesota Press, 1993).

13. David Roediger, *Toward the Abolition of Whiteness: Essays on Race, Politics, and the Working Class* (New York: Verso, 1994).

14. John Hartigan, Jr., "Locating White Detroit," in *Displacing Whiteness: Essays in Social and Cultural Criticism*, edited by Ruth Frankenberg (Durham: Duke University Press, 1997), p. 204.

15. Barbara Flagg, "Transparently White Subjective Decision Making," in *Critical White Studies: Looking Behind the Mirror* edited by Richard Delgado and Jean Stefancic (Philadelphia: Temple University Press, 1997), p. 220.

16. Ian F. Haney López, *White by Law: The Legal Construction of Race* (New York: New York University Press, 1996), p. 157.

17. Henry A. Giroux, "White Squall: Resistance and the Pedagogy of Whiteness," *Cultural Studies* (1997) 11 (3): 383.

18. See Ashley W Doane, Jr., "Dominant Group Ethnic Identity in the United States: The Role of 'Hidden' Ethnicity in Intergroup Relations," *Sociological Quarterly* 38 (3): 375–97.

19. See Charles A. Gallagher, "Redefining Racial Privilege in the United States," *Transformations* 8, no. 1 (spring 1997): 28–39.

20. Cornet West, "The New Cultural Politics of Difference," in *The Cultural Studies Reader*, edited by Simon During (New York: Routledge, 1993), p. 212.

21. Paul M. Sniderman and Thomas Piazza, *The Scar of Race* (Cambridge: Harvard University Press, 1993). Sniderman and Piazza found that whites were quite willing to change their minds about racial policy issues when presented with a counterargument.

22. Henry A. Giroux, *Channel Surfing: Race Talk and the Destruction of Today's Youth* (New York: St. Martin's Press, 1997), p. 108.

23. See *Race Traitor*, edited by Noel Ignatiev and John Garvey (New York: Routledge, 1996).

24. See Charles A. Gallagher, "White Racial Formation: Into the Twenty-First Century," in *Critical White Studies: Looking Behind the Mirror*, edited by Richard Delgado and Jean Stefancic (Philadelphia: Temple University Press, 1997).

25. Jennifer L. Hochschild, *Facing Up to the American Dream* (Princeton: Princeton University Press, 1995), p. 68.

26. Michael Omi and Howard Winant, *Racial Formation in the United States: From the 1960s to the 1990s* (New York: Routledge, 1994), p. 71.

27. Cited in David Roediger, *The Wages of Whiteness: Race and the Making of the American Working Class* (New York: Verso, 1991), p. 1.

Beginning Where We Are

Feminist Methodology in Oral History

KATHRYN ANDERSON, SUSAN ARMITAGE,
DANA JACK, AND JUDITH WITTNER

> Our means of knowing and speaking of ourselves and our world are writ-
> ten for us by men who occupy a special place in it . . . In learning to speak
> our experience and situation, we insist upon the right to begin where we
> are, to stand as subjects of our sentences, and to hear one another as the au-
> thoritative speakers of our experience.[1]

INTRODUCTION

Oral history is a basic tool in our efforts to incorporate the previously overlooked lives, activities, and feelings of women into our understanding of the
past and of the present. When women speak for themselves, they reveal hidden realities: new experiences and new perspectives emerge that challenge
the "truths" of official accounts and cast doubt upon established theories.
Interviews with women can explore private realms such as reproduction,
child rearing, and sexuality to tell us what women actually did instead of
what experts thought they did or should have done. Interviews can also tell
us how women felt about what they did and can interpret the personal meaning and value of particular activities. They can, but they usually do not.

Our fieldwork shows us that oral history has only skimmed the surface
of women's lives. Women have much more to say than we have realized.
As oral historians, we need to develop techniques that will encourage
women to say the unsaid. We also need to move beyond individual accounts
to make much more systematic use of our interviews. Here, then, we propose an interdisciplinary feminist methodology to achieve these goals.

This paper is the result of a series of collaborations. Initially, historians
Kathryn Anderson and Susan Armitage worked together on the Washington Women's Heritage Project exhibit, which illustrated the everyday lives
of women with photographs and with excerpts from oral history interviews.
Their assumption was that Washington women shared a set of values—a female subculture—but this hypothesis proved more difficult to document
than they had expected. Although both feminist scholarship and their own

personal sense of self told them that relationships with others have always been a central component of female activity and identity, Anderson and Armitage found that existing oral histories provided very little direct support for this assumption. It was much easier to document activities than feelings and values. Surprised by this finding, each historian pursued the question further. Anderson's critical scrutiny of her own oral history interviews revealed a strong bias *against* just the sort of information we had hoped to find and led her to reformulate her questions and interview goals. Anderson turned to a colleague, psychologist Dana Jack, and found useful insights in her work and the work of other feminist psychologists. Thus our first interdisciplinary connection was made, and we developed a perspective on women's historical activity that incorporated a methodology to explore and validate personal feelings.

While Anderson was thinking about personal experience, Armitage had begun to try to put women's experience into a wider context.[2] She was concerned, in particular, with finding a way to generalize from the individual to the common experience. She wondered how much the feelings and values of one individual woman can tell us about female values. Is there really a set of common feelings and values that women of a particular culture, class, or historical period can be said to share? Are there cross-class and cross-race commonalities? How can personal feelings be compared, without resort to sociological "schedules" and rigid interview formats? Just as Armitage was beginning to worry seriously about these questions, she was fortunate to find, in Judith Wittner, a feminist colleague who was thinking about similar questions within a sociological framework. Thus was forged the second interdisciplinary connection, as the life history tradition in sociology was brought to focus upon the wider questions raised by women's oral history.

The final collaboration brings us together to tell from our originally separate disciplinary perspectives how we have forged an interdisciplinary approach to the oral history of women's lives.

THEORETICAL FRAMEWORK

Recent feminist scholarship has been sharply critical of the systematic bias in academic disciplines, which have been dominated by the particular and limited interests, perspectives, and experiences of white males. Feminist scholars have insisted that the exploration of women's distinctive experiences is an essential step in restoring "the multitude of both female and male realities and interests" to social theory and research.[3]

Assembling women's perspectives seemed necessary to feminist scholars because women's experiences and realities have been systematically different from men's in crucial ways and therefore needed to be studied to fill large gaps in knowledge. This reconstitution of knowledge was essential because of a basic discontinuity: women's perspectives were not absent simply as a result of oversight but had been suppressed, trivialized, ignored, or reduced to the status of gossip and folk wisdom by dominant research traditions institutionalized in academic settings and in scientific disciplines. Critical analyses of this knowledge often showed that masculinist biases lurked beneath the claims of social science and history to objectivity, universal relevance, and truth.[4]

The injunction to study women's realities and perspectives raised methodological as well as substantive issues. Dominant ideologies distorted and made invisible women's real activities, to women as well as to men. For example, until recently it was common for women to dismiss housework as "not real work." Yet, unlike most men, women also experienced housework as actual labor, as a practical activity that filled their daily existence. In effect, women's perspectives combined two separate consciousnesses: one emerging out of their practical activities in the everyday world and one inherited from the dominant traditions of thought. Reconstructing knowledge to take account of women, therefore, involves seeking out the submerged consciousness of the practical knowledge of everyday life and linking it to the dominant reality.

The perspectives of two feminist scholars, Marcia Westkott and Dorothy Smith, have especially influenced our thinking about oral history. Westkott provides us with a basic approach to individual consciousness. She describes how traditional social science assumes a fit between an individual's thought and action, "based on the condition of freedom to implement consciousness through direct activity." But within a patriarchal society, only males of a certain race or class have anything approaching this freedom. Social and political constraints customarily have limited women's freedom; thus in order to adapt to society while retaining their psychological integrity women must simultaneously conform to and oppose the conditions that limit their freedom.[5]

In order to understand women in a society that limits their choices, we must begin with the assumption that what they think may not always be reflected in what they do and how they act. Studying women's behavior alone gives an incomplete picture of their lives, and the missing aspect may be the most interesting and informative. So we must study consciousness, women's sphere of greatest freedom; one must go behind the veil of outwardly conforming activity to understand what particular behavior means to her, and reciprocally to understand how her behavior affects her consciousness and activity.[6]

Dorothy Smith has argued that feminist sociology must "begin where we are" with real, concrete people and their actual lives if it is to do more than reaffirm the dominant ideologies about women and their place in the world. Smith suggests examining how these ideological forms structure institutions and shape everyday life; her "institutional ethnography" begins with the actual daily lives of women and moves from there to examine how their activities appear in organizational processes. As an example, Smith examines the articulation of two forms of women's work, mothering and teaching, to show in what ways the organizational processes of institutionalized education organize how women in these positions work with children, and the effect of institutional education in standardizing their activities, making them "accountable within the institutional context," and rendering invisible any education work that cannot be accounted for within the documentary record.[7]

From the point of view of feminist scholarship on women, therefore, oral history should involve more than simply gathering accounts from informants, itself a difficult process involving considerable skill. These bits of evidence we collect—subjectively reconstructed lives—contain within them formidable problems of interpretation. What theoretical conclusions to draw from these accounts is the additional and enormous task that oral historians face. Using the insights provided by feminist scholars, we explore in the following pages what it means to develop in oral history a feminist methodology situated in women's experiences and perspectives.

THE PROBLEM OF MEANING (KATHRYN ANDERSON)

As I was interviewing women in Whatcom County for the Washington Women's Heritage Project, a public archive, my colleague Dana Jack was conducting confidential interviews with depressed women for a study of women's development. In the process of sharing what we were learning about women from their interviews, both of us gained valuable insights as to how women understand their lives.[8]

I became aware, as I reviewed my early interviews, that my research questions were more sophisticated than my interview questions; I had not probed deeply enough or listened attentively enough to satisfy my curiosity about how women interpret their existence.

Why have not historians, and especially historians of women, pursued the subjective experience of the past more rigorously? My own interviews and those of others show a definite preference for questions about activities and facts and a conspicuous lack of questions about feelings, attitudes, values, and meaning. Traditional historical sources tell us more about what happened and how it happened than how people felt about it and what it meant to them. As historians, we are trained to interpret meaning from facts. But oral history gives us the unique opportunity to ask people directly How did it feel? What did it mean?

Activity is, undeniably, important to document; but a story restricted to action and things is incomplete. Oral history can tell us not only how people preserved meat but whether the process was fun or drudgery, whether it was accompanied by a sense of pride or failure. The unadorned story of what people did tells us more about the limitations under which they operated than the choices they might have made. With oral history we can go further; we can *ask* what the person would rather have been doing.

Reviewing my interviews, I have found that my training in the history of facts and action triumphed over my awareness of a decade of historical research pointing to the importance of relationships and consciousness in women's lives and kept me from hearing the reflections that women were clearly willing to share.

Although I asked what seemed at the time to be enlightened questions about relationships, I now see how often I shied away from emotionally laden language to more neutral questions about activity. My first interview with Elizabeth illustrates the point. We had been talking about her relationships with her mother and half sister when she offered the following:

> I practically had a nervous breakdown when I discovered my sister had cancer, you know; it was kind of like knocking the pins—and I had, after the second boy was born, I just had ill health for quite a few years. I evidently had a low grade blood infection or something. Because I was very thin and, of course, I kept working hard. And every fall, why, I'd generally spend a month or so being sick—from overdoing, probably.

Instead of acknowledging and exploring further her reflections upon the physical and mental strains of her multiple roles, my next question followed my imperative for detailing her role on the farm: "What kind of farming did you do right after you were married?"

Elizabeth is a farm woman who was a full partner with her husband in their dairy farm and has continued an active role as the farm has switched to the production of small grains. Her interview has the potential of giving us valuable information about the costs incurred by women who combined child rearing and housework with an active role in the physical labor and business decisions of the farm. It also suggests something of the importance of relationships with family and close friends in coping with both roles. The interview's potential is severely limited, however, by my failure to encourage her to expand upon her spontaneous reflections and by my eagerness to document the details of her farming activity. Not until later did I realize that I do not know what she meant by "nervous breakdown" or "overdoing." The fact that other farm women used the same or similar terms to describe parts of their lives alerted me to the need for further clarification. Now I wish I had let her tell me in her own words of the importance of the relationship with her sister and why its possible loss was such a threat.

Later in the same interview I did a better job of allowing her to expand upon her description—only to deflect the focus from her experience once again. Elizabeth was telling me how hard it was to be a full partner in the field and still have full responsibility for the house:

> This is what was always so hard, you know. You'd both be out working together, and he'd come in and sit down, and I would have to hustle a meal together, you know. And that's typical.

> *How did you manage?*

> Well, sometimes, you didn't get to bed till midnight or after, and you were up at five. Sometimes when I think back to the early days, though, we'd take a day off, we'd get the chores done, and we'd go take off and go visiting.

Was that typical? Neighbors going to visit each other after the chores were done?

While Elizabeth was telling me how she managed, I was already thinking about patterns in the neighborhood. My first question had been a good one, but by asking about what other people did, my next one told her that I had heard enough about her experience. The two questions in succession have a double message: "Tell me about your experience but don't tell me too much." Part of the problem may have been that even while I was interviewing women I was aware of the need to make sense of what they told me. In this case, the scholar's search for generalizations may have interfered with the interviewer's need to listen to an individual's experience.

If we want to know how women feel about their lives, then we have to allow them to talk about their feelings as well as their activities. If we see rich potential in the language people use to describe their daily activities, then we have to take advantage of the opportunity to let them tell us what that language means. "Nervous breakdown" is not the only phrase that I heard without asking for clarification. Verna was answering a question about the relationship between her mother and her grandmother.

> It was quite close since my mother was the only daughter that was living. My grandmother did have another daughter, that one died. I didn't know it until we got to working on the family tree. My mother was older than her brother. They were quite close. They worked together quite well when it would come to preparing meals and things. They visited back and forth a lot.

Her answer gave several general examples of how the closeness was manifested, but now I want to know still more about what Verna means when she describes a relationship as "close" twice in a short answer and what her perception of this relationship meant to her. My next question asked, instead, for further examples of manifestations: "Did they (grandparents) come to western Washington because your parents were here?"

Even efforts to seek clarification were not always framed in ways that allowed the interviewee to reflect upon the meaning of her experience. Elizabeth was answering a question about household rules when she was a child and commented: "My mother was real partial to my brother because, of course, you know that old country way; the boy was the important one." My question "How did her partiality to the brother show?" elicited some specific examples, but none of a series of subsequent questions gave her an opportunity to reflect upon how this perception affected her understanding of herself and her place in the family.

A final example from Verna's interviews illustrates the best and the worst of what we are trying to do. Her statement is the kind of powerful reflection upon her role as a mother that could only have emerged from a comfortable and perceptive interview. The subsequent question, however, ignores all of the emotional content of her remarks.

Yes. There was times that I just wish I could get away from it all. And there were times when I would have liked to have taken the kids and left them someplace for a week—the whole bunch at one time—so that I wouldn't have to worry about them. I don't know whether anybody else had that feeling or not, but there were times when I just felt like I needed to get away from everybody, even my husband, for a little while. Those were times when I would maybe take a walk back in the woods and look at the flowers and maybe go down there and find an old cow that was real gentle and walk up to her and pat her a while—kind of get away from it. I just had to it seems like sometimes . . .

Were you active in clubs?

Two realizations emerge from this somewhat humbling experience of recognizing the inadequacy of what, on other levels, are extremely useful interviews: (1) oral historians should explore emotional and subjective experience as well as facts and activities; (2) oral historians should take advantage of the fact that the interview is the one historical document that can ask people what they mean.

To accomplish the first of these, we need more and better questions about relationships of all kinds, questions that explore feelings of competency—when women feel good about what they have done and how they have done it—as well as feelings of incompetence, when they feel like failures or that things have gone wrong, and why. Oral historians need to be sensitive to women's perceptions of their choices and how they feel about their responses. We also need to be sensitive to what women value and why. When women reveal feelings or experiences that suggest conflict, we need to explore what the conflict means and what form it takes. Finally, we need general questions that allow women to reflect upon their experience and choose for themselves which experiences and feelings are central to their sense of their past.

The language women use to explore the above topics will be all the richer when they have ample opportunity to explain and clarify what they mean. We need to ask for explanations and examples of words and phrases like "support," "close," "sisterhood," "tomboy," "visiting," and "working together." With letters and diaries we can only infer what individuals mean by the language they use; with oral history interviews we can simply ask them.

The oral historian will never be as exclusively concerned as the psychologist with questions of self-concept and consciousness, but we can do much better than we have done to document questions of value and meaning in individuals' reflections upon their past. We must learn to help women to tell their own stories as fully, completely, and honestly as they desire.

LEARNING TO LISTEN (DANA JACK)

As I interviewed depressed women to try to understand their experience, I encountered a different set of problems from those described by Kathryn.

My difficulty lay not in finding the "right" questions to ask, but in my ability to hear and interpret what women were saying about their psychological experience. The women told stories of the failure of relationships, and inability to connect with the person(s) with whom they wanted to achieve intimacy. These were the expected stories, predicted by existing models, and the temptation was to interpret the stories according to their agreement with or deviance from existing concepts and norms for "maturity" and "health." However, when the woman, instead of the researcher, is considered the expert on her own psychological experience, women's stories challenge existing standards and concepts. These norms are biased in their equation of maturity with self-reliance and autonomy, and are ideas impoverished by a history of male interpretation of female experience.

Within psychology, researchers have been reluctant to trust the reliability of subjective accounts of disturbed people, including depressed women. The reluctance is due to at least two major factors. First, the Freudian emphasis on the unconscious and the defensive maneuvers of the ego suggests that normal people's explanations for their behavior or emotions cannot be trusted. This stance holds true even more strongly in the case of psychopathology. The clinical view is that the person is repressing painful and/or threatening material and cannot give an accurate explanation of his/her psychological state; the person's behavior and emotions must be explained by experts. Thus the issue of interpretation becomes critical for the data we collect through oral interviews. Secondly, clinicians consider that the very nature of depressive illness causes the person to exaggerate the negative aspects of his/her life. Distortion becomes part of the illness, and women's descriptions of negative aspects cannot be considered as reliable. Again, the person has been eliminated as a valid interpreter of his/her knowledge. These two concerns have been called into doubt by research that independently verified the truth of depressed women's accounts by objective measures of outside events. Two studies, one by George W. Brown and Tirril Harris of depressed women,[9] and another by Deborah Belle of women in poverty,[10] have established the reliability of depressed women's descriptions of their lives.

The critical questions for oral interviewers are whose story is the woman asked to tell, who interprets it, and in what contexts? The subject's story (the data) is the result of an interaction between two people. The personality and biases of the researcher clearly enter into the process to affect the outcome. Is it the woman's understanding of her own experience that is sought, or is the researcher structuring the interview so that the subject tells a story that conforms to the researcher's orientation? If the goal of the interview is to encourage the woman to tell her own story, to speak in her own terms, then how one asks questions, and with what words, becomes critical to the outcome of the interview.

The oral interview not only allows women to articulate their own experiences but also to reflect upon the meaning of those experiences to them. It provides a picture of how a woman understands herself within her world, where and how she places value, and what particular meanings she attaches to her actions and locations in the world.

Oral interviews allow us to hear, if we will, the particular meanings of a language that both men and women use but which each translates differently. For women, the ability to value their own thought and experience is hindered by self-doubt and hesitation when private experience seems at odds with cultural myths and values concerning how a woman is "supposed" to think and feel. Looking closely at the language and the particular meanings of important words women use to describe their experience allows us to understand how women are adapting to the culture within which they live.

To explore women's experience of depression, I designed a longitudinal study that included interviews with a group of twelve women clinically diagnosed as depressed. Because I did not want to structure their thoughts about their experience of depression with my own ideas, I started with the question, "Can you tell me in your own mind what led up to your experience of depression?" Starting with their initial answers, I explored what they said using their own words to ask them to elaborate, or else I asked them to explain what they meant by a term.

Accepting the premise that we have a great deal to learn from women's stories about both their psychology and their history, how do we proceed with analysis? For me, the critical step was to learn to listen in a new way. As I listened to the woman's self-commentary, to her reflection upon her own story, I learned about her adaptation to the particular historical and relational world she was living in, especially her adaptation to the stereotypes to which she tried to conform. I listened with an awareness that the women's self-reflection is not just a private, subjective act. The categories and concepts we use for reflecting upon and evaluating ourselves come from a cultural context, one that has historically demeaned and controlled women's activities. So an exploration of the language and the meanings women use to articulate their own experience leads to an awareness of the social forces and the ideas affecting them. Observed from the outside through their behavior, depressed women are called passive, dependent, masochistic, compliant, and victimized by learned helplessness. Yet, agreeing with Marcia Westkott that we must go behind the veil of outwardly conforming activity in order to understand how behaviors affect women's consciousness and their self-concept, I found a different way to understand depression.[11] Basically, what became evident through listening to the women's self-reflection was the activity required in order to be passive, to live up to the stereotype of the "good" woman, particularly the good wife.

How do we listen to interviews without immediately leaping to interpretations suggested by prevailing theories? Content analysis provides the first step: it tells us what is there, what themes dominate the interviews . But the step that allows us to challenge existing formulations and to uncover what the women are feeling and saying is the step of exploring the dynamics of a person's thought through the use of language. By probing the meaning of the words women use to describe themselves and their experience, we can begin to employ an analysis of the social forces that affect their consciousness. In this way we can begin to understand Nancy Cott's observation that "the meaning which women ascribe to their own behavior is reducible neither to the behavior itself nor to the dominant ideology. It is derived from women's consciousness which is influenced by the ideas and values of men, but is nevertheless uniquely situated, reflective of women's concrete position within the patriarchal power structure."[12]

Women's concrete position as subordinates creates a possibility for self-evaluation that vacillates between "me" and "not me." On one level, women often accept the stereotypes that define them as dependent, passive, giving, compassionate and gentle. Yet these concepts are negatively valued in the wider society and are often impossible to live up to. Thus concepts that shape self-experience are often demeaning and self-alienating to women and at the same time are both valued and devalued by women who understand themselves in society's terms. With such a perspective on the woman's self -reflection, we can listen more perceptively to how she adjusts to her world and its expectations of her as a woman.

Listening to the women's interviews, I first noticed how they continually socialized their feelings: they judged not only how they were acting, but also how they were thinking and feeling.[13] The standard that they continually failed to meet (in their own minds) was a generalized image of how women *should* think and feel, informed by the wider culture and by the examples of their own families.

For example, psychologists consider depressed women to be overdependent upon their relationships for a sense of self and self-esteem. But if we look at how depressed women understand dependence, and how their evaluation of themselves as dependent affects their self-perception and their actions, the concept is cast in a new light. In a first interview with a thirty-three-year-old depressed woman, about seven minutes into the interview the following interchange occurred. The woman was talking about her feelings about herself, her problems, and how she felt she had "lost a lot of myself" through the activities of being a wife and a mother. In her self-understanding, the issue of dependence was central and problematic:

> You know, I'm basically a very dependent person to start with. And then you get me married and tied down to a home and not working . . .

Asked what she meant by dependent, she responded:

> I like closeness. I like companionship. I like somebody, and intimate closeness, even with a best friend. I was always so close to my mother. . . . I was used to that all through my childhood, having an intimate closeness . . . someone that shared my feelings, my fears, my doubts, my happiness, my achievements, my failures. And I've never had that with my husband. I can't talk to him on those levels. . . . He lives in a very concrete, day to day, black and white world. But I've always been used to channeling a lot of my energies into more deep levels of intimacy with people, and sharing. . . .

And so I guess when I say I'm a dependent person, I guess I mean that I like having a closeness. I have a need for a deep intimate level of friendship with somebody.

How is that dependent?

Maybe it isn't. But I do have that need for closeness, and I've always, sometimes I've, sometimes I get frustrated with myself that I have to have that, you know. I look at other people that seem so self-sufficient and so independent and so—I don't know—I just have always needed a closeness. And maybe I identified that as dependency.

Does that have a negative kind of connotation to you?

It never used to, but since I've been married I realize it's kind of a negative thing to be that way. Because I've tried to bury that. And so I guess that has also contributed to a lot of my frustrations.

Saying that she "had been feeling that my need for intimacy and my need for that kind of a deep level of friendship or relationships with people was sort of bad," she began "to believe there was something the matter with me." In her attempt to "bury" her needs for closeness, she revealed the activity required to be passive, to try to live up to self-alienating images of "today's woman."

One sees how this woman's healthy capacity for intimacy, a hallmark of adult maturity, has been held up to her by the culture and by her husband as a weakness. Yet, women's capacity for intimacy, their orientation toward relationships, has recently been reinterpreted by feminist scholars as arising out of a developmental history which differs from that of males. The self-in-relation theorists consider that women and men have different ego capacities, strengths, and vulnerabilities based upon the fact that they form a gender identity either of sameness or difference in relation to the female primary caretaker. These revisionist theorists are redefining women's orientation toward their relationships as a central, positive, and crucial aspect of psychological development and functioning beyond childhood.[14] In the interview, one can also see how this woman has judged her feelings against a standard that says that to need closeness makes one dependent, that one should be able to be self-sufficient and autonomous. Further, she reflects upon her own experience, her capabilities, and her needs not from the basis of who she is and what she needs but in terms of how her husband sees her and how the culture sees her. This process of self-alienation is often deepened in therapy when the therapist identifies the woman's problem as being too dependent upon the husband and urges her to separate more and to do things for herself. Her capacity for closeness and intimacy goes unacknowledged as a strength and is presented to her as something that she must overcome in order to adjust to her relationship. Rather than a failure of the husband's response, the problem is identified as her "neediness."

For the researcher using oral interviews, the first step is to ask the meaning of words in order to understand them in the subject's own terms. If a researcher went into this interview with the traditional notion of dependence in mind, s/he would find the hypothesis that depressed women are overdependent confirmed. Instead, when one listens, one hears how women use the language of the culture to deny what, on another level, they value and desire. We must learn to help women tell their own stories, and then learn to listen to those stories without being guided by models that restrict our ability to hear.

DEVELOPING THEORY FROM ORAL HISTORY (JUDITH WITTNER)

For very good reasons, oral histories have become important vehicles for research about women. Finding out about women's actual lives deepens the critique of existing knowledge by documenting the inadequacy of past assumptions. Often, women's life stories highlight the ways in which concepts and methods that claim the status of science in our respective fields are partial and subjective and make women's experience difficult to observe or to take seriously. Therefore, the seemingly simple task of description often forces us to give up old frameworks and develop new ones better grounded in women's realities. For example, until the 1970s sociologists routinely assumed that work and family relations were two separate domains, linked only by the common participation of employed fathers. But the analytic separation of work and family life obscured the character of the everyday lives of ordinary housewives. Sociologists studying housewives found that new conceptual frameworks were necessary to understand the tasks and situations that structured women's lives in households.

Women's life stories are equally important to theory building. As descriptions of social life from the vantage point of women accumulate, they show that we must change our theories of society to incorporate the activities and perspectives of women. Indeed, learning about these invisible and neglected areas of experience grounds our attempts to develop new understandings and helps us to formulate better social theories. If we are to reconstruct theoretical accounts of society by seriously including women, we must begin to situate each individual woman's life story in its specific social and historical setting and show how women's actions and consciousness contribute to the structuring of social institutions. We need to go directly to women to learn about their part in the production and reproduction of society. We cannot have adequate theories of society without them. The women interviewed by Anderson and Jack grappled with ideas about solitude and independence in the context of society-wide changes in women's situations and in their consciousness. Their conflicts expressed the meaning of contrasting and contradictory social pressures in personal terms. Their reports described how they understood the social relationships and institutions that made up the worlds they lived in and how they acted to preserve or restructure those relations. We need to show how the conflicts, hopes, and fears of these and other women spurred them to action or kept them from it, and what difference this state of affairs made to them and to the worlds they inhabit.

In pursuing these goals we should not be too quick to dismiss the insights of generations of scholars in our fields. Our research often teaches us to distrust the traditions and techniques of our respective disciplines and to argue that conventional divisions between disciplines are part of a system that deflects attention from women's settings and women's concerns. But often, I believe, we go too far in rejecting or ignoring research traditions that, despite their lack of direct concern with women, offer important ideas and research tools for women's studies. In order to build truly interdisciplinary approaches, it is important that we become familiar with these theories and methods so that we may adapt them to our own purposes.

For example, in my own discipline of sociology there have been significant attempts to overcome the influence of dominant ideologies by developing theories and methods of research that treat humans as active subjects and that consider the part meaning plays in social life. Despite the often greater visibility and prestige of abstract theories and quantitative analysis, the idea that meaning informs social action and is a critical element in its study has been a theme running through the history of sociology. Following Max Weber, this tradition is often referred to as the *verstehen* approach.

Sociologists in this tradition assumed that people's perspectives and subjective interpretations informed and organized their courses of action. They did not treat subjective orientations as biases to be eliminated from their studies, as did quantitatively oriented sociologists—quite the opposite. Subjectivity was central to their understanding of social action. In their view, people were constantly interpreting their situations and acting in terms of the meanings or perspectives they developed within particular situations and from specific positions within organizations and groups. They viewed society as a plurality of interacting and competing groups, each of which developed collective solutions to the problems encountered in their shared situations. In such a society there was no neutral vantage point but only the different viewpoints generated within variously situated collectivities. For example, Howard Becker has written:

> Italian immigrants who went on making wine for themselves and their friends during prohibition were acting properly by Italian immigrant standards, but were breaking the law of their new country (as, of course, were many of their Old American neighbors). Medical patients who shop around for a doctor may, from the perspective of their own group, be doing what is necessary to protect their health by making sure they get what seems to them the best possible doctor, but from the perspective of the physician, what they do is wrong because it breaks down the trust the patient ought to put in his physician. The lower-class delinquent who fights for his "turf" is only doing what he considers necessary and right, but teachers, social workers, and police see it differently.[15]

Sociologists such as Becker have focused upon how people actively dealt with situational contingencies and resolved the problems they met as they pursued their goals, using and changing these situations for their own purposes as well as adapting to them. According to this perspective, it was not structure that "determined" action. Rather, actors in similar situations were understood to develop shared perspectives or definitions of their situation and to act in terms of these definitions.

Subjective accounts were useful to sociologists for many of the same reasons that they are important in women's studies research today. Both oral historians and sociologists often depend upon these to uncover aspects of social life that had been socially invisible and to analyze and interpret social reality from a new vantage point. These sociologists were concerned with socially marginal people and groups such as women and with the theoretical understanding of marginalizing processes such as the production of deviant statuses. Certainly these substantive and theoretical concerns bring them close to students of women's lives.

Efforts to develop methods reflecting an interest in subjective meaning and those capable of providing an empirical foundation from which to elaborate and refine the theory span the history of sociology in the United States since World War I. Members of the first sociology department at the University of Chicago developed the use of life histories and were also greatly influenced by anthropological field techniques. Over time, these techniques of participant observation were transformed into approaches suited to studying groups and lifeways in urban settings. By the 1940s, quantitative methods and grand theories dominated the field, and the use of personal accounts declined. Still, many sociologists continued to base their research on subjective accounts and wrote extensively on the theoretical and methodological issues raised by these data. These sociologists have been called or call themselves symbolic interactionists, naturalists, or humanists. Their work generally includes the use of participant observation techniques and unstructured, intensive interviews. Much of this work was published during the 1950s and 1960s.[16] Today a growing number of sociologists have returned to this literature for its approaches to collecting and analyzing subjective accounts.[17]

Several issues treated in this body of literature are useful as guides in thinking through the problems of an oral history for women. First, interactionists showed why it was necessary to give up the claim that real science is disinterested and neutral by linking meanings or "perspectives" to social positions. Dominant perspectives were not "truer" to reality but were the perspectives of dominant (more powerful, more legitimate) groups.[18] This interactionist approach can help us to articulate more completely the sources of women's alternative perspectives and to understand how women make use of these alternatives in their everyday lives.

Second, interactionists treated the social order as a negotiated order emerging out of social interaction. Social organization is the outcome of this intentional action, as people collectively and individually try to work out day-to-day solutions to problems they encounter in concrete situations.[19] Their studies of the practical activities involved in the daily production of social life should be of interest to us as we gather evidence about women's daily lives and attempt to understand its significance as historical data.

Third, interactionists rarely saw subordinates as victims but rather looked at how they carved out areas of autonomy despite their formal lack of power. For example, Gresham Sykes showed that in certain respects it was inmates who ran prisons, and guards who depended upon their cooperation to do their jobs.[20] So, too, we must guard against regarding our informants as passive victims, a perspective in direct contradiction to our desire to see women as subjects actively constructing history.

Fourth, interactionists viewed society in terms of processes rather than structures and viewed social institutions as the product of interaction over time. As a result, they introduced history into their analysis of society. In particular, they looked at biographies as historical accounts, detailing the movements of individuals through institutions in patterned sequences, called "moral careers" because accompanied by transformations in identity and perspective.[21] By focusing attention on the dialectical relationship between the construction of identities and the construction of institutions, the career concept allowed sociologists to observe the process of "structuration" by moving analytically between personal accounts and institutional histories.[22] As we try to draw the connections between women's daily lives and the structures that limit and oppress them, surely such concepts will be useful additions to our methods and our thought.

I have barely touched upon some of the many suggestive ideas provided by this sociology. My object here has been to stress the value of a particular branch of sociology to the study of women and to suggest that oral historians acquaint themselves with this work. I do not intend to suggest that this literature has all the answers we are looking for. Indeed, it can be accused of the distortions and biases apparent in most scholarship that predates the feminist movement in academia. Certainly women's studies needs techniques that can help to show what has been taken for granted about women's lives and to provide sources of information to help us ask more relevant questions and undertake new lines of research. We must develop methods specific to our interests and problems. We need to construct our theories out of the actual experiences of women. Nevertheless, I believe that sociologists can teach us some of what we want to know about this work.

CONCLUSION (SUSAN ARMITAGE)

One of the assumptions shared by the authors of this paper is that there are profound differences in the ways that men and women view the world and their places in it. Fifteen years ago such an assertion by feminist scholars would have been virtually unthinkable. We were still so intimidated by Freud's famous dictum "biology is destiny" that the very notion of difference inevitably smacked of inequality, but as feminist scholarship has developed, and in particular as researchers have listened carefully to what they have heard in oral interviews, the *fact* of difference has become inescapable.[23] We are just at the beginning of knowing what that difference means. We do know, from a variety of sources, that women's sense of themselves in relationship to family and work is different from that of men. In the Washington Women's Heritage Project we identified this attitude in the high value women place on relationships; others have spoken of women's "embeddedness" in both family and work.[24] Historian Joan Kelly in one of her last articles explored the theoretical implications of this insight, calling it "The Doubled Vision of Feminist Theory."[25] Kelly challenged the nineteenth-century division of society into private and public spheres, arguing that "Women's place is not a separate sphere or domain of existence but a position within social existence generally." Recognizing women's true place leads to an awareness of the ways in which, for each gender, "our personal, social and historical experience is seen to be shaped by the *simultaneous operation* of relations of work and sex." Just as Westkott explored the "doubleness" of the individual female consciousness (as women simultaneously adapt to male social structures and reject them), so Kelly allows us to see the public roles of women as expressions of "doubleness" in which private and public concerns are always intertwined. As we unravel these meanings, we will understand much more fully than we do now not only how women have lived and understood their lives but how our social theory must change to accommodate this hidden reality.

Finally, the preceding pages show the growing complexity of feminist scholarship. Our paper includes critiques of accepted methodologies in history, psychology, and sociology. All three are revealed as inadequate to describe the reality of women's experience as we have come to understand it through many different kinds of feminist research in the past fifteen years. We certainly do not claim to understand fully the contours and complexities of women's lives, but we have enough knowledge to be certain that uncritical use of old methodologies will hinder rather than help our future investigations. Thus we regard it as essential that careful scrutiny be applied to the assumptions that we carry into the oral history interview. We propose a definite structuring of oral history methods to achieve the goals of feminist research. As Anderson and Jack have shown, we will not find out about women's consciousness unless we ask. We will need to incorporate considerable psychological awareness and listening skills into our interviews in order to succeed.[26] The stance we adopt toward our completed interviews is equally crucial. The desire of feminist researchers to make sure that women are the subjects and not the objects of study is laudable but difficult to accomplish. Here we need the sophisticated sociological awareness of the reciprocal relationships between individual and institution developed by interactionist sociologists and their followers. This range of skills makes it virtually mandatory that future women's oral history projects be conducted by interdisciplinary teams.

Why bother? Why not just continue our present uncritical interview methods? The answer, of course, is that they do not reflect the insights of the new feminist scholarship. The old methods will not tell us what we now know we can learn about women if we ask the right questions.

NOTES

1. Dorothy Smith. Women and psychiatry. In *Women Look at Psychiatry: I'm not Mad, I'm Angry*, ed. Dorothy Smith and Sara David (Vancouver: Press Gang Pub., 1975), 2.

2. See Susan Armitage "The Next Step," in Special Women's Oral History Two issue of *Frontiers: A Journal of Women Studies* 8 (1, 1983) 3–8.

3. Marcia Millman and Rosabeth Moss Kanter, *Another Voice: Feminist Perspectives on Social Life and Social Science* (New York: Anchor Press/Doubleday, 1975), viii.

4. See Dale Spender, *Men's Studies Modified: The Impact of Feminism on the Academic Disciplines* (Oxford, N.Y.: Pergamon Press, 1981).

5. Marcia Westkott, "Feminist Criticism of the Social Sciences," *Harvard Educational Review* 49 (November 1979): 422–30.

6. For a fuller explanation see Dana C. Jack, "Clinical Depression in Women: Cognitive Schemas of Self, Care, and Relationships in a Longitudinal Study" (Ph.D. diss., Harvard University, 1984), chap. 2.

7. Dorothy Smith, "A Sociology for Women," in *The Prism of Sex: Essays in the Sociology of Knowledge*, ed. Julia Sherman and Evelyn Beck (Madison: University of Wisconsin Press, 1979); and Smith, "Institutional Ethnography," unpublished manuscript, n.d.

8. Kathryn Anderson and others, interviews for the Washington Women's Heritage Project, Center for Pacific Northwest Studies, Western Washington University, Bellingham, Washington. In the following account, two interviews from the collection are cited: interview with Elizabeth Bailey, 1 July 1980; interview with Verna Friend, 31 July 1980.

9. George W. Brown and Tirril Harris, *The Social Origins of Depression: A Study of Psychiatric Disorder in Women* (London: Tavistock Publications, 1978).

10. Deborah Belle, ed., *Lives in Stress: Women and Depression* (Beverly Hills: Sage Publications, 1982).

11. Jack, "Clinical Depression in Women."

12. Nancy Cott, "Passionlessness: The Interpretation of Victorian Sexual Ideology, 1790–1850," *Signs* 4 (1978): 219–36, as explained by Westkott in "Feminist Criticism," 429.

13. Arlie Russell Hochschild, "Emotion Work, Feeling Rules, and Social Structure," *American Journal of Sociology* 85 (November 1979): 551–75.

14. See especially Nancy Chodorow, *The Reproduction of Mothering: Psychoanalysis and the Sociology of Gender* (Berkeley: University of California Press, 1978).

15. Howard Becker, *Outsiders: Studies in the Sociology of Deviance* (New York: Free Press, 1963), 14–15.

16. Members of the first sociology department at the University of Chicago wrote thousands of life histories during the 1920s and 1930s. An interesting treatment of Chicago life histories can be found in James Bennett's book *Oral History and Delinquency: The Rhetoric of Criminology* (Chicago: University of Chicago Press, 1981).

Norman Denzin discusses the relation between symbolic interactionist theory and methods in *The Research Act: A Theoretical Introduction to Sociological Methods* (Chicago: Aldine Pub. Co., 1978). Everett Hughes provides important insights on how to study the connections between institutions and individuals in essays collected in *The Sociological Eye: Selected Papers*, 2 vols. (Chicago: Aldine Pub. Co., 1971). The work of his student Howard S. Becker has been centrally important to this tradition. See especially, *Sociological Work: Method and Substance* (Chicago: Aldine Pub. Co., 1970), a collection of his essays on method, and his introduction to Clifford Shaw's classic life history, *The Jack-Roller: A Delinquent Boy's Own Story* (Chicago: University of Chicago Press, 1966). Becker is credited with developing the labeling theory of deviance. David Matza defines and discusses "naturalistic" sociology in *Becoming Deviant* (Englewood Cliffs, N.J.: Prentice-Hall, 1969), in which he appraises the work of Becker and others. A bibliography that includes the work of many other sociologists employing subjective accounts can be found in R. Bogdan and S. Taylor, *Introduction to Qualitative Research Methods: A Phenomenological Approach to the Social Sciences* (New York: John Wiley and Sons, 1975). M. Hammersley and P. Atkinson, in *Ethnography, Principles in Practice* (London: Tavistock, 1983), provide a more recent annotated bibliography of ethnographic texts.

17. See, for example, Ken Plummer, *Documents in Life: An Introduction to the Problems and Literature of a Humanistic Method* (London: Allen and Unwin, 1983); A. Faraday and K. Plummer, "Doing Life Histories," *Sociological Review* 27 (November 1979): 773–92; Daniel Bertaux, ed., *Biography and Society: The Life History Approach in the Social Sciences* (Beverly Hills, Calif: Sage Publications, 1981); Philip Abrams, *Historical Sociology* (Somerset, Eng.: Open Books, 1982); Clem Adelman, ed., *Uttering, Muttering: Collecting, Using and Reporting Talk for Social and Educational Research* (London: Grant McIntyre, 1981); and the previously cited Hammersley and Atkinson, *Ethnography, Principles in Practice*.

18. See Becker, "Whose Side Are We On?" in *Sociological Work* for a clear statement of this position.

19. Many studies describe how social order is negotiated on a daily basis by subordinates and superordinates in organizational settings. See, for example, Julius Roth, *Timetables: Structuring the Passage of Time in Hospital Treatment and Other Careers* (Indianapolis: Bobbs Merrill, 1963); Erving Goffman, *Asylums: Essays on the Social Situation of Mental Patients and Other Inmates* (New York: Anchor Press/Doubleday, 1961); Gresham Sykes, *Society of Captives: A Study of a Maximum Security Prison* (Princeton, N.J.: Princeton University Press, 1958); Howard Becker, Blanche Geer, Everett Hughes, and Anselm Strauss, *Boys in White: Student Culture in Medical School* (New Brunswick, N.J.: Transaction Books, 1983); and Peter Berger, *The Human Shape of Work: Studies in the Sociology of Occupations* (New York: Macmillan, 1964).

20. Sykes, *Society of Captives*.

21. The career concept was first articulated by Everett Hughes in several essays collected in *The Sociological Eye*. See in particular his essay in that volume "Cycles, Turning Points, and Careers." Others who have commented on the concept or developed it in case studies include Howard Becker, "The Career of the Chicago Public School Teacher," *American Journal of Sociology* 57 (March 1952): 470–77; "Notes on the Concept of Commitment," *American Journal of Sociology* 66 (July 1960): 32–40; Howard Becker and Blanche Geer, "Latent Culture: A Note on the Theory of Latent Social Roles," *Administrative Science Quarterly* 5 (September 1960): 304–13; Howard S. Becker, Blanche Geer, and E. C. Hughes, *Making the Grade: The Academic Side of College Life* (New York: John Wiley and Sons, 1968); Howard S. Becker and Anselm

L. Strauss, "Careers, Personalities, and Adult Socialization," *American Journal of Sociology* 62 (November 1956): 253–63; and three previously cited works: Becker et al., *Boys in White*; Goffman, *Asylums*; and Abrams, *Historical Sociology*.

22. Abrams, *Historical Sociology*.

23. The first major work clearly to take this as a premise was Carol Gilligan's *In a Different Voice: Psychological Theory and Women's Development* (Cambridge: Harvard University Press, 1982).

24. See in particular Barbara Noble and May Whelan, "Woman and Welfare Work: Demystifying the Myth of Disembeddedness," in *Sex/Gender Division of Labor: Feminist Perspectives* (Minneapolis: University of Minnesota Center for Advanced Feminist Studies and Women's Studies, 1983) and the papers of Italian feminists Luisa Passerini and Adele Pesce at the International Conference on Oral History and Women's History, Columbia University, November, 1983.

25. Joan Kelly, "The Doubled Vision of Feminist Theory: A Postscript to the 'Women and Power' Conference," *Feminist Studies* 5 (Spring 1979): 216–27.

26. For a clear explanation of the process of the psychological interview, see Pamela Daniels and Kathy Weingarten, *Sooner or Later: The Timing of Parenthood in Adult Lives* (New York: W. W. Norton, 1982), 315–22.

Understanding Domestic Service through Oral History and the Census

The Case of Grand Falls, New Foundland

INGRID BOTTING

INTRODUCTION

Though the work of recent Canadian feminist, working-class, and social historians has revealed a great deal about the lives and experiences of previously neglected individuals and groups, our understanding of certain areas remains vague and incomplete. One area about which we have an insufficient understanding concerns the work and migration experiences of domestic servants, who by the late nineteenth and early twentieth centuries were primarily female and represented the largest job group of women wage earners. In 1891, around 41 per cent of all wage earning women worked as domestics in Canada, a percentage that dropped to around 18 per cent in 1921, rising again during the 1930s.[1] The case studies by Canadian women's historians such Marilyn Barber and Varpu Lindström Best, writing of domestic service in the 1980s, have demonstrated that most of these domestics were single working-class women, many of them immigrants from Britain and continental Europe (35 percent in 1911), and others migrated from Canada's rural regions to urban centres where they found situations.[2] This research also provided some initial insight into the variety of domestics' work experiences. While live-in domestics were generally isolated in the household, lacked worker protection, earned low wages, and were vulnerable to exploitation, their working conditions, wages, and experiences varied regionally and along ethnic lines. Equally important, the number of domestics in relation to the entire female workforce also varied regionally, depending on factors such as supply and demand and the availability of alternative forms of wage work for women.

Notably, more Canadian and American feminist scholars have explored domestic service in the contemporary period than they have in historical terms.[3] These scholars, who are primarily social scientists, have generally written of domestics through the lens of immigration. At root of their interpretations has been a concern with the fact that despite transformations in the labour market, changing gender ideologies, capitalist restructuring, and the women's movement, domestic service has persisted into the present as women's work and continues to encompass relations of domination and subordination in many aspects of public policy, legislation, and in human relationships. A number of case studies by sociologists and anthropologists writing of paid domestic work in an international context, also in the contemporary period, have shown that it is no longer possible to assume a universal pattern for domestic service; it has followed, and continues to follow, the flow of capital and labour in a global economy.[4] Few Canadian historians of women's work have examined closely any regional variation in patterns of domestic employment historically, and one area that deserves much more attention is the self-definition of former domestics who performed this work in the decades between World War I and World War II.

Since my research centres on understanding domestic servants' work and migration experiences in Newfoundland in the interwar years through the use of two fairly traditional sources, the census and oral history, it is necessary to explain briefly why there has been a gap in the feminist historical literature on domestic servants. First, over the past decade and a half feminist labour historians have produced fewer studies of women workers' experiences than they had during the 1970s and 80s, when the new social history, combined with a second wave feminist commitment to understanding women as agents of change, influenced their research agendas. Much of the recent scholarship has taken a broader approach, focussing on the ways in which gender relations were influenced by, and influenced, social change in terms of shifting religious, political, and moral discourses at specific moments in time.[5] In Canada, as elsewhere, some feminist historians have been influenced by poststructuralist approaches to understanding gender, which has raised the question of whether it is possible to understand women's experience "separate from the cultural discourses constructing the experience."[6] This scepticism about more "traditional" feminist methodologies, and the debates around the issue of what constitutes gender has meant a movement away from specific groups of women workers.[7] Second, and more specific to domestic service, the nature of the historical sources has shaped historians' approaches to the topic. Domestic servants rarely unionized, their work was generally temporary, and it remained largely hidden in the household. Thus, North America historians have had to rely on records produced by employment agencies, immigration authorities, and court records to document the work patterns and struggles of domestic servants. Rarely have scholars had access to documentary sources that would enable them to develop a thorough profile of domestics and their employers to combine with oral accounts.[8]

My current research explores the lives and migration experiences of domestics who migrated to the pulp and paper mill town of Grand Falls, Newfoundland, between 1909 and the onset of World War II in 1939. This work traces women from countryside to company town, into the household—as workplace—and then into their married lives, drawing primarily on oral history and on manuscript census schedules, the availability of which has presented me with a rare occasion to study the circumstances of domestics within the household.

Newfoundland is located on the most easterly point of North America. Along with the mainland territory of Labrador, it has been a province of Canada since 1949. In the late fifteenth century, European countries began using the island as a fishing station for the lucrative cod fishery. In time, Newfoundland was eventually settled by Europeans, primarily English, Irish, and French, and by the early nineteenth century, it had become a settled colony. The permanent population continued to grow and settle on different parts of the island, forming a necklace of communities around the coast. Thereafter, most of the population growth was by natural increase and the fishery remained the mainstay of the economy. Faced with a declining fishery and swelling numbers of fishers seeking winter relief after 1870, successive governments sought to diversify the economy by promoting railway building and industrialization based on the exploitation of the island's mineral and forest resources. As a result of this policy shift, several mines began operation, as well as two pulp and paper mills; one at Grand Falls in the island's interior opened in 1909, and the other opened at Corner Brook on the island's west coast in the early 1920s. Despite these attempts at landward development, Newfoundland's economy remained marginalized and unevenly developed throughout the period. Industrial enclaves such as Grand Falls co-existed with a fishery-based economy in which people's livelihoods had been based on a mix of subsistence agriculture, logging, sealing, hunting and trapping, as well as household production of foodstuffs and other basic necessities. The rural economy was cashless and it relied on merchant credit and the truck system.

Newfoundland's peculiar constitutional history, the details of which are outside of the scope of this essay, has meant that the Newfoundland manuscript census is accessible. These census schedules, which include the years 1921, 1935, and 1945, are the only mid-twentieth century source of its kind that are open to researchers in North America. In all other North American jurisdictions such material is closed, generally by statutory provisions. For example, the latest year for which the manuscript census is available in Canada is 1901. Unlike the aggregate census reports, which provide only statistical data, and did not always include calculations on domestic servants, the manuscripts are an invaluable source for documenting the extent to which women took such employment, as well as the types of households that employed live-in help. The manuscript censuses are also critical for examining the historical circumstances of gender divisions within the household, which is a crucial site for an evaluation of domestic service. For instance, the decisions of daughters, widowed women, and, less frequently, married women, to leave home to find domestic work were shaped by their household circumstances. The demand for live-in help was also shaped by material and social circumstances of the household. Factors such as number and age of children, income, the health of wives, and social status contributed to an increase in demand.

Recognizing that choice of subject and the availability of sources do not encompass a feminist methodology, I planned to incorporate interviews with former domestics into my research agenda to move beyond a discussion of the structural determinants of these women's oppression, such as poverty, low wages, and vulnerability to exploitation. Serendipitously, the recent dates for which the censuses were available afforded me the opportunity to interview some of the women who were enumerated in them, presenting a rare opportunity to work with the census and oral history simultaneously. While the accessibility of the schedules for 1921, 1935, and 1945 made the type of research I wanted to do possible, access to these sources also raised numerous ethical questions. For instance, these documents were private at the time of their creation and many of the individuals enumerated are still alive. Over the course of my research I also determined that such ethical issues—such as the researcher's privileged knowledge about people's backgrounds and past experiences—are similar to the questions feminist historians and social scientists have raised about research relationships in oral history.[9] My initial assumptions about the distinctiveness and compatibility of the census and oral history became increasingly blurred throughout the research process.

This paper explores the ways in which the manuscript census and oral history are compatible insofar as they both stem from complex relationships of power and privilege between investigator and subject. I explore how existing ideology and practice regarding gender roles, as well as the cultural, economic, and social character of Newfoundland during the 1920s and 1930s, needed to be kept in mind when using both of these sources in a reflexive manner. I also explain how the uneasy place of paid housework in the social relations of production was key in guiding ethical and methodological concerns throughout the process of this project, especially in terms of census categories and women's self definition of their employment. I have integrated a discussion of the applicability of the problems I encountered into a broader feminist research agenda throughout the paper. With some notable exceptions, few academics have examined the Newfoundland and Labrador manuscript censuses in a critical and systematic manner.[10] The following paper thus teases out some of the questions I encountered about these sources over the course of my research without necessarily providing answers to them.

CONTEXT

In 1903, the Newfoundland government granted enormous concessions to Britain's preeminent newspaper barons, the Harmsworth Brothers, to build the mill town of Grand Falls where no previous European settlement existed in the island's interior. The company town, strictly governed by the Anglo Newfoundland Development Company's (AND Company) paternalistic management practices, operated as a closed and unincorporated town until 1961. From the outset the mill owners made every effort to establish a permanent community by accommodating families. Most of the workforce was recruited locally; however, the company hired men from Canada, the United States and Great Britain to fill managerial and the more skilled elite mill jobs. Grand Falls introduced the social relations of industrial capitalism to a previously non-industrialized region, which had major implications for gender relations. Wage labour, the male breadwinner ideology, the separation of home and work, and consumption, which were central features of the company town, stood in sharp contrast to life in the outlying districts, where home and work were largely indistinguishable; men, women, and children contributed to the production of the product, albeit under unequal conditions, and the economy centred on merchant credit instead of on the cash nexus. Over the course of my research I came to a greater understanding that domestics straddled both of these economies, and, to a lesser extent, so did the residents who hired them. These findings may not have been apparent through an analysis of the census alone.

Though domestic service was inextricably linked to Newfoundland's slow and sporadic settlement process, by the nineteenth century daughters of fishing families began to supply the demand for domestics on and off the island. Newfoundland differed from other North American regions because there was generally a labour surplus on the island throughout the early twentieth century. Government was not involved in recruiting immigrant women to supply the demand for domestics. Gender divisions in the patriarchal inshore fishery generally meant that daughters left their households, especially in periods of economic crisis. As sociologist Barbara Neis has suggested, factors such as male preference in the ownership of fishing gear, property and traditional knowledge, and male inheritance practices pushed many women out of fishing households.[11] Young women left home for places like New York and Boston in the northeastern United States, and Montreal, Halifax, and Sydney in Canada to find work. Others stayed on the island and went to St. John's—the island's largest urban centre—or they found situations in smaller centres on the island. When young women worked in fishery-based communities, they were generally engaged in fishery-related work and domestic work, for which they were paid by credit or in kind.

Within this context of women's work, my research aimed to identify the women who moved to Grand Falls and to understand how they perceived their experience working there, and how that work and migration experience shaped the decisions they made for the rest of their lives. Did moving to Grand Falls for a brief period before marriage change the outlook of these women on gender relations, work, consumption, or leisure, representing a break with their rural past? Did they view their paid housework as low status, and their position in the labour market and within the household as exploited? My initial research questions were shaped by my academic assumptions about gender inequality in the labour market, where domestic service has been understood simultaneously as a "respectable" occupation for working-class daughters, and as one of the most restrictive and least preferred jobs for young women.[12] The oral data combined with the census, however, painted a different and more fluid picture.

THE CENSUS

I began my research by identifying women who were enumerated as domestic servants in the 1935 manuscript census for the community of Grand Falls. I constructed a database to render the microfilm format of the manuscripts into machine readable form. The manuscript census portrays families in residential units, providing information on kinship relationships, name, household status, birth place, religion, present occupation, literacy, wages, and marital status. The results of my preliminary analysis of the 1935 census year were surprising to the extent that popular histories of Grand Falls and the AND Company literature failed to mention the strong presence of young women in the town's history of work, culture, or in community development. As with other resource-based communities, Grand Falls was considered a man's town. While the converted paper manufacturing industry that prevailed in other North American regions relied on female labour, pulp and paper generally did not. In fact, one of the Newfoundland government's rationales for supporting pulp and paper development was that the AND Company had promised to provide jobs to local men. As economic historian David Alexander once stated, steady employment for wages in Newfoundland became known as a "Grand Falls Job."[13] The snapshot provided by the census indicated a large presence of women in this town working in a variety of capacities, even though their wages were typically only a fraction of men's, and their work was either part-time or of a temporary nature.

As I expected, the census provided both a quantitative and qualitative foundation for the research, since I had the manuscript version at my disposal and since my research objectives did not centre on number crunching. Domestic servants made up the largest job category for any worker (male or female) in Grand Falls in 1935. As Table 12.1 indicates, the participation of single women in the workforce increased over the first three decades of the twentieth century. Single women represented 15 per cent of the wage earning population in 1921, increasing to 21 per cent in 1935, and 22 per cent in 1945. By far the greatest number of women wage earners performed paid domestic work, mostly live-in, in households or in the town's few hotels and boarding houses.

In a town like Grand Falls, work was most obviously divided along gender lines. In the 1920s, some young men gained access to mill jobs through their fathers, others secured permanent work after working on mill construction. Daughters of mill workers generally got part time clerical jobs, or jobs in the town's expanding retail sector; they rarely, if at all, worked as domestics. Married women did unpaid domestic labour in the household, which was partly due to the fact that a marriage bar was strictly enforced

TABLE 12.1 Single Women's Employment, Grand Falls, 1921–1945

Sectors Employing Women	1921	1935	1945
office/clerical	25	33	81
retail	29	49	77
service	114	153	81
teachers/nurses	13	25	39
other	8	7	41
total number of women workers	189	267	319
total Grand Falls Workforce	1246%	1250%	1444%
percentage of women in the workforce	15%	21%	22%
percentage of domestic servants in total woman workforce	60%	57%	25%

Source: Manuscript censuses, Newfoundland, Grand Falls, 1921, 1935, 1945

by the AND Company. While the 1935 census consistently indicated a blank for the occupation of married women in the schedules, other sources not surprisingly revealed that elite and non-elite married women engaged in a wide range of voluntary and philanthropic activities in the community. They also provided unpaid care for children, elderly relatives, husbands, and in some cases cooked and cleaned for boarders, who were generally distant relatives. While these patterns of employment generally persisted into the 1930s, union officials and the town's elite expressed concern over the next generation of Grand Falls residents being able to find employment. As the population stabilized, the local economy remained undiversified, and the labour market narrowed, a division of labour based on migration status and gender had begun to intensify a trend which partly explained an increase in the number of domestics.

In Newfoundland, internal migration towards industrial enclaves such as Grand Falls characterized the Depression decades of the 1920s and 1930s, as barriers to outmigration and a crisis in the fishery increased demographic pressure on towns that offered the possibility of paid employment. During the 1930s, Grand Falls was viewed by British government officials, and by its own elite population, as "an oasis in a desert of tribulation."[14] Within this context, two other groups, distinguished by their exclusion from permanent residency in the town (albeit for different reasons), earned wages in Grand Falls. One group consisted of male mill workers who did construction and contract work on a temporary basis for the company. These men generally migrated in and out of the town as wage work became available, some of them setting up temporary dwellings in Grand Falls Station, a shanty town that gradually emerged and expanded during the 1930s just outside the boundaries of Grand Falls. The other group consisted of domestic servants.

In 1921, domestics represented 60 per cent of the total female workforce, dropping slightly to 57 per cent in 1935. The percentage of domestics fell

more substantially to 25 per cent in 1945 for a number of reasons including
the fact that during World War II, Americans and Canadians built bases on
the island which provided wage work for men and women. The unevenness of the aggregate census data make it difficult to find out if these percentages were comparatively high. According to Nancy Forestell's sampling
of the manuscript census for the city of St. John's, domestics represented
around 40 per cent of the female workforce (in 1921 and 1935), a percentage
she suggests was higher than in Canada, where there was a chronic servant
shortage and a wider range of job opportunities for young single women
during the same time period.[15]

In Grand Falls the majority of domestics worked in non-elite households.
A census analysis of every household that employed a domestic (I was able
to avoid sampling because of the relatively small population) indicated that
employers of domestics included mill management, professionals, skilled
workers, and labourers. Around 20 per cent of all households hired live-in
domestics and almost no domestic work was done on a live-out basis until
the 1940s. The domestics were overwhelmingly young (between the ages of
15 and 25), single, and from rural regions of the island. In 1935, they earned
on average $10 a month, which generally varied according to the household
circumstances of employers. Wages for domestics working in Grand Falls
were relatively low—they were comparable to the earnings of domestics
working in certain regions of Canada at the turn of the century. Even though
the 1935 census did not include specific data on the birthplace of residents,
oral history and an analysis of the birthplace data contained in the 1921 and
1945 census schedules indicated that these women were migrants from rural
fishing and logging communities located along the island's northeast coast.
In fact, they generally came from the same communities as the town's permanent residents. In cases where the enumerator recorded household status,
it appeared that some of these women were related to their employers.

THE CENSUS AS ORAL HISTORY?

The manuscript census proved useful in developing a demographic and occupational profile of Grand Falls at a particular moment in time. A closer
look at the occupational categories contained in the census not surprisingly
suggests that the population had been robbed of its fluidity. As historians
of women's work have argued, aspects of work such as skill and wages
should not be viewed as objective categories. Rather, they are ideological
constructs which should not be divorced from the historical particularity
of the situation, or from the gender ideology of those creating the records.
Did the profile of these women gleaned from the census records represent
hegemonic knowledge about the status of domestic servants in this small
community?

There has been an international literature on the social construction of
statistics which challenges our acceptance of these records as quantitative
by examining the circumstances of their creation.[16] In addition, Canadian

historians Bettina Bradbury, Peter Baskerville and Eric Sager, for example, have explored social change, patterns of men's, women's, and children's paid and unpaid work and unemployment during periods of industrialization in Canada by using the manuscript censuses.[17] In so doing they have highlighted the benefits and limitations of the nineteenth century censuses, and more recently, the 1901 manuscript censuses as historical sources. Their studies remind us that the workforce helped construct the census when they responded to the enumerator's questions about employment, an approach to the source that raises questions similar to those asked by feminist scholars about oral history.[18]

Feminist scholars who have used oral history have also been long advocating methodologies which consider women's own perceptions of their experiences, not to be measured solely against the written word. As Susan Geiger stated:

> Researchers tend to regard information generated by "experts" and found in libraries, archives or universities as "reliable." If we insist that the validity of women's oral accounts must be evaluated against existing knowledge, then we are not being feminist in our methodology.[19]

A few decades ago feminist historians began to use oral history as a form of questioning the tenets of a discipline that ignored the views of subordinate groups and individuals. As one influential feminist collective argued, "personal narratives of nondominant social groups are often particularly effective sources of counterhegemonic insight because they expose the viewpoint embedded in the dominant ideology as particularist rather than universal."[20] More recently, Canadian women's historians have drawn on current debates in the social sciences to develop more reflexive methodologies and to scrutinize oral history as a source in the same way they exercise source criticism with documentary evidence.[21] Joan Sangster's recent study of wage earning women in Peterborough, Ontario, for example, has fruitfully woven oral evidence with other sources to trace the historical complexity of women's wage earning experiences in the context of the full cycle of their lives.[22] Sangster and others have shown that results from interviews can call into question the categories in which women's lives have been made to fit, and that women have often been contradictory in their beliefs and actions. Interestingly, these methods of source criticism resemble those methods used by British historians of women's work, such as Edward Higgs and Bridget Hill, who have argued that the nineteenth century occupational censuses are best understood as a qualitative representation of what a male-dominated political and economic elite viewed as significant about labour and women's and men's social and economic status in society.[23]

I drew on this literature to scrutinize the Newfoundland manuscript censuses in order to get behind the written word and to consider the relations of power and privilege that shaped those records. My preliminary investigation revealed that the relations of power and privilege in the creation of the 1935 Newfoundland census operated in at least three interdependent ways. First, the census was ultimately a product of the colonial relationship between Newfoundland and Britain, and this relationship had a direct bearing on how patterns of paid and unpaid work were revealed in the schedules. When the 1935 census was taken, Newfoundland had recently lost responsible government status and an appointed Commission of Government took over Newfoundland's affairs under suspended democratic conditions.[24] In 1935 in the midst of world-wide Depression, the Commission of Government enacted hastily the census with a view to taking an inventory of employment and unemployment on the island and to document school attendance, which was not legislated until 1942. The Commissioners were less interested in the details of the local situation in 1935 than the Newfoundland government had been when it took the census in 1921. For instance, in 1921 the government took special care to develop an accurate system of counting the population because educational and road grants were allocated to each settlement according to its population. This policy meant that the census schedules of 1921 contained detailed data on the birthplace of residents, facilitating an early account of internal migration patterns on the island.

The Secretary of Public Welfare's *Interim Report* of the 1935 census stated that the forms used by the enumerators were "obtained from the United Kingdom and the Dominion of Canada," a seemingly benign statement when taken out of context.[25] The enumerators used the categories on those forms when they collected their household and community-based data. Those categories were based on the economies of Britain and Canada, which, while distinct from each other, had both industrialized earlier than Newfoundland's economy, which was an economy based on household production, occupational pluralism, and a strong and complex informal economy, operating symbiotically with the commercial economy.[26]

Second, the categories used by the state to define women's place within the household may have revealed more about the gender ideology of the dominant society than they did about the reality of men's and women's lives in Newfoundland. For example, in 1935 the enumeration was done in one summer month, but "in 1921 the enumeration was spread over a period of six months, from July to December." Interestingly, the Secretary of Public Health and Welfare implicitly believed that enumeration over one month was a sign of progress, for cost cutting dictated the 1935 census compilation. The Secretary also took great pains to have compilers "checking A and B sheets i.e.: names of persons temporarily absent and temporarily employed in various Districts, and placing them in their proper districts."[27] Keeping in mind that the state did not gather data for the benefit of social historians, the method of compiling used in 1935 resulted in an under-representation of the extent to which temporary outmigration was woven into women's and men's daily lives, contributing further to the undercounting of domestic servants. Most likely the 1935 census enumeration over one month provided a more accurate profile of mill workers who had steady, year-round employment than it did for domestics. Equally important, many of the young women listed in the Grand Falls census as domestic servants remained linked to their household economies in rural communities. For example, the former domestics I interviewed generally stressed that they sent most of their cash wages home to their parents (more specifically to their mothers). The fact that cash was scarce in Newfoundland during this period suggests that these young women were not necessarily making a permanent move from home. Some of them were working in Grand Falls as part of the seasonal round and the 1935 census may have listed many of them in their temporary summertime employment.

The time of the year the census was taken is crucial for understanding patterns of work in Newfoundland. Throughout the 1930s the nature of work in the fishing economy revolved around the occupational pluralism of men, and to a lesser extent of women. Men generally engaged in a number of subsistence activities, which they combined with temporary outmigration for wage work in Canada and in the United States, varying over the course of a year. In periods of male absence from home, wives, sons, and daughters performed those tasks that would have generally fallen to men. In households where daughters were not needed, they generally "shipped out" to work for a nearby fishing family, where their paid domestic work was contingent on the weather, the seasons, and the immediate survival needs and strategies of the family for whom they worked. In a place like Grand Falls, such factors had less of an influence on the rhythms of housework. Rarely has domestic service been integrated into studies of occupational pluralism and the Newfoundland economy.[28]

Many of the women who came to Grand Falls to work as domestics worked for their own relatives. Such arrangements, negotiated through families, were masked by the census category domestic servant, which most historians have generally described as a cross-class and a cross-racial/ethnic working arrangement.[29] An analysis of all census years also indicated that the wives of the town's elite employed domestics more consistently than mill workers' wives did. Oral history revealed that family life-cycle factors such as number of children, age of children, health of wives, ability to pay, and number of boarders, determined when a mill worker's wife hired household help.

The third relationship of power and privilege centres on the enumerator's place in the community and local politics. It is highly probable that most residents had a personal knowledge of the Grand Falls enumerator, and they may have shaped their responses to questions about income, employment and social relationships within the household accordingly. In 1935 a local newspaper published an article encouraging residents to cooperate with the enumerator, reporting that "many people regard him [the enumerator] as a preying busy-body—they misconceive the purpose of a census and are unwilling to give the desired information." This scepticism may have been due in part to the fact that during the 1930s, the state was becoming an increasingly large presence in the lives of the population than ever before. In responding to an acute economic crisis on the island, the

Commission of Government was concerned about, and fixated on, getting people off public relief. During this period, the government appointed magistrates and other inspectors to evaluate residents' eligibility for relief, which fishers often relied on over the winter months. My archival research, in fact, revealed that the enumerator for Grand Falls had written the Department of Public Health and Welfare with comments on living conditions in a nearby town, indicating that he had scrutinized households while taking the census.[30]

The interaction between the enumerator and the individual household member at the door would also have mediated the way that women's domestic labour was enumerated in the census. As a researcher it is impossible to know who answered the enumerators questions at the door, but it was possible to imagine how that relationship played itself out through a close look at different household circumstances as they were conveyed in the census schedules. If a male head of household was responding for all household members and was asked, for example, the identity or relationship of the young single woman living in the household to himself, he may have chosen domestic servant as the simplest explanation to define a much more complex relationship. As mentioned above, Grand Falls was a closed town and the company strictly regulated who could live there.

The schedules' category "domestic servant," which was sometimes inscribed in the schedules as "maid," "housekeeper," or the more active designation "in service" (usually appearing beside the names of fishers daughters who were working in Grand Falls), encompassed a much broader range of experience than even the manuscript census could reveal. A qualitative assessment of the census, oral history, and other documentary research indicated a variety of experiences for Grand Falls domestics. Some of them moved there temporarily to work for relatives, some of them left their homes for the first time to earn much needed cash, while others moved to Grand Falls after gaining considerable experience working as domestics in other communities. Some women stayed for only the summer or winter, depending on when they were needed at home.

ORAL HISTORY

I made no allusions to "sisterhood" in planning the interview component of my research. Feminist historians, and sociologists and anthropologists in particular, have written and reflected extensively on research relationships, their limitations, and the effects of those relationships on scholarship.[31] These scholars generally agree, "that a [feminist] research relationship is a particular kind of association, at least with respect to the work being done in its context."[32] They have also pointed to the barriers that inevitably exist between the researcher and the informant and generally agree that feminist academics should devise reflexive methods of data collection and interpretation not necessarily to overcome these barriers, but to approach the research as honestly as possible and to be aware of the inequalities that may exist between ourselves and the women whose voices we want to hear.

As a newcomer to the field of women's oral history, I initially dwelt on the polarities between myself and the women I was going to interview. I thought that because I was a non-Newfoundlander, and because I was an academic from St. John's, the women I contacted would be sceptical of my intentions. Throughout the 1960s and 1970s, Newfoundland was visited by anthropologists and sociologists to document what they saw as a dying culture, or the last vestige of tradition untouched by the industrial capitalist world. They collected songs, oral tradition, or artifacts, and then they left. This precedent contributed to my hesitancy in approaching possible informants. I intended to adopt an interactive approach, so that women would be the subjects and not the objects of my research. I ambitiously thought the interview process would serve as a vehicle for these women to value the paid and unpaid work they did, and to draw those accomplishments to the attention of their families. In that regard I decided I would provide copies of the tapes to them.

Due to financial and time constraints, I had to confine my research to interviewing those women who had stayed in Grand Falls, or remained connected to that community. After my preliminary research trip to the town, I decided a snowball sample would be the best approach, both ethically and practically—it would be less of an intrusion if I contacted women through word of mouth rather than identifying them through the census. In any case, women enumerated as domestic servants in the census would have been virtually untraceable because most of them married and changed their names. I did not realize at the time that this approach made a considerable impact on my research because the sample population was contained geographically and historically by its continuous relationship to the town. After the labour market became more or less saturated during the 1930s, over the next few decades there was little in-migration to Grand Falls. Many of the pioneering residents, or their sons and daughters, still live there. When I began my fieldwork, most of my initial contacts were members of the community's elite. They were the individuals to whom I had been referred, and most of them remembered those women who first came to Grand Falls as domestics, and helped distinguish these women from those who grew up in the town. Over the years a stigma about women's paid domestic work had developed and it became increasingly apparent to me that this uneasiness was going to limit the number of women who were willing to talk to me about their past work experiences.

I devised two separate questionnaires: one for former employers of domestics and the other for former domestics. I intended to use the questionnaires as general guidelines, while trying to keep the interview as open-ended as possible. As I progressed in my research I came to understand that employers and domestics did not necessarily encompass two distinct groups. The mother of one woman I interviewed had moved to Grand Falls in the 1910s to work as a domestic servant in a mill workers' household, later finding a situation as a live-in domestic in one of the town's few working-man's hotel. This woman married a mill worker and she and her husband stayed in Grand Falls. After her marriage she hired a number of domestic servants in her own household. Her daughter, Gertrude L., described the hiring process as follows:

> the people she would hire were from Fox Harbour (her birthplace). They would write to mother. . . . It was just some place to come and stay . . . it didn't cost very much . . . all my life we always had a maid. . . . They were very very nice, most of them were relatives anyway.[33]

Gertrude L. was typical of mill workers' daughters in the 1920s and 1930s in that she never worked as a domestic servant herself. I found no evidence of mill workers' daughters taking situations either in the town or in other urban centres. In fact, one former domestic told me that "domestic help usually came from outside Grand Falls because Grand Falls wasn't a place you'd go in and find working girls in there."[34] Gertrude L. also grew up with a different set of expectations than women of her cohort who grew up in coastal communities. Daughters of mill workers went to school longer than young women who grew up in the outlying communities, and while marriage was their key expectation growing up, some of them furthered their training after they finished school. Gertrude L. mentioned she was intent on being a nurse when she was young and her parents had the money to send her away to school. She also stated that when she got married she could not boil water, because other women had always cooked and cleaned for her when she was growing up and when she was away at school. When I began interpreting Gertrude L.'s recollections I had difficulty knowing whether her statement that "most of them were relatives anyway" was an apology for living in a household that employed domestics or whether her comments reflected the way the labour market for domestic servants worked. Was it a moral economy based on kinship responsibilities between women during a period when the Newfoundland economy had reached a crisis? The 1935 census data had indicated a gender imbalance favouring women in the 19 to 25 age cohort 106 women for every 100 men), which seemed unusual for a single resource town that relied mainly on male labour.

Sarah C., who had grown up in the northeast coast fishing community of Musgrave Harbour, had first left her parents' home to take a position in St. John's, where she gained several years of experience working as a domestic servant.[35] She was later offered a job as a cook in the household of one of the AND Company managers. Sarah C. also married a mill worker, whom she met through the girl next door. She and her husband, a timekeeper in the mill, lived in a company house for the remainder of their lives, where they raised four children. In response to a question about what she did within marriage, Sarah C. told me that she sold baking from her kitchen in Grand Falls and that she always "had a girl" working for her. She did not see the same irony I had in the fact that within her marriage she found herself on the other side of the social equation, as an employer of domestics. I asked her how she felt about hiring domestics herself after she had worked as a servant for nine years, a question to which she replied, "I had to treat them like I'd like to be treated," and "I wouldn't do anything to hurt their feelings or put obstacles in their way." In this case, was her initial silence more significant than the response I solicited? Was the servant/employer relationship distinct when the employer and employee shared a similar gender, class, and ethnic background? Was it a different relationship when mill managers and professionals, who were generally from elsewhere, hired domestic servants? By asking each questions over the course of my research, I began to rethink the central focus of the project, placing more emphasis on employers than I had previously thought I would.

By beginning my research process with the census, I made a choice as to what was the defining moment in these women's lives: their move to Grand Falls, as they were enumerated in the census at a particular time. Was I wrong? On the one hand, the job category domestic servant represented a commonality for these women. On the other hand, within that category their experiences varied immensely and called into question my assumptions about skill, stigma, and the uneasy place of paid domestic work in women's memories from both sides of the employee-employer relationship.

One significant aspect of former domestics' self-definition was that when I asked them about housework and their ability to perform it, they spoke confidently and sometimes downplayed the arduous aspects of the work. One former domestic, for example, stated, "it was just like playing a game when you're used to doing it."[36] In general, what these women had in common was a general recollection that working in domestic service was a continuity in their lives. They never stopped "working," even when they were no longer earning wages for their labour, suggesting that in their own minds there was little division between paid and unpaid work in their lives. Surprisingly, their experience in domestic service formed a distinct memory of their lives, but they did not necessarily perceive the work and migration experience in Grand Falls as a key transformation. When they spoke about living in the community, however, their reflections indicated that they often felt lonely, isolated, and left out. I found that it was not only important to ask questions about the nature of the work, but that I learned most about these women when I integrated questions into the interviews that bridged the gap between the workplace (even if the workplace and the household were one and the same) and their status in the community more generally. Questions about their lives before and after their migration to Grand Falls also proved enlightening, highlighting further the static nature of the census schedules.

For example, Martina L. moved to Grand Falls in the early 1930s to take a job after she had worked as a domestic in a number of smaller communities near her northeast coast home. She told me that her uncle was a mill worker in Grand Falls and he had found her a situation working in a household where the wife was "sickly while having her baby." Four years later Martina L. met a man who was working as a temporary AND Company mill employee, whom she soon married. Since her husband was not on the permanent company pay roll, he did not have access to a company house.

Thus, like the majority of Grand Falls domestics, Martina L. left the town for good. The couple moved to her husband's home community of Sweet Bay, on the island's northeast coast, to live in his elderly parents' house, where she provided unpaid care for them until they died. When she spoke about the difference between her four-year experience as a servant in Grand Falls and her life within marriage in Sweet Bay, she stated: "In Grand Falls I only did housework, in Sweet Bay I had to do outdoor work and indoor work," underlining the distinction between working in a town where housework took place primarily within the home and goods for consumption were purchased in stores, and women's lives in rural communities where they were engaged in household production.

Another commonality among former domestics was the wide range of skills and experience that they brought with them to Grand Falls. The young women who grew up outside the town generally did not experience childhood in the same way that the children who grew up in Grand Falls did. It was common for most of them to be engaged in household production from a young age. Factors such as their mothers' health, the number of daughters in the household, family's need for cash, and kinship connections to mill employees and their wives shaped the experiences that they brought to their situations in Grand Falls.

Stella B., the second oldest daughter in a family from a small northeast coast community, was required to do most of the domestic work in her parents' household before she moved to Grand Falls. Her father was often absent from home because he fished from a schooner on the coast of Labrador. Stella B.'s oldest sister had moved to St. John's to work as a servant and her younger sister had a physical disability. Significantly, her mother had considerable problems with her health and was bedridden most of the time. Stella B. recalled that her mother could only do light work around the house. Light work encompassed household chores that did not involve arduous physical labour. Heavy work involved scrubbing laundry, tending the garden, cleaning the stove, bringing in wood and water, scrubbing the floor boards.

Most of the skills Stella B. acquired at home were put to use for wages when she moved to Grand Falls for a few months of every year. There, she worked for two families until she married. When she lived at home, however, she was the only girl who "went out with the men working." She salted herring, cast caplin with her brother, and cultivated potatoes.[37] She recalled that her father purchased clothes for her at Christmas in return for her labour in the garden and on the lakes. One of her weekly chores around her parents' house was to prepare the Sunday noon meal on Saturday night. She made bread for ten people every two days in her parents' home and never balked at the task, which was simplified in Grand Falls by smaller families and the availability of yeast in stores. While Stella B. went directly to Grand Falls from her parents' home, a number of other women I interviewed had moved to the mill town after working for a number of years in households near their parents' home community. For these women, going to Grand Falls did not prove to be a dramatic or shocking transition in their memories.

CONCLUSION

In this paper I have outlined the various ways in which my research project evolved by considering the comparability of the manuscript censuses and oral history: the process of developing a reflexive methodology to deal with these two potentially problematic sources opened up a number of possibilities for understanding the relevance of domestic labour in the lives of women such as Stella B., Martina L., and Gertrude L. The accessibility of the manuscript censuses provided me with the only extant documentary evidence of domestic servants, who have remained outside of dominant interpretations of social relations and economic development in the early twentieth century. Such a study would have been impossible if I had had to rely solely on the aggregate tabulations. However, the kinds of questions that I began to ask to understand the self-perceptions of former domestics were linked closely to, and shaped by, the limitations of my two key sources. My questions were also shaped by the fact that oral history and census material are both products of human interaction. Over the course of my research, I began to realize that the relationships of power and privilege, which were key in the creation of both the manuscript census and oral history, were not only relationships of inequality between men and women. They were also relationships of inequality between women of different backgrounds, and between researcher and informant, and they were embedded in the process of historical and cultural change within Newfoundland at particular moments in time. The ethical and methodological considerations guiding my research were inextricably linked to an understanding of the place of paid housework within and outside of the lives of former domestics.

NOTES

I would like to thank the Social Sciences and Humanities Research Council of Canada (SSHRC), and the Institute of Social and Economic Research (ISER), Memorial University of Newfoundland, and the J.R. Smallwood Research Foundation for providing financial support for my doctoral research.

1. Paul Phillips and Erin Phillips, *Women and Work: Inequality in the Canadian Labour Market*, Revised Edition (Toronto: James Lorimer and Company, Publishers, 1993), p. 17.

2. Marilyn Barber, "The Women Ontario Welcomed: Immigrant Domestics for Ontario Homes, 1870–1930," Alison Prentice and Susan Trofimenkoff, eds., *The Neglected Majority: Essays in Canadian Women's History, Vol. II* (Toronto: McClelland and Stewart, 1985); Varpu Lindstrom Best, *Defiant Sisters: A Social History of Finnish Immigrant Women in Canada* (Toronto: Multicultural History Society of Ontario, 1988); and D.A. Muise, "The Industrial Context of Inequality: Female Participation in Nova Scotia's Paid Labour Force, 1871–1921," *Acadiensis*, vol. 20, no. 2 (Spring 1991).

3. Agnes Calliste, "Canada's Immigration Policy and Domestics from the Caribbean: The Second Domestic Scheme," in Elizabeth Comack and Stephen Brickley, eds., *The Social Basis of Law*, 2nd Ed. (Halifax: Garamond Press, 1991); Mary Romero, *Maid in the U.S.A.* (New York and London: Routledge, 1993); Sedef Arat-Koc, "Immigration Policies, Migrant Domestic Workers, and the Definition of Citizenship in Canada," in V. Satzewich, ed., *Deconstructing a Nation: Immigration, Multiculturalism and Racism in '90s Canada* (Halifax: Fernwood Publishing, 1992); and Audrey Macklin, "On the Inside Looking In: Foreign Domestic Workers in Canada," in Wenona Giles and Sedef Arat-Koc, eds., *Maid in the Market Women's Paid Domestic Labour* (Halifax: Fernwood Publishing, 1994); and Abigail Bakan and Daiva Stasiulis, eds., *Not One of the Family: Foreign Domestic Workers in Canada* (Toronto: University of Toronto Press, 1997).

4. See especially the essays in Roger Sanjek and Shellee Colen, eds., *At Work in Homes: Household Workers in World Perspective* (Washington: American Ethnological Society, 1990).

5. It is beyond the scope of this paper to examine this historiographical shift in great detail. For examples of recent approaches, see Cecilia Morgan, *Public Men and Virtuous Women: The Gendered Languages of Religion and Politics in Upper Canada, 1791–1850* (Toronto: University of Toronto Press, 1996), and Carolyn Strange, *Toronto's Girl Problem: The Perils and Pleasures of the City, 1880–1930* (Toronto: University of Toronto Press, 1995)

6. Joan Scott's *Gender and the Politics of History* (New York: Columbia University Press, 1988) has been central to debates about gender and experience in Canadian women's history. See Joan Sangster, "Beyond Dichotomies: Re-Assessing Gender History and Women's History in Canada," *left history*, vol. 3, no. 1 (Spring/Summer 1995) for a lively discussion on the debate about the importance of poststructuralism in the Canadian historical literature on women. See Pat Armstrong and M. Patricia Connelly, "Feminism and Political Economy: An Introduction," *Studies in Political Economy 30* (Autumn, 1989) for an appeal for more historical studies on Canadian women's experiences in terms of regionality, gender, class, and ethnicity.

7. For a thorough discussion on using "women's experiences" in the writing of Canadian women's history, see Ruth Roach Pierson, "Experience, Difference, Dominance and Voice in the Writing of Canadian Women's History," in Karen Offen, Ruth Roach Pierson, and Jane Rendall, eds., *Writing Women's History: International Perspectives* (Bloomington and Indianapolis: Indiana University Press, 1991).

8. Some feminist scholars (mainly American) have integrated oral history into their studies of domestics to show how servants' actions and protests have effectively changed the nature of the occupation over time. The shift from live-in to live-out, among certain groups of domestics, has represented one of the most significant changes. See Evelyn Nakano Glenn, *Issei, Nisei, War Bride: Three Generations of Japanese American Women in Domestic Service* (Philadelphia: Temple University Press, 1986); Elizabeth Clark Lewis, *Living In, Living Out: African American Domestics in Washington, D.C.: 1910–1940* (Washington and London: Smithsonian Institution Press, 1994) and Mary Romero, *Maid in the U.S.A.*

9. The essays in Sherna Berger Gluck and Daphne Patai, eds., *Women's Words: The Feminist Practice of Oral History* (New York and London: Routledge, 1991) offer detailed reflections on the ethical issues of doing oral history. See in particular, the essay by Daphne Patai, "U.S. Academics and Third World Women: Is Ethical Research Possible?"

10. For one of the few existing accounts of domestics' work experiences in St. John's, see Nancy Forestell, "Women's Paid Labour in St. John's Between the Two World Wars" (unpublished MA thesis, Memorial University of Newfoundland, 1987), especially Chapter 4. See also Forestell's related published work, where she draws heavily on the manuscript censuses, "'Times Were Hard': The Pattern of Women's Paid Labour in St. John's Between the Two World Wars. *Labour/Le Travail*, 24 (Fall 1989).

11. Barbara Neis, "From 'Shipped Girls' to 'Brides of the State': The Transition from Familial to Social Patriarchy in the Newfoundland Fishing Industry," *Canadian Journal of Regional Science*, vol. 16, no. 2 (Summer 1993).

12. In a recent study, Magda Fahrni explored the notion of "respectability" and domestic service in Canada. While she found that employers hired servants to maintain bourgeois respectability, and domestic service was viewed as a respectable occupation for working-class girls, her study importantly examined the "convergences and disparities" between these two visions of respectability in light of domestic-mistress relationships. See Magda Fahrni, "'Ruffled' Mistresses and 'Discontented' Maids: Respectability and the Case of Domestic Service, 1880–1914," *Labour/Le Travail*, 39 (Spring 1997), p. 70.

13. David Alexander, *Atlantic Canada and Confederation: Essays in Canadian Political Economy*, compiled by Eric W. Sager, Lewis R. Fischer, and Stuart O. Pierson (Toronto: University of Toronto Press, 1983), p. 64.

14. *Newfoundland Royal Commission 1933 Report* (London: HSMO, 1933).

15. Nancy Forestell, "'Times Were Hard'."

16. See Ian Hacking, *The Social Construction of What?* (Cambridge, Massachusetts: Harvard University Press, 1999) for a theoretical discussion of this issue. See also Donald A. MacKenzie, *Statistics in Britain 1865–1930: The Social Construction of Scientific Knowledge* (Edinburgh: Edinburgh University Press, 1981).

17. See Bettina Bradbury, *Working Families: Age, Gender, and Daily Survival in Industrializing Montreal* (Toronto: McClelland and Stewart Inc., 1993) for a discussion of censuses in Canada between 1861 and 1891. For an extensive discussion of the creation of the 1901 Canadian census, see Peter Baskerville and Eric W. Sager, *Unwilling Idlers: The Urban Unemployed and Their Families in Late Victorian Canada* (Toronto: University of Toronto Press, 1998), pp. 195–216.

18. Peter Baskerville and Eric Sager, *Unwilling Idlers*, p. 196.

19. Susan Geiger, "What's So Feminist about Women's Oral History?" *Journal of Women's History*, vol. 2, no. 1 (Spring, 1990), p. 174.

20. Personal Narratives Group, ed., *Interpreting Women's Lives: Feminist Theory and Personal Narratives* (Bloomington: Indiana University Press, 1989), p. 7.

21. See the essays in Shema Berger Gluck and Daphne Patai, eds., *Women's Words: The Feminist Practice of Oral History*.

22. Joan Sangster, *Earning Respect: The Lives of Working Women in Small-Town Ontario, 1920–1960* (Toronto: University of Toronto Press, 1995). For a detailed discussion of the issues Sangster encountered in using oral history, see "Telling Our Stories: Feminist Debates and the Use of Oral History," *Women's History Review*, vol. 3, no. 1 (1994).

23. See Marilyn Warring, *If Women Counted: A New Feminist Economics* (New York: Harper Collins, 1988) for a riveting discussion about economic statistics and the undervaluing of women's unpaid work globally. For a discussion on the manuscript census and women's work in Britain, see Edward Higgs, "Women, Occupations and Work in the Nineteenth-Century Censuses," *History Workshop Journal*, 23

(Spring 1987), and Bridget Hill, "Women, Work and the Census: A Problem for Historians of Women," *History Workshop Journal*, 35 (Spring 1993).

24. Peter Neary, *Newfoundland in the North Atlantic World, 1929–1949* (Kingston and Montreal: McGill-Queen's University Press, 1988).

25. Department of Public Health and Welfare, *Interim Report: Census of Newfoundland and Labrador, 1935* (St. John's, 1936), p. 2.

26. The historical literature on Newfoundland's economy is too vast to list here. For an important description of the symbiotic relationship between the informal and commercial economies see Rosemary Ommer, "Merchant Credit and the Informal Economy: Newfoundland, 1919–1929," in *Historical Papers* (Canadian Historical Association: Ottawa, 1989).

27. Memorandum, Department of Public Health and Welfare, n.d., Provincial Archives of Newfoundland and Labrador (PANL), GN38, S6-1-5A, file 5, 1935.

28. One of the first scholars to describe domestic service as an aspect of women's work in Newfoundland was Ellen Antler in "Fisherman, Fisherwoman, Rural Proletariat: Capitalist Commodity Production in the Newfoundland Fishery," unpublished PhD dissertation, University of Connecticut, 1981.

29. Using a gender sensitive approach to population studies, British women's historians Di Cooper and Moira Donald have revealed a great deal about the kinship connections between domestics and employers in a British suburb. Di Cooper and Moira Donald, "Households and 'Hidden' Kin in Early Nineteenth-Century England: Four Case Studies in Suburban Exeter, 1821–1861," *Continuity and Change*, vol. 10, no. 2 (1995).

30. Correspondence from Census Enumerator (Windsor Vicinity) to Department of Public Health and Welfare, 3 December 1945, PANL, GN38, S6-1-7, File 14. Note that the same individual enumerated the community of Grand Falls in 1935.

31. Sherna Berger Gluck and Daphne Patai, eds., *Women's Words*.

32. Susan Geiger, "What's So Feminist about Women's Oral History," p. 175.

33. Interview with Gertrude L., Grand Falls, 1997.

34. Interview with Martina L., St. John's, Newfoundland, 1997.

35. Interview with Sarah C., Grand Falls, 1997.

36. Interview with Martina L.

37. Interview with Stella B., Summerford, Newfoundland, 1997.

CHAPTER 13

Focus Groups

DAVID L. MORGAN

INTRODUCTION

Although some form of group interviewing has undoubtedly existed for as long as sociologists have been collecting data (e.g., Bogardus 1926), the last decade has produced a remarkable surge of interest in group interviews generally and focus groups in particular. Much of this interest first surfaced in the mid-1980s. In 1987, Robert Merton published remarks that compared his pioneering work on "focused interviews" (Merton & Kendall 1946) with marketers' uses of the focus group, while John Knodel and his collaborators (Knodel et al 1987) published a summary of their focus group research on demographic changes in Thailand. The next year produced two book-length treatments of focus groups by social scientists (Krueger 1988/1994, Morgan 1988). This initial burst of interest was followed by another texts (Stewart & Shamdasani 1990, Vaughn et al 1996), a reissuing of Merton et al's original manual (Merton et al 1956/1990), an edited collection of more advanced material (Morgan 1993a), and at least two special issues of journals (Carey 1995, Knodel 1995).

The current level of interest in focus group interviews is evident from searches of *Sociological Abstracts*, *Psychological Abstracts*, and the *Social Science Citation Index*. All of these sources show a steady growth in research using focus groups, indicating that well over a hundred empirical articles using focus groups appeared in refereed journals during 1994 alone. These searches also show interesting patterns in the use of focus groups. In particular, a content analysis of the materials from *Sociological Abstracts* revealed that over 60% of the empirical research using focus groups during the past decade combined them with other research methods, although the proportion of studies that relied solely on focus groups has been increasing in recent years. Hence, this review pays attention to uses of focus groups both as a "self-contained" method and in combination with other methods. Before examining the uses of focus groups, however, I examine how focus groups are related to group interviews in general.

FOCUS GROUPS AND GROUP INTERVIEWS

This chapter defines focus groups as a research technique that collects data through group interaction on a topic determined by the researcher. This definition has three essential components. First, it clearly states that focus groups are a research method devoted to data collection. Second, it locates the interaction in a group discussion as the source of the data. Third, it acknowledges the researcher's active role in creating the group discussion for data collection purposes.

While this definition is intentionally quite broad, each of its three elements does exclude some projects that have occasionally been called focus groups. First, focus groups should be distinguished from groups whose primary purpose is something other than research; alternative purposes might be: therapy, decision making, education, organizing, or behavior change (although focus groups that are primarily for data collection may have some of these outcomes as well). Second, it is useful to distinguish focus groups from procedures that utilize multiple participants but do not allow interactive discussions, such as nominal groups and Delphi groups (these techniques are reviewed in Stewart & Shamdasani 1990). Finally, focus groups should be distinguished from methods that collect data from naturally occurring group discussions where no one acts as an interviewer. The distinction here is not whether the group existed prior to the research, but whether the researcher's interests directed the discussion, since focus groups are often conducted with existing groups (Morgan 1989).

Lying behind this effort to define focus groups is the fundamental question of whether focus groups should be distinguished from other types of group interviews. In one camp are those who use an inclusive approach that treats most forms of group interviews as variants on focus groups. In another camp, however, are those who use an exclusive approach that treats focus groups as a narrower technique not to be confused with other types of group interviews. One version of the exclusive approach, which is particularly common in marketing research (Greenbaum 1988, 1993, McQuarrie 1996), is a statement that focus groups must meet some specified set of criteria, typically that they consist of structured discussions among 6 to 10 homogeneous strangers in a formal setting. The problem with this approach is that it fails to demonstrate any advantages of either limiting the definition of focus groups to studies that meet these criteria or excluding group interviews that deviate from them.

In contrast to such unthinking reliance on an exclusive definition of focus groups, Frey & Fontana (1991) have created a typology that locates focus groups as one among several categories of group interviews. The typology includes some that the present definition already distinguishes from focus groups (nominal and Delphi groups and observations of naturally occurring groups), and some (brainstorming groups and field interviews in naturally occurring settings) that the current definition would treat as variations on focus groups. (See Khan & Manderson 1992 for a similar but more anthropologically based typology). One way to assess the usefulness of a typology such as Frey & Fontana's is to ask if it can determine whether a particular group interview is or is not a focus group. According to the dimensions that define their typology, group interviews are something other than focus groups if they: (i) are conducted in informal settings; (ii) use nondirective interviewing; or (iii) use unstructured question formats. Yet applied demographers such as Knodel (1987, 1995) have held focus group interviews throughout the world and have concluded that they can be adapted to a wide variety of settings and culture practices. Similarly, social science texts on focus groups (Krueger 1993, Morgan 1988, Stewart & Shamdasani 1990) describe ways to conduct focus groups with more or less directive interviewing styles and more or less structured question formats, depending on the purposes of the particular project. It would thus, in actual practice, be quite difficult to apply Frey & Fontana's typology to determine whether any given group interview was or was not a focus group.

In the long run, the question of whether sociologists should use a more inclusive or exclusive definition of focus groups will depend on which approach maximizes both the effective application of available techniques and the innovative development of new techniques. For the present, this remains an open question. Consequently, this chapter follows an inclusive approach that treats focus groups as a set of central tendencies, with many useful variations that can be matched to a variety of research purposes.

CURRENT USES FOR FOCUS GROUPS

This review necessarily concentrates on the uses of focus groups by sociologists. Still, it should be obvious that focus groups, like other qualitative methods, are used across a wide variety of different fields. Other disciplines in which focus groups are relatively widespread include communication studies (Albrecht et al 1993, Staley 1990), education (Brotherson & Goldstein 1992, Flores & Alonzo 1995, Lederman 1990), political science (Delli Carpini & Williams 1994, Kullberg 1994), and public health (Basch 1987). Outside of academia, focus groups are well known to be popular in marketing (Goldman & McDonald 1987, Greenbaum 1993), where they have been used for everything from breakfast cereals (Templeton 1987) to political candidates (Diamond & Bates 1992). This acceptance in applied marketing has not, however, carried over to the academic field of marketing (McQuarrie 1990), although there does seem to be a trend toward more methodological research in this field (McDonald 1993, Nelson & Frontczak 1988).

Given the breadth of possible applications of focus groups and group interviews, it is hardly surprising that they have found uses in many of the specialty areas that interest sociologists, including: aging (Knodel 1995, Duncan & Morgan 1994), criminology (Sasson, 1995), medical sociology (Morgan & Spanish 1985, McKinlay 1993), political sociology (Gamson 1992), social movements (Cable 1992), and the sociology of work (Bobo et al 1995). In addition, many applications of focus groups do not fit within the neat, traditional boundaries of sociology's subdisciplines. For example, Shively's (1992) study of how American Indians and Anglos responded to cowboy movies used focus groups within a cultural studies framework; Jarrett's (1993, 1994) work on low-income, African American women combined elements of family sociology, inequality, and race and ethnicity; and Pinder-hughes' (1993) investigation of racially motivated violence mixed elements of urban sociology, criminology, and race relations.

Despite this wide-ranging interest in focus groups, they have found more currency within several specific areas of sociological interest. In particular, marketing's legacy of using focus groups to hear from consumers has carried over into their use in the development and evaluation of programs ranging from substance abuse (Lengua et al 1992) to curricular reform (Hendershott & Wright 1993). Program development efforts use focus groups to learn more about the potential targets of these programs in order to reach them more effectively. This use often occurs under the explicit rubric of "social marketing," which applies tools such as focus groups to socially valued goals, as in Bryant's (1990) program to encourage breast feeding among low-income women. On the program evaluation side, focus groups have become an important tool in qualitative evaluation research, including not only post-program evaluation, but also needs assessment and strategic planning (Krueger 1994).

Two specific research areas where the applied use of focus groups has had a major and continuing link to sociology are family planning and HIV/AIDS. The application of focus groups to research on fertility first emerged in the early 1980s (e.g. Folch-Lyon et al 1981). These studies typically sought a better understanding of knowledge, attitudes, and practices with regard to contraception in the Third World; in particular, advocates of a social marketing approach to contraceptives (Schearer 1981) argued that focus groups could supplement the kind of attitudinal data that surveys produced. Since that time, focus groups have been an important source of data on fertility and family planning preferences around the world, as in the work of Ward et al (1991) in Guatemala, Honduras, and Zaire, or Knodel et al (1987) in Thailand. This established application in the study of sexual behavior also led to the use of focus groups in research on the spread of HIV, both in the Third World (Irwin et al 1991) and the West (Kline et al 1992, Pollak et al 1990).

An important theme that reappears in many of these uses of focus groups is their ability to "give a voice" to marginalized groups. For example, in early HIV/AIDS research (Joseph et al 1984), epidemiologists used focus groups to gain a better understanding of at-risk groups with whom they had little prior experience, such as gay and bisexual men. Focus groups have thus been used in many applied settings where there is a difference in perspective between the researchers and those with whom they need to work. Others have argued, however, that the value of focus groups goes well beyond listening to others, since they can serve as either a basis for empowering "clients" (Magill 1993, Race et al 1994) or as a tool in action and participatory research (Hugentobler et al 1992, Padilla 1993). Similarly, feminist researchers have noted the appeal of focus groups because they allow participants to exercise a fair degree of control over their own interactions (Nichols-Casebolt & Spakes 1995, Montell 1995).

USES IN COMBINATION WITH OTHER METHODS

As noted at the outset of this review, a content analysis of *Sociological Abstracts* revealed that a majority of the published research articles using focus groups combined them with other methods. Further examination of the specific combinations of focus groups with other methods showed that the most frequent pairings were with either in-depth, individual interviews or surveys. Between these two, the use of focus groups with individual interviews is the more straightforward, since both are qualitative techniques. (This does not, however, imply that the two methods are interchangeable; the following section contains a comparison of individual and group interviews.) Investigators' reasons for combining individual and group interviews typically point to the greater depth of the former and the greater breadth of the latter (Crabtree et al 1993). For example, individual interview studies have used follow-up group interviews to check the conclusions from their analyses and to expand the study populations included in the research (Irwin 1970). This strategy has the advantage of getting reactions from a relatively wide range of participants in a relatively short time. In a complementary fashion, focus group studies have used follow-up interviews with individual participants to explore specific opinions and experiences in more depth, as well as to produce narratives that address the continuity of personal experiences over time (Duncan & Morgan 1994). This strategy has the advantage of first identifying a range of experiences and perspectives, and then drawing from that pool to add more depth where needed. Thus, depending on the varied needs that a qualitative study has for breadth and depth, there is little difficulty in combining individual and group interviews.

While studies that bring together focus groups and surveys are one of the leading ways of combining qualitative and quantitative methods, such designs also raise a complex set of issues, since the two methods produce such different kinds of data. Morgan (1993c) presented a conceptual framework to clarify these issues by distinguishing four ways of combining qualitative and quantitative methods in general and focus groups and surveys in particular. The four ways of combining the methods are based on which method received the primary attention and whether the secondary method served as a preliminary or follow-up study.

Thus, the first combination contains studies in which surveys are the primary method and focus groups serve in a preliminary capacity. Survey researchers typically use this design to develop the content of their questionnaires. Because surveys are inherently limited by the questions they ask, it is increasingly common to use focus groups to provide data on how the respondents themselves talk about the topics of the survey. Although this practice has long been common in marketing research, systematic publications in this area did not appear until social scientists renewed their interest in focus groups (Fuller et al 1993, O'Brien 1993, Zeller 1993b). Still, this is an area that is just beginning to receive attention, and many issues are only now arising, such as the need to find other means of pursuing focus group insights that are not amenable to survey research (Laurie 1992, Laurie & Sullivan 1991). At present, this is easily the most common reason for combining focus groups and surveys.

In the second combination, focus groups are the primary method while surveys provide preliminary inputs that guide their application. Studies following this research design typically use the broad but "thin" data from surveys to assist in selecting samples for focus groups or topics for detailed analysis. With regard to sampling, Morgan & Zhao (1993) and O'Connor et al (1992) both used surveys of medical records to divide a larger population into different "segments" that they then compared using separate sets of focus groups. With regard to analysis, Morgan (1994) and Shively (1992) both illustrated the use of findings from a brief preliminary survey with focus group participants to guide the more detailed interpretive analysis of the data from the group discussions. Compared to the first combination, studies that use surveys as a secondary method to assist focus group research are relatively rare.

The third combination once again uses surveys as the primary method, but the focus groups now act as a follow-up that assists in interpreting the survey results. One increasingly common use for qualitative follow-up methods, including focus groups, is to recontact survey respondents for illustrative material that can be quoted in conjunction with quantitative findings. More interesting from a methodological perspective are efforts to clarify poorly understood results, such as Knodel's (1987) and Wolff et al's (1993) efforts to account for fertility rates and education levels in Thailand, Morgan's (1989) investigations of the ineffectiveness of social support among recent widows, and Harari & Beaty's (1990) deeper probing of surface similarities in the survey responses of black workers and white managers in South Africa under apartheid. Among the four combinations, these designs are the second most frequent, but they have yet to receive any systematic methodological attention.

The final combination of surveys and focus groups uses focus groups as the primary method and surveys as a source of follow-up data. One such application would examine the prevalence of issues or themes from the focus groups. For example, Nichols-Casebolt & Spakes (1995:53) followed up their focus groups by locating secondary data from surveys that showed policy makers "the scope of the problems associated with the issues identified by the participants." Another possibility would be to survey a large number of sites to determine where the results from a more limited focus group study might be most immediately transferable. But studies that employ designs from this fourth combination are easily the rarest of this set. One likely reason that those who conduct focus group studies seldom do smaller follow-up surveys is their desire to avoid any implication that quantitative data are necessary to "verify" the results of the qualitative research. In other words, the issues that accompany combining methods from different "paradigms" (Lincoln & Guba 1985) involve not just technical considerations, but epistemological and political issues as well (Bryman 1988). Still, the current popularity of work from the first combination, where focus groups aid in developing surveys, demonstrates the potential value of combining focus groups with quantitative methods. It thus seems likely that research using various combinations with surveys will continue to be not only one of the major uses of focus groups but also one of the most practical ways of bringing together qualitative and quantitative methods.

HOW FOCUS GROUPS COMPARE TO OTHER SOCIOLOGICAL METHODS

Despite the increasingly widespread use of focus groups as a method within sociology and the other social sciences, virtually all this work has occurred in the past ten years. This "newcomer" status has encouraged comparisons between focus groups and the various traditional methods in each of these areas, but researchers have offered two very different reasons for comparing methods. One reason for comparing focus groups to more familiar methods has been to determine whether the two methods produce equivalent data. According to this view, focus groups are most useful when they reproduce the results of the standard methods in a particular field. A different reason for comparing focus groups to existing methods has been to locate the unique contributions that each can make to a field of studies. According to this view, focus groups are most useful when they produce new results that would not be possible with the standard methods in a particular field. There is an obvious paradox here, as focus groups cannot produce results that are simultaneously the same as and different from results of familiar techniques. Unfortunately, the failure to recognize these divergent goals has limited the cumulative knowledge from studies that compare focus groups to other methods. Nonetheless, these comparisons are useful for summarizing the strengths and weaknesses of focus groups.

COMPARISONS TO SURVEYS

In one of the earliest reports of a major social science application of focus groups, Folch-Lyon et al (1981) also included a detailed comparison to a survey on the same topic. This study investigated attitudes toward contraception in Mexico using two independent research teams. One team conducted 44 focus groups with some 300 participants, while the other did household surveys with over 2000 respondents. Overall, the authors had little difficulty in matching the investigation of their substantive topics across the two methods; their results showed an overwhelming convergence. As Stycos (1981) pointed out, however, most of Folch-Lyon et al's judgments about the convergence between the two methods were based on subjective assessments of the correspondence of the findings; fortunately, more recent efforts have used more systematic comparisons.

Ward et al (1991) compared survey and focus group results from three studies on family planning in Guatemala, Honduras, and Zaire. For each of their three studies, they matched topic areas where methods contained similar questions, and they judged results from the two methods to be similar when "they would lead to the same conclusions" (p. 272). Based on explicit comparisons across a total of 60 variables, they found that the results from the two methods were: (i) highly similar for 30% of the variables; (ii) similar, but focus groups provided more information for 42% of the variables; (iii) similar, but surveys provided more information for 17%; and (iv) dissimilar for 12% of the variables. The biggest difference found between the methods was the ability of the focus groups to produce more in-depth information on the topic at hand.

In another systematic comparison of survey and focus group results, Saint-Germain et al (1993) reported on two studies of the barriers to breast cancer screening services for older Hispanic women in the southwestern United States. To assess the comparability of the results, the authors rank-ordered a list of barriers according to how often survey respondents had experienced each, and then they compared this to a rank-order of how often each barrier was mentioned in the focus groups. Saint-Germain et al's conclusions (1993:363) matched those of Ward et al: "The findings of the focus group interviews, in most cases, confirmed the findings of the previous population surveys. In many cases, the focus group interviews went beyond the information obtained in the survey, amplifying our understanding of the various facets of barriers to breast cancer screening and specifying more exactly how some of the barriers work in practice."

Although each of these studies emphasized the convergence of the results from focus groups and surveys, a consistent set of differences did occur in all three studies. First, the survey interview setting limited what respondents said about sensitive topics, in comparison to what they revealed in focus groups. Second, the differences in response options meant that surveys were better able to elicit yes/no answers about specific behaviors and experiences, even though the forced-choice format of the survey items limited what respondents could say on general attitude areas, in comparison to the more open-ended discussions in the focus groups. Finally, Ward et al explicitly noted that all of these comparisons used only the variables that occurred in both studies, thus downplaying the fact that the surveys typically covered many more topics than did the focus groups. There was thus a key tradeoff between the depth that focus groups provided and the breadth that surveys offered.

COMPARISONS TO INDIVIDUAL INTERVIEWS

Fern's (1982) work on the relative productivity of individual interviews and focus groups was one of the very few methodological studies that involved a head-to-head comparison between the two methods. Using an "idea generation" task, Fern compared focus groups to an equivalent number of aggregated responses from individual interviews (i.e. "nominal groups"). He determined that each focus group participant produced only 60% to 70% as many ideas as they would have in an individual interview; he also had raters judge the quality of ideas from the two methods, and again an advantage appeared for individual interviews. These results clearly argue against the notion that focus groups have a "synergy" that makes them more productive than an equivalent number of individual interviews. Instead, the real issue may well be the relative efficiency of the two methods for any given project. For example, Fern's results suggest that two eight-person focus groups would produce as many ideas as 10 individual interviews. As Crabtree et al (1993) have pointed out, however, a number of logistical factors, such as location of the interviews, the mobility of the participants, the flexibility of their schedules, would determine which study would actually be easier to accomplish.

The major issue in studies of individual and group interviews has not, however, been the number of ideas they generate, but the comparability of the results they produce. Wight (1994) reported one of the rare studies on this issue. The study involved both group and individual interviews with the same adolescent males concerning their sexual experiences, and systematic variation in which of the two types of interviews was done first. Wight concluded that the greatest number of discrepancies occurred between reports of boys who participated in individual interviews first and then in focus groups, while boys who started in group interviews gave similar accounts in subsequent individual interviews. Kitzinger (1994a, b) reported that the conclusions about the results from her study on HIV issues validated those of Wight's, although she also found that the difference between individual and group interviews was limited to heterosexual males. Kitzinger thus argued against a generalized effect of groups on conformity, and she called for more attention to how such processes are affected by the group's composition, the topic, the relationship of the interviewer to the group, and the general context of the interview.

Kitzinger (1994b: 173) also reached the more general conclusion that, "Differences between interview and group data cannot be classified in terms of validity versus invalidity or honesty versus dishonesty. . . . The group data documenting macho or sexual harassing behaviour is no more 'invalid' than that showing the research participants' relatively acceptable behaviour in interview settings." It thus seems a safe conclusion that, if one searches, one is bound to find differences in how some interviewees talk about some topics in individual versus group interviews. For those cases where we are interested only in a specific social context, this interest will determine which form of data is more valid. In general, however, the existence of differences between what is said in individual and group interviews is as much a statement about our culture as our methods, and this is clearly a research topic of interest in its own right.

STRENGTHS AND WEAKNESSES OF FOCUS GROUPS

One benefit of comparing focus groups to other methods is a more sophisticated understanding of the strengths and weaknesses of focus groups. For example, rather than just listing exploratory research as a strength of focus groups, it is now necessary to note that individual, nominal interviews can be a more effective technique for idea generation (Fern 1982) and that surveys can be more effective for determining the prevalence of any given attitude or experience (Ward et al 1992). Comparisons to other methods have thus led to the conclusion that the real strength of focus groups is not simply in exploring what people have to say, but in providing insights into the sources of complex behaviors and motivations (Morgan & Krueger 1993).

Morgan & Krueger also argued that the advantages of focus groups for investigating complex behaviors and motivations were a direct outcome of the interaction in focus groups, what has been termed "the group effect" (Carey 1994, Carey & Smith 1994). An emphasis on the specific kinds of interactions that occur in focus groups is also an improvement over vague assertions that "synergy" is one of their strengths. What makes the discussion in focus groups more than the sum of separate individual interviews is the fact that the participants both query each other and explain themselves to each other. As Morgan & Krueger (1993) have also emphasized, such interaction offers valuable data on the extent of consensus and diversity among the participants. This ability to observe the extent and nature of interviewees' agreement and disagreement is a unique strength of focus groups. A further strength comes from the researcher's ability to ask the participants themselves for comparisons among their experiences and views, rather than aggregating individual data in order to speculate about whether or why the interviewees differ.

The weaknesses of focus groups, like their strengths, are linked to the process of producing focused interactions, raising issues about both the role of the moderator in generating the data and the impact of the group itself on the data. With regard to the role of the moderator, Agar & MacDonald (1995) used discourse analysis to compare the conversations between interviewers and interviewees in a single focus group and a set of individual interviews. They concluded that the dynamics of the individual interviews put more burden on the informants to explain themselves to the interviewer, while the moderator's efforts to guide the group discussion had the ironic consequence of disrupting the interaction that was the point of the group. Saferstein (1995) also used discourse analysis to make a similar point about moderator control in a comparison of focus groups and naturally occurring talk at a job site. In particular, he noted that it is the moderator, rather than the ongoing work of the group, that determines the agenda and form of the discussion. Both of these articles directly questioned the assertion that focus groups mimic a conversation among the participants, and each independently suggested that a meeting would be a better analogy, due to the control exercised by the moderator.

Although the issues that Agar & MacDonald (1995) and Saferstein (1995) raised are of most concern with more directive styles of moderating, there is no denying that the behavior of the moderator has consequences for the nature of the group interviews. But the issue of interviewer effects is hardly limited to focus groups, as is shown in work from both survey research (Fowler & Mangione 1990) and individual interviewing (Mischler 1986). All of these issues point to the importance of understanding the range of variation that is possible across different styles of moderating, a range discussed in the following section.

In terms of weaknesses that are due to the impact of the group on the discussion itself, Sussman et al (1991) used a design from small group research and administered questionnaires before and after focus groups to find out if the discussions changed the participants' attitudes. They found the predicted "polarization" effect—attitudes became more extreme after the group discussion. The magnitude of this effect was small, however, as it accounted for only 4% of the variance in attitude change; this may be significant in an analysis of variance, but it is not likely to skew the results of most focus group research. Nonetheless, the point is well taken that we know little about how group members affect each other, and research designs from the social psychological study of small groups can offer useful tools for investigating this issue.

A final weakness due to the impact of the group on its participants concerns the range of topics that can be researched effectively in groups. Because group interaction requires mutual self-disclosure, it is undeniable that some topics will be unacceptable for discussion among some categories of research participants. At present, however, assertions about this weakness of focus groups are based more on intuition than data, since there are no empirical investigations of the range of topics or participants that either can or cannot be studied with group interviews. In particular, claims that focus groups are inappropriate for "sensitive topics" seem to ignore the widespread use of group interviewing to study sexual behavior in all forms. Further, the growing use of focus groups with cultural minorities and marginalized groups suggests that experience is the best predictor of where focus groups will and will not work. Fortunately, several of the researchers who have worked with sensitive topics and minority groups have written about their use of focus groups in these settings (Jarrett 1993, 1994, Hoppe et al 1995, Hughes & DuMont 1993, Kitzinger 1994a, b, Zeller 1993a), and only time will tell how widely these techniques apply to other topics and populations.

RESEARCH DESIGNS FOR SOCIOLOGICAL APPLICATIONS OF FOCUS GROUPS

As the previous sections demonstrate, sociologists and other social scientists have used focus groups in many ways for many purposes. Yet, if there are many ways of doing focus groups, then how does a practicing researcher make choices between doing focus groups one way versus another? And how does an outside reviewer determine whether a focus group project was done in a proper and effective fashion? The emerging consensus is that these issues can be resolved through an emphasis on research design in focus groups.

An emphasis on research design has advantages both for the field of focus groups as a whole and for individual investigators. For the field of focus groups, Morgan (1992a) has argued that an emphasis on research design would generate explicit principles that would replace the "rules of thumb" that have guided past practice. Thus, rather than simply asserting that focus groups should consist of structured discussions among 6 to 10 homogeneous strangers in a formal setting, an emphasis on research design would systematically investigate the implications of conducting more structured versus less structured discussions, of using smaller versus larger groups, etc. For the individual investigator, such research design principles would provide a means for linking the purposes of the research and the specific procedures that best achieve these purposes. For example, in his research on the political consciousness of ordinary citizens, Gamson (1992) first noted that his procedures departed from the prevailing rules of thumb when he used loosely moderated groups of four to six familiar acquaintances who met at one of the participants' homes; he then justified each of these design decisions by stating why it would produce data better suited to his purposes.

In considering the set of issues involved in designing focus group research, it is useful to distinguish between decisions that apply to the research project as a whole (i.e. project-level design issues), and those that apply to the conduct of a particular group (i.e. group-level design issues). While decisions at the project level specify the kinds of data that the focus groups should produce, group-level design decisions largely determine how to conduct the groups in order to produce such data. In particular, many of the group-level decisions are related to issues of group dynamics that help to ensure a productive discussion.

PROJECT-LEVEL DESIGN ISSUES

Standardization

As a project-level design issue, standardization addresses the extent to which the identical questions and procedures are used in every group. At one extreme would be an emphasis on "emergence" that lets the questions and procedures shift from group to group in order to take advantage of what has been learned in previous groups. At the other extreme, a project could begin by determining a fixed set of questions and procedures that would apply throughout. Of course, standardization is actually a matter of degree, and even standardized designs allow minor variations that accommodate the unique aspects of each group, in order to avoid what Merton et al (1990) called the fallacy of adhering to fixed questions.

Although nothing like a census of focus group designs among sociologists exists, it is quite clear that the majority of these research projects have used a fixed research design that relied on a consistent set of predetermined questions and procedures. This tendency toward standardized research designs has not gone unexamined. Orosz (1994) has argued that this aspect of focus groups is inconsistent with many of the key tenets of qualitative research, while Brotherson & Goldstein (1992) made the case for pursuing standardization within an emergent research design. According to the present argument for making decisions according to research design principles, whether to standardize the questions and procedures in a focus group project should not be based on past tradition, within either the more standardized practices of focus group researchers or the less standardized approach favored by practitioners of other qualitative methods. Instead, it should be based on a conscious assessment of the advantages and disadvantages of standardization with regard to the goals of a particular project.

The great advantage of standardization, and its most common justification, is the high level of comparability that it produces across groups. This comparability is particularly valuable when the goal of the research is to compare the responses of different categories of participants (see the discussion of segmentation in the next section). As Knodel (1993) pointed out, standardization has the particular advantage of facilitating the analysis of focus groups by allowing for direct comparisons of the discussions from group to group. The obvious disadvantage of standardization is that one must live with whatever questions and procedures were chosen prior to entering the field, which would be inimical to many truly exploratory applications of focus groups.

Morgan (1993c) has described two types of designs that combine the advantages of more standardized and more emergent designs (see Morgan 1992b for a partial application of these procedures). The first such design breaks the project into phases that move from less standardized to more standardized groups. This has the advantage of allowing the early groups in the project to take a more exploratory approach, which then serves as the basis for developing a later set of standardized questions and procedures grounded in the data themselves. The second compromise design organizes the questions in each group according to a "funnel" pattern that begins with a fixed set of core questions and then proceeds to a variable set of specific issues. This has the advantage of maintaining comparability across groups for the first part of each discussion but allowing the later section of each group to vary according to the emergent needs of the research.

Sampling

Focus group research reveals its historical association with marketing research by using the term "segmentation" to capture sampling strategies that consciously vary the composition of groups. This use of segmentation to create groups that consist of particular categories of participants is a long-standing practice, as illustrated by Folch-Lyon et al's (1981) study on family planning, where they composed groups that were as homogeneous as possible by sex, age, marital status, contraceptive use, socioeconomic status, and geographical location. The most obvious kinds of segmentation capture something about the research topic itself. For example, if gender differences were of interest, then one might conduct separate groups of men and women, or an evaluation study might segment the groups into more frequent and less frequent users of the program in question.

Segmentation offers two basic advantages. First, it builds a comparative dimension into the entire research project, including the data analysis. For example, Folch-Lyon et al (1981) analyzed their data according to the categories described above and found the most wide-ranging differences between groups of men and women, with some additional differences between groups in rural and urban areas. Second, segmentation facilitates discussions by making the participants more similar to each other. For example, even if the behavior of men and women does not differ greatly on a given topic, discussion still may flow more smoothly in groups that are homogeneous rather than mixed with regard to sex. The same logic applies to dividing groups according to the age, race, or social class of the participants, although the value of segmenting to facilitate a free-flowing discussion obviously depends on the research topic.

The obvious disadvantage of segmentation is that it can greatly multiply the number of groups. As Knodel (1993) pointed out, it is seldom wise to run just one group per segment, since what one learns about that segment is confounded with the group dynamics of that unique set of participants. As Knodel also noted, however, using multiple segmentation criteria can produce acceptable designs that have only one group "per cell" in the overall design, as long as there are multiple groups in each separate segment (e.g. there may be several groups of women, several rural groups, and several groups of older participants, but only one group of older, rural women). Even so, using multiple segmentation criteria can easily lead to projects that involve large numbers of focus groups, like the 44 groups conducted by Folch-Lyon et al (1981).

Number of Groups

The most common rule of thumb is that most projects consist of four to six focus groups. The typical justification for this range is that the data become "saturated" and little new information emerges after the first few groups, so that moderators can predict what participants will say even before they say it (Zeller 1993b). Morgan (1992a) has suggested that diversity in either the participants or the range of topics to be covered will increase the number of groups necessary to achieve saturation. For example, Kitzinger wished to hear about views on AIDS from a wide range of different populations and thus conducted 52 groups, while Gamson (1992) wanted each of his groups to give their opinions on four different political issues and thus conducted 37 groups in order to produce enough discussion on each topic.

As the previous section noted, using multiple segments will increase the number of groups needed, which is a special case of diversity in the study population. Projects that use a lower level of standardization will also typically need more groups, since this produces more variation in the topics that are raised group to group. The connection between the number of groups and issues of standardization and segmentation raises the question of how different aspects of research design for focus groups intersect—a topic addressed at the end of this section.

GROUP-LEVEL DESIGN ISSUES

Level of Moderator Involvement

The presence of a moderator is one of the most striking features of focus groups. Groups in which the moderator exercises a higher degree of control are termed "more structured," and Morgan (1992a) has called attention to two senses in which a group can be more structured. First, it can be more structured with regard to asking questions, so that the moderator controls what topics are discussed (e.g. directing attention away from what are deemed less important issues). Second, it can be more structured with regard to managing group dynamics, so that the moderator controls the way that the participants interact (e.g. trying to get everyone to participate equally in the discussion). Both of these aspects of moderator involvement can be elements of the research design.

With regard to the moderator's involvement in asking questions, a less structured discussion means that the group can pursue its own interests, while a more structured approach means that the moderator imposes the researcher's interests, as embodied in the questions that guide the discussion. A key factor that makes groups more or less structured is simply the number of questions. Thus, if the average focus group lasts 90 minutes, and the moderator has the responsibility for covering a great many questions during that time, then the moderator will be heavily involved in controlling the group's discussion. Unfortunately, there is currently little consensus about what constitutes a more structured or less structured approach to questioning. For example, Lederman (1990:123) characterized a guide that contained five broad questions as "quite structured," while Byers & Wilcox (1991:65) termed a guide with 17 specific questions "relatively unstructured."

One possible cause for this confusion is the failure to distinguish between structure that controls questioning and structure that controls group dynamics. In managing group dynamics, a less structured approach allows participants to talk as much or as little as they please, while a more structured approach means that the moderator will encourage those who might otherwise say little and limit those who might otherwise dominate the discussion. Although most marketing approaches to focus groups (e.g. Greenbaum 1993) have typically advocated a more structured control of group dynamics, many social science approaches have explicitly favored a less directive style of interviewing (e.g. Krueger 1994, Merton et al 1990). Morgan's (1988) instructions for how to conduct "self-managed" groups, in which the moderator does not even sit at the same table as the participants, probably represent the extreme in social science advocacy of less structured approaches to group dynamics.

In general, marketing researchers, more than social science researchers, prefer research designs with high levels of moderator involvement that impose more structure with regard to both asking questions and managing group dynamics. Morgan (1988) has suggested that this reflects a difference between the marketing goal of answering questions from an audience of paying customers and the social science goal of generating new knowledge for an audience of peer reviewers. To the extent that this broad generalization does hold, it is a nice illustration of the general principle that research designs should follow from research goals. This conclusion—that approaches to moderating should be linked to research goals—is strongly supported by one of the few instances of systematic research that evaluates differences in moderator style (McDonald 1993). Further, it implies that arguments about whether moderators should use a more or less structured approach are meaningless unless one specifies the goals of the research.

Group Size

The number of participants who are invited to a focus group is one element of the research design that is clearly under the researcher's control. Morgan (1992a) reviewed the bases for determining group size, concluding that smaller groups were more appropriate with emotionally charged topics that generated high levels of participant involvement, while larger groups worked better with more neutral topics that generated lower levels of involvement. On the one hand, a smaller group gives each participant more time to discuss her or his views and experiences on topics in which they all are highly involved. On the other hand, a larger group contains a wider range of potential responses on topics where each participant has a low level of involvement. In addition, small groups make it easier for moderators to manage the active discussions that often accompany high levels of involvement and emotional topics, whereas large groups are easier to manage when each participant has a lower level of involvement in the topic.

This last point once again raises an issue that involves the intersection of two different design principles, group size and moderator involvement. Although it is generally the case that design dimensions cannot be considered in isolation from each other, current knowledge about how design issues impinge on each other is limited to a few obvious considerations. In addition to the linkage between group size and moderator involvement, earlier portions of this section noted connections between standardization and sample segmentation, and between the number of groups and both standardization and segmentation. There is thus an increasing but still limited stock of knowledge about how design issues go together. This limitation is understandable, given that most of the explicit investigations of research design in focus groups have come from social scientists and consequently reflect only a decade or so of activity.

DATA QUALITY CONCERNS

The basic goal in specifying research designs for focus groups is to ensure that the research procedures deliver the desired data. Despite the best research designs, however, things can still go wrong due to poor planning or the inappropriate implementation of otherwise optimal designs. Krueger (1993) and Morgan (1995) have both noted that data quality depends on a number of factors, including whether the researcher locates enough participants, selects appropriate samples, chooses relevant questions, has a qualified moderator(s), and uses an effective analysis strategy.

Standards for reporting on research procedures are one practical step to improve the quality of focus group research. At present, the reporting of focus group procedures is a haphazard affair at best. Based on the studies reviewed for this chapter, the following is one effort to develop such standards. First, to learn the overarching context for the research, readers should know whether a standardized set of questions and procedures applied throughout the project. Then, most basically, readers should know the number of groups conducted and the size range of these groups. There should also be information on the group composition, including relevant background data on the participants. In particular, when groups were divided into different sample segments, there should be information on the basis for this sampling strategy and the number of groups per segment. Regardless of whether the study used segmentation, it is important to report the sources for locating participants and other information about recruitment procedures. In terms of the interview itself, thorough summaries of the question content are needed; surprisingly, many current publications say very little about the questions that were asked. Similarly, most current reports say little about moderating, and useful information would include concrete descriptions of the degree of structure that the moderator(s) imposed, how many moderators were used, and what their training and qualifications were. Finally, ethical issues need to be discussed, and, although the field as a whole has been slow to address ethical concerns in focus group research, there now is at least one discussion of this topic (Smith 1995).

This kind of information would aid not only reviewers in judging the quality of the research design and procedures but also other researchers in adapting these practices into future work. For both of these purposes, it would be highly desirable for research reports to go beyond merely presenting factual information to including justifications for the more crucial design decisions. This process of making public the basis for our decisions about why to do focus groups one way and not another is a vital step in the growth of our field.

FUTURE DIRECTIONS FOR FOCUS GROUPS

The steady increase in the use of focus groups over the past decade clearly demonstrates that sociologists and other social scientists have found them to be a useful and practical method for gathering qualitative data. The leading role that sociologists have played in this field has been most evident in methodological research on focus groups, which has given sociologists a major influence on both their current uses and future directions. In terms of future directions, a group of social science researchers participated in focus groups, funded in part by the American Sociological Association, that led to a statement on "Future Directions for Focus Groups" (Morgan 1993b). Not surprisingly, several of the specific topics considered there have been echoed here, such as the need to set standards for focus groups and the need to further define the strengths and weaknesses of the method.

The major theme raised in the focus group discussions on future direction was the need to do more research on focus groups as a method, and several of the studies reviewed here provide concrete examples of how to accomplish this. For example, both Agar & MacDonald (1995) and Saferstein (1995) demonstrate the value of discourse analysis for investigating interactions between moderators and participants. Sociologists who have experimented with discourse analysis (e.g. Gamson 1992) have concluded that the time and expense spent in producing such data have little value for substantive analyses of what was said in groups. Yet, methodological analyses of how things are said in focus groups may well be a more profitable use of these tools. Another potentially useful technique from another field is Sussman et al's (1991) application of procedures from small group research. As Morgan & Krueger (1993) note, however, it is important not to confuse the standard decision-making paradigm in small groups research with the data gathering goals of focus groups. One particularly promising aspect of the Sussman et al procedures is the post-group questionnaire, and other focus group researchers (Pies 1993, Swenson et al 1992) have used this technique to investigate not only the impact that the discussion had on the participants, but also their feelings about the discussion, including the extent to which they were able to share their true opinions on the topics they discussed. One final promising technique for methodological research on focus groups is McDonald's (1993) use of an archive of focus group transcripts to investigate how differences in project goals were linked to differences in moderator style. Unfortunately, qualitative researchers have been slower in archiving their work than their quantitative counterparts; still, the opportunity to compare the qualitative procedures of multiple investigators across multiple topics would be an exciting opportunity that should not be limited to focus groups.

Data analysis is another topic for future work on focus groups. To date, most discussions of how to analyze focus groups have occurred within broader discussions of the method (e.g. Knodel 1993), and only one article is specifically dedicated to analysis of issues (Bertrand et al 1992). Although it is true that many of the analytic issues in focus groups are the same as in other qualitative methods, it is also true that focus groups raise some unique issues, such as the ongoing debate about the circumstances under which the unit of analysis should be the groups, the participants, or the participants' utterances (Carey & Smith 1994, Gamson 1992, Morgan 1995). In addition, focus groups offer some special opportunities for the application of computer technologies in the analysis of qualitative data (Javidi et al 1991).

Beyond such strictly methodological concerns, there are also promising new uses for focus groups. The most notable of these involves researchers who are more actively engaged with the participants and their concerns. In an earlier section, this was summarized as an increasing interest in focus groups among those who pursue goals such as empowerment or approaches such as action and participatory research. Underlying many of these efforts is a desire to break down the division between using groups as a means for gathering data and as a means for educating, mobilizing, or intervening with participants. This matches a widespread concern in the social sciences about the artificiality of the division between researchers and those who are researched. This issue is especially relevant for focus groups, since they have been widely touted (e.g. Morgan & Krueger 1993) as a means for helping to bridge the gap between those in authority and the people they control.

One question about focus groups that has remained unasked, however, is why they have reemerged with such popularity at this particular time. One segment of our future work on focus groups should thus go beyond practical concerns with the method itself to ask about their place within the history of sociology—especially since this is the discipline that is self-consciously charged with the study of humans in groups. Part of the present popularity of focus groups may indeed be due to their unique advantages for addressing such contemporary issues as empowerment and diversity. Whether this is true or not, it is clear that focus groups are both being shaped by the directions that our discipline is taking and playing a role in shaping those directions.

REFERENCES

Agar, M., J. MacDonald. 1995. Focus groups and ethnography. *Hum. Organ.* 54:78–86.

Albrecht, T.L., and G.M. Johnson, J.B. Walther. 1993. Understanding communication processes in focus groups. See Morgan 1993a, pp. 51–64.

Basch, C.E. 1987. Focus group interview: an underutilized research technique for improving theory and practice in health education. *Health Educ. Q.* 14:411–48.

Bertrand, J.E., J.E. Brown, and V.M. Ward. 1992. Techniques for analyzing focus group data. *Eval. Rev.* 16:198–209.

Bobo, L., C.L. Zubrinsky, J.H. Johnson, and M. L. Oliver. 1995. Work orientation, job discrimination, and ethnicity: a focus group perspective. *Res. Social. Work* 5:45–55.

Bogardus, E.S. 1926. The group interview. *J. Appl. Sociol.* 10:372–82.

Brotherson, M.J., and B.L. Goldstein. 1992. Quality design of focus groups in early childhood special education research. *J. Early Interv.* 16:334–42.

Bryant, C.A. 1990. The use of focus groups in program development. *Natl. Assoc. Pract. Anthropol. Bull.* 39:1–4.

Bryman, A. 1988. *Quality and Quantity in Social Research*. London: Unwin Hyman.

Byers, P.Y., and J.R. Wilcox. 1991. Focus groups: A qualitative opportunity for researchers. *J. Bus. Comm.* 28:63–78.

Cable, E.S. 1992. Women's social movement involvement: the role of structural availability in recruitment and participation processes. *Sociol. Q.* 33:35–50.

Carey, M.A. 1994. The group effect in focus groups: planning, implementing, and interpreting focus group research. In *Critical Issues in Qualitative Research Methods*, ed. J Morse, pp. 225–41. Thousand Oaks, CA: Sage.

Carey, M.A. 1995. Issues and applications of focus groups. *Qual. Health Res.* 5:413–530 (Special issue).

Carey, M.A, and M. Smith. 1994. Capturing the group effect in focus groups: a special concern in analysis. *Qual. Health Res.* 4:123–127.

Crabtree, B.F., M.K. Yanoshik, W.L. Miller, and P.J. O'Connor. 1993. Selecting individual or group interviews. See Morgan, pp. 137–49.

Delli Carpini, M.X., and B. Williams. 1994. The method is the message: focus groups as a method of social, psychological, and political inquiry. *Res. Micropolit.* 4:57–85.

Diamond E., and S. Bates. 1992. *The Spot: The Rise of Political Advertising on Television.* Cambridge, MA: MIT Press. 3rd ed.

Duncan M.T., and D.L. Morgan. 1994. Sharing the caring: family caregivers' views of their relationships with nursing home staff. *The Gerontologist* 34:235–44.

Fern, E.F. 1982. Focus groups: a review of some contradictory evidence, implications, and suggestions for future research. *Adv. Consumer Res.* 10:121–26.

Flores, J.G., and C.G. Alonso. 1995. Using focus groups in educational research. *Eval. Rev.* 19:84–101.

Folch-Lyon E., L. de la Macorra, and S.B. Schearer. 1981. Focus groups and survey research on family planning in Mexico. *Stud. Fam. Plan.* 12:409–32.

Fowler F.J., and T.W. Mangione. 1990. *Standardized Survey Interviewing.* Thousand Oaks, CA: Sage.

Frey, J.H., and A. Fontana. 1991. The group interview in social research. *Soc. Sci. J.* 28:185–87. See also Morgan 1993a, pp. 20–34.

Fuller, T.D., J.N. Edwards, S. Vorakitphokatorn, and S. Santhat. 1993. Using focus groups to adapt survey instruments to new populations: experience from a developing country. See Morgan 1993, pp. 89–104.

Gamson, W.A. 1992. *Talking Politics.* Cambridge, UK: Cambridge Univ. Press.

Goldman, A.E., and S.S. McDonald. 1987. *The Group Depth Interview: Principles and Practice.* Englewood Cliffs, NJ: Prentice Hall.

Greenbaum, T.L. 1993. *The Practical Handbook and Guide to Focus Group Research.* Lexington, MA: Lexington. Rev. ed.

Harari, O., and D. Beaty. 1990. On the folly of relying solely on a questionnaire methodology in cross-cultural research. *J. Manage. Issues* 2:267–81.

Hendershott, A., and S. Wright. 1993. Student focus groups and curricular review. *Teach. Sociol.* 21:54–59.

Hoppe, M.J., E.A. Wells, D.M. Morrison, M.R. Gillmore, and A. Wilsdon. 1995. Using focus groups to discuss sensitive topics with children. *Eval. Rev.* 19:102–14.

Hugentobler, M.K., B.A. Israel, S.J. Schurman. 1992. An action research approach to work-place health: integrating methods. *Health Educ. Q.* 19:55–76.

Hughes, D., and K. DuMont. 1993. Using focus groups to facilitate culturally anchored research. *Am. J. Community Psychol.* 21:775–806.

Irwin, J. 1970. *The Felon.* Englewood Cliffs, NJ: Prentice Hall.

Irwin, K., J. Bertrand, N. Mibandumba, K. Mbuyi, and C. Muremeri, et al. 1991. Knowledge, attitudes, and beliefs about HIV infection and AIDS among healthy factory workers and their wives, Kinshasa, Zaire. *Soc. Sci. Med.* 32:917–30.

Jarrett, R.L. 1993. Focus group interviewing with low-income, minority populations: a research experience. See Morgan 1993a, pp. 184–201.

Jarrett, R.L. 1994. Living poor: family life among single parent, African-American women. *Soc. Probl.* 41:30–49.

Javidi M, L.W. Long, M.L. Vasu, and D.K. Ivy. 1991. Enhancing focus group validity with computer assisted technology in social science research. *Soc. Sci. Comput. Rev.* 9:231–45.

Joseph, J.G., C.A. Emmons, R.C. Kessler, C.B. Wortman, K. O'Brien, et al. 1984. Coping with the threat of AIDS: an approach to psychosocial assessment. *Am. Psychol.* 38:1297–302.

Khan, M.E., and L. Manderson. 1992. Focus groups in tropical diseases research. *Health Policy Plan* 7:56–66.

Kitzinger, J. 1994a. The methodology of focus groups: the importance of interaction between research participants. *Sociol. Health Illn.* 16:103–21.

Kitzinger, J. 1994b. Focus groups: method or madness. In *Challenge and Innovation: Methodological Advances in Social Research on HIV/AIDS*, ed. M Boulton, pp. 159–75. New York: Taylor & Francis.

Kline, A., E. Kline, and E. Oken. 1992. Minority women and sexual choice in the age of AIDS. *Soc. Sci. Med.* 34: 447–57.

Knodel, J. 1993. The design and analysis of focus group studies: a practical approach. See Morgan 1993a, pp. 35–50.

Knodel. J, A. Chamratrithirong, and N. Debavalya. 1987. *Thailand's Reproductive Revolution: Rapid Fertility Decline in a Third-World Setting*. Madison, WI: Univ. Wisc. Press.

Krueger, R.A. 1993. Quality control in focus group research. See Morgan 1993a, pp. 65–85.

Krueger, R.A. 1988/1994. *Focus Groups: A Practical Guide for Applied Research*. Thousand Oaks, CA: Sage, 2nd ed.

Kullberg, J.S. 1994. The ideological roots of elite political conflict in post-Soviet Russia. *Eur. Asia Stud.* 6:929–53.

Laurie, H. 1992. Multiple methods in the study of household research allocation. In *Mixing Methods: Qualitative and Quantitative Research*, ed. J Brannen, pp. 145–68. Brookfield, VT. Aveburr.

Laurie, H., and O. Sullivan. 1991. Combining qualitative and quantitative data in the longitudinal study of household allocations. *Sociol. Rev.* 39:113–30.

Lederman, L.C. 1990. Assessing educational effectiveness: the focus group interview as a technique for data collection. *Commun. Educ.* 39:117–27.

Lengua, L.J., M.W. Roosa, E. Schupak-Neuberg, M.L. Michaels, C.N. Berg, and L.F. Weschler. 1992. Using focus groups to guide the development of a parenting program for difficult-to-reach, high-risk families. *Fam. Relat.* 14:163–68.

Lincoln, Y.S., and E.G. Guba. 1985. *Naturalistic Inquiry*. Thousand Oaks, CA: Sage.

Magrill, R.S. 1993. Focus groups, program evaluation, and the poor. *J. Sociol. Soc. Welfare* 20:103–14.

McDonald, W.J. 1993. Focus group research dynamics and reporting: an examination of research objectives and moderator influences. *J. Acad. Mark. Sci.* 21:161–68.

McKinlay, J.B. 1993. The promotion of health through planned sociopolitical change: challenges for research and policy. *Soc. Sci. Med.* 36:109–17.

McQuarrie, E.F. 1990. Review of: Morgan, *Focus Groups as Qualitative Research,* and McCracken, *The Long Interview. J. Mark. Res.* 13:114–17.

McQuarrie, E.F. 1996. *The Market Research Toolbox.* Thousand Oaks, CA: Sage.

Merton, R.K. 1987. The focussed interview and focus groups: continuities and discontinuities. *Public Opin. Q.* 51:550–66.

Merton, R.K., M. Fiske, and P.L. Kendall. 1956/1990. *The Focused Interview.* New York: Free Press. 2nd ed.

Merton, R.K., and P.L. Kendall. 1946. The focussed interview. *Am. J. Sociol.* 51:541–57.

Mischler, E.G. 1986. *Research Interviewing: Context and Narrative.* Cambridge, MA: Harvard Univ. Press.

Montell, F.B. 1995. *Focus group interviews: a new feminist method.* Presented at Annu. Meet. Am. Sociol. Assoc., Washington, DC.

Morgan, D.L. 1988. *Focus Groups as Qualitative Research.* Thousand Oaks, CA: Sage.

Morgan, D.L. 1989. Adjusting to widowhood: do social networks really make it easier? *Gerontologist* 29:101–7.

Morgan, D.L. 1992a. Designing focus group research. In *Tools for Primary Care research,* ed. M. Steward, et al., pp. 177–93. Thousand Oaks, CA: Sage.

Morgan, D.L. 1992b. Doctor caregiver relationships: an exploration using focus groups. In *Doing Qualitative Research in Primary Care: Multiple Strategies,* ed. B. Crabtree, W. Miller, pp. 205–30. Thousand Oaks, CA: Sage.

Morgan, D.L. 1993a. *Successful Focus Groups: Advancing the State of Art.* Thousand Oaks, CA: Sage.

Morgan, D.L. 1993b. Future directions for focus groups. See Morgan 1993a, pp. 225–44.

Morgan, D.L. 1993c. *Focus groups and surveys.* Presented at Annu. Meet. Am. Sociol. Assoc., Pittsburg, PA.

Morgan, D.L. 1994. *Seeking diagnosis for a family member with Alzheimer's disease.* Presented at Annu. Meet. Am. Sociol. Assoc., Los Angeles, CA.

Morgan, D.L. 1995. Why things (sometimes) go wrong in focus groups. *Qual. Health Res.* 5:515–22.

Morgan, D.L., and R.A. Krueger. 1993. When to use focus groups and why. See Morgan 1993a, pp. 3–19.

Morgan, D.L., and M.T. Spanish. 1985. Social interaction and the cognitive organization of health-relevant behavior. *Sociol. Health Illness* 7:401–22.

Morgan, D.L., and P.Z. Zhao. 1993. The doctor-caregiver relationship: managing the care of family members with Alzheimer's disease. *Qual. Health Res.* 3:133–64.

Nelson, J.E., and N.T. Frontczak. 1988. How acquaintanceship and analyst can influence focus group results. *J. Advert.* 17:41–48.

Nichols-Casebolt, A., and P. Spakes. 1995. Policy research and the voices of women. *Soc. Work Res.* 19:49–55.

O'Brien, K.J. 1993. Improving survey questionnaires through focus groups. See Morgan 1993a, pp. 106–17.

O'Connor, P.J., B.F. Crabtree, and N.N. Abourizk. 1992. Longitudinal study of a diabetes education and care intervention. *J. Am. Board Fam. Practice* 5:381–87.

Orosz, J.F. 1994. *The use of focus groups in health care service delivery: understanding and improving the health care experience.* Present at Qual. Health Res. Conf., Hershey, PA.

Padilla, R. 1993. Using dialogical methods in group interviews. See Morgan 1993, pp. 153–66.

Pies, C. 1993. *Controversies in context: ethics, values, and policies concerning NORPLANT*. PhD thesis. Univ. Calif. Berkeley.

Pinderhughes, H. 1993. The anatomy of racially motivated violence in New York City: a case study of youth in southern Brooklyn. *Soc. Probl.* 40:478–92.

Pollak, M., G. Paicheler, and J. Pierret. 1992. AIDS: a problem for sociological research. *Curr. Sociol./La Sociol. Contemp.* 40:1–134.

Race K.E., D.F. Hotch, and T. Packer. 1994. Rehabilitation programs evaluation: use of focus groups to empower clients. *Eval. Rev.* 18:730–40.

Saferstein, B. 1995. *Focusing opinions: conversation, authority, and the (re)construction of knowledge*. Presented at Annu. Meet. Am. Sociol. Assoc., Washington, DC.

Saint-Germain, M.A., T.L. Bassford, and G. Montano. 1993. Surveys and focus groups in health research with older Hispanic women. *Qual. Health Res.* 3:341–67.

Sasson, T. 1995. *Crime Talk: How Citizens Construct a Social Problem*. Hawthorne, NY: Aldine.

Schearer, S.N. 1981. The value of focus groups research for social action programs. *Stud. Fam. Plan.* 12:407–8.

Shiverly, J.E. 1992. Cowboys and Indians: perceptions of Western films among American Indians and Anglos. *Am. Sociol. Rev.* 57:725–34.

Smith, M. 1995. Ethics in focus groups: a few concerns. *Qual. Health Res.* 5:478–86.

Staley, C.S. 1990. Focus group research: the communication practitioner as marketing specialist. In *Applied Communication Theory and Research*, ed. D O'Hair, G Kreps, pp. 185–201. Hillsdale, NJ: Erlbaum.

Steward, D.W., and P.N. Shamdasani. 1990. *Focus Groups: Theory and Practice*. Thousand Oaks, CA: Sage.

Stycos, J M. 1981. A critique of focus groups and survey research: the machismo case. *Stud. Fam. Plan.* 12:450–56.

Sussman, S., D. Burton, C.W. Dent, A.W. Stacy, and B.R. Flay. 1991. Use of focus groups in developing an adolescent tobacco use cessation program: collective norm effects. *J. Appl. Soc. Psychol.* 21:1772–82.

Swenson, J.D., W.F. Griswold, and P.A. Klieber. 1992. Focus groups: method of inquiry/ intervention. *Small Groups Res.* 23:459–74.

Templeton, J.F. 1987. *Focus Groups: A Guide for Marketing and Advertising Professionals*. Chicago: Probus.

Ward, V.M., J.T. Bertrand, and L.F. Brown. 1991. The comparability of focus groups and survey results. *Eval. Rev.* 15:266–83.

Wight, D. 1994. Boys' thoughts and talk about sex in a working class locality of Glasgow. *Sociol. Rev.* 42:702–37.

Wolff, B., J. Knodel, and W. Sittitrai. 1993. Focus groups and surveys as complementary research methods: a case example. See Morgan 1993a, pp. 119–36.

Zeller, R.A. 1993a. Focus group research on sensitive topics: setting the agenda without setting the agenda. See Morgan 1993a, pp. 167–83.

Zeller, R.A. 1993b. Combining qualitative and quantitative techniques to develop culturally sensitive measures. In *Methodological Issues in AIDS Behavioral Research*, ed. D. Ostrow and R. Kessler, pp. 95–116. New York: Plenum.

Why Urban Parents Resist Involvement in Their Children's Elementary Education*

PETER MCDERMOTT AND JULIA ROTHENBERG

Experienced teachers are well aware of the benefits of family involvement in children's education. In the past, parental support was always thought to be a critical component of education, and teachers assumed, whether accurately or not, that families supported their efforts and expectations for children's learning. Yet in contemporary society issues about parental support and involvement are complicated by diverse family arrangements and vast socio-cultural differences among classroom teachers, children and families. In particular, urban families are often marginalized from everyday school life by poverty, racism, language and cultural differences, and the parents often perceive that public education is designed for children from middle class, white families at the expense of others (Oakes & Lipton, 1999).

Many researchers have examined the challenges of involving low-income urban families in their children's education. Comer, Haynes, Joyner and Ben-Avie (1996) have shown how parent involvement in the most poverty stricken urban schools can improve a building's psychological climate for learning and children's academic performance. Delpit (1992) argued that families should serve as cultural informants for teachers to interpret children's behaviors. McCarthey (2000) explained how family involvement in education is influenced by culture, income, language, and the adults' perceptions of school and family responsibilities.

It is widely known that low-income urban parents are reluctant to be involved in their children's education. Hoover-Dempsey and Sandler (1997) identified three psychological factors contributing to this problem. First, the family's perceptions of their role and responsibility in their children's education is the most important factor predicting parental involvement. Middle class parents, for example, feel that they should collaborate with school efforts. But low-income families often perceive themselves as outside the school system and feel it is the school's responsibility to do the teaching. Second, parental feelings of efficacy contribute to their involvement in their children's school. Parents who believe they can make a difference in their children's education are more likely to visit and participate in school activities than those who feel ineffective. Third, some schools are more welcoming than others, and the extent to which schools make parents feel comfortable and valued contributes to the adults' participation in their children's education. Schools serving low income, ethnically diverse neighborhoods, Hoover-Dempsey and Sandler argued, must make greater efforts to welcome families, because those are the parents who often feel excluded because of differences in their ethnicity, income, and culture.

There are a variety of reasons why low income urban parents resist involvement in school activities, but certainly cultural and communication differences between teacher and families lie at the heart of the problem. Au and Mason (1981) found that when teachers' conversation styles match that of the community, children are more able and eager to participate in classroom activities. Heath (1983) discovered that children will achieve more when their home language patterns and values for literacy resemble that of the school. Cazden (1988) showed that teachers who are familiar with children's conversational styles, including the uses of silence, are more successful in their instruction than teachers who are not.

Urban teachers often lack knowledge and respect of the ethnicities and cultures of the children they teach. Baker, Kessler-Sklar, Piotrkowski and Parker (1999) discovered that teachers often have limited knowledge of what parents do at home to help children in school. Pianta, Cox, Taylor and Early (1999) found that most teacher communication with low income families consists of "low intensity" letters and flyers with little face-to-face interaction with the parents. Moreover, as their number of African American and Latino children increased in a school, fewer "high intensity" teacher contacts with families ever took place. Linek (1997) argued that many urban teachers possess a "We-Them" attitude toward urban parents and do not view them as collaborators in children's education. Valdez (1996) found that even well-meaning teachers do not recognize the impact of family beliefs and values about schooling; consequently, some parent education projects, such as those designed for Mexican American immigrants, do more harm than good because they do not build on the families' cultural capital. Recently, Nieto (1999) and Bloom, Katz, Slosken, Willet and Wilson-Keenan (2000) have emphasized that teachers must establish respectful and trusting social relationships with children and families, and this is essential for any efforts to improve urban education.

Recent research indicates that family resistance to school involvement can be reversed. This can be accomplished when teachers actively develop an understanding of children's cultural backgrounds, and when teachers make sustained and creative efforts to collaborate with families. Edwards, Pleasants, and Franklin (1999) show how "family stories" can inform classroom teachers about children's literary backgrounds—family stories about children's reading experiences have helped teachers discard stereotyped notions of literacy in the inner cities. Nistler and Maiers (2000) demonstrated how urban families can become successful collaborators in primary grade children's literacy learning. Like Delpit's notion of cultural informants, Nistler and Maiers argue that urban families can provide teachers with "talent, energy, and insight" (p. 671) about children's learning. They described how parents who were scheduled to participate each Friday in classroom literacy activities became empowered and real contributors to their children's education.

For nearly ten years we have worked with an urban after school literacy program where our graduate and undergraduate students have tutored children (McDermott, Rothenburg, & Gormley, 1999). Yet throughout this time we did not consciously elicit parental concerns about their involvement in local public schools. Our practica students held individual parent conferences to discuss children's literacy growth, and each spring we held a "Literacy Celebration" where children shared their reading and writing with their families. Yet we never asked the parents about the extent of their participation in their children's schooling. Recently, we also wondered what our best cooperating teachers said about urban family involvement in school. Consequently in this study we examined the following questions: (1) What do low-income parents say about their involvement in their children's education? (2) In what ways do low-income parents and teachers agree or differ about family involvement in school activities? By investigating answers to these questions we might find ways to better prepare new teachers for urban schools. In addition, as we grow in our own understanding of effective family involvement, we can influence the local public schools' relationship with the low-income families with whom our students work.

METHOD

This study generates from several that we have recently conducted about teaching in high poverty urban schools. In the first study we used a rating scale of best teachers and a Likert survey of teachers from high poverty buildings (McDermott & Rothenberg, 1999). In the second study (McDermott & Rothenberg, 2000) we conducted qualitative focus group interviews of teachers, children, and parents in low-income settings. This present paper reports our findings from the focus groups with urban parents and teachers.

THE SETTING

The setting for this study is an intrinsic component of our method. We conducted the study in a small Northeastern city. Like many cities throughout the Northeast, this city had undergone a collapse of its century old textile industry. As its factories moved out, downtown buildings that previously contained bustling restaurants and department stores closed. The city's population decreased from nearly 100,000 at the turn of the 20th century to about 60,000 at the present time. The drop in the city's size has coincided with a growth in the African American and Latino population.

The college is located in the city's downtown neighborhood. One block away are four high rise public housing buildings, home to approximately four hundred families. Ninety-five percent of the children living there are African American and Puerto Rican. There is a good deal of interaction between the college community and the residents of the housing project. Much of this interaction takes place in the context of practica required in the college students' course work.

One urban school district and an after-school arts and literacy program, in particular, served as the physical and social context for the study. A few years ago the city school district integrated its elementary schools. The elementary building serving the downtown housing project had become highly segregated with low-income children of color. Consequently, the district decided to bus children from the downtown housing project to a more affluent elementary school that is located on the hill in one of the city's remaining middle class neighborhoods.

DATA COLLECTION

Our qualitative methods evolved from the first part of a previous study (McDermott & Rothenberg, 1999). That study incorporated a selection of teachers in urban and rural low-income schools, based on observation and reports from informants in each school. Our definition of a good teacher was one who, at any level of teaching, created and cultivated ongoing learning. We administered a survey of teaching practices and beliefs, using a Likert measurement scale. Among the highly ranked results, which included the important of both structure and flexibility, personal warmth and empathy, respect for children and their cultures, and knowledge of subject matter, there were several anomalies. The teachers, who were mostly white, decried children's dialects and grammar, felt that children should never use home language in school. The teachers did not believe that their participation in the community was important to their teaching.

We decided to investigate the teachers' opinions about language and community participation further. Consequently, we developed a focus group of four teachers from the original 25 who completed the Likert survey. Based on previous research (Madriz, 2000; Morgan, 1988) we felt that a focus group, consisting of teachers we knew well, would allow us to explore contradictions and complexities of the teaching beliefs from the survey.

One of the focus group discussions examined teachers' perceptions about parent involvement. The poverty levels of the schools where the teachers worked ranged from 83% to 90%. African American and Latino children comprised one third to one half the student population in the urban buildings. During the focus group the teachers produced additional comments that were similar to the results from the Likert survey. We met with the four teachers twice for about 90 minutes each, on May 15 and October 16 of 1998. Two of the teachers taught first grade and two were newly appointed assistant principals in two high poverty elementary buildings. One teacher dropped out after the first meeting because of a back injury.

We designed our parent focus group to generate discussion with the least intrusion of power elements that might be introduced by us. We decided to use a study room in the apartments where the parents lived, that was a block from our college. We chose focus groups as our method because of its valued use with marginalized participants, in this case people who are minorities, women, and of lower socioeconomic status (Madrix, 2000). Methodologically, we placed ourselves in the framework of standpoint research because we viewed this group as constructivist, developing their own knowledge and ways of working with it, both within and outside the group (Olesen, 1994).

We had additional reasons for using focus groups as our research method: We selected focus groups because we anticipated that they would offer a non-threatening and comfortable social context when interviewing people who have been alienated from the public education system. The goal of the focus groups was to describe and explain the points of view of inner city parents and teachers about urban education. We anticipated that the social support and camaraderie of focus groups might help the parents when conversing with us, who are college faculty, European Americans, and outsiders to their socio-cultural communities. Furthermore, we thought that our social roles and color might inadvertently serve as a communication barrier between ourselves and the low-income parents we wanted to interview. Consequently, we thought a group interview context might be more comfortable and supportive for the parents as we discussed their children's education. Labov (1972) used a similar research strategy when he interviewed inner city adolescents in his classic sociolinguistic study of dialect. We knew that recent educational research texts (Gay, 1996; Krathwohl, 1997) discussed focus groups as valid and efficient methods for data collection.

We experienced some difficulty scheduling the parent groups. Although the first one proceeded as scheduled, only one parent attended the second scheduled meeting. That parent explained that the others had already attended a housing project meeting the previous night, and that was why, she thought, no one else came. It took two more weeks before we could identify a night that other parents might come, and at that meeting five parents attended. We met with them on June 10, 1999, and May 25, 2000. We first sent the parents a flyer asking to meet and discuss their thoughts about their children's best teachers. We did this because we wanted to conduct the focus groups in a positive manner and not use the meetings as gripe sessions. At the first year's focus group seven women, including three African American, three Latina, and one European American participated. In the second year five parents attended; three were Latina, one African American and one European American. The majority of the women attending were in their late twenties. A few were in their mid-thirties and there was one older parent of about 45 years of age. The first year's focus group lasted for one and a half hours, and the second about one hour. We contacted the parents through the after-school arts and literacy project where our college students tutored children. Teachers from the arts and literacy program helped us contact the parents, but we also relied on one parent who helped us schedule the meeting nights.

When we met with the teachers we questioned them about their thoughts pertaining to cultural responsiveness, language diversity, and methods of teaching in low-income schools. We used different kinds of questions with the parent focus group: (1) Have your children had really good teachers and what were they like? (2) What do you think the principal should tell teachers to assist them with their teaching? (3) What kinds of things should new teachers know when teaching in city schools? And for the second year we added, (4) what do you think teachers should do to help parents feel comfortable about attending school events?

One researcher interviewed the parents and the other served as an outside reader of the field notes. Both researchers participated in the teacher focus groups. During the focus groups we wrote verbatim and paraphrased entries about what the respondents said. Afterwards these notes were typed and filled-in with contextual information. We analyzed the notes by testing for emerging categories, patterns, and themes that we detected (Lincoln & Guba, 1985). During the first focus group, the parents built upon what each other said and the conversation became rich and energetic. In the first focus group in particular, the parents expressed frustration and anger about their relationships with school personnel. In the second focus group, some of the parents expressed more contentment and comfort with their children's teachers and the assistant principal. Pseudonyms are used throughout the paper.

RESULTS

We first present data from our teacher focus group, and then share our findings from the parents. Data representing salient moments from these focus groups discussions are presented. That is, we offer data that revealed the frustrations and conflict expressed by the participants in the study. This data is representative of the information and emotional tone shared and displayed during the focus group discussions with the urban parents and teachers.

Data from the Teacher Focus Groups

This focus group consisted of some of the best urban teachers we knew. We had worked with them for many years, and they were well respected by other college faculty and colleagues in their schools. Yet, even this well regarded group admitted an overall lack of success at involving urban families in school events.

The teachers recognized the importance of parental involvement in children's education, but they knew they were unsuccessful in this aspect of their teaching. They thought the mobility of low-income urban people contributed to their lack of involvement in school activities. Diane said that the composition of children in many classrooms changed by half over the course of an academic year. Dorothy agreed, saying that the transience of families, as well as their own alienation from the public educational system, explained the lack of family involvement in school events. "Maybe the difference is that in my school's community the families are transitional. Parents are new to the community and many of them move in and out of it (over the course of the school year) . . . "

Frustration characterized many of the teachers' statements about parental involvement. "We have trouble getting them to conferences. . . . They are always working," Meg complained. The teachers acknowledged the importance of involving parents in family literacy events, but they admitted they had little success with it. "We need to teach parents again . . . we have tried [to teach them about literacy activities] . . . but many of the parents are so young, and they are afraid to come to school because of their own [poor] school experiences."

Dorothy gave specific examples of the lack of parental involvement in her school's recent Open House: " . . . this year I only had five out of 19 parents attend. Last year it was worse, with only one parent attending. So, I don't know."

The teachers thought the lack of family involvement in school was an increasing problem. They sensed that parents had become more resigned and removed from the impersonal forces of large city school district. They thought that many parents felt urban schools were unresponsive to their children's learning needs. They felt there was a general deterioration in family involvement as children progressed through school. "In first grade, more parents are actively involved . . . they are still clinging to their children . . . but in a few years they have bought into the system and they have accepted their children's problems and accepted the system [for good and bad]."

Yet unlike many other teachers from high poverty schools who often give up, this group still held high standards for children's learning. They supported Meg's comment, "All the children are going to leave my classroom reading!"

Meg shared her frustration about getting parents to attend school conferences, but said she would no longer accept excuses: "They may have good excuses for not coming to school, but they are not good enough for me anymore! " Yet at the same time, she said it was her responsibility to make sure children learn in her classroom. She did not scapegoat and said that she frequently wakes up at four in the morning to plan ideas for her teaching.

Teachers shared interesting comments about culture and teaching. They said they tried to integrate children's cultural experiences into their lessons. Meg matter of factly said, "You have to include children's language into your teaching . . . at my school we have 28 ESL children from Asia, Africa, and South American countries . . . schools are getting more students from other countries and teachers are incorporating these cultural experiences into their lessons." Dorothy elaborated, "It is the right thing to do. A few years ago several of our teachers received a teacher grant for 'Walk a Mile in My

Shoes.' " This was a faculty and student collaboration to study cultural and ethnic differences in their schools. The teachers discussed the importance of selecting literature that illustrated the children's cultural backgrounds. Dorothy gave one example of tying literature to children's linguistic backgrounds, "There is a book I like to read to my children. It is by Lois Erhart and it is bilingual." Teachers stressed the importance of integrating children's cultural knowledge throughout the curriculum. Diane explained that she used social studies to discuss children's cultural backgrounds by using music, food, literature, dance . . . and guest speakers. "I even integrate cultural knowledge into science," Diane proudly added.

Data from the Parent Focus Group

The data in this section comes from the voices of six mothers who participated in our focus groups. The women are as follows: Mrs. Herrera, a Latina immigrant from Puerto Rico; Mrs. Davis, an older African American woman; Mrs. Taylor, an African American woman who recently finished her degree at a local university; Mrs. Howard, an African American woman; Mrs. Figuerra, a young monolingual parent from Puerto Rico, and Mrs. Evers, the only white woman in the group.

The women said they were very concerned about their children's education. They also said that their children have benefited from some good classroom teachers. Several parents, in both the first and second year focus groups, spoke about a kindergarten teacher who was particularly kind to their children; although she was strict teacher, she looked for positive qualities in each child. Mrs. Herrera, said, "Mrs. DeSantis loves children." When asked how she knew that, Mrs. Herrera said, "She hugs and kisses them!" Although this might seem incidental to being a good teacher, the parents frequently discussed the importance of teachers being respectful and loving of their children. Displaying respect for children and their work such as hugging in kindergarten and praising in upper grades may be more important when teaching children in low-income families than middle class ones whose families are already well established and connected in the communities.

Other parents agreed about their experiences with Mrs. DeSantis, whom they all liked. This teacher frequently sent notes home to the parents. This teacher, Mrs. Evers said, " . . . affirmed my child . . . Mrs. DeSantis is really good." Mrs. Evers added that this teacher taught her daughter, Liz, to express her feelings: "Mrs. De Santis drew 'happy faces' on her work . . . she sent notes home about Liz and kept me informed." Another mother, Mrs. Taylor said, "She gives positive reinforcement . . . she recognized my child as 'star of the month!' " They said Mrs. DeSantis even came to visit the housing project to see the after-school program. Mrs. Evers said, "Mrs. DeSantis stayed in contact with me, even after Liz was promoted to the next grade . . . Mrs. DeSantis left space on her notes for me to write back . . . She emphasized choices for kindergartners. But some people say too rigid . . . Keeps them at their desks, but I like her."

Parents believed it was essential that teachers were positive with their children. Good teachers complimented children frequently about their work and made children feel good about being in school. Mrs. Taylor said, "I like it when teachers look for the positive in kids . . . Everyone has something positive . . . Children pick up on it . . . Children like compliments . . . Teachers need to look for the positive." Conversely, the parents repeatedly spoke about how the communication they typically received from school was negative. They shared anecdotes about school suspensions, placement of their children in special education programs, and retention. Mrs. Taylor, a particularly articulate mother, shared her frustration with her daughter's school: She was " . . . sick of hearing the word 'immaturity' " . . . this word was a code (word) to retain kids . . . it was used to retain children of color . . . They track my child by saying she is immature . . . It is the same negativity!" Mrs. Taylor told the other parents they should not feel "intimidated by school . . . I know they don't make you feel comfortable . . . They throw language at you . . . How many black kids did Piaget study? It makes you feel uncomfortable . . . teachers should communicate so you understand . . . teachers need to be creative . . . build on what my daughter knows . . . I had some fights with her teacher . . . Parents should not back off . . . I don't care what they (the teachers) think of me . . . "

In the second focus group parents shared a coping strategy for interacting with the teachers. In last year's focus group Mrs. Herrera said she was nervous and uncomfortable when visiting the school. When she went to the school her English became awkward, and she could not understand what the principal or classroom teacher told her. So this year she brings her own interpreter, a teacher from the arts and literacy program!

Evidently, the school also improved its strategies for working with families from the housing project. The assistant principal, for instance, came down from the school to visit the housing projects several times. He helped with the bus and he removed dead pigeons from under the bridge that were frightening the children. The parents said this "showed that he cared" to come to the river and visit their community.

Parents appealed for good communication skills in their children's teachers. The best teachers communicated frequently through notes and telephone conversations with the parents. Parents liked teachers who sent home weekly newsletters or notes. They appreciated phone calls and loved it when teachers visited the afternoon tutoring program in the housing project, as a guidance counselor and kindergarten teacher had recently done. Parents discussed how communication difficulties were a major problem with their children's school. Mrs. Howard said, "Last year I didn't know that my child was doing poorly . . . the report card said everything was good, yet at the end of the year, she said my child needed to be left back . . . this year the same thing is happening . . . they keep telling me everything is good until the end of the year, he is left back." Mrs. Taylor echoed a similar feeling about her child's teacher, "Same thing with Tonya, I didn't know . . . they never let you know . . . never once told me she wasn't doing well . . . they don't tell me what's going on . . . this year I know how my daughter is doing." Mrs. Taylor said, "No mother wants to hear her child is doing badly. I want to know how to help . . . constructive criticism . . . come up with a plan!"

The parents confirmed what the teachers in our focus group said about parent involvement in school events—parents were so busy it was difficult for them to visit. Of course, there was more to it than that. Many of the parents worked. However, their jobs consisted of low wage, low skill employment. So although most worked, they were employed in poorly paid positions, that offered few benefits or security. Consequently, none of them had cars, and to visit the school required a great deal of planning to take time from work and arrange for transportation. It was not simply a matter of jumping into a car and driving up to the school for an hour. Moreover, the parents felt anxious about visiting the school. They generally perceived schools as racist institutions. For example, some parents thought their children were "singled-out" whenever there was a problem in school. Given these issues as well as others, it is no wonder that they have been "always busy" and unable to attend school events.

"Parents have something to do all the time," Mrs. Evers explained. "So teachers should send home notes." "Each child is an individual," she added. "Teachers should call the mother if there is a bad day . . . maybe the mother can work with the child . . . they should give information to the mother . . . let the parent know, nip it in the bud." Mrs. Evers continued, "Some teachers show favoritism . . . sometimes it is the way they talk with children." Mrs. Davis added, "My child says, 'they dis me.' Parents should nip it in the bud!"

We often needed to redirect discussion during the first focus group because of the negative tone of much to what parents said. At that time parents spoke far more about negative experiences with urban teachers than positive. Unanimously, the parents said they felt unwelcome and uncomfortable in the school to which their children were bussed. They complained that many of the teachers "spoke down" to them, some "brushed them off," and others did not answer their questions. Mrs. Howard shared how she felt a teacher was disingenuous to her and her daughter, Alena. The family has a genetic eye disorder that has been passed down through at least three generations, but she said it had no relationship to intelligence. In February of this year the third grade teacher said Alena needed to be retained. "My child came to school in January, but in February they told me she should be left back—only one month and they decided this! They never gave her a chance . . . stigmatized!"

Parents in the first focus group said teachers did not like being questioned about their teaching methods. They spoke about the principal who did not speak respectfully with them. They wished the school used interpreters to help with Spanish speaking parents. All the parents wanted to be part of their children's education, but they felt excluded because of negative attitudes they perceived in teachers. Mrs. Herrera said, "I feel like dumb going to the school . . . I'm not comfortable . . . I don't feel welcome . . . They don't interpret for me . . . Teachers look at us as beggars . . . " Parents said the teachers have poor communication skills and lack respect for Latino and African American people.

Good communication skills and respect for children and their families reappeared as the most desirable teacher characteristic for these parents. These qualities ran throughout the focus group discussion and were evidenced in each of their anecdotes. The parents also wanted teachers who knew how to teach their children well. They wanted teachers who would be "kind but strict," and they did not want their children "babied." Their children needed to be "pushed to the limit," but done in ways to make "learning fun." For example, like learning a "rap song would be fun!" "Some teachers," Mrs. Taylor said, "baby the kids so much the children believe they are inferior."

The parents also discussed culture and teaching. Mrs. Taylor said, "New teachers should be aware of not just reading 'white' books . . . they should make an effort to celebrate 'Kwansa' because more families are doing it and children should share it . . . teachers should look into the holidays . . . they [teachers] should visit here." Mrs. Figuera said (as interpreted by Mrs. Herrera), "It is harder on the Spanish-speaking children to read cursive, so teachers should also print."

Three important topics repeatedly appeared throughout our with the parents: 1) Teachers need to display respect and love for children. 2) They should communicate frequently with families, and this can be done through notes, newsletters, and telephoning the mothers at home or work. 3) Teachers should visit their community because this shows interest and care for children and their families.

DISCUSSION

In recent presentations at the meetings of the American Educational Research Association (e.g., Allexsaht-Snider, 2000; Gunn-Morris, 2000; Hoover-Dempsey, Walker, Jones, & Reed, 2000) researchers reported difficulties that teachers experienced in working closely with urban parents. These papers explained that teachers need a whole new set of skills and new psychological dynamics for engaging urban parents in meaningful discussions about their children and their children's learning, especially for children with learning difficulties. Urban teachers reported that their administrators supported neither their efforts nor their problems when it came to parents. Administrators would bow to the easiest solution, and encourage them to avoid future problems with parents. There are very real issues, particularly if, as we believe, engagement with parents is important for low-income children to succeed and for meaningful school reform in low-income urban schools.

This year we are beginning a study with novice teachers, introducing skills, issues, and experiences in working with low income, urban parents.

But we find it increasingly difficult to fit into our syllabi, already crowded with new standards, and all that we want and need to teach. This points further to the need for longer teacher preparation programs and more experiences for novice teachers directly in schools while being mentored. It is vital that this experience occurs during the preparation program, given the ambivalence of many schools toward parent engagement.

Urban school districts know the influence families have on children's education. Yet, except in a few rare cases, urban districts are notoriously ineffective at involving parents in school activities. The teachers in our focus group, whom we believed were highly experienced and skilled, admitted they had little success at involving urban families in their children's education. As one teacher said, "They [parents] are always busy."

Our data revealed the urban mothers who participated in our focus groups said they were very concerned about their children's education. They also indicated in many ways that the schools were not welcoming or considerate of their circumstances. Parents from our first year's focus group revealed a surprising point of view about school involvement—they deliberately decided to withdraw from school activities because they thought the school was racist.

Many of the parents' comments indicated that they perceived the school as representing the values and interests of established white America and not the needs of low-income people of color. We suspect the parents assumed a "We-Them" attitude about their children's teachers, similar to what teachers assumed of them. Whether fairly or not, the parents perceived the public school to be unwelcoming, and social interaction with teachers became painful encounters. Even during our second focus group, when parents were far more positive about the school's efforts, some parents thought teachers unfairly blamed their children for classroom incidents because they lived in public housing and were bussed to school.

The urban teachers expressed frustration with parental involvement. Although they believed in family participation, they despaired at improving it. However, the teachers did not know that parents deliberately decided to stop supporting school events. Even on seemingly straightforward issues, such as homework, the teachers did not understand the parents' perspective. Teachers complained parents did not help children with their schoolwork, but the parents explained they did not know what homework teachers assigned their children. This frustration and anger felt by the parents were indications of the gulf existing between the community and school.

A year later, there were indications of improvement in the communication between parents and the school. Parents praised the vice-principal who visited their community, and they said one of the teachers visited the after-school arts and literacy program. Parents said these visits showed they cared about the children. There was additional evidence that the parents were learning how to better communicate with the school. Last year one of the parents said the school should provide an interpreter for teacher conferences, but this year she brought her interpreter with her whenever she visited the building. However, even though communication had improved, parents continued to be wary of the school's ability to help.

Social relationships are what drive parents' perceptions of their children's school. There are already so many social barriers between the school and the families due to differences in skin color, ethnicity, culture, and language that the parents are highly sensitive to whether teachers respect their children. The parents said they could recognize when teachers do not appreciate their children. Given the frequency in which this issue emerged in our focus groups, it is clear that teachers' ability to convey kindness and respect for children and their families is essential for their classroom effectiveness and any family support that they might obtain.

Urban parents are more likely to participate in school activities when they feel their children are respected, and their communities and heritages are valued. Yet the parents admitted that they often were busy and could not attend school events. This is, perhaps, why they valued frequent communication from the teachers. However, when parents perceived that the teachers did not like their children, they would not participate or contribute in school activities.

Schools are responsible for establishing open communication with parents. Yet, we learned that teachers, even the exemplary ones, expected parents to communicate with the schools in middle class ways, such as telephoning them, visiting, and writing notes. But parents in our focus group felt vulnerable with school authority, and they could not comfortably communicate with teachers in ways that white, middle class families were accustomed. These urban parents did not have cars and could not easily visit the school. Some of them spoke English hesitantly, and most, we infer, felt anxious about their own writing.

Urban schools need alternative ways of connecting and communicating with parents who live in high poverty areas. For example, the conventional "Parents Night" might be placed at a community room in the neighborhood where families live. Schools with children who are acquiring English should plan for interpreters when parents attend conferences and other school events. While some of the parents are bilingual, we know their anxiety about visiting school still blocks their ability to understand what teachers say to them.

Teacher education programs must prepare new teachers to work effectively with parents. New teachers need to learn a variety of strategies and skills to involve urban parents in their children's education. Teachers must learn to communicate clearly and sensitively with adults of different ethnic and cultural backgrounds. They must learn strategies that allow parents to collaborate in their children's education; evidence from other studies indicates that exemplary teachers view families as collaborators in their children's education (Alvarez & Williams, 1998; Ladson-Billings, 1994) and not as clients or adversaries.

White, middle class teachers must learn to build trusting and respectful relationships with low-income people of color, and these strategies will differ from what they are accustomed. Teachers should learn about the ethnicities of the children they teach and develop culturally sensitive ways of connecting and establishing good relationships within those communities.

Communicating effectively in multiethnic communities is essential for today's teachers. From the very beginning of their practica placements prospective teachers should learn the importance of parental participation in children's education and ways to bring it about. Prospective teachers must acquire both "low and high intensity" strategies for communicating and working with urban parents. Introductory course work should help students understand their own values and attitudes about diversity. The same course work should provide them opportunities to see and hear what urban life is like for families in high poverty neighborhoods. After acquiring a better understanding of themselves and others, prospective teachers can develop communication strategies that can make a difference when teaching in urban classrooms.

Methods course work should provide opportunities for prospective teachers to learn how to write effective notes, letters, and newsletters to families. Prospective teachers must learn how to display their value and respect for the cultural backgrounds of the children they teach. They need to learn how schools should be transformed so that cultural and ethnic diversity is celebrated throughout the school year; such celebrations should be evident the moment one walks into a building and its classrooms. Teachers should learn to display books and media representing children's cultural backgrounds. Frequent notes and letters to families acknowledging children's strengths are also helpful.

Urban schools might make greater use of "looping" models of instruction. With "looping" children remain with the same teacher for two years. So, for example, a first grade teacher would move-up to second grade to follow her students as they are promoted. The advantage of looping in terms of family involvement is that teachers will have greater opportunity to construct long lasting relationships with parents and family members. Less learning time will be lost at the beginning of a school year because the classroom teacher already knows the children and their families.

Prospective teachers must learn how to conduct effective parent conferences. They should learn conversational strategies that focus on children's positive qualities as well as identify ways they might grow and be helped at home. Teacher education programs should encourage prospective teachers to visit urban communities. Although many urban neighborhoods are plagued by violence, there are ways teachers can safely visit; for example, teachers might visit community centers, churches and after-school programs. Teachers can attend cultural events that are held in urban neighborhoods. These are all gestures that will may help break social and ethnic barriers and foster understanding and respect between family and schools.

From this study we learned the great value of constructing strong, trusting relationships with families and children. Nieto (1999) and Ladson-Billings (1994) argue that meaningful relationships between teachers and the urban communities lie at the heart of effective urban teaching, and the results of our study support their argument. Unfortunately, some of the parents in our study lacked trust and respect for their children's school. We have also learned that teacher education programs must do much more for helping prospective teachers learn about the urban families and neighborhoods of the children they will teach.

NOTE

*We presented an earlier version of this paper at the Twelfth Annual Conference on Ethnographic and Qualitative Research in Education, State University of New York at Albany, June 9–10, 2000.

REFERENCES

Allexsaht-Snider, M. 2000. *Families, schools and communities: Research & practice*. Paper presented at the meetings of the American Educational Research Association, New Orleans LA, April 2000.

Alvarez, T., and D. Williams. 1998. *African-American and Latino teachers' perspectives on successful inner-city teaching*. Ethnography in Education Research Forum, University of Pennsylvania Center for Urban Ethnography, Philadelphia PA, March 5–7.

Au, K.H., and J.M. Mason. 1981. Social organizational factors in learning to read: The balance of rights hypothesis. *Reading Research Quarterly* 17(1): 115–52.

Baker, A., S. Kessler-Sklar, C. Piotrkowski, and F. Parker. 1999. Kindergarten and first-grade teachers' reported knowledge of parents' involvement in their children's education. *The Elementary School Journal* 99: 367–379.

Bloom, D., L. Katz, J. Solsken, J. Willet, and J. Wilson-Keenan. 2000. Interpellations of family and classroom literacy practices. *Journal of Educational Research* 93: 155–163.

Cazden, C. 1988. *Classroom discourse: The language of teaching and learning*. Portsmouth, NH: Heinemann Publications.

Comer, J., N. Haynes, E. Joyner, and M. Ben-Avie, eds. 1996. *Rallying the whole village: The Comer process for reforming education*. NY: Teachers College Press.

Delpit, L. 1992. Education in a multicultural society: Our future's greatest challenge. *Journal of Negro Education* 61: 237–249.

Edwards, P., H. Pleasants, and S. Franklin. 1999. *A path to follow: Learning to listen to parents*. Portsmouth, NH: Heinemann.

Gay, L. 1996. *Educational research: Competencies for analysis and application* (5th Ed.). NY: Merrrill.

Gunn-Morris, V. 2000. *Preparing for family involvement*. Paper presented at the meetings of the American Educational Research Association, New Orleans, LA, April.

Heath, S.B. 1983. *Ways with words: Language, life, and work in communities and classrooms*. Cambridge: Cambridge University Press.

Hoover-Dempsey, K., and H. Sandler. 1997. Why do parents become involved in their children's education. *Review of Educational Research* 67: 3–42.

Hoover-Dempsey, K., and J. Walker, K. Jones, and R. Reed. 2000. *Teachers involving parents (TIP): An inservice teacher education program for enhancing parental involvement.* Paper presented at the Annual Meeting of the American Education Research Association, New Orleans, LA.

Krathwohl, D. 1997. *Educational and social science research: An integrated approach* (2nd Ed.). New York: Longman.

Labov, W. 1972. *Language in the inner city: Studies in the black English vernacular.* Philadelphia: University of Pennsylvania Press.

Ladson-Billings, G. 1994. *The dream keepers: Successful teachers of African American children.* San Francisco: Jossey Bass.

Lincoln, Y., & E. Guba. 1985. *Naturalistic inquiry.* Beverly Hills, CA: Sage Publications.

Linek, W., T. Rasinski, and D. Harkins. 1997. Teacher perceptions of parent involvement in literacy education. *Reading Horizons* 38: 90–106.

Madriz, E. 2000. Focus groups in feminist research, pp. 835–850 In *Handbook of Qualitative Research* (2nd Ed.), ed. N. Denzin and Y. Lincoln. Thousand Oaks, CA: Sage Publications.

McCarthey, S. (2000). Home-school connections: A review of the literature. *The Journal of Educational Research*, 93, 145–153.

McDermott, P. and J. Rothenberg. 2000.*Triangulating data about exemplary urban teachers with focus groups.* Paper Presented at the 21st Annual Ethnography in Education Research Forum Center for Urban Ethnography University of Pennsylvania, March 3–5.

McDermott, P. & J. Rothenberg. 1999. *Teaching in high poverty, urban schools—Learning from practitioners and students.* Paper presented at the Annual Meeting of the American Education Research Association, Montreal, Canada, April 19–23. (ERIC Document Reproduction Service No. ED 408 346)

McDermott, P., J. Rothenberg, and K. Gormley. 1999. The impact of community and school practica on new urban teachers. *The Educational Forum* 63: 180–185.

Morgan, D.L. 1988. *Focus groups as qualitative research.* Newbury Park, CA: Sage Publications.

Neito, S. 1999. *The light in their eyes: Creating multicultural learning communities.* New York: Teachers College Press.

Nistler, R., and A. Maiers. 2000. Stopping the silence: Hearing parents' voices in an urban first-grade family literacy program. *The Reading Teacher* 53: 670–680.

Oakes, J., and M. Lipton. 1999. *Teaching to change the world.* Boston: McGraw Hill.

Olesen, V. 1994. Feminisms and models of qualitative research, pp. 158–174 in *Handbook for Qualitative Research*, ed. N.K. Denzin and Y.S. Lincoln. Thousand Oaks: Sage Publications.

Pianta, R., M. Cox, L. Taylor, and D. Early. 1999. Kindergarten teachers' practices related to the transition to school: Results of a national survey. *Journal of Teacher Education* 100: 71–86.

Valdez, G. 1996. *Con respecto: Bridging the distances between culturally diverse families and schools: An ethnographic portrait.* New York: Teachers College Press.

PART III

UNOBTRUSIVE METHODS, VISUAL RESEARCH, AND CULTURAL STUDIES

Unobtrusive qualitative methods rely on nonliving forms of data generally subsumed under the category "texts." Major advantages to working with these forms of data are that they are noninteractive and exist independent of the research process (Reinharz, 1992:147–48). These qualities of texts add a built-in dimension of authenticity to the qualitative research process. Researchers do not produce data specifically for research but rather investigate existing cultural texts, hence the term "unobtrusive." Data can range from historical archival documents to current cultural texts. Historically, "content analysis" constituted the primary practice within unobtrusive methods. Generally this involved the examination of written textual artifacts. Typically, researchers using content analysis were considered little more than "bean counters"; however, quantitative researchers, on their own and in conjunction with qualitative practice, have repeatedly shown the importance of content analysis as a method of gaining "hard data" on macro-processes. These efforts have been effective in not only creating new knowledge but also directly impacting social policy.

The traditional quantitative practice of content analysis is an important part of social scientific practice. The strength of this method is that it enables researchers to examine patterns and themes within the artifacts produced by a culture. In other words, researchers analyze preexisting data in order to reveal large-scale, or macro, processes. The quantitative practice of content analysis is important because researchers are able to present their findings on clear and concise charts and tables, frequently in the form of statistics. This is a powerful tool when attempting to call attention to systemic practices of inequality and/or attempting to alter public policy. In terms of contributing to our knowledge about social inequality, quantitative content analysis has been a staple method for analyzing the socialization process, which is the process by which people internalize the norms and values of their culture. For example, Brabant and Mooney (1997) analyzed "sex-role stereotyping" in the Sunday comics, ultimately revealing the biased ways in which males and females are portrayed in relation to housework (Wysocki, 2001:248–49). While an analysis of comics may at first glance seem trivial, Briabant and Mooney used their 3-year longitudinal study as an example of gender-role socialization. Comics are directed at children and accordingly are a valuable example of how our artifacts teach larger ideas about what it means to be male or female. The power of Brabant and Mooney's work lies in its use of "found" data and the ability of the researchers to reduce their findings to clear quantitative results.

Likewise, traditional content analysis has been used to help shape public policy by calling our attention to systemic inequalities in need of transformation. The problem in question is frequently related to the way we socialize citizens. Content analysis has revealed a range of biases in school textbooks and in standardized testing procedures. This practice has a relatively long history in the social sciences. For example, James A. Banks (1969) conducted a quantitative content analysis of American textbooks in order to examine how these materials portrayed African Americans. Through a careful coding process, where terms and phrases from the books were placed into code categories (hence the misnomer "bean counting"), Banks revealed large-scale patterns in the representation of African Americans in the American school system (a primary institution of socialization). More recently Wysocki and Harrison (1991) conducted a content analysis of periodicals in order to reveal patterns of AIDS representation. This process of data collection enabled the researchers to effectively examine the way knowledge about AIDS is transmitted to children and teenagers. These kinds of research are often used in changing public policy—whether the change is a reevaluation of standard textbooks or a reexamination of sex and drug education. But content analysis and newer forms of unobtrusive methods can do more than reveal patterns and themes. They can also help researchers to *explain* macro social processes.

Over the past 25 years there has been a huge surge in the development and practice of unobtrusive methods, which are now frequently used to analyze written, visual, audio, and audiovisual texts. Qualitative researchers working in a range of epistemological traditions have been at the forefront of the effort to develop and implement these new methodologies. The rapid increase in the qualitative practice of unobtrusive methodologies is inextricably linked to a growing academic interest in cultural studies and related programs such as American studies and African American studies.

UNOBTRUSIVE METHODS AND CULTURAL STUDIES

The postmodernist critique of social science knowledge production has been one the most significant factors in the expanded academic interest in cultural studies that has increased the use of unobtrusive methodologies. Postmodern theory has thus informed the development of cultural studies as a distinct sphere of inquiry. The ideas contained in the theoretical frameworks of postmodernism and cultural studies often are explored and evidenced best using unobtrusive methodologies. In other words, postmodern theory is informed through unobtrusive methods explicitly illustrating the profound link between theory and methods in the actual practice of social scientific research. Perhaps the most significant recent contribution to critical scholarship is Michel Foucault's (1978) assertion that power and knowledge are linked, together forming a complex web of power-knowledge relations. In essence, Foucault explains that all knowledge is contextually bound and specifically produced within a field of shifting power relations. Scholars must interrogate cultural texts and discursive practice (i.e., the specific ways that language is used within texts) in order to reveal traces of the dominant worldview embedded within the artifact as a result of the process by which it was produced. This is a theoretical position that is enabled by unobtrusive methodologies. Foucault advocates an archeological method of inquiry to unravel how a text assumed its present form (Prior, 1997). This specific technique relies on tracing the artifact's process of production.

Some researchers have given names, or terminology, to the tenets of cultural studies theory. Roland Barthes (1957, 1998) argues for the necessity of semiological analyses of representations. Barthes developed a tri-partite system detailing how people, places, times, and events (the signified) are distilled into signifiers (concepts) that are then planted in a host of signs (representations). This process gives culturally specific interpretive practices the appearance of nature or fact. In other words, researchers must analyze the signs or representations produced within a culture in order to deconstruct the process of meaning construction that created them, which necessarily occured within a power-charged context. Semiological analysis focuses on unraveling social processes of making meaning. Here again we can see how theory is enabled, exemplified, and elaborated by a particular set of methodological practices. The recent widespread use of unobtrusive methods by researchers working within the growing field of cultural studies, from postmodernist and other critical theoretical positions, makes sense as we look at how these theoretical positions are informed by these practical forms of data collection.

Why study texts? What does it mean to say that power-knowledge relations are embedded within the text? Stuart Hall (1981), a pioneer in the field of cultural studies, explains that cultural texts not only reflect the social world, but also are a part of the process of constituting social reality. Representations are the end-products of cultural work and embody ideological practice (Hall, 1981). In this view it is clear that texts do not mirror our cultural history but rather help to shape it. It is within cultural texts that hegemony is enacted, contested, resisted, and challenged. Complex power-knowledge relations are enshrined in cultural texts. To put it differently, the "order of things" is embodied in cultural representations (Prior, 1997). Critical scholars' growing engagement in cultural studies is based in these theoretical assumptions about the nature of texts and the active part they play in the social world. Lindsay Prior explains that we can "know the world through the representational orders contained within the text" (1997:67). Prior (1997) argues for the importance of looking at texts as primary sites of empirical study for qualitative analysts. Texts, notes Prior, are representations that need to be "explained and accounted for through discursive rules and themes that predominate in a particular socio-historical context." (p 70).

The "knowing subject" has traditionally been used as the starting point of both qualitative and quantitative research (Prior, 1997). We saw this in Part II, where a variety of qualitative field methods and methods of interview were reviewed. Those methods rely on generating data from individuals and small groups. Unobtrusive methods are useful when researchers are interested in going "beyond the world of individuals" (Prior, 1997:61). There are many different reasons for wanting to use preexisting texts as the starting point in the research process. It may be an epistemological decision based on the assumptions within cultural studies already addressed. Alternately, many critical scholars explain that individuals are themselves "imprinted" by their culture's power-knowledge relations and thus that researchers must use representational products as their starting point in order to more accurately examine social power (Taylor, 1987). Texts are cultural products (Prior, 1997). In other words, because knowledge is situated in a complex arrangement of power relations, individuals living in the social order have been impacted by discursive practices, thus shading how they view the context they live in. In this epistemological conceptualization people are socialized into a "common sense" ideology through which they may unknowingly give partial consent to their own oppression within a hierarchical society (Gramsci, 1994). In order to understand the social world and, more specifically, how meanings are created and social power is enacted, researchers must go beyond "imprinted" individuals and deconstruct cultural texts. By referring to individuals as "imprinted" we simply mean to call attention to the fact that all individuals are deeply impacted by their social environment, even on levels that they may not be fully cognizant of. The cultural contexts we live in act as partial screens that mediate how we interpret our behaviors and attitudes, as well as those of others. Accordingly, individuals are "imprinted," to varying degrees, with the dominant worldview. Let us consider an example.

If a researcher were to approach you, present you with a variety of pop images and ask you to interpret the images of women in a variety of popular magazines he or she presents you with, how would you go about performing the task? How would you respond to questions about attractiveness and body ideals? Given that you live in the context where these images circulate and have thus been exposed to comparable images over an extended period of time, it is fair to assume that the very images you are now being asked to respond to are also mediating your perception of attractiveness and body ideals. A qualitative researcher interested in going beyond the perception of individuals whose vision is inevitably already influenced by societal norms may use the texts themselves as the starting point for research. By deconstructing preexisting images of women in popular magazines, a researcher is interrogating the process by which the images came to be and how they represent prevailing arrangements of social power.

Beyond engagement with critical theoretical frameworks, a qualitative researcher may simply design a study where unobtrusive methods best suit the research goals—which, of course, is always linked to a researcher's epistemological and theoretical orientation.

TEXTS AS A STARTING POINT

Unobtrusive methods are frequently used in multimethod qualitative designs to augment data from field research or interviewing; however, the growth of cultural studies has caused many qualitative researchers to use unobtrusive measures as a stand-alone method. Critical analyses of texts are no longer only adjuncts to field methods but now constitute a starting point for research (Prior, 1997:65). Let us consider an example and compare the differences in research objectives and data when unobtrusive methods are used as an augment versus a starting point.

A qualitative researcher might be interested in studying body image issues within a hierarchically structured society—such as patriarchal culture. Let us be more specific and say that the researcher is interested in the relationship between the American mass media and gendered body image issues cultivated within that society. A preliminary literature review would probably reveal that adolescent to college-age females are most visibly impacted by body ideals constructed in the media in terms of eating/dieting attitudes and behaviors. Accordingly, a researcher may decide to study girls. The researcher would begin with a primary research question such as "What is the relationship between media images and female body ideals?" One approach to this question would be to conduct in-depth interviews with adolescent girls and ask them to discuss how they experience body image and how they feel their experience is shaped or reflected by the media. The researcher may ask how the girls feel about their own bodies when they see media images of models and actresses and how their attitudes impact their behavior. Using this research design, data is collected from selected individuals—they are the starting point of the research project. What is gained from this form of inquiry is a body of data that reflects how individual girls feel about and are impacted by certain kinds of media images. A qualitative researcher interested in how mass-mediated images *themselves* reflect and constitute normative body images within a given culture, as opposed to how individuals subjectively relate to such images, might find content analysis to be the appropriate methodological choice.

> Qualitative research in this context, then, is not so much a question of deciding what a given text or textual extract might mean to a thinking subject as a matter of analysing the origins, nature or structure of the discursive themes by which the text has been produced (Prior, 1997:66).

A qualitative researcher might select a representative sample of fashion magazines and analyze the textual and visual components in order to unravel the processes by which certain body image ideals—and, furthermore, gendered differences within these normative ideals—have emerged. If gendered differences are evidenced, as previous research has shown (Hesse-Biber, 1996), the researcher can begin to examine how access to channels of mass communication impacts the creation of ideal representations which not only reflect but also shape the world (Prior, 1997:71). In other words, where these images are produced, and, whether or not only a limited number of citizens have access to image production technologies, impacts the diversity of mass-mediated images, but how? In what ways do these cultural processes impact images of masculinity and femininity? How are gendered norms reinforced or challenged? Unlike the researcher conducting in-depth interviews, in this context the researcher is interested in contributing to our knowledge of how body ideals are created and reflected by the mass media. The focus here is then on the *cultural processes* that construct beauty ideals. In the age of mass media such processes occur within that realm. This removes the point of origin from individuals such as interviewees who, because they live in a social context, have been "imprinted"/impacted by the media images that circulate around them. This is not to imply that one method is better than the other, but rather they are a closer fit to different research objectives.

As discussed in Part I, the research method should always have a "tight fit" with the researcher's goals and epistemological position. In-depth interviews and other forms of interactive research can also be used in conjunction with content analysis in a multimethod design. This allows a researcher to examine large-scale processes of body image formation and individual impact. For example, let us again consider our example of studying images of female attractiveness and body ideals within popular magazines. A multimethod approach to this project would generate data from multiple perspectives. Such a design could be carried out in two phases. In one phase the researcher would conduct a content analysis of the magazine images in order to (1) create a thick description of the female appearance standards that circulate in the texts, and (2) investigate the gendered social power embedded in the images. In the second phase the researcher would conduct in-depth interviews with a representative sample of the women the magazines are targeting, such as college-age women, in order to ascertain information pertaining to the following themes: (1) descriptions of their own ideals of female appearance, (2) how they have arrived at their standards, (3) what cultural pressures influence their attitudes, and (4) how they interpret and cope with cultural ideals of attractiveness. Answers relating to the first theme will allow the researcher to compare the images within popular magazines from the first phase to the standards of attractiveness held by the women for whom such images are mainly intended. The latter themes add depth to the research by examining how large-scale cultural standards of beauty subjectively impact young women. In this instance we can see how a multimethod design would produce multiple layers of data by allowing the researcher to ask a broader range of questions in regard to one general topic.

Content analysis can also serve as a method of gaining preliminary data that can direct future qualitative research such as methods of interview. Denna Harmon and Scott B. Boeringer provide an excellent example of how to use content analysis in order to generate data in an emergent field of inquiry.

Harmon and Boeringer were interested in conducting a qualitative study of sexual content on the Internet. As Web-based forms of pornography are relatively new they decided to use content analysis as a method of gaining baseline data that other researchers could later use. After a review of Internet Web sites, they decided to collect 200 "postings" from a Web site with explicit sexual content. As they deemed four postings "unusable" they ended up with a sample of 196 "postings" collected over a 2-week period. The chapter by Chris Mann and Fiona Stewart addresses the strengths and weaknesses of analyzing preexisting computer documents. Using a line-by-line method of analysis Harmon and Boeringer assigned each line of text a "code." For example, "pedophilia" and other "fetishes" were among the codes selected as reflective of certain lines of text. In the end they were astounded by the extent to which "nonconsensual" expressions dominated the "postings." The research process and findings were so troubling that one of the researchers sought a professional "debriefing" from a university counselor. It is often important for qualitative researchers to do so, as they are often faced with personal concerns as they conduct research projects. In field research the nature of relationships formed with research participants is a constant concern for the qualitative researcher. Likewise, researchers conducting in-depth interviews with adolescent girls on body image issues may be troubled if they discover that respondents have eating disorders or disorderly eating habits. The qualitative researcher engaged in content analysis is not immune to these challenges. The research topic and researcher personality often dictate the toll a project has on the researcher. This is not meant to discourage qualitative practice; these challenges specific to qualitative research also carry their own rewards.

As the Harmon and Boeringer study analyzed data in an emergent field, its findings can be used to direct future researchers interested in computer pornography. As qualitative researchers are typically interested in how social meaning is generated and experienced, Harmon and Boeringer situate their findings within studies on the "effect of" pornography. They are careful to point out that computers are an interactive medium differing from magazines and videotapes. The differences between interactive simulated computer pornography and interactive simulated exotic dancing may also be of interest to researchers working in this field. More research needs to be conducted to understand how this form of pornography impacts attitudes about sexuality and sexual violence and the relationship between these narratives and sexual (violent and nonviolent) behaviors. In this case qualitative methods of interview could elaborate on and contextualize the data yielded from content analysis.

In addition to storing preexisting "documents," computers offer qualitative researchers other methods of gathering textual data. Researchers can analyze ongoing interactions that appear in text form. For example, a researcher can observe chat room discussions. In doing so a researcher performs "discourse analysis" (Mann and Stewart, 2000). This is where a researcher analyzes language-based conversation. The data appears as a line-by-line text although it occurs in the form of ongoing real-time conversation. By analyzing computer-driven conversations, researchers are able to be "voyeurs" in their observation of interaction (Mann and Stewart, 2000). The presence of the researcher does not need to be revealed and the dialogue would be occurring regardless of the research, thus maintaining the principles of "unobtrusive" research. The difference here between traditional content analysis and discourse analysis is in the form of the data. In the latter, conversations and all of their particularities are available for analysis.

So far we have been focusing on forms of content analysis that use written text as data. As cultural studies and critical scholarship have expanded, new questions have been raised about how the various image-driven venues of the mass media both reflect and constitute the social world. In accord with these emergent areas of interest, other forms of media also serve as data for the qualitative researcher. Audiovisual data present a range of analytical possibilities and research challenges. Let us return to our example of body image and the media in order to examine how audiovisual data might be used in order to reveal the processes by which gendered body image ideals are created and distributed.

AUDIOVISUAL DATA AS A "MULTIPLE FIELD"

Diana Rose used audiovisual data to study representations of "madness" on British television. Let us use her framework to examine how one might study gendered representations of body image within television or film. It is important to bear in mind that any form of data collection and analysis always involves a process of reduction. This is particularly relevant to qualitative researchers because they generate large amounts of descriptive data that must be reduced for purposes of analysis. It is worth noting that some researchers conducting oral histories do publish unedited transcripts of their data; however, this is very rare, and researchers generally simplify their data. Rose explains this as a process of "translation" whereby one medium (or language) is translated into another (2000:246–47). During this process of translation some material is inevitably excluded. As critical scholars influenced by the postmodern critique of the social sciences remind us, what is left out is as important as what remains. These are choices the qualitative researcher makes, and as the Harding article in Part I explains, accounting for the "context of discovery" is a critical component of reflexive practice. Rose encourages researchers to remember that they can never "fully" represent the text, so they must be explicit about the fit between their choices and research goals (2000:247).

The process of translation that occurs when working with audiovisual data is particularly complex because the medium contains multiple parts: visual, sound, dialogue. Rose refers to this as a "multiple field" requiring simplification as it is transformed into a body of written data and eventually a written report (2000:246). Let us take our example and, following Rose's model, examine how we might study body image using television as our data source.

The researcher must first select which television programs (or films) are going to be analyzed. If representations of body image and their relationship to girls' identity development is the research topic, relevant shows aimed toward that audience (such as *Dawson's Creek*, *Gilmore Girls*, and *Buffy the Vampire Slayer*) might be analyzed. A representative sample can be chosen in multiple ways. For example, a certain number of episodes or episodes appearing in a determined time frame could be used. An alternative method might be to select a particular time of day and television network and analyze the shows contained within it. How do qualitative researchers make sense of the data sources once they have chosen them? How do we extract the data we are interested in? More specifically, how do we reveal and interpret multimedia narratives relating to body image?

Commonly, researchers working with audiovisual data create a definition of the representation they are looking for. In Rose's case she developed a definition of a depiction of "madness." In our example, the researcher would have to develop a definition of an extract depicting "body image." The form the definition takes is up to the researchers, so they must make the reasons for their definitional choices explicit. The definition of a representation of body image might be something like this: a reference to physicality including weight, general appearance, clothing, and attractiveness. After creating a working definition of the depictions one is looking for, the unit of analysis must be defined. The term "unit of analysis" refers to a piece of data. This is relatively simple when conducting a content analysis of written documents. In such a case the unit of analysis would typically be a sentence. In the Harmon and Boeringer study the units of analysis were individual lines of text. Audiovisual data such as television shows present a greater challenge to the researcher determining the unit of analysis. This is because audiovisual materials are mixed-media, including visual, sound, and dialogue operating in conjunction with each other. Rose used the change of camera shot as a method of marking the units of analysis. Scene change is a typical demarcation.

The decision on what to code is also more complex when working with a "multiple field." Rose suggests considering the following possibilities: posture, demeanor, colors, lighting, position of people in shot, and number of people in shot. The selection of material to be coded should be guided by the research goals. In our example codes might include the following: posture; relation of bodies in shot; references to weight, appearance, clothing, height, and attractiveness; the tone of references; and reactions to such references. Following Rose's model, the researcher would create two columns:

visual and verbal. For each unit of analysis (i.e. scene/camera change), the verbal dialogue and corresponding visual containing one or more of the codes would be noted. In other words, for each scene the researcher could extract lines or phrases of dialogue containing relevant codes and also make descriptive notes about the simultaneous visual imagery. As with other qualitative methods, the researcher produces "illustrative extracts" (Rose, 2000:247). Using this method the researcher is able to study audiovisual data as other narrative form. By isolating the material pertaining to body image the researcher examines whether "body image" is narrated differently than other topics. Are stories of the body and body ideal told in particular ways? This is how Rose examined depictions of "madness" on British television.

THE VARIED FORMS OF IMAGE-BASED RESEARCH

Analyzing visual representations is another possibility for the qualitative researcher. This analysis can be performed in multiple ways. The researcher interested in the relationship between media images and gendered body image ideals might analyze a sample of magazine images. In our example, fashion magazines or magazines aimed at a teen audience might be most appropriate. Visual analysis can be conducted in conjunction with text-based content analysis, or the visual images can be examined in isolation. The visual images within magazines are generally photographs. As Jon Prosser and Dona Schwartz explain, photographs can be conceived of in two distinct ways: as "visual records" or as "visual diaries."

Conceptualizing photographs as "visual records" implies that they represent some aspect of the social world—they enhance memory. In other words, they are material records. By framing photographs as "visual diaries" the images serve the unobtrusive qualitative researcher as "field notes" imbued with their producer's standpoint. Building on Paul Byers's (1966) statement that "cameras don't take pictures [; people do]," visual diaries acknowledge that photography (along with other means of producing visual documents) is a *medium,* just as film and television are (Prosser and Schwartz, 1998). This brings reflexivity into active practice (Prosser and Schwartz, 1998). The way image-based data is categorized impacts how the data is treated. Researchers working from critical perspectives such as feminism, multi-cultural theory, postmodernism, and poststructuralism are more inclined to view images as visual diaries.

> The notion of photographs as a visual diary reintroduce[s] the researcher and the qualities of the medium into the research process (Prosser and Schwartz, 1998:8).

The current surge in cultural studies has made this the primary way of viewing image-based texts. In this view "found photographs" and other pre-existing visual representations are often contextualized during analysis (Prosser and Schwartz, 1998). Situating photographic texts is very common within historical sociology. By analyzing images of the body in magazines aimed at young female consumers, researchers can begin to unravel how normative body ideals are formed, distributed, and consumed, and how magazines ultimately create a cultural beauty ideal. This analysis can be situated within a discussion of the power of visual images, which are processed differently than language-based texts.

Qualitative researchers also engage in *interactive* visual research. This is when a researcher acts as a photographer. In this instance, the research method would not be considered "unobtrusive." A researcher may take photographs as a part of data collection. This can augment traditional field methods or the primary method of data collection. The issues that permeate other field methods also crop up when the researcher takes photographs. Researchers must gain access, consider reactivity (or researcher effect), and make decisions about whether or not to disclose their identity (Prosser and Schwartz, 1998). Photographs can be useful in both practice and presentation because they give a sense of "being there" in a way that other methods of expression, such as writing, do not (Prosser and Schwartz, 1998). When used as a part of field research the same choices must be made regarding how a researcher will conceptualize the data, as a record or a diary. When conceived of as a visual diary, photographs can be a powerful supplement to written field notes.

Computers also present both qualitative and quantitative researchers with a range of new methodological options. Survey research is a typical part of quantitative practice because it yields an abundance of quantifiable responses. Survey researchers can now use e-mail surveys where respondents answer via the "reply" button. Research indicates no significant difference in responses to surveys conducted by paper and those conducted by e-mail (Mann and Stewart, 2000). Likewise, Web-based surveys are also useful in ensuring each respondent receives an identical questionnaire (Mann and Stewart, 2000). These methods are likely to be used by quantitative researchers seeking large quantities of data that are reducible to a table or set of statistics. Qualitative researchers can also use computer-directed methods of data collection in the form of semistructured interviews. This methodology enables researchers to interview respondents located in other geographic regions, allowing for fewer "practical" constraints in sample selection. While qualitative interviews are generally very personal and depend on a rapport between the researcher and respondent, computer-based interviewing adds a dimension of anonymity to the process. This may be useful when discussing challenging subjects such as body image attitudes and related behaviors.

CONCLUSION

As with all research methods, the selection of unobtrusive, visual, and computer-based methods depends on a researcher's goals and epistemological position. These methods can be used in isolation or in triangulation with other qualitative and/or quantitative methods. The postmodern critique of knowledge construction and the recent explosion of cultural studies have served as the impetus to growing research in these areas. Unobtrusive methods remain an attractive way of "going beyond the world of individuals" in order to explore larger questions about how power and knowledge interact within a particular social order.

Regardless of the theoretical position from which research is conducted, unobtrusive methods are an important tool for asking and answering questions about the social structure. These methodologies allow social science scholars to examine macro-processes through empirical analyses. In the same vein, quantitative researchers have made important contributions to our awareness of the themes and patterns embedded within the products of our culture. They have also used this form of knowledge construction to help shape social policies, thus reinforcing the link between scholarly practice and social activism. Qualitative researchers have expanded this tradition by helping not only to reveal systemic processes, but also to contextualize them. Accordingly, the qualitative practice of unobtrusive methods has immeasurably added to our cumulative knowledge about cultural and institutional practices. Many of these macro-processes would not be discernible if other methods of data collection were used.

Finally, a built-in strength of these methodologies lies in the data themselves. Because the data generated by these methodologies are preexisting and noninteractive, unobtrusive methods produce findings with an added dimension of "naturalness" and/or "authenticity." When making the leap from scholarly practice to social activism, these qualities of "the text" are a powerful tool of persuasion. We encourage researchers to always fit the method to the research question in order to most effectively conduct their research, and as we hope you see in the readings in this section, unobtrusive methods and other forms of textual research allow researchers to ask and answer a wide range of pertinent sociological and interdisciplinary questions in new and interesting ways.

BIBLIOGRAPHY

Banks, James A. 1976. A content analysis of the Black american in text-books. In M. Patricia Golden (Ed.), *The research experience* (pp. 375–383). Itasca, IL: F. E. Peacock.

Barthes, Roland. 1998. Myth today. In Susan Sontag (Ed.), *A Barthes reader* (pp. 93–149). New York: Hill and Wang.

Brabant, S., and L. A. Mooney. 1997. Sex role stereotyping in the Sunday comics: A twenty year update. In *Sex Roles, 37* (3–4), 269–281.

Byers, P. 1964. Still Photography in the Systematic Recording and Analysis of Behavioural Data. *Human organisation.* Vol. 23, pp. 78–84.

Foucault, Michel. 1978. *The history of sexuality: An introduction. Volume 1.* New York: Random House.

Gramsci, Antonio. 1994. *Letters from prison: Volume one* (Frank Rosengarten, Ed., and Raymond Rosenthal, Trans. New York: Columbia University Press.

Hall, Stuart. 1981. Notes on deconstructing "The popular." In R. Samuel (Ed.), *People's history and socialist theory*. London: Routledge.

Harmon, Denna, and Scot B. Boeringer. 1997, September. A content analysis of Internet-accessible written pornographic depictions. *Electronic journal of sociology*, 3(1).

Hesse-Biber, Sharlene. 1996. *Am I thin enough yet? The cult of thinness and the commercialization of identity*. New York: Oxford University Press.

Mann, Chris, and Fiona Stewart. 2000. Chapter 4 : Introducing online methods. In *Internet communication and qualitative research: A handbook for researching online* (pp. 65–98). London: Sage.

Prior, Lindsay. 1997. Following in Foucault's footsteps: Text and context in qualitative research. In David Silverman (Ed.), *Qualitative research: Theory, method and practice* (pp. 63–79). London: Sage.

Prosser, Jon, and Dona Schwartz. 1998. Photographs within the sociological research process. In Jon Prosser (Ed.), *Image-based research: A sourcebook for qualitative researchers* (pp. 115–130). London: Falmer Press.

Rose, Diana. 2000. Analyses of moving images. In Martin W. Bauer and George Gaskell (Eds.), *Qualitative researching with text, images and sound: A practical handbook* (pp. 246–262). Thousand Oaks, CA: Sage.

Taylor, C. 1987. Interpretation and the sciences of man. In P. Rabinow and M.W. Sullivan (Eds.), *Interpretive social science: A second look* (pp. 33–81). London: University of California Press.

Reinharz, Shulamit. 1992. *Feminist methods in social research*. New York: Oxford University Press.

Wysocki, Diane Kholos. 2001. *Readings in social research methods*. Belmont, CA: Wadsworth/Thomson Learning.

Wysocki, Diane Kholos, and Rebecca Harrison. 2001. AIDS and the Media: A Look at How Periodicals Influence Children and Teenagers in their Knowledge of AIDS. In Diane Kholos Wysocki (Ed.), *Readings in social research methods*. (pp. 261–267). Wadsworth/Thomson Learning.

Following in Foucault's Footsteps

Text and Context in Qualitative Research

LINDSAY PRIOR

THE DOMAIN OF THE KNOWING SUBJECT

There are no Lele books of theology or philosophy to state the meaning of the [pangolin] cult. The metaphysical implications have not been expressed to me in so many words by Lele, nor did I even eavesdrop on a conversation between diviners covering this ground. Indeed I have recorded that I started on the cosmic patterning approach to Lele animal symbolism because I was frustrated in my direct inquiries seeking reasons for their food avoidance (Douglas, 1966: 204).

Pick up almost any text on research design or on the nature of the social research process in general and you will immediately notice that the discussion is predicated on the presence of what we might call a knowing subject. Almost invariably, your chosen research manual will suggest that the knowing subject be questioned, queried, interrogated and enticed into revealing to the investigator some conscious aspect of social life or social behaviour. In order to achieve this aim the manual will probably offer instruction on such things as how to compose questionnaires and scales, how to check for reliability and validity, and how to administer the instruments. Sometimes the intending researcher will be encouraged to become an active participant in the social milieu that she or he has elected to study. In which case the researcher will be instructed in how to enter the 'field', how to find informants and negotiate with gatekeepers, and how, eventually, to analyse the resultant data that the knowing subject divests.

This focus on the knowing subject is characteristic of both quantitative and qualitative research—and it is, perhaps, one of their few points of commonality. Thus, big survey research is just as ready to embrace the knowing subject as is small-scale qualitative research. So the *British Household Panel Survey* (Buck et al., 1994), for example, is built around approximately 10,000 subjects who are closely questioned on such topics as diverse as their attitudes to work, their voting intentions, domestic plans and housing choices. Somewhat surprisingly, however, given the pride of place that the knowing subject is awarded, you will discover that the raw data generated by individual subjects are ultimately of little interest to the researcher. So quantitative researchers, in particular, usually seek to reconstruct the answers they get from individual respondents in terms of a wider mesh, and will therefore aggregate the personal data in a search for such things as class, generational, gender or ethnic 'effects'—none of which can, of course, be attributed to any individual.

In like manner, qualitative researchers also take the knowing subject as their starting point. Indeed, in one of the seminal texts of ethnographic method Malinowski once argued that the guiding theme of anthropological research should be to 'grasp the native's point of view, his relation to life, to realise *his* vision of *his* world' (Malinowski, 1922: 25). And these very same words are often paraphrased in more modern texts on qualitative research. Thus Bogdan and Taylor, for example, talked about the need for the phenomenologically inclined researcher to 'see things from [a participant's] point of view' (1975: 14). Bryman, meanwhile, says that 'the most fundamental characteristic of qualitative research is its express commitment to viewing events, action, norms, values, etc., from the perspective of the people who are being studied' (1988: 61). Yet, as with the quantitative researcher, the ultimate goal of the qualitative researcher is rarely, if ever, the mere replication of the 'native's point of view', for usually the ethnographer's eye is focused on a broader target. That target can vary from being something as vast and amorphous as another 'culture' (Malinowski, 1944), or as intricate as a symbol system (Geertz, 1984), to something as localized as a 'moral order' (Garfinkel, 1967a), or as apparently mundane as 'the common-sense world of daily life' (Schutz, 1962).

This dependence of the social sciences on the knowing subject, however, has itself been consistently questioned during the final decades of the twentieth century. Thus, Charles Taylor, for example, in an essay entitled 'Interpretation and the sciences of man', has railed against an epistemology that predicates the source of social scientific knowledge on 'the impressions imprinted on the individual subject' (1987: 61). Taylor's individual subject is, of course, the selfsame one who is randomly sampled and questioned and interrogated and asked to self-report and introspect in the very worthy cause of providing social scientific data. But according to Taylor little of such introspection, self-reporting and questioning touches the core of social life because social life is established on mutual social relations of various kinds. That is to say, it is established on forms of collective activity or praxis, and if that is so then it must follow that social science research has to confront a dimension of human activity that cannot be contained in the consciousness of the isolated subject. In short, it has to look at something that lies beyond the world of atomistic individuals.

This plea for a focus on something other than the thinking subject has also been a marked feature of the work of Michel Foucault—perhaps one of the most influential of all late twentieth-century thinkers. For example, in his Foreword to the English edition of *Les Mots et les Choses*, Foucault argued that his analysis was to be based 'not [on] a theory of the knowing subject, but rather [on] a theory of discursive practice' (1970: xiv). Consequently, one of the guiding themes of Foucault's entire *oeuvre* involved the rejection of the 'author' as the source and origin of textual knowledge, whilst in place of authorial intent and design, Foucault attempted to examine the discursive rules through which knowledge comes to be produced, encoded and displayed. For, according to him, it is only by means of such rules that any 'author' can claim a legitimacy to speak, write and authoritatively pronounce on a given topic in the first instance.

Texts and textual knowledge form the centrepiece of this chapter, and many of the texts to which I shall make reference may be described as texts without authors—such as statistical tables, certificates, records and reports from government departments. That is not to say that such things are other than human creations, but in the same way that it would be erroneous to credit a given performance of a Beethoven symphony solely to Beethoven, or a single performance of *Hamlet* to Shakespeare, then it is equally fallacious to credit textual materials of the type mentioned below to an identifiable creator—a subject. Of course, texts are far from being neglected in qualitative research. Indeed, the role of text is often given pride of place in sociological studies of interaction (see, e.g. Strauss, 1987). What I shall argue for here, however, is that the study of text need not be subordinated to studies of interaction, nor need texts be regarded as a mere adjunct to the empirical analysis of subjects; still less do we need to seek out the 'meaning' or authorial intent of texts. Texts can constitute a starting point for qualitative analysis in their own right, and to expand on this theme I shall begin by describing some ways in which we can study texts as representations.

TEXT AS REPRESENTATION

In 1903 Durkheim, together with his nephew Mauss, published a series of papers entitled *Primitive Classification* (Durkheim and Mauss, 1963). The papers were subtitled 'a contribution to the study of collective representations'. Although the empirical detail contained in *Primitive Classification* is flawed, it remains an interesting and worthwhile publication because it focuses on how human beings think with things. More directly, it focuses on aspects of classification and how concepts of time and space are reflected in and constituted through aspects of social organization. So Durkheim and Mauss, for example, analysed the ways in which the so-called 'clan system' of the Pueblo Indians reflected and constituted their concepts of orientation (namely north, south, east, west, zenith, nadir and centre). In cultural anthropology this basic idea was followed through in numerous and diverse contexts. Hence, the internal layout of domestic dwellings, the layout of a dining table, the order in which food is served, the order of a procession, the ways in which items of personal dress are combined or the ways in which animals are described might all be used to represent the structure of a conceptual, or classificatory, scheme. Some years ago Mary Douglas collected some interesting examples on this elemental theme in her *Rules and Mean-*

ings (1973). More recently, Sahlins (1995), in his study of Captain Cook in Hawaii, has extended this line of discussion to say something about the limits of psychologistic interpretations of intent, as against a structuralist analysis of order in general.

This notion that human beings often choose to think with things (including the sea routes of Captain Cook) rather than with abstract ideas and notions was followed through with particular force in the anthropological work of Claude Lévi-Strauss. So in his study of *Totemism*, for example, he focused not on the personal subjective meaning which statements held for individuals, but on how things are arranged. Thus when the Nuer say that twins are 'one person' or twins are 'birds', we should not, according to Lévi-Strauss (1969: 151-3), take such statements as literal description, nor as reflecting the misunderstandings of some primitive mind, but regard them instead as the concrete representation of a covert classificatory system. In other words there is little point in seeking out the subjective meaning of Nuer statements about twins and birds, but everything to be gained by analysing the rules concerning how such statements are related. This same fascination with classificatory schemes also tended to dominate the work of Foucault during the 1960s. Which is why, perhaps, he opened *The Order of Things* with a discussion of a 'certain Chinese encyclopaedia' (cited by Jorge Luis Borges) which classified animals as (a) belonging to the Emperor . . . , (k) drawn with a very fine camel hairbrush . . . , (n) that from a long way off look like flies, and so on.

As the reference to Borges's encyclopaedia suggests, in most literate cultures the order of things is often displayed and represented in text as well as in artefacts. The classification of flora and fauna in a biological taxonomy, the classification of constellations in a star atlas, the classification of human beings in a text of physical anthropology, or the classification of diseases in a nosology. Often such schemes of classification can appear as bizarre as the Chinese encyclopaedia invented by Borges. Thus, some years ago I recall seeing the causes of insanity listed in the 1901 *Census of Ireland*. A partial list is as follows: 'Disappointment, love and jealousy, terror, grief, reverse of fortune, religious excitement, study, pride, sunstroke, childbirth, . . . seduction'. It is a puzzling mixture by any standards (and the reference to sunstroke in Ireland was a source of considerable and long-lasting hilarity to one of our Guyanese students). Yet in looking at such taxonomies we should not rush to the conclusion that the order of causation is somehow incoherent, incomplete or lacking in rigour. On the contrary we should treat each text as coherent simply because it is there, lying before us as a unified object. The task of the researcher is therefore to investigate 'archaeologically', as Foucault might say, the innumerable accidents and myriad twists and turns of human practice that have brought the text to its present form. Qualitative research in this context, then, is not so much a question of deciding what a given text or textual extract might mean to a thinking subject as a matter of analysing the origins, nature and structure of the discursive themes by means of which the text has been produced.

Textually ordered knowledge packages and stabilizes the order of things as they appear within a wider realm of discourse. Indeed, a text instructs us how to see the world, how to differentiate the parts within it, and thereby provides the means by which we can engage with the world. One might even argue that in many spheres of human practice one can only know the world through the representational orders contained within text. Perhaps I could provide an example. I am looking at *Norton's 2000.0 Star Atlas* (Ridpath, 1989). The atlas represents the shape of the universe as we currently understand it, and it describes that universe mainly by reference to the constellations (Pisces, Orion, Cygnus, and so on). These constellations are very clearly human constructions in the sense that they exist only in the annals of human culture. (Thus, no one, I think, would argue that the stars in Andromeda belong together in anything other than a star atlas made by earth-persons.) More importantly, of course, the atlas informs us how we should 'observe' the night sky. It tells us what to 'see', it structures our observation and our understanding. Moreover, as its maps and projections of the universe change from one edition to another, so do our perceptions of that same universe. In that respect the text takes ontological precedence over what is observed and discovered by an observer.

A star atlas is not the only kind of text that structures observation, of course. Lynch and Woolgar (1990) offer many other examples of representations that serve to construct scientific and other objects of human attention. For example, their book includes references to the use of ornithological field guides, and visual images of evolutionary theory. In this section, however, I intend to concentrate on a particularly authoritative representation of the world's diseases—a nosology. I shall begin with a reference to the ninth edition of the World Health Organization's (WHO) nosology on causes of disease—which I shall refer to as the *ICD*, the *International Classification of Diseases* (World Health Organization, 1977). Furthermore, for the purposes of this chapter I shall elect to examine the *ICD* in the context of causes of death.

Table 15.1 provides a summary of causes of death. I have laid out the table in terms of the seventeen separate chapters which appeared in the ninth edition of the *ICD*. I have also added some empirical detail of the death rates appropriate to each category for Belfast, 1993 (though any town, region or nation would have sufficed as an example).

It is, of course, interesting to know that causes of death can be classified at all when one considers the myriad things that can precede a death. It is even more interesting to consider what can and what cannot be regarded as a relevant cause of human fatality. Thus we can see at once, for example, how the vision of death expressed herein is, in the main, one predicated on the human body, its biological subsystems and the diseases to which they fall prey. There is thus no reference to ill-luck, malfeasance or misfortune, nor to more mundane ideas such as poverty or old age or exhaustion here.

Now, one way to begin our investigation of this frame would be to ask some questions about its origins. That is to say, to first ask about its ge-

TABLE 15.1 The Causes of Death by World Health Organization Nosological Categories, Belfast, 1993.

Chapter	Nosological Category	Deaths Per 100,000 Both Sexes, All Ages
I	Infectious and parasitic diseases	3.58
II	Neoplasms (sub-classified by anatomical site)	315.14
III	Endocrine, nutritional and metabolic diseases and immunity disorders	5.73
IV	Diseases of the blood and blood forming organs	1.79
V	Mental disorders	6.08
VI	Diseases of the nervous system and sense organs	14.32
VII	Diseases of the circulatory system	541.12
VIII	Diseases of the respiratory system	241.73
IX	Diseases of the digestive system	5.01
X	Diseases of the genitourinary system	2.86
XI	Complications of pregnancy and childbirth	0.0
XII	Diseases of the skin and subcutaneous tissue	2.51
XIII	Diseases of the musculoskeletal system and connective tissue	2.86
XIV	Congenital anomalies	7.88
XV	Conditions originating in the perinatal period	2.51
XVI	Symptoms, signs and ill-defined conditions	2.86
XVII	External causes of injury and poisoning	52.29

Source: Annual Report of the Registrar General, Northern Ireland, 1995

nealogy (to use a term much favoured by Foucault). And at the broadest level one would be drawn to study a system of medicine that sought to describe and understand disease in terms of what might be called anatomical lesions. In his *The Birth of the Clinic*, Foucault examined such a localizing anatomical discourse as historically peculiar and opened his study with the following claim. 'For us, the human body defines, by natural right, the space of origin and of distribution of disease. . . . But this order of the solid, visible body is only one way—in all likelihood neither the first, nor the most fundamental—in which one spatializes disease' (1973: 3). Foucault did not, of course, have the *ICD* taxonomy of disease in mind when he wrote that passage, but his words have a particular resonance when one considers the table of death that lays before us.

For practical research activities of course it would be unrealistic to suggest that qualitative researchers can immediately turn themselves into broadbrush historians of medical discourse or whatever. It is not, however, unrealistic to suggest that qualitative researchers can and should ask questions about the points at which certain terms in a classificatory framework, such as this, appear and disappear. When, for example, did such items as 'old age' and decrepitude as causes of death disappear from the *ICD* list? Was poverty ever regarded as a legitimate cause of death? Which diseases and anatomical subsystems have disappeared from the list during the twentieth century and which disorders and subsystems have newly appeared? (The tenth edition of the *ICD*, for example, has introduced new chapters for diseases of the eye and the ear, and added behavioural disorders to Chapter V [World Health Organization, 1992].) How might the concept of violence (as in deaths from violence) have changed and altered during the mid- or late twentieth century?

It is comparatively easy to discover the answers to such questions by consulting the different editions of the *ICD*—starting with the current, tenth, edition and working backwards as far as is required. (The first *ICD* was published in 1903.) In fact, in relation to most of the questions listed above, I have already provided the answers (Prior, 1989).

If one were to follow through on such a genealogical trek one would also discover, among other things, that until the tenth edition of the *ICD*, each disease and possible cause of death was placed into one of 999.99 categories. So all known causes of death could be numbered in a system from 0.01 to 999.99. (In the most recent edition of the *ICD* [World Health Organization, 1992] the classification has been changed somewhat so that each anatomical category contains causes divided into 99.9 subdivisions, thus enhancing the possibilities for expansion within each anatomical subsystem.) I recall being asked on one occasion what would happen if a new disease were discovered—would there then be 1,000 causes of disease and death? The answer, of course, must be 'no', because the *ICD* classification is no more a mirror image of some independent empirical reality than are the classificatory systems of flora and fauna used by the Nuer or the Tallensi that Lévi-Strauss discusses in his *Totemism*. The *ICD* is simply a grid for organizing things—in this case a grid constructed on and around the human frame. It is not a reflection of some external reality in that sense, but rather a representation of what is assumed to exist. It is, if you like, a simulacrum rather than a reflection.

As well as examining the relationship of one *ICD* chapter to another we can of course zoom in to a different level of detail and ask questions about particular types of disease, such as, say, mental illnesses. The *ICD* naturally contains a subclassification of such illnesses. It is headed by reference to organic diseases and ends with a reference to unspecified mental disorder. As well as examining the order in which these various illnesses are arranged, one of the tasks of the genealogist would be to trace the points at which certain illnesses have been admitted into the nosology and others expelled from it. So, for example, in the *ICD*, mental illnesses used to be classified under the heading of diseases of the nervous system—they are now separated as mental and behavioural disorders—and we can legitimately ask at what point were 'nervous diseases' separated from mental disorders. (For an answer see Prior, 1993.) Or again, we might look at *The Diagnostic and Statistical Manual* (*DSM*) of the American Psychiatric Association (1994), which is perhaps even more influential as a classificatory system in psychiatry than is the *ICD*. In which case we might begin by noting that its classificatory principles concentrate on symptoms rather than 'causes' and it therefore presents us with a somewhat different image of the range of mental disorders from that contained in the *ICD*. In addition, of course, we can also ask questions about the genealogy of specific diagnostic terms and concepts, and investigate the different points at which they appear and disappear in the nosology of the *DSM*. (So we might, for example, be interested to note when 'behaviour' as a category first appears in the *DSM*, or the point at which homosexuality was removed from it.)

These nosological frameworks provide just two examples of a genre of representations—texts without authors. These are not, of course, the only examples of such texts. I could therefore have presented a life table as an example of a textual representation, and asked questions about its categorizations and the genealogy of its conceptual structure. In which case I would have been drawn to examine mathematical (mainly probabilistic) representations against medical ones. Or, again, I could have chosen, say, a textbook discussion of schizophrenia and carried out a similar exercise—looking at how the features of the disorder have changed and altered in different editions of key psychiatric texts. Or had I been interested in sociological representations of class and occupation, I could have set about examining the changing classification of occupations in the United Kingdom using, say, the *Classification of Occupations*.

Overall, then, classificatory systems provide a fruitful terrain for the qualitative researcher. For each use of the template and each revision of the score produces a new schema, and with it a new image of the world. By examining the rules of revision and the nature of the new and the discarded components, the qualitative researcher can determine how the world is ordered and reordered. In short, one can discover how people think with things.

TEXT AS PRODUCT

I suggested, above, that a representation should be understood not as a true and accurate reflection of some aspect of an external world, but as something to be explained and accounted for through the discursive rules and themes that predominate in a particular socio-historical context. The task of the researcher is to disentangle the rules of association by means of which the representation is structured, the genealogy of the various elements contained in the text (such as the points at which new terms and concepts enter the text), and the image of 'reality' which the text projects. Foucault, of course, denied that representations were representations *of* anything in particular, and merely referred to the process of similitude—implying that there were no such things as ultimate reference points (in the external world, say) to which the representations corresponded. For our purposes, however, we can leave that argument in abeyance, and turn instead to the question of how representations are produced.

In his *The Archaeology of Knowledge*, Foucault (1972) pointed out that discourse not only restricts, limits and arranges what can and cannot be said about the phenomena within its domain; it also empowers (and disempowers) certain agents to speak on this or that question of fact. In many respects one might say that discourse empowers certain agents to create representations, and thereby to authoritatively pronounce on the shape and form of the world.

To expand on this theme I would like to examine an issue that has occupied the sociological imagination ever since Durkheim published his infamous study of suicide in 1897. It concerns the nature of suicide statistics as representations. For convenience, I shall structure my discussion in relation to the question of whether such statistics ought to be considered as a resource for sociological study or as a 'topic' for investigation. (The distinction between topic and resource was, I think, first explicated by Zimmerman and Pollner [1971], though not in the context of examining suicide statistics.)

In his *Suicide*, Durkheim (1952), rather like ourselves, was somewhat concerned to sidestep the investigation of a knowing subject. That is to say, he was keen to offer social rather than psychological explanations of suicide, and he wished to avoid referring to the motives and dispositions of victims. (However, it is sometimes argued that in his rush to avoid examining interpretations of 'knowing subjects', Durkheim frequently interjected his own interpretations into the data—but I leave that aside.) In place of the individual and personal, therefore, Durkheim wished to establish the primacy of the collective. Moreover, during his quest for the collective, Durkheim turned to an examination of contemporary suicide statistics—which he called upon as a resource for establishing the presence of 'collective' effects.

Understandably, perhaps, Durkheim took such statistics to offer a fair and accurate representation of events in the world—that is, to offer a reasonably accurate count of suicide events. What he failed to consider and investigate, however, was the manner in which such statistics were produced. It was (and is) a failure regularly compounded during the twentieth century by all kinds of social scientific investigators. As for sociology, it was only during the 1960s that researchers turned with any enthusiasm to the issue of whether suicide statistics should be regarded as a resource for study at all. Subsequently it was argued that such statistics should, perhaps, be more properly treated as a topic for investigation than as a resource for study. In other words, sociologists should turn their attention away from regarding suicide statistics as a mirror on the world and instead examine the ways in which they are assembled and produced.

J.D. Douglas (1967), for example, sought to emphasize how the imputation of suicide demanded a study of situated or contextual meanings. For without such a study how could anyone differentiate between a suicide, an accident or a homicide? (Perhaps I should point out that in most cases of violent death, all that is discovered is a corpse. The cause of death for that corpse always remains a matter to be negotiated—usually and principally, though not entirely, through the procedures of coroners and other legal officials.) Indeed, when later investigators (such as Atkinson, 1978; Taylor, 1982) examined the matter of suicide imputation via their empirical investigations, they brought forth endless examples of the ways in which suicide verdicts are manufactured from all kinds of strange and interesting background expectancies. Thus, in English law, before a decision of suicide is formally arrived at, relatives, pathologists, coroners, witnesses, friends, associates, jurors, and so on, have to impute (to a greater or lesser degree) an intention of self-harm to the deceased. The procedures by means of which they fulfil that task can form a rich seam for sociological research.

To show how difficult it can be to identify a death as a suicide, I have provided below three coroner's summary statements on three 'unnatural' deaths. The written summaries contain details of what the coroner regarded as being relevant to the cases in question. In each case, take care to note the primary cause of death.

CASE ONE

Death of a woman aged sixty-two years. The causes of death were given as:

I(a) Overdose of pentobarbitone
II   Hypertension and Chronic Bronchitis.

The coroner's description of what he considered to be the relevant detail is as follows:

The deceased suffered from her nerves and from angina and was addicted to sleeping tablets. On November 17th, she went to bed at about 5:15 p.m. and at about 7 p.m. her husband gave her something to eat and then left for his club. When he returned at midnight he found the deceased dead on the bedroom floor, leaning against the bed.

CASE TWO

Death of a woman aged fifty-eight years. The causes of death were given as:

I(a) Poisoning by alcohol and chlordiazepoxide (Librium)

The coroner stated of this death:

The deceased lived alone and was last seen alive by a neighbour on the morning of November 13th. She was found dead by her nephew at about 3.30 p.m. the same day, lying over the television set in her living room.

CASE THREE

Death of a woman aged sixty-two years. The causes of death were given as:

I(a) Poisoning by Maprotiline

The coroner's summary description is as follows:

The deceased suffered from depression for 5 years for which she had received hospital and out-patient treatment. On October 23rd, her husband was admitted to hospital and she visited him there the following Saturday. At 6.30 p.m. she was visited by her grandson at her home. The next day she failed to pay her customary visit to her daughter who alerted the police. At the request of her daughter, the police made a forced entry into the deceased's house and found her laying dead in bed with several empty packets of Ludiomil nearby.

Each of these texts could, of course, be used as starting points for research in their own right. We might justifiably ask, for example, why the coroner considers reference to such things as 'nerves' and 'depression' as relevant to his 'findings' and not, say, reference to the financial background of the deceased on the day. Or why there is no reference to suicide notes, while there is to visitors. However, just to concentrate on the problems involved in classifying such deaths perhaps you would like to lay your bets now on which, if any, of the three cases were regarded as suicide. I have listed the official decision of each case at the end of the chapter.[1]

The imputation of suicide in cases such as these is important, because in Northern Ireland, where the relevant events occurred, there are no court or coroners' verdicts on such matters as suicide—simply a record of findings. (Sometimes a coroner will scribble in pencil the single word 'suicide', 'accident' or 'homicide' on the back of the certificate. However, he or she is not obliged to do so and it has no legal basis, for 'verdicts' were abolished in 1982.) The ultimate decision about whether a death is a suicide or whatever is therefore a task for a coding clerk, and the coding clerk has no more information on the matter than what is included above. For example, and in terms of the tenth edition of the *ICD*, the coding clerk has to decide whether to code the deaths as cases of, say, X41 (accidental poisoning), or X61 (intentional self-poisoning). What is more, in the event of case two another complication arises—namely, the reference to alcohol poisoning—which leaves open the possibility of coding the death as X45 or X65. You can deduce quite easily that statistics on such things as suicide and accident and even such finer distinctions as alcohol-related accidents are very much products of these coding activities, and that when we multiply the coding process by hundreds of cases, the cumulative effects will be significant.

Now, asking questions about how text is produced, under what conditions, according to which rule books and by what kinds of people is therefore fundamental to the analysis of representational products. In terms of the example which I have chosen, I would go further and argue that studying the technical organizational processes by means of which the text is produced is directly related to the representational product which social scientists commonly use as a research resource. To clarify this point perhaps we can turn to consider Figure 15.1.

Figure 15.1 contains at least two representations of the suicide rate in Northern Ireland between 1968 and 1993: the upper trace, which makes the suicide rate look volatile and rising, and the lower trace, which makes it look relatively smooth and predictable. (The different effects are achieved merely by using different scales.) By concentrating solely on the upper trace, however, we can see that there was a marked variability in rates after 1982. Indeed, following the abolition of verdicts in 1982, the graphical representation of the suicide rate shows a notable year on year variability and a significant rise over the rate for the 1970s. (There had also been a change in legal practice at the end of the 1960s which, I believe, can be linked to the

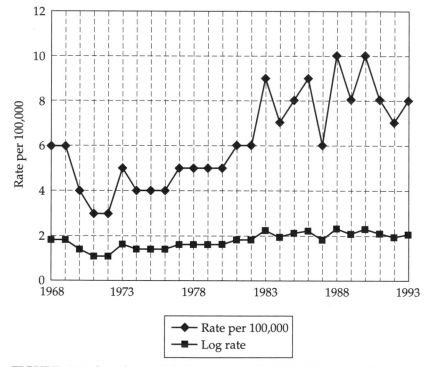

FIGURE 15.1 Suicides in Northern Ireland, 1968–1993, per 100,000 at midyear estimates of population. Annual Reports of Registrar General, Northern Ireland.

apparent decrease in the suicide rate during the early 1970s.) In other words changes in the rate are at the very least coincident with changes in the human practices through which the representation has been produced. In fact one might argue that as the agents entitled to pronounce on a death as a 'suicide' change, then so too does the graphical pattern. As researchers, we could probably carry out parallel exercises for crime, economic and all other kinds of statistical product.

Naturally, having produced a representation of suicide, crime, accidents, the movement of prices or whatever, others endow it with meaning. Thus, for almost every fluctuation in a graph or table of events there will be a nascent social theorist waiting in the wings to explain it. In the case of suicides in Northern Ireland, for example, various individuals have attempted to explain the fluctuations by reference to such things as the 'troubles', unemployment, changing roles of masculinity, and moral decline in general. Such a hermeneutics of representation indeed has its place, and to illustrate how that might be followed through I would like to end with a brief consideration of the hermeneutics of the 'subject'.

THE SUBJECT OF TEXT

1 P: Tell me Freddie. How do you feel in your nerves today?

2 F.—I feel upset.

3 P: You feel upset Freddie? Why is that tell me?

4 F: Control of me. I feel like a thick sound from a plate. Dolphin
5   been drove into the cooking room. There must be some kind
6   of connection (. . . inaudible).

7 P: A sound from a plate? What sort of sound is it Freddie?

8 F.—Sound. Teacup. Rattle of a tea cup. Hold on my body
      (. . . inaudible).

9 P: Tell me Freddie. How do you get on with the other patients?

As the information contained in line 9 might suggest, this extract is taken from an interview between a psychiatric 'patient' and a health professional. The professional was a psychiatrist, and as was explained to the researcher just before the interview took place, the psychiatrist was intending to assess Freddie's 'mental state'. Yet whatever his intentions, there is no doubt that we as sociologists could analyse this interchange in numerous ways. For example, had I given more data on the way in which the interview was structured in relation to time and conversational emphasis, we could have set about analysing the manner in which the patient-doctor relationship is created and constructed in the course of the interview. Or we could have looked at the ways in which, say, the symptoms of psychoses are constructed in and through the interview session. (That is to say, we could examine the ways in which the psychiatrist draws out the 'symptoms' by using a specific and deliberate scheme of questioning.) We might even be tempted to search for the meanings embodied in the interchange and perhaps go on to question the psychiatrist about his interpretation of Freddie's responses. Had we done so he would have referred at some point to such things as 'first-rank symptoms' and the nature of schizophrenic reactions, and so on. Indeed, were we to look at Freddie's 'chart' (medical file) we would see that previous interviews with Freddie have usually been written up and summarized in terms of his expressing reactions considered typical of a schizophrenic condition.

Psychiatric interviews and the records which they have generated have constituted the subject of study for numerous sociological inquiries (e.g. Byrd, 1981; Garfinkel, 1967b; Hak, 1992). Most of the discussions have been concerned with looking at how such records are assembled and how what has been 'put together' relates to some external point of reference; that is to say, how the records 'fit' with organizational requirements (Byrd, 1981; Garfinkel, 1967b), or how they are composed so as to express instances of some idealized representation of a psychiatric trait (Schegloff, 1963), or even how they relate to the requirements of professional practice (Hak, 1992). Naturally, any one of these routes into the analysis of records has a place in the armoury of the qualitative researcher, and some of them have been discussed elsewhere in this volume. Here, however, I would like to pick up on a Foucauldian theme and show how such records are used to manufacture the 'subjects' of sociological inquiry.

In his later work, such as *Discipline and Punish* (1977), Foucault became fascinated with the exercise of what he called power/knowledge. In particular he focused on how specific forms of power/knowledge (such as medical or juridical discourse) impinged on human beings so as to manufacture docile, pliant and disciplined bodies. That is to say, Foucault was interested, among many other things, in the manner in which discourse and its associated forms of daily human practice combined to manufacture *subjects*. In talking of records, for example, he thereby mentions how 'the carefully collated life of mental patients or delinquents' functioned as a procedure of objectification and subjection (1977: 192).

The carefully collated life of psychiatric patients is of course written in many registers. Thus, as well as being written up in a psychiatric 'chart', Freddie is also written up in nursing care notes and social work records. In each case the discourse that describes him is drawn together from different threads. Thus, the psychiatrist, in large part, draws his threads from the vade-mecum knowledge contained in psychiatric texts. Nurses draw on one of many of their 'models of nursing', and social workers draw their threads from their professional texts. In the case of Freddie, for example, the nurses described him primarily in terms of his 'activities of daily living' (ADL). Indeed, in some respects one could say that he was described as a functioning machine whose communication skills, everyday living skills, hygiene skills, and so on, were graded and scaled. One of the major tasks of the nursing staff involved assessing Freddie in terms of such scales, and having made notes on his 'deficiencies', they subsequently drew plans of nursing action to correct the perceived shortcomings.

In such ways Freddie, as a subject of sociological inquiry, might be said to have been more properly constructed in text than in action. This is so because the text (i.e. the records) has a permanence, combined with an easy possibility of transfer through time and space so as to fix Freddie's identity more firmly than any episodic encounter in, say, a psychiatric ward. Thus Freddie was often referred to as a 'schizophrenic' even during those periods when none of the first-rank (or even lesser) symptoms of schizophrenia were evident. Naturally, his psychiatric notes—which fixed and stabilized his biography—followed him wherever he went.

RESEARCHING TEXT

In *The Archaeology of Knowledge* (1972: 138–9) Foucault draws a distinction between document and monument. Archaeology, he says, 'does not treat discourse as *document*, as a sign of something else . . . it is concerned with discourse in its own volume, as a *monument*'. Archaeology, then, is not an interpretive discipline, 'it does not seek, a better-hidden discourse', but instead seeks to analyse the structure of discourse in its own terms. In order to undertake such an analysis, it is not always necessary to interrogate authors or other thinking subjects. (Indeed, such humanism would have been anathema to Foucault.) Instead we are free to focus on such issues as the rules concerning what can and cannot be thought, the ways in which knowledge can be represented, the nature of the grid by means of which thought is expressed and classified, and the rules concerning who is, and who is not, entitled to pronounce on the nature of a given phenomenon.

It is not, of course, always easy to translate Foucault's work into a set of methodological precepts that can be followed by the empirical researcher. Moreover, it may seem to some that I have been curiously selective in my exposition of his work. In reply to that, however, I can do no better than quote Foucault himself. 'All my books', he stated, 'are little tool boxes. If people want to open them, to use a particular sentence, a particular idea, a particular analysis like a screwdriver or a spanner . . . so much the better!' (1995:720). In that generous vein, perhaps I could end by mentioning the work of someone who, although he was not specifically influenced by Foucault, nevertheless might be said to have provided some further clues as to how discursive regimes may be investigated in an empirical manner.

The someone is Phillippe Ariès, who, in his *The Hour of Our Death* (1981) and *Images of Man and Death* (1985), sought to examine Western attitudes towards death from the Middle Ages to the present. In so doing he demonstrated how such varied phenomena as the layout of cemeteries, the nature of a liturgy, the arrangement of human bodies, the style and content of painting, icons and other text intertwined and interconnected to express coherent discourses on death. Unfortunately, and all too frequently, Ariès also interjected himself, as a knowing subject, into the interpretive frame. Despite that, however, his work served to illustrate how qualitative research can not only start with the investigation of things (rather than persons), but can also examine links and connections between objects that cannot speak, yet nevertheless bear messages. In the preceding sections, I hope only that I have gone some way towards showing how the investigation of such connections might begin.

NOTES

1. The respective verdicts were accident, accident, suicide.

REFERENCES

American Psychiatric Association. 1994. *Diagnostic and statistical manual: Mental disorders* (4th edn). (*DSM-IV*). Washington, DC: American Psychiatric Association.

Ariès, P. 1981. *The hour of our death*, trans. H. Weaver. New York: Knopf.

Ariès, P. 1985. *Images of man and death*, trans. J. Lloyd. Cambridge, MA: Harvard University Press.

Atkinson, J.M. 1978. *Discovering suicide: Studies in the social organization of death*. London: Macmillan.

Bogdan, R. and S. J. Taylor. 1975. *Introduction to qualitative research methods: A phenomenological approach to the social sciences*. New York: Wiley.

Bryman, A. 1988. *Quantity and quality in social research*. London: Unwin Hyman.

Buck, N., J. Gershuny, D. Rose, and J. Scott, eds. 1994. *Changing households: The British household panel survey 1990–1992*. Colchester, Essex: ESRC Research Centre.

Byrd, D. E. 1981. *Organizational constraints on psychiatric treatment: The outpatient clinic*. Greenwich, CT: JAI Press.

Douglas, J. D. 1967. *The social meanings of suicide*. Princeton: Princeton University Press.

Douglas, M. 1966. *Purity and danger: An analysis of concepts of pollution and taboo*. London: Routledge and Kegan Paul.

Douglas, M., ed. 1973. *Rules and meanings: The anthropology of everyday knowledge*. Harmondsworth: Penguin.

Durkheim, É. 1952. *Suicide: A study in sociology*, trans. J.A. Spaulding and G. Simpson. London: Routledge and Kegan Paul.

Durkheim, É. and M. Mauss. 1963. *Primitive classification*, trans. R. Needham. London: Cohen and West.

Foucault, M. 1970. *The order of things: An archaeology of the human sciences*, trans. A. Sheridan. London: Tavistock.

Foucault, M. 1972. *The archaeology of knowledge*, trans. A.M. Sheridan Smith. London: Tavistock.

Foucault, M. 1973. *The birth of the clinic*, trans. A. Sheridan. London: Tavistock.

Foucault, M. 1977. *Discipline and punish*, trans. A. Sheridan. Harmondsworth: Penguin.

Foucault, M. 1995. *Dits et ecrits*, 1954–88, Vol. 2, ed. D. Defert and F. Ewald. Paris: Gallimard.

Garfinkel, H. 1967a. Studies of the routine grounds of everyday actions, pp. 35–75 in *Studies in Ethnomethodology*. Englewood Cliffs, NJ: Prentice Hall.

Garfinkel, H. 1967b. Good organizational reasons for bad clinical records, pp. 186–207 in *Studies in Ethnomethodology*. Englewood Cliffs, NJ: Prentice Hall.

Geertz, C. 1984. From the native's point of view: On the nature of anthropological understanding, pp. 123–136 in *Culture Theory*, eds. R.A. Shweder and R.A. LeVine. Cambridge: Cambridge University Press.

Hak, T. 1992. Psychiatric records as transformations of other texts, pp. 138–155 in *Text in context: Contributions to ethnomethodology*, eds. G. Watson and R.M. Seiler. London: Sage.

Lévi-Strauss, C. 1969. *Totemism*, trans. R. Needham. Harmondsworth: Penguin.

Lynch, M. and S. Woolgar, eds. 1990. *Representation in scientific practice*. Cambridge, MA: MIT Press.

Malinowski, B. 1922. *Argonauts of the western pacific*. London; Routledge.

Malinowski, B. 1944. *A scientific theory of culture and other essays*. Chapel Hill: University of North Carolina Press.

Prior, L. 1989. *The social organization of death: Social practices and medical discourse in Belfast*. Basingstoke: Macmillan.

Prior, L. 1993. *The social organization of mental illness*. London: Sage.

Ridpath, I., ed. 1989. *Norton's 2000.0 Star Atlas and reference handbook* (18th edn). Harlow: Longman.

Sahlins, M. 1995. *How natives think, about Captain Cook, for example*. Chicago: University of Chicago Press.

Schegloff, E.A. 1963. Toward a reading of psychiatric theory, *Berkeley Journal of Sociology* 8: 61–91.

Schütz, A. 1962. Common-sense and scientific interpretation of human action, pp. 3–47 in *Collected Papers* Vol. 1, ed. M. Natanson. The Hague; Martinus Nijhoff.

Strauss, A.L. 1987. *Qualitative analysis for social scientists*. Cambridge: Cambridge University Press.

Taylor, C. 1987. Interpretation and the sciences of man, pp. 33–81 in *Interpretive Social Sciences: A Second Look*, eds. P. Rabinow and M.W. Sullivan. London: University of California Press.

Taylor, S. 1982. *Durkheim and the study of suicide*. London: Macmillan.

World Health Organization 1977. *Manual of the international statistical classification of diseases, injuries and causes of death*, 2 vols (9th edn). Geneva: WHO.

World Health Organization 1992. *International statistical classification of diseases and related health problems*, 3 vols (10th edn). Geneva: WHO.

Zimmerman, D.H. and M. Pollner. 1971. The everyday world as a phenomenon, pp. 80–103 in *Understanding Everyday Life*, ed. J.D. Douglas. London: Routledge and Kegan Paul.

CHAPTER 16

Photographs within the Sociological Research Process

JON PROSSER AND DONA SCHWARTZ

Any discussion of using photographs in the research process should begin by considering researchers' underlying epistemological and methodological assumptions, since they orientate the way we conduct our studies. How research proceeds also depends on the orientation provided by an academic discipline, e.g., sociology, anthropology, psychology; the theoretical framework guiding the study, e.g., material culture, phenomenology, symbolic interaction, and feminist theory; the researcher's role, i.e., ethnographer, historian, advocate, biographer, evaluator and interpreter; and personal attributes such as skills, experiences, values and beliefs. These many variables shape the way we design our studies, our views of what constitutes data, and the kinds of conclusions we draw. Uncertainty surrounding the research act, a consequence of recent critiques launched by post-modernists and exponents of new approaches to ethnography, compounds the problems posed by these complex contextual issues. Debates regarding the appropriate relationship of theory to practice, a quandary inherent in any research process, reflect the difficult times in which qualitative researchers work. While recent discussions usefully foreground critical issues facing social scientists, they sometimes threaten to undermine the entire research enterprise and seem to suggest that we surrender our efforts to the truths put forth by fiction.

Discussions of these underpinning issues rarely encompass the use of images, unsurprisingly, since so little has been written regarding the role photographs can play in the research process. In addition, widespread assumptions that photographic images offer a transparent 'window on the world' has discouraged critical analysis of the medium. Just as recent debates have raised questions about the neutral status of data collected by social scientists and the conclusions they yield, so too has photography come under closer scrutiny. Even among practitioners whose livelihood hinges upon the factuality of the photographic image—photojournalists, documentarians, and many scientists—the malleability of photographs has injected formerly secure fields with a healthy dose of circumspection. We take heed of the ongoing dialogues and the arguments put forward by different factions from a variety of fields of endeavour, but, rather than throw out the baby with the bath water, our purpose here is to suggest productive approaches to using photographs in social science research, while simultaneously acknowledging the contingent nature of the empirical research we ourselves conduct. We have elected to discuss a selection of issues that help us do field work, building on an empirical tradition within image based research initially espoused in the 1960s and 70s by Sol Worth, Howard Becker, John Collier, Jr., and Jay Ruby.

We undertake this task because, as image based researchers, we have discovered the valuable contribution photographs can make, both in the practice and presentation of our work. Like our field notes and other forms of empirical data, photographs may not provide us with unbiased, objective documentation of the social and material world, but they can show characteristic attributes of people, objects, and events that often elude even the most skilled wordsmiths. Through our use of photographs we can discover and demonstrate relationships that may be subtle or easily overlooked. We can communicate the feeling or suggest the emotion imparted by activities, environments, and interactions. And we can provide a degree of tangible detail, a sense of being there and a way of knowing that may not readily translate into other symbolic modes of communication. So, despite the irksome complexity of travelling through contested territory, the new knowledge yielded by the innovative methods we suggest makes the journey beneficial.

Consider this:

> I am walking along a city street. In one pocket I have a camera and a notebook and in the other two lenses and extra rolls of film. A young couple are peering into a jeweller's shop. I take out the camera and begin shooting, using the wide angle lens and a slow shutter speed to freeze the couple and turn other shoppers into a blur, suggesting and emphasising the couple's stillness and intimacy. I change to a short telephoto, shift position, and shoot against the light to accentuate their intimacy and body language. The couple's reflection in the window catches my eye and I switch to a standard lens and shoot some more, aware that the image is analogous to a theoretical concept derived from interviews with other couples conducted earlier in the study. I put the camera away, take out my notebook and . . .

No doubt you could, whatever your discipline or theoretical persuasion (but assuming some experience in conducting qualitative research), provide a reasonable account of the *processes* and *techniques* preceding the activity, which were used during the event described, and also those following the 'shoot.' You will be aware that a research focus, a flexible research design and an understanding of theoretical sampling provide me with a rationale to be doing what I'm doing in the place I'm doing it; you will also be aware that I made three different types of photographs, perhaps for different applications; you recognise that I collected interview data prior to taking photographs and that further data based on an analysis of these and other data may lead to further, more focused data collection; and you correctly surmise that this will lead to a formal report—a case study perhaps—in which the photographs, presented in the form of visual quotes, will be used in conjunction with other evidence to support a particular theory or working hypothesis. You are aware of this because there are certain elements commonly applied to a wide range of qualitative studies. Researchers using photographs span multifarious disciplines but share common understandings about what constitutes a 'qualitative' study and that the overall aim is to contribute to a body of knowledge by marshalling evidence to answer research questions. The defining characteristics which shape the way we design and conduct our studies could be described as holistic, contextually well defined, field orientated; design is emergent and progressively focused, naturalistic and non-interventionist; interpretative, working hypotheses emerge from the data; interpretations are validated by triangulation, multiple realities or single view (adapted from Stake, 1995:48).

In this chapter we aim to 'unpack', explore and refine the meanings of such terms with regard to image based research with one important caveat described earlier: we will focus attention on methodology and the ways in which theory informs and legitimates practice. The remainder of the chapter will, therefore, consider key facets of conducting research involving photography: *research design, data collection,* and briefly, *analysis.*

RESEARCH DESIGN

Research design makes explicit a plan for conducting a study, proffers a model and justification for establishing the validity of data and inferences drawn from them, and implicitly indicates a researcher's ability to successfully conduct a study. Research design should be made explicit so that others may gain insight into how the study was conducted and, more importantly, judge its worth. Any design of research operates within a discipline or across disciplines, takes into account the purpose of the study and deploys a particular set of research strategies.

Orthodox qualitative research design offers a 'blueprint' for the conduct of research, incorporating, according to Marshall and Grossman (1995: 38) the overall approach and rationale; site and sample collection; the researcher's role; data collection methods; data management; analysis strategy; trustworthiness features; and the time management plan. The future status and acceptability of image based research may depend on working within a relatively conservative framework whilst exploring alternative modes of enquiry which are image orientated yet sensitive to orthodox researchers' methodological concerns. Researchers using photographs in their work lack alternative over-arching research designs that provide models of good or innovative practice and a rich 'menu' of alternatives. Other more established approaches, for example designs for auto/biographical studies, historical research, or case studies, are sufficiently well rehearsed to indicate potential variations of strategy and probable data collection methods. Image based researchers have not routinely explicated their research designs and few models of good practice exist outside of anthropology and ethnography.

Bateson and Mead (1942), Byers (1964), Collier (1979), and Collier and Collier (1986), among others, provide models and insights into research design for anthropological and ethnographic studies. Good examples of research design within visual sociology are more difficult to find. An interesting discussion of how to conduct a study, however, is given by Rieger (1996) in a paper which reflects on the relationship between visual change and social change. He uses examples of changes in peoples' lives and to the landscape of small towns in the U.S. and over an extended period to illustrate the ways in which various photographic strategies, combined with traditional qualitative and quantitative data, are able to provide a robust research design. He provides, for example, 'picture portraits' of changes to a mining town over a 100-year period, and juxtaposes Dorothea Lange's famous 'Migrant Mother' image of 1936 with an image exhibiting a similar structure taken in 1979. Within Rieger's paper are features important to the design of a sociological study: *theoretical underpinnings* (such as the relationship between visual change and social change) are employed and act as a framework within which the study 'sits'; there is a *rationale* for combining research strategies; various visual *methods* are discussed (for example, repeating photographs of the same site over time, repeating photographs of participants in the change process, and re-photographing activities, processes or functions); complementary non-visual methods are applied (for example examining statistics on changes in population and employment); the use of triangulation of various indicative data to add *trustworthiness* of findings is discussed; and the *problems* (such as determining what constitutes an indicator of social change) and *limitations* of data and findings are aired. An image based approach, as Reiger points out, "must adhere to the same standards of evidence and inference" (1996:45) demanded of traditional non-image based research and it should make logical connections that start with a study's initial research questions and extend through to its conclusions.

Not all research designs follow the kind of structured approach Rieger describes. If research design is *"colloquially . . . an action plan for getting from here to there"* (Yin, 1994:19), as long as important methodological signposts are present many paths can be travelled. Some designs emphasise the flexibility that distinguishes qualitative research from other approaches. Harper (1992), in a case study of 'Willie,' an auto mechanic living in New York's 'Northern County,' takes a more responsive and reflexive stance than Rieger. Through Willie, Harper explores the decline of skilled manual labour and the kinds of knowledge lost in the process. As the study unfolds the reader senses a degree of empathy between the researcher and his subject that exceeds the norm in traditional participant observation, and we are left with the feeling that the study is as much a statement about Harper as Willie.

One key signpost in research design is how and by what criteria data are to be interpreted. Here Harper draws on grounded theory (Glaser and

Straus, 1967) to allow theory to emerge from the data but he adds commentary distinguishing Willie's 'emic,' or insider understandings, from the 'etic' sociological framework he uses to characterise that world in terms that have resonance and significance for social scientists.

> I have studied Willie's work from several angles, but the categories I have ended up with are my own. In naming and classifying its elements, I have separated out aspects of Willie's taken-for-granted world, presented them back to him in discussions we have recorded, and finally used them to translate Willie's experienced world in terms that those unfamiliar with the culture can understand (Harper, 1992:9)

Rieger and Harper offer two quite different but legitimate approaches to research design. However, the outcomes are similar in that they instill a level of confidence in the veracity of their images that is missing in many visual sociologists' work. Whatever research design is put forward as a methodological 'blueprint' of conduct during the research process, the overarching concern must be with enhancing the trustworthiness of findings and the scope and clarity of the constructs developed. Research design translates epistemological principles into pragmatic decisions and explains the choices we make.

DATA COLLECTION

Important steps in formulating any study involve identifying, locating and gaining access to an appropriate research site and the sources of data it can yield. Before qualitative researchers begin to mine a site for the data it holds, we need to consider how we present ourselves to our subjects. Many qualitative methods texts examine the relative advantages and disadvantages of assuming an overt or covert role, of participant observation or observation alone (Bogdan and Taylor, 1984; Lincoln and Guba, 1985), but we consider these dichotomies overly abstract simplifications of the complex relationships formed in the field. The choices we make regarding the roles we play in the field raise a host of procedural and ethical issues, many of which have been outlined in recent critiques of qualitative work. These issues become even more salient when considered within the context of visual research strategies.

Cameras in hand, visual researchers generally take a more pragmatic stance than other fieldworkers, because we need to employ methods that enable us to produce images capable of generating useful data. Recognising the added complexity introduced when making images in the course of conducting research, we also feel compelled to consider issues regarding 'empowerment' (of subjects), and 'ownership' (of data and findings), especially in regard to photographs. We accept that making pictures can be a threatening act (amply demonstrated by the metaphors photography invokes: we 'load,' 'aim' and 'shoot') that yields an artificial product, an artefact of the idiosyncratic relationship among photographers and subjects, the medium, and the cultural expectations it generates. We also make the assumption that the appearances of naturally occurring objects, events and behaviours provide a gateway to the taken-for-granted and reflects deeply embedded and therefore unquestioned aspects of culture which are critical to studies of society. Therefore, it is incumbent upon us to devise multiple strategies and roles for photographers that allow us to produce images that further our attempts to study the everyday world. While we cannot envision methods that guarantee photographs uncontaminated by reactivity between photographers and subjects, unbiased by cultural expectations shaping the act of making pictures, or unmediated by the characteristics of the technology itself, we do propose to build upon the uniquely iconic capacity of photography to usefully represent the particularities of a specific moment in time and space.

There are a hierarchy of questions to pose when considering the issues of access and role. The nature of the research question, even taken at a pragmatic level, is of paramount importance. A mature female researcher photographing a young man's world or a white middle class academic making a video of low income Hispanics may both claim that as 'outsiders' they have 'critical distance' on the problem at hand. This approach has credibility since 'critical distance' allows them to treat as problematic that which is taken-for-granted—as did Robert Frank (1955) in 'The Americans.' Conversely, outsider status may prevent researchers from penetrating a protected domain. We must consider and make explicit the benefits and disadvantages our own positions engender, and the ways in which cameras hinder or help our attempts to gain access.

An alternative to maintaining a distinct separation between 'outsider' researchers and their subjects is to build a bridge between them. Worth and Adair (1972) adopted this approach when they taught the technology of filmmaking to Navajo Indians so that they themselves could represent their traditions and rituals. Worth and Adair hoped that by offering them the means to visually depict their own culture the Navajo would provide an emic account offering the insider's perspective. Worth and Adair did encounter and acknowledge problems with their approach. Since film was not an indigenous representational medium available to the Navajo prior to their study, the researchers attempted to teach film production from a neutral perspective, unbiased by the cultural codes and conventions Worth and Adair themselves had internalized. The Navajo were asked to narrate their culture using an alien communicative medium. Nevertheless, *Through Navajo Eyes* presents an innovative research model that has been imitated in both academic and professional milieus.

Data can be collected covertly, 'under cover.' Photographers may hide themselves from public view, or choose a telephoto lens that allows shooting a scene from a distant berth. Some research questions encourage such a strategy. For example, time samples can be compiled at a particular locale in order to establish patterns of use or activity. But researchers who hope to gain access and be welcomed by members of communities may place future relationships at risk if they begin by employing what appear to be surveillance techniques. What happens further down the line when the 'spy' is discovered? Such revelations can compromise researchers' credibility and, consequently, trust may be impossible to cultivate. In most instances surveillance photography provides only superficial data which can be easily construed the result of 'outsider arrogance.' Covert photography more often reveals researchers' discomfort with their own photographic activity than it does insights into the daily lives of their subjects.

The nature of the research question should determine strategies for gaining access to subjects and constructing the researcher/photographer's role, but subjects' own social positions factor into the equation. When qualitative researchers make their agendas explicit they often depend on subjects' willingness to be studied, and members of different social groups may view the research process (and the researcher) with varying degrees of scepticism. And different populations have unequal defence mechanisms to ward off the intrusions researchers inevitably introduce. In some situations, the power differential between the researcher and the researched may make an overt approach untenable, as Taylor (1989: 66–7) points out:

> You will find many ethnographic studies of relatively powerless groups, such as school-children, the sick and handicapped, gays or dope smokers, but very few, if any, of powerful groups such as leading politicians, senior civil servants or military chiefs. This is not because sociologists are not interested in power and how it is used. They are. It is simply because sociologists (and other potential observers) are not normally granted access to centres of power. The only knowledge we have of what goes on in some powerful groups comes when one of the participants makes disclosures and even then, in the UK at least, there are problems in getting such revelations published. The problem of access illustrates that what can be achieved through participant observation is strictly limited. (Taylor, 1989:66–7)

This scenario repeats itself in many guises and encourages visual researchers to use covert and devious means to gain access to data. While we acknowledge that elites wield greater power to limit outsiders' access to their social domains, we must also recognise valid ethical and moral restrictions, like religious proscriptions, individuals' and groups' rights to privacy, or threats to security, health or safety. For example, in a comparative study of the daily lives of mothers of different U.S. social classes, Schwartz spent several months locating and interviewing wealthy women, most of whom declined to participate in a photographic study, or were later urged to decline by their husbands. Among the more compelling reasons cited was one couple's genuine fear that publishing photographs of their children could conceivably lead to a kidnapping attempt. It bears noting, however, that economically disadvantaged mothers were equally hesitant to be photographed, although they harboured quite different anxieties. The knowledge that powerful groups are likely to deny access to qualitative researchers, especially camera-toting fieldworkers, increases the likelihood that visual sociologists will adopt a covert stance and employ hidden cameras or craft personae resembling despised paparazzi who stalk celebrities in search of valuable photo opportunities. While going covert may yield usable photographic data, it undermines possibilities for participant observation, an important check on whether the researcher has captured participant's experiences. The flip side of the coin is, of course, the inability of powerless groups and individuals to protect themselves from intrusion. Researchers too often tend to shirk these moral dilemmas; the concrete issues they raise should be addressed in the design and implementation of research strategies so that we do not infringe upon the rights of our subjects.

Deciding on an appropriate role is only the beginning of 'getting in and staying in' the field. All qualitative researchers confront the process of establishing rapport with subjects, but cameras present additional complexities for subjects and researchers alike. Because photography is a popular hobby and photographs pervade Western industrialised societies, our subjects are likely to be familiar with both making and viewing photographic images. Snapshooting provides a template for subjects' ability to understand what visual sociologists do and the equipment they use. But as visual sociologists, we often present ourselves as professionally trained camera users and because we photograph a variety of objects, people, and events in the course of research, subjects may implicitly compare visual sociologists with photojournalists as part of their own process of classifying and thereby understanding what is taking place. In the course of our field experiences, the authors have been initially construed curious amateurs, professional freelance photographers, journalists and artists. While none of these classifications accurately reflect the role we intend to play, these common sense understandings provide a useful starting point for conversation, in the course of which we can clarify our goals and procedures. Whatever the opening, whether discussions of our activities, our equipment, or the weather, these first encounters with community members can (and should) be used to lay the groundwork for future data collection. Our identity as friend or foe is often established during these initial exchanges.

The introduction of the camera to participants can take place on the first day as a 'can opener' (Collier and Collier, 1986; Schwartz, 1989a) or over a period of time using a 'softly softly' approach (Prosser, 1992). The 'softly softly' approach, in this case, initially entailed walking around the sampling site with a camera in its 'out of the case over the shoulder like a piece of jewellery' mode, followed by 'safe' photography of buildings, and only much later was 'serious' photography attempted when participants were accustomed to photography taking place. Whether the camera comes out immediately or gradually, visual sociologists need to confidently perform the tasks necessary to make pictures and they should handle equipment with apparent ease. Photographers who act nervous or lack self-confidence usually convey those feelings to the people around them and, consequently, their activities may become suspect. In the initial stages of a research project qualitative researchers with little photographic experience do well to begin by mapping the physical surround. This accomplishes several tasks simultaneously: it allows the photographer to ease into the new setting and role; it makes the photographer visible to community members, opening opportunities for interaction; and it provides a visual catalogue of the physical setting in which the fieldwork take place. Not only must visual sociologists feel comfortable with themselves as photographers, they must also be attuned to the comfort levels displayed by subjects. Insensitive photographers who lack the ability act and react to significant 'others' as they themselves act and react to them will damage the quality of their data and compromise their ability to maintain rapport, a necessity if the researcher hopes to remain in the field.

Both the camera and the photograph are flexible tools used to collect data in various ways. In this section we will explore a small range of possibilities. *Found photographs*, like found or historical documents, are useful for 'backward mapping' but often lack important contextual information such as the relationship between the photographer and the subject, why a photograph survived when others did not, and the photographer's intention in making the image. How can we interpret an image or assess its significance without its context? Alternative forms of data and methods which illuminate, confirm or disconfirm are used to complement initial interpretation of found images. Found photographs, whatever their age and history, may be enlightening or misleading if viewed without an 'encompassing structure' (Trachtenberg, 1989). The 'encompassing structure' may come in the form of an analytical framework or constituent data, i.e., from contemporary writings, field notes, auto/biographical details about the photographer or participants. Historical, political, social and cultural information often aid our interpretation by elaborating the milieu from which a found photograph emerged. But, as in any qualitative study, all data have their limitations and there is danger in over extrapolation, of claiming what cannot be justified. The skills of the historian and archivist extend to us the possibility of judging the significance of found photographs. For example, an important icon of the Spanish Civil war that had been reproduced in *Life* magazine in 1936, 'Death of a Loyalist Soldier' by Robert Capa, was thought to be a 'set up' during the 1970s. However, an amateur historian found evidence that suggested the photograph was authentic and subsequent 'police work' reestablished the trustworthiness not only of the icon but also of Capa himself.[1]

Researcher generated images are widely used as a 'visual record' or as a 'visual diary.' While these two terms may seem synonymous we see an important, if fine-grained, distinction between them, a distinction that reflects differing positions with regard to the capacities of photography to provide an 'unbiased' record of a reality. When viewed as visual records, researchers depend upon photography's capacity to provide extra-somatic 'memory.' The ability of the camera to record visual detail without fatigue suggests that 'camera notes' may be superior to the field notes recorded by tired social scientists. Even when we become weary or muddled the camera can continue, so long as film and batteries are refreshed. The visual records produced by the indefatigable camera can be organised, catalogued and analysed at a later date. Thus, the camera's reproductive and mimetic qualities can be used in two basic ways, first as an adjunct or complement to an ethnographic field diary, or, second, to systematically record visual detail with emphasis on reproducing objects, events, places, signs and symbols, or behavioural interactions.

Creating a so-called 'visual diary' carries a somewhat different set of connotations that build upon an alternative conceptualisation of the photographic medium itself. As Paul Byers (1966) asserted early in the game, "cameras don't take pictures," people do. Even though cameras don't tire, the social scientists pressing the shutter release do, and the degree of perspicacity we marshal by the end of a field encounter may affect both what we include or omit, and the way in which we render the activities in front of the lens. Besides the person/machine issue looms a larger critique of factual uses of photography. Choices of types of supplies and equipment make a difference in the view of the world photography can offer. Large or medium format cameras depict the world differently than a thirty-five millimetre; the lens we choose to employ may either collapse or expand space and impart a different feeling to the viewer. The use of natural or artificial light, colour or black and white film stocks, and myriad other choices shape the nature of the depictions we create. Add to this laundry list such concerns as the aesthetic predisposition of the photographer, his or her own level of sensitivity to objects and events before the lens, and degree of facility with the medium, and the sanctity of the photographic image as a visual record is assailed. All of these factors contribute to the production of photographic images.

The notion of photographs as visual diary reintroduces the researcher and the qualities of the medium into the research process. That is, a diary is a self-reflexive and media-literate chronicle of the researcher's entry, participation in, and departure from the field. The images generated within this paradigm are acknowledged to be the unique result of the interaction of a certain researcher with a specific population using a particular medium at a precise moment in space and time. Reviewing these many variables in the photographic process more clearly distinguishes the notion of a visual record from that of visual diary. Consonant with these different views, when considered and constructed as visual records, photographs may offer greater potential as comparative data, uncontaminated by the idiosyncrasies different photographers might introduce. On the other hand, photographs intended as diaries of field experiences may better encode researchers' inferences (see Schwartz, 1993, for an example of the visual diary approach). Whatever belief qualitative researchers espouse regarding the medium, whether they make visual records or visual diaries, we advocate researchers making their approach explicit so that colleagues can better judge the conclusions they present. The argument we are making parallels a distinction made by Worth (1980) between 'records of' and 'records about' culture. Records of culture are the documents made by members of a culture themselves, while records about culture are the documents made by outsiders.

Taking this point a step further, Ruby (1976) suggests that the images made by anthropologists may be usefully viewed as records of the culture of visual anthropologists, while simultaneously considered records about the culture of so-called others.

Researcher generated photographs are commonly used during data collection as an interview device. This is commonly referred to as 'photo-elicitation' and takes many differing forms including interviews with individuals, with groups, with children, and those who respond more easily to visual, rather than lexical, prompts. We have described elsewhere (Schwartz 1989b: 120–121) an important addendum to the use of photographs as an interview device:

> Viewing photographic imagery is a patterned social activity shaped by social context, cultural conventions, and group norms. In order to present photographs to informants for purposes of photo-elicitation, some foreknowledge of the respondents' group's use of photographs is required so that methodological strategies can be planned, and the resulting data assessed within the context of informants' shared meanings. (Schwartz, 1989b:120–1)

Although not a homogeneous set of practices, in its conventional form (see Harper, 1988; Schwartz 1989a; Walker and Weidel, 1985) photo-elicitation can be described as a single photograph or sets of photographs assembled by the researcher on the basis of prior analysis and selected with the assumption that the chosen images will have some significance for interviewees. The photographs are shown to individuals or groups with the express aim of exploring participants' values, beliefs, attitudes, and meanings, and in order to trigger memories, or to explore group dynamics or systems. Of course researchers in different disciplines, with distinct epistemological assumptions may approach photo-elicitation differently. A less conventional use of photo-elicitation in sociology draws its inspiration from psychology, using photographs as a projective technique similar to that of incomplete sentences or inkblots. This approach, however, does not draw on the ambiguous nature of an image but is purposefully provocative and disruptive and is intended to elicit suppressed views. Prosser (1992) provides an example of this approach in an educational setting. A photograph entitled 'Pupil Graffiti' was shown to staff in a secondary school. The photograph is of a book whose title was altered from its original *Nine Modern Poets, An Anthology* to *Nine Nude Puffs in an Orgy*. As anticipated, when shown the photograph, staff *reacted* and reacted differently, providing insights that other, more passive means, may not have achieved.[2] The aim was to stimulate comment not on the content of the photograph but what is intimate to the interviewees that is 'triggered' by the photograph. Photo-elicitation used in this way can be provocative but is not necessarily aggressive.

Regardless of the strategy the researcher adopts, the chosen approach must be consistent with the way in which photography has been conceptualised at the outset. Photographs conceived and constructed as records will most likely be used according to a different logic than photographs made as part of the researcher's self-reflexive visual diary. While either approach can yield useful interview prompts, visual researchers need to understand both the processes of encoding meaning in which they have engaged, and informants' approaches to decoding photographic meaning. Researchers are often clear about their intentions as they go about constructing a set of images to use in the course of interviews, but they may just as often be surprised (pleasantly or disappointingly) by the nature of the responses their photographs generate. Confessions regarding serendipitous or disastrous interchanges rarely make their way into research narratives. Since many people spend time looking at photographs—in the press, in advertising, in family albums, in galleries—researchers need to carefully explain the similarities or differences between the interview setting and these other familiar viewing events so that subjects can be better informed about the task at hand. It is then the researcher's responsibility to interpret and assess the nature of respondents' interactions with the photographs used for elicitation, and to incorporate those conclusions into the data to be analysed.

Analysis

Analysing photographic data in qualitative research, as with textual data, is a series of inductive and formative acts carried out throughout the research process. As with other qualitative research strategies, visual researchers begin the task of analysis in the course of field research so that new inferences can be exploited before the fieldwork ends. Caldarola (1985) elaborates a plan for integrating photography into ethnographic research that includes regular viewing sessions with informants. In this way visual data can be validated as research proceeds and used to generate new inferences that inform future data gathering. All data have strengths and limitations but poor data, that is, data that are invalid, implausible, or untrustworthy, are not worth analysing. The initial problem for the interpreter of photographs is how to ensure their plausibility and believability. Because cameras do not take pictures (Byers, 1966) the fallibility and selectivity of the picture maker must be scrutinised. Full contextual detail (if this is ever possible) enables the trustworthiness and limitations of photographs to be assessed and this means having an understanding of both the external and internal photocontext. Such contexts are multi-faceted, reflecting the academic discipline, research paradigm and theoretical framework the researcher works within; the extent of disparity between the picture taker's culture (and the interpreter's) ethnicity, religion, gender, class, and values and the object of the photograph; the micro-context that shapes the particular dynamic relationship between 'taker' and 'taken'[3]; and picture theory. Picture theory is of growing importance to visual sociologists because it takes representation as problematic. It investigates the differences and relationship between images and words, or as Mitchell (1994: 5) explains, "the interactions of visual and verbal representation in a variety of media, principally literature and the visual arts"; and questions the relationship between representations on two-dimensional surfaces and their connection with issues of power, values and social influences. Any analysis of photographs without information elaborating the macro and micro contexts is generally unacceptable since image production and image reception informs our understanding of those photographs.

There are numerous theoretical and practical approaches to analysing photographs. One approach is the 'doctrine of signs' which draws on the work of Barthes' *Elements of Semiology* (1964) and denotation-connotation pairing, the semiotics of Peirce, or more recently socio-semiotics (Gottdiener, 1995). At the opposite end of the spectrum Collier (1979) suggests:

> We should first approach photographs *openly* (Hall, 1974) in order to respond to their holistic content. We could call this initial experience "listening to the visual voice of imagery"; the researchers respond with all their senses open so that they may be more deeply affected by documentary realism. (Collier, 1979)

Between structuralist and hermeneutical investigation are more specific approaches to interpretation. In addition to Caldarola (1985), Ruby (1976) critiques how anthropologists derive meaning from photographs, suggesting new and innovative approaches to visual anthropology; Collier and Collier (1986: 178) provide a four stage generic analytical model applicable to a wide range of research topics; Ball and Smith (1992) describe general theoretical approaches to interpreting images; Collier (1979) suggests three broad approaches to interpreting photographs depending on the nature of the enquiry—macro analysis and open enquiry, structured and micro analytical study, and micro image analysis of behaviour; and Chalfen provides a good example of an analytical framework within a substantive area. A common thread running through each approach is the way it moves the analyst toward theory generation (substantive rather than grand theory) and the testing of emergent ideas.

Interpretation of any photographic data requires a theoretical framework. A framework aids management of large amounts of (visual) data by providing logic for sorting, organising, indexing and categorisation. The interpretative process begins well before viewing a photograph, and takes place, for example, when decisions are made as to *what* and *how* the photographs are to be taken. Harper (1992) honestly describes these early faltering analytical steps that are part and parcel of any photographic study:

> The first photographs I took at the shop lacked any coherence from Willie's perspective. They were really photos by an interested outsider, seeing the exotic forms in the routine of the shop. Howard Becker would say I lacked a theory, which in his terms is 'a set of ideas with which you can make sense of a situation while you photograph it. The theory tells you when an image contains information of value, when it communicates something worth communicating. It furnishes the criteria by which worthwhile data and statements can be separated from those that contain nothing of value, that do not increase our knowledge of society.' (Harper, 1992:12)

Harper adapts, realigns and refines his approach and moves on, illustrating the flexibility and non-linearity of analytic induction required in qualitative studies.

Making sense of photographs is also dependent on what sort of social explanation or intellectual puzzle is to be resolved. Consider, for example, two separate photographs of two deputy principals of similar status and carrying out similar roles in an English secondary school.

The photographs were taken to provide data for a *comparative* study of working practices, to explore the similarities and differences in the deputy principals' working practices. They are two 'slices' of constituent data (constituent in that they require separate interpretation informed by the context in which the images were made, and the particular questions being asked of them) which were contrasted with each other and other data sets. A starting point for analysis would be to consider the photographs in terms of what Collier and Collier (1986: 47) call a 'cultural inventory': "The spatial configuration of otherwise ordinary objects, common to a mass society, may often reflect or express the cultural patterns and values of distinct cultural groups." Each office contains proxemic information (measurements of space), numerical information, information on the level of technology available, and information on décor aesthetics. The layout of objects in space is not arbitrary but tells us a great deal about the deputy principals, about who they are, what they do, and how they behave in their rooms.

Choosing an analytical framework must be guided by the same logic that undergirds the visual researcher's overall approach. We reiterate that researchers must themselves be clear about the way they conceptualise photographs and their role in research so that methodological strategies can be consistently employed throughout. Photographs prepared as visual records will trigger a different analytic strategy than will photographs intended as visual diaries. Worth's (1980) distinction between records *of* and records *about* culture, which built upon his and John Adair's *Through Navajo Eyes*, exemplifies the kind of theoretical clarity and circumspection we advocate, both for visual researchers in particular and qualitative researchers in general. These same concerns must govern the use of photographs in the presentation of research. While detailed discussion of this issue remains beyond the scope of the present chapter, suffice it to say that the agenda set forth by Ruby in 1976 has yet to be completed. Visual researchers need to attend closely to the ways in which their images are used in the display and/or publication of their findings.

CONCLUSION

As with any overview we have been both selective and brief in our outline of research procedures, resulting in some important omissions. We have not discussed, for example, notions of 'sampling,' 'representation' or 'ethics.' In this chapter we elected to focus on a narrow set of issues that have helped

us conduct fieldwork: *research design; data collection,* and *analysis.* Nevertheless these issues are crucial to planning and implementing visual research,
and our discussion will inform, if not enable, new researchers to enter the
field. Image based research as social enquiry is developing and refining both
its theory and methodology. In this chapter we have discussed key methodological issues and we have tried to balance theoretical frameworks with
practical insights. A central theme throughout has been to illustrate how different theoretical assumptions and different phases of the research process
require the deployment of distinct photographic strategies in order to provide a visual orientation to qualitative research.

NOTES

1. Jay Ruby circulated, via the Visual Communications Discussion Group (VIS-
COM@TEMPLE.EDU, the following message taken from the New York Times, Sunday,
September 1996: "The decisive moment, when it was taken in 1936, it was called one
of the great war photographs ever. In the mid-70s it was called a great fake. Now Robert
Capa's spectacular image of the Spanish Civil War, a picture of a Loyalist militiaman
falling as he is fatally shot in the head, is being rehabilitated. The picture was supposed
to have been taken in Cerro Muriano on September 5. So, an amateur historian named
Mario Brotons went to the military archives in Madrid and Salamanca and found that
only one man died at Cerro Muriano on September 5: Frederico Borrell, a mill worker
from Alcoy. From there, Rita Grosvenor picked up the pieces. She tracked down Frederico's brother's widow, who confirmed that the picture was of Frederico. Richard Whe-
len, Mr Capa's biographer, said, 'It has the ring of truth.'"

2. Principal of the school, on seeing the photograph took a stance commensu-
rate with his role, said he "felt threatened" and believed showing it to pupils would
lead to further "vandalism," whilst the art teacher (taking a similar 'role' orientated
stance) thought it most "creative" and wished more pupils demonstrated such talent. It is interesting but peripheral that to Prosser the graffiti represented the darker
unpleasant side of pupil culture and their perception of sexuality. Any member of
the staff who saw the photograph did not raise this interpretation.

3. Because people make pictures, not cameras, personal reactivity needs to be considered. Researchers bring to any study, skills, knowledge, past experiences, abilities,
personal values, beliefs, enthusiasms, which are embedded in a culture which directs
not only their visual perception and what they study, but the way they conduct that
study. Hagaman (1996), in *'How I Learned Not to Be a Photojournalist'* offers a rare but
valuable insight into how she (a photojournalist) produced images useful for sociological purposes. She describes how she put to one side her journalistic skills that produced
images with the required impact and drama and learned to be a visual sociologist.

REFERENCES

Ball, M.S. and G.W.H. Smith. 1992. *Analysing visual data.* Newbury Park, Sage.
Bateson, G. and M. Mead. 1942. *Balinese character.* Special Publications of the New
    York Academy of Sciences, Vol. II.
Barthes, R. 1964. *Elements of semiology.* New York, The Noonday Press.

Bogdan, R. and S. Taylor. 1984. *Introduction to qualitative research methods,* New York, John Wiley.

Byers, P. 1964. Still photography in the systematic recording and analysis of behavioural data. *Human Organisation* 23: 78–84.

Byers, P. 1966. Cameras don't take pictures. *Columbia University Forum* 9: 27–31.

Caldarola, V. 1985. Visual contexts: A photographic research method in anthropology. *Studies in Visual Communication.* 11(3): 33–53.

Collier, J. 1979. Evaluating visual data. In *Images of Information,* ed. Jon Wagner. Beverly Hills, Sage Publications.

Collier, J. and M. Collier. 1986. *Visual anthropology: Photography as a research method.* Albuquerque, University of New Mexico Press.

Frank, R. 1955. *The Americans.* New York, Aperture.

Glaser, B. G. and A. L. Strauss. 1967. *The discovery of grounded theory.* Chicago. Aldine.

Gottdiener, M. 1995. *Postmodern semiotics. Material culture and the forms of postmodern life.* Oxford, Blackwell.

Hagaman, D. 1996. *How I learned not to be a photojournalist.* University Press of Kentucky.

Harper, D. 1988. Visual sociology: Expanding the sociological vision. *The American Sociologist* 19(1): 54–70.

Harper, D. 1992. *Working knowledge. Skill and community in a small shop.* Berkeley, University of California Press.

Lincoln, Y. S. and E. G. Guba. 1985. *Naturalistic enquiry.* Newbury Park. Sage.

Marshall, C. and G. B. Grossman. 1995. *Designing qualitative research.* London, Sage.

Mitchell, W. J. T. 1994. *Picture theory: Essays on verbal and visual representation.* Chicago, University of Chicago Press.

Prosser, J. 1992. Personal reflections on the use of photography in an ethnographic case study. *British Educational Research Journal* 18(4): 397–411.

Rieger, J. H. 1996. Photographing social change. *Visual Sociology* 11(1): 5–49. International Visual Sociology Association.

Ruby, J. 1976. In a pic's eye: Interpretive strategies for deriving significance and meaning from photographs. In *Afterimage* (March): 5–7.

Schwartz, D. 1989a. Legion Post 189: Continuity and change in a rural community. *Visual Anthropology* 2: 103–133.

Schwartz, D. 1989b. Visual ethnography: Using photography in qualitative research. *Qualitative Sociology* 12(2).

Schwartz, D. 1993. Superbowl XXVI: Reflections on the manufacture of appearance. *Visual Sociology* 8(1): 23–33.

Stake, R. E. 1995. *The art of case study research.* Thousand Oaks, Sage.

Taylor, R. 1989. Research in child abuse. In *Investigating Society,* ed. R. Burgess. London, Longman Educational.

Trachtenberg, A. 1989. *Reading American photographs: Images as history, Mathew Brady to Walker Evans.* New York: Hill and Wang, The Noonday Press.

Walker, R. and J. Weidel. 1985. Using photographs in a discipline of word, pp. 191–216 in *Field methods in the study of education,* ed. R. Burgess. Lewes, Falmer Press.

Worth, S. 1980. Margaret Mead and the shift from visual anthropology to the anthropology of visual communication. *Studies in Visual Communication* 6(1): 15–22.

Worth, S. and J. Adair. 1972. *Through Navajo eyes: Explorations in film communication and anthropology.* Albuquerque University of New Mexico Press.

Yin, R.K. 1994. *Case study research: Design and Methods.* Beverly Hills, Sage.

CHAPTER 17

Analyses of Moving Images

DIANA ROSE

In this chapter, I will discuss a method for analysing television and other audiovisual material. The method was developed specifically to look at representations of madness on television and, inevitably, some of what I have to say will be specific to that topic. However, much of it has a more general application in that it consists of a set of concepts and techniques that can guide the analysis of many social representations in the audiovisual world.

Part of the general applicability of the method derives from its theoretical foundation. Indeed, conceptual argument is critical at each point in the development of the technique. I shall begin, therefore, by saying something about the theoretical foundations of this method, confining myself at this point to the most general level.

What precisely are audiovisual media like television? Is television like radio with pictures? I would argue not. Apart from the fact that radio itself is not simple, audiovisual media are a complex amalgam of meanings, images, techniques, shot framing, shot sequence and much more. It is therefore imperative to take this complexity into account when carrying out an analysis of its content and structure.

Every step in the process of analysing audiovisual materials involves translation. And every translation involves decisions and choices. There will always be viable alternatives to the positive choices made, and what is left out is as important as what is present. Choice in a multiple field is especially important when analysing a complex medium where translation will usually take the form of simplification.

There can never be an analysis that captures a single truth of the text. For instance, in transcribing televisual material, decisions have to be made about how to describe the visuals, whether to include pauses and hesitations in speech, and how to describe special effects such as music or changes in lighting. Different theoretical orientations will lead to different choices about what to select for transcription, as I shall show below.

As already argued, there is no way to collect, transcribe and code a data set that will be 'true' to the original text. The question then is to be as explicit as possible about the means that have been used for the various modes of translation and simplification. Bernstein (1995) has suggested that we call the text 'L1' (the L standing for language) and the coding frame 'L2'. The resultant analysis is then an interaction between L1 and L2. It is a translation from one language to another and, for Bernstein, it has rules or procedures. The problem with this model is that it assumes only two steps. Or, perhaps, it assumes that processes of selecting, transcribing and coding data can be seen as a single language. However, the distinction does make clear that there can be no simple reflection of the data set in the final analysis. Processes of translation do not produce simple copies but proceed interactively to a new outcome.

Let us take an example, again from the field of transcription. Potter and Wetherell (1987) have proposed a method for transcribing speech. They make much of the importance of describing pauses and hesitations and the length of these silences in their description. Is this 'truer' than a simple word-for-word transcription? I would argue not. What about inflection and cadence (see, for example, Crystal and Quirk, 1964)? And more important for present purposes, what about the visual aspects of communication? Kinesics is an approach described by Birdwhistell (1970) but rarely used. It describes the non-verbal dimensions of communication. An emphasis on speech or discourse can never include these features. Saussure recognized this long ago when he said that semiotics is the science of signs, and signs are not limited to the realms of speech and writing.

To turn to the analysis of media, Wearing (1993), following Potter and Wetherell, analysed press reports of a murderer deemed to be insane. The analysis stayed wholly at the level of the text, ignoring layout, headlines, photographs and positioning in relation to other stories. Wearing insisted that a new portrayal had been produced by the intertwining of two discourses—the journalistic and the psychiatric. We have to say that media representations are more than discourses. They are a complex amalgam of text, written or spoken, visual images and various techniques for inflecting and sequencing the speech, the pictures and the positioning of these two.

The point is not that there is a way of capturing all these nuances to produce a truer representation. It is rather that some information will always be lost, other information may be added, and so the process of analysing speech and pictures is like a translation from one language to another. At the same time, it will usually entail a simplification when the immediate text is as complex as television. The end product will usually be a simplification as well—a set of illustrative extracts, a table of frequencies.

There are cases where analysis exceeds the text, in both length and complexity. Many works of literary criticism take this form, Barthes's (1975) *S/Z* being a case in point. In the work of Birdwhistell (1970), mentioned above, it took two years and a whole book to analyse a two-minute sequence of a person lighting and smoking a cigarette. Perhaps this shows the absurdity of trying to capture everything intrinsic to the immediate text in the analytic work.

Further, and as already argued, televisual materials are not defined by text alone. The visual dimension involves techniques of camera and direction that are only secondarily textual. They produce meanings, to be sure, but these meanings are generated by specialist techniques.

Rather than aim for an impossible perfection, we need to be very explicit about the techniques we use to select, transcribe and analyse data. If these techniques are made explicit, then the reader has a better opportunity of judging the analysis that has been undertaken. Because of the nature of translation, there will always be space for opposition and conflict. An explicit method provides an intellectual and practical open space where analyses can be debated.

For the rest of this chapter, I will describe a method for analysing television and endeavour to make this description as explicit as possible. This method was devised specifically for analysing representations of madness on British television. Whilst the method is not confined to this subject area, madness is the topic I shall use for my examples. In the course of this, a few theoretical points, which I believe are general, will be addressed.

SELECTING THE PROGRAMMES

The first task is sampling and selecting material for recording off air. Which programmes are selected will depend on the topic area and the theoretical orientation. For instance, a researcher may be particularly interested in a topic covered mostly by documentary programmes. S/he may even have advance knowledge of broadcasts to do with the topic. Even with this level of knowledge, the selection process is not transparent. What to leave out is just as important as what to include and will affect the resultant analysis. The questions of omission and absence were central to the early semioticians (Barthes, 1972). Theoretical and empirical choices influence the selection of programmes or stories which are not self-evident examples of the topic being considered.

A common way of selecting programmes is to do a broad sweep of prime time coverage and then pick out coverage of the topic of interest. This, of course, means viewing the entire data set, which can be a very lengthy process. With prime time coverage the number of hours to watch is in the hundreds. Gerbner and his team (Signorelli, 1989) have used this method to study representations of violence on prime time over a 20-year period in the United States. This is also the route I chose to look at representations of madness on television.

Within the process of recording there are at least two steps. The first is when and how much prime time to record. I selected an eight-week period in early summer of 1992 and recorded prime time on BBC1 and ITV, these being the popular channels. The news was routinely recorded as were two soap operas, two drama serials and two situation comedies from each channel. Documentaries were also included.

The choice of dates was pragmatic. Different results may have been revealed had the recording taken place in autumn or winter. Televisual media are affected by the annual cycle. This would have been more important if the object of analysis had been political stories. It should be noted that random sampling would not overcome this problem since the 'population' is not homogeneous.

The next problem was the selection of extracts depicting madness. When is a representation a representation of madness? For instance, the Glasgow Media Group (Philo, 1996) included agony columns and chat shows in their analysis of media coverage of madness. I used a much tighter definition, following Wahl:

> I would favour, for example, the presence, within the media presentation, of a specific psychiatric label (including slang designations such as 'crazy,' 'madman' etc., as well as formal diagnoses such as schizophrenia or depression) or indication of receipt of psychiatric treatment as the appropriate criteria. (1992: 350)

It is important to be explicit about the reasons for choosing a definition such as Wahl's. The choice to take definite mental illness as the focus of the work has an ethical basis. Such is the scope of the net of psychiatry today that almost any human problem can become its subject. But it is those with the most severe problems who are outcast and excluded, and this may be affected by how they are represented in the media. Hence there is an ethical concern to focus on mental distress serious enough to come to the attention of a psychiatrist. Such ethical concerns, particularly when they are also to do with social exclusion, may well apply to other excluded groups also.

The final problem with selecting the data set concerns metaphors. Mental illness terminology is routinely used as tease and insult: 'You're a raving nutter'; 'Who is this loony schizo?'; 'She's mad about the boy.' These uses of mental illness terminology are important for the overall representation of madness on television. They were noted in the analysis to be described here.

Metaphoric use of mental illness terminology can be more tightly or more lightly connected with other representations of madness. There remains the question of what metaphoric uses to include. However, if language is a system, then signs belonging to one context appearing in a completely different one will still carry some of the weight of the initial meaning. At first sight, the famous phrase 'She's mad about the boy' seems to have little to do with psychiatric disorder. But the term 'mad,' generic for centuries, is still tinged with notions of extreme and excess, and even emotional danger, when located in its new context.

The question of definition would have to be decided for any analysis of prime time television, and there are certainly other topics (such as physical disability) where metaphor would be an issue. Defining what counts as a representation of the topic of interest will involve theoretical choices but also ethical choices, as has been discussed.

TRANSCRIPTION

The purpose of transcription is to generate a data set that is amenable to careful analysis and coding. It translates and simplifies the complex image on the screen. Early researchers did not have video recorders (Nunnally,

1961) and coded straight from air. It would be possible to do this with a coding frame of only two or three dimensions, but anything more detailed requires the capture of the medium in the written word. This, as has been said repeatedly, is a form of translation.

It is important to decide on the unit of analysis. This is a point made strongly by conversation analysts (Silverman, 1993) and those who have produced computer techniques for analysing qualitative data, such as ETHNOGRAPH and NUD*IST. In the study I am using for purposes of illustration, the unit of analysis was taken to be the camera shot. When a camera switched content, a new unit of analysis began. The definition of the unit of analysis was therefore basically visual.

Conversation analysts or discourse theorists typically take the unit of analysis to be a line, sentence or paragraph. Thus the unit is speech-based. Mindful of the importance of non-verbal aspects of audiovisual texts, I chose the unit of analysis on the basis of visuals but also, pragmatically, because in the vast majority of cases these are relatively simple to work with. There is a place for pragmatism in complex analyses.

Television is an audiovisual medium and there must be some way of describing the visual as well as the verbal dimension. I have emphasized the visual dimension and it is now time to look at this in a little more detail. It is impossible to describe everything on the screen, and I would argue that the transcription decisions should be theory driven. In the study on madness, it was proposed theoretically that mental illness was stigmatized, seen as different and excluded. It was further proposed that the televisual representation of this would often take the form of single, isolating shots and scrutinizing close-ups. Therefore, it was decided to code the camera angle for each unit of analysis (each camera shot), and also to code how many people appeared in each shot. This was to test the idea that mentally distressed people are photographed differently from those not so diagnosed. In this case, the procedure can indeed be seen as a form of hypothesis testing (Kidder and Judge, 1986).

Different theoretical orientations would lead to different choices about how to select and transcribe. For instance, the structuralist/psychoanalytic tradition represented by the journal *Screen* would tell a different story (Cowie, 1979; MacCabe, 1976). Screen theorists focus on the level of symbols, especially those to do with gender and sexuality, and unconscious relationships. So, they have done detailed work on shot-reverse-shot sequences which work to establish relationships between characters. The camera 'sets the scene' for the relationship by filming first one character, then the second from the first's point of view, and then the first from the second's point of view. The study on madness did not look at individual shot sequences because there was nothing in the theory to suggest this would be important. It is open, nonetheless, to question the choices made from a different theoretical orientation. There may have been occasions where shot-reverse-shot sequences signalled difficulty and closeness, but my decision was to focus the visual part of the analysis on camera angle.

Mood and the expression of difference can also be represented through lighting and music and other effects. Shadowy photography implies something dangerous that should be hidden, and eerie music contrasts with the light-heartedness of most music on television. Should people with mental distress be filmed in shadowy shots, or with a background of haunting music, this again emphasizes difference.

Camera angle, single versus group shots, lighting and music are all conventions of film and television. Indeed, haunting music can be referring directly to the filmic conventions of horror movies. There is a diagetic space with its own conventions. A structuralist analysis would focus on this space in its specificity. However, the method I propose is one of contrasts. We want to investigate whether a certain group in society and a certain condition—mentally ill people and their associated illness—is represented differently from 'ordinary' folk who appear on television at the same time.

Gilman (1982) has carried out very detailed work on visual representations of the mad person since the middle ages. He focuses on art and sculpture rather than moving images. Posture, demeanour, gesture, size and much more were important to this endeavour. The analysis has some similarities with the Screen theorists mentioned above.

There are yet other aspects of the visual dimension of television which could have been coded: for example, the colours of clothes, with dark colours implying depression, and even the relative position of characters in two-shots and group shots. For instance, it became evident with one depressed character that she was always in a 'lower' position than one of the other key characters in the story. If he was standing, she was sitting; if he was sitting, she was reclining. These aspects were not systematically noted in the transcription, but they could have been.

Other topics, other theoretical positions will require the selection of different aspects of the visual text for transcription. What is important is that the criteria for selection should be explicit and have a conceptual grounding. It should be conceptually and empirically explicit as to why certain choices were made and not others.

In the light of these choices, material was selected, recorded and transcribed. The transcription is in two columns and camera shots are signalled by paragraph breaks. The left-hand column describes the visual aspect of the story, in the terms proposed above, and on the right is a verbatim transcription of the verbal material.

What do we mean by 'verbatim'? Not that every pause, hesitation, false start and silence should be noted. There would be times when these things are important. Even with representations of madness, it could be hypothesized that mentally ill people are marked off by different rates, inflections and tone of their discourse. These supra-linguistic features are significant from some theoretical points of view, and are significant on some occasions from nearly all theoretical points of view. In cases other than madness, it might be of the first importance to include these factors. It was decided, however, that what was paramount was the semantic content of television's discourse on madness, and therefore the transcription was verbatim but omitted the kinds of phenomena stressed by conversation analysts.

The content does not stand alone, nonetheless. We shall see in the next section that each story was analysed as to its narrative structure. Whilst this is strictly a matter of coding and not transcription, it is important to point out that structure was not ignored.

Two examples of transcripts from the data on representations of madness on television are given as follows. The first is fairly straightforward: it was easy to transcribe. The second is an extract from the most difficult story in the entire data set. It is theoretically important that the story was difficult to transcribe, since it embodied ideas of chaos, transgression and difference. This locks into the theory that guided the coding frame, as we shall see in the next section. The camera codes are discussed later and given in Table 17.1.

Devising a Coding Frame

The full coding frame is given in Figure 17.1. It has a hierarchical structure in line with the proposition that representations of madness on television will signify at more than one level. This section will concentrate, however, on the theory underlying the coding frame and its epistemological status. I shall make no attempt to spell out in words what exists in diagrammatic form.

Bernstein's L2 is the coding frame proper or the language of description. The coding frame used in the study of representations of madness on television was very complex, and I would like to make two main points. First, this instrument is theoretically grounded. Secondly, it is designed so that theoretical derivations can be refuted. Let us take these two points in sequence.

The theory used, and modified, was Moscovici's (1984, 1994) work on social representations. One of the central tenets of the theory is that social representations function to make the unfamiliar more familiar. This point has also been made about televisual representations by Roger Silverstone (1981). My argument is that, from this point of view, madness is a special

TABLE 17.1 Visual Analysis: Camera Angle Codes

ECU	Extreme Close-up
CU	Close-up
MCU	Medium close-up
MW	Medium Wide
WA	Wide angle
Tracking	Camera follows action
Environment	Shot other than a person

'The Bill', ITV, 28 May 1992

Visual	**Verbal**
Front of hotel, forensics, PO, DI comes out, another DI enters frame, both MW	DI1: Ian DI2: Hello, Jack, how are you? Fill me in. DI1: Morgan's at the hospital now. He looks fit for all three killings. He's an alcoholic with a history of psychiatric disorder, no previous for violent offences. DI2: How did you get onto him? DI1: Your Sergeant R found personal possessions belonging to the victim, PH. I suppose he could have found her body by the railway line and then robbed it. Much more likely he killed her before dumping her there. DI2: And our girl AA is very nearly his latest victim. DI1: Yeah. Must have put up one heck of a fight. Otherwise.

'Casualty', BBC1, 4 July 1992

Woman with arm in sling sitting MCU, man pacing, leaps on her, man CU then ECU, attacks her, she struggles Woman rises, man grabs her, bites her, ECU, attacks	Man: . . . evil, fixes darling, ebony black devils. You know what I'd like to do with them? I'd like to bite the bastards' heads off and put them between my
	Wo1: Get away from me.
Staff come running, WA	Man: Growls. Screams.
Nurse in cubicle with 2nd Wo, second nurse enters, exit both nurses	Nurse: Ash, quick, there's a bloke gone berserk out here. Come on.
Staff struggling with man, WA, Wo1 led away, distressed, everyone screaming	Wo1: Oh my arm, my arm, oh, oh oh, my God, oh.
Camera tracking scene *Wo1 and two nurses pass cubicle occupied by Wo2, MCU, she exits, moves across corridor and picks up bottle sitting on trolley. She walks past scene with man who now has a blanket over his head* *Other people come to control man, WA*	Charge nurse (Charlie): Calm down calm down Nurse: Easy. Charlie: Don't just stand there Man: I'm choking. Charlie: Alright, alright. Take it easy. Alright, alright.
Charlie starts to remove blanket from man's head *Blanket removed, man lying on, ground WA*	Porter: No, I, I wouldn't. Man: I'm going to faint. Charlie: All right. Alright. I'm going to take it off now. Now you behave yourself. Man: All right . . . (inaudible) . . . lovely.
Man punches Charlie in the face, WA *Aerial shot chaos*	Charlie: Oh! Man: Oh!
Wo2 exiting hospital, police officers pass her and enter MW	(No speech)

A
Scene-setting

1 Neutral												2 Disruption	
a	b	c	d	e	f	g	h	i	j	k	l	m	n
Danger	Law	Obsessed	Strange	Maniac	Sick	Neglect	Distress	Cope	Sucess	Help	Comedy	Victim	Misc.

B
Narrative description

1	2	3
Present a to n as above	Reconstruction a to n as above	Neutral/gossip

C
Explanation

1	2	3	4	5
Stress/trauma	Medical	Insanity	Neglect	Miscellaneous

D
Resolution

1 Absent					2 Present				
a	b	c	d	e	a	b	c	d	e
Problems in law and order	Sickness	Neglect	Failure	Misc.	Law and order	Health	Support	Success	Misc.

Figure 17.1 Coding frame with fear narrative elements: scene-setting, narrative description, explanation and resolution.

case. For social and psychological reasons, representations of mental ill health, be they in the media or as everyday conversation, *maintain madness in an unfamiliar position*. Familiarization, social or psychological, does not structure the representational field of madness. There are two reasons for this. First, the content of many representations emphasizes danger, menace and threat. The mad killer or psychotic murderer is a distinguishable theme in the British media. But more than this, the structure of the representations around madness is unstable. There are myriad meanings of madness that resist fixity and threaten in a semiotic sense. Meaning is ruptured by chaos and transgression.

Moscovici has a concept of anchoring. A new, and unfamiliar, social object will be made more familiar by being assimilated to one that is already familiar. My argument is that madness either is not assimilated at all and stands excluded, or is assimilated to other objects that are never quite made familiar, such as people with learning disabilities, people with physical disabilities, people or things who take part in the monstrous.

What does this mean for a coding frame? The coding frame was derived from two sources: the theory referred to above, and also preliminary reading of the data. In 157 hours of prime time, there were six hours of material relevant to mental health. These are the six hours that were transcribed and influenced the design of the coding frame.

So far, we have conceptualized the coding of content. But many forms of text and textual practice have a discernible structure. This is often referred to as narrative form (Chatman, 1978; Todorov, 1977). Narrative structure refers to the form of a story in that it has an identifiable beginning where the state of play changes, a middle where the different forces play out their roles, and an end where outstanding issues are tied up. This end of the story is often referred to as 'narrative closure.' There is also an issue around 'voice' in narrative and the identity of the narrator. This issue was not included as it seems less relevant to the television text than to, for instance, the novel.

Television stories partake of narrative structure. In line with the theory of semiotic instability outlined above, I was interested to know whether stories about madness were narratively distinguishable from those which were about other topics. For example, do they exhibit narrative closure?

The coding frame, then, had a hierarchical structure with the top of each hierarchy being a narrative element (see Figure 17.1). The body of the story was coded according to 14 content categories, a large number being required to capture the multiple, shifting meanings of madness. Presence or absence of resolution, and type of resolution were also coded.

I have put forward the idea that madness and other objects of difference and exclusion disrupt semiotic certainty by being made up of multiple, conflicting, shifting meanings. At the same time they threaten because some of these meanings are dangerous. What if this theory were wrong? Qualitative research is often criticized for seeing only what it wants to see. But the theory can be disconfirmed. For instance, it would be open to a critic to argue that surely the dominant meaning of mental illness, in our culture if not in the media, is precisely 'illness.' In this case, the present analysis would reveal a high proportion of units in the 'sickness' category and very few units allocated to other codes. Medicine would be the dominant discourse around mental illness on television, and this meaning would be general and would anchor the 'mental' half of 'mental illness.' This is not what was found. However, the structure of the coding frame makes it possible to find an overarching discourse and thus to disconfirm the theory that difference is also made up out of semiotic slippage and, sometimes, a chaos of meanings (see the 'Casualty' extract).

The method of contrasts, used with the visual material, also holds the possibility of disconfirming the conceptualization. It would, for example, be possible to find that there was no difference whatsoever in the camera angles used to film people designated mentally ill when compared with those without the designation. So, the proposal that filming techniques mark off the mad person as different, isolated and excluded, would have to be rejected.

The Mechanics of Coding

I shall begin with the verbal dimension of the text. The coding frame described above has basically three levels, and it is highly likely that other coding frames designed for use with audiovisual material will have more than one level. I have labelled the first level with a capital letter, the second with a number, and the third with a lower-case letter. Codes look like this:

A2a   scene-setting, disruption, danger

B2f   narrative description, reconstruction, illness

C1   explanation, stress (the 'explanation' codes have only two levels)

D1c   resolution, absence, neglect

Each unit of analysis (camera shot) is allocated a code. There will be occasions when a single code does not fully capture the density of meaning in the unit, and in these cases two or even three codes need to be allocated.

There is an issue here of reliability. As we have said, the process of coding is a process of translation. The researcher is interpreting the meaning of each unit of analysis. Although the interpretations are constrained by both theory and the coding frame, it does make sense to ask whether other coders would have come to the same conclusion.

An exercise was then undertaken to see what the degree of commonality might be when eight separate people coded three selected stories. The level of agreement ranged from 0.6 to 0.78. The level of agreement was directly related to how familiar the coder was with the theory and the coding frame. Whilst this touches on one of the thorniest problems with assessing reliability, it shows that the coding procedure is at least replicable. From the epistemological point of view which I have been using, the coders were using a common set of translation procedures to turn the transcript into a series of codes. The crucial point is that this set of translation procedures is made explicit and available to inspection in the diagram of the coding frame (see Figure 17.1).

To turn now to the visual dimension. Here things are simpler as, once the selection choices were made, the transcription and coding were more straightforward. First, the camera angle of each shot in the data set is coded. Secondly, a note is made of whether the shot is a single shot, a two-shot (two people in frame) or a group shot. Finally, a count is made of the number of shots that use shadowy lighting and the number of times music is used and its nature.

The codes for visual analysis can be seen at work in the extracts. They are, in fact, transcribed and coded in one movement. While there are infinite gradations in filming characters, television does make use of some conventions in photography. This is to our benefit since it is known that, for instance, the close-up is an emotional and scrutinizing shot. On the other hand, the medium close-up and medium wide shots often signify authority (as with newscasters and experts). The full set of visual codes can be found in Table 17.1.

The method of contrasts entails a comparison between the camera angles typically used to film those designated mad and to film those not so designated. Since the conventions of the shots are partially known, this allows an inference as to whether mentally distressed people are being signified differently to others in the visual code.

Usually, the two modes of visual and verbal will tell the same story, since this is a convention of television. However, there is the possibility of conflict or contradiction (or irony and sarcasm) between the two: for instance, a picture of a homely grandmother with a child on her lap as the reporter's voice-over describes her double murder of her neighbour's children. It will normally be clear which of the modes carries the weight of the meaning but, where there is evenly balanced conflict, this should be noted.

Tabulating the Results: The Question of Numbers

The outcome of the processes described above will be tables of frequencies. To this extent, the procedure is a form of content analysis dating back to the seminal paper of Berelson (1952) and described in various collections throughout the 1950s and 1960s (for a relatively recent example see Krippendorff, 1980).

Content analysis has been criticized by media theorists such as Allen (1985) and only partially accepted by researchers such as Leiss et al. (1986). This critique derives from semiological approaches to texts. It is said that numbers cannot be meaningfully applied to significations and that simple counts of appearances of a word or theme in the text ignore structure and context. The detail which can be extended to a semiotic reading of a text is well illustrated by Barthes's S/Z (1975). Here is an instance where the translation does not constitute a simplification but is a book-length exegesis on a short story.

Let us take the criticisms in turn. The first is the proposition that meanings cannot be counted. That is to say, that meanings are always context-specific and allocating a number to semantic units suggests a spurious equivalence of different instances. Meanings are not discrete and even values are too ineffable to be measured.

Osgood (1957) was one of the first to count meanings. It is noteworthy that Osgood developed a theory of meaning that was neo-behaviourist in orientation so that, while focusing on the text, he could claim that his analysis was theoretically grounded. The most important tool that was produced by this approach was the semantic differential (Osgood et al., 1957). This is eschewed by more literary-based forms of analysis.

While the theory today looks absurd, this is a first example of the attempt at quantitative semantics within a defined theoretical framework.

Osgood had a neo-behaviourist theory of meaning. The method described above has its theoretical roots in notions of social representation (Moscovici, 1984; Jodelet, 1991). Numbers in tables, then, are not free-floating but are anchored to a conceptual perspective. What a number signifies depends upon the nature of the empirical material and the nature, too, of the language of description. There is nothing unusual in this. Mathematics uses theories, including theories that deal with chance, randomness and probability.

So, what exactly does it mean to count representations, meanings or other techniques of imaging? Table 17.2 shows the outcome of the analysis of representations of madness for the first two narrative elements (scene-setting and narrative description) for the news. The table should be read like a map. It shows the points of emphasis and stress and the points of lack and absence in the news data. It would not be sensible to say there was 'twice as much danger as sickness' although a metric reading of the figures would come to that conclusion. It makes more sense to say that danger dominated themes of sickness, and that the lack of themes of success and coping say something significant about how mental health problems are represented on

TABLE 17.2 Examples of Results of Content Analysis in Tabular Form: Distribution of Frequencies of Semantic Elements in Scene-Setting and Description Shots on the News.

	Danger	Law	Obsessed	Strange	Maniac	Sick	Neglect
No. of units	168	60	9	1	3	84	63
% total (N = 697)	24.1	8.6	1.3			12.1	9.0

	Distress	Cope	Success	Help	Comic	Victim	Misc.
No. of units	28	8	9	25	0	7	67
% total (N = 697)	4.0	1.2	1.3	3.6		1.0	9.6

the news. What is absent is just as important as what is present, as semioticians have taught us.

I have said before that it was possible, with the visual material, to employ a method of contrasts. Since both mentally ill and mentally well people appear in the programming, their visual depiction can be compared. Table 17.3 shows such a comparison. It will be noted that the chi-square statistic is employed, which seems to say that the numericization of the data amounts to more than maps. It is easier to assign true numbers to visual data because of the conventions discussed above. Even here, the view holds that numbers are not rigid indicators but species of signs. Nonetheless, high significance levels are telling.

Now to the criticism that content analysis ignores structure. This criticism stands. If we have learned anything from Chomsky, it is that structure carries meaning. And this has been accepted in the above analyses. Since we are dealing with audiovisual material, structure has been conceptualized in terms of narrative form. Indeed, many semioticians have used this concept, deriving as it does from the work of Propp (1969) and Lévi-Strauss (1968). Narrative structure on television is often open—for example, in soap operas, to keep up the suspense. But the analysis of narrative structure in the representation of people designated mad showed that lack of narrative closure was the norm. This, of course, adds weight to the idea that representations of madness on television are chaotic and resist the fixity of anchors. Here we see representations as often structureless. Table 17.4 shows the results of the analysis of narrative structure in drama programmes. The majority of sequences have either no ending at all or no restoration of social harmony.

The other method of presenting data is to use illustrative quotations. In an analysis where the method is theoretically grounded and where data are also presented numerically, it is arguable that exemplary quotations can be used to illustrate and confirm or disconfirm the theoretical and methodological propositions. In other words, rules for the selection of illustrative quotations can be themselves conceptually grounded. This means that it is

TABLE 17.3 Example of Tabular Results of Visual Analysis: Type of Shot and Character in the Soap Opera Coronation Street

Type of Shot	Mrs. Bishop*	Mr. Sugden**	Others	Total
ECU/CU	45	8	9	62
MCU	42	33	41	116
MW	22	36	16	74
Other	22	9	3	34
Total	131	86	69	286

Chi-Square = 45.6; d.f. = 6; $p < 0.001$.

* suffering a mental breakdown

** a friend who tries to help

TABLE 17.4 Narrative Structure: Frequency Distribution of Types of Narrative Sequence in Television Drama

As can be seen from the coding frame, stories were coded according to their structure. Each unit was assigned a code and then the story structure was summarized. This table presents the codes and results for drama.

A1	scene-setting neutral
A2	scene-setting disruptive
B1	narrative description in the present
B2	narrative description in the form of reconstruction of events
B3	neutral facts (news) or gossip (drama)
C	explanation
D1	resolution with absence of social harmony
D2	social harmony restored

Narrative Sequence	No
A2/B1/D1	29
A2/B1/D2	4
A2/B1	12
B1/D1	19
B1/D2	7
B1 only or B3 only	28
A2 only	8
D1 only	3
D2 only	4
Other	7
Total	121

not necessary to choose illustrative quotations randomly. Rather, they should be selected to both verify and disconfirm the conceptual principles and the numerically presented aspect of the empirical data.

CONCLUSION

This chapter has tried to do two things. First, I have tentatively proposed some methods for analysing television and other audiovisual material. Some of the techniques put forward should be adapted for contents other than madness. But secondly, I have tried to draw out the epistemological pitfalls and ethical consequences of this type of analysis.

At risk of repetition, I will say that each step in the analysis of audiovisual material is a translation and, usually, a simplification. There can be no perfect reading of the text. The point, then, is to be explicit about the theoretical, ethical and practical grounds of the technique and open up a space where the work itself can be debated and judged.

STEPS IN THE ANALYSIS OF AUDIOVISUAL TEXTS

1. Choose a theoretical framework and apply it to the empirical object.
2. Select a sampling frame—time or content based.
3. Select a means of identifying the empirical object in the sampling frame.
4. Construct rules for the transcription of the data set—visual and verbal.
5. Develop a coding frame based on the conceptual analysis and preliminary reading of the data set: to include rules for the analysis of both visual and verbal material; to contain the possibility of disconfirming the theory; to include analysis of narrative structure and context as well as semantic categories.
6. Apply the coding frame to the data, transcribed in a form amenable to numerical translation.
7. Construct tables of frequencies for units of analysis, visual and verbal.
8. Apply simple statistics where appropriate.
9. Select illustrative quotations to complement numerical analysis.

REFERENCE

Allen, R. 1985. *Speaking of soap operas.* Chapel Hill, NC: North Carolina Press.

Barthes, R. 1972. *Critical essays.* Evanston, IL: Northwestern University Press.

Barthes, R. 1975. *S/Z.* London: Cape.

Berelson, B. 1952. *Content analysis in communication research.* Chicago, IL: Glencoe Free Press.

Bernstein, S. 1995. *Pedagogy, symbolic control and identity.* London: Taylor and Francis.

Birdwhistell, R. L. 1970. *Kinesics in context: Essays on body–motion communication.* Harmondsworth: Penguin.

Chatman, S. 1978. *Story and discourse: Narrative structure in fiction and film.* Ithaca, NY and London: Cornell University Press.

Cowie, E. 1979. The popular film as a progressive text. *m/f* 3: 59-82.

Crystal, D. and R. Quirk. 1964. *Systems of prosodic and paralinguistic features in English.* London: Mouton.

Gilman, S. 1982. *Seeing the insane.* New York: Wiley.

Jodelet, D. 1991. *Madness and social representations.* Hemel Hempstead: Harvester Wheatsheaf.

Kidder, L. and C. Judge. 1986. *Research methods in social relations.* 5th edn. New York: CBS.

Krippendorff, K. 1980. *Content analysis: An introduction to its methodology.* London: Sage.

Leiss, W., S. Kline, and S. Jhally. 1986. *Social communication in advertising.* Toronto: Methuen.

Levi-Strauss, C. 1968. *Structural anthropology*. Harmondsworth: Allen Lane.

MacCabe, C. 1976. Theory and film: principles of realism and pleasure. *Screen* 17: 7–27.

Moscovici, S. 1984. The phenomenon of social representations, pp. 3–69 in *Social Representations*, ed. R.M. Farr and S. Moscovici. Cambridge: Cambridge University Press.

Moscovici, S. 1994. Social representations and pragmatic communication. *Social Science Information* 33(2): 163–77.

Nunnally, J. 1961. *Popular conceptions of mental health*. New York: Holt, Rinehart and Winston.

Osgood, C. 1957. The representational model and relevant research methods, pp. 33–88 in *Trends in Content Analysis*, ed. I. de S. Pool. Urbana, IL: University of Illinois Press.

Osgood, C., G. Suci, and P.H. Tannenbaum. 1957. *The measurement of meaning*. Urbana, IL: University of Illinois Press.

Philo, G., ed. 1996. *Media and mental distress*. London: Longman.

Potter, J. and M. Wetherell. 1987. *Discourse and social psychology*. London: Sage.

Propp, V. 1969. *The morphology of the folktale*. Austin, TX: University of Texas Press.

Signorelli, N. 1989. The stigma of mental illness on television. *Journal of Broadcasting and Electronic Media* 33(3): 325–31.

Silverman, D. 1993. *Interpreting qualitative data: Methods for analysing talk, text and interaction*. London: Sage.

Silverstone, R. 1981. *The message of television: Myth and narrative in contemporary culture*. London: Heinemann.

Todorov, T. 1977. *The poetics of prose*. Oxford: Blackwell.

Wahl, O. 1992. Mass media images of mental illness: a review of the literature. *Journal of Community Psychology* 20: 343–52.

Wearing, M. 1993. Professional discourse and sensational journalism: media constructions of violent insanity. *Australian Journal of Communication* 20(1): 84–98.

CHAPTER 18

Introducing Online Methods

CHRIS MANN AND FIONA STEWART

The main tools of data collection favoured by qualitative researchers are interviewing, observation and document analysis. Interviewing is the most widely applied technique for conducting systematic social enquiry in academic, clinical, business, political and media life (Holstein and Gubrium, 1997) and qualitative research is well established in this area. 'Interviewing' can take a number of forms, so it is perhaps better thought of as a collection of related methods. The primary distinction is between standardized (structured) and non-standardized (unstructured) interviews. Non-standardized interviews can be further subdivided into individual (or one-to-one) and group interviews (often called focus groups). A wide range of techniques for generating and analysing data from face-to-face (FTF) interviews with individuals and groups has been developed over time (see Briggs, 1986; Fontana and Frey, 1994; Lincoln and Guba, 1985; McCracken, 1988).

Observational techniques are also widely used in conventional qualitative research, frequently in conjunction with some form of interviewing. Finally, there are forms of data collection where there is a lower level of interaction with the researcher and a stronger emphasis on documentary analysis, such as journals, diaries and autobiographical approaches (see Chamberlain and Thompson, 1998; Flick, 1998; Gluck and Patai, 1991; Reinharz, 1992).

These different research methods have costs and benefits at both practical and methodological levels, and one of the main purposes of this chapter is to investigate whether, and to what extent, computer-mediated communication (CMC) can reduce the cost of these methods and/or increase the benefits. We shall begin this investigation by considering:

- how these methods are used in a conventional format;
- the advantages and disadvantages of attempting to conduct such methods online.

An essential aspect of this discussion is the place of practical expertise. When collecting data, the qualitative researcher-as-*bricoleur* picks and chooses from the tools of this methodological trade (Denzin and Lincoln, 1994: 2). In most forms of conventional research, methods of data collection are well established and training manuals and courses are readily available. However, there are additional challenges for researchers who wish to collect data online.

Researchers may have differing levels of experience with computers. In addition, technology is progressing very quickly. There are pros and cons associated with the use of electronic interaction in a research design, and some studies would clearly not be suited to this medium. However, once a researcher has decided that CMC is the way forward, the first practical step is to ensure that the researcher and all respondents have access to the required technology and the confidence to use it. Then researchers need to consider the logistics and mechanics of arranging and conducting qualitative research online with individuals and groups.

In this chapter we discuss such issues in relation to

- standardized interviews in the form of email and Web-page-based surveys;
- non-standardized forms of online one-to-one interviewing;
- 'observation' of virtual communities; and
- the collection of personal documents online.

The aim is to provide sufficient information to (a) spur online research initiatives and (b) give a basis for methodological discussion of online research.

STANDARDIZED INTERVIEWS

In structured interviews, interviewees are asked standardized questions with a limited set of response categories. Conventional surveys often take place face-to-face (FTF) or over the telephone; others may be in the form of a self-completion questionnaire. Responses are recorded according to a pre-established coding scheme and are generally analysed statistically (Fontana and Frey, 1994). Frequently, and especially when paper based, standardized interviews are referred to as 'surveys.'

There has been a long history of debate regarding the place in qualitative research of methods which have been characterized as involving numbers rather than words (Miles and Huberman, 1994: 15). Beginning with Max Weber (1922), some qualitative researchers have not excluded quantitative measurements a priori, but have used them where appropriate and with necessary caution. Epistemological and philosophical discussion relating to qualitative and quantitative research continues (Becker, 1996; Bryman, 1988). Recent formulations suggest that, when 'method' is understood as a procedure, tool or technique, there is no one method or set of methods which would define an enquiry as qualitative (Schwandt, 1997). If we distinguish qualitative research questions as those which focus on the form/nature of phenomena, there will be times when additional contextual information is relevant. Allowing that apparently simple, factual questions can be more difficult than they seem (see Wilson [1996] for a discussion) qualitative researchers may still have recourse to, for instance, demographic information.

While some researchers retain a qualitative-quantitative distinction at the level of practical data collection (May, 1993), many others are prepared to combine methods in the research design if this strategy addresses the research question (Brannen, 1992; Miles and Huberman, 1994). A qualitative researcher may purposefully adopt 'multiple research strategies' (Burgess, 1993) as part of a process of triangulation (Denzin, 1970), or as part of a cumulative process in the search for qualitative understanding (Reinharz, 1992). Williams *et al.* (1988: 15), who consider methods for new media as mainly extensions of existing methods, also suggest that 'the new media researcher should consider alternative methods, or even multiple methods, and attempt a triangulation of methods'. (See Mixed Methods section later in this chapter.) Accordingly, as some qualitative researchers will include standardized interviews in their repertoire of methods, we shall consider the impact of CMC on this form of data collection. The challenges faced by researchers who have attempted structured interviews online have been more extensively documented than many of the other methods we discuss. Studies of online surveys began to be published from the end of 1995 (for reviews see Comley, 1996; Witmer *et al.*, 1999) and offer considerable practical insight for any researcher who intends to use CMC in this way.

Email Surveys

In an email survey the questions are usually sent to respondents as the text of a conventional email message. To complete the survey, respondents use the 'reply' facility of their email system and add their answers to the text of the returned message. The answers received can then be typed into an analysis program in the same way as for a conventional survey. Alternatively, a program can be written that interprets the emailed responses and reads the answers directly into a database, offering significant savings in terms of data entry. Commercial survey creation programs[1] are available that, as well as assisting in producing the text of a survey, can carry out this interpretation of replies, provided the survey has been completed correctly (see also Smith, 1997).

Text-based email surveys are convenient for the respondent because they require no facilities or expertise beyond those that they use in their day-to-day mail communication. However, because only text can be used, the survey can appear dry and uninteresting. Email in its simplest form cannot be used to transmit extended characters such as pound signs (£) and does not allow formatting of text (such as bold and italics, different fonts, etc.). In addition, although the researcher may ask the respondent to use a particular format for the reply, this is completely under the control of the individual and cannot be imposed. There is nothing to prevent the user from answering outside the boxes, from selecting three choices where only one is required or from deleting questions or altering their format. The researcher may still be able to interpret what the respondent means, as with a badly completed paper questionnaire, but the need to edit responses removes the advantages of automated data entry and can greatly increase the per-case costs.

If all potential respondents are using more modern email systems that can understand HTML,[2] then these problems can be alleviated by using an HTML-based email survey. Because HTML only uses standard text characters, the survey is still sent as the text of an email. But because the email system interprets the HTML commands, the message can be laid out in an attractive way. In addition, the researcher has control over the user's responses: answers can only be typed in text entry boxes and, if only one choice is required, only one will be accepted. HTML-based email combines these advantages of Web-based surveys (see below) with the direct response of email. However, until HTML-enabled email systems become more common, these benefits are only possible if the survey will be covering a defined population where the researcher knows what system respondents are using.

A third possibility is to present the survey not as the email message itself but as a file (for example, a word processor document or a spreadsheet) which is attached to the email. The respondent opens the attached file, completes the survey using the relevant program, saves the file and then attaches the saved file to a return email. This gives control over the appearance of the survey, but completion and return require more technical ability of the respondents. In addition, respondents must all have access to the program (such as Microsoft Word or Microsoft Excel) in which the attached document was created. As with HTML-based mail the approach is only suitable for a defined population where the researcher knows the abilities of respondents or can provide training and support.

Some of these problems can be overcome by using survey creation software to produce a self-contained interactive survey program.[3] The program file is emailed as an attachment. Respondents run the program (for example, by double-clicking the attachment icon) and are then shown the survey questions in an attractive graphical interface which most users should find easy to understand. The program may be able to check users' responses and may allow personalized routes to be taken through the questions, producing an elegant, responsive and efficient survey. No other software needs to be available on respondents' computers, and the survey program can produce a formatted answers file which can be mailed back to the researcher for automated input to a database. However, there are a number of limitations. A program created for the Windows operating system will not run on a Macintosh and vice versa. This limits the number of respondents who can use the program, or introduces numerous complexities associated with having two versions of the same survey program. Even with a single operating system there may be unexpected technical difficulties when trying to run the program on the wide range of computers likely to be used by respondents. (Couper et al. [1999] found problems with all seven of their pre-test subjects.) The program files produced may be large (in the case of Couper *et al.*, approaching 1Mb) which may result in unacceptable volumes of Internet traffic and may be beyond the size permitted for incoming email attachments. Indeed, some organizations may prohibit the receipt of any programs as email attachments because of fears about viruses.

Because of these problems, most of the email surveys reported to date have used the straightforward text-based route. Email surveys have been used to study small-scale homogeneous groups of online users (Parker, 1992; Smith, 1997; Tse *et al.*, 1995; Winter and Huff, 1996) and, more recently, as a method for administering a large national survey in the United States (Sheehan and Hoy, 1999). Studies report widely differing comparative response rates between postal mail and email survey returns (Sheehan and Hoy, 1999; Smith, 1997; Witmer et al., 1999). Sheehan and Hoy suggest that lower email response rates may be associated with the unfamiliarity of the technology—but this is rapidly changing, and among some sections of society use of email is already almost universal.

Schaefer and Dillman (1998) conducted an experimental study in which they compared three mixed mode, multiple contact email procedures with a survey using conventional mail methods. The population for the experiment, the permanent faculty of Washington State University, received four contacts: a prenotice, the questionnaire, a thank you/reminder and a replacement questionnaire. One group received all contacts by email, a second group received the prenotice on paper and all other contacts by email (unless they responded by requesting a paper survey), a third group received the thank you/reminder on paper and other contacts by email, and the control group received all contacts on paper. The authors reported no significant difference in the response rates of the all-paper and all-email groups (both around 58 per cent), though the email questionnaires were returned significantly faster. Email responses were more complete, especially for open ended questions, and the email survey achieved much longer responses to open ended questions than the paper version (a finding of particular interest to qualitative researchers). Schaefer and Dillman concluded that, 'this study suggests the viability of a standard E-mail method based on techniques found successful in mail survey research' (1998: 392), though they recommend that it be combined with paper methods in a mixed-mode design to ensure that respondents who do not have (or do not wish to use) email are not excluded.

However, Couper *et al.* (1999) reported less successful results from their comparison of mail and email surveys of employees of five US government agencies. Their methodology was similar to Schaefer and Dillman, though their questionnaire was longer. Couper *et al.* reported an overall response rate of 71 per cent for the paper questionnaire sent by conventional mail but only 43 per cent for the email version, with very different patterns between different agencies. The difference in response rates may have been partly due to the fact that many employees, despite being automatically allocated an email address, did not in fact use email and hence never received the questionnaire. (Schaefer and Dillman, on the other hand, were able to validate the addresses of their email sample by a number of means.) Couper *et al.* also put part of the variation between agencies down to technical problems; some agencies use an email system which converts messages over a certain size (such as the questionnaire) into attachments, and a number of employees reported that they had received attachments but didn't know what to do with them. (This problem was also reported by Comley [1996] who had to split his survey into two emails.) About 21 per cent of all email respondents did not make use of the reply feature as intended, using a word processor or text editor instead. Twenty seven per cent of responses required editing before they could be added to the database, leading the authors to conclude that, 'we did not experience the cost savings expected from e-mail' (1999: 53).

Despite these problems, Couper *et al.* 'remain optimistic about the potential for e-mail as an alternative to the traditional mail survey' (1999: 54). As they point out, the success of an email survey may depend on many factors and there is a need to explore in greater detail the factors that affect nonresponse and measurement errors in email surveys.

Web-Page-Based Surveys

Schaefer and Dillman commented that their experiment with email surveys 'revealed the possibility that [these] represent only an interim surveying technology' (1998: 392). Many researchers are turning their attention to the World Wide Web as a more suitable medium for administering questionnaires[4] (for further information see Comley, 1996; Kehoe and Pitkow, 1996; Coomber, 1997; O'Connor and Madge, 2000; and for a comparison with email surveys, Patrick et al., 1995).

A Web-page-based survey has the advantage that it appears identical (subject to the browser used) to all respondents. The survey can be given an attractive appearance utilising text formatting, colours and graphics. It is also easy for respondents to complete, typically by selecting responses from predefined lists or entering text in boxes and then simply clicking a 'Submit' button when finished. The data received by the researcher are in a completely predictable and consistent format, making automated analysis possible without the editing that may be necessary with text-based email.

The disadvantages of using the Web relate to the technical knowledge required to set up the survey. The researcher must have (or be able to call on) expertise in HTML[5] in order to create the Web pages. Survey creation programs[6] can provide 'what you see is what you get' editing of pages, removing much of the mystery of HTML, but identifying and learning a suitable program presents another hurdle to be overcome. Once the pages have been created, space on a host Internet server[7] must be arranged (this may be available as part of an internet service provier (ISP) package) and the pages must be uploaded to the server. Uploading usually requires an file transfer protocol (FTP) program; a possible source of this may be the ISP, or the relevant facilities may be provided as part of the survey creation program. A numeric address and password for the server will be required (obtainable from the ISP), together with a steady nerve in the face of advancing jargon. Finally, it will be necessary to identify the full, correct unique resource locator (URL, http://address) for the Web pages so that respondents to the survey can find them.

Unfortunately, that's not quite it. When the user clicks the 'Submit' button on the survey page it activates a small program, known usually as a 'script', that transfers their answers to the host server. The script is held on the host and the page designer must ensure that the correct script is being used by the Web page, and is in the correct place on the server. Advice can be obtained from the ISP or other sources, but will usually include the terms 'CGI' or 'Perl,' and by now the avalanche of acronyms may have overwhelmed the courageous researcher. As Smith (1997, *online*) concluded in her review of online surveys, 'the lack of standardization among operating systems, servers and browsers creates a challenging milieu in which a researcher must be technologically savvy as well as methodologically sound.'

Despite these problems, Web-page-based surveys offer significant advantages (which we discuss next) in terms of reach, speed and economy. Consequently they seem certain to become more and more common, especially for commercial market research. Smith (1997, *online*) predicted that Web survey software would soon become an indispensable research tool, 'along with or even instead of analytical tools like SPSS.' It may not be long before the creation of Web survey pages is routinely taught in social science research methods courses.

Advantages/Disadvantages of Conventional and Online Standardized Interviews

When we consider the advantages/disadvantages of conventional and online standardized interviews, it is in terms of their narrowly defined role in qualitative research. We suggest that, for qualitative researchers, structured interviews are useful when focused and specific contextual information is required and cost, time, reach (possible range of context) and/or anonymity are an issue. Accordingly, we shall compare and contrast conventional and online versions of this technique in terms of these four factors.

COST. Discussions about cost are relevant within and between conventional and online standardized interview methods. Conventional self-administered questionnaires are generally considered more economically viable than labour-intensive FTF or phone interviews. However, CMC can cut costs further. Email offers substantial savings as it eliminates paper and is cheap to send. Although Web-based surveys can involve initial start-up costs, once these have been met the costs for implementation and analysis of the survey are minimal (Sheehan and Hoy, 1999). However, researchers need to ensure that both they and the participants understand what is involved in terms of the costs of acquiring expertise.

TIME.   Within conventional methods, self-completion surveys are considered time effective. But CMC offers even greater time benefits. Comley's (1996) study directly comparing email, postal mail and Web survey options showed that increased speed was a major advantage in the use of email. Schaefer and Dillman's (1998) study confirmed that email questionnaires were returned faster than their paper equivalents.

Web-page-based surveys can speed up responses even further (Comley, 1996; Smith, 1997); studies have shown that hundreds of responses may be generated over a single weekend (Sheehan and Hoy, 1999) and there are anecdotal accounts of 'thousands of responses' being received within a few hours (Gjestland, 1996). However, researchers may need to set aside a considerable period of time for solving technical problems before implementation of an online survey (Couper et al., 1999) and even during it. Smith remarked with frustration that, in her Web-based survey, a Javascript[8] pop-up 'thank you' message did not work (although it had worked when initially tested) and respondents did not receive acknowledgement that their data had been successfully submitted. She then had to spend time deleting redundant information. She added:

> One respondent reported that every other question in Part 1 of his questionnaire was missing . . . This remains a mystery. (1997: *online*)

Email surveys can also consume time if the researcher has to search around for addresses, if many addresses turn out to be invalid and if the form of the survey has to be explained to participants.

REACH (EXTENSION OF CONTEXT).   One drawback to all FTF interviews is that they generally involve organizational problems. If qualitative researchers want to set in-depth studies within a wider context, arranging multiple standardized FTF interviews may present logistical problems. Phone interviews (Cannell, 1985; Sykes and Hoinville, 1985) have the potential to increase the geographical reach of researchers, but there are financial considerations, and problems remain when interviews need to cross time zones.

With the caveat that Internet use is variable worldwide, Web-page-based and email surveys offer considerable advantages in terms of increased reach by collapsing boundaries of time and space (Bachmann et al., 1996; Mehta and Sivadas, 1995). Email surveys can only be sent to known addresses; but if that address is a group, a single transmission can reach many people. A drawback to this is that surveys posted to one population (a newsgroup, for instance) may be forwarded to other populations, resulting in confusion about the source of responses (Coomber, 1997).

Use of the Web is growing rapidly as the information available on it proliferates, but the very attractiveness of the Web is causing some employers, in particular, to consider controlling access to it. Evidence at present is anecdotal but it seems likely that, in a work setting, fewer people have access to the Web than to email. The Web is arguably now the most popular application on home computers, but since completion of a Web-page-based survey requires the user to be online the whole time it may be less attractive than an email survey which can be completed offline. On the other hand, since access to Web pages is usually available to anyone who knows (or finds) their URL, it can be difficult to prevent people who are not part of the target population from completing the survey, or to prevent multiple submissions by the same person. Pages can be password protected, but this adds another technical challenge for the researcher and complicates the administration of the survey.

Nevertheless, because they can be completed by anyone who accesses the relevant page, Web-based polls generate very high rates of response (Kehoe and Pitkow, 1996). This points to increasing reach in terms of the potential diversity of participants (Sheehan and Hoy, 1999). On the other hand, it may be supposed that respondents are homogeneous in terms of their familiarity with Web usage—in which case online surveys may only offer understanding of limited, and specific, contexts.

A further complicating factor is the strong bias against survey research among some computer cultures that has been reported by Kendall (1999) and Paccagnella (1997). Paccagnella noted that many of the most interesting virtual communities are proud of their exclusive culture. A stranger wanting to do academic research is sometimes seen as an unwelcome arbitrary intrusion. Kendall concluded that her research about 'mudding' (use of multi-user [MU*] environments); would have been unlikely to have received sufficient responses following a rash of poorly conceived surveys sent out by mudding college students (1999: 71).

Finally, if the aim of the survey is to provide a wider context, it is essential to ensure that desired participants do actually respond to research enquiries. This begins with recruitment. Simply advertising the research on a Web page is not sufficient. The researcher would need to be pro-active by, perhaps, posting information to appropriate online groups (see Coomber, 1997). Decisions would have to be made regarding the use of specific survey clearing house sites, invitations to participants posed to user groups, and direct email contact (see Walther and Boyd, 2000).

In sensitive areas response rates will also be related to the next factor we consider: concerns about anonymity (Coomber, 1997).

ANONYMITY. The focus of some qualitative studies emphasizes the need for anonymity. When sensitive information is needed from a wide range of people, an anonymous survey may be a suitable complement to the in-depth component of the research.

Here privacy is a paramount concern. In a virtual environment, where an 'aura of suspicion' surrounds the stranger-to-stranger communication associated with survey research (Smith, 1997), research trust and credibility are essential. Smith noted that many of the respondents in her email survey had been 'extremely interested' in how she had acquired their names and addresses, and many had verified her identity and credentials before participating. Another practical difficulty is that participants using Bulletin

Board Systems (BBSs) and Internet Relay Chat (IRC) may fail to complete surveys correctly (or at all) because it is the anonymity of the medium that they most value (Myers, 1987).

Reviewers of survey research distinguish anonymity issues for email and Web-page-based standardized interviews (Smith, 1997; Sheehan and Hoy, 1999) with email being seen as a less protected medium. When respondents use the 'reply' function of their email programs to return completed surveys, the message carries their name and email address in its header. It is possible to send messages through an anonymous remailer which strips messages of their original headers and replaces them with something else, so that the originator of the message becomes virtually untraceable (Lee, 1996).[9] Unfortunately, this anonymity may then act as a cover for multiple responses from one person.

In principle, Web surveys allow for anonymity since respondents can choose whether to include their names. Once again, this can become a problem as 'ballot stuffers' can make multiple responses. In addition, as the Web is an open medium, unwanted participants, who are not part of the target sample, might respond. If these problems are circumvented by employing password protection of a survey site, anonymity again becomes an issue. Practical details for setting up a Web survey when anonymity is a paramount concern are discussed by Coomber (1997).

Different issues of anonymity may come into play when researchers are investigating virtual communities in which participants adopt online personae. For instance, standardized interviews may be used as part of an ethnography of virtual communities. Here, personae responding to standardized interviews may be 'deliberate and elaborate fabrications' (Walther, 1992: 3). Paccagnella has questioned the meaning of socio-demographic data obtained through structured online questionnaires in these circumstances:

> What is really happening, for example, when SweetBabe, a regular participant in IRC channel #netsex and one of the hypothetical cases from our survey sample, tells us that her real name is Mary, she's thirty years old and she works as a secretary? It is wise to suppose that, more than providing us some (if any) actual information about Mary's real life, such an answer could help to understand better SweetBabe's symbolic universe, her online self-representation, her social values and relationships . . . from a phenomenological standpoint, SweetBabe and her social world are for us much more real than this supposed Mary about whom we actually know absolutely nothing. (1997: *online*)

In fact, issues of anonymity and authenticity remain the core methodological stumbling block for researchers using online methods.

In structured interviews the researcher attempts to control the interview by standardizing questions and constraining responses. It is in non-standardized interviews that the focus moves from the pre-formulated ideas of the researcher to 'the meanings and interpretations that individuals attribute to events and relationships' (May, 1993: 94). It is this emphasis which leads many practitioners to refer to such interviews as qualitative—and it is to these methods we now turn.

NON-STANDARDIZED INTERVIEWS

Once we move outside tightly structured survey interviews, the interview continuum is very wide (see Briggs, 1986; Lincoln and Guba, 1985). These methods offer different levels of qualitative depth as, depending upon the interview form, participants have more or less opportunity to answer questions in their own terms (May, 1993: 92–94). The choice of interview method usually depends upon the research question itself, or upon the qualitative approach which informs the overall research design (for classifications of qualitative studies see Creswell, 1998; Tesch, 1990). Working online, less structured interviews with individuals are usually conducted by email, or by 'chatting' one-to-one using real-time software.

The Qualitative Interview Spectrum

At one end of the non-standardized interview spectrum is the semi-structured interview. This may be fairly formalized, using an interview protocol organized into specific thematic areas, or it may branch out tangentially from a small selection of more open-ended questions. Such interviews are more like conversations between equal participants than standardized interviews (Garfinkel, 1967). Supplementary questions (sometimes called probes) are introduced in a spontaneous manner to seek further clarification and elaboration of answers (Wilson, 1996). The main advantage of such interviews is to offer 'purposive topical steering' (Flick, 1998: 106) as the format allows interviewers to track the issues which are of most interest to themselves. In contrast, 'squarely at the qualitative end of the research spectrum' (May, 1993: 94), unstructured or 'in-depth' interviews place greater emphasis on the subjective experiences of individuals (Denzin, 1989; Clandinin and Connelly, 1994).

Interviewers who favour in-depth methods are often skeptical about how far subjective experiences may be accessed even in relatively flexible semi-structured interviews (Flick, 1998: 98). There is a concern that the interview may reflect the researcher's own agenda too closely. With in-depth interviews, it is participants who structure the form and content of extensive reflective responses (sometimes called narratives) evoked by a broad initial enquiry from the interviewer. Although the interviewer provides the focus of the interview, there is generally an emphasis on the 'stories' that people tell, the 'voice' of the person within the story, and the narrator as the prime 'knower' of self (Seidman, 1991).

There are also differences of style and emphasis between in-depth interviews depending upon the purpose of the interview, and its place within different disciplines. Methods include such forms as the long interview (McCracken, 1988), oral history (Portelli, 1998), the life story (Chanfrault-Duchet,

1991), the psychological voice-centred interview (Brown and Gilligan, 1992), feminist personal narratives (Gluck and Patai, 1991; Middleton, 1993), and the narrative interview (see Flick, 1998). Cross-national, interdisciplinary perspectives and debates about research practice in a variety of these approaches may be found in Chamberlain and Thompson (1998).

Non-standardized Interviews Online

Debates about qualitative interviewing are not only relevant in terms of discussing conventional methods, but also inform discussion about the possible place of the Internet as a research tool. For instance, we have seen that a key challenge in the design of a qualitative study is to find a balance between interview methods which give participants 'the floor' and those which allow interviewers to pursue their own research enquiries.

The experiences of researchers who have used CMC to interview illustrate that, as in conventional studies, it is possible to achieve different degrees of balance online depending on the purpose of the study and the methodological perspective of the interviewer. O'Connor and Madge (2000), who carried out semi-structured online interviews with real-time focus groups, reported being delighted with the results because the groups successfully developed key themes introduced in an earlier questionnaire. Here the emphasis is on the interviewer's purposes. Bennett, who conducted in-depth interviews, also used real-time chat (one-to-one). She found she preferred chat to either FTF or email alternatives because it enabled an equitable research balance to be established from the beginning of the interaction. She valued the immediacy of the real-time response not only for the speed with which her own enquiries could be addressed but also because it allowed a negotiation of meaning between herself and her 'co-researchers' (while also avoiding the potential embarrassment of FTF interaction).

Researchers who have carried out non-standardized interviews using asynchronous CMC are divided about their success. Hodkinson (2000) experienced semi-structured email interviews as excessively question structured and formal. He felt unable to achieve the fruitful mutual interaction he enjoyed when conducting in-depth interviews FTF. Partly as a consequence, a number of his email interviews involved few exchanges and participants did not become as engaged as he hoped. In contrast, in the Graduates of the Millennium project, Mann was confident that semi-structured email interviews conducted sequentially over a three-year period had allowed both the student participants and herself to explore their own agendas.

Ferri, who focused on women with learning disabilities, and Anders, who investigated women with disabilities in higher education, both sought 'invisible' stories of women's experience within a frame of identity politics. Here, the emphasis of the research balance was firmly on the subjective experiences of participants. Anders conducted email interviews over a full year. Although discussions developed broadly from three 'staggered' questionnaires, the women were invited to reshape/reframe these questions in any way they preferred. Anders was delighted with the richness of the resulting dialogue (between 10 and 100 hours with each individual over the year). Finally Ferri (2000) set out to explore 'the potential of electronic mail to transgress boundaries between the researcher and the researched, and the product and the process of constructing knowledge.' She regularly collected messages from each participant in her 'closed' discussion list and then circulated everyone's contributions with all identifying material removed. The ensuing asynchronous discussion fora yielded 'very interactive, complex and rich data.' Ferri found working online 'an amazing way to bring people together and to facilitate participatory research' (1999, personal communication). The studies described in this section suggest that CMC can be adapted to interviews across the qualitative spectrum.

Practicalities of Organizing Non-standardized Interviews

A number of challenges are shared by all non-standardized interview approaches using CMC. As discussed above, there are considerable logistical difficulties with structured interviewing and many of these issues carry over to less structured methods. Whether working online or FTF, there are practicalities of accessing, financing and having the competence to use the relevant technology, whether recording and transcribing equipment, the phone, or the Internet. Similarly, whether using standardized or non-standardized methods, all interviewers have to make choices about sampling, gain access to participants, make initial contact, give a rationale for the investigation, build trust or credibility, persuade participants to respond, and give clear instructions about the interview process. However, at almost every stage of the interview process there are vital procedural differences which distinguish interviews which seek qualitative depth from those which identity the frequency or distribution of phenomena. We shall discuss these differences in terms of sampling, access, making contact and giving instructions in non-standardized one-to-one interviews.

Sampling Strategies in Non-standardized Interviews

As we saw above, surveys tend to focus on numerical 'reach.' In qualitative interviews sampling is more focused; the challenge is to find individuals who have experienced the phenomenon under study and are prepared to be involved (Miles and Huberman, 1994: 119). Rather than looking for representativeness, 'purposeful' sampling strategies are generally adopted (see Patton, 1990). The interviewer's 'purpose' is associated with the methodological approach taken (Creswell, 1998: 112–113). For instance, a biographical interviewer might seek a unique individual, ethnographers might seek a cultural group to which they are strangers, a case study researcher might seek a sample showing the widest range of relevant characteristics (the 'maximum variation' of sites or participants). Purposive sampling is often constrained by logistical difficulties and traditional and online methods have different strengths and weaknesses in this area.

Considerations in Conventional Sampling

In conventional research, sampling decisions involve geographic and other practical considerations. In most studies, interviewers need to make travel arrangements; schedule (and frequently reschedule) the times, dates and venues of meetings; set up recording equipment (often in less than ideal environments); and keep in mind transcription costs. These issues may dictate choice of site. Multiple sites increase organizational complexities which might deter the interviewer working alone. Even within single sites,[10] the research design might point to multiple interviews, with the potential for further logistical problems if different participants are available for interview in the same time slot.

Arranging 'sufficient' interviews is a further serious methodological and hence logistical challenge in different approaches to qualitative interviewing (Creswell, 1998). Researchers seeking the maximum variation of characteristics between sites, or between participants, may realize that the number of planned interviews is escalating. Sometimes a decision is made to limit the scope of the enquiry if the interview arrangements threaten to become too costly or time-consuming. There is some consensus that theoretical sampling approaches such as grounded theory require between twenty and thirty hour-long interviews, and these are often on different sites to allow comparisons to be made (Creswell, 1998; Douglas, 1985). In-depth interviews might require fewer people but each interview may be time-consuming (McCracken, 1988). As one researcher involved in narrative interviews commented, 'the problem of telling one's own life is that one knows too much' (Larson, 1997: 456). When 'long' interviews can last from two to four hours, ten participants might be considered reasonable (Creswell, 1998), but this is a conservative estimate. In a study of female academics in Canada, a group of five interviewers conducted 200 such interviews (Acker and Feuerverger, 1999).

In addition, there may need to be flexibility with regard to extending the interview base. For instance, with grounded theory, data are collected from a range of interviews until a particular theoretical category is 'saturated'; that is, until nothing new can be learned (Glaser and Strauss, 1967). Apart from the original interviews arranged, the researcher might need to move quickly to set up new interviews if a theoretical category needs to be refined further. The analysis of 'sufficient' numbers of interviews also involves financial considerations. With in-depth interviews the financial burden of recording, transcribing and analysing huge amounts of unstructured rich textual material is often underestimated. It is also a common place for budget costcutting.

Another consideration for conventional researchers is to be able to offer a secure, private and familiar environment where personal issues might be explored. This is particularly the case when the interviewing is sensitive (Lee, 1993). For instance, Wilson (1996) chose to interview people who had been in long-term residential care in their own homes. However, in some situations, participants might be cautious about inviting interviewers into their homes (women, the elderly, people who fear public exposure) or might not have access to private living space (if living in prisons, refuges, etc.). In conventional interviewing the alternative is usually to meet in public places, which can be noisy and lack privacy, or in non-familiar settings organized by the researcher. These options are clearly not ideal for conducting non-standardized interviews which seek to explore subjectivities in depth.

Sampling Online

How might online interviewing address these problems? Assuming that both interviewer and participants have ready access to online communication, many of the factors discussed above are not an issue when using email as an interview method. The interviewer rarely needs to travel; organizing recording equipment and costing for transcription is unnecessary; the asynchronous nature of most email interaction allows participants great flexibility in terms of the frequency and length of their responses; access to a computer in a personal environment can offer both privacy and familiarity; and, in areas where email use is ubiquitous, techniques such as 'snowballing' (finding one participant through another) can locate additional interviewees with the minimum of time and energy. So, in the online environment, there are fewer of the constraints associated with conventional research as many of the difficulties of accessing multiple, and geographically disparate, real-life sites disappear.

In addition, the global range of the Internet opens up the possibilities of studying projects which might have seemed impracticable before. In one study, CMC allowed the interviewer to widen the geographic scope of her in-depth interviews with gay fathers to include participants not only in the United Kingdom, but also in New Zealand, Canada and the United States (Dunne, 1999).

Online interviewing was also an appropriate choice for studying the translocal and transnational subculture of the Goths (Hodkinson, 2000). In this latter study, the global reach of the research, and the established Internet culture of the participants, meant that purposive sampling was like fishing in a very big pond. If participants did not respond, or dropped out after answering an initial set of questions, Hodkinson merely tried somebody else.

However, the overall patchiness of computer access and skills would certainly limit the possibility of purposive sampling in many areas of real life (although not of course of virtual communities). It might well defeat the aim of some interviewers, particularly in areas like oral history, to actively seek out lives in order to open up the possibility for self-expression among previously marginalized groups such as women in the family, the old, the institutionalized and hospital patients (Bornat, 1994). Even if some individuals had occasional use of email, time constraints on computer access could mitigate against longer interviews and, if computer access were limited to public venues issues of privacy remain. Although silent communion with a computer screen in a cybercafe might attract less attention than an FTF interview in a coffee bar, the possibility of passers-by reading intimate thoughts may inhibit many potential participants (Creswell, 1998).

There is another aspect of access which has a deep resonance for online research. In principle, the virtual interviewer could camouflage aspects of personal identity such as class, age, gender and ethnicity in order to make previously limited or proscribed access possible. However, there is strong evidence that people do make attributions about others from information which is inadvertently (as well as consciously) transmitted online.

It is possible to circumvent social cues which might be suggested by names or email addresses by, for instance, opening an 'iname' account. This allows the user to choose a context-free username (which can be almost anything) together with the domain name: iname.com.[11] Another possibility is to interview in teams. Here, characteristics such as age, gender and ethnicity may be variously represented. In the Graduates of the Millennium (GOTM) project, the two interviewers initially involved were a young man and a middle-aged woman. Both names were appended to all emails so the identity of an individual participant's interviewer was unclear. However, other interviewers may prefer to utilize CMC as a cloak for the real-life self, and this clearly involves ethical considerations as well as implications for data.

Problems of Access in Non-standardized Interviews

A consideration related to sampling decisions is whether the site(s) chosen require the researcher to go through a gatekeeper who controls access to participants. Gatekeepers can grant or withhold permission to conduct research in their jurisdiction, be that a prison, a family, a golf club, a student society or a multi-national business. In their concern to protect their own interests and those of the group, gatekeepers may refuse access altogether or restrict it to particular areas, times or events (Foster, 1996). This may be less of a problem if the experience or process being studied takes place in multiple sites. Because the research is not focused on a particular site it may be acceptable to contact participants directly (Seidman, 1991: 35).

These issues take on different aspects in online research. As we have seen, using email makes the option of using multiple sites more feasible, so, if avoiding one key all-powerful gatekeeper was a priority, there would be fewer logistical problems to prejudice that option. In addition email permits direct access to individuals without the use of intermediaries. This is particularly the case where researchers are investigating public sites with which they are already familiar, such as specific academic or business environments. There are also special interest sites where users consciously seek to make contact with each other. As Hodkinson noted:

> I used a combination of Web-searches and hypertext links, to collect the e-mail addresses of several Goth bands from various parts of the world, and

then sent them all an e-mail which introduced my research, and requested an online interview. In fact, finding e-mail addresses was one of the most convenient aspects of using the net. Every Web-site and every e-mailing list post contains the address of the individual responsible for it, making it possible to make contact instantly. The interconnectedness between E-mail addresses, Web site URLs and newsgroups were especially useful. (1999: personal communication)

However, it can be much more difficult to access individuals outside familiar contexts. As it is unlikely that an accurate national, or preferably international, register of email addresses will be established, problems of access remain. In the online world both moderators (the people who intercept and decide on the legitimacy of messages sent to a newsgroup or mailing list) and Webmasters/postmasters (the people who run www/email servers and have the power to give away email addresses) have the potential to act as gatekeepers.

For instance, when Foster (1994: 94) attempted to contact people through mailing lists and interest groups some moderators, 'quite rightly, took the view that my survey was not germane to the main business of the group, blocked it, and courteously informed me of this.' In another study, Smith-Stoner and Weber (2000) had to persuade teaching universities to announce their desire to interview women distance learning students through 'system wide broadcasts' in their institutions. Some institutions refused to do this. Cole (2000), however, was successful in gaining permission from the Web site manager of the United States 'Promise Keepers' movement, allowing him to follow up email addresses for potential participants. As we shall see in the next section, where we discuss how a researcher might make contact with participants, the relational style of a qualitative researcher might have an impact at each stage of the access process.

Making Contact in Non-standardized Interviews

The question of *how* to gain access to participants is more crucial in qualitative than quantitative approaches to interviewing. The stress placed on the researcher as the human instrument of research means there is a greater degree of closeness and personal involvement between interviewer and participants. This relationship is crucial to the success of the research and it develops from the very beginning of the research process. As Seidman (1991:31) noted, the way interviewers gain access to potential participants and make contact with them can affect every subsequent step in the interviewing process. To a much greater degree than in standardized interviews, the 'communicative competencies' (Flick, 1998: 55) and the perceived social and personal characteristics of the researcher are salient issues.

Current research suggests that interviewers experience email as an easy and efficient means of initial communication with contacts, whether they are subsequently interviewed in person or online. Cole (2000) arranged his FTF interviews with Promise Keepers in this way. Similarly, Hodkinson arranged offline and online interviews with his Goth contacts, through formal and informal email networking:

One e-mailing list appeal for volunteers for off-line interviews resulted in my conducting two tape recorded group discussions. In another, numerous e-mail exchanges with an individual I met fleetingly at a Goth festival resulted in a place to stay, and a guide for an important off-line research trip to Leeds. I have found that the Internet is particularly suited to establishing the first contact in such eventual networks of respondents. (1999: personal communication)

Another approach is to place strategic advertisements in appropriate newsgroups, mailing lists or BBSs. Bennett (1998) found her male participants by advertising in groups such as alt.acadia and soc.men, stressing that she was seeking extended interaction in a confidential one-to-one exchange. Dunne (1999), who was seeking a generally invisible population marginalized in both mainstream and gay culture (gay fathers), included her email address in publicity leaflets and journals.

Locating participants is only the first step. Given the emphasis on relationship building, a key consideration in online research is whether text-based email communication is able to establish sufficiently close contact with potential participants, in the early stages of the research, to secure their collaboration (Seidman, 1991: 31). In conventional research, making initial contact with participants usually involves writing a letter or phoning, often followed by a first contact visit. These introductory moves can be a daunting experience if interviewers are shy, have difficulties in self-presentation, or act awkwardly on the phone (Seidman, 1991). Making first contact using CMC might alleviate these pressures slightly: email is a less intrusive medium than the phone as it almost never interrupts the receiver (possibly minimizing the chance of an initial irritated response), and it requires less attention to formalities than a letter (although in some situations formality would remain the most suitable approach).

It could be argued that email messages at least hold their own with the phone and the letter as a means of projecting an ideal introductory style, incorporating, 'seriousness but friendliness of tone, purposefulness but flexibility in approach, and openness but conciseness in presentation' (Seidman 1991: 38).

Giving Instructions in Non-standardized Interviews

A final step in the early stages of arranging qualitative interviews is conveying the form and purpose of the research to new recruits. Whether the preliminaries are discussed by letter or phone, the interviewer using conventional methods is generally able to clear up any remaining misunderstandings FTF. Qualitative interviews which are arranged and then conducted online have to rely on text to put across the broad and finer points of the research, to spell out the interview protocol and to arrange any other 'housekeeping' details such as flagging the arrival of follow-up information (Foster, 1994).

In one study where semi-structured online interviews were to follow a brief online demographic survey, the researchers stressed that 'advance organizers' were essential to clarify the research procedure. Phrases such as: 'This is the second step in the interview process. After you return the survey we will begin he interview' were used to talk participants through each stage of the research (Smith-Stoner and Weber, 2000: 6). However, the interviewers found that, because online instructions required more context and explanations than conventional research, there was a danger that the interactions became too long and convoluted:

> Two computer screens full of text seems to be most effective in getting respondents to explain and elaborate on responses. Scrolling back and forth on the screen with longer posts can become confusing and result in topics being missed. (2000: 9)

Another issue, which is clearly relevant at all stages in online interviewing, is the precise verbal formulation of instructions and questions. As Smith-Stoner ruefully reported,

> We are used to saying 'A picture paints a thousand words'. In reality, online, 'A word paints a thousand pictures' (quote from Eric Berkowitz, a fellow student) so we have to allow for that. We asked people about 'meaningful learning' and they said they didn't understand the questions. When we eliminated that as a question and asked: 'What were you passionate about?' they used the word 'meaningful'. So we had to tinker a lot with the words. (1999: personal communication)

As we have seen, there are problems with some aspects of setting up online qualitative interviews for, as with conventional research, 'various methods may produce different problems, suspicions and fears in different persons' (Flick 1998: 58). However, in suitable contexts, online qualitative interviewing does seem to offer the possibility of minimizing some logistical problems in the research design. This is important because, 'every step the interviewer takes to ease the logistics of the process is a step toward allowing the available energy to be focused on the interview itself' (Seidman, 1991: 39).

OBSERVATIONAL TECHNIQUES

For the qualitative researcher, observational work offers another means to understand the social meanings which are constitutive of and reflected in human behaviour. Observational work can have advantages over interviews. Foster's (1996) comprehensive overview of these advantages suggested that: information about human behaviour can be recorded directly without having to rely on the retrospective or anticipatory accounts of others; observers may see the familiar as strange, noting features of the environment/behaviour that participants may not be able to see; patterns and regularities in the environment may be observed and analysed over time; observation can give access to information about people who are busy, deviant or hostile to taking part in research (Foster, 1996: 58).

With these aims in mind, there are multiple options for observational approaches. Researchers may 'themselves participate in the activities of the group they are observing (participant observation); they may be viewed as members of the group but minimize their participation; they may assume the role of observer without being part of the group; or their presence may be concealed entirely from the people they are observing' (Frankfort-Nachmias and Nachmias, 1996: 207).

Clearly, currently available text-based CMC is not an appropriate method for research which seeks to observe the 'real' world. However, recent studies, which focus on virtual communities, begin to challenge the basis of terms such as 'observation' and 'natural contexts' as used in traditional research.

OBSERVATION OF LINGUISTIC BEHAVIOUR

How might we begin to conceptualize observation of the constructed environment of the Internet? Let us consider the foci of observation in real life. Frankfort-Nachmias and Nachmias (1996: 210) identified four areas of observational interest: non-verbal behaviour (body language and particularly facial expressions), spatial behaviour (issues of physical closeness and distance), linguistic behaviour (both what is said and how) and extralinguistic behaviour (rate of speaking, loudness, tendency to interrupt, pronunciation). Using currently available technology only one of these four options, that is linguistic behaviour, seems to be a clear focus for observation via the Internet. Indeed, for these purposes, 'the Internet is a research setting par excellence, practically irresistible in its availability' (Jones, 1999: 13). Although researchers and participants are not 'visually or auditorially present' (Ferrara et al., 1991: 14), researchers may also observe non-verbal and extralinguistic behaviour exhibited in 'emoticons' (Metz, 1994) and paralinguistic and non-linguistic cues such as 'electronic paralanguage':

> expressives such as used in comic strips (eg, 'humpf'), multiple vowels to represent intonation contours (eg, 'sooooo'), multiple punctuation marks (eg, 'well how did things go yesterday????' (to express exaggerated questioning or surprise), use of asterisks for stress (eg 'please call—we've *got* to discuss'). (Murray,1988: 11)

Language Analysis in Experimental Settings

Assuming that a qualitative researcher sets out to 'observe' linguistic behaviour online, a key methodological issue becomes relevant. Qualitative researchers focus on 'natural' as opposed to contrived research settings. The preference is to observe participants in the 'field,' which is generally interpreted as the site where social action takes place whether the researcher is there or not (Schwandt, 1997). To observe participants in artificial set-tings is seen to diminish the possibility of attaining *verstehen* or empathic understanding.

However, a great deal of the research which has looked at linguistic behaviour using CMC has been conducted in experimental settings. Paccagnella (1997) has given a detailed and insightful review of literature which has identified the limitations of experimental designs from the perspective of qualitative researchers. For instance, Baym (1995a) points out that experimental findings rarely draw attention to the nature of the group or the individual participants who have taken part in interaction; the task the group was required to accomplish; the kind of CMC used (particularly if it was synchronous or asynchronous communication); and the time the group spent interacting. As Paccagnella (1997) notes, time constraints seem to be a particular source of flaws in experimental studies.

A meta-analysis of previous research (Walther *et al.*, 1994) argues that time-controlled group interaction (communication exchanges were often only 30 minutes long) could be held responsible for the different way that CMC has been characterized in artificial as opposed to field studies. These authors conclude that being asked to complete a task in a given time, in a context where participants have minimal knowledge of the other people involved and little expectation of future interaction, can hardly be considered a parallel to observing the social richness and interactional complexity of an established online group. Paccagnella concluded his review of experimental observation of discourse in online communities with the following words: 'the invitation issued by Robert Park in the first half of this century to get the seat of our pants dirty by real research conducted out of the classrooms and laboratories is still valid' (1997: *online*).

Discourse Analysis in Naturalistic Settings

Can studying the 'naturalistic' linguistic and extralinguistic behaviour of interactive online communities further the deeper aims of qualitative research, which are to study participants' 'ideas, attitudes, motives and intentions, and the way they interpret the social world'? (Foster, 1996: 61).

Ethnomethodological approaches to social enquiry, such as conversational and discourse analysis,[12] are broadly concerned with how people construct their own definition of a social situation (see Schwandt, 1997: 44–45). These methods focus on ordinary, mundane, naturally occurring talk to reveal the way meaning is accomplished by everyone involved. Qualitative researchers with an interest in these approaches can 'observe' the natural conversations of various kinds of newsgroups, synchronous conferencing (using real-time chat), and MU* formats. By 'lurking' unseen they are able to watch the interaction without intervening in any way.

Some examples of studies which have observed conversations online are Denzin (1999), who used conversational analysis to interpret the gendered 'narratives of self' in a newsgroup focusing on 'recovery' from alcoholism; Rodino (1997), who looked at the multiple, sometimes contradictory, ways in which users 'performed' gender on an IRC channel; and Paccagnella

(1997), who studied the 'logs and messages' of an Italian virtual community named Cyberpunk. There are differences in scale in such research. Paccagnella recorded and archived messages every month for eighteen months. He was then able to conduct searches for particular situations, for example, the dialogues between specific groups of actors, in a given period, on a particular topic. His constructivist interpretation of Cyberpunk involved analysing nearly 10,000 messages from 400 users. Rodino qualitatively analysed text from observations made over a much shorter ten-week period:

> Most of these observations were recorded. I made observations by entering chat channels and lurked (entered no text). I watched interactions on chat channels: #boston, #chat, #chatzone, #gaysex, #hottub, #ircbar, #romance, #talk, #teenchat, #texas, #truthdare. (1997: *online*)

Denzin (1999) also intensively analysed threads of conversation as particular topic areas in a newsgroup were elaborated by participants.

All these studies sought to understand cultural meanings and the complexity of daily social experience through dense deep readings of cybertext discourse. This observation of online communities attempted to 'make visible the cultural apparatuses and biographical histories that allow such talk to be produced and understood' (Denzin 1999: 122).

However, Paccagnella (1997) has identified some ways in which qualitative analysis of online discourse might lack some of the analytic breadth that is possible when FTF conversations are observed. Referring to Marvin (1995), he points out that, as in FTF interaction, there is a dynamic dimension to conversational turn-taking in CMC. The time taken typing, and the delays between turn-taking (which can be a few seconds in synchronous CMC or several days in asynchronous options), can shape the mood of the interaction. This information is often lost in the analysis.

Second, the logs or messages ignore the context of speech: 'the actual experiences of individual participants at their own keyboards in their own rooms all around the globe.' Finally, Paccagnella cites Reid (1995), who points out that CMC discourse is not intended for people uninvolved directly in the interaction. Perhaps even more than in FTF conversation, CMC loses part of its sense and meaning when reread afterward by those who had not been involved.

Clearly, CMC offers an excellent site for qualitative researchers who 'observe' discourse online. While some discourse analysts (like Denzin) lurk (observe unknown), others (like Paccagnella) participate in the online interaction. Participant observers of virtual communities may emphasize dialogue or may seek an ethnographic account of specific online cultures.

We shall now discuss how qualitative researchers might investigate virtual communities as cultures. For, in cyberspace as in real life, 'man is an animal suspended in webs of significance he himself has spun' (Geertz, 1973: 5).

PARTICIPANT OBSERVATION

One definition describes FTF participant observation like this:

> As a methodology for ethnographic field work, participant observation is a procedure for generating understanding of the ways of life of others. It requires that the researcher engage in some relatively prolonged period of participation in a community, group, and so on . . . Broadly conceived, participant observation thus includes activities of direct observation, interviewing, document analysis, reflection, analysis, and interpretation. (Schwandt, 1997)

What would it mean to understand a way of life in a virtual community? Kendall identified the following areas where the social meanings of online participants might be explored: (a) changing meaning and perceptions of Internet usage for various groups, (b) cultural and subcultural affiliations of Internet users, and (c) explorations of political action and affiliation online (1999: 63). In all these areas participant observation of CMC interaction is seen to be a key way forward (Sharf, 1999: 244), a view stated strongly by Kendall:

> Much as my personal biases lead me in that direction, I would never have the audacity to suggest that all social science research projects ought to include participant observation. Yet with regard to research on interactive online forums, I recommend just that. (1999: 57)

Certainly data that gives insight into online groups from the perspective of those involved are becoming increasingly available. At some level all researchers who comment on virtual communities of which they are part are participant observers (Horn, 1998; Rheingold, 1994; Turkle, 1995). Findings from some qualitative studies emphasize the ethnographic status of their descriptions of specific virtual worlds (for example, Baym, 1992; Kendall, 1999; Meyer and Thomas, 1990; Myers, 1987; Reid, 1991; Sharf, 1999). As with FTF research, online participant studies will be extended in time (often over years), for

> Reaching understandings of participants' sense of self and of the meanings they give to their on-line participation requires spending time with participants to observe what they do on-line as well as what they say they do. (Kendall, 1999: 62)

The cultures which are investigated may be as diverse as a Usenet group devoted to discussing soap operas (Baym, 1992, 1995b); a breast cancer mailing list (Sharf, 1999); an online version of a real-life subculture (Hodkinson, 2000); and an interactive social forum (MU*) conceptualized by participants as a virtual bar (Kendall, 1999).

Negotiating Access in Participant Observation

Participant observation is, above all, concerned with access. There are some immediate practical bonuses about making initial access to venues in cyberspace. In contrast to the real-time world, it lends itself to 'hanging around' (lurking) in situations where a person's presence is normally brief or transient (Foster, 1996). In conventional observational research there are also practical difficulties in recording and writing about a setting at the same time as observing it, and time lags in recording observations can allow inaccuracies and distortion. This is clearly not a problem online.

In cyberspace the physical presence of both researchers and participants is concealed. For instance, this allowed Sharf (1999), out of general interest and curiosity, to subscribe to, and to lurk on, a mailing list called the Breast Cancer List. After a few weeks she began to collect interesting postings but without any specific objective in mind. Some months later, when she realized that her casual interest had turned into a developing research project, she became an 'active' participant of the group. Sharf's experience has parallels with FTF participant research, where a researcher may pose as a real participant (perhaps a novice)—or, if more openly, as an 'acceptable marginal member' (Hammersley and Atkinson, 1995).

However, there are clear differences in FTF situations. Here, even more than with interviews, ascribed characteristics such as age, gender or ethnicity might limit access, or contribute to the researcher being defined as an insider or outsider. For instance, in J. Foster's (1990: 168) ethnography of petty crime, 'being small, young and female was a decided advantage,' while in Liebow's (1967: 249) study of street corner men in the United States, 'colour' was a nonnegotiable factor. 'They saw, first of all, a white man. In my opinion, this brute fact of colour, as they understood it in their experience and as I understood it in mine, irrevocably and absolutely relegated me to the status of outsider.' P. Foster (1996: 72) accepted that, 'as a 40-year-old white male, I would find it difficult to present myself as a young 'rap' music enthusiast, or develop close peer-type relationships with school pupils, or directly access the world of radical feminists.'

The potential for moving beyond these limitations is certain to become a central issue in qualitative online research in general, and in participant observation in particular. As Turkle (1995: 228) has noted, 'Life on the screen makes it very easy to present oneself as other than one is in real life,' allowing identities to be 'flexible, swappable and disconnected from real-world bodies' (Shields, 1996: Introduction).

Hodkinson's online participatory study of Goth culture provided an intriguing counterbalance to accepted conventional research practices in which gaining acceptance might involve dressing in acceptable ways and/or behaving in ways that don't alienate the group. Although some researchers might see online participation as a means to move beyond the signs and significations of appearance, Hodkinson showed that this could work the other way:

> The most obvious badge of subcultural status—one's physical appearance—becomes devoid when one is communicating with a group of strangers communicating only by e-mail. Therefore, in such forums, the purple and pink

streaks in my hair, my piercing, make-up and subculturally distinctive clothing, which have been so useful to most of my research became redundant.
In such a situation one must establish subcultural capital—or insider
status—only through what one writes. (1999: personal communication)

At a later point in his research Hodkinson found a way of bringing his appearance back into the equation by publishing photographs of himself on
his own Web site, and advertising it on Goth fora.

In conventional research, access may also be difficult if a physical environment or certain forms of behaviour are inaccessible or difficult to observe. Many people assume that the social world of cyberspace is readily accessible once there is technological mastery but, once users have more
experience, they begin to realize that the online world also has its hidden
areas. These may be areas of place.

For instance, Kendall (1999: 70) investigated an online forum known as
'BlueSky.' In the course of her research she realized that some participant
observers may have made limited assumptions about the character of online communities because they had never penetrated beyond the most public and easy-to-find interactive 'rooms' and had only interacted with other
'newbies'. She pointed out that, 'regulars who seek a quiet place to convene
with friends build their own rooms, which allows them to control access.'
It is only researchers who both 'find' these secret places, and who then negotiate access, who begin to grasp the boundaries of the community.

There may also be hidden areas relating to the levels of insider status
which are reached. Hodkinson discovered that his ready acceptance as
a Goth in real life did not give him immediate access to Goth behaviour
online:

> Regardless of one's involvement in the Goth scene off-line, acceptance in
> their exclusive on-line forums can take considerable time to earn. Further-
> more, it requires the learning of particular sets of norms for on-line behav-
> iour distinct from the values of the subculture as a whole. Nevertheless, on-
> line forums are useful in that one is able to 'lurk' (read without posting) for
> a period of time, and pick up the described norms of behaviour. Having
> done this, I gradually became more adept and confident at communicating
> with the groups in a way which was consistent with these unwritten rules.
> Furthermore, I found that I became able to convey written details which re-
> vealed my status as a subcultural insider. (1999: personal communication)

As Hodkinson grew to delight in and to accept his new status as a Cyber-
goth it would seem that (as in some FTF studies) he did risk 'going native.'
In other words, the changed balance of insider-outsider might have an impact on the ways he finally described and analyzed data (see Kerr and Hiltz,
1982).

Issues of identity penetrate all levels of CMC research but, with regard
to participant observation, they have also been a pertinent issue for FTF research. In sensitive or volatile real-life settings there may be very real difficulties in coping with the consequences if a researcher's identity and pur-

poses are discovered. Some commentators suggest that, in the online environment, people need not fear any 'real' repercussions from their actions. The way seems open to participate in any virtual community, and to publicize findings from any kind of participant research, without considering the possibly painful outcome of personal exposure. However, there is no doubt that if online research focuses on such areas as money laundering, bribery in global companies or terrorism the researcher could not rely on the dubious security offered by electronic communication systems for protection from the consequences of deciding to 'publish and be damned!'

Ethical Issues in Participant Observation

Complete participation in field research has been justified on the grounds that it makes possible the study of inaccessible groups or groups that do not reveal to outsiders certain aspects of their lives. However, in CMC, as in FTF research, there are serious considerations regarding the invasion of privacy. As discussed above, Sharf did not set out to study the Breast Cancer mailing list. Once she realized that her research interests were being engaged she decided to 'contextualize' herself by mailing posts explaining that she was interested in breast cancer as well as being an academic researcher, for

> In retrospect, I believe I had a sense early in that it was prudent to let fellow list members know that I had two reasons for participating in this forum. (1999: 249)

Sharf's sensitivity to the ethical dimensions of participant research was sharpened by her understanding of the highly personal nature of the Breast Cancer List postings and the fact that many subscribers were coping with the disease themselves. Yet, even without these additional dimensions, ethical issues relating to the secret collection of data remain.

COLLECTING PERSONAL DOCUMENTS

While subjective experiences may be collected from interviews (see above), qualitative researchers also use personal documents to increase their understanding of participants who shaped history and culture and were shaped by it (Chamberlain and Thompson, 1998). Such documents might include (a) diaries or journals which can record day-to-day events or fragments of experience and (b) written autobiographies. While diaries and journals are 'ongoing records of practices and reflections on those practices' (Connelly and Clandinin, 1988: 34), autobiographical writing attempts to 'write' the whole life. Researchers use autobiographical materials to find a written record of someone's life in the person's own terms (Creswell, 1998). They seek someone 'distinctive for her or his accomplishments and ordinariness or who sheds light on a specific phenomenon or issue being studied' (Denzin, 1989: 111).

Solicited Documents

Personal documents can be solicited from participants in many walks of life. In conventional research they have been used to record the subjective experiences of participants whose unfamiliar lifestyle, or whose individual responses to a way of life, may be outside the experience of and/or inaccessible to the researcher. For instance, they allow a researcher to explore young people's experiences of education and the family (Mann, 1998), or an inmate's subjective experiences of imprisonment (Cohen and Taylor, 1977).

One practical benefit of this approach is that different participants can record events that may be in a closed access location, or going on simultaneously in a single location. When life histories, autobiographical material and diary work are requested and presented online these benefits increase: access to participants (and hence range of experience) is wider and multiple sites and/or locations may be involved.

Soliciting personal documents in conventional research also has disadvantages. Some authors have noted that the method asks a great deal of participants. They are, in effect, asked to be 'co-researchers' (Burgess, 1993); a commitment like writing a diary on a regular basis can become onerous and people may give up (Lee, 1993: 115). There are also communication difficulties. On the one hand, a participant's handwriting may be difficult to read. On the other, the researcher may need to put across detailed instructions about how to focus observations.

How might these challenges transfer to an online context? Clearly, handwriting would no longer be an issue. Some issues, such as gaining and retaining the co-operation of participants, remain. As with conventional research, the effectiveness of the method would depend, to a great extent, on the personal response of participants to the whole idea of writing in this way. Not everyone would want to do it and, from a sampling point of view, there may be differences in those who do. Here are a range of responses from some Graduates of the Millennium students to a general query about whether they might be interested in keeping a journal of their university experiences:

> I spend a lot of time E-mailing and so I think the diary approach would be a fairly good idea for me. Just let me know what aspects of my life at Cambridge and my thoughts on them you're interested in, and I'll let you know.

> I am sure I will be far too busy or at least absent minded to keep up any sort of diary response, but I shall be happy to answer all of your specific enquiries.

> Sorry—I'll have zero initiative about topics myself but I'll answer any questions y'all might have.

> I'll do it—But just remember to give me a prod now and then to get me thinking. Writing a commentary on life to someone who will listen to whatever you say is surprisingly difficult.

Diary methods have been used by university staff to monitor the wellbeing and intellectual progress of students involved in long-distance learning.[13] As with Mann's study, not all students volunteered to participate and some (the minority) kept a handwritten diary, which they submitted at the end of the course module, rather than sending regular email entries. This has enabled Furneaux, the lecturer and researcher involved, to compare traditional and email diaries, identifying the pros and cons she associates with using the diary as an interview method:

Pros

- Subjects can dash off a few thoughts as they occur to them, it doesn't require a lot of time on any one occasion.

- It's easy to set up and does not require subjects to expend much energy to send you your data.

- They don't have previous diary entries in front of them as they write, so you get authentic thoughts at that point of time, 'unpolluted' by previous entries.

- You get insights into individual students' thinking/lives you rarely get on a campus-based course (and we are a department that has a lot of staff/student contact and support). They mention minutiae/details they'd never tell you in a tutorial, especially about their personal lives/circumstances.

Cons

- Receiving regular entries from subjects, it is tempting to 'reply', if only to acknowledge receipt of the e-mail. This can turn into more of a two-way correspondence than a diary and can interfere with the methodology. Also, if for any reason the researcher stops replying then the entries can stop too.

- Subjects write more in conventional diaries, and can look back at and refer to what they have written previously—it makes for a more coherent whole to analyze.

- It's a new genre for everyone and some people take to it more readily than others. Some write a glorious 'stream of consciousness flow'—everything and anything that occurs to them at that point in time. Pure gold! Others can write a rather stilted cross between a factual narrative and a report about the study they have done/plan to do. This is not very informative!

- You are asking quite a lot of people—they have to remember to keep sending dairy entries at regular intervals over a period of time. Some send more than others, which makes it hard to compare them for analysis purposes, as you have entries from different people on different occasions. (1999: *personal communication*)

Furneaux concluded that traditional diaries give a sense of a story unfolding, while emailed entries are more like 'snap-shots' at particular points in time. In addition, while some traditional diary entries were very short—'I didn't do anything today'—all emailed entries were at least a paragraph long. This suggests that the rapid note-taking style of much email correspondence might diminish the feeling of being burdened by the task of writing journal entries regularly.

Furneaux and Mann both recognized the relish, depth and flair shown in the outpourings of some email diarists. Although an online journal/ diary is not always appropriate, it may offer some participants a highly successful vehicle for being deeply reflective. There is a general awareness that people are often more willing to 'interface' with a computer screen than talking directly (Thu Nguyen and Alexander, 1996). Why should this be? Why is it a commonplace experience that 'it is much easier to articulate thoughts to a screen than a person' (GOTM student)? Thu Nguyen and Alexander (1996) claim that it is human computer interaction which allows individuals to project and realize their thoughts. Matheson and Zanna (1990) suggest there are two reasons for this. Computer users are relaxed and reflective because they feel less inhibited by the possible evaluation of others. They also seem more aware of their private selves. The intimate nature of typed, informal communication seems to increase a person's concentration on their own reactions and opinions. In particular people seem to be in tune with covert aspects of themselves, such as personal feelings, attitudes, values and beliefs (Matheson, 1992).

There is certainly empirical evidence supporting the view that users may experience a sense of symbiosis with the computer. 'Rather than the computer/human dyad being a simple matter of self versus other, there is, for many people, a blurring of the boundaries between the embodied self and the PC' (Lupton, 1995: 98). Some authors describe the loss of self-consciousness as they write and the deep connection with the screen:

> A pen now feels strange, awkward and slow in my hand, compared to using a keyboard. When I type, the words appear on the screen almost as fast as I formulate them in my head. There is, for me, almost a seamless transition of thought to word on screen. (Lupton 1995: 97)

> I don't even feel I am typing . . . I am thinking it, and there it is on the screen . . . I feel totally telepathic with the computer. (Quoted in Turkle, 1984: 211)

A student from the Graduates of the Millennium study echoes these sentiments: 'in a way, although it's a computer screen, it brings out a lot more than speaking to someone does.' It seems that, for a certain period, a totally absorbed writer may be only marginally aware of the eventual participant. As Gibson noted some years ago, 'everyone I know who works with computers seems to develop a belief that there's some kind of actual space behind the screen, someplace you can't see but you know is there' (cited in Kitchin, 1998: 17). It seems possible that the 'space behind the screen' may be a way of conceptualizing an individual's dialogue with their own mind. 'We are searching for a home for the mind and heart. Our fascination with computers is more erotic than sensuous, more deeply spiritual than utilitarian' (Heim, 1992: 61, cited in Lupton, 1995). As thoughts, hopes and history are typed onto the keyboard they reassemble as neat, accessible text on the screen. This ability of the computer to reflect persons back to themselves opens up the possibility that for some individuals CMC journals may be an ideal method to generate rich data about the subjective self, a self accessed in what may be experienced as an almost transparent process of relating to one's own consciousness.

Unsolicited Documents

Personal documents in conventional research may also be obtained from other sources such as private collections, archives and libraries. Access to personal documents in CMC is at a stage of transition. While extended texts (such as autobiographical writing) might be consciously stored on a computer or as printouts, 'letters' written online have a more ephemeral quality than those written on paper. One example of a series of letters and journal entries which were stored and later published is Ruth Picardie's reflections/correspondence written in the last stages of her illness (1998). However, the Internet offers huge advantages in terms of finding unsolicited materials from public online sites. For instance, DejaNews allows an archival search for all recorded newsgroup entries to be conducted. On the Web, hypertext links also allow users to look deeper into aspects of the content made available in any one document. In addition, innovations in methods of electronic storage and dissemination of written materials may eliminate the challenge of collecting written documents from geographically dispersed sites, or those to which access is limited or forbidden. On the other hand, issues of copyright remain and may present even greater problems than documents retrieved in more conventional ways, as the legislation is constantly changing.

In terms of documentary analysis, conventional methodological challenges relating to the authenticity of documents (forgery, mistaken authorship, falsification, propaganda) and the agenda of the writer remain (Finnegan, 1996; Scott, 1990). However, there are exciting prospects for discussing these issues online with enthusiasts all over the world.

MIXED METHODS

Many qualitative researchers use a multi-method approach in their investigations in order to examine different levels of the same situation or to focus on different aspects of the same phenomenon (Dillabough, 1999; Luttrell, 1999; Mann, 1998). However, CMC studies may offer further opportunities and challenges for mixed-method research. Above all, informed commentators (Fielding and Lee, 1999: personal communication) identify the development and convergence of technologies as a major opportunity for future research.

As data become increasingly digital in form the boundaries between data sources and manipulation processes will weaken. Qualitative software packages already have SPSS export facilities, survey researchers are more aware of automatic text processing, and qualitative and quantitative data taken from the Web can be 'dropped' into analytic software with ease. The technological developments are crucial as researchers who study interaction on the Internet itself tend to use a combination of methods (Garton *et al.*, 1999; Rice and Rogers, 1984). For instance, Garton *et al.* suggest that forms of self-reporting (such as interviews and diaries) may readily access perceptions of media use, while observation or electronic data gathering may be better for measuring actual use of the Internet (see Schiano, 1997).

There are other mixed-method precedents. In some studies, questionnaires, in either conventional (Dunne, 1999) or online versions (O'Connor and Madge, 2000; Seymour *et al.*, 1999; Smith-Stoner and Weber, 2000), may be followed by online semi-structured interviews. Semi-structured interviews may be combined with solicited diary materials (Mann, 1998). Online interviews, or participant observation of groups online, may be accompanied by 'documentary' analysis of newsgroup or list materials (Paccagnella, 1997; Sharf, 1999) or popular conventional journals (Cushing, 1996). Mixing CMC methods with FTF methods may be particularly important if researchers wish to investigate differences and/or similarities between online and offline interaction. For instance, Stewart *et al.* (1998) were able to compare the efficacy of FTF and virtual focus groups with young people. By using FTF and email interviews Hodkinson (2000) was able to access, and make comparisons between, a subculture which had real-life and virtual domains.

Alternatively, researchers may seek to access, in real life, participants who frequent virtual worlds (Turkle, 1995). Correll (1995) used a three-way methodology to study an online community and its processes. First, she observed the daily traffic between patrons at a virtual cafe, occasionally asking them to explain various actions or conversations. Second, she interviewed twelve patrons using semi-structured interviews via private email. Finally, she interviewed eight patrons in two FTF group sessions. Similarly, Kendall (1999) combined three years of participant observation and analysis of online documentary material with FTF interviews and participation in FTF gatherings. Kendall noted that, 'The ability to access off-line environments provides useful information between online and off-line interaction, but such access may not always be feasible' (1999: 71).

CONCLUSION

This chapter is advisedly called an introduction to online methods. We have attempted to contextualize online approaches within the conventional research canon, but we are aware that we have only mapped in the possibilities for Internet research at the most superficial level. Different disciplines, and different traditions within these disciplines, will, no doubt, capitalize on innovatory practices discussed here and take online research into hitherto uncharted territory. The potential for development and diversity is immense.

NOTES

1. In March 2000 these included MaCATI (www.senecio.com), Survey Internet (www.aufrance. com), Survey Said (www.surveysaid.com), Survey Select (www. surveyselect.com), Survey Solutions (www.perseus.com) and SurveyTracker (www. surveytracker.com). MaCATI's editing program is for the Macintosh only and it has versions of its data collection program for the Mac, Windows and Java. All other programs run under Windows only. Smith (1997) has pointed out that, while Web survey development software is increasingly available, packages have huge variations in terms of price, function and server compatibility. It remains to be seen which, if any, of these packages will become the standard.

2. HTML stands for HyperText Markup Language—the coding system used to create pages which can be displayed by Web browsers. It consists of a series of 'tags' which give instructions to the browser about how to display the text. For example, the text '⟨b⟩bold words⟨/b⟩ and ⟨i⟩italic words⟨/i⟩' would be displayed by a Web browser (or HTML-enabled email system) as:

bold words and *italic words*

However, if the same text was read using a standard email system, all the characters would be displayed exactly as typed:

⟨b⟩bold words⟨/b⟩ and ⟨i⟩italic words⟨/i⟩

HTML documents were originally created by typing the tags using a text editor. However, it is increasingly common to create HTML using 'what you see is what you get' editing programs where the author applies the formatting required (such as bold or italic) and the program automatically adds the relevant tags.

3. For example, Perseus SurveySolutions Interviewer; see www.perseus.com.

4. The best-known Web survey is Georgia Tech's Graphics, Visualization, and Usability Centre (GVU) which uses repeat participation to map current and changing Internet user characteristics and attitudes (see Kehoe and Pitkow, 1996, and www.gvu.gatech.edu/user_surveys/). Over 55,000 respondents were involved in the first five surveys and new versions of the survey are sent out biannually.

5. See note 2.

6. See note 1.

7. In this context, a server is a large computer which forms part of the worldwide network of permanently-connected computers that is the Internet. Your pages are held on your host server. When someone requests a page, the request is routed to your host server and the page information is passed back to their computer via the network.

8. Javascript is a programming language which can be used to make Web pages more interactive.

9. Increasingly, the administrators of remailers are charging for their services. However, it is still possible to send anonymous email free of charge—www.anonymizer.com offers this service.

10. A single site is one where 'an intact culture-sharing group has developed shared values, beliefs, and assumptions' (Creswell, 1998: 114).

11. For more details see: www.iname.com.

12. See Silverman (1993) for a summary of differences between approaches.

13. The study was carried out by Clare Furneaux at the Centre for Applied Language Studies, University of Reading, Reading RG6 6WB, UK (http://www.rdg.ac.uk/AcaDepts/cl/CALS/furneaux.html).

REFERENCES

Baym, N. 1995a. The emergence of community in computer mediated communication, pp. 139–163 in *Cybersociety: Computer-Mediated Communication and Community*, ed. S. Jones. Thousand Oaks, CA, and London: Sage.

Baym, N. 1995b. From practice to culture on Usenet, pp. 29–52 in *The Culture of Computing*, ed. S. Star. Oxford: Blackwell.

Bennet, C. 1998. *Men Online: Discussing Lived Experiences on the Internet*. Unpublished Honours Dissertation, James Cook University, Townsville, Australia.

Bornat, J. 1994. Is oral history auto/biography? *Auto/Biography?* (publication of the British Sociological Society Study Group on Auto/Biography), 3(1).

Brannen, J. 1992. *Mixing Methods: Qualitative and Quantitative Research*. Aldershot: Avebury.

Chamberlain, M. and Thompson, P. 1998. *Narrative and Genre*. London and New York: Rutledge.

Chanfrault-Duchet, M. 1991. Narrative structures, social models, and symbolic representation in the life story, pp. 77–93 in *Women's Words*, eds. S. Gluck and D. Patai. New York and London: Routledge.

Cohen, S. and Taylor, L. 1977. Talking about prison blues. In C. Bell and H. Newby (eds.), *Doing Sociological Research*. London: Allen & Unwin.

Cole, R. 2000. Promising to be a man: Promise Keepers' organizational construction of masculinity, in *Men Wrestling with Commitment: The Promise Keepers, Masculinity, and Christianity*, ed. D. Claussen. Jefferson, NC: MacFarland.

Comley, P. 1996. The use of the Internet as a data collection method [Online]. Available: http://www.sga.co.uk/esomar.html.

Coomber, R. 1997. Using the Internet for survey research. *Sociological Research Online* [Online], 2. Available: http://www.socresonline.org.uk/socresonline/2/2/2.html.

Creswell, J. 1998. *Qualitative Inquiry and Research Design: Choosing among five traditions*. Thousand Oaks, CA, and London: Sage.

Denzin, N. 1999. Cybertalk and the method of instances, in *Doing Internet Research*, ed. S. Jones. Thousand Oaks, CA, and London: Sage.

Douglas, J. 1985. *Creative Interviewing*. Beverly Hills, CA: Sage.

Dunne, G. 1999. *The Different Dimensions of Gay Fatherhood: Exploding the Myths*. Report to the Economic and Social Research Council. London: London School of Economics.

Fielding, N. and Lee, R. 1998. *Computer Analysis and Qualitative Research*. London and Thousand Oaks, CA: Sage.

Finnegan, R. 1992. *Oral Traditions and the Verbal Arts: A Guide to research practices*. London: Routledge.

Flick, U. 1998. *Introduction to Qualitative Research*. London and Thousand Oaks, CA: Sage.

Fontana, A. and Frey, J. 1994. Interviewing: The art of science. In N. Denzin and Y. Lincoln (eds.), *Handbook of Qualitative Research*. London: Sage.

Foster, J. 1990. Observational research, in *Data Collection and Analysis*, ed. R. Sapsford and V. Jupp. London and Thousand Oaks, CA: Sage.

Frankfor-Nachmias, C. and Nachmias, D. 1996. *Research Methods in the Social Sciences*. London and Sydney: St Martin's Press.

Garfinkel, H. 1967. *Studies in Ethnomethodology*. London: Routledge and Kegan Paul.

Geertz, C. 1973. *The Interpretation of Cultures*. New York: Basic Books.

Gjestland, L. 1996. Net? Not yet. *Marketing Research*, 8:26–29.

Glaser, B. and Strauss, A. 1967. *The Discovery of Grounded Theory: Strategies for Qualitative Research.* New York: Aldine De Gruyter.

Gluck, S. and Patai, D. 1991. *Women's Words: The Feminist Practice of Oral History.* New York and London: Routledge.

Hammersly, M. and Atkinson, P. 1995. *Ethnography: Principles in Practice.* New York: Routledge.

Heim, M. 1992. The erotic ontology of cyberspace, pp. 59–80 in *Cuberspace: First Steps,* ed. M. Benedikt. Cambridge, MA: MIT Press.

Holstein, J. and Gubrium, J. 1997. Active interviewing, pp. 113–130 in *Qualitative Research Theory, Method and Practice,* ed. D. Silverman. London and Thousand Oaks, CA: Sage.

Horn, S. 1998. *Cyberville: Clicks, Culture and the Creation of an Online Town.* New York: Warner Books.

Jones, S. (ed.) 1999. Studying the net: Intricacies and issues, pp. 1–29 in *Doing Internet Research,* ed. S. Jones. Thousand Oaks, CA, and London: Sage.

Kehoe, C. and Pitkow, J. 1996. Surveying the territory: GVU's five WWW user surveys. *The World Wide Web Journal,* 1.

Kendall, L. 1999. Recontextualizing Cyberspace: Methodological considerations for on-line research, pp. 57–75 in *Doing Internet Research,* ed. S. Jones. Thousand Oaks, CA, and London: Sage.

Lee, R. 1993. *Doing Research on Sensitive Topics.* London and Newbury Park. CA: Sage.

Lincoln, Y. and Guba, E. 1985. *Naturalistic Inquiry.* Beverly Hills, CA: Sage.

Lupton, D. 1995. The embodied computer/user. *Body and Society,* 1: 97–112.

Mann, C. 1998. Family fables, pp. 81–99 in *Narrative and Genre,* eds. M. Chamberlain and P. Thompson. London and New York: Routledge.

May, T. 1993. *Social Research, Methods and Processes.* Buckinham: Open University Press.

McCracken, G. 1988. *The Long Interview.* Newbury Park, CA: Sage.

Metz, M. 1994. Computer-mediated communication: Literature review of a new context. *Interpersonal Computing and Technology* [Online], 2(2): 31–49. Available: http://www.lib.ncsu.edu/stacks/i/ipct/ipct-v2n02-metz-computermediated.txt

Miles, M. and Huberman, A. 1994. *Qualitative Data Analysis: A Sourcebook of New Methods.* Thousand Oaks, CA: Sage.

Middleton, S. 1993. *Educating Feminists: Life Stories and Pedagogy.* New York: Teacher's College Press.

O'Connor, H. and Madge, C. 2000. *Cyber-parents and Cyber-research: Exploring the Internet as a Medium for Research.* University of Leicester: Centre for Labour Market Studies.

Paccagnella, L. 1997. Getting the seat of your pants dirty: Strategies for ethnographic research on virtual communities. *Journal of Computer-Mediated Communication* [Online], 3(1). Available: http://www.ascusc.org/jcmc/vol3/issue1/paccagnella.html.

Portelli, A. 1998. Oral history as genre, pp. 142–160 in *Narrative and Genre,* eds. M. Chamberlain and P. Thompson. London and New York: Routledge.

Reinharz, S. 1992. *Feminist Methods in Social Research.* New York: Oxford University Press.

Rodino, M. 1997. Breaking out of binaries: Reconceptualizing gender and its relationship to language in computer-mediated communication. *Journal of Computer-Mediated Communication* [Online], 3(3). Available: http://www.ascusc.org/jcmc/vol13/issue3/rodino.html.

Schaefer, D. and Dillman, D. A. 1998. Development of a standard e-mail methodology: Result of an experiment. *Public Opinion Quarterly*, 2: 378–397.

Schwandt, T. 1997. *Qualitative Inquiry: A Dictionary of Terms*. Thousand Oaks, CA, and London: Sage.

Scott, J. 1990. *A Matter of Record*. Cambridge: Polity Press.

Schiano, D. 1997. Convergent methodologies in cyber-psychology: A case study. *Behavior Research Methods, Instruments and Computers*, 29: 270–273.

Seidman, I. 1991. *Interviewing as Qualitative Research*. Columbia University: Teacher's College.

Sharf, B. 1999. Beyond netiquette: The ethics of doing naturalistic research on the Internet, in *Doing Internet Research*, ed. S. Jones. Thousand Oaks, CA, and London: Sage.

Sheehan, K. and Hoy, M. 1999. Using e-mail to survey Internet users in the United States: Methodology and assessment. *Journal of Computer-Mediated Communication* [Online], 4(3). Available: http://www.ascusc.org/jcmc/vol4/issue3/sheehan.html.

Smith, C. 1997. Casting the Net: Surveying an Internet population. *Journal of Computer-Mediated Communication* [Online], 3(1). Available: http://www.ascusc.org/jcmc/vol3/issue1/smith.html.

Smith-Stoner, M. and Weber, T. 2000. *Developing Theory Using Emergent Inquiry: A Study of Meaningful Online Learning for Women*. Unpublished doctoral dissertation, California Institute of Integral Studies (E-mail: mssrn@aol.com).

Turkle, S. 1995. *Life on the Screen: Identity in the Age of the Internet*. London: Weidenfeld and Nicolson.

Walther, J. and Boyd, S. 2000. Attraction to computer-mediated social support, in *Communication Technology and Society: Audience Adoption and Uses of the New Media*, eds. C. Lin and D. Atkin. New York: Hampton Press.

Weber, M. 1922. *Gesammelte Aufsatze zurWissenschaftslehre*. Tubingen: Mohr.

Wilson, M. 1996. Asking questions, pp. 94–121 in *Data Collection and Analysis*, eds. R. Sapsford and V. Jupp. London: Sage in association with The Open University.

Winter, D. and Huff, C. 1996. Adapting the Internet: Comments from a women-only electronic forum. *American Sociologist*, 27: 30–54.

Witmer, D. and Katzman, S. 1997. On-line smiles: Does gender make a difference in the use of graphic Accents? *Journal of Computer-Mediated Communication* [Online], 2(4). Available: http://jcmc.mscc.huji.ac.il/vol2/issue4/witmer1.html.

CHAPTER 19

A Content Analysis of Internet-Accessible Written Pornographic Depictions

DENNA HARMON AND SCOT B. BOERINGER

Concerns over the availability of sexually explicit material in what has come to be termed "cyberspace" have recently blossomed into a national debate on the subject. Attempts to restrict access to the sexual side of the Internet have expanded to involve universities, access providers, and the Federal Government, which enacted substantial new restrictions upon Internet content as part of the 1995 Telecommunications Reform Bill. These restrictions, which were ruled unconstitutional recently by the Supreme Court, were enacted in part due to research suggesting that the Internet is a veritable smorgasbord of pornographic entertainment, available to anyone, regardless of age, with a computer and Internet access. While there are serious questions regarding the research project which provided much of the press and governmental officials' information on the subject, the issue is important enough to warrant more research before the social science community can claim to be informed. This project assesses the content of images contained in one of the more commonly accessible Usenet newsgroups: alt.sex.stories.

THE INTERNET AND USENET NEWSGROUPS

The Internet, as it presently exists, is a interconnected network of computers owned by government, business, and education. Originally a small number of government and education computers interconnected for the purpose of exchanging defense-related data, the Internet has exploded in size in the last five years; some estimates today place the number of primary, or server, Internet computers approaching ten million. Personal computers linked to these servers account for at least ten times that number. The data that are transmitted over the Internet consist mainly of electronic mail messages and file transfers, where data is transmitted from one computer to another. For example, banks can transmit information between branches, end users can download software for their own computers, and business transactions may be performed. Another major aspect of the Internet is the dissemination of information to a large audience through an aspect of the Internet called Usenet. Usenet, or the User's Network, began in the early 80's as a way for users and programmers of the UNIX operating system to exchange information and ideas, but quickly grew to include discussions and information about a wide variety of topics. The Usenet architecture is that of a bulletin board system: users can leave messages "on" the board, where they can be read by others. Each topic has its separate board, thus Usenet today has upwards of 15,000 bulletin boards, or "newsgroups". Online services such as Compuserve, America Online, and Prodigy, as well as most other Internet access providers, have access to the Usenet newsgroups, including the groups dealing with sexual topics.

There are newsgroups on Usenet dealing with almost any topic: sports, computing, politics, recreation, education, and sex are all represented on this system. While the overwhelming majority of Usenet groups do not deal with sexual material, some of the most widely accessed groups have names clearly indicating their sexual focus, such as

alt.sex "alt" is short for alternative; a heading given to groups which may not fall into one of the other categories, such as "rec" (recreation), "comp" (computing), or "soc" (social/social science).

alt.sex.fetish.feet

alt.sex.pedophilia

alt.binaries.pictures.erotica (a newsgroup containing binary pictures)

However, one group which claims a general focus on sexual topics is alt.sex.stories. This group is purported to be one of the most frequently read newsgroups on the Internet (Elmer-Dewitt, 1993), a fact which is difficult to substantiate because of the difficulty in monitoring "lurkers" (people who do not post stories but simply read them). At any rate, alt.sex.stories is intended as a newsgroup where amateur sexually oriented written material is posted for viewing by others. As there is no particular slant evidenced by the title of the group, this material is likely to be varied in nature, encompassing a variety of sexual topics and material. The topics of each story are sometimes posted in the subject line of the posting, which is available in the groups directory. Some of these abbreviated indications of story content are: pedo (pedophilia), pain, torture, n/c (non-consensual), beast (bestiality), f/m (heterosexual), m/m (male/male sex), f/f (female/female sex), and variations on the last two themes, such as m/m/m, f/m/m/m, f/f/f/m, etc.

An extensive literature review on the subject of Internet-accessible depictions of this nature reveals very few systematic research projects. An upsurge of interest in computer pornography and the alt.sex.* bulletin boards has been expressed in several articles in the mainstream press (Elmer-Dewitt, 1993, 1994, 1995; Turner, 1990). A recent research project conducted at Carnegie-Mellon University (Rimm, 1995) examined hundreds of thousands of images of online pornography, but these were almost exclusively photographic images, and were overwhelmingly culled from examination of private dial-up bulletin boards, rather than from Usenet images. Another project dealing with Internet pornography (Mehta and Plaza, 1994) also dealt with Internet graphic images. To date, there has been no published analysis of written pornography on the Internet.

As the Internet becomes more widely used, and as literally millions of people now have access to the Usenet groups, there is an increased need for a systematically conducted analysis of this material instead of pure speculation upon content and effects. It is also important to realize just how easy it is to access these new groups. From most university computer systems or Internet-linked home computers, it only takes a few mouse clicks and entered commands to access these Usenet groups.

METHODS

In planning this study, several methodological decisions were made. First, due to the lack of prior research in this area, primary data collection was essential. The principal investigator (the first author) performed a content-analysis of 196 stories, categorizing each story by its content by what appeared to be common themes in the postings: pedophilia, homoerotic, nonconsensual sex, pain, bondage, torture, and other fetishes. Most stories contained more than one element being categorized. For example, a story about an adult man forcing sex upon a young female child would be categorized as "pedophilic" and "nonconsensual sex." Any other unusual or interesting aspects of each posting were recorded by the researcher.

A second methodological decision made by the researchers was to consider each posting as a separate piece of data for analysis purposes, due to the fact that some stories might consist of several postings over time periods as long as a few months. Thus rather than 196 separate *stories*, the analysis consisted of 196 separate *postings*. Postings on alt.sex.stories which constituted narrative "stories" were considered valid data. Any posting which was in reply to a posted story or a request for a story to be reposted was ignored for the purposes of this research. It was also decided that the most important element was the existence of discrete types of material in each story, thus no effort was made to calculate percentages of each story spent on each topic or even the number of times an element was present in each story.

There was no attempt to place the data collection within any specific time-frame or time period. It was decided that a sample of two hundred stories would provide adequate data for a content analysis. As such, the principal investigator (PI) began data collection at a convenient time during the semester. Once the project was begun, all stories which were copied to the alt.sex.stories group on the news server (the server location is not being disclosed for reasons of confidentiality) were downloaded and analyzed for content until the sample size had been reached. The data collection took approximately two weeks, thus there were approximately one hundred usable postings posted per week to the newsgroup. Four postings were deemed unusable (incomplete or duplicates), thus 196 postings were retained for analysis.

Results

The results of this analysis were quite interesting in several respects (see Table 19.1). The most prevalent element was the non-consent element, which was present in 40.8% of the stories. The non-consent element consists of stories of rape, child molestation, forced slavery, mind control, and other similar themes.

The next most common element, present in 35.7% of stories, was the female/female homosexuality element. This not only included interpersonal relationships defined as lesbian, but female/female sexual encounters that include a male or males as well. This is not a surprising statistic considering the popularity of pornographic movies that contain female/female sex.

Twenty-four percent of stories analyzed included some element of bondage and 23.5% included some form of discipline, while 21.9% of the stories contained some element of intentionally inflicted pain. Stories in this category contained mild inflictions of pain such as spanking. Only incidences of pain that did not cause any permanent damage were included in this category.

A rather disturbing finding was that 19.4% of analyzed stories contained at least one incidence of pedophilic sex. The majority of these stories involved very young children having intercourse and oral sex repeatedly with one or more adults. Frequently, the adults depicted in the postings were sexually involved with more than one child per posting.

The torture element, which was present in 11.7% of the stories, involved very violent, sadistic types of sexual activity. Story plots ranged widely, from a man who tortures women by pulling out their toe nails and smashing their

**TABLE 19.1 Percentages
by Category**

Category	Percentage of Stories
Nonconsent	40.8
Homosexual acts	36.7
Bondage	24
Discipline	23.5
Pain	21.9
Pedophilia	19.4
Torture	11.7
Group sex	8.2
Furry	5.1
Mind control	5.1
Incest	4.6
Bestiality	1

feet while engaging in sexual activity with them, to a story about a rapist who would pour molten plastic into his victims' vaginas while video-taping the incident.

Other specific fetish behaviors were noted as well. The most prevalent of these were the following: Group sex was present in 8.2 % of the stories. 5.1% of the stories involved an interesting, yet relatively undocumented fetish known as "furry." This fetish involves various sexual activities with anthropomorphized animals such as weasels and cats. These animals possess extensive human qualities such as speech, cognition, and walking upright. 5.1% of stories involved some kind of mind control (such as hypnosis, the use of mythical mind control machines or drugs) used to acquire sex and/or sex slaves. 4.6% of the stories contained some incidence of incest between close family members. The remainder of the sub-elements in the other fetishes category each comprise 2% or less of the total percentage of this element within the analysis.

Implications

The implications of this research are interlinked with existing research upon the effects of pornography. Potential effects of the pornography available on the Internet can only be generalized from existing research on effects of pornography. An overview of research upon the effects of pornography indicates that while the effects of "erotica" and non-violent pornography seem to be minimal, the effects of violent pornography upon subjects' attitudes towards women, coercive behavior, and realistic view of sex might be extensive and detrimental (Donnerstein and Linz, 1986; Boeringer, 1994). However, little research has been done upon the effects of written pornography at all. In one study, no effect was found for the exposed group as opposed to the control group; however, the study utilized "erotica" as opposed to hard-core written pornography (Malamuth et al., 1980). In another study, Slade (1980) found that video pornography was relatively nonviolent compared to written pornography. Existing research done using pictorial pornography and film indicates that aggressive pornography does have a detrimental effect upon the attitudes (and possibly actions) of subjects exposed to it (Donnerstein and Linz, 1986; Demare, et al., 1988). However, in all likelihood little experimental research has ever been done using pornography as violent or as deviant as some of the postings available on this Internet newsgroup. This is understandable considering the ethical problems of exposing subjects to such materials and the possible permanent effects that subjects might suffer. The extreme violence and brutality sometimes present in postings on the Internet cannot be over-emphasized when discussing the potential effects upon viewers—especially young viewers. The PI of this study found it necessary to seek professional debriefing through the counseling services offered at the university after conducting this analysis. Caution and careful preparation is advised in expanding and replicating this research.

A literature search in the area of cognitive and perceptual psychology also presents some interesting implications where computer pornography is concerned. Some researchers have found that subjects who are computer literate and view computers in a positive manner some times absorb information more quickly and view it as more interesting than the same information presented on paper (Wang, 1989). It seems reasonable to assume that if someone is spending time on the Internet that they are computer literate and, more likely than not, view computers in a somewhat positive way. The interactive nature of computers as opposed to the static nature of pictorial, film, and text pornography could also play a role in a possible *increase* in effect upon the viewer. Future research should focus on this possibility.

REFERENCES

Boeringer, S. 1994. Pornography and sexual aggression: Associations of violent and nonviolent depictions with rape and rape proclivity. *Deviant Behavior* (July–Sep.).

Demare, D., J. Briere, and H. Lips. 1988. Violent pornography and self-reported likelihood of sexual aggression. *Journal of Research in Personality* 22: 140–153.

Donnerstein, E., and D. Lintz. 1986. Mass media sexual violence and male viewers: Current theory and research. *American Behavioral Scientist* 29: 601–618.

Elmer-Dewitt, P. 1993. Orgies on line. *Time* 61 (31 May).

_____. 1994. Censoring cyberspace: Carnegie Mellon's attempt to ban sex from its campus computer network sends a chill along the info highway. *Time* 102 (21 November).

_____. 1995. On a screen near you: Cyberporn. *Time*, 3 (July): 38–45.

Malamuth, N.M., S. Haber, and S. Feshbach, S. 1980. Testing hypothesis regarding rape: Exposure to sexual violence, sex differences, and the "normality" of rapists. *Journal of Research in Personality* 14: 121–137.

Mehta, M. D., and D. E. Plaza. 1994. A content analysis of pornographic images on the Internet. Paper presented at symposium, Free Speech and Privacy in the Information Age. University of Waterloo.

Rimm, Martin. 1995. Marketing pornography on the information superhighway. *Georgetown Law Journal* 83: 5.

Turner, J.A. 1990. Messages in questionable taste. *The Chronicle of Higher Education*, A13.

Wang, Z. 1989. The human computer interface hierarchy model and strategies in system development. *Ergonomics*. 32: 1392–1400.

PART IV

ANALYSIS, INTERPRETATION, AND THE WRITING OF QUALITATIVE DATA

Ethnographer Michael Agar distinguishes between analysis and interpretation by noting:

> In ethnography . . . you learn something ("collect some data"), then you try to make sense out of it ("analysis"), then you go back and see if the interpretation makes sense in light of new experience ("collect more data"), then you refine your interpretation ("more analysis"), and so on. The process is dialectic, not linear (Agar, 1980:9).

Data analysis is a reflexive part of the research process and comes directly out of your data collection. The two processes are "highly transactional, each activity shedding new light on the other," and I would caution you here about completing one process in its entirety without at all engaging in the other (Ely, Vinz, Downing, and Anzul, 1997: 165). As you move from one stage of your research to the other, be certain to not shut the door on subsequent collections, analyses, and interpretations. Be open to revisiting the field and rethinking your ideas. As Lofland and Lofland (1984) argue, the most productive research is that which allows "analysis and data collection [to] run concurrently for most of the time expended on the project" (quoted in Ely, et al. 1997:164).

Several questions may arise as you ponder the process of transforming your data from your initial observations or interviews into what Harry Wolcott terms "intelligible accounts" (Wolcott, 1994:1). How do you know if you focused on the major themes contained in your interview material or ethnographic fieldwork account? Do the categories of analysis you have chosen make sense in light of the data you've gathered? With what type of analysis should you proceed? As qualitative researchers accumulate many pages of text, they are constantly faced with important decisions, such as whether or not they should continue collecting more data for their study and what type of analysis is most appropriate. As quantitative researchers want to stay as close to their data as possible as well as to utilize the volumes of material they have worked so hard to collect, they may find it helpful to use a computerized software program to analyze their data. Such a tool can be very helpful to the analytic process of an ambitious researcher, as it alleviates the strain of organizing and sorting what can become thousands of codes and categories.

However, important analysis and interpretation issues can arise when using such a tool. If we consider Mills's contention that "the procedures are neither 'scientific' nor 'mechanistic': qualitative analysis is 'intellectual craftsmanship'" (quoted in Ely et al., 1997:164), it is difficult to see how automated, advanced technology can play a part. Should a researcher employ a computer software program at all? After all, isn't analysis more of an art form? Will the software program interfere with the creative process of analysis? Will using a computer software program distance researchers from their data?

These are only some of the fundamental questions researchers may face as they begin the process of turning their interviews and ethnographic observations into a book or article. Qualitative researchers' analytic work is more difficult because they are working not with numbers or statistics but with unanalyzed textual data that can total thousands of pages. Miles and Huberman note:

> A chronic problem of qualitative research is that it is done chiefly with words, not with numbers. Words are fatter than numbers and usually have multiple meanings. This makes them harder to move around and work with. Worse still, most words are meaningless unless you look backward or forward to other words. . . . Numbers, by contrast, are usually less ambiguous and may be processed with more economy. . . . Small wonder, then that most researchers prefer working with numbers alone, or getting the words they collect translated into numbers as quickly as possible. . . . [However] converting words into numbers, then tossing away the words gets a researcher into all kinds of mischief. . . . Focusing solely on numbers shifts our attention from substance to arithmetic, and thereby throws out the whole notion of qualitativeness; one would have done better to have started with numbers in the first place (1984:54–55).

Here you can see the fundamental tension between qualitative and quantitative research. Which is better—words or numbers? We are qualitative types, ourselves, and we will not spend time defending the merit of our chosen methodology. Rather, we will give you, our reader, a foundation affording you the ability to analyze and interpret the value of the qualitative approach for yourself.

ANALYSIS AND INTERPRETATION

In order to build theory and potentially draw conclusions from their data, researchers engage in a process called "coding," which is the central part of qualitative data analysis and involves extracting meaning from collected textual materials. If we were to describe how the process is actually performed it would sound something like this: Coding usually consists of describing "themes" or "ideas" in "chunks "or "segments" of text in the data and labeling them with a short name or sometimes even a number. Coding is the analytic strategy many qualitative researchers employ in order to locate key themes, patterns, ideas, and concepts within their data.

While it can be a time-consuming and labor-intensive process, close, critical coding is a fundamental part of good, strong research. Analyzing qualitative data from in-depth interviews, field notes, magazines, or oral histories, for example, presents a distinct challenge for the qualitative researcher. There are many different forms of analyses with many different goals, all depending on the stated research question and qualitative method utilized. Let us consider two distinct examples to elucidate this discussion of coding.

If I wish to study the characteristics of language, more specifically the gender-role bias in textbooks for preschoolers, I might want to conduct a content analysis study, which is defined as research examining "patterns of symbolic meaning within written text, audio visual, or [an]other communication medium" (Neuman, 2000:506) . I would specify the nature of the sampling frame and the type of textbooks selected, and I would be attuned to the presence or absence of certain gender role terms, coding those expressions accordingly. In this way, I might set forth a predefined coding scheme for analyzing my data. I might even want to test some specific hypotheses concerning reasons for the rise and fall of certain gender-role stereotypes over specified time periods. As I see patterns or themes emerging from my generated codes, I might begin to develop some kind of meaning about them. It is at this point that I might begin to jump back and forth between my roles as data coder, analyzer, and interpreter.

The procedures for this analysis would be closely aligned with quantitative techniques in that I would be interested in counting the number of occurrences of certain words and/or phrases in the text. This would be a qualitative-deductive analysis, which allows me to select codes and categories before engaging in any type of coding or sorting process.

If, on the other hand, I wanted to conduct a set of intensive interviews with a small sample of individuals who lost loved ones in the events of September 11, 2001, in order to explore how they are coping with their lives in the wake of this tragedy, I would probably start with a set of general, open-ended interview questions. My coding procedure would be much more open-ended and "holistic." My goal would be to gain insight and understanding into the lives of these individual survivors. I would not have a predefined set of coding categories. My analysis procedure would be inductive and would require my immersion in the text until themes, concepts, or dimensions of concepts emerged from the data. I would especially look for the common ways or patterns of behavior whereby individuals cope with trauma.

These studies exemplify two different types of strategies which range from more structured to less structured, the former being a deductive approach to social research and the latter being an inductive one. It is important to note here that in deductive research, the researcher moves from abstract ideas to empirical data through hypothesis testing and that in inductive research the researcher moves in the opposite direction, from empirical details to generalized theory or principles (Neuman, 2000: 508–11).

When we talk about analysis you may get the feeling that the discussion is progressing in ways and with terms that are somewhat technical and procedural, and you are right. Analysis usually begins with the determination of descriptive codes within the data that will eventually generate a set of key concepts or themes and ultimately allow the researcher to build on those themes to construct or validate some type of theory.

In the following segment of text below, we have taken an excerpt from one of many interviews with college-age women concerning their eating patterns and disordered eating habits (See Hesse-Biber, 1996).

Case #2 (Text/Segment/Chunk)

Text:	Code:
I always wanted to be the thinnest,	Thinnest, Prettiest
the prettiest. I wanted to look like	look like girls in magazines
the girls in the magazines. I'm	boys will love me
going to have so many boyfriends,	positive body image
and boys are going to be so in love	provides economic resources
with me, I won't have to work and	Thin Rationale
I'll be taken care of for the rest of	Thin as a means of security
my life	Media creates Standards

As you can see, in the illustration above the first few codes listed are "literal" codes, meaning that the words also appear within the text. These are fairly descriptive code categories. As we go down the code list, the codes become much more interpretive, or what has been termed "analytical." These codes are not tied as tightly to the text itself, but rather they begin to rely on the researcher's insights for drawing out interpretation. This type of coding depends on what we call "focused coding." A " focused" coding procedure allows for the building and clarifying of concepts. In "focused" coding a researcher examines all the data in a category, compares each piece of data with every other piece, and finally builds a clear, working definition of each concept. Such concepts are then assigned "codes" (Charmaz, 1983:117).

Focused coding further requires that a researcher develop a set of analytical categories rather than just topically label data. Modifying code categories becomes important in the development of more abstract code categories that aid in the generation of theoretical constructs. This process is in turn essential to the generation of theory-building. One would begin to do this type of coding only after examining a number of interviews, retrieving the text associated with similar passages of text from other interviews, and determining whether any common themes occur.

To refer again to the preceding example: I retrieved the text for several eating-disordered interviews like this one, and in fact I discovered that some common themes did emerge. Two themes I noted at the bottom were "thinness as a means of security" and "media creates standards." "Thinness as a means of security" really encompasses some of the concerns expressed by the interviewee—that she wants to have a boyfriend, love, and money and be taken care of. In fact, examining other interviews uncovered a range of other reasons respondents wanted to be thin such as: "thin as healthy," "thin as empowering," and so on. This eventually led me to develop an even larger code category I termed "thin rationales," of which the code category "thinness as a means of security" was a subset. A second, larger category, "media creates standards" (of behavior), was developed in a similar manner.

Kathy Charmaz's article, "Grounded Theory," provides one type of analysis model for generating meaning from qualitative data. She provides us with a concise, step-by-step set of analysis instructions that assist in the development of "progressively more abstract conceptual categories to synthesize, to explain and to understand" data (Charmaz, 1995:28). She takes the reader through the process of collecting data, analyzing, and writing memos, and she shows that grounded theory analysis starts with and stays close to the data. All of these parts of the analysis work interactively, which means that data collection and data analysis go hand in hand. As illustrated earlier, as one collects the data one is analyzing the data (Charmaz, 1995: 28–32). The researcher derives analytic categories not from preconceived ideas or theories, but rather from what is directly happening in the empirical world (Charmaz, 1995: 32).

When I was doing the interviews for my eating disorders study, I was constantly hearing and thinking about how strongly the media influenced girls' desires to be thin. Even if I tried, I could not divorce my data collection from my analysis, for I was constantly engaged with the recurring issues and ideas when I was interviewing and listening.

One begins the more formal process of analysis, says Charmaz, by doing "open coding." This consists of reading the text line by line. One begins by carefully coding each line, sentence, and paragraph. The questions one should ask during this process are

- "What is going on?
- What are people doing?
- What is the person doing?
- What do these actions and statements take for granted?
- How do structure and context serve to support, maintain, impede or change these actions and statements?" (Charmaz, 1995: 38)

As the process continues, the researcher may begin to see more developed codes, that is, focused codes, especially through the process of writing memos about codes. A memo helps bridge the gap between coding and the first draft of analysis. It helps "elaborate processes, assumptions and actions" that are entrenched in codes (Charmaz, 1995: 42–43). By writing memos codes can be raised to the level of "category." Indeed, memo writing is an integral part of the grounded theory process, as it assists researchers in elaborating on their ideas regarding their data and code categories. Ideally, memo writing takes place at all points in the analysis process. Reading through and sorting memos can also aid researchers in integrating their ideas and may even serve to illuminate additional ideas and relationships in the data. Let us look at an example of memo writing done during the study of girls and body image (Hesse-Biber, 1996):

Memo on Attitudes toward appearance

> Overall, appearance seemed to occupy a central place in these girls' estimation of themselves and others. For example, when asked how important appearance was to them, many of the girls said that it was very important. Some asserted that it was the most important aspect of their self-concept. For instance, one girl said that her ideal woman was defined more by her looks than by her character. Other girls said that they were obsessed with and anxious about their appearance. Many responded to the questions about how much they cared or were worried about their appearance by saying that they really cared what others thought about their appearance. Many of the girls expressed overall negative feelings about their bodies. A significant proportion of girls expressed moderate concern. Several girls talked about the overall pressures they experience from peers and family to "look good." The girls spoke about how competitive they were with other girls when it came to appearance. Girls seem to be comparing themselves against an ideal uniform standard.

The memo written by the researcher during the process of data collection takes the idea contained within codes, such as "thin rationales," and helps the researcher develop larger data categories from interaction with respondents. This descriptive data reflects the researcher's impressions and analysis.

The idea of a grounded theory approach, which we mentioned earlier, can be summarized in the following way: A grounded theory approach to social research helps researchers read carefully through their data; it helps them uncover the major categories/concepts lodged deeply within their data; and it ultimately brings to light the properties of these categories and their interrelationships.

The grounded theory approach of coding represents one end of the qualitative continuum. While it can be employed by researchers working from multiple standpoints, including feminism, it can be broadly categorized as a postpositivist approach to analysis and interpretation. Charmaz's postpositivist framework is at one end of a continuum, and postmodernist and poststructuralist interpretive styles are at the other. Postmodernist approaches represent critical methods of analysis—attentive to the power imbued within any knowledge construction. Researchers with what Denzin calls a "postmodern sensibility" view traditional interpretive criteria *themselves* as highly problematic or as inherently biased in ways that perpetuate and validate hierarchical ways of creating knowledge. In other words, postmodernists believe that the positivist tradition produces knowledge that is inattentive to how social power impacts the research process and the construction of social meaning in society. Postmodernists do not impose preexisting theoretical frameworks on data, such as code categories and replicable methods of analysis, but rather let the world speak for itself. As such, qualitative researchers working from a postmodern sensibility are highly concerned with voice, authorship, and multiple perspectives. They seek to create situated and partial truths that reveal themselves through fluid and reflexive practice. Likewise, poststructuralists unravel meaning through a process of critical and reflexive deconstruction—not with the intent to reconstruct and thereby impose another theoretical framework their data, but rather to expose and naturally transform it.

There is no one right way to proceed with analysis. As C. Wright Mills noted early on, qualitative analysis is, after all, "intellectual craftsmanship" (Mills, 1959, cited in Tesch, 1990:96). As Renata Tesch notes, qualitative analysis can and should be done 'artfully' (Guba and Lincoln, 1981: 185), even 'playfully' (Goetz and LeCompte, 1984: 172), but it also requires a great amount of methodological knowledge and intellectual competence" (Tesch, 1990:97). Norman K. Denzin further argues in "The Art and Politics of Interpretation" that there is an "art of interpretation."

> This may also be described as moving from the field to the text to the reader. The practice of this art allows the field-worker-as-*bricoleur* . . . to translate what has been learned into a body of textual work that communicates these understandings to the reader (2000: 313–314).

As the researcher changes caps from data collector to analyzer to interpreter to writer during the research process, it becomes evident that qualitative data analysis is an "eclectic" and even "cyclic" activity (Tesch, 1990: 95–7, cited in Ely et al., 1997: 163). There is no right or wrong way to synthesize data, and often the researcher jumps back and forth between collection, analysis, and writing. Hats come on and off, and sometimes sit one on top of the other. The facets of qualitative research must continually be refined and revisited during all phases of the research process.

To assist in the never-ending task of data analysis, researchers often make use of modern technology. This is the current trend in qualitative research. A researcher's analysis can be greatly enhanced by the use of computer software packages. As Fielding and Lee note in their article "Computer Analysis and Qualitative Research" the work of researchers over the past two decades is being transformed by computerized software programs. Innovations such as CAQDAS (Computer Assisted Qualitative Data Software) help "acquire, store and manage data" and are becoming a "palpable presence" in the qualitative field of research (Fielding and Lee, 1998:1).

Software programs can be grouped into two main categories. The first category is "generic software," which consists of programs that were not specifically designed for qualitative research. There are three types of software in this category: (1) "word processors," which assist the researcher with typing and sorting out field notes and/or interviews *and* developing an organizing scheme for these data; (2) "text retrievers," which quickly sort through a range of data to find a specific pattern or "string" of characters in the data to enable the researcher to identify themes and/or topics within a large body of data; and (3) "textbase managers," which are large database systems that allow for the retrieval of semistructured information which is entered into "records" and "fields" (Fielding and Lee, 1998:6–8).

The second category of software is specifically designed for qualitative data analysis; this category encompasses "dedicated qualitative analysis packages." These packages fall into four types (1) "code and retrieve" programs," (2) "code-based theory building programs," (3) conceptual network buildings, and (4) "textual mapping software." Code and retrieve programs allow codes to be assigned to particular segments of text and make for easy recovery of categories using sophisticated "Boolean search functions," which search using terms and the operands "and, or, not." Code-based theory building programs allow the researcher to analyze the systematic relationships among the data, the codes, and the code categories. Some programs provide a rule-based systems approach which allows for the testing of hypotheses in the data, while others allow for a visual representation of the data. Last, conceptual network building and textual mapping software programs allow researchers to draw links between code categories in their data, which may be viewed as an "add-on" feature to the code-based theory building programs (Fielding and Lee, 1998:9–11).

Fielding and Lee note that the field of qualitative software development has grown over time and that there is a growing and extensive national and international community of software users. They even go so far as to claim that we may be witnessing the "last generations of qualitative social researchers who still analyze their data 'mainly by hand'" (Fielding and Lee, 1998:1). Unsurprisingly, the growing usage of computer software programs as tools in qualitative analysis raises a number of methodological and theoretical concerns regarding data analysis and interpretation of qualitative data.

Sharlene Hesse-Biber's article, "Unleashing Frankenstein's Monster? The Use of Computers in Qualitative Research," discusses five fears about the use of computer software in qualitative research that are frequently expressed. The first of these fears is that computer programs will separate the qualitative researcher from the creative process. Hesse-Biber notes that some analysts liken the experience of doing qualitative work to artistic work—"just as the artist prefers a brush or pencil and paper, so too do some qualitative researchers" (Hesse-Biber, 1995:27). The use of computer technology is seen as incompatible with artistic processes.

With the advent of more advanced qualitative software features, such as the ability to test hypotheses with artificial intelligence, there is the additional fear of "data dredging." This is using technology to do one's thinking by having the software automatically code the data. This overdependence on technology could possibly result in the absence of significant theoretical input from the researcher (Hesse-Biber, 1995:27).

Furthermore, computer software programs have been criticized for skewing the distinction between quantitative and qualitative analysis. Hesse-Biber argues that the line between quantitative and qualitative analysis will be blurred by imposing the logic of survey research onto qualitative research and by sacrificing in-depth analysis for larger sample sizes. Such concerns stem from the fact that computer software programs now permit the easy coding and retrieval of large numbers of documents. For many of the new software programs, there is no limit on the number of files or size of data that can be handled and synthesized. Because the volume of data now collected for some qualitative studies is comparable to that of quantitative methods, a potential fear that qualitative research will be reduced to quantitative research is often discussed. Similarly qualitative researchers can also generate counts of the occurrence of codes or concepts in their data, which can be linked up via a matrix to a statistical software program and analyzed quantitatively, further blurring the line between the two methods.

Another fear related to this current computer controversy is that computer usage might dictate the definition of a particular field of study. Software program structures often set requirements for how a research project should proceed. This raises concerns among some critics that computer software programs will determine what types of questions are asked as well as how the specific data analysis will be performed.

An additional fear is that researchers will now have to be more accountable for their analysis. Computer programs for analyzing qualitative data require researchers to be more explicit in the procedures and analytical processes through which they produce their data and interpretations. Asking qualitative researchers to be more overt about their methodology and holding their interpretations accountable to tests of validity and reliability will raise some controversies, such as the following: Should there even be strict tests of validity and reliability for qualitative data? It is important to understand that most qualitative researchers are often not explicit about the exact way in which they arrived at their findings. If computer programs require a strict detailing of this process, several issues of interpretation may arise, especially if secondary analyses of the same data are undertaken (Hesse-Biber, 1995:27–33).

In struggling with this tension, Hesse-Biber (1995:31) argues that at present it is difficult to follow the exact methodology used in many qualitative studies. If procedures are made more detailed so that secondary analyses are possible, several more issues are bound to arise: How do we resolve differences in interpretation of the same data? Whose interpretation is correct? Are several interpretations possible, and if so, under what conditions?

Finally, Hesse-Biber discusses the fear that confidentiality will be sacrificed through the use of multimedia data. When audio or visual data are used in a research study it becomes difficult for a researcher to ensure that the identity of the respondent will be secure. Hesse-Biber asks: "What if someone recognizes a respondent? What if data are lost or stolen? There are also negative unintended consequences of utilizing visual data in qualitative analysis" (Hesse-Biber, 1995:32).

Computers hold out the promise of revolutionizing the way in which researchers conduct their analysis, but they also contain a set of caveats for the qualitative analyst. Researchers who use these programs should assess their strengths and weaknesses as well as the implications of using computer software programs to analyze qualitative data. Researchers need to decide in what manner and to what extent they want to use computer software as a tool for data analysis. While technological programs cannot replace human thinking, they certainly can assist with some of complex aspects of qualitative research.

As we transition from problems with data collection and coding to issues of interpretation and writing up research results, more questions begin to emerge concerning the interpretation of qualitative data. At the heart of this discussion are issues of power and control over the interpretation process.

Early traditional qualitative researchers followed a "scientific" model of research that patterned research procedures along the lines of the natural sciences by following the tenets of positivism. It was imperative that researchers be "objective," that is, not allow their values to enter into the research process. In this model of research the scientist remains "objective" in order to gain a "true" understanding of the reality. It was as if the "reality" or "true" picture would emerge if only the researcher would be faithful to the scientific tenet of "objectivity."

In "An End to Innocence: The Ethnography of Ethnography," John Van Maanen presents the early ethnographic attitude that says one should always "let the ethnographer speak for the data," with very little or no input from the researched as far as the interpretation of findings went.

> There once was a time—some might say a dreamtime—when ethnography was read as a straight-ahead cultural description based on the firsthand experience an author had with a strange (to both author and reader) group of people. Those who wrote ethnographies may have had their doubts about what the adventure of fieldwork taught them and just how "being there" resulted in an ethnography, but few doubts surfaced in their written products. It seemed as if an ethnography emerged more or less naturally from a simple stay in the field. One simply staked out a group, lived with them for awhile, took notes on what they said and did, and went home to write it all up. If anything, ethnography looked like a rather pleasant, peaceful, and instructive form of travel writing (Van Maanen, 1995:1).

Yet little by little the central tenet of ethnography—the authority of the ethnographic representation—has come under intense criticism. As Van Maanen notes, "a kind of ethnography of ethnography" is emerging through textual study, and "new understandings are gradually altering the way we think about cultural representation practices both past and present" (Van Maanen, 1995:17). Ethnographers are increasingly being scrutinized for har-

boring preconceived notions about subjects or cultures and anticipating theoretical connections within data. New questions are being raised, including
"What role does the researcher play in the process of interpreting his/her
data? Should the qualitative researcher allow his or her feelings to enter into
the interpretation process? Whose point of view is the ethnographer really
representing with his or her data?" (Van Maanen, 1995:16–17).

In light of such criticism, Van Maanen argues that there are limits to
ethnographic representation. Rereading and reinterpreting texts may very
well elucidate new analysis from different standpoints. By revisiting classic
ethnographic studies like "People of the Plains" or "Ashanti Character," cultural anthropologists, for example, have been able to refute ideas that the
portrayed groups were isolated, powerless peoples (Van Maanen, 1995:19).
Instead, "re-presentations" of this kind have actually shown them to be anything but "timeless or beyond the reach of contemporary society" (Van Maanen, 1995:19). Such an example "remind us of the limits of representational
possibilities and makes a strong argument to counter any faith in a simple
or transparent world that can be known with any certainty" (Van Maanen,
1995:18–19).

Much of qualitative research deals with observation and interviewing,
and it is a method that requires the constant interaction of the researcher
and the researched. The researcher can impact the research process at
multiple points along the research path—from the choice of research
project/problem to the research design to the analysis and interpretation of
findings.

It is important to recognize that there are important power dynamics
within interviewer/interviewee relationships that can affect the interpretation of research results. One of the central issues we examine in this section
is the extent to which power relations between the researcher and researched
exist and impact the interpretation process.

In thinking about this specific problem in the research process, one might
ask, How much power should the researcher have in determining whose
voice will be heard in the interpretation of research findings? Some critics
of traditional qualitative research analyses—especially those who have experienced oppression in terms race, class, age, gender, and sexuality—are
concerned about presenting the lived experiences and points of view of the
"other" in the text, stories, or narratives. Dorothy Smith, for example, recognizes that the discipline of sociology as a whole has long discredited the
authority of feminist-based knowledge. In advocating a standpoint epistemology, she argues for knowing a society from within, which is an approach
that could help the researcher interpret the data of the "other" more effectively. In other words, in order to understand a society we must access data
from those who constitute that society. As a hierarchical society produces
different standpoints based on both achieved and ascribed characteristics,
data must be gathered from the variety of standpoints produced in a given
culture. Smith notes that in order to unlock a sociology specifically for
women, one must get inside their experiences to gain situated knowledge.

While researchers "can never escape the circles of [their] own heads," they need to use research as a mode of discovering and rediscovering society from within. The goal of standpoint epistemology is therefore not a reiteration of what it is already known, but rather "an exploration of what passes beyond that knowledge and is deeply implicated in how it is" (Smith, 1974, cited in Lemert, 1999:390).

As a qualitative researcher attempts to get inside of and understand subjective experiences, one might question the feasibility of achieving such an understanding. For instance, can a white, middle-aged, male researcher effectively relate to and accurately convey the life of a black, lesbian teenager? Many disagree about this. It is crucial to point out that the tension between the researcher and the researched is part of an ongoing power struggle, and negotiating such identity politics is certainly a process that requires close attention and sensitivity.

While feminist research methods do challenge traditional, positivist approaches to social inquiry, we must not assume that power dynamics do not affect the collection, analysis, and interpretation of data. Such relations cut across boundaries of age, race, class, and gender and cannot be ignored during the research process. Daphne Patai argues that in order to balance frequently disparate power relations, many feminist scholars seek to return their research to the communities that made it possible, but they do so in a manner that reinforces traditional inequalities and hierarchies. They may do this as a "feel good measure" to reconcile power imbalances, and they may also abandon intellectual responsibilities in order to gain the trust and approval of their subjects, compromising academic interpretation for a degree of "sisterhood" among subjects (Patai, 1991:147).

These questions of power and interpretation are of central importance in Katherine Borland's contribution, " 'That's Not What I Said': Interpretive Conflict in Oral Narrative Research." In this piece she explores the range of interpretive difference she encounters as she conducts an oral narrative with her grandmother, Beatrice (Bea) Hanson. She asks her grandmother to relate the story of her trip with her father to the Bangor, Maine, Fair Grounds' race track forty-two years ago. Borland is interested in understanding the different levels of "meaning making" that take place in the telling and interpretation of oral narratives, and she struggles with how to present her own work in a fashion that "grants the speaking woman interpretive respect without relinquishing [her] responsibility to provide [her] own interpretation of her experience" (Borland, 1991:64). For traditional ethnographers, it was commonplace to exclude the subject from the process of post-field interpretation. More recently, however, feminist researchers like Borland are seeking to empower these women by giving voice and value to their lives. Yet in combining the subject's perspective with academic and authoritarian perspectives, a researcher like Borland may find herself in conflict. What happens when the researcher and researched disagree?

As Borland interviews her grandmother, she creates a "first-level narrative story"—that is, the story her grandmother tells her conveys the particular way her grandmother constitutes the meaning of the event. There is, however, a second level of meaning to the narrative. This is the meaning the researcher constructs. It is the meaning of the narrative that is filtered through the personal experience and expertise of the researcher, Bea's granddaughter. Borland interprets her grandmother's story, but as she listens to the narrative, she reshapes it by filtering the story through her own life experiences and outward experiences, keeping in mind the expectations of her scholarly peers, to whom, she notes, "we must display a degree of scholarly competence." Borland uses a gender-specific theoretical lens to interpret her grandmother's story as a feminist account. However, her grandmother does not agree with Borland's interpretation because she does not consider herself a feminist. After reading her granddaughter's interpretation of the narrative, Bea says that her story has suffered a "sea of change" and that she has been misrepresented. Borland admits that if she had consulted with her grandmother during her analysis and before her actual write-up then maybe Bea would not have felt robbed of "textual authority" (Borland, 1991:73).

Borland raises issues of authority over and ownership of narratives, asking who has the right to interpret narrative accounts. For Borland the answer lies in a type of delicate balancing act. Borland shows her interpretation to her grandmother, and it is in the process of exchange of ideas that the interpretation begins. It is clear that no story should remain "unmediated"—that is, the storyteller's viewpoint ought to be present within the interpretation. While not all conflicts can be resolved, Borland feels it is important that researchers be challenged by the narrator's point of view, and vice versa. It is in the exchange of points of view that one may begin to see new ways of understanding the data (Borland, 1991:63–73).

WRITING

As the previous discussion points out, when performing qualitative research the researcher is constantly bouncing back and forth between the phases of analysis and interpretation. It is difficult to demarcate where one process begins and the other ends. However, there does come a point in a study when researchers have to take what they have for data, analysis, and interpretation, and begin the write-up. They spend memorable moments—or months—bonded to their computers, pondering material and framing a discussion. What are they going to produce from all of their hard labor? What words will they choose? How will they present their findings?

Norman Denzin notes that "writing is not an innocent practice," but rather is a tool that helps change the world (2000:898). The writer has stakes and intentions, and it is virtually impossible to separate the spheres of writing and interpretation from each other. Writing is a powerful interpretative form of discourse that has a "material presence in the world" and that can be "central to the workings of a free democratic society" (Denzin, 2000:898–99). As language is an influential cultural force, writing becomes a researcher's means of communicating and passing on valuable information and interpretation to a wider public audience.

When researchers are ready to begin the writing phase of their research project, they should be mindful of how connected their writing will be to the process of interpretation with which they are constantly engaged. In effect, writing and interpretation can be considered one and the same process. As there can be multiple tales from the field, they are charged with writing just one of them, but they should not lose sight of the notion that other representational possibilities exist. Van Maanen brought critique to bear on the traditional ethnography and made modern researchers attuned to the idea that singular tales of field studies are limited at best. Many stories can be told from a field experience. Many voices can be heard, and some inevitably are left out. In this regard, Van Maanen makes "a strong argument to counter any faith in a simple or transparent world that can be known with any certainty" (1995:18).

In this refutation Denzin argues that a new genre of writing is erupting in the postmodern era. Different styles are being tested by researchers and journalists alike, and they insist that facts need to be considered social constructions (Denzin, 2000:899). While the traditional "logico-scientific mode" of social research yearns for empirical proof and "universal truth conditions," the test now is to deconstruct such rationality (Richardson, 1995: 201). It is our contention that there is no one truth out there, one experience, or one beginning, middle, or end to a story. Likewise, the lines of reality are continually being blurred by researchers who struggle with exactly how to write their up their research. What should the standards be? In this fluid world of interpretative writing, how can they represent the other without somehow representing themselves?

Knowing that writing is not a " 'true' representation of an 'objective' reality," such postmodern researchers continually question who the audience is and what their goals are (Richardson, 1995:199). Writing does involve ethical, moral, and personal decisions, and how one chooses to formulate language creates value, bestows meaning, and constitutes the form of the subjects and objects that emerge from a study (Shapiro, 1985–1986, cited in Richardson, 1995:199). In this way, writing also allows the wider audience the chance to develop what C. Wright Mills calls the "sociological imagination" by seeing the social context around which personal experiences have been framed (Mills, 1959, quoted in Richardson, 1995:216). Indeed, "people everywhere experience and interpret their lives in relation to time," and when writing allows them to understand the sociohistorical context of their lives, they are better able to "gauge their 'own fates'" (Richardson, 1995:207, 215). This is what Mills called the promise of sociology, and it is why writing can take on different meanings for different people.

Researchers like Laurel Richardson, who advocates the use of the narrative as a means of communicating the sociological, contribute to this so-called blurring of social reality. Richardson considers writing a "method of inquiry" whereby the researcher is in continual dialogue with his or her data, analysis, and interpretation (1998:345). Richardson advocates for an experimental "postmodern" approach to writing. One example of this writing is a "narrative of the self" that is a personalized account of the researcher's lived experiences from the field whereby the reader can have the opportunity to "relive" the "imaginative renderings" of events with the writer (1998:356). Richardson (1998) suggests a range of writing tips concerning how to engage in experimental forms of interpretation and she offers concrete writing suggestions, along with exercises, for qualitative researchers. In her discussion of the narrative as a useful mode of "reasoning and representation," Richardson argues that we, as sociologists, need to consider alternative forms of writing (1995:200). To marginalize the narrative as a way of expressing the social experience is to do all of society a great disservice. Social science writing influences our public discussions of politics, policy, identity, and transformation, and the narrative can help with these debates. The narrative form is a means of telling a story that "reflect[s] the universal human experience of time and link the past, present, and future" (Richardson, 1995:218). It combines literature with history, as well as the individual with the communal. It makes "individuals, cultures, societies, and historical epochs comprehensible as wholes" as it allows people to see themselves as part of a larger system (Richardson, 1995:200). The narrative can stimulate liberating civic discussion about important social concerns by allowing readers to use their "sociological imaginations" to "reveal personal problems as public issues, to make possible collective identity and collective solutions" (Richardson, 1995:216).

In presenting their interpretation of society through writing, researchers today are increasingly using narrative accounts of everyday life, real-life dialogue, multiple points of view, and a plain, sparse style (Harrington, 1997, cited in Denzin, 2000:899). Writers may be either present as narrators or participants or invisible in the text, but at all moments their interpretative voice is being communicated. They are producing a "symbolic tale, a parable that is not just a record of human experience" (Denzin, 2000:902). It is a tale that helps the readers as well as the researchers discover moral truths and multiple viewpoints about an issue. Although they may seek to communicate the story of another to a wider audience, their presence, their ideas, and their interpretation are being felt throughout.

In the spirit of civic transformation, ethnographic writing is today used as a means of public education to "create moral compassion and help citizens make intelligent decisions and take public action on private troubles that have become public issues" (Denzin, 2000:901). Writing can serve as the material that incites the public to meaningful judgment and subsequent action, and in essence helps transform the civic society (Charity, 1995, quoted in Denzin, 2000:901).

Postmodern writing practices have sought to capture some of those lost voices. Women, for instance, have often been silenced in enthographic studies, and attention has been focused on male studies (Clough, 1992, cited in Van Maanen, 1995:2). Attention to feminist issues only recently has unearthed a great deal of subject matter recognizing women's presence and problems in society. It is only through such research that action can now be taken to remedy such plights, and it is important that such writing be continually forthcoming. The language and experiences need to be actualized in words to bring forth increasing awareness of the problem. As Denzin notes, such writing demonstrates an "affectionate concern for the lives of people," and it is through this type of writing that social change can be propelled (Denzin, 2000:899). The language of the author can produce it, but the experiences of "the other" can direct it. Both voices undoubtedly will be interwoven into the script and ultimately work together to empower those who need the silence broken.

BIBLIOGRAPHY

Agar, Michael. 1980. *The professional stranger: An informal introduction to ethnography.* New York: Academic Press.

Berger Gluck, Sherna, and Daphne Patai. 1991. *Women's words: The feminist practice of oral history.* New York: Routledge.

Borland, Katherine. 1991. " 'That's not what I said!: Interpretive conflict in oral narrative research" pp. 63–75. In Sherna Berger Gluck and Daphani Patai (Eds.) *Women's Words: The Feminist Practice of Oral History* New York: Routledge.

Charity, A. 1995. Doing public journalism. New York: Guilford.

Charmaz, Kathy. 1995. Grounded theory. In Jonathan Smith, Ron Harroe and Luk Van Langenhov (Eds.), *Rethinking methods in psychology* (pp. 27–49). London: Sage.

Charmaz, Kathy. 1983. The grounded theory method: An explication and interpretation. In R. M. Emerson (Ed.), *Contemporary field research: A collection of readings.* (pp. 109–126). Prospect Heights, IL: Waveland Press.

Clough, Patricia. 1992. *The ends of ethnography.* Newbury Park, CA: Sage.

Denzin, Norman. 2000. The practices and politics of interpretation. In Norman Denzin and Yvonna Lincoln (Eds.), *Handbook of qualitative research.* Thousand Oaks, CA: Sage.

Ely, Margot, Ruth Vinz, Maryann Downing, and Margaret Anzul. 1997. *On writing qualitative research: Living by words.* London: Farmer Press, 1997.

Fielding, Nigel, and Raymond Lee. 1998. Introduction: Computer analysis and qualitative research. In *Computer analysis and qualitative research.* London: Sage.

Goetz, Judith P. and Margaret D. LeCompte. 1984. *Ethnography and qualitative design in educational research.* Orlando, FL: Academic Press.

Guba, Egon and Yvonna Lincoln. 1981. *Effective evaluation.* San Francisco: Jossey-Bass.

Harrington, W. (Ed.). 1997. A writer's essay: Seeking the extraordinary in the ordinary. In *Intimate journalism* (pp. xvii–xlvi). Thousand Oaks, CA: Sage.

Hesse-Biber, Sharlene. 1995. Unleashing Frankenstein's monster: The use of computers in qualitative research. *Studies in Qualitative Methodology* (Volume 5). Westport, CT: JAI Press.

Hesse-Biber, Sharlene. 1996. *Am I thin enough yet? The cult of thinness and the commercialization of identity.* New York: Oxford University Press.

Lemert, Charles (Ed.). 1999. *Social theory: The multicultural and classical readings* (2nd ed.). Boulder: Westview Press.

Lofland, J., and Lofland, L.H. 1984. *Analyzing social settings: A guide to qualitative observation and analysis.* Columbus: Ohio State University Press.

Matthew B. Miles and A. Michael Huberman. 1984. *Qualitative data analysis.* Beverly Hills, CA: Sage.

Mills, C. Wright. 1959. *The sociological imagination.* Oxford: Oxford University Press.

Neuman, William Lawrence. 2000. *Social research methods: Qualitative and quantitative approaches* (4th ed.). Needham, MA: Allyn & Bacon.

Patai, Daphne. 1991. U.S. academics and third world women: Is ethical research possible? pp. 137–153 in *Women's Words: The Feminist Practice of Oral History,* eds. S. B. Gluck & D. Patai. New York: Routledge.

Richardson, Laurel. 1995. Narrative and sociology. In John Van Maanen (Ed.), *in Representation in ethnography.* Thousand Oaks, CA: Sage.

Richardson, Laurel. 1998. Writing: A method of inquiry, pp. 345–371 in *Collecting and Interpreting Qualitative Materials,* eds. N. K. Denzin & Y. S. Lincoln. Thousand Oaks, CA: Sage.

Shapiro. M. 1985–1986. Metaphor in the philosophy of the social sciences. *Cultural Critique, 2,* 191–194.

Smith, Dorothy. [1974] 1990. Knowing women from within: A woman's standpoint. In *The conceptual practices of power: A feminist sociology of knowledge* (pp. 21–24). Boston: Northeastern University Press.

Tesch, R. 1990. *Qualitative research: Analysis types and software tools.* London: Falmer Press.

Van Maanen, John. 1995. An end to innocence: The ethnography of ethnography. In *Representation in ethnography.* Thousand Oaks, CA: Sage.

Wolcott, Harry F. 1994. *Transforming qualitative data: Description, analysis and interpretation.* Thousand Oaks, CA: Sage.

Wolcott, Harry. 1995. Making a study "more ethnographic." In John Van Maanen (Ed.), *Representation in ethnography.* Thousand Oaks, CA: Sage.

An End to Innocence

The Ethnography of Ethnography

JOHN VAN MAANEN

There once was a time—some might say a dreamtime—when ethnography was read as a straight-ahead cultural description based on the firsthand experience an author had with a strange (to both author and reader) group of people. Those who wrote ethnographies may have had their doubts about what the adventure of fieldwork taught them and just how "being there" resulted in an ethnography, but few doubts surfaced in their written products. It seemed as if an ethnography emerged more or less naturally from a simple stay in the field. One simply staked out a group, lived with them for awhile, took notes on what they said and did, and went home to write it all up. If anything, ethnography looked like a rather pleasant, peaceful, and instructive form of travel writing.

For some readers of ethnography—myself included—the apparent freedom from rigid methodological rules associated with fieldwork and the blissful disregard that many ethnographic writers displayed for high-flying abstractions in their papers and monographs seemed to provide a wonderful excuse for having an adventurous good time while operating under the pretext of doing serious intellectual work. Certainly for me the ethnographer's way of knowledge appeared in this dreamtime to be less arcane, more concrete, and far more intimate and respectful than count-and-classify survey work or building and testing off-the-shelf theoretical models. All that was required, it seemed, was a steady gaze and hand, a sturdy and thick notebook, and plenty of time to spare.

No more. The master trope these days appears to be *J'Accuse!* Ethnography is no longer pictured as a relatively simple look, listen and learn procedure but, rather, as something akin to an intense epistemological trial by fire. Boon (1982), for instance, takes ethnography to task for its reliance on unquestioned cultural conceits ("ours" not "theirs"). Rosaldo (1989) sternly chides ethnography for its unwarranted claims of objectivity, whereas Clifford (1988) points to its inevitable but treacherous subjectivity. Clough (1992) indicts ethnography for its gendered silences and partiality. Denzin (1988) faults ethnography for its failure to abandon the scientific posturing associated with modernism or essentialism, and Said (1989) considers ethnography's link to the empire discrediting yet difficult to shed. For these reasons and more, the cultural representation business has become quite tricky. Nor does it seem to matter much whether one goes to the headwaters of the Amazon or to the corner tavern in search of others sufficiently different from one's self to ethnographically realize. Just what is required of ethnography today is by no means clear, and among its producers and consumers alike, restlessness is the norm.[1]

Such restlessness, however, has not brought the enterprise down. And, like any other social practice, the techniques and results of ethnography—though to be fair, not so much its aims—have long been subject to question. The very term ethnography carries several meanings whose gradual and contested emergence must be appreciated to understand the current epistemological moans and groans. The trade has persisted over time not by pushing away critique but by absorbing it, thus maintaining certain ethnographic traditions by stretching them to embrace novel interests and practices. Some of these ethnographic traditions—notably those associated with fieldwork, the culture concept(s), and the pursuit of what is so often presented as the empathetic understanding of the other—are now so strongly articulated, so associated with recognized, hard, and intractable questions, and so enlivened by various interpretive strategies that deep or paradigmatic change is difficult if not impossible to imagine.

Broadly conceived, ethnography is a storytelling institution. It is one that carries a good deal of cultural legitimacy because its stories are commissioned and approved by the leading scientific and educational organizations of the day. Ethnography claims and is granted by many if not most of its readers a kind of documentary status on the basis that someone actually goes "out there," draws close to people and events, and then writes about what was learned *in situ*. It is, by and large, the ethnographer's direct personal contact with others that is honored by readers as providing a particularly sound basis for reliable knowledge. Put in cartoon form, an ethnographer is something of a Supertourist who visits a group of natives in their natural habitat and brings back the news of their way of life. This cartoon is, of course, a view of ethnography more common outside than inside ethnographic circles. Most ethnographers would offer a considerably more nuanced, sophisticated, and perhaps skeptical perspective on their trade. Nonetheless, these general understandings and expectations do play a part in what at any given time will be read as a proper ethnography.

The full measure of the ethnography industry includes the ceaseless production of authoritative monographs, exhaustive reviews of the literature(s), method manuals, encyclopedias of concepts and theories, meta-critical expositions, themed anthologies, experimental writings, annotated bibliographies, established and quasi-established journal publications, formal presentations of talks and papers presided over by a number of academic societies, and so forth. Little wonder that novelties and new directions can be readily absorbed.[2] Over long periods of time, everything may change, but from day to day, ethnographic practices seem much the same. In other words (my words), the center may not hold, but it appears rather formidable at any given time. This is especially true of the sense of vocational purpose or mission carved out and claimed as distinctive by those in the trade to write about one culture in terms of another. Thus, even when ethnography is racked by debate—as it is today—it continues to remain ethnography so long as what is being debated is not whether or not the work should go on but how best to go on with such work.[3] Consider, in more detail, the scope and shape of contemporary ethnography.

FIELDWORK, TEXTWORK, AND HEADWORK

In the most general sense, ethnography refers to the study of the culture(s) a given group of people more or less share. The term is double-edged for it points to both a method of study and a result of such study. When used to indicate a method, ethnography typically refers to fieldwork conducted by a single investigator—the fabled though slightly oxymoronic participant observer—who "lives with and lives like" those who are studied for a lengthy period of time (usually a year or more). When used to indicate a result, ethnography ordinarily refers to the written representation of culture. Contemporary students of culture emphasize the latter usage and thus look to define ethnography in terms of its rhetorical features such as the topical, stylistic, documentary, evidentiary, and argumentative choices made by an author and displayed in a text.

To understand the move toward rhetoric is to also appreciate three rather distinct activity phases or moments associated with ethnography.[4] The first moment concerns the collection of information or data on a specified (or proposed) culture. The second refers to the construction of an ethnographic report or account and, in particular, to the specific compositional practices used by the ethnographer to fashion a cultural portrait. The third moment of ethnography occurs with the reading and reception of an ethnographic text across various audience segments. Each phase raises distinctive and problematic concerns for the subjects, the producers, and the consumers of ethnography.

By far the most attention within ethnographic circles has been paid to its first moment—fieldwork. This live-in form of social research is both a product of and a reaction to the cultural studies conducted in the mid to late nineteenth century (Stocking 1987, 1992). Early ethnography is marked by more than a little distance between the researcher and researched. The mostly British ethnographers of the day based much of their cultural representations not on firsthand study but on their readings of documents, reports, and letters originating from colonial administrators, members of scientific expeditions, missionaries, traders, adventurers and, perhaps most important, far-away correspondents guided by questions posed by their stay-at-home pen pals.[5] It was not until the early twentieth century that ethnographers began to enter and stay for more than brief periods in the social worlds of those of whom they wrote. The modern and more or less foundational form of fieldwork as advocated but not always practiced by Malinowski ([1922] 1961, 1–25) required of an ethnographer the sustained, intimate, and personal acquaintance with what the "natives" say and do—in today's vernacular, what "cultural members" say and do. Malinowski's marching orders for fieldworkers were characteristically blunt and to the point: "Find out the typical ways of thinking and feeling, corresponding to the institutions and culture of a given community and formulate the results in the most convincing way" (p. 3).

There is (and was), however, a good deal of variation in terms of just how a fieldworker goes about finding things out and, perhaps more critical, just how such gentle or hard-nosed detective work leads to a convincing written description of culture. In regard to fieldwork, current practices include techniques such as intensive and representative interviewing, working closely and almost exclusively with a few "key" informants, designing and administering local surveys, observing and participating in everyday routines and occasioned ceremonies engaged in by those studied, collecting samples of member talk and action across a range of social situations, and so on. Indeed, there is now an enormous literature designed to help novice or veteran fieldworkers carry out various forms of ethnographic research (e.g., Friedlich 1970; Hammersley and Atkinson 1983; Spradley 1979; Werner and Schoepfle 1986).

Yet much of the good advice offered in fieldwork manuals defies codification and lacks the consensual approval of those who produce ethnographies. Fieldnotes, for example, are more or less *de rigueur* in terms of recording what is presumably learned in the field, but there is little agreement as to what a standard fieldnote—much less a collection of them—might be (Sanjek 1990). Moreover, how one moves from a period of lengthy field study to a written account based on such study is by no means obvious. Despite seventy or so years of practice, fieldwork remains a sprawling, highly personal, and therefore quite diverse activity (Kuper 1977; Lofland 1974; Stocking 1992).

The second moment of ethnography—"writing it up"—has by and large been organized and dominated by a genre called "ethnographic realism" (Clifford and Marcus 1986; Van Maanen 1988). It is, however, a genre that has itself undergone changes over time from a relatively unreflective, closed, and general ("holistic") description of native sayings and doings to a more tentative, open, and partial interpretation of member sayings and doings (Geertz 1973). Still, realism—for some quite defensible reasons remains a governing style for a good deal of ethnography, descriptive or interpretive (Jacobson 1991). The genre itself is marked by a number of compositional conventions including, for example, the swallowing up and disappearance of an author in the text, the suppression of the individual cultural member's perspective in favor of a typified or common denominator "native's point of view," the placement of a culture within a rather timeless ethnographic present, and a claim (often implicit) for descriptive or interpretive validity based almost exclusively on the author's own "being there" experience (fieldwork).

The most unapologetic realist styles foster an impression that ethnography is a clear, unmediated record of a knowable world. It is washed by a thick spray of objectivity. Aesthetic visions are downplayed because artful delights and forms are often seen by writers and readers alike to interfere with the presentation of what is really there in a given social world. Realism, of course, depends heavily on current cultural codes as to what counts as really real. Thus prevailing ideas as to the nature of the studied world and the acceptable kinds of explorable differences between "them" and "us" as well as the easy accessibility of the writing and its insistent certainty contribute to what might be called a Studio Portraiture form of realism—tightly framed, sharply focused, unnaturally bright, and shadowless.[6]

Some ethnographers, though by no means all, have expressed a degree of dissatisfaction with ethnographic realism (Marcus and Cushman 1982). Much of the initial discontent was generated by readers and critics from outside ethnographic circles who wondered just how personal experience could serve as the basis for a real, bona fide scientific study of culture. As a response to these self-appointed "real scientists," some ethnographers tried to make visible—more accurately, textualize—their discovery practices and procedures (Agar 1980). A degree of ironic embarrassment followed, for it seemed the more scientific ethnographers tried to be by writing about their methods, the less scientific those methods appeared. Such embarrassment accompanies many scientific fields these days, not just ethnography (Latour 1987). But one consequence of the ethnographic introspection of the 1960s and 1970s has been the spread of a methodological self-consciousness and a concern for reflexivity that has not gone away. Nor has guilt and anxiety expressed in some of the early inward-turning work gone away either. If anything, the moral ambiguity and political complicity associated with ethnography has grown ever more obvious and problematic in the shrinking and increasingly interconnected post-colonial world.[7]

In the wake of this heightened self-consciousness, alternatives to ethnographic realism have emerged. One, in particular, is now rather well developed. "Confessional ethnography" is a genre of fieldworkers' trials and tribulations that moves a reader's attention from the signified (the studied culture) to the one who, quite literally, signifies (the ethnographer).[8] The research process itself—fieldwork— becomes the focus of an ethnographic text. Its composition rests on moving the fieldworker to center stage and displaying how the writer came to know a given social world. Although often set apart from an ethnographer's realist accounts, confessional ethnography may nonetheless convey a good deal of the same sort of cultural information and speculation put forth in conventional realist works but in a more personalized and historically-situated fashion (e.g., Dumont 1978; Rabinow 1977). Thus what began as an attempt to shore up the ethnographic trade and make it safe for science turned out to have almost the opposite effect. It cracked open established representational practices and ushered in a period of increasing textual experimentation in ethnography.

Consider, for example, three other forms of ethnographic writing. Each of these forms, like the confessional, have isolated precedents to be found deep in the ethnographic archives but, as a genre, each contrasts sharply with the ethnographic realism and have been taken up by more than a few contemporary writers for just that reason. "Dramatic ethnography" rests on the narration of a particular event or sequence of events of obvious significance to the cultural members studied. These ethnographies present unfolding stories and rely more on techniques drawn from literary fiction and personal essays than from plain-speaking, documentary techniques—the style of nonstyle—drawn from scientific reports (e.g., Erickson 1976; Shore 1982). "Critical ethnographies" provide another genre wherein the represented culture is located within a larger historical, political, economic, social, and symbolic context than is said to be recognized by cultural members. This pushes the writer to move beyond traditional ethnographic interests and frameworks when constructing the text (e.g., Willis 1977; Nash 1979; Traweek 1988; Foley 1990). As a final illustration, "self-" or "auto-ethnographies" have emerged in which the culture of the writer's own group is textualized. Such writings often offer a passionate, emotional voice of a positioned and explicitly judgmental fieldworker and thus obliterate the customary and, ordinarily, rather mannerly distinction between the researcher and the researched (e.g., Hayano 1982; Young 1991).[9]

A good deal of the narrative variety now visible in ethnographic writing is also a consequence of the post-1960s spread of the specialized and relatively insular disciplinary aims of anthropology and, to a lesser extent, sociology. Growing interest in the distinctly modern idea of culture—as something held by all identifiable groups, organizations, and societies—has put ethnography in play virtually everywhere. No longer is ethnography ordered and organized principally by geographic region, society, community, or social group. Adjectival ethnographies have become quite common, and libraries are now well stocked with works in medical ethnography, school ethnography, occupational ethnography, organizational ethnography, family ethnography, and many more. One result of these intellectual and territorial moves of both at-home and away ethnography has been a noticeable increase in the novel and provisional forms in which ethnography is cast. Purists may regard this proliferation of styles as a dilution or, worse, a bastardization of the trade, but others—myself included—take this upswing in ethnographic styles as a welcome offering of alternatives (some good, some not so good) to certain taken-for-granted and seemingly calcified representational techniques of both realist and confessional writings.

This expansion of ethnographic interests, methods, and styles is, of course, a product of the third moment of ethnography—the reading of ethnographic texts by particular audiences and the kinds of responses these texts appear to generate among those audiences. Of interest here are the categories of readers an ethnographer recognizes and courts through the topical choices, analytic positioning, and composition practices displayed in a text. Take, for illustrative purposes, three loosely demarked audience categories. Collegial readers are those who follow specific ethnographic domains most avidly. They are surely the most careful and critical readers of one another's work and the most familiar with the past and present of ethnography. General social science readers provide a second category but operate outside ethnographic circles. These are readers attracted to a particular ethnographic work because the presumed facts (less often, the arguments) conveyed in the work help further their own research agendas. Perhaps as a result of their exploitative aims, they are often the least tolerant of the breaching of narrative conventions in ethnography. Finally, there are some who read ethnography more for pleasure than professional enlightenment. Certain ethnographic works put forth in *mirable dictu*—lucid, straightforward language—attract a large, unspecialized lay audience for whom the storytelling and allegorical elements of an ethnography are salient. Such readers look for a familiar format—a traveler's tale, a romantic adventure, a personal journal, an investigative report, or, perhaps most frequently, a widely acclaimed ethnographic classic(s) of the past—when appraising the writing. Ironically, the ethnographer charged with being a novelist manqué by colleagues and other social scientists is quite likely to be the ethnographer with the largest number of readers.

For each reader segment, particular ethnographic styles are more or less attractive.[10] Collegial readers may take in stride what those outside the field find inelegant, pinched, and abstruse. Yet the growing segmentation across collegial readers may also suggest that many are puzzled as to what their nominal ethnographic colleagues are up to with their relatively odd topical choices, particularistic research techniques, peculiar theoretical concerns, and occasionally distinctive prose styles. This creates something of a dilemma because it suggests that not only is there considerable distance between the general reader and the ethnographic specialist but that the distance between differing segments of ethnographic specialists themselves is growing. Although ethnography is itself in little or no danger of vanishing, the ethnographic community is now a very splintered—however splendored—thing.

Still, the trade prospers—at least numerically in terms of those who identify with the qualitative fieldwork traditions of ethnography. Those eager to do backyard or far-away fieldwork, to put culture to print, and to read about it in some form or other are probably more numerous than ever. But, as I want this quick and quirky review to suggest, just how a culture is rendered intelligible in the first moment of ethnography and, in the second moment of ethnography, passed on in a fashion that persuades others of its value and truth when read in the third moment of ethnography are now matters of considerable concern and debate. New questions are being asked of ethnography. Experimental works are being composed. Many if not most of the representational techniques of realist (alternatively, classical) ethnography are now seen by many as dated, naive, and, in a certain light, both professionally and socially indefensible.

In short, one might say that the cat is out of the bag and it seems unlikely that the sort of "just do it" innocence (and spirit) that once characterized ethnography will ever return. The very partiality, self-limitations, paradigm conceits, and institutional constraints are now simply too well known to be ignored (or, for that matter, overcome). Moreover, an acute textual awareness has developed in some circles based on close literary readings of ethnographic work. From such readings comes the view that an ethnographic truth is, like any truth (including this one), a rhetorical category whose meaning and shape varies with the contingencies of history and circumstance.

This is not, as some traditionalists might argue, the beginning of an inevitable slide into solipsism, relativism, or (gasp) nihilism—an "anything goes" approach to contemporary ethnography. My reading of the current turn toward text and language in ethnography is governed by a belief that holds rhetoric, broadly defined, to be the medium through which all truths or certainties are established (and shaken). Thus, for example, to look closely at well-received or persuasive ethnographic texts, to their compositional practices rather than through them to the worlds they portray is to examine how a culture becomes a substantial reality for a given set of readers and perhaps beyond. By looking at representational choices and their changes over time is to learn (among other things) just how ethnographers construct differences of various kinds. These surface differences may flatter or shatter the expectations held by readers but to move beyond a surface reading is to force an ethnography to tell a different story than it was intended to tell—a story about its makers and takers rather than its subjects. Not all texts will emerge with credit from such readings, but, depending on the text and reader, some will, and presumably by paying attention to the way those works are put together we will learn more about the art (and science) of our representational trade.

DECONSTRUCTION RECONSTRUCTED

To examine the compositional practices of ethnography requires setting some sort of limit about what counts as an ethnography in the first place. Because I have come to regard the breakdown of standard ethnographic topics, borders, and styles as something to celebrate, not mourn, I cannot take a very hard line on this matter. Suffice it to say that a text is axiomatically an ethnography if it is put forth by its author as a nonfiction work intended to represent, interpret, or (perhaps best) translate a culture or selected aspects of a culture for readers who are often but not always unfamiliar with that culture. Giving such works close textual attention will not alter their status as ethnographies. Elliot Liebow's (1967) *Talley's Corner* is an ethnography whether or not anyone likes it and would still be an ethnography even if no one liked it. But *Talley's Corner* can also be read for its own sake, thus directing attention to the text itself—to such features as authorial voice, topical choice and arrangement, the use of master and minor tropes, the elid-

ing of time, narrative conventions, rhetorical thrusts, truth claim
forth.

As I suggested earlier, the increased interest in the second and ѡ.ѡ.
ments of ethnography reflects a relatively recent intellectual shift within
ethnographic circles. This shift toward text is, of course, part of a much wider
scholarly turn toward meaning and language wherein the relationship ordinarily held to obtain between a desciption and the object of such description is reversed. The ordinary or commonsensical view holds that the objects of the world are logically prior and thus limit and provide the measure
of any description. Vocabulary, text, and representation of any intendedly
nonfictional sort must be constrained by fact. But, as virtually all ethnographers now realize (however much they may complain), language has been
promoted in the intellectual scheme of things. Language is now auditioning
for an *a priori* role in the social and material world, a role that carries constitutional force—bringing facts into consciousness and therefore being. No
longer then is something like culture or, for that matter, atoms and quarks
thought to come first while our understandings, models, or representations
of culture, atoms, or quarks come second. Rather, our representations may
well come first, allowing us to selectively see what we have described.[11]

This reverse argument has gradually wormed its way into various ethnographic communities. It is quite common these days to state rather matter-
of-factly that the language and models that ethnographers have available to
them—the conceptual tools that precede the doing of ethnography—shape
what will be seen in the field, written in a report, and read by those who
purchase their texts. If, for example, the prominent linguistic categories available to urban ethnographers include various forms of social disorganization,
it is likely that they will also look for events associated with city life in just
these terms. Violence, drug taking, and crime thus become indicators of disorganization. The representational details and patterns of their work will
follow from what writers feel fit a given category. If the representational language that typifies the research community is full of concepts like deviance,
disintegration, and decline all drawn, say, from textbook sociology—an
ethnographic study of city life will produce events that fit these very features rather than events that fit features associated with different concepts
such as displacement or destablization as drawn, respectively, from the vocabulary of postmodernism or critical theory.[12]

The point of consequence is that simply to describe this reversal—
related perhaps to what Rabinow (1986) calls "the desire to anthropologize
the West"—is also to display the problem that ethnographic representations
currently face. Ideas about empirical evidence, objectivity, reason, truth, coherence, validity, measurement, and fact no longer provide great comfort or
direction. If such concepts are relative, not absolute, they are always con-
testable in whatever form they appear—although this is not to say that such
concepts are thereby rendered irrelevant or unthinkable.

Again, this reversal is not a terribly controversial issue these days—at
least among most practicing ethnographers. The priority of the signifier over

the signified, the placing of implicit quotation marks about terms such as "truth" and "reality" (hedges from which these words are unlikely to ever escape), and the now problematized foundations of some of our most sacred concepts (from "self" to "society") are all ideas that have been absorbed and, if not canonized, at least recognized by ethnographers as presenting troublesome epistemological issues with which we as writers must in some fashion deal. What remains to be seen, however, is just how this turn toward language alters—if at all—traditional ethnographic practices in the field, behind the desk, and in the library or easy chair.

At first glance, fieldwork traditions seem to be securely in place despite the in-house hammering they have taken in both anthropology and sociology. Ethnographers still claim a good deal of their authority on firsthand experience. While hardly the boastful and brash experiential positivism of an earlier era, fieldwork nonetheless continues to be held responsible—at least partially—for the written account of a studied group. Indeed, ethnographers remain inextricably linked to their people, their turf, and their culture. This tight connection between authors and authored is based on the continuing faith that what is learned in the field will somehow outweigh or counterbalance the anticipation of theory and other preconceptions carried by fieldworkers.

This has long been the case. Thus, in anthropology, Evans-Prichard (1940) remains tied to the Neur, Firth (1936) to the Tokopia, Geertz (1973) to the Balinese, and Rosaldo (1980) to the Ilongots. To a lesser degree, it is also true of sociology (in the United States), where Whyte (1943) is closely linked to the street corners of North Boston, Goffman (1961) to mental hospitals and inmates, Manning (1977, 1980) to the city police, and Becker (1982) to the producers, exhibitors, curators, and dealers (among others) who make up various cosmopolitan art worlds. Marcus (1994: 521) calls this the "one tribe, one ethnographer" rule and considers it a domain or territorial rule remarkable for its apparent staying power. Certainly, there are important disciplinary figures in ethnography not so directly linked to specific social domains, but their contributions to ethnography—although not to cultural theory—are often regarded as fragile and speculative because they are not embedded in an intense, lengthy, and hence presumably rich field experience.[13]

The tenacity of this position is strong—so strong that the idea of something like an ethnographic revolution or breakthrough is itself a rather improbable and odd notion. The object of ethnography is seen as simply too much "out there." Traditionally, fieldwork implies either discovery (going where no one has gone before) or elaboration (building on and extending the pioneering cultural portraits of others by others). Overturning previous representations is not often claimed, and restudies of the same group of people by different ethnographers are rare indeed.[14] Cultural theory may proceed disjunctively, contentiously, by lurches or so-called paradigm shifts, but not ethnography. Advancement in an ethnographic domain comes cumulatively through the steady elaboration of a given culture itself subject to temporal shifts brought about by known (or, in principle, knowable) internal or external changes. Thus the ethnographic writings of outmoded theorists can continue to instruct even if the conceptual frameworks surrounding such accounts are considered hopelessly behind the times.

Yet little by little this unifying faith in the lasting value of ethnographic representations—although not fieldwork—is being questioned as ethnographic texts themselves are put to close examination. A kind of ethnography of ethnography is emerging through textual study, and new understandings are gradually altering the way we think about cultural representation practices both past and present. Yet having new or transformed categories available to describe ethnographic practices does not necessarily alter those practices. Reading, analyzing, and writing about an ethnographic work is not the same thing as creating one, and few if any recipes for improved performance are likely to follow directly from textual analysis. A good deal of the work to date has been to pick apart or deconstruct various texts, to search for the ways they fail to make the points they are trying or claiming to make. But the result of this work does not provide a better way to do ethnography. It does, however, remind us of the limits of representational possibilities and makes a strong argument to counter any faith in a simple or transparent world that can be known with any certainty.

By and large, these deconstructive efforts have been aimed at the most persuasive and respected ethnographic writings of the past (Clifford and Marcus 1986; Geertz 1988). The result is not itself an ethnography but a critique of one (or more). Occasionally, however, ethnography itself starts from an analysis or deconstruction of previous representations of a given culture (including but not limited to ethnographic ones). This textual orientation is relatively new and provides something of an ironic twist to the fashionable idea that culture can be studied "as if" it were a text by suggesting that culture might not amount to much more than a text in the first place. There is perhaps poetic justice here, for the ethnographers of one generation find themselves treated by those of the next generation as "others" and subjected to something of the same rough and tumble exigencies of cultural representation that they put their own people through. Students of culture these days may be less likely to call for a Festschrift for their mentor than to call into question their mentor's work.

Cultural anthropology provides a number of splendid examples of this re-reading of the ethnographic past. Classical ethnographies of remote, invisible, or otherwise "out of the way" people have become increasingly unpersuasive, in part because the presumption of the great divide between modern and traditional communities has broken down and in part because the idea of a bounded, independent, undisturbed, and self-contained society is today suspect (Geertz 1994). Thus descriptions of the "People of the Plains" or the "Ashanti Character" are repositioned as representations of a relatively powerless, displaced, and sometimes despised people who are nonetheless altogether agile and adaptive out of necessity. The point driven home in these re-presentations is that the group portrayed is anything but isolated, timeless, or beyond the reach of contemporary society. The wistful assumption of "one place, one people, one culture" no longer holds the ethnographic imagination in check. This is made quite clear in what Marcus (1994) calls the "messy texts"of a deterritorialized, open-ended, and "new" ethnography that attempts to foster an idea of how lives around the globe may be contrasted yet still interconnected.

Important messy texts do not lament the loss of the anthropological object but, in fact, invent a more complex object whose study can be as revelatory and as realistic as the old. Consider, as an exemplar, Kondo's (1990) subtle portrait of everyday life on the shop floor of a small, family-owned factory in Tokyo and the multiple, gendered, and crafted "selves" that seem to emerge in such a context. Consider also Tsing's (1994) dense, occasionally hesitant but always moving treatment of a much abused and marginalized Indonesian group she calls "The Meratus." Both authors are explicitly critical of previous "holistic" representations that have settled on those of whom they write and the encrusted fiction that these people reside in a pristine, encapsulated "natural" community—a cultural island—whose traditions persist outside the contemporary world.

Back home in North America, anthropologists are also at work on new objects of study. Consider here Fjellman's (1992) collage-like and code-cracking *Vinyl Leaves*, a representation of DisneyWorld cast off in a slapdash and breathless postmodern style, or Moffatt's (1989) embracing of Margaret Mead's imagery in *The Coming of Age in New Jersey*, a vivid, emotionally charged representation of what Moffatt saw and heard during his stay in the dormitories of Rutgers University in the mid-1980s. These works violate the image of the ethnographer as the intrepid traveler who journeys to exotic locales to bring back the news of the native while at the same time they challenge realist codes of representation reflecting prevailing ideas of the "other" because the other is none other than ourselves.

Defamiliarization is something of an emerging strategy for ethnographic representation. Nowhere is this more apparent than in recent work that examines reader responses to a variety of cultural products including, centrally, texts. Take, for instance, Lutz and Collins's (1992) close reading of the *National Geographic* and its romantic, upbeat, glossy, and unabashed see-for-yourself style so popular in the United States where the color photograph is taken as a particularly sound measure of reality. Lutz and Collins manage to make the magazine tell a different story than the one to which we are accustomed—a story about the makers and readers of the *National Geographic* rather than the subjects of its photographic gaze. Similar tales are constructed by Radway (1984) and Liebes and Katz (1990) about, in turn, the readers of formula romance novels and the culturally diverse viewers of the epic television series *Dallas*. These writings produce what I think are profoundly ambiguous images of all-too-familiar cultural objects and thus push ethnography into the rather novel but altogether useful role of making the familiar strange rather than the strange familiar.

The reception to topical and narrative innovations in ethnography varies no doubt across audience segments, but many of us are reading experimental texts and wondering about their possibilities and relevance to what we are currently doing. Yet we also know that if the experimental turns paradigmatic, the future of our trade may be in grave jeopardy for we would be left with nowhere in particular to go and with no visible models for our craft. This is, I think, unlikely because style, not genre, is immediately at issue, and, in point of fact, few ethnographers are writing experimental—or even messy—texts.

Nor is it the case that all ethnographic conventions are currently up for grabs. What would it mean, for example, if we were not to accept certain settled ethnographic practices? Would it mean that we would not go to the field to conduct our studies? Would it mean that we would not take notes when in the field? Would it mean that we would not try to publish our work in scholarly outlets and be responsive to colleagues and professional peers? Or, sin of sins, would it mean that we would not read and acknowledge the previous work done in a given ethnographic domain?

Questions of this sort are almost (but not quite) purely imaginary for they suggest lines of action that are more or less unthinkable for anyone self-identified as an ethnographer. The issue at hand is not to evaluate the options for there are none (at least now). These are practices an ethnographer follows because they constitute membership in a community of ethnographers. They are not practices offered up for approval or disapproval. No one says to the would-be ethnographer, "Hey, listen up now, we usually go to the field for a year or so and then write up what we learn. Do you think you can live with that?" To the contrary, the would-be ethnographer becomes an ethnographer by doing the same sort of things others in the trade have done before and so discovers the obligatory ways through which writings we call ethnographies are produced. The normative aspects of ethnography are not piled on top of a set of everyday practices but come—kit and caboodle—with them. Ask ethnographers to justify their reliance on fieldwork and they will be as befuddled by the question as plumbers are when asked to justify their use of a plunger or wrench.

This is not to say that the conventions associated with either the first, second, or third moment of ethnography are unshakable or cast in stone. Both Stocking (1983) and Clifford (1983) track several highly significant changes in ethnographic practices. Most of us would now agree that all ethnographies owe whatever persuasive power they can muster to contingent social, historical, and institutional forces, and no meta-argument can question this contingency. But when it comes to constructing a particular ethnography, this sublime contingency offers very little aid because any particular ethnography offered up to readers must make its points by the same means that were present before the contingency was recognized—through the hard work of presenting evidence, providing interpretations, elaborating analogies, invoking authorities, working through examples, marshalling the tropes, and so on. The nature of ethnographic evidence, interpretation, and authority may, of course, all change modestly or radically over time, but the appeal of any single ethnography will remain tied to specific arguments made within the text and referenced to a particular, not general, sub-stantive and methodological situation.

What I am claiming, of course, is the possibility that we can assert both the textuality of the ethnographic facts and the factuality of ethnographic texts. We can do so because the two claims lie in quite different domains. To say, for instance, that ethnographic facts are socially constructed (yawn) is a general claim and not one that can be applied willy-nilly to particular facts. A certain fact is flimsy or firm on the basis of the arguments presented (and received) on its behalf. When such facts are recognized as question-able, the arguments and views based on them are discredited also. Textual-ity replaces factuality but only after previous views have been dislodged and new facts move into place. These new facts are as firm as the old but are supported by a new and different perspective. It is a little like recog-nizing that the explanation of a joke is not itself funny but at the same time realizing that knowing so does not help one construct hilarious one-liners.

The work at the coal face of ethnography goes on therefore in much the same way as it did before textuality came into vogue. Evidence must be of-fered up to support arguments whose pedigree must be established in a way that will convince at least a few readers that the author has something cred-ible to say. Changes in attitude are always possible, and what is persuasive to one generation may look ludicrous to another. To some perhaps, the tex-tuality and factuality of ethnography is paradoxical. But, following Fish (1989), I think the paradox vanishes with the realization that ethnography—like literary theory, law, molecular biology, astronomy, or astrology—does not remain the same because its facts, methods, genres, theories, and so forth all survive the passage of time but because in the midst of change an audi-ence still looks to it for the performance of a given task. In the case of ethnog-raphy, what we continue to look for is the close study of culture as lived by particular people, in particular places, doing particular things at particular times.[15]

NOTES

1. This much procrastinated chapter began as a brief introduction to the articles that made up a special issue of the *Journal of Contemporary Ethnography* published in 1990 (vol. 22, no. 1) on "The Representation of Ethnographic Research." It ran five pages and was titled "Great Moments in Ethnography." The introduction has grown and its name has changed, but its intent remains the same: to set up and off the same articles—plus two—that comprised the special issue. I must thank Peter Manning and Mitch Allen for pushing this project forward and encouraging me to rework my skimpy introduction into something that resembles—in length if not in quality—the other chapters in this book.

2. This, of course, raises the question of how any single scholar can possibly keep up with such a large and ever expanding literature. The answer in principle and in practice is that he or she can't, for the potentially relevant ethnographic ma-terials (on a society, region, or people) are overwhelming and new journals, new the-

ories, new problems, new topics, new concepts, and new critiques of older works multiply with each passing year. Moreover, scholars must now know not only their Marx, Weber, and Durkheim but also be familiar with the works of Gramsci, Baktin, Habermas, and Rorty and *au courant* with the fashionable French such as Bourdieu, Derrida, and Foucault. Even fieldwork itself has grown increasingly textual as materials that were once routinely ignored, such as government records, novels, biographies, popular magazine articles, and news reports, are now treated by many ethnographers as important source materials. It seems the best we can do these days is to selectively pursue and cultivate an ever diminishing proportion of the relevant literature that comes our way and assume an attitude of benign neglect toward the rest. Stocking (1992: 362–65) has some sharp but discouraging observations to make on the difficulties of keeping up with the field in cultural anthropology, as do many of the authors represented in Faradon's (1990) collection of essays on localizing strategies in ethnography.

3. Much of the debate turns on what to make of the sacred heart of ethnography, the culture concept. Some critics, notably those with intellectual roots in deconstructive literary criticism, regard the idea of a distinct, bounded, and unifying culture in today's world as little more than a superstition carried over from nineteenth-century discourse and argue that an "incredulity toward metanarratives" should characterize all social study (Lyotard 1984). Other critics within the many folds of ethnography also regard the culture concept as something of an embarrassing colonial artifact in serious need of repair (Fabian 1983; Marcus and Fischer 1986). Nonetheless, despite the critical fire, there is still an insistance in almost all camps that any serious study of social life must be grounded ethnographically. The debate is then not so much about the doing of ethnography as it is about the conceptual positioning of such work. Hannerz (1992) provides one of the more useful anthropological reworkings of the culture concept in the context of a postmodern, information-intensive world. See also Griswold's (1994) sociological treatment of culture in a rapidly changing age. Both authors jettison unicultural perspectives in favor of multicultural ones emphasizing polycentrism, local innovation, and widespread cultural diffusion.

4. The term "moments" may be confusing. Denzin and Lincoln (1994: 7–11), for example, use the term to denote particular historical periods in the development of an intellectual field—in their subject case, the emergence of qualitative research techniques in the social sciences. My use of the term refers to the stages through which a particular ethnography must pass—fieldwork, publication, and consumption. The latter stage is justified on the grounds that an unread ethnography is not, properly speaking, an ethnography at all. For a more elaborate treatment of these stages, see Van Maanen (forthcoming).

5. These pen pal arrangements were aided by the guidebook *Notes and Queries in Anthropology* first published in 1874 with the subtitle *"for use of travellers and residents in uncivilized lands"* and revised regularly, without the subtitle, into the mid-twentieth century. The idea was to provide the armchair ethnographer's pen pal, the so-called man on the spot, with a set of questions to pose to local informants (Stocking 1983). The goal was to standardize the slabs of information gathered by the men on the spot. These slabs were sent home to be pondered, interpreted, and eventually written up by a "real" ethnographer.

6. I have in mind as Studio Portraiture work some of the more scientifically oriented or formal ethnographies written, it seems, to track, illustrate, and document a particular theory of the social world. Baumgartner's (1988) *The Moral Order of a Sub-*

urb provides, for example, an intrigrung portrait of the "cordial detachment" that marks contemporary American life. The work is, however, one that allows few interpretive doubts to slip into view. All people, events, and circumstances represented by the author neatly fit her analytic categories. Halle's (1993) *Inside Culture* is another example of ethnographic scholarship that is tied closely to a given culture theory. I hasten to add that I find considerable value in both works, but both are also remarkable for their unblinking use of realist conventions.

7. The rise and fall of Project Camelot and the Thailand Controversy forced ethical and political issues out in the open and injected an important self-consciousness into fieldworkers operating far from home (Horowitz 1967; Wakin 1992). In the postcolonial world, the observer is perhaps as destabilized as the observed. No longer comforted and protected by colonial power, ethnographers face radically different problems entering, staying, and leaving the field (let alone learning in the field). Reflexive, self-critical, dialogic approaches to ethnography seem a contemporary necessity. For some recent and highly personalized perspectives on many of the changes that cultural anthropology has undergone in the postcolonial period, see the autobiographic essays collected by Fowler and Hardesty (1994).

8. A joke by Marshall Salhins and reported by Marcus (1994, 569) is worthy of inclusion here: "But as the Fijian said to the New Ethnographer, 'That's enough talking about you, let's talk about me!'" Self-discovery and personal quest are to be sure a part of ethnography but, as the joke suggests, such matters are not to be pushed too far—at least in writing. Where exactly the limits of ethnographic reflexivity are to be found remains a most open question.

9. The text only hints at the kinds of ethnographic experimentation now occurring. Nigel Barley (1983, 1986), for example, develops a kind of "comedy ethnography" based on some of his fieldwork misadventures. Hebdige (1979, 1987) works out a version of "hip-hop ethnography" put forth in the very pop culture idiom that is the subject of his study. Frolick (1990) uses the voice of an invented character "Luke" to shape a "fictional ethnography" about spiritual healing in the United States. These works are hardly conventional, but they all carry strong ethnographic sensibilities and contribute to the genre bending now taking place. What most experimental works display is a resistance to received analytic categories and concepts; thus the subject and lines of study are kept open and unsettled. Objectivity, if it is claimed at all, is of a highly situated sort and the writing is impressionistic rather than interpretive (Van Maanen 1988: 101–24).

10. Taste in ethnography results from what is no doubt a complex interaction involving ethnographers, their mentors, their students, their subjects, their critics, and their readers (increasingly their subjects as well). The process is rather decentered and beyond the grasp of any one group to fully control or monitor—although, until recently, ethnographers themselves probably held the upper hand. Most of us, it seems, follow the traditions in which we were trained and are thus committed generationally and institutionally to a particular perspective, objectivity, research etiquette, and topical, if not stylistic, preference. For instance, sociological fieldworkers operating in the Chicago School traditions often define within a complex society the equivalent of a bounded little island society and go about studying and writing about it in quite similar (and traditional) ways whether it is a street gang, a fitness center, a police agency, a first-year medical school class, or an engineering division of a Fortune 500 company. Appreciation of ethnographic work created in the Chicago School shadow depends on how much one has already accepted and absorbed Chicago School ideas and approaches and just how directly one can trace one's own

intellectual roots back to the founders and other legendary Chicago figures (e.g., from Becker to Hughes to Parks). On the Chicago School of sociology and its distinctive ethnographic tastes, see Bulmer (1984) and Fine, ed. (forthcoming).

11. This language-first switch produces a most culturally relative version of reality and suggests that perception is as much a product of imagination as imagination is a product of perception. Reality, then, emerges from the interplay of imaginative perception and perceptive imagination. Language and text provide the symbolic representations required for both the construction and communication of conceptions of reality and thus make the notions of thought and culture inseparable. Because culture comes to us in large measure through ink on a page, the careful examination of previous cultural representations is a necessary analytic step. The textual turn in ethnography comes from the perhaps belated recognition that any cultural portrait exists within a context of already existing portraits. New writings are to varying degrees parasitic on old writings and few, if any, contemporary ethnographic subjects are completely unknown. This leads some writers such as Marcus (1994) and Clifford (1988) to argue that ethnographers should abandon the idea that there are new worlds to discover and concentrate instead on the deconstruction and reconstruction of social worlds already—in different ways—represented. An engaging example of some textually focused ethnography is found in Dorst's (1989) *The Written Suburb*.

12. This is not to say that the assumptions that undergird postmodernism or critical theory are themselves beyond suspicion. They too rest on unexamined assumptions. At any level, the tools of revisionist analysis are vulnerable to the same kind of deconstruction they claim to perform on a targeted writing. This can produce something of an intellectual funhouse where authors, texts, concepts, riddles, labels, theories, and phrases (both catchy and stilted) bounce off one another. To wit, following Dumont's (1986) example, a reader can track Rabinow's (1986) deconstruction of Clifford's (1982) deconstruction of Leenhardt's (1937) ethnography (in French) of the New Caledonians. Where the New Caledonians themselves come out in this intertextual blender is anyone's guess, for, as deconstructionists are only too happy to point out, there are no ultimate standards on which to test the validity of any given reading. No matter how deep a writer may go in questioning the arguments of previous work, there will remain in the offered work arguments whose clarity and strength depend on the same kind of historical, institutional, and personal factors shown to influence and hence undermine the work of others. Although reading what Derrida (1976) calls the "text in the text" certainly raises problems for ethnographers, it does not solve them. Ironically, as Fish (1993) forcefully suggests, the more one is persuaded by deconstructive arguments, the less one can do with them. At most, deconstruction can be used to refute the truth claims of others, but it cannot be used to make new truths. Such is the state—and point—of deconstruction.

13. To date, the "one tribe, one ethnographer" rule fits anthropologists more closely than sociologists. Although Sahlins's classic *bon mot* "sociologists study the West and anthropologists get the rest" still holds, its sweep is perhaps less encompassing today than yesterday as anthropologists become repatriated and sociologists earn frequent flier miles. Yet it is still the case that anthropologists more so than sociologists are likely to visit and revisit a field site over a full career, thus developing not only deep and lasting personal ties to a community but also a relatively keen appreciation for the various kinds of social changes that mark "their" community over time. On some of the distinctive features of extensive, long-term, single-site fieldwork, see Foster et al. (1979) and Fowler and Hardesty (1994).

14. This is not to say that representational disagreements are nonexistent in ethnography. Certainly, there have been some quite spectacular disputes on just whose representation of a people is most trustworthy (e.g., Redfield vs. Lewis 1964; Mead vs. Freeman 1983; Whyte vs. Boelen 1992). Yet these debates are rare and work largely as exceptions that prove the "one ethnographer, one tribe" rule.

15. By concluding on such a note, I am asserting that ethnographers are at their best when mucking around the empirical base camps of social science than when perched (always precariously) on some theoretical mountain top. This has, I think, always been the case. What may have changed in the past ten or so years is that the mists surrounding the base camps are gradually clearing. Gone perhaps are the illusions of progress by theory, by formal models, by positivism (or antipositivism), by methodological purity, and so on. With no fixed, natural, objective, or universal criteria to guide ethnography up to the mountain top, there is no alternative but to get down to the specific studies that make up the field(s) and acknowledge that ethnographic values, criteria, and perspectives spring from the specific interests and histories of ethnographic writers. These can never be placed above criticism, of course, as ethnographic writers are beings—human beings—who are everywhere and always socially situated and purposive. For some far more eloquent versions of this zero-point argument, see Bruyn (1966), Gans (1982), Rosaldo (1989), and Whyte (1994).

REFERENCES

Agar, M. 1980. *The professional stranger*. New York: Academic Press.

Barley, N. 1983. *The innocent anthropologist*. New York: Holt.

———. 1986. *Ceremony*. New York: Holt.

Baumgartner, M. P.1988. *The moral order of a suburb*. New York: Oxford University Press.

Becker, H. S. 1982. *Art worlds*. Berkeley: University of California Press.

Boelen, M. A. M. 1992. Street corner society: Cornerville revisited. *Journal of Contemporary Ethnography* 21:13–42.

Boon, S. A. 1982. *Other tribes, other scribes*. Cambridge: Cambridge University Press.

Bruyn, S. T. 1966. *The human perspective in sociology*. Englewood Cliffs, NJ: Prentice Hall.

Bulmer, M. 1984. *The Chicago School of sociology*. Chicago: University of Chicago Press.

Clifford, J. 1982. *Person and myth: Maurice Leenhardt in the Melanesian world*. Berkeley: University of California Press.

———. 1983. On ethnographic authority. *Representations* 1:118–46.

———. 1988. *The predicament of culture*. Cambridge, MA: Harvard University Press.

Clifford, J., and G. E. Marcus, eds. 1986. *Writing culture*. Berkeley: University of California Press.

Clough, P. 1992. *The ends of ethnography*. Newbury Park, CA: Sage.

Denzin, N. 1988. *Interpretive interactionism*. Newbury Park, CA: Sage.

Denzin, N., and Y. Lincoln. 1994. Introduction, pp. 1–17 in *The Handoook of Qualitative Research*, ed. N. Denzin and Y. Lincoln. Thousand Oaks, CA: Sage.

Derrida, J. 1976. *On grammatology*. Translated by G. C. Spivak. Baltimore: Johns Hopkins University Press.

Dorst, J. 1989. *The written suburb*. Philadelphia: University of Pennsylvania Press.

Dumont, J. P. 1978. *The headman and I*. Austin: University of Texas Press.

———. 1986. Prologue to ethnography or prolegomena to anthropology. *Ethos* 14:344–67.

Erickson, K. 1976. *Everything in its path*. New York: Simon & Schuster.

Evans-Prichard, E. E. 1940. *The Nuer*. Oxford: Oxford University Press.

Fabian, J. 1983. *Time and the other*. New York: Columbia University Press.

Faradon, R., ed. 1990. *Localizing strategies*. Edinburgh: Scottish Academic Press.

Fine, G. A., ed. Forthcoming. *The second Chicago school?* Chicago: University of Chicago Press.

Firth, R. 1936. *We, the Tikopia*. London: Allen & Unwin.

Fish, S. 1989. *Doing what comes naturally: Change, rhetoric and the practice of theory in literary and legal studies*. New York: Oxford University Press.

———. 1993. *There's no such thing as free speech . . . and it's a good thing too*. New York: Oxford University Press.

Fjellman, S. 1992. *Vinyl leaves*. Boulder, CO: Westview.

Foley, D. E. 1990. *Learning capitalist culture*. Austin: University of Texas Press.

Foster, G. M., T. Scudder, E. Colson, and R. Kemper, eds.1979. *Long-term field research in social anthropology*. New York: Academic Press.

Fowler, D. D., and D. L. Hardesty, eds. 1994. *Others knowing others*. Washington, DC: Smithsonian Institution Press.

Freeman, D. 1983. *Margaret Mead and Samoa*. Cambridge, MA: Harvard University Press.

Freilich, M. 1970. *Marginal natives*. New York: Harper & Row.

Frolick, F. 1990. *Healing powers*. Chicago: University of Chicago Press.

Gans, H. J. 1982. The participant observer as a human being, pp. 221–233 in *Field Research*, ed. R. G. Burgess. London: Allen & Unwin.

Geertz, C. 1973. *The interpretation of cultures*. New York: Basic Books.

———. 1988. *Works and lives*. Stanford, CA: Stanford University Press.

———. 1994. Life on the edge. *New York Review of Books*, 7 April, 3–4.

Goffman, E. 1961. *Asylums*. Garden City, NY: Anchor.

Griswold, W. 1994. *Cultures and societies in a changing world*. Thousand Oaks, CA: Pine Forge Press.

Halle, D. 1993. *Inside culture*. Chicago: University of Chicago Press.

Hammersley, M., and P. Atkinson. 1983. *Ethnography*. London: Tavistock.

Hannerz, U. 1992. *Cultural complexity*. New York: Columbia University Press.

Hayano, D. M. 1982. *Poker faces*. Berkeley: University of California Press.

Hebdige, D. 1979. *Subcultures*. London: Methuen.

———. 1987. *Cut'n'mix*. London: Methuen.

Horowitz, I. L. 1967. Project Camelot. In *Ethics, Politics and Social Research*, ed. G. L. Sjoberg. London: Routledge & Kegan Paul.

Jacobson, D. 1991. *Reading ethnography*. Albany: State University of New York.

Kuper, A. 1977. *Anthropology and anthropologists*. London: Routledge & Kegan Paul.

Kondo, D. 1990. *Crafting selves*. Chicago: University of Chicago Press.

Latour, B. 1987. *Science in action*. Cambridge, MA: Harvard University Press.

Leenhardt, M. 1937. *Do Kamo: La personne et la mythe dans la monde mélanésien*. Paris: Gallimard. (Trans. by B. Gulati as *Do Kamo: Person and myth in the Melanesian world*, University of Chicago Press, 1979)

Leibes, T., and E. Katz. 1990. *The export of meaning*. New York: Oxford University Press.

Lewis, O. 1964. *Life in a Mexican village: Tepozilan revisited*. Urbana: University of Illinois Press.

Liebow, E. 1967. *Talley's corner*. Boston: Little, Brown.

Lofland, J. 1974. Styles of reporting qualitative field research. *American Sociologist* 9:101–11.

Lutz, C., and J. Collier. 1992. *Reading National Geographic*. Chicago: University of Chicago Press.

Lyotard, J. 1984. *The postmodern condition*. Minneapolis: University of Minnesota Press.

Malinowski, B. [1922] 1961. *Argonauts of the Western Pacific*. New York: E. P. Dutton.

Manning, P. K. 1977. *Police work*. Cambridge: MIT Press.

———. 1980. *The narc's game*. Cambridge: MIT Press.

Marcus, G. E. 1994. What comes (just) after "post"? The case of ethnography, pp. 565–582 in *The Handbook of Qualitative Research*, ed. N. Denzin and Y. Lincoln. Newbury Park, CA: Sage.

Marcus, G. E., and D. Cushman. 1982. Ethnographies as text. *Annual Review of Anthropology* 11:25-69.

Marcus, G. E., and M. Fisher. 1986. *Anthropology as cultural critique*. Chicago: University of Chicago Press.

Moffatt, M. 1989. *Coming of age in New Jersey*. New Brunswick, NJ: Rutgers University Press.

Nash, J. 1979. *We eat the mines and the mines eat us*. New York: Columbia University Press.

Rabinow, P. 1977. *Reflections on fieldwork in Morocco*. Berkeley: University of California Press.

———. 1986. Representations are social facts, pp. 234–261 in *Writing Culture*, ed. J. Clifford and G. E. Marcus. Berkeley: University of California Press.

Radway, J. A. 1984. *Reading the romance*. Chapel Hill: University of North Carolina Press.

Rosaldo, R. 1980. *Ilongot headhunting, 1883–1974*. Stanford, CA: Stanford University Press.

———. 1989. *Culture and truth*. Boston: Beacon.

Said, E. W. 1989. Representing the colonized. *Critical Inquiry* 15:205–25.

Sanjek, R., ed. 1990. *Fieldnotes*. Ithaca, NY: Cornell University Press.

Shore, B. 1982. *Sala'ilua: A Samoan mystery*. New York: Columbia University Press.

Spradley, J. P. 1979. *The ethnographic interview*. New York: Holt, Rinehart & Winston.

Stocking, G. W., ed. 1983. *Observers observed*. Madison: University of Wisconsin Press.

———. 1987. *Victorian anthropology*. New York: Free Press.

———. 1992. *The ethnographer's magic*. Madison: University of Wisconsin Press.

Traweek, S. 1988. *Beamtimes and lifetimes*. Cambridge, MA: Harvard University Press.

Tsing, A. L. 1994. *In the realm of the diamond queen*. Princeton, NJ: Princeton University Press.

Van Maanen, J. 1988. *Tales of the field: On writing ethnography*. Chicago: University of Chicago Press.

———. Forthcoming. Ethnography. In *Encyclopedia of the Social Sciences*, vol. 2, ed. by A. Kuper and J. Kuper. London: Routledge.

Wakin, E. 1992. *Anthropology goes to war*. Madison: University of Wisconsin Center for Southeast Asia Studies.

Werner, O., and G. M. Schoeptle. 1986. *Systematic fieldwork*. 2 vols. Newbury Park, CA: Sage.

Whyte, W. F. 1943. *Street corner society*. Chicago: University of Chicago Press. (Republished in 1955 with method appendix)

———. 1994. *Participant observer*. Ithaca, NY: Cornell University Press.

Willis, P. 1977. *Learning to labour*. London: Routledge & Kegan Paul. (U.S. edition, 1981, Columbia University Press)

Young, J. 1991. *An inside job*. Oxford: Oxford University Press.

The Art and Politics of Interpretation

NORMAN K. DENZIN

> Once upon a time, the Lone Ethnographer rode off into the sunset in search of his "native." After undergoing a series of trials, he encountered the object of his quest in a distant land. There he underwent his rite of passage by enduring the ultimate ordeal of "fieldwork." After collecting "the data," the Lone Ethnographer returned home and wrote a "true" account of "the culture."
>
> RENATO ROSALDO,
> *CULTURE AND TRUTH*, 1989

> I have been working to change the way I speak and write.
>
> BELL HOOKS, *YEARNING*, 1990

In the social sciences there is only interpretation. Nothing speaks for itself. Confronted with a mountain of impressions, documents, and field notes, the qualitative researcher faces the difficult and challenging task of making sense of what has been learned. I call making sense of what has been learned the *art of interpretation*. This may also be described as moving from the field to the text to the reader. The practice of this art allows the field-worker-as-*bricoleur* (Lévi-Strauss, 1966, p. 17) to translate what has been learned into a body of textual work that communicates these understandings to the reader.

These texts, borrowing from John Van Maanen (1988), constitute tales of the field. They are the stories we tell one another. This is so because interpretation requires the telling of a story, or a narrative that states "things happen this way because" or "this happened, after this happened, because this happened first." Interpreters as storytellers tell narrative tales with beginnings, middles, and ends. These tales always embody implicit and explicit theories of causality, where narrative or textual causality is presumed to map the actual goings-on in the real world (Ricoeur, 1985, p. 4). How this complex art of interpretation and storytelling is practiced is the topic of this chapter.

The history of qualitative research in the social sciences reveals continual attempts to wrestle with this process and its methods. In this chapter I

review several of these methods, or traditions, paying special attention to
those that have been employed in the most recent past, including the constructivist,[1] grounded theory, feminist, Marxist, cultural studies, and poststructural perspectives.[2] I examine problems generic to this process, and
briefly allude to my own perspective, interpretive interactionism (Denzin,
1989). I conclude with predictions concerning where the art and politics of
interpretation will be 10 years from now.

THE INTERPRETIVE CRISIS IN THE SOCIAL SCIENCES

The following assumptions organize my analysis. First, the social sciences
today face a crisis of interpretation, for previously agreed-upon criteria from
the positivist and postpositivist traditions are now being challenged (Guba,
1990b, p. 371; Rosaldo, 1989, p. 45). This crisis has been described as poststructural and postmodern, a new sensibility regarding the social text and
its claims to authority. Describing this new situation, Richardson (1991) observes, "The core of [this] sensibility is doubt that any discourse has a privileged place, any method or theory a universal and general claim to authoritative knowledge" (p. 173).

Second, each social science community (Fish, 1980) has its own criteria
for judging the adequacy of any given interpretive statement. These criteria
will be grounded in the canonical texts the community takes to be central
to its mission. What works in one community may not work in another. Patricia Hill Collins (1990) contends, for example, that the Eurocentric, masculine positivist epistemology asks African American women to "objectify
themselves, devalue their emotional life, displace their motivations for furthering knowledge about Black women, and confront in an adversarial
relationship those with more social, economic and professional power"
(p. 205).

Third, this crisis can be resolved only from *within* social science communities. It is doubtful that a new set of criteria shared by all points of view
will, can, or should be developed. This means that "once the privileged veil
of truth is lifted, feminism, Afro-American, gay, and other disparaged discourses rise to the same epistemological status as the dominant discourse"
(Richardson, 1991, p. 173).

Fourth, increasingly, the criteria of evaluation will turn, as Richardson
notes, on moral, practical, aesthetic, political, and personal issues—the production, that is, of texts that articulate an emancipatory, participative perspective on the human condition and its betterment.

Fifth, as Clough (1992, p. 136) argues, the problems of writing are not
different from the problems of method or fieldwork. It is not the case, as
some may contend, that the above problems can be answered only through
new forms of writing. These new writing forms function primarily as sources
of validation for a reinvigorated empirical science. They direct attention
away from the ways in which the experimental text can perpetuate new
forms and technologies of knowledge and power that align qualitative re-

search with the state. The insistence that writing and fieldwork are different cannot be allowed (Clough, 1992, p. 136).

The age of a putative value-free social science appears to be over. Accordingly, sixth, any discussion of this process must become political, personal, and experiential. Following John Dewey, I believe that the methods for making sense of experience are always personal. Life and method are inextricably intertwined. One learns about method by thinking about how one makes sense of one's own life. The researcher, as a writer, is a bricoleur. He or she fashions meaning and interpretation out of ongoing experience. As a bricoleur, the researcher uses any tool or method that is readily at hand. I discuss, then, the politics, craft, and art of experience and interpretation.

FROM FIELD TO TEXT TO READER

Moving from the field to the text[3] to the reader is a complex, reflexive process. The researcher creates a field text consisting of field notes and documents from the field. From this text he or she creates a research text, notes and interpretations based on the field text, what David Plath (1990) calls "filed notes." The researcher then re-creates the research text as a working interpretive document. This working document contains the writer's initial attempts to make sense out of what has been learned, what Clandinin and Connelly term "experiencing experience." The writer next produces a quasi-public text, one that is shared with colleagues, whose comments and suggestions the writer seeks. The writer then transforms this statement into a public document, which embodies the writer's self-understandings, which are now inscribed in the experiences of those studied.[4] This statement, in turn, furnishes the context for the understandings the reader brings to the experiences being described by the writer. Reading and writing, then, are central to interpretation, for, as Geertz (1973, p. 18) argues, interpretation involves the construction of a reading of an event, both by the writer and by the reader. To paraphrase Geertz, a good interpretation takes us into the center of the experiences being described.

Such interpretations, however, may not take us to the heart of the matter, as these matters are understood in the everyday world. Here is Rosaldo (1989) describing, in anthropological terms, the daily family breakfast at the home of his prospective parents-in-law: "Every morning the reigning patriarch, as if just in from the hunt, shouts from the kitchen, 'How many people would like a poached egg?' Women and children take turns saying yes or no. In the meantime the women talk among themselves and designate one among them the toast maker" (pp. 46–47).

Rosaldo (1989) says of this account, "My rendition of a family breakfast in the ethnographic present transformed a relatively spontaneous event into a generic cultural form. It became a caricatured analysis . . . the reader will probably not be surprised to hear that my potential in-laws laughed and laughed as they listened to the microethnography . . . about their family breakfast" (p. 48). Rosaldo employs terms that Geertz (1983) would call experience-distant, or second order. Terms and phrases such as *reigning patri-arch* and *in from the hunt* may work for the anthropologist talking to another anthropologist, but they lack relevance and meaning for Rosaldo's prospective new family.

Interpretation is an art; it is not formulaic or mechanical.[5] It can be learned, like any form of storytelling, only through doing. Indeed, as Laurel Richardson argues, writing is interpretation, or storytelling. Field-workers can neither make sense of nor understand what has been learned until they sit down and write the interpretive text, telling the story first to themselves and then to their significant others, and then to the public.

A situated, writing self structures the interactions that take place among the writer, the text, and the reader. The writer presents a particular and unique self in the text, a self that claims to have some authority over the subject matter that is being interpreted. However, the rules for presenting this self are no longer clear. Krieger (1991) comments: "The challenge lies in what each of us chooses to do when we represent our experiences. Whose rules do we follow? Will we make our own? Do we . . . have the guts to say, 'You may not like it, but here I am'?" (p. 244).

INTERPRETATION AS STORYTELLING

The storytelling self that is presented is always one attached to an interpretive perspective, an "espoused theory" (Argyris & Schön, 1974, p. viii) that gives the writer a public persona. Four major paradigms (positivist and post-positivist, constructivist, critical) and three major perspectives (feminist, ethnic models, cultural studies) now structure qualitative writing. The stories qualitative researchers tell one another come from one or another of these paradigms and perspectives.

These paradigms and perspectives serve several functions for the writer. They are masks that are hidden behind, put on, and taken off as writers write their particular storied and self-versions of a feminist, gay-lesbian, Afro-American, Hispanic, Marxist, constructionist, grounded theory, phenomenological, or interactionist text. They give the writer a public identity. These masks direct the writer into specific theoretical and research traditions, what Argyris and Schön (1974) call "theories-in-use" (p. viii). Each tradition has its own taken-for-granted and problematic writing style.

These masks offer scenarios that lead writers to impose a particular order on the world studied. For example, if the paradigm is positivist or postpositivist, the writer will present a text that stresses variables, hypotheses, and propositions derived from a particular theory that sees the world in terms of causes and effects (see Guba & Lincoln, 1989, p. 84). Strauss and Corbin (1990) offer a simple example: "Conditions of intense pain will be followed by measures taken to relieve pain" (p. 111). Here antecedent conditions (intense pain) produce subsequent actions (measures to relieve the pain).

If the paradigm is constructivist, the writer will present a text that stresses emergent designs and emergent understandings. An interpretive, or phenomenologically based, text would emphasize socially constructed realities, local generalizations, interpretive resources, stocks of knowledge, intersubjectivity, practical reasoning, and ordinary talk.

A writer working from a feminist standpoint paradigm (1998) will attempt to tell a situated story stressing gender, reflexivity, emotion, and an action orientation (Fonow & Cook, 1991, p. 2), examining, for example, how "the ideology of the 'single parent' [organizes] multiple sites (parent-teaching contact) in education" (Smith, 1992, p. 97). Similarly, a Marxist or emancipatory text will stress the importance of terms such as *action, structure, culture,* and *power,* which are then fitted into a general model of society (Carspecken & Apple, 1992, p. 513).

WRITING ISSUES: SENSE MAKING, REPRESENTATION, LEGITIMATION, DESIRE

Any discussion of how the researcher moves from the field to the text must address a host of issues or problems closely related to storytelling traditions. These issues group into four areas. (Each problem works its effects on the field, research, and interpretive texts that lay the foundation for the writer's final, public document.) These problems may be conceptualized as phases, each turning on a different issue, and each turning back on the others, as in Dilthey's (1900/1976) hermeneutic circle. They may be named and called the interpretation, or sense-making, representation, legitimation, and desiring phases of moving from field to text to reader. They interact with each other as the writer wrestles with them in the field, research, interpretive, and public phases of textual construction.

Sense Making

The first issue concerns how the writer moves from and through field notes into the actual writing process (into the research and interpretive texts), making decisions about what will be written about, what will be included, how it will be represented, and so on. A considerable literature surrounds this process (see Wolcott, 1990, for a review; see also Sanjek, 1990). For example, Strauss and Corbin (1990, p. 197) direct investigators in this field and research text phase to write memos, as well as theoretical, operational, and code notes concerning conceptual labels, paradigm features, emerging theoretical understandings, and visual representations of relationships between concepts and analytic terms. Richardson discusses other forms of anticipatory interpretive writing, including observation, methodological, theoretical, and personal notes that are kept in an ongoing journal.

Representation

The second area speaks to such topics as voice, audience, the "Other," and the author's place in the reflexive texts that are produced (see Geertz, 1988; Krieger, 1991; Richardson, 1990, 1992; Rose, 1990; Van Maanen, 1988). To paraphrase Brady (1991, p. 5), there is more than one way to do representation. Representation, of course, is always self-presentation. That is, the Other's presence is directly connected to the writer's self-presence in the text. The Other who is presented in the text is always a version of the researcher's self. Krieger (1991) argues: "When we discuss others, we are always talking about ourselves. Our images of 'them' are images of 'us'" (p. 5). This can occur poetically, as in Laurel Richardson's (1992) poem "Louisa May's Story of Her Life." Richardson has Louisa May say of herself:

> *I grew up poor in a rented house*
> *in a very normal sort of way*
> *on a very normal sort of street*
> *with some very nice middle-class friends. (p. 127)*

Here Richardson's poetic self poetically presents Louisa May's truncated life story.

Representation turns on voice and the use of pronouns, including first-person statements. Patricia Hill Collins (1990) describes her use of pronouns:

> I often use the pronoun "our" instead of "their" when referring to African-American women, a choice that embeds me in the group I am studying instead of distancing me from it. In addition, I occasionally place my own concrete experience in the text. To support my analysis, I cite few statistics and instead rely on the voices of Black women from all walks of life. (p. 202)

Frequently writers are positioned outside, yet alongside, those Others they write about, never making clear where they stand in these hyphenated relationships that connect the Other to them. When Others are not allowed to speak, they remain "an absent presence without voice" (hooks, 1990, p. 126). There are major problems with this approach to "Othering," and it has been extensively criticized (Denzin, 1990). In such situations it is best to let Others do their own talking. However, even when "we" allow the Other to speak, when we talk about or for them, we are taking over their voice. A multivoiced as opposed to single-voiced text can partially overcome this issue (see Bakhtin, 1986; also Collins, 1990).

Legitimation

The third problem centers on matters of epistemology, including how a public text legitimates itself, or makes claims for its own authority. Traditional foundationalist topics such as reliability, validity, and generalizability may be encountered here (see Hammersley, 1992; Lather, 1993). The postmodern sensibility doubts foundational arguments that seek to anchor a text's authority in such terms. A more local, personal, and political turn is taken. On this, Seidman (1991) is informative: "Instead of appealing to absolutist justifications, instead of constructing theoretical logics and epistemic casuistries to justify a conceptual strategy . . . I propose that we be satisfied with local, pragmatic rationales for our conceptual [interpretive] approaches" (p. 136; see also Lather, 1993).

Desire

There is still a fourth problem, or phase, in this project, given in the subtitle to Howard S. Becker's influential 1986 book, *Writing for Social Scientists: How to Start and Finish Your Thesis, Book, or Article*. This problem circles back on the first, making decisions about what will be written. But it goes deeper and refers to the writing practices that field-workers deploy: how one moves from a blank page (or screen) to a written text, one sentence after another, building an emergent, reflexive interpretation of the subject matter at hand (see Richardson, 1998; also see Becker, 1986; for an interpretation of Becker's strategies, see Clough, 1992, chap. 5). The topic, to borrow Roland Barthes's (1975) phrase, is the pleasure of the text. Or, as Laurel Richardson (1998: 347) says, "How do we create texts that are vital?"

A vital text is not boring. It grips the reader (and the writer). A vital text invites readers to engage the author's subject matter. Many qualitative research texts are boring. Writers have been taught to write in a particular style, a style that takes the "omniscient voice of science, the view from everywhere." (1998: 347). The postmodern sensibility encourages writers to put themselves into their texts, to engage writing as a creative act of discovery and inquiry. However, engaging or boring writing has more to do with the writer than with the paradigm or perspective that is employed.

I turn now to the problems generic to the sense-making, representation, legitimation, and desiring phases of writing. This will involve additional consideration of the relationship between the writer and the text.

TWO MODELS OF THE WRITER

The foregoing discussion has separated, or isolated, four phases of writing. Although analytically useful, this formulation conveys a sometimes heroic, romantic picture of the writer and the text. It presumes a writer with the guts to tell it like it is, to put him- or herself on the line, so to speak. It presumes a socially situated (and isolated), unique writer who has the courage and authenticity to write a bold new text. This writer first experiences, feels, and thinks. Having had the experience, this bold writer then writes, deploying one or more narrative traditions in the story he or she tells.[6]

This model makes writing an expressive, and not a productive, process. It romanticizes the writer and his or her experiences. It distances experience from its expressions. Sense making, interpretation, representation, and claims for legitimacy are all part of the same process. They can be separated only artificially.

Interpretation is a productive process that sets forth the multiple meanings of an event, object, experience, or text. Interpretation is transformative. It illuminates, throws light on experience. It brings out, and refines, as when butter is clarified, the meanings that can be sifted from a text, an object, or a slice of experience. So conceived, meaning is not in a text, nor does interpretation precede experience, or its representation. Meaning, interpretation, and representation are deeply intertwined in one another.

Raymond Carver (1989), the short story writer, describes it this way. Writing is an "act of discovery" (p. 25). The writer deals with moments of experience. The writer brings all of his or her powers, "intelligence and literary skill" (p. 27) to bear on these moments to show how "things out there really are and how he [or she] sees those things—like no one else sees them" (p. 27). This is done "through the use of clear and specific language; language that will bring to life the details that will light up the story for the reader . . . the language must be accurately and precisely given" (p. 27).

Experimental writing, Carver argues, is "original." "The real experimenters have to Make It New . . . and in the process have to find things out for themselves . . . writers want to carry news from their world to ours" (p. 24). This means that "absolutely everything is important" (p. 38), including where the writer puts the "commas and periods" (p. 38). The writer invests experience with meaning, showing how everything has suddenly become clear. What was unclear before has "just now become clear" (p. 23). Such understandings emerge in moments of sudden awakening. The writer brings this sense of discovery and awakening to the reader.

Writing, then, relives and reinscribes experience, bringing newly discovered meanings to the reader. No cheap tricks, Carver (1989, p. 23) says, no gimmicks. Writing must bring news of the world to the reader. In writing, the writer creates this world. He or she fills it with real and fictional people. Their problems and their crises are brought to life. Their lives gone out of control are vividly described. Their lives, suddenly illuminated with new meanings and new transformation of self, are depicted.

What is given in the text, what is written, is made up and fashioned out of memory and field notes. Writing of this order, writing that powerfully reinscribes and re-creates experience, invests itself with its own power and authority. No one else but this writer could have brought this new corner of the world alive in this way for the reader.

Thus are expressive (romantic) and productive views of writing mutually complementary. The field-worker must be a committed writer, but the stories that are boldly told are those that flow from a commitment not to shock, or brutalize, or alienate the reader (Carver, 1989, p. 24). Experimentation is not an excuse or a "license to be careless, silly or imitative" (p. 24).

THE WRITING PROCESS

Understanding and mystery are central to the writing project. Carver's writer unravels a mystery, discovering and then understanding what was previously hidden and unclear. He or she cuts to the heart of an experience, disclosing its immediate, as well as deep, symbolic and long-lasting meanings for the people involved. This suggests that the writer accurately describes a hidden or submerged reality that the text brings to light. So conceived, a text establishes its own verisimilitude. It tells the truth. But there are complicated relations among truth, reality, and the text (see also Lincoln & Denzin, 1998). Every writing genre has its own laws of verisimilitude.

For example, verisimilitude is the theme of the murder mystery. "Its law is the antagonism between truth and verisimilitude" (Todorov, 1977, p. 86). In a murder mystery, the murderer must appear to be innocent and the innocent person must be made to appear guilty. "The truth has no verisimilitude, and the verisimilitude has no truth" (Todorov, 1977, p. 86). The end of the narrative must, of course, resolve this tension or contradiction. It must show the apparently innocent person to be guilty, and the apparently guilty party to be innocent. Only in the conclusion to the mystery, as Todorov (1977) notes, do truth and verisimilitude coincide. Thus is truth only and always a "distanced and postponed verisimilitude" (p. 88). Truth is a textual production.

So in the end, clear description, as defined by a genre, provides the basis for interpretation, understanding, and verisimilitude. That is, an event or process can be neither interpreted nor understood until it has been well described. However, the age of "objective" description is over. We are, as Lather (1991, p. 91) argues, in the age of inscription. Writers create their own situated, inscribed versions of the realities they describe.

There is more than one way to do a description-as-an-inscription. Thin description simply states a set of facts (Geertz, 1973, pp. 9–10; Ryle, 1968, pp. 8–9), for example:

> X drank a cup of coffee at 9:30 a.m. on Wednesday February 3 as he e-mailed a message to his editor and co-editor.

Here is a thick description, taken from a Carver short story, "So Much Water So Close to Home" (1989). The action described in this passage sets the context for the nervous breakdown of the woman who narrates the story. Four men have gone to the mountains on a fishing trip.

> They parked the car in the mountains and hiked several miles to where they wanted to fish. They carried their bedrolls, food and cooking utensils, their cards, their whisky. The first evening at the river, even before they could set up camp, Mel Dorn found the girl floating face down in the river; nude, lodged near the shore in some branches. He called the other men and they all came to look at her. They talked about what to do . . . one of them thought they should start back to the car at once. The others stirred the sand with their shoes and said they felt inclined to stay. They pleaded fatigue, the late hour, the fact that the girl 'wasn't going anywhere.' In the end they all decided to stay. (pp. 186–187)

A thin description simply reports facts, independent of intentions or circumstances. A thick description, in contrast, gives the context of an experience, states the intentions and meanings that organized the experience, and reveals the experience as a process. Out of this process arises a text's claims for truth, or its verisimilitude.

Ethnography, Geertz (1973, p. 10) suggests, is thick description, a "written representation of a culture" (Van Maanen, 1988, p. 1). Field-workers inscribe social discourse. They write it down, turning a passing event into something that now exists in its inscriptions (Geertz, 1973, p. 19). What is written down is itself interpretive, for the researcher interprets while writing, attempting in the process to rescue the " 'said' I of such discourse from its perishing occasions and fix it in perusable terms" (Geertz, 1973, p. 20). The intent is to create the conditions that will allow the reader, through the writer, to converse with (and observe) those who have been studied.

Building on what has been described and inscribed, interpretation creates the conditions for authentic, or deep, emotional understanding. Authentic understanding is created when readers are able to live their way into an experience that has been described and interpreted. Early in his research on Ilongot headhunters, Rosaldo (1989) explained the headhunting ritual with exchange theory. He presented his theory to an older Ilongot man named Insan:

> What did he think, I asked, of the idea that headhunting resulted from the way that one death (the beheaded victim's) canceled another (the next of kin). He looked puzzled, so I went on to say that a victim of a beheading was exchanged for the death of one's own kin. . . . Insan reflected a moment, and replied that he imagined somebody could think such a thing . . . but that he and other Ilongots did not think any such thing. (pp. 3–4).

Fifteeen months after his wife Michelle's tragic death in the field, Rosaldo returned to his headhunting materials. There, attempting to deal with his own rage, he found the meaning of the Ilongot ritual, and the rage that headhunting addressed. He states, "Either you understand it or you don't" (pp. 1–2). Unless you have had the experience, you cannot understand it.

Interpretation is done, of course, by an interpreter, or storyteller. There are two types of interpreters: people who have actually experienced what has been described, and those who are often ethnographers, or field-workers, so-called well-informed experts. These two types (local and scientific) of interpreters often give different meanings to the same set of thickly described/inscribed experiences. Local interpreters use experience-near concepts—words and meanings that actually operate in the worlds studied (Geertz, 1983, p. 57). These individuals seek emic, or contextual, situated understandings. Scientific interpreters frequently use experience-distant terms—words whose meanings lie in the observer's theory (Geertz, 1983, p. 57). They produce etic, or abstract, noncontextualized interpretations. Geertz (1973) clarifies the goal in this situation:

> [We] set down the meaning particular social actions have for the actors whose actions they are . . . stating as explicitly as we can manage, what the knowledge thus attained demonstrates about the society in which it is found. . . . Our double task is to uncover the conceptual structures that inform our subject's acts, the "said" of social discourse, and to construct a system of analysis . . . [which reveals] what is generic to those structures. (p. 27)

Thick descriptions and inscriptions create thick interpretations.[7] Thick interpretations interpret thick descriptions, in terms of the local theories that are structuring people's experiences.

In nearly all situations, individuals are able to articulate interpretive stories, or working theories, about their conduct and their experiences. These theories-as-stories are contained in the oral and cultural texts of the group and are based on local knowledge—that is, what works for them (Geertz, 1983). These pragmatic theories give meaning to problematic experiences. The interpreter attempts to uncover these theories, showing how they work in the lives of the individuals studied.

THE TEXT, ITS AUTHORITY, AND STYLE

A text and an author's authority can always be challenged. This is so for three reasons. First, stories can always be told (inscribed) in different ways, and the Others who are spoken for may offer different tellings of their story. Second, all texts are biased productions. Many reflect patriarchal, male, interpretive biases (Collins, 1990, pp. 203–206). Third, the interpretive criteria that an author employs may be questioned, and the logic of the text that is assembled may be called into doubt. I will briefly discuss each of these points.

Different Tellings

In a recent article, W. A. Marianne Boelen (1992) criticizes William Foote Whyte's classic study *Street Corner Society* (1943) on several grounds. She notes that Whyte did not know Italian, was not an insider to the group studied, did not understand the importance of the family in Italian group life, and, as a consequence, seriously misrepresented many of the facts in "Cornerville" society. Whyte (1992) has disputed Boelen's charges, but they linger, especially in light of Doc's (Whyte's key informant) estrangement from Whyte. But unnoticed in the Whyte-Boelen exchange is the fact that no permanent telling of a story can be given. There are only always different versions of different, not the same, stories, even when the same site is studied.[8]

Writing Styles

There are several styles of qualitative writing, several different ways of describing, inscribing, and interpreting reality. Each style creates the conditions for its own criticism. Some version of the realist tale, or style, however, predominates. The realist tale attempts to make the subject's world transparent, to bring it alive, to make it visible (Clough, 1992, p. 132). There are three prevailing realist styles: mainstream, interpretive, and descriptive.

Mainstream realist writing presents thick and thin descriptions of the worlds studied, giving accounts of events, persons, and experiences. These texts assume the author can give an objective accounting, or portrayal, of the realities of a group or an individual. Such texts often utilize experience-distance concepts, such as kinship structure, to explain a group's way of life. Mainstream realism leads to the production of analytic, interpretive texts that are often single voiced.

Interpretive realism describes those texts where authors insert their personal interpretations into the life situations of the individuals studied. Clifford Geertz's (1973) study of the Balinese (which uses thick description) frequently privileges Geertz's interpretations. For example, he states: "In the cockfight, man and beast, good and evil, ego and ideology . . . fuse in a bloody drama of hatred, cruelty, violence and death" (p. 442). Here experience and its meanings are filtered through the researcher's, not the subject's, eyes.

In descriptive realism the writer attempts to stay out of the way and to allow the world being described to speak for itself. Of course, this is impossible, for all writing is interpretive. However, the impulse is to tell a multivoiced story (see, for example, Bruner & Gorfain, 1991; Ulmer, 1989). The excerpt from the Carver story quoted above is an example of this form of storytelling.[9]

Bias

Viewing the world through the male voice and gaze, too many writers equate masculinity with objectivity and femininity with subjectivity. In general, as Reinharz (1992) observes, "quantitative research defines itself as hard, firm, real . . . and strong . . . [and] defines qualitative research as soft, mushy, fuzzy, and weak" (p. 295). But all texts are biased, reflecting the play of class, gender, race, ethnicity, and culture, suggesting that so-called objective interpretations are impossible.

The Logic of the Text

Any social text as a story can be analyzed in terms of its treatment of five paired terms:

1. the real world of lived experience and its representation in the text;
2. the text itself and the author, including the author's voice (first person, third person);
3. lived experience and its representation in the text (transcriptions from interviews and so on); and
4. subjects and their intentional meanings
5. the reader and the text (see Van Maanen, 1988, p. 6).

In telling a story, the author attempts to weave a text that re-creates for the reader the real world that was studied. Subjects, including their actions, experiences, words, intentions, and meanings, are then anchored inside this world as the author presents experience-near, experience-distant, local, and scientific theories of it. Readers take hold of this text and read their way into it, perhaps making it one of the stories they will tell about themselves. They develop their own naturalistic generalizations and impressions, based on the tacit knowledge and emotional feelings the text creates for them (see Stake, 1983, p. 282).

As a narrative production, interpretive writing is like fiction. It is created out of the facts of experience (things that did occur, might have occurred, or could occur). The story that is told often turns the researcher into a masculinized hero who confronts and makes sense of the subject's life situation. This situation is frequently conceptualized as a struggle that locates the subject's experiences within the primordial contexts of work, family, kinship, and marriage. This struggle is given meaning by the writer of the text, who becomes the only person authorized to represent the subject's story. The story that is finally told becomes the researcher's accomplishment, his or her self-fashioned narration of the subject's story (Clough, 1992, p. 17).

AN ANALYSIS OF INTERPRETIVE PRACTICES

To summarize: The art of interpretation produces understandings that are shaped by genre, narrative, stylistic, personal, cultural, and paradigmatic conventions. I turn next to a review of the major paradigms and perspectives that now structure qualitative research writing practices: positivist and postpositivist, constructivist, critical (Marxist, emancipatory), and poststructuralist—including ethnic, feminist, and cultural studies—models. I select an exemplar from each tradition.[10] Qualitative research is now in its "fifth moment," writing its way out of writing culture.

GROUNDED THEORY AS AN INTERPRETIVE STYLE (POSTPOSITIVISM)

The grounded theory perspective reflects a naturalistic approach to ethnography and interpretation, stressing naturalistic observations, open-ended interviewing, the sensitizing use of concepts, and a grounded (inductive) approach to theorizing, which can be both formal and substantive. Strauss and Corbin (1990) outline the criteria for judging a grounded theory study. They preface their discussion thus: "The usual canons of 'good science' should be retained, but require redefinition in order to fit the realities of qualitative research" (p. 250). These usual canons of good science are significance, theory observation compatibility, generalizability, consistency, reproducibility, precision, and verification. Strauss and Corbin argue, for example, that if a similar set of conditions exists, and if the same theoretical perspective and the same rules for data gathering and analysis are followed, two researchers should be able to reproduce the same theoretical explanations of a given phenomenon.

Investigators should be able to provide information on the sample (including theoretical variations), core categories, key events and incidents, hypotheses, and negative cases that emerged and were pursued during the research process. The empirical grounding of a study (its grounded theory) should be judged by the range, density, linkages between, and systematic relatedness of its theoretical concepts, as well as by the theory's specificity and generality. Strauss and Corbin (1990) urge that these criteria be followed so that readers can "judge the credibility of [the] theory" (p. 258).

The grounded theory perspective is the most widely used qualitative interpretive framework in the social sciences today.[11] Its appeals are broad, for it provides a set of clearly defined steps any researcher can follow (see also Prus, 1991). Its dangers and criticisms, which arise when it is not fully understood, are multiple. There may be a flood of concepts unattached to the empirical world, and the analyst may get lost in coding and category schemes. Just exactly what a theory is, is also not clear (see Woods, 1992, p. 391). Some suggest that because the facts of a theory are always theory laden, a theory can only ever discover and hence ground itself (Lincoln & Guba, 1985, p. 207). The overemphasis on theory has also been criticized, including the use of previous theory as a guide to research and the attempts to make previous theory more dense (but see Gerson, 1991, p. 285). This preoccupation with prior theory can stand in the way of the researcher's attempts to hear and listen to the interpretive theories that operate in the situations studied. The perspective's affinities with positivism have also been criticized (Roman, 1992, p. 571). There is also a textual style that frequently subordinates lived experience and its interpretations to the grounded theorist's reading of the situation.

At the same time, grounded theory answers to a need to attach the qualitative research project to the "good science" model. Yet the perspective continues to fit itself to feminist and other poststructural, postmodern interpretive styles (Star, 1991).

CONSTRUCTIVISM AS AN INTERPRETIVE STYLE

The constructivist program of Lincoln, Guba, and others represents a break with the postpositivist tradition, while retaining (at one level) a commitment to the grounded theory approach of Strauss and associates.[12] A good constructionist interpretation (text) is based on purposive (theoretical) sampling, a grounded theory, inductive data analysis, and idiographic (contextual) interpretations. The foundation for interpretation rests on triangulated empirical materials that are trustworthy. Trustworthiness consists of four components: credibility, transferability, dependability, and confirmability (these are the constructionist equivalents of internal and external validity, reliability, and objectivity; Lincoln & Guba, 1985, p. 300).[13]

Trustworthy materials are subjected to the constant comparative method of analysis that grounded theory deploys, that is, comparing incidents applicable to categories, integrating categories and their properties, delimiting and writing the theory. These materials are then developed into a case report that is again subjected to a comprehensive member check and an external audit. This done, the study is ready for public release (Lincoln & Guba, 1985, p. 381).

These constructivist interpretive strategies address many of the perceived problems in grounded theory, including the theory- and value-laden nature of facts, ambiguities in incidence, and category analysis. The paradigm, while disavowing the ontology, epistemology, and methodologies of postpositivism (Guba, 1990a, p. 27), sustains, at one level, Strauss and Corbin's commitment to the canons of good science. Hence the enormous commitment to methods and procedures that will increase a text's credibility, transferability, dependability, and confirmability.

Feminists, liberation theologists, Freirian critical theorists, and neo-Marxists may criticize the paradigm for not being ideological enough (Lincoln, 1990, p. 83). However, it is moving in these directions, as the authors seek a language and a set of practices that more fully celebrate and implement the moral, ethical, and political dimensions of social research (Lincoln, 1990, p. 86). Still, some would contend that it (like grounded theory) has yet to engage fully the new sensibilities flowing from the poststructural and postmodern perspectives.

CRITICAL THEORY AS AN INTERPRETIVE STYLE

There are multiple critical theory and participatory action frameworks (Guba, 1990a, p. 25). All share a critical realist ontology, a subjectivist epistemology, and a dialogic, transformative, ethnographic methodology (Guba, 1990a, p. 25). This often produces a criticism of traditional, naturalistic ethnographies (Roman, 1992, p. 558).

There are two distinct traditions within the cultural studies, critical theory model. One school, following Paulo Freire (1982, p. 30), regards concrete reality, dialectically conceived, as the starting point for analysis that examines how people live their facts of life into existence. The other school reads social texts (popular literature, cinema, popular music) as empirical materials that articulate complex arguments about race, class, and gender in contemporary life. Some scholars merge the ethnographic and textual approaches, examining how cultural interpretations are acted on and given meaning in concrete local cultural communities. Such work moves back and forth between concrete ethnographic texts and the content, semiotic, and narrative analysis of systems of discourse—for example, a particular television show or a film.

Critical inquiry is theory driven by neo-Marxist and cultural studies models of the raced, classed, and gendered structures of contemporary societies (Carspecken & Apple, 1992, pp. 541–42). An emancipatory principle drives such research, which is committed to engaging oppressed groups in collective, democratic theorizing about "what is common and different in their experiences of oppression and privilege" (Roman, 1992, p. 557). A constant focus is given to the material and cultural practices that create structures of oppression.

A critical text is judged by its ability to reveal reflexively these structures of oppression as they operate in the worlds of lived experience. A critical text thus creates a space for multiple voices to speak; those who are oppressed are asked to articulate their definitions of their situations. For some, critical theory must be testable, falsifiable, dialogic, and collaborative (Carspecken & Apple, 1992, pp. 547–548). Others reject the more positivist features of this formulation (Roman, 1992, p. 558). Dorothy Smith (1992, p. 96), for example, evaluates a text by its ability to reveal the invisible structures of oppression in women's worlds.

Thus a good critical, emancipatory text is one that is multivocal, collaborative, naturalistically grounded in the worlds of lived experience, and organized by a critical, interpretive theory. Such formulations have been criticized for their tendency to impose their voices and values on the groups studied (Quantz, 1992, p. 471), for not being reflexive enough, and for being too theoretical (top-down theory), too preoccupied with theory verification (Roman, 1992, p. 571), and not sufficiently aware of postmodern sensibilities concerning the text and its social construction (Clough, 1992, p. 137).

These approaches, with their action criteria, politicize qualitative research. They foreground praxis, yet leave unclear the methodological side of the interpretive process that is so central to the grounded theory and constructionist approaches.

POSTSTRUCTURAL INTERPRETIVE STYLES

I will discuss three poststructural interpretive styles: those connected to the standpoint and cultural studies perspectives (Clough, 1992; Denzin, 1989; Lather, 1991, 1993; Smith, 1992; see also Olesen, 1998), those articulated by women of color (Collins, 1990; hooks, 1990), and my own approach, interpretive interactionism. Each of these perspectives is intimately connected to the critical and emancipatory styles of interpretation.

Style 1: Women of Color

Collins (1990, pp. 206–219) offers four criteria of interpretation, which are contrasted to the positivist approaches to research. Derived from an Afrocentric standpoint, her criteria focus on the primacy of concrete lived experience, the use of dialogue in assessing knowledge claims, the ethic of caring, and the ethic of personal accountability.

Experience as a criterion of meaning directs attention to black sisterhood, to the stories, narratives and Bible principles embodied in black church and community life. Concrete black feminine wisdom is contrasted to knowledge without wisdom: "A heap see, but a few know" (Collins, 1990, p. 208). Wisdom is experiential, cultural, and shared in the black feminine community. Dialogue, bell hooks argues, is humanizing speech. Black feminists assess knowledge claims through discourse, storytelling, connected dialogue in a group context. This emphasis on dialogue is directly translated into the black feminist text. Zora Neale Hurston, for example, located herself inside the folktales she collected, and carried on extensive dialogues with them, thus creating a multivocal text (Collins, 1990, p. 214).

Dialogue extends to the ethic of caring, which suggests that "personal expressiveness, emotions and empathy are central to the knowledge validation process" (Collins, 1990, p. 215). This ethic values individual uniqueness and the expression of emotionality in the text, and seeks writers who can create emotional texts that others can enter into. The ethic of personal accountability makes individuals accountable for their values and the political consequences of their actions.

These four criteria embody a "self-defined Black women's standpoint using an Afrocentric epistemology" (Collins, 1990, p. 219). They call into question much of what now passes for truth in methodological discourse. They articulate criteria that stand in vivid contrast to those criteria contained in the grounded theory, constructionist, critical, and emancipatory traditions.

Style 2: Poststructural Feminist Interpretive Styles

Fonow and Cook (1991, pp. 2–13) suggest that four interpretive themes structure feminist research: an emphasis on researcher and textual reflexivity; an action and praxis orientation; an attention to the affective, emotional components of research; and concrete grounding in immediate situations. Lather (1991) extends this discussion. Her argument is threefold. First, feminist research challenges narrative realism, and the traditional naturalistic ethnography, because there is now an "uncertainty about what constitutes an adequate depiction of reality" (p. 91). As noted above, Lather argues that the age of description has ended. We are, as we have always been, in the moment of inscription, wherein writers create their own situated versions of the worlds studied. Accordingly, the social text becomes a stage, or a site where power and knowledge are presented. This means, third, we must explore alternative ways of presenting and authorizing our texts.

Lather (1993) then turns to a discussion of five new forms of validity, different ways of authorizing a text. These new forms are called reflexive, ironic, neopragmatic, rhizomatic, and situated validity. Each enacts a multivoiced, reflexive, open-ended, emotionally based text that is action, or praxis, based. For Lather and others in this tradition, theory is interpretation. There is no break between empirical activity (gathering empirical materials, reading social texts) and theorizing. Theory as interpretation is always anchored in the texts that it analyzes and reads. Conceptualizing theory-as-interpretation or theory-as-criticism means that the writer employs a style that immediately connects a theoretical term to its referent. For example, ideology is given in a popular culture text, or desire is present in a Madonna pose. Rosaldo (1989) provides an example; here the text merges with its subject matter—criticism and interpretation are not separated:

> My anger at recent films that portray imperialism with nostalgia informs this chapter. Consider the enthusiastic reception of *Heat and Dust*, *A Passage to India*, *Out of Africa*, and *The Gods Must Be Crazy*. The white colonial societies portrayed in these films appear decorous and orderly, as if constructed in accord with the norms of classic ethnography. . . . Evidently a mood of nostalgia makes racial domination appear innocent and pure. (p. 68)

Style 3: Interpretive Interactionism

I turn now to a brief exposition of another interpretive style, what I have elsewhere termed *interpretive interactionism* (Denzin, 1989). Interpretive research begins and ends with the biography and the self of the researcher. The events and troubles that are written about are ones the writer has already experienced and witnessed firsthand. The task is to produce "richly detailed" inscriptions and accounts of such experiences.

The focus of the research is on those life experiences (epiphanies) that radically alter and shape the meanings persons give to themselves and their life projects. In epiphanies, personal character is manifested and made apparent. By recording these experiences in detail, and by listening to the stories people tell about them, the researcher is able to illuminate the moments of crisis that occur in a person's life. Having had such experiences, the individual is often never quite the same again. (Examples of epiphanies include religious conversions, divorces, incidents of family violence, rape, incest, murder, and loss of a job.)

Sartre's (1963, pp. 85–166) progressive-regressive method of analysis organizes the interpretive process. The investigator situates a subject, or class of subjects, within a given historical moment. Progressively, the method looks forward to the conclusion of a set of acts or experiences undertaken by the subject. Regressively, the method works back in time to the historical, gender, class, race, cultural, biographical, and emotional conditions that moved the subject forward into the experience that is being studied.

Interpretive materials are evaluated by their ability to illuminate phenomena as lived experience. Such materials should be based on thickly contextualized materials that are historical, relational, and processual. The core of these materials will be the personal experience stories subjects tell one another. These stories should be connected to larger institutional, group, and cultural contexts, including written texts and other systems of discourse (cinema, music, folklore). The understandings that are put forth should engulf all that has been learned about the phenomenon. The moral biases that organize the research should be made evident to the reader. The competing models of truth and interpretation (rationality and emotionality) that operate in the subject's situations should be revealed. The stories that are presented to readers should be given in the language, feelings, emotions, and actions of those studied.[14]

CRITICISMS OF POSTSTRUCTURALISM

Poststructural, postmodern, feminist texts have been criticized because of their interpretive criteria. Critics complain that there is no way to evaluate such work because traditional, external standards of evaluation (internal and external validity, reliability, objectivity) are not followed. This means, the argument goes, that there is no way to evaluate a good or bad poststructural, feminist text. Others argue that the feminist and poststructural text imposes an interpretive framework on the world, and does not allow subjects to speak. These criticisms come, of course, from the positivist and post-positivist traditions.

These criticisms are rejected on several grounds. First, they are seen as not reflecting an understanding of the new postmodern sensibility, which doubts and challenges any attempt to legitimate a text in terms of positivist or postpositivist criteria. Such criteria represent attempts to bring legitimacy and authority to the scientific project. Science, in its traditional forms, is the problem. Knowledge produced under the guise of objective science is too often used for purposes of social control (Clough, 1992, p. 134). The criteria of evaluation that poststructuralists employ answer to a different set of problems and to a different project. They seek a morally informed social criticism, a sacred version of science that is humane, caring, holistic, and action based (see Reason, 1993; see also Lincoln & Denzin, 1998).

Poststructuralists celebrate uncertainty and attempt to construct texts that do not impose theoretical frameworks on the world. They seek to let the prose of the world speak for itself, while they remain mindful of all the difficulties involved in such a commitment. They, more than their postpositivist counterparts, are sensitive to voice and to multiple perspectives.

MULTIPLE INTERPRETIVE COMMUNITIES

There are many ways to move from the field to the text, many ways to inscribe and describe experience. There are multiple interpretive communities that now circulate within the many terrains of qualitative research. These communities take different stances on the topics treated above, including the matters of writing, description, inscription, interpretation, understanding, representation, legitimation, textual desire, and the logic and politics of the text.

A simplistic approach to the many paradigm dialogues that are now occurring (Guba, 1990a) might use the old-fashioned distinctions between humanists and scientists, between the "tender-minded" and the "tough-minded," to borrow William James's (1908/1978, pp. 10–13) terms. Such distinctions are displayed in Table 21.1. But critical analysis soon makes this pretty picture messy. On the surface, critical, emancipatory, feminist, interactional, poststructural, and postmodern researchers belong to the tender-minded interpretive community. Following James, they are more intuitive, emotional, and open-ended in their interpretive work. Some are quite dogmatic about this. But many critical theorists write realist texts, are hard-nosed empiricists, work within closed theoretical systems, and follow the canons of good science.

In the same vein, positivists, postpositivists, grounded theorists, and constructivists appear to belong to the tough-minded interpretive community. They are hard-nosed empiricists, system builders, often pluralistic in their use of theory, and skeptical of nonsystematic theory and empirical work. But there are feminists who use grounded theory methods and produce traditional-looking texts, based on foundational criteria. There are

TABLE 21.1 Two Interpretive Communities

Tender-Minded	Tough-Minded
Intuitive	Hard-nosed empiricists
Emotional	Rational, cognitive
Open-ended texts	Closed texts, systems
Interpretation as art	Interpretation as method
Personal biases	Neutrality
Experimental texts	Traditional texts
Antirealism	Realist texts
Antifoundational	Foundational
Crticism	Substantive theory
Science-as-power	Good science canons
Multivoiced texts	Single-voiced texts

tough-minded constructivists who are antirealist and antifoundational, and who regard interpretation as more art than method.

Clearly, simplistic classifications do not work. Any given qualitative researcher-as-*bricoleur* can be more than one thing at the same time, can be fitted into both the tender- and the tough-minded categories. It is clear that in the fifth (and sixth) moments of qualitative research, the concerns from each of James's two communities work alongside and inform one another. Accordingly, it can be argued that the following contradictory understandings operate in this broad field we have called qualitative research.

Interpretation is an art that cannot be formalized. Scholars are increasingly concerned with the logic of the text, especially the problems involved in presenting lived experience and the point of view of the Other. Many are preoccupied with the biases in the emotional stories they tell and are drawn to experimental forms of writing; some reject mainstream narrative realism. It is common for texts now to be grounded in antifoundational systems of discourse (local knowledge, local emotions). These texts tell emancipatory stories grounded in race, class, and gender. Personal experience is a major source of empirical material for many, as are cultural texts and materials gathered via the ethnographic method. More than a few researchers expose their writerly selves in first-person accounts, and many are attempting to produce reader-friendly, multivoiced texts that speak to the worlds of lived experience. It is becoming commonplace for qualitative researchers to be advocates of the moral communities they represent, while attempting to participate directly in social change.

At the same time, there are those who remain committed to mainstream realism. They write texts that adhere to complex sets of methodological principles connected to postpositivist foundational systems of meaning ("good science"). Their texts are grounded in concrete empirical materials (case studies) and are inductively interpreted through the methods of grounded theory or variations thereof. Existing theories, both substantive and formal, structure inquiry, which is organized in a rigorous, stepwise manner.

Finally, there are conflicting views and disagreements on the very topic of interpretation itself. The immediate, local, personal, emotional biases of many lead them to tell stories that work outward from the self to society. These writers are writing to make sense of their own lives. Others write to make sense of "another's" life. In the end it is a matter of storytelling and the stories we tell each other.

INTO THE FUTURE

Of course, persons who do interpretations feel uncomfortable doing predictions. But where the field of interpretation, the art and politics of telling stories, will be in 10 years should be addressed. If the past predicts the future, and if the decade of the 1980s and the first half of the 1990s are to be taken seriously, then interpretation is moving more and more deeply into the regions of the postmodern sensibility. A new postconstructivist paradigm may emerge. This framework may attach itself to a new and less foundational postpositivism and a more expansive critical theory framework built on modified grounded theory principles.

Epistemologies of color will proliferate, building on Afrocentric (Collins), Chicana (Rosaldo, Chabram-Daernersesian, Anzaldua), Native American, Asian (Trinh T. Minh-ha), Third World (Spivak), and other minority group perspectives. More elaborated epistemologies of gender (and class) will appear, including "queer theory" (Seidman, 1993), and feminisms of color. These interpretive communities will draw on their minority group experiences as the basis of the texts they write, and they will seek texts that speak to the logic and cultures of these communities.

These race-, ethnicity-, and gender-specific interpretive communities will fashion interpretive criteria out of their interactions with the postpositivist, constructivist, critical theory, and poststructural sensibilities. These criteria will be emic, existential, political, and emotional. They will push the personal to the forefront of the political, where the social text becomes the vehicle for the expression of politics.

This projected proliferation of interpretive communities does not mean that the field of qualitative research will splinter into warring factions, or into groups that cannot speak to one another. Underneath the complexities and contradictions that define this field rest three common commitments. The first reflects the belief that the world of human experience must be studied from the point of view of the historically and culturally situated individual. Second, qualitative researchers will persist in working outward from their own biographies to the worlds of experience that surround them. Third, scholars will continue to value and seek to produce works that speak clearly and powerfully about these worlds. To echo Raymond Carver (1989, p. 24), the real experimenters will always be those who Make It New, who find things out for themselves, and who want to carry this News from their world to ours.

And so the stories we tell one another will change and the criteria for reading stories will also change. And this is how it should be. The good stories are always told by those who have learned well the stories of the past, but who are unable to tell them any longer because those stories no longer speak to them, or to us.

NOTES

1. Here I deal with the constructivism of Guba and Lincoln, not the social constructionism of Gergen. Schwandt compares and contrasts these two frameworks.

2. See the relevant chapters in the *Handbook of Qualitative Research* that take up each of these traditions, including those in Volume 1 (*Landscape of Qualitative Research*) by Fine (Chapter 4), Guba and Lincoln (Chapter 6), Schwandt (Chapter 7), Kincheloe and McLaren (Chapter 8), Olesen (Chapter 9), Fiske (Chapter 11), and Marcus (Chapter 12); those in Volume 2 (*Strategies of Qualitative Inquiry*) by Atkinson and Hammersley (Chapter 5), Holstein and Gubrium (Chapter 6), and Strauss and Corbin (Chapter 7); and those in Volume 3 (*Collecting and Interpreting Qualitative Materials*) by Altheide and Johnson (Chapter 10) and Richardson (Chapter 12).

3. Rosaldo (1989) argues that anthropological doctrine presents this as a three-step process, involving preparation, knowledge, and sensibility, but cautions that "one should work to undermine the false comfort it can convey. At what point can people say that they have completed their learning or life experience?" (p. 8).

4. Mitch Allen and Yvonna Lincoln clarified these steps for me.

5. Yvonna Lincoln suggests that this may have been less the case in earlier historical moments, when realist tales were organized in terms of well-understood conventions.

6. I am deeply indebted to Meaghan Morris for her help in clarifying the meanings in this section.

7. Elsewhere I have offered a typology of descriptions and interpretations, including descriptions that are primarily micro, macro, biographical, situational, interactional-relational, incomplete, glossed, pure, and interpretive, and interpretations that are thin, thick, native, observer based, analytic, descriptive-contextual, and relational-interactive (Denzin, 1989, pp. 99, 111–120).

8. The Whyte-Boelen exchange is similar, in these respects, to earlier controversies in this area, including the famous Redfield-Sanchez and Mead-Freeman debates over who got it right—the original, classic study or the reinvestigation of the same site by a later researcher.

9. Mainstream, interpretive, and descriptive realist stories may be supplemented by more traditional and experimental formats, including confessional ("the problems I encountered doing my study") and impressionistic ("dramatic and vivid pictures from the field") tales of the field (Van Maanen, 1988), as well as personal memoirs of the field experience (Stoller & Olkes, 1987), narratives of the self (see Ellis & Bochner, 1992; Ellis & Flaherty, 1992; Ronai, 1992), fiction texts (Stewart, 1989), and ethnographic dramas and performance texts (McCall & Becker, 1990; Richardson & Lockridge).

10. These, of course, are my interpretations of these interpretive styles.

11. The presence is greatest, perhaps, in education, the health sciences, and communication, but also in sociology, less so in anthropology. When one peels back the layers of discourse embedded in any of the numerous qualitative guides to interpretation and theory construction, the core features of the Strauss approach are present, even when Strauss and associates are not directly named.

12. It argues that the facts for any theory are always interpreted and value laden, that no theory can ever be fully tested (or grounded), and an interactive relationship always exists between the observer and the observed. A dialectical, dialogic hermeneutic posture organizes inquiry that is based on thick descriptions of action and subjective experience in natural situations.

13. Specific strategies and criteria are attached to each of these components. Credibility is increased through prolonged field engagement, persistent observation, triangulation, peer debriefing, negative case analysis, referential analysis (Eisner's term for cinematic methods that provide a record of social life), and member checks (talking to people in the field). Thick description provides for transferability, whereas dependability can be enhanced through the use of overlapping methods, stepwise replications, and inquiry (dependability) audits (the use of well-informed subjects) (Lincoln & Guba, 1985, p. 316). Confirmability builds on audit trails (a "residue of records stemming from inquiry"; p. 319) and involves the use of written field notes, memos, a field diary, process and personal notes, and a reflexive journal.

14. The five steps to interpretation (Denzin, 1989, p. 27) should be followed: deconstruction, capture, bracketing, construction, contextualization.

REFERENCES

Argyris, C., and D. A. Schön. 1974. *Theory in practice.* San Francisco: Jossey-Bass.

Bakhtin, M. M. 1986. *Speech genres and other essays.* Austin: University of Texas Press.

Barthes, R. 1975. *The pleasure of the text.* New York: Hill & Wang.

Becker, H. S. 1986. *Writing for social scientists: How to start and finish your thesis, book, or article.* Chicago: University of Chicago Press.

Boelen, W. A. M. 1992. *Street corner society*: Cornerville revisited. *Journal of Contemporary Ethnography* 21: 11–51.

Brady, I., ed. 1991. Introduction, pp. 3–36 in *Anthropological Poetics*, ed. I. Brady. Savage, MD: Rowman & Littlefield.

Bruner, E. M., and P. Gorfain. 1991. Dialogic narration and the paradoxes of Masada, pp. 117–206 in *Anthropological Poetics*, ed. I. Brady. Savage, MD: Rowman & Littlefield.

Carspecken, P. F., and M. Apple. 1992. Critical research: Theory, methodology, and practice, pp. 507–554 in *The Handbook of Qualitative Research in Education*, eds. M. D. LeCompte, W. L. Millroy, & J. Preissle. New York: Academic Press.

Carver, R. 1989. *Fires.* New York: Vantage.

Clandinin, D. J. and F. M. Connelly. 1998. Personal experience methods, pp. 150–178 in *Collecting and Interpreting Qualitative Materials*, eds. N. K. Denzin & Y. S. Lincoln. Thousand Oaks, CA: Sage.

Clough, P. T. 1992. *The end(s) of ethnography: From realism to social criticism.* Newbury Park, CA: Sage.

Collins, P. H. 1990. *Black feminist thought: Knowledge, consciousness and the politics of empowerment.* New York: Routledge.

Denzin, N. K. 1989. *Interpretive interactionism.* Newbury Park, CA: Sage.

Denzin, N. K. 1990. Harold and Agnes: A feminist narrative undoing. *Sociological Theory* 8: 198–216.

Dilthey, W. L. 1976. *Selected writings.* Cambridge: Cambridge University Press. (Original work published 1900)

Ellis, C., and M. G. Flaherty, eds. (1992). *Investigating subjectivity: Research on lived experience.* Newbury Park, CA: Sage.

Ellis, C., and A. P. Bochner. 1992. Telling and performing personal stories: The constraints of choice in abortion, pp. 79–101 in *Investigating subjectivity: Research on lived experience,* eds. C. Ellis & M. G. Flaherty. Newbury Park, CA: Sage.

Fine, M. 1998. Working the hyphens: Reinventing self and other in qualitative research, pp. 130–155 in *The Landscape of Qualitative Research,* eds. N. K. Denzin & Y. S. Lincoln. Thousand Oaks, CA: Sage.

Fish, S. 1980. *Is there a text in this class? The authority of interpretive communities.* Cambridge, MA: Harvard University Press.

Fiske, J. 1998. Audiencing: Cultural practice and cultural studies, pp. 359–378 in *The Landscape of Qualitative Research,* eds. N. K. Denzin & Y. S. Lincoln. Thousand Oaks, CA: Sage.

Freire, P. 1982. *Pedagogy of the oppressed.* New York: Continuum.

Fonow, M. M., and J. A. Cook. 1991. Back to the future: A look at the second wave of feminist epistemology and methodology, pp. 1–15 in *Beyond Methodology: Feminist scholarship as lived research,* eds. M. M. Fonow & J. A. Cook. Bloomington: Indiana University Press.

Geertz, C. 1973. *The interpretation of cultures: Selected essays.* New York: Basic Books.

Geertz, C. 1983. *Local knowledge: Further essays in interpretive anthropology.* New York: Basic Books.

Geertz, C. 1988. *Works and lives: The anthropologist as author.* Stanford, CA: Stanford University Press.

Gerson, E. M. 1991. Supplementing grounded theory, pp. 285–302 in *Social Organization and Social Process: Essays in Honor of Anselm Strauss,* ed. D. R. Maines. New York: Aldine de Groyter.

Guba, E. G. 1990a. The alternative paradigm dialog, pp. 17–30 in *The Paradigm Dialog,* ed. E. G. Guba. Newbury Park, CA: Sage.

Guba, E. G. 1990b. Carrying on the dialog, pp. 368-378 in *The Paradigm Dialog,* ed. E. G. Guba. Newbury Park, CA: Sage.

Guba, E. G., and Y. S. Lincoln. 1989. *Fourth generation evaluation.* Newbury Park, CA: Sage.

Hammersley, M. 1992. *What's wrong with ethnography? Methodological explorations.* London: Routledge.

hooks, b. 1990. *Yearning: Race, gender, and cultural politics.* Boston: South End.

James, W. 1978. *Pragmatism and the meaning of truth.* Cambridge, MA: Harvard University Press. (Original work published 1908)

Kincheloe, J. L. and P. L. McLaren. 1998. Rethinking critical theory and qualitative research, pp. 260–299 in *The Landscape of Qualitative Research,* eds. N. K. Denzin & Y. S. Lincoln. Thousand Oaks, CA: Sage.

Krieger, S. 1991. *Social science and the self: Personal essays as an art form.* New Brunswick, NJ: Rutgers University Press.

Lather, P. 1991. *Getting smart: Feminist research and pedagogy with/in the postmodern.* New York: Routledge.

Lather, P. 1993. Fertile obsession: Validity after poststructuralism. *Sociological Quarterly* 35.

Lincoln, Y. S. 1990. The making of a constructivist: A remembrance of transformations past, pp. 68–87 in *The Paradigm Dialog*, ed. E. G. Guba. Newbury Park, CA: Sage.

Lincoln, Y. S., and E. G. Guba. 1985. *Naturalistic inquiry.* Beverly Hills, CA: Sage.

Lincoln, Y. S. and N. K. Denzin. 1998. The fifth moment, pp. 407–429 in *The Landscape of Qualitative Research*, eds. N. K. Denzin & Y. S. Lincoln. Thousand Oaks, CA: Sage.

Lévi-Strauss, C. 1966. *The savage mind* (2d ed.). Chicago: University of Chicago Press.

Manning, P. K. and B. Cullum-Swan. 1998. Narrative, content, and semiotic analysis, pp. 246–247 in *Collecting and Interpreting Qualitative Materials*, eds. N. K. Denzin & Y. S. Lincoln. Thousand Oaks, CA: Sage.

McCall, M., and H. S. Becker. 1990. Performance science. *Social Problems* 32: 117–132.

Olesen, V. 1998. Feminisms and models of qualitative research, pp. 300–332 in *The Landscape of Qualitative Research*, eds. N. K. Denzin & Y. S. Lincoln. Thousand Oaks, CA: Sage.

Plath, D. 1990. Fieldnotes, filed notes, and the conferring of note, pp. 371–384 in *Fieldnotes: The Makings of Anthropology*, ed. R. Sanjek. Albany: State University of New York Press.

Prus, R. C. 1991. *Road hustler* (exp. ed.). New York: Steranko.

Quantz, R. A. 1992. On critical ethnography (with some postmodern considerations), pp. 447–505 in *The Handbook of Qualitative Research in Education*, eds. M. D. LeCompte, W. L. Millroy, & J. Preissle. New York: Academic Press.

Reason, P. 1993. Sacred experience and sacred science. *Journal of Management Inquiry* 2: 10–27.

Reinharz, S. 1992. *Feminist methods in social research.* New York: Oxford University Press.

Richardson, L. 1990. *Writing strategies.* Newbury Park, CA: Sage.

Richardson, L. 1991. Postmodern social theory: Representational practices. *Sociological Theory* 9: 173–179.

Richardson, L. 1992. The consequences of poetic representation: Writing the other, rewriting the self, pp. 125–137, in *Investigating Subjectivity: Research on Lived Experience*, eds. C. Ellis & M. G. Flaherty. Newbury Park, CA: Sage.

Richardson, L. 1998. Writing: A method of inquiry, pp. 345–371 in *Collecting and Interpreting Qualitative Materials*, eds. N. K. Denzin & Y. S. Lincoln. Thousand Oaks, CA: Sage.

Richardson, L., and E. Lockridge. 1991. The sea monster: An ethnographic drama. *Symbolic Interaction* 14: 335–340.

Ricoeur, P. 1985. *Time and narrative.* Vol. 2. Chicago: University of Chicago Press.

Roman, L. G. 1992. The political significance of other ways of narrating ethnography: A feminist materialist approach, in pp. 555–594, *The Handbook of Qualitative Research in Education*, eds. M. D. LeCompte, W. L. Millroy, & J. Preissle. New York: Academic Press.

Ronai, C. R. 1992. The reflexive self through narrative: A night in the life of an erotic dancer/researcher, in *Investigating Subjectivity: Research on Lived Experience*, eds. C. Ellis & M. G. Flaherty. Newbury Park, CA: Sage.

Rosaldo, R. 1989. *Culture and truth: The remaking of social analysis.* Boston: Beacon.

Rose, D. 1990. *Living the ethnographic life.* Newbury Park, CA: Sage.

Ryle, G. 1968. *The thinking of thoughts* (University Lectures, No. 18). Saskatoon: University of Saskatchewan.

Sanjek, R. 1990. *Fieldnotes: The makings of anthropology.* Albany: State University of New York Press.

Sartre, J.-P. 1963. *Search for a method.* New York: Alfred A. Knopf.

Seidman, S. 1991. The end of sociological theory: The postmodern hope. *Sociological Theory* 9: 131–146.

Seidman, S. 1993. *Embattled Eros: Sexual politics and ethics in contemporary America.* New York: Routledge.

Smith, D. 1992. Sociology from women's perspective: A reaffirmation. *Sociological Theory* 10: 88–97.

Stake, R. 1983. The case study method in social inquiry, *Evaluation Models,* eds. G. Madaus, M. Scriven, & D. Stufflebeam. Boston: Kluwer-Nijhoff.

Star, S. L. 1991. The sociology of the invisible: The primacy of work in the writings of Anselm Strauss, pp. 265–284, in *Social Organization and Social Process: Essays in Honor of Anselm Strauss,* D. R. Maines. New York: Aldine de Gruyter.

Stewart, J. 1989. *Drinkers, drummers and decent folk: Ethnographic narratives of Village Trinidad.* Albany: State University of New York Press.

Stoller, P., and C. Olkes. 1987. *In sorcery's shadow.* Chicago: University of Chicago Press.

Strauss, A. L., and J. Corbin. 1990. *Basics of qualitative research: Grounded theory procedures and techniques.* Newbury Park, CA: Sage.

Todorov, T. 1977. *The poetics of prose.* Ithaca, NY: Cornell University Press.

Ulmer, G. 1989. *Teletheory.* New York: Routledge.

Van Maanen, J. 1988. *Tales of the field: On writing ethnography.* Chicago: University of Chicago Press.

Whyte, W. F. 1943. *Street corner society: The social structure of an Italian slum.* Chicago: University of Chicago Press.

Whyte, W. F. 1992. In defense of *Street Corner Society. Journal of Contemporary Ethnography* 21: 52–68.

Wolcott, H. F. 1990. *Writing up qualitative research.* Newbury Park, CA: Sage.

Woods, P. 1992. Symbolic interactionism: Theory and method, pp. 336–404 in *The Handbook of Qualitative Research in Education,* eds. M. D. LeCompte, W. L. Millroy, & J. Preissle. New York: Academic Press.

CHAPTER 22

Writing: A Method of Inquiry

LAUREL RICHARDSON

> The writer's object is—or should be—to hold the
> reader's attention. . . . I want the reader to turn
> the page and keep on turning to the end.
>
> **BARBARA TUCHMAN,** *NEW YORK TIMES,*
> **FEBRUARY 2, 1989**

In the spirit of affectionate irreverence toward qualitative research, I consider writing as a *method of inquiry*, a way of finding out about yourself and your topic. Although we usually think about writing as a mode of "telling" about the social world, writing is not just a mopping-up activity at the end of a research project. Writing is also a way of "knowing"—a method of discovery and analysis. By writing in different ways, we discover new aspects of our topic and our relationship to it. Form and content are inseparable.

I have composed this chapter into two *equally* important, but differently formatted, sections. I emphasize the *equally* because the first section, an essay, has rhetorical advantages over its later-born sibling. In the first section, "Writing in Contexts," I position myself as a reader/writer of qualitative research. Then, I discuss (a) the historical roots of social scientific writing, including its dependence upon metaphor and prescribed formats, and (b) the postmodernist possibilities for qualitative writing, including experimental representation. In the second section, "Writing Practices," I offer a compendium of writing suggestions and exercises organized around topics in the text.

Necessarily, the chapter reflects my own process and preferences. I encourage researchers to explore their own processes and preferences through writing—and rewriting and rewriting. Writing from our Selves should strengthen the community of qualitative researchers and the individual voices within it, because we will be more fully present in our work, more honest, more engaged.

WRITING IN CONTEXTS

I have a confession to make. For 30 years, I have yawned my way through numerous supposedly exemplary qualitative studies. Countless numbers of texts have I abandoned half read, half scanned. I'll order a new book with

473

great anticipation—the topic is one I'm interested in, the author is someone I want to read—only to find the text boring. Recently, I have been "coming out" to colleagues and students about my secret displeasure with much of qualitative writing, only to find a community of like-minded discontents. Undergraduates are disappointed that sociology is not more interesting; graduate students confess that they do not finish reading what has been assigned because it is boring; and colleagues express relief to be at long last discussing qualitative research's own dirty little secret: Our empire is (partially) unclothed.

Speaking of this, and in this way, risks identifying my thoughts with that dreadful genre, *putdownism*. But that is not the emotional core or intention of my remarks. Rather, I want to raise a serious problem. Although our topics often are riveting and our research carefully executed, our books are underread. Unlike quantitative work, which can carry its meaning in its tables and summaries, qualitative work depends upon people's reading it. Just as a piece of literature is not equivalent to its "plot summary," qualitative research is not contained in its abstracts. Qualitative research has to be read, not scanned; its meaning is in the reading.

Qualitative work could be reaching wide and diverse audiences, not just devotees of the topic or the author. It seems foolish at best, and narcissistic and wholly self-absorbed at worst, to spend months or years doing research that ends up not being read and not making a difference to anything but the author's career. Can something be done? That is the question that drives this chapter: How do we create texts that are vital? That are attended to? That make a difference? One way to create those texts is to turn our attention to writing as a method of inquiry.

I write because I want to find something out. I write in order to learn something that I didn't know before I wrote it. I was taught, however, as perhaps you were, too, not to write until I knew what I wanted to say, until my points were organized and outlined. No surprise, this static writing model coheres with mechanistic scientism and quantitative research. But, I will argue, the model is itself a sociohistorical invention that reifies the static social world imagined by our nineteenth-century foreparents. The model has serious problems: It ignores the role of writing as a dynamic, creative process; it undermines the confidence of beginning qualitative researchers because their experience of research is inconsistent with the writing model; and it contributes to the flotilla of qualitative writing that is simply not interesting to read because adherence to the model requires writers to silence their own voices and to view themselves as contaminants.

Qualitative researchers commonly speak of the importance of the individual researcher's skills and aptitudes. The researcher—rather than the survey, the questionnaire, or the census tape—is the "instrument." The more honed the researcher, the greater the possibility of "good" research. Students are trained to observe, listen, question, and participate. Yet they are trained to conceptualize writing as "writing up" the research, rather than as a method of discovery. Almost unthinkingly, qualitative research training validates the mechanistic model of writing, even though that model shuts down the creativity and sensibilities of the individual researcher.

One reason, then, that our texts are boring is that our sense of self is diminished as we are homogenized through professional socialization, through rewards and punishments. Homogenization occurs through the suppression of individual voices. We have been encouraged to take on the omniscient voice of science, the view from everywhere. How do we put ourselves in our own texts, and with what consequences? How do we nurture our own individuality and at the same time lay claim to "knowing" something? These are both philosophically and practically difficult problems.

Postmodernist Context

We are fortunate, now, to be working in a postmodernist climate (see, e.g., Agger, 1990; Lehman, 1991; Lyotard, 1979). Postmodernism has affected all the disciplines and has gained ascendancy in the humanities, arts, philosophy, and the natural sciences. Disciplinary boundaries are regularly broken. Literary studies are about sociological questions; social scientists write fiction; sculptors do performance art; choreographers do sociology; and so on. (See, for literary criticism, Eagleton, 1983; Morris, 1988. For philosophy, see Hutcheon,1988; Rorty,1979; Nicholson,1990. For physics, Gleick, 1984. For mathematics, Kline, 1980. For arts, Trinh, 1989. For communications, Carey, 1989. For social sciences, Clifford & Marcus, 1986; Clough, 1992; Denzin, 1986, 1991; Fiske & Schweder, 1986; Geertz,1983; Marcus & Fischer,1986; Richardson,1991; Seidman & Wagner, 1991; Turner & Bruner, 1986. For education, Lather, 1991.)

The core of postmodernism is the *doubt* that any method or theory, discourse or genre, tradition or novelty, has a universal and general claim as the "right" or the privileged form of authoritative knowledge. Postmodernism *suspects* all truth claims of masking and serving particular interests in local, cultural, and political struggles. But postmodernism does not automatically reject conventional methods of knowing and telling as false or archaic. Rather, it opens those standard methods to inquiry and introduces new methods, which are also, then, subject to critique.

The postmodernist context of doubt distrusts all methods equally. No method has a privileged status. The superiority of "science" over "literature"— or, from another vantage point, "literature" over "science"—is challenged. But a postmodernist position does allow us to know "something" without claiming to know everything. Having a partial, local, historical knowledge is still knowing. In some ways, "knowing" is easier, however, because postmodernism recognizes the situational limitations of the knower. Qualitative writers are off the hook, so to speak. They don't have to try to play God, writing as disembodied omniscient narrators claiming universal, atemporal general knowledge; they can eschew the questionable metanarrative of scientific objectivity and still have plenty to say as situated speakers, subjectivities engaged in knowing/telling about the world as they perceive it.

A particular kind of postmodernist thinking that I have found especially helpful is *poststructuralism* (for an overview, see Weedon,1987). Poststructuralism links language, subjectivity, social organization, and power. The centerpiece is language. Language does not "reflect" social reality, but produces meaning, creates social reality. Different languages and different discourses within a given language divide up the world and give it meaning in ways that are not reducible to one another. Language is how social organization and power are defined and contested and the place where our sense of selves, our *subjectivity*, is constructed. Understanding language as competing discourses, competing ways of giving meaning and of organizing the world, makes language a site of exploration, struggle.

Language is not the result of one's individuality; rather, language constructs the individual's subjectivity in ways that are historically and locally specific. What something means to individuals is dependent on the discourses available to them. For example, being hit by one's spouse is experienced differently if it is thought of within the discourse of "normal marriage," "husband's rights," or "wife battering." If a woman sees male violence as "normal" or a "husband's right," then she is unlikely to see it as "wife battering," an illegitimate use of power that should not be tolerated. Experience is thus open to contradictory interpretations governed by social interests rather than objective truth. The individual is both site and subject of discursive struggles for identity. Because the individual is subject to multiple and competing discourses in many realms, one's subjectivity is shifting and contradictory, not stable, fixed, rigid.

Poststructuralism thus points to the *continual cocreation of self and social science*; they are known through each other. Knowing the Self and knowing "about" the subject are intertwined, partial, historical, local knowledges. Poststructuralism, then, permits—nay, invites—no, incites us to reflect upon our method and explore new ways of knowing.

Specifically, poststructuralism suggests two important things to qualitative writers: First, it directs us to understand ourselves reflexively as persons writing from particular positions at specific times, and second, it frees us from trying to write a single text in which everything is said to everyone. Nurturing our own voices releases the censorious hold of "science writing" on our consciousness, as well as the arrogance it fosters in our psyche. Writing is validated as a method of knowing.

Historical Contexts: Writing Conventions

Language, then, is a constitutive force, creating a particular view of reality and of the Self. Producing "things" always involves value—what to produce, what to name the productions, and what the relationship between the producers and the named things will be. Writing "things" is no exception. No textual staging is ever innocent (including this one). Styles of writing are neither fixed nor neutral but reflect the historically shifting domination of particular schools or paradigms.

Having some sense of the history of our writing practices helps us to demystify standard practices and loosen their hold on our psyches. Social scientific writing, like all other forms of writing, is a sociohistorical construction and, therefore, mutable.

Since the seventeenth century, the world of writing has been divided into two separate kinds: literary and scientific. Literature, from the seventeenth century onward, was associated with fiction, rhetoric, and subjectivity, whereas science was associated with fact, "plain language," and objectivity (Clifford, 1986, p. 5). Fiction was "false" because it invented reality, unlike science, which was "true," because it simply "reported" "objective" reality in a single, unambiguous voice.

During the eighteenth century, assaults upon literature intensified. John Locke cautioned adults to forgo figurative language lest the "conduit" between "things" and "thought" be obstructed. David Hume depicted poets as professional liars. Jeremy Bentham proposed that the ideal language would be one without words, only unambiguous symbols. Samuel Johnson's dictionary sought to fix "univocal meanings in perpetuity, much like the univocal meanings of standard arithmetic terms" (Levine, 1985, p. 4).

Into this linguistic world the Marquis de Condorcet introduced the term *social science*. He contended that "knowledge of the truth" would be "easy and error almost impossible" if one adopted precise language about moral and social issues (quoted in Levine, 1985, p. 6). By the nineteenth century, literature and science stood as two separate domains. Literature was aligned with "art" and "culture"; it contained the values of "taste, aesthetics, ethics, humanity, and morality" (Clifford, 1986, p. 6), and the rights to metaphoric and ambiguous language. Given to science was the belief that its words were objective, precise, unambiguous, noncontextual, nonmetaphoric.

But because literary writing was taking a second seat in importance, status, impact, and truth value to science, some literary writers attempted to make literature a part of science. By the late nineteenth century' "realism" dominated both science and fiction writing (Clough, 1992). Honoré de Balzac spearheaded the realism movement in literature. He viewed society as a "historical organism" with "social species" akin to "zoological species." Writers deserving of praise, he contended, must investigate "the reasons or causes" of "social effects"—the "first principles" upon which society is based (Balzac, 1842/1965, pp. 247–249). For Balzac, the novel was an "instrument of scientific inquiry" (Crawford, 1951, p. 7). Following Balzac's lead, Émile Zola argued for "naturalism" in literature. In his famous essay "The Novel as Social Science," he argued that the "return to nature, the naturalistic evolution which marks the century, drives little by little all the manifestation of human intelligence into the same scientific path." Literature is to be "governed by science" (Zola, 1880/1965, p. 271).

Throughout the twentieth century, crossovers—uneasy and easy, denied and acknowledged—have characterized the relationship between science and literary writing. Today, scholars in a host of disciplines are involved in tracing these relationships and in deconstructing scientific and literary writing (see Agger, 1989; Atkinson, 1990; Brodkey, 1987; Brown, 1977; Clough, 1992; Edmondson, 1984; Nelson, Megill, & McCloskey, 1987; Simons, 1990). Their deconstructive analyses concretely show how all disciplines have their own set of literary devices and rhetorical appeals, such as probability tables, archival records, and first-person accounts.

Each writing convention could be discussed at length, but I will discuss only two of them—metaphor and writing formats. I choose these because I believe they are good sites for experimenting with writing as a method of inquiry (see the section "Writing Practices," below). Thinking critically about social science's metaphors and writing formats helps break their brake on our pens and word processors.

METAPHOR.   A literary device, *metaphor*, is the backbone of social science writing. Like the spine, it bears weight, permits movement, is buried beneath the surface, and links parts together into a functional, coherent whole. As this metaphor about metaphor suggests, the essence of metaphor is the experiencing and understanding of one thing in terms of another. This is accomplished through comparison (e.g., "My love is like a green, green toad") or analogy (e.g., "the evening of life").

Social scientific writing uses metaphors at every "level." Social science depends upon a deep epistemic code regarding the way "that knowledge and understanding in general are figured" (Shapiro, 1985–1986, p. 198). Metaphors external to the particular piece of research prefigure the analysis with a "truth-value" code belonging to another domain (Jameson, 1981). For example, the use of *enlighten* to indicate imparting or gaining knowledge is a light-based metaphor, what Derrida (1982) refers to as the "heliocentric" view of knowledge, the passive receipt of rays. Immanent in these metaphors are philosophical and value commitments so entrenched and familiar that they can do their partisan work in the guise of neutrality, passing as literal.

Consider the following statements about theory (examples inspired by Lakoff & Johnson, 1980, p. 46):

- What is the *foundation* of your theory?
- Your theory needs *support*.
- Your position is *shaky*.
- Your argument is *falling apart*.
- Let's *construct* an argument.
- The *form* of your argument needs buttressing.
- Given your *framework*, no wonder your argument *fell apart*.

The italicized words express our customary, unconscious use of the metaphor "Theory is a building." The metaphor, moreover, structures the actions we take in theorizing and what we believe constitutes theory. We try to build a theoretical structure, which we then experience as a structure, which has a form and a foundation, which we then experience as an edifice, sometimes quite grand, sometimes in need of shoring up, and sometimes in need of dismantling or, more recently, deconstructing.

Metaphors are everywhere. Consider *functionalism, role* theory, *game* theory, *dramaturgical analogy, organicism, social evolutionism,* the social *system, ecology, labeling* theory, *equilibrium, human capital,* the *power elite, resource mobilization,* ethnic *insurgency, developing* countries, *stratification,* and *significance* tests. Metaphors organize sociological work and affect the interpretations of the "facts"; indeed, facts are interpretable ("make sense") only in terms of their place within a metaphoric structure. The "sense making" is always value constituting—making sense in a particular way, privileging one ordering of the "facts" over others.

WRITING FORMATS.   In addition to the metaphoric basis of social scientific writing, there are prescribed writing formats: How we are expected to write affects what we can write about. The referencing system in the social sciences, for example, discourages the use of footnotes, a place for secondary arguments, novel conjectures, and related ideas. Knowledge is constituted as "focused," "problem" (hypothesis) centered, "linear," straightforward. Other thoughts are extraneous. Inductively accomplished research is to be reported deductively; the argument is to be abstracted in 150 words or less; and researchers are to identify explicitly with a theoretical label. Each of these conventions favors—creates and sustains—a particular vision of what constitutes sociological knowledge. The conventions hold tremendous material and symbolic power over social scientists. Using them increases the probability of one's work being accepted into "core" social science journals, but is not *prima facie* evidence of greater—or lesser—truth value or significance than social science writing using other conventions.

Additional social science writing conventions have shaped ethnographies. Needful of distinguishing their work from travelers' and missionaries' reports as well as from imaginative writing, ethnographers adopted an impersonal, third-person voice to explain an "observed phenomenon" and trumpet the authenticity of their representations. John Van Maanen (1988) identifies four conventions used in traditional ethnographies, or what he calls "realist tales." First, there is *experiential author(ity)*. The author as an "I" is mostly absent from the text, which talks about the people studied; the author exists only in the preface, establishing "I was there" and "I'm a researcher" credentials. Second, there is *documentary style,* with a plethora of concrete, particular details that presume to represent the typical activity, pattern, or culture member. Third, *the culture members' point of view* is claimed to be presented through their accounts, quotations, explanations, language, cultural clichés, and so on. And fourth, the author claims *interpretive omnipotence.* The ethnographer's "no-nonsense" interpretations of the culture are claimed as valid. Many of the classic books in the social sciences are realist tales. These include Kai Erikson's *Everything in Its Path* (1976), William

Foote Whyte's *Street Corner Society* (1943), Elliot Liebow's *Tally's Corner* (1967), and Carol Stack's *All Our Kin* (1974).

Other genres of qualitative writing—such as texts based on life histories or in-depth interviews—have their own sets of traditional conventions (see Mischler, 1991; Richardson, 1990). In these traditional texts, the researcher proves his or her credentials in the introductory or methods section, and writes the body of the text as though the quotations and document snippets are naturally there, genuine evidence for the case being made, rather than selected, pruned, and spruced up for their textual appearance. Like ethnography, the assumption of scientific authority is rhetorically displayed in these qualitative texts. Examples of traditional "life-story" texts include Lillian Rubin's *Worlds of Pain* (1976), Sharon Kaufman's *The Ageless Self* (1986), and my own *The New Other Woman* (Richardson, 1985).

Experimental Writing

In the wake of feminist and postmodernist critiques of traditional qualitative writing practices, qualitative work has been appearing in new forms; genres are blurred, jumbled. I think of them as *experimental representations*. Because experiments are experimental, it is difficult to specify their conventions. One practice these experiments have in common, however, is the *violation of prescribed conventions*; they transgress the boundaries of social science writing genres.

Experimental representation is an emergent and transgressive phenomenon. Although some people are uncomfortable with it both as an idea and as a practice, I highly recommend experimental writing as a method of knowing. Because experimentation is taking place in (because of?) the postmodernist context, experimentation can be thought about within that frame. Working within the "ideology of doubt," experimental writers raise and display postmodernist issues. Chief among these are questions of how the author positions the Self as a knower and teller. For the experimental writer, these lead to the intertwined problems of subjectivity/authority/authorship/reflexivity, on the one hand, and representational form, on the other.

Postmodernism claims that writing is always partial, local, and situational, and that our Self is always present, no matter how much we try to suppress it—but only partially present, for in our writing we repress parts of ourselves, too. Working from that premise, we are freed to write material in a variety of ways: to tell and retell. There is no such thing as "getting it right," only "getting it" differently contoured and nuanced. When experimenting with form, ethnographers learn about the topic and about themselves what is unknowable, unimaginable, using prescribed writing formats. So, even if one chooses to write a final paper in a conventional form, experimenting with format is a practical and powerful way to expand one's interpretive skills and to make one's "old" materials "new."

We can deploy different forms for different audiences and different occasions. Some experimentation can be accomplished simply by writing the same piece of research for an academic audience, a trade book audience, and the popular press (see Richardson, 1990). The potential for alternative forms of representation, however, goes way beyond those stagings.

Social scientists are now writing "narratives of the self" (e.g., Ellis, 1992, 1993; Geertz, 1988; Kondo, 1990; Krieger, 1991; Ronai, 1992; Steedman, 1986; I. K. Zola, 1983), fiction (see Frohock, 1992; Stewart, 1989; Wolf, 1992), poetry (e.g., Brady, 1991; Diamond, 1981; Patai, 1988; Prattis, 1985; Richardson, 1992a), drama (Ellis & Bochner, 1992; Paget, 1990; Richardson, 1993; Richardson & Lockridge, 1991), "performance science" (McCall & Becker,1990), "polyvocal texts" (e.g., Butler & Rosenblum, 1991; Krieger, 1983; Schneider, 1991), "responsive readings" (see Richardson, 1992b), "aphorisms" (E. Rose, 1992), comedy and satire (e.g., Barley, 1986, 1988), visual presentations (e.g., Harper, 1987), mixed genres (e.g., Dorst, 1989; Fine, 1992; hooks, 1990; Lather, 1991; Linden, 1992; Pfohl, 1992; D. Rose, 1989; Stoller, 1989; Trinh, 1989; Ulmer, 1989; Walkerdine, 1990; Williams, 1991; Wolf, 1992), and more. It is beyond the scope of this chapter to outline or comment on each of these experimental forms. Instead, I will address a class of experimental genres that deploy literary devices to re-create lived experience and evoke emotional responses. I call these *evocative representations*. I resist providing the reader with snippets from these forms because snippets will not do them justice and because I hope readers will read and experiment for themselves. l do describe some texts, but I have no desire to valorize a new canon. Again, *process* rather than product is the purpose of this chapter.

Evocative experimental forms display interpretive frameworks that demand analysis of themselves as cultural products and as methods for rendering the sociological. Evocative representations are a striking way of seeing through and beyond sociological naturalisms. They are powerful tools in the "writing as analysis" tool chest. Casting sociology into evocative forms reveals the underlying labor of sociological production and its rhetoric, as well as its potential as a human endeavor, because evocative writing touches us where we live, in our bodies. Through it we can experience the self-reflexive and transformational process of self-creation. Trying out evocative forms, we relate differently to our material; we know it differently. We find ourselves attending to feelings, ambiguities, temporal sequences, blurred experiences, and so on; we struggle to find a textual place for ourselves and our doubts and uncertainties.

One form of evocative writing is the *narrative of the self*. This is a highly personalized, revealing text in which an author tells stories about his or her own lived experience. Using dramatic recall, strong metaphors, images, characters, unusual phrasings, puns, subtexts, and allusions, the writer constructs a sequence of events, a "plot," holding back on interpretation, asking the reader to "relive" the events emotionally with the writer. Narratives of the self do not read like traditional ethnography because they use the writing techniques of fiction. They are specific stories of particular events. Accuracy is not the issue; rather, narratives of the self seek to meet literary criteria of coherence, verisimilitude, and interest. Because narratives of the self are staged as imaginative renderings, they allow the field-worker to exaggerate, swagger, entertain, make a point without tedious documentation, relive the experience, and say what might be unsayable in other circumstances. Writing these frankly subjective narratives, ethnographers are somewhat relieved of the problems of speaking for the "Other," because they are the Other in their texts.

In *ethnographic fictional representations*, another evocative form, writers define their work as fiction, as products of the imagination. The writers are seeking a format in which to tell a "good story"; that story might be about the self, but more likely it is about the group or culture studied. In addition to the techniques used by self-narrators, ethnographic fiction writers draw upon other devices, such as flashback, flashforward, alternative points of view, deep characterization, tone shifts, synecdoche, dialogue, interior monologue, and, sometimes, even the omniscient narrator. The ethnographic setting encases the story, the cultural norms are seen through the characters, but the work is understood as fiction. Although writing up qualitative research as fiction frees the author from the constraints of science, competing with "real" fiction writers is chancy. And if the author wants the work to have an impact for social change, fiction may be a rhetorically poor way to stage the research. But it may just be a good way for the writer to see the material from different points of view.

A third evocative form is *poetic representation*. A poem, as Robert Frost articulates it, is "the shortest emotional distance between two points"—the speaker and the reader. Writing sociological interviews as poetry displays the role of the *prose trope* in constituting knowledge. When we read or hear poetry, we are continually nudged into recognizing that the text has been constructed. But all texts are constructed—prose ones, too; therefore, poetry helps problematize reliability, validity, and "truth."

When people talk, whether as conversants, storytellers, informants, or interviewees, their speech is closer to poetry than it is to sociological prose (Tedlock, 1983). Writing up interviews as poems honors the speaker's pauses, repetitions, alliterations, narrative strategies, rhythms, and so on. Poetry may actually better represent the speaker than the practice of quoting snippets in prose. Further, poetry's rhythms, silences, spaces, breath points, alliterations, meter, cadence, assonance, rhyme, and off-rhyme engage the listener's body, even when the mind resists and denies it. "Poetry is above all a concentration of the power of language which is the power of our ultimate relationship to everything in the universe. It is as if forces we can lay claim to in no other way become present to us in sensuous form" (DeShazer, 1986, p. 138). Settling words together in new configurations lets us hear, see, and feel the world in new dimensions. Poetry is thus a *practical* and *powerful* method for analyzing social worlds.

Ethnographic drama is a fourth evocative genre. Drama is a way of shaping an experience without losing the experience; it can blend realist, fictional, and poetic techniques; it can reconstruct the "sense" of an event from multiple "as-lived" perspectives; and it can give voice to what is unspoken, but present, such as "cancer," as portrayed in Paget's (1990) ethnographic drama, or abortion, as in Ellis and Bochner's (1992) drama. When the material to be displayed is intractable, unruly, multisited, and emotionally laden, drama is more likely to recapture the experience than is standard writing.

Constructing drama raises the postmodern debate about "oral" and "written" texts. Which comes first? Which one should be (is) privileged, and with what consequences? Why the bifurcation between "oral" and "written"? Originating in the lived experience, encoded as field notes, transformed into an ethnographic play, performed, tape-recorded, and then reedited for publication, the printed script might well be fancied the definitive or "valid" version, particularly by those who privilege the published over the "original" or the performance over the lived experience. What happens if we accept this validity claim? Dramatic construction provides multiple sites of invention and potential contestation for validity, the blurring of oral and written texts, rhetorical moves, ethical dilemmas, and authority/authorship. It doesn't just "talk about" these issues, it *is* these issues.

A last evocative form to consider is *mixed genres*. The scholar draws freely in his or her productions from literary, artistic, and scientific genres, often breaking the boundaries of each of those as well. In these productions, the scholar might have different "takes" on the same topic, what I think of as a postmodernist deconstruction of triangulation.

In traditionally staged research we valorize "triangulation" (for discussion of triangulation as method, see Denzin, 1978; for an example, see Statham, Richardson, & Cook,1991). In that process, a researcher deploys "different methods"—such as interviews, exploration of census data, and document checking—to "validate" findings. These methods, however, carry the *same domain* assumptions, including the assumption that there is a "fixed point" or "object" that can be triangulated. But in postmodernist mixed-genre texts, we do not triangulate; we *crystallize*. We recognize that there are far more than "three sides" from which to approach the world.

I propose that the central image for "validity" for postmodernist texts is not the triangle—a rigid, fixed, two-dimensional object. Rather, the central image is the crystal, which combines symmetry and substance with an infinite variety of shapes, substances, transmutations, multidimensionalities, and angles of approach. Crystals grow, change, alter, but are not amorphous.

Crystals are prisms that reflect externalities and refract within themselves, creating different colors, patterns, arrays, casting off in different directions. What we see depends upon our angle of repose. Not triangulation, crystallization. In postmodernist mixed-genre texts, we have moved from plane geometry to light theory, where light can be both waves and particles.

Crystallization, without losing structure, deconstructs the traditional idea of "validity" (we feel how there is no single truth, we see how texts validate themselves); and crystallization provides us with a deepened, complex, thoroughly partial, understanding of the topic. Paradoxically, we know more and doubt what we know.

We see this crystallization process in several recent books. Margery Wolf, in *A Thrice-Told Tale* (1992), takes the same event and tells it as fictional story, field notes, and a social scientific paper. John Stewart, in *Drinkers, Drummers and Decent Folk* (1989), writes poetry, fiction, ethnographic accounts, and field notes about Village Trinidad. Valerie Walkerdine's *Schoolgirl Fictions* (1990) develops/displays the theme that "masculinity and femininity are fictions which take on the status of fact" (p. xiii) by incorporating into the book journal entries, poems, essays, photographs of herself, drawings, cartoons, and annotated transcripts. Ruth Linden's *Making Stories, Making Selves: Feminist Reflections on the Holocaust* (1992) intertwines autobiography, academic writing, and survivors' stories in a Helen Hooven Santmyer Prize in Women's Studies book, which was her dissertation. Patti Lather's *Getting Smart: Feminist Research and Pedagogy with/in the Postmodern* (1991), a winner of the American Educational Studies Critics Choice book award, displays high theory and transcript, pedagogue and students. John Dorst's *The Written Suburb* (1989) presents a geographic site as site, image, idea, discourse, and an assemblage of texts.

In some mixed-genre productions, the writer/artist roams freely around topics, breaking our sense of the externality of topics, developing our sense of how topic and self are twin constructs. With the artful self in display, the issues of constructedness and authorial responsibility are profiled. Susan Krieger's *Social Science and the Self: Personal Essays on an Art Form* (1991) is a superb example. The book is "design oriented," reflecting Krieger's attachment to Pueblo potters and Georgia O'Keefe, and, as she says, it "looks more like a pot or a painting than a hypothesis" (p. 120). Trinh T. Minh-ha's *Woman, Native, Other* (1989) breaks down writing conventions within each of the essays that constitute the book, mixing poetry, self-reflection, feminist criticism, photographs, and quotations that help readers experience post-coloniality. John Van Maanen's *Tales of the Field* (1988) analyzes examples of realist, confessional, and impressionist narratives. Stephen Pfohl's *Death at the Parasite Cafe* (1992) employs collage strategies and synchronic juxtapositions, blurring critical theory and militant art forms. Anthologies also reflect these mixed genres. Carolyn Ellis and Michael Flaherty's *Investigating Subjectivity: Research on Lived Experience* (1992) is one example, and the series *Studies in Symbolic Interaction* is another.

Whither and Whence?

The contemporary postmodernist context in which we work as qualitative researchers is a propitious one. It provides an opportunity for us to review, critique, and re-vision writing. Although we are freer to present our texts in a variety of forms to diverse audiences, we have different constraints arising from self-consciousness about claims to authorship, authority, truth, validity, and reliability. Self-reflexivity unmasks complex political ideological agendas hidden in our writing. Truth claims are less easily validated now; desires to speak "for" others are suspect. The greater freedom to experiment with textual form, however, does not guarantee a better product. The opportunities for writing worthy texts—books and articles that are "good reads"—are multiple, exciting, and demanding. But the work is harder. The guarantees are fewer. There is a lot more for us to think about.

One thing for us to think about is whether writing experimentally for publication is a luxury open only to those who have academic sinecure. Can/should only the already tenured write in experimental modes? Are the tenured doing a disservice to students by introducing them to alternative forms of writing? Will teaching them hereticisms "deskill" them? Alienate them from their discipline? These are heady ethical, pedagogical, and practical questions. I struggle with them in my teaching, writing, and collegial discussions. I have no definitive answers, but I do have some thoughts on the issues.

First, there are many different avenues open for the sociological writer (see Denzin, 1994; Richardson, 1990). There is no single way—much less "right" way—of staging a text. The same material can be written for different audiences—positivists, interactionists, postmodernists, feminists, humanities professors, cultural studies scholars, policy makers, and so on. That is why it is called *material*. Like wet clay, it is there for us to shape. What are our purposes? What are our goals? Whom do we want to reach? What do we want to accomplish? If you are a graduate student, your likely purpose is the approval of your Ph.D. dissertation by your committee; if you are an untenured academic, your concern is probably the acceptance of an article by a mainline journal. Writing for those purposes is one way of knowing the material and one way of communicating with one kind of reader. Writing in standard ways does not prevent us from writing in other ways. We cannot write every way, for every purpose, at the same time. Most important, once we understand how to stage a dissertation or journal article rhetorically, we are more likely to get it accepted, get tenured, or the like. Even liberatory and radical messages can be published in conservative journals, if the writer follows the rules (Agger, 1990). Consequently, deconstructing traditional writing practices is a way of making writers more conscious of writing conventions, and, therefore, more competently able to meet them and to get their messages into mainstream social science.

Second, writing is a process of discovery. My purpose is not to turn us into poets, novelists, or dramatists—few of us will write well enough to succeed in those competitive fields. Most of us, like Poe, will be at best only almost poets. Rather, my intention is to encourage individuals to accept and nurture their own voices. The researcher's self-knowledge and knowledge of the topic develops through experimentation with point of view, tone, texture, sequencing, metaphor, and so on. The whole enterprise is demystified. Even the analysis paralysis that afflicts some readers of postmodernism is attenuated when writers view their work as process rather than as definitive representation.

Third, writing practices can improve traditional texts because writers relate more deeply and complexly to their materials. The writer understands the material in different ways. The deepened understanding of a Self deepens the text. The text will be less boring because the writer will be more consciously engaged in its production, more present to self and others.

Finally, contemporary experimental writing is a harbinger; qualitative research has been and will continue to be changed by and through it. High-grade journals—such as *The Sociological Quarterly, Symbolic Interaction, Journal of Contemporary Ethnography, and Qualitative Sociology*—already publish experimental pieces. The annual *Studies in Symbolic Interaction* showcases evocative writing. Presses such as Routledge, University of Chicago, University of Michigan, University of Indiana, University of Pennsylvania, Rutgers University Press, and Sage Publications regularly publish experimental work by both well-known and lesser-known authors. Traditional ethnographers write more reflexively and self-consciously (see Thorne, 1993). Even those opposed to postmodernism legitimate it through dialogue (Whyte, 1992). Throughout the social sciences, convention papers include transgressive presentations. Entire conferences are devoted to experimentation, such as the "Redesigning Ethnography" conference at the University of Colorado, which featured speakers from different disciplines. At least two well-respected interpretive programs—at the University of Illinois (under Norman Denzin) and at the University of South Florida (under Arthur Bochner and Carolyn Ellis)—are teaching about representational issues. All of these changes in academic practices are signs of *paradigm changes*.

In the 1950s, the sociology of science was a new, reflexively critical area. Today, the sociology of science undergirds theory, methods, and interdisciplinary "science studies." In the 1960s, "gender" emerged as a theoretical perspective. Today, gender studies is one of the largest (if not the largest) subfield in social sciences. In part, science studies and gender studies thrived because they identified normative assumptions of social science that falsely limited knowledge. They spoke "truly" to the everyday experiences of social scientists. The new areas hit us where we lived—in our work and in our bodies. They offered alternative perspectives for understanding the experienced world.

Today, the postmodernist critique is having the same impact on social sciences that science studies and gender have had, and for similar reasons. Postmodernism identifies unspecified assumptions that hinder us in our search for understanding "truly," and it offers alternative practices that work. We feel its "truth"—its moral, intellectual, aesthetic, emotional, intuitive, embodied, playful pull. Each researcher is likely to respond to that pull differently, which should lead to writing that is more diverse, more author centered, less boring, and humbler. This is a time of transition, a propitious moment. Where this experimentation will eventually take us, I do not know, but I do know that we cannot go back to where we were.

WRITING PRACTICES

Writing, the creative effort, should come first—at least for some part of every day of your life. It is a wonderful blessing if you will use it. You will become happier, more enlightened, alive, impassioned, light hearted and generous to everybody else. Even your health will improve. Colds will disappear and all the other ailments of discouragement and boredom. (Ueland, 1938/1987)

In what follows, I suggest some ways of using writing as a method of knowing. I have chosen exercises that have been productive for me and my students because they demystify writing, nurture the researcher's voice, and serve the process of discovery. I wish I could guarantee them to bring good health as well! The practices are organized around topics discussed in the text.

Metaphor

Using old, wornout metaphors, although easy and comfortable, after a while invites stodginess and stiffness. The stiffer you get, the less flexible you are. You invite being ignored. In less metaphoric terms, if your writing is clichéd, you will not stretch your own imagination (ouch! hear the cliché! hear the cliché of me pointing out the cliché!) and you will bore people.

1. In standard social scientific writing, the metaphor for theory is that it is a "building" (structure, foundation, construction, deconstruction, framework, form, and so on). Consider a different metaphor for theory, such as "theory as a tapestry" or "theory as an illness." Write a paragraph about theory using your metaphor. (See above for examples of "theory as building.") Do you "see" differently and "feel" differently about theorizing when you use an unusual metaphor?

2. Consider alternative sensory metaphors for "knowledge" other than the heliocentric one mentioned above. What happens when you rethink/ resense "knowledge" as situated in "voice"? In touch?

3. What metaphors do you use in your writing? Take a look at one of your papers and highlight your metaphors and images. What are you saying through metaphors that you did not realize you were saying? What are you reinscribing? Do you want to? Can you find different metaphors that change how you "see" ("feel"?) the material? Your relationship to it? Are your mixed metaphors pointing to confusion in yourself or to social science's glossing over of ideas?

4. Take a look at George Lakoff and Mark Johnson's *Metaphors We Live By* (1980). It is a wonderful book, a compendium of examples of metaphors in everyday life and how they affect our ways of perceiving, thinking, and acting. What everyday metaphors are shaping your knowing/writing? What alternative ones can you find?

Writing Formats

1. Choose a journal article that you think exemplifies the writing conventions of the mainstream of your discipline. Then write a two- to four-page analysis of that article. How is the argument staged? Who is the presumed audience? How does the paper inscribe ideology? How does the author claim "authority" over the material? Where is the author? Where are "you" in this paper? Who are the subjects and who are the objects of research here?

2. Choose a journal article that exemplifies excellence in qualitative research, and write a two- to four-page analysis of that article. How has tbe artide built upon normative social science writing? How is authority claimed? Where is the author? Where are "you" in the article? Who are the subjects and who are the objects of research here?

3. Choose a paper you have written for a class or that you have published that you think is pretty good. How did you follow the norms of your discipline? Were you conscious of doing so? How did you stage your paper? What parts did your professor/reviewer laud? How did you depend upon those norms to carry your argument? Did you elide over some difficult areas through vagueness, jargon, calls to authorities, or other rhetorical devices? What voices did you exclude in your writing? Who is the audience? Where are the subjects in the paper? Where are you? How do you feel about the paper now? About your process of constructing it?

Experimental Writing

An excellent way to open yourself up to experimental writing is to learn from creative writers. They have much to teach us about writing, and about ourselves. Even if you chose to write a fairly traditional text, the creative writing experience will enrich that text.

1. Join or start a writing group. This could be a writing support group, a creative writing group, a poetry group, a dissertation group, or another kind. (For dissertation and article writing, see Becker, 1986; Fox, 1985; Richardson, 1990; Wolcott, 1990.)

2. Work through a creative writing guidebook. Natalie Goldberg (1986, 1990), Rust Hills (1987), Brenda Ueland (1938/1987), and Deena Metzger (1993) all provide excellent guides.

3. Enroll in a creative writing workshop. This experience is valuable for both beginning and experienced researchers. Here is testimony from Barrie Thorne (personal communication, September 2, 1992), an experienced, compelling, and traditionally inclined ethnography writer: "Taking a weekly creative writing class from Deena Metzger has been an important part of this quest. She encourages connecting with the unconscious, reaching for unusual verbs and evocative concrete detail, and exploring the emotional side of writing."

4. Use "writing up" field notes as an opportunity to expand your writing vocabulary, habits of thought, and attentiveness to your senses, and as a bulwark against the censorious voice of science. Where better to develop your sense of self, your voice, than in the process of doing your research? Apply creative writing skills to your field notes. I turn again to Barrie

Thorne's description and testimony, not only because it is instructive, but because she writes within mainstream ethnographic tradition:

> Field notes . . . have a private and intimate character; one can innovate, make false starts, flare up with emotions without feeling an anonymous audience at one's shoulder. . . . As I write field notes, I push for full description, avoiding sociological jargon, staying close to what I saw, while letting my imagination roam around the event, searching for patterns and larger chains of significance (as they occur to me, I write these analytic hunches in capital letters in parentheses).

5. Some of us are more "choked" than Barrie Thorne in our field note writing, and we may need other devices to free our writing. For some it may mean rethinking what we have been taught about objectivity, science, and the ethnographic project. What works for me is to give different labels to different content. Building upon Glaser and Strauss's (1967) work, I use four categories, which you may find of value:

- *Observation notes* (ON): These are as concrete and detailed as I am able to make them. I want to think of them as fairly accurate renditions of what I see, hear, feel, taste, and so on.
- *Methodological notes* (MN): These are messages to myself regarding how to collect "data,"—who to talk to, what to wear, when to phone, and so on. I write a lot of these because I like methods, and I like to keep a process diary of my work.
- *Theoretical notes* (TN): These are hunches, hypotheses, poststructuralist connections, critiques of what I am doing/thinking/seeing. I like writing these because they open up my text—my field note text—to alternative interpretations and a critical epistemological stance. It is a way of keeping me from being hooked on my "take" on reality.
- *Personal notes* (PN): These are feelings statements about the research, the people I am talking to, myself doing the process, my doubts, my anxieties, my pleasures. I do no censoring here at all. I want all my feelings out on paper because I like them and because I know they are there anyway, affecting what/how I lay claim to knowing. Writing personal notes is a way for me to know myself better, a way of using writing as a method of inquiry into the self.

6. Keep a journal. In it, write about your feelings about your work. This not only frees up your writing, it becomes the "historical record" for writing a narrative of the self.

7. If you wish to experiment with evocative writing, a good place to begin is by transforming your field notes into drama. See what ethnographic rules you are using (such as fidelity to the speech of the participants, fidelity in the order of the speakers and events) and what literary ones you are invoking (such as limits on how long a speaker speaks, keeping the "plot" moving along, developing character through actions). Writing dramatic presentations accentuates ethical considerations. If you doubt that, contrast writ-

ing up an ethnographic event as a "typical" event with writing it as a play, with you and your hosts cast in roles that will be performed before others. Who has ownership of spoken words? How is authorship attributed? What if people don't like how they are characterized? Are courtesy norms being violated? Experiment here with both oral and written versions of your drama.

8. Experiment with transforming an in-depth interview into a poetic representation. Try using only the words, rhythms, figures of speech, breath points, pauses, syntax, and diction of the speaker. Where do you figure in the poem? What do you know about the interviewee and about yourself that you did not know before you wrote the poem? What poetic devices have you sacrificed in the name of science?

9. Experiment with writing narratives of the self. Keep in mind Barbara Tuchman's warning: "The writer's object is—or should be—to hold the reader's attention. . . . I want the reader to turn the page and keep on turning to the end. This is accomplished only when the narrative moves steadily ahead, not when it comes to a weary standstill, overlaced with every item uncovered in the research" (in the *New York Times*, February 2, 1989).

10. Consider a fieldwork setting. Consider the various subject positions you have or have had within it. For example, in a store you might be a salesclerk, customer, manager, feminist, capitalist, parent, child, and so on. Write about the setting (or an event in the setting) from several different subject positions. What do you "know" from the different positions? Next, let the different points of view dialogue with each other. What do you discover through these dialogues?

11. Consider a paper you have written (or your field notes). What has been left out? Who is not present in this text? Who has been repressed? Who has been marginalized? Rewrite the text from that point of view.

12. Write a story about the "self" from your point of view (such as something that happened in your family or in your seminar). Then, interview another participant (such as a family or seminar member) and have that person tell you his or her story of the event. See yourself as part of the other individual's story in the same way he or she is part of your story. How do you rewrite your story from the other person's point of view? (This is an exercise used by Carolyn Ellis.)

13. Collaborative writing is a way to see beyond one's own naturalisms of style and attitude. This is an exercise that I have used in my teaching, but it would be appropriate for a writing group as well. Each member writes a story of his or her life. It could be a feminist story, success story, quest story, cultural story, professional socialization story, realist tale, confessional tale, or whatever. All persons' stories are photocopied for the group. The group is then broken into subgroups (I prefer groups of three), and each subgroup collaborates on writing a new story, the collective story of its members. The collaboration can take any form: drama, poetry, fiction, narrative of the selves, realism, whatever the subgroup chooses. The collaboration is shared with the entire group. All members then write about their feelings about the collaboration and what happened to their stories, their lives, in the process.

14. A variant on exercise 13 is for each member to tape-record his or her own story and for other members to create a written text out of the oral one (a technique used by Art Bochner). The "originator" of the story then comments upon the others' telling. This is a good way to break down oral and written codes.

I hope these exercises are helpful. I hope you find new ways to experiment. I hope we all do.

> Willing is doing something you know already—there is no new imaginative understanding in it. And presently your soul gets frightfully sterile and dry because you are so quick, snappy, and efficient about doing one thing after another that you have no time for your own ideas to come in and develop and gently shine. (Ueland, 1938/1987, p. 29)

Happy writing and rewriting!

REFERENCES

Agger, B. 1989. *Reading science: A literary, political and sociological analysis.* Dix Hills, NY: General Hall.

Agger, B. 1990. *The decline of discourse: Reading, writing and resistance in postmodern capitalism.* Bristol, PA: Falmer.

Atkinson, P. A. 1990. *The ethnographic imagination: Textual constructions of reality.* London: Routledge.

Balzac, H. de. 1965. Preface to *The human comedy,* from *At the sign of the cat and racket* (C. Bell, Trans., 1897; original work published 1842), pp. 246–254 in *The Modern Tradition: Backgrounds of Modern Literature,* eds. R. Ellman & C. Feidelson, Jr. New York: Oxford University Press.

Barley, N. 1986. *Ceremony: An anthropologist's misadventures in the African bush.* New York: Henry Holt.

Barley, N. 1988. *Not a pleasant sport.* New York: Henry Holt.

Becker, H. S. 1986. *Writing for social scientists: How to finish your thesis, book, or article.* Chicago: University of Chicago Press.

Brady, I., ed. 1991. *Anthropological poetics.* Savage, MD: Rowman & Littlefield.

Brodkey, L. 1987. *Academic writing as social practice.* Philadelphia: Temple University Press.

Brown, R. H. 1977. *A poetic for sociology.* Cambridge: Cambridge University Press.

Butler, S., and B. Rosenblum. 1991. *Cancer in two voices.* San Francisco: Spinsters.

Carey, J. W. 1989. *Communication as culture: Essays on media and society.* Cambridge: Cambridge University Press.

Clifford, J. 1986. Introduction: Partial truths, pp. 1–26 in *Writing Culture: The Poetics and Politics of Ethnography,* eds. J. Clifford & G. E. Marcus. Berkeley: University of California Press.

Clifford, J., and G. E. Marcus, eds. 1986. *Writing culture: The poetics and politics of ethnography.* Berkeley: University of California Press.

Clough, P. T. 1992. *The end(s) of ethnography: From realism to social criticism.* Newbury Park, CA: Sage.

Crawford, M. A. 1951. Introduction. In *Old Goriot*, ed. H. de Balzac. NewYork: Penguin.

Denzin, N. K. 1978. *The research act.* New York: McGraw-Hill.

Denzin, N. K. 1986. A postmodern social theory. *Sociological Theory* 4: 194–204.

Denzin, N. K. 1991. *Images of postmodern society.* Newbury Park, CA: Sage.

Denzin, N. K. 1994. Evaluating qualitative research in the poststructural moment: The lessons James Joyce teaches us. *Qualitative Studies in Education* 7: 295–308.

Derrida, J. 1982. *The margins of philosophy* (A. Bass, Trans.). Chicago: University of Chicago Press.

DeShazer, M. K. 1986. *Inspiring women: Reimagining the muse.* New York: Pergamon.

Diamond, S. 1981. *Totems.* Barrytown, NY: Open Book.

Dorst, J. D. 1989. *The written suburb: An American site, an ethnographic dilemma.* Philadelphia: University of Pennsylvania Press.

Eagleton, T. 1983. *Literary theory: An introduction.* Minneapolis: University of Minnesota Press.

Edmondson, R. 1984. *Rhetoric in sociology.* London: Macmillan.

Ellis, C. (forthcoming). *Final negotiations.* Philadelphia: Temple University Press.

Ellis, C. 1993. Telling a story of sudden death. *Sociological Quarterly* 34: 711–730.

Ellis, C., and A. P. Bochner. 1992. Telling and performing personal stories: The constraints of choice in abortion, pp. 79–101 in *Investigating Subjectivity: Research on Lived Experience,* eds. C. Ellis & M. G. Flaherty. Newbury Park, CA: Sage.

Erikson, K. T. 1976. *Everything in its path: Destruction of the community in the Buffalo Creek flood.* New York: Simon & Schuster.

Fine, M. 1992. *Disruptive voices: The possibility of feminist research.* Ann Arbor: University of Michigan Press.

Fiske, D. W., and R. A. Schweder, eds. 1986. *Metatheory in social science: Pluralisms and subjectivities.* Chicago: University of Chicago Press.

Fox, M. F., ed. 1985. *Scholarly writing and publishing: Issues, problems, and solutions.* Boulder, CO: Westview.

Frohock, F. 1992. *Healing powers.* Chicago: University of Chicago Press.

Geertz, C. 1983. *Local knowledge: Further essays in interpretive anthropology.* New York: Basic Books.

Geertz, C. 1988. *Works and lives: The anthropologist as author.* Stanford, CA: Stanford University Press.

Glaser, B. G., and A. L. Strauss. 1967. *The discovery of grounded theory: Strategies for qualitative research.* Chicago: Aldine.

Gleick, J. 1984. Solving the mathematical riddle of chaos. *New York Times Magazine,* 10 June, 30-32.

Goldberg, N. 1986. *Writing down the bones: Freeing the writer within.* Boston: Shambala.

Goldberg, N. 1990. *Wild mind: Living the writer's life.* New York: Bantam.

Harper, D. 1987. *Working knowledge: Skill and community in a small shop.* Chicago: University of Chicago Press.

Hills, R. 1987. *Writing in general and the short story in particular.* Boston: Houghton Mifflin.

hooks, b. 1990. *Yearning: Race, gender, and cultural politics.* Boston: South End.

Hutcheon, L. 1988. *A poetics of postmodernism: History, theory and fiction.* New York: Routledge.

Jameson, F. 1981. *The political unconscious.* Ithaca, NY: Cornell University Press.

Kaufman, S. 1986. *The ageless self: Sources of meaning in later life.* Madison: University of Wisconsin Press.

Kline, M. 1980. *Mathematics: The loss of certainty.* New York: Oxford University Press.

Rondo, D. 1990. *Crafting selves.* Chicago: University of Chicago Press.

Krieger, S. 1983. *The mirror dance: Identity in a women's community.* Philadelphia: Temple University Press.

Krieger, S. 1991. *Social science and the self: Personal essays on an art form.* New Brunswick, NJ: Rutgers University Press.

Lakoff, G., & Johnson, M. (1980). *Metaphors we live by.* Chicago: University of Chicago Press.

Lather, P. 1991. *Getting smart: Feminist research and pedagogy within the postmodern.* New York: Routledge.

Lehman, D. 1991. *Signs of the times: Deconstruction and the fall of Paul de Man.* New York: Poseidon.

LeVine, D. N. 1985. *The flight from ambiguity: Essays in social and cultural theory.* Chicago: University of Chicago Press.

Liebow, E. 1967. *Tally's corner: A study of Negro street corner men.* Boston: Little, Brown.

Linden, R. R. 1992. *Making stories, making selves: Feminist reflections on the Holocaust.* Columbus: Ohio State University.

Lyotard, J.-F. 1979. *The postmodern condition: A report on knowledge* (G. Bennington & G. Masumi, Trans.). Minneapolis: University of Minnesota Press.

Marcus, G. E., and M. J. M. Fischer. 1986. *Anthropology as cultural critique: An experial moment in the human sciences.* Chicago: University of Chicago Press.

McCall, M., and H. S. Becker. 1990. Performance science. *Social Problems* 32: 117–132.

Metzger, D. 1993. *Writing for your life: A guide and companion to the inner worlds.* New York: HarperCollins.

Mischler, E. G. 1991. *Research interviewing: Context and narrative.* Cambridge, MA: Harvard University Press.

Morris, M. 1988. *The pirate's fiancee: Feminism, reading, and postmodernism.* NewYork: Verso.

Nelson, J. S., A. Megill, and D. N. McCloskey, eds. 1987. *The rhetoric of the human sciences: Language and argument in scholarship and human affairs.* Madison: University of Wisconsin Press.

Nicholson, L. J., ed. 1990. *Feminism/postmodernism.* New York: Routledge.

Paget, M. 1990. Performing the text. *Journal of Contemporary Ethnography* 19: 136–155.

Patai, D. 1988. Constructing a self: A Brazilian life story. *Feminist Studies* 14: 142–163.

Pfohl, S. J. 1992. *Death at the Parasite Café: Social science (fictions) and the postmodern.* New York: St. Martin's.

Prattis, l., ed. 1985. *Reflections: The anthropological muse.* Washington, DC: American Anthropological Association.

Richardson, L. 1985. *The new other woman: Contemporary single women in affairs with married men.* New York: Free Press.

Richardson, L. 1990. *Writing strategies: Reaching diverse audiences.* Newbury Park, CA: Sage.

Richardson, L. 1991. Postmodern social theory: Representational practices. *Sociological Theory* 9: 173–180.

Richardson, L. 1992a. The consequences of poetic representation: Writing the other, rewriting the self, pp. 125–140 in *Investigating Subjectivity: Research on Lived Experience*, C. Ellis & M. G. Flaherty. Newbury Park, CA: Sage.

Richardson, L. 1992b. Resisting resistance narratives: A representation for communication. *Studies in Symbolic Interaction* 13: 77–83.

Richardson, L. 1993. The case of the skipped line: Poetics, dramatics and transgressive validity. *Sociological Quarterly* 34: 695–710.

Richardson, L., and E. Lockridge. 1991. The sea monster: An "ethnographic drama." *Symbolic Interaction* 14: 335–340.

Ronai, C. R. 1992. The reflexive self through narrative: A night in the life of an erotic dancer/researcher, pp. 102–124 in *Investigating Subjectivity: Research on Lived Experience*, eds. C. Ellis & M. G. Flaherty. Newbury Park, CA: Sage.

Rorty, R. 1979. *Philosophy and the mirror of man*. Princeton, NJ: Princeton University Press.

Rose, D. 1989. *Patterns of American culture: Ethnography and estrangement*. Philadelphia: University of Pennsylvania Press.

Rose, E. 1992. *The werald*. Boulder, CO: Waiting Room.

Rubin, L. B. 1976. *Worlds of pain: Life in the working-class family*. New York: Basic Books.

Schneider, J. 1991. Troubles with textual authority in sociology. *Symbolic Interaction* 14: 295-320.

Seidman, S., and D. Wagner, eds. 1991. *Postmodernism and social theory*. New York: Basil Blackwell.

Shapiro, M. 1985-1986. Metaphor in the philosophy of the social sciences. *Cultural Critique* 2: 191–214.

Simons, H. W. 1990. *Rhetoric in the human sciences*. London: Sage.

Stack, C. B. 1974. *All our kin: Strategies for survival in a black community*. New York: Harper & Row.

Statham, A., L. Richardson, and J. A. Cook. 1991. *Gender and university teaching: A negotiated difference*. Albany: State University of New York Press.

Steedman, K. 1986. *Landscape for a good woman: A story of two lives*. New Brunswick, NJ: Rutgers University Press.

Stewart, J. 1989. *Drinkers, drummers and decent folk: Ethnographic narratives of Village Trinidad*. Albany: State University of New York.

Stoller, P. 1989. *Taste of ethnographic things: The senses in anthropology*. Philadelphia: University of Pennsylvania Press.

Tedlock, D. 1983. *The spoken word and the work of interpretation*. Philadelphia: University of Pennsylvania Press.

Thorne, B. 1993. *Gender play*. New Brunswick, NJ: Rutgers University Press.

Trinh T. M.-H. 1989. *Woman, native, other: Writing postcoloniality and feminism*. Bloomington: Indiana University Press.

Turner, V., and E. M. Bruner, eds. 1986. *The anthropology of experience*. Champaign-Urbana: University of Illinois Press.

Ueland, B. 1987. *If you want to write: A book about art, independence and spirit*. Saint Paul, MN: Graywolf. (Original work published 1938)

Ulmer, G. 1989. *Teletheory: Grammatology in the age of video*. New York: Routledge.

Van Maanen, J. 1988. *Tales of the field: On writing ethnography*. Chicago: University of Chicago Press.

Walkerdine, V. 1990. *Schoolgirl fictions*. London: Verso.

Weedon, C. 1987. *Feminist practice and poststructuralist theory*. New York: Basil Blackwell.

Whyte, W. F. 1943. *Street corner society: The social structure of an Italian slum*. Chicago: University of Chicago Press.

Whyte, W. F. 1992. In defense of *Street corner society. Journal of Contemporary Ethnography* 21: 52-68.

Williams, P. J. 1991. *The alchemy of race and rights: Diary of a law professor.* Cambridge, MA: Harvard University Press.

Wolf, M. 1992. *A thrice-told tale: Feminism, postmodernism, and ethnographic responsibility.* Stanford, CA: Stanford University Press.

Wolcott, H. F. 1990. *Writing up qualitative research.* Newbury Park, CA: Sage.

Zola, E. 1965. The novel as social science, pp. 270–289 in *The Modern Tradition: Backgrounds of Modern Literature,* eds. R. Ellman & C. Feidelson, Jr. New York: Oxford University Press. (Original work published 1880)

Zola, I. K. 1983. *Missing pieces: A chronicle of living with a disability.* Philadelphia: Temple University Press.

CHAPTER 23

Grounded Theory*

KATHY CHARMAZ

This chapter addresses the question that most beginning qualitative researchers ask: "How can I gather good data and then what should I do with
it?" Starting out on a qualitative research project is an exciting challenge but
can be a daunting venture. You can learn to do good qualitative research.
Sometimes students and professional social scientists alike believe that an
insightful qualitative study only results from the researcher's extraordinary
talents. They are wrong. Good qualitative research results from hard work
and systematic approaches. That means gathering enough data, synthesiz-
ing them, and making analytic sense of them.

Grounded theory methods provide a set of strategies for conducting rigorous qualitative research. These methods make the strategies of gifted qualitative researchers explicit and available to any diligent novice. Using
grounded theory methods expedites your research, enables you to develop
a cogent analysis, and prompts your excitement about and enjoyment of doing research. This chapter will help plan your data collection and give you
strategies for handling your data analysis.

In the following pages, I introduce the grounded theory method and
show how a novice can apply its basic procedures. Throughout the discussion, I illustrate points by drawing upon my recent social psychological
study of experiencing chronic illness. To begin, I provide a short discussion
of the logic of grounded theory to explain its basic premises and strategies
and to locate it within qualitative research more generally. Next, I discuss
data collection objectives and strategies to show how to generate useful data.
Then I move on to coding qualitative data and describe how creating categories early in the research shapes subsequent data collection. A discussion
of memo-writing follows because it is the crucial intermediate step between
data collection and writing drafts of papers. Last, I compare the procedures
of the grounded theory approach with traditional logico-deductive research
design to clarify their differences.

THE LOGIC OF GROUNDED THEORY

Defining Grounded Theory

What are grounded theory methods? They are a logically consistent set of
data collection and analytic procedures aimed to develop theory. Grounded

theory methods consist of a set of inductive strategies for analyzing data. That means you start with individual cases, incidents, or experiences and develop progressively more abstract conceptual categories to synthesize, to explain, and to understand your data and to identify patterned relationships within it. You begin with an area to study. Then, you build your theoretical analysis on what you discover is relevant in the actual worlds that you study within this area.

Grounded theory methods provide systematic procedures for shaping and handling rich qualitative materials although they may also be applied to quantitative data. Grounded theory methods allow novices and old hands alike to conduct qualitative research efficiently and effectively because these methods help in structuring and organizing data-gathering and analysis. The distinguishing characteristics of grounded theory methods (see Charmaz 1983; 1990; Glaser and Strauss 1967; Glaser 1978; 1992; Strauss 1987; Strauss and Corbin 1993) include (1) simultaneous involvement in data collection and analysis phases of research, (2) creation of analytic codes and categories developed from the data, not from preconceived hypotheses, (3) the development of middle-range theories to explain behavior and processes, (4) memo-making, i.e., writing analytic notes to explicate and fill out categories, the crucial intermediate step between coding data and writing first drafts of papers, (5) theoretical sampling, i.e., sampling for theory construction, not for representativeness of a given population, to check and refine the analyst's emerging conceptual categories, and (6) delay of the literature review. I will address each of these characteristics throughout the chapter. For the moment consider how these characteristics compare with other methods. Most fundamentally, grounded theory methods explicitly unite the research process with theoretical development. Hence, the rigid division of labor between empiricists and theorists breaks down. Similarly, grounded theory methods blur the often rigid boundaries between data collection and data analysis phases of research. Furthermore, grounded theory methods undermine definitions of qualitative analysis as only intuitive and impressionistic and of quantitative analysis as exclusively rigorous and systematic. A major contribution of grounded theory methods is that they provide rigorous procedures for researchers to check, refine, and develop their ideas and intuitions about the data. In addition, these methods enable the researcher to make conceptual sense of large amounts of data. A grounded theory analysis starts with data and remains close to the data. Levels of abstraction are built directly upon the data and are checked and refined by gathering further data (cf. Glaser, 1978; Glaser and Strauss 1967; Henwood and Pidgeon 1992; Strauss 1987). In this way, grounded theory studies yield dense conceptual analyses of empirical problems and worlds.

For what kinds of research questions are grounded theory methods appropriate? Barney G. Glaser and Anselm L. Strauss, the creators of grounded theory (1967; see also Glaser 1978; 1992; Strauss 1987; Strauss and Corbin 1990), might answer, 'Every kind.' Grounded theory methods are suitable for studying individual processes, inter-personal relations, and the reciprocal effects between individuals and larger social processes. For example, these methods are useful for studying typical social psychological topics such as motivation, personal experience, emotions, identity, attraction, prejudice, and inter-personal cooperation and conflict.

A Brief History of Grounded Theory Methods

Grounded theory methods emerged from the fruitful collaboration of sociologists Glaser and Strauss (1965; 1967; 1968; Strauss and Glaser 1970) during the 1960s. From its beginnings as a social science to the present, sociology has had a long qualitative tradition of ethnographic fieldwork and case studies (see, for example, Athens 1989; Biernacki 1986; Denzin 1987a; 1987b; Fine 1986; Glaser and Strauss 1965; 1968; Goffman 1959; 1961; 1963; Hochschild 1983; Lofland 1966; Park 1950; Park and Burgess 1921; Shaw 1930/1966; Snow and Anderson 1993; Thomas and Znaniecki 1918; Whyte 1943/1955). However, by the 1960s that tradition had eroded as sophisticated quantitative methods gained dominance and beliefs in scientific logic, objectivity, and truth supported and legitimized reducing qualities of human experience to quantifiable variables. Proponents of quantification relegated qualitative research to a preliminary exercise to refine quantitative instruments. Simultaneously, a growing division occurred between theory and research. At that time, theory informed quantitative research through the logico-deductive model of research, but this research seldom led to new theory construction.

Glaser and Strauss (1967) challenged (1) the arbitrary division of theory and research, (2) the prevailing view of qualitative research as primarily a precursor to more "rigorous" quantitative methods by claiming the legitimacy of qualitative work in its own right, (3) the belief that qualitative methods were impressionistic and unsystematic, (4) the separation of data collection and analysis phases of research, and (5) the assumption that qualitative research only produced descriptive case studies rather than theory development. They articulated explicit analytic procedures and research strategies that previously had remained implicit among qualitative researchers. Previously, qualitative researchers had taught generations of students through a combination of mentoring and direct field experience (cf. Rock 1979). Glaser and Strauss changed that oral tradition by offering a clear set of written guidelines for conducting qualitative research. The epistemological assumptions, logic, and systematic approach of grounded theory methods reflect Glaser's rigorous quantitative training at Columbia University. The intimate link to symbolic interaction (cf. Denzin 1995) stems from Strauss' training at the University of Chicago with Herbert Blumer and Robert Park. Through their influence, Strauss adopted both the pragmatist philosophical tradition with its emphasis on studying process, action, and meaning and the Chicago legacy of ethnographic research (see esp. Blumer 1969; Mead 1932; 1934; 1936; 1938; Park 1950; Park and Burgess 1921).

As Glaser and Strauss (1967) have argued, grounded theory methods cut across disciplines. These methods have been widely adopted in education, evaluation research, nursing, and organizational studies (see, for example, Chenitz and Swanson 1986; Guba and Lincoln 1989; Martin and Turner 1986; Price 1994; Stern 1994; Turner 1981). Some grounded theorists (Charmaz 1990; 1993; 1994; forthcoming) subscribe to interpretative views of the research process as created through the researcher's disciplinary and theoretical proclivities, relationships with respondents, and the interactional construction and rendering of the data. However, leading grounded theorists (Glaser and Strauss 1967; Strauss 1987; Strauss and Corbin 1990) portray their methods as compatible with traditional positivistic assumptions of an external reality that researchers can discover and record. As such, I have long argued that grounded theory can bridge traditional positivistic methods with interpretative methods in disciplines like psychology that embraced quantification (Charmaz 1986). Similarly, Rennie et al. (1988) propose that grounded theory methods can resolve the growing crisis in confidence concerning methods in psychology. To them, grounded theory offers systematic approaches for discovering significant aspects of human experience that remain inaccessible with traditional verification methods. Because grounded theory methods are designed to study processes, these methods enable psychologists to study the development, maintenance, and change of individual and interpersonal processes. By borrowing and adapting Glaser's (1978) emphasis on basic social and social psychological processes, psychologists can also gain a deeper understanding of psychological processes.

The Place of Grounded Theory in Qualitative Research

How then, do grounded theory methods fit with other qualitative research? Grounded theory methods bridge interpretative analyses with traditional positivist assumptions because they are used to discover research participants' meanings; they assume an empirical enterprise, and they provide a set of procedures to follow (see Bigus, Hadden, and Glaser 1994; Charmaz 1983; 1986; 1990; Glaser 1978; Glaser and Strauss 1967; Henwood and Pidgeon 1992; Rennie et al. 1988; Strauss 1987; Strauss and Corbin 1990). These methods can be employed in any approach ranging from highly interpretative to structured positivist analyses. Interpretative analyses attempt to describe, explain, and understand the lived experiences of a group of people (cf. Denzin 1989; Giorgi 1995). The interpretative tradition relies on knowledge from the "inside." That is, this tradition starts with and develops analyses from the point of view of the experiencing person (see also Bigus 1994). Such studies aim to capture the worlds of the people by describing their situations, thoughts, feelings and actions and by relying on portraying the research participants' lives and voices. Their concerns shape the direction and form of the research. The researcher seeks to learn how they construct their experience through their actions, intentions, beliefs, and feelings.

Positivistic assumptions, in contrast, lead to studies from the "outside," or those studies that rely substantially more on the observer's concerns and interpretations of the research participants' behavior. Positivistic assumptions rest on notions of a describable, predictable world that is external to the observer and from which discoveries may be made. Grounded theory methods can be used by researchers who subscribe to realist, objectivist assumptions as well as by those who subscribe to interpretative, constructionist perspectives. According to Van Maanen (1988), a realist rendering of the data is characterized by the absence of the author from most of the text and by the unquestioned authority of the researcher to portray the research participants, to document their lives minutely, and to interpret them and their worlds objectively. Van Maanen (1988) casts grounded theory studies into realist works whether they begin with interpretative or positivistic assumptions. He does so because grounded theorists typically provide dispassionate, objectivist accounts of their data and assume that by being objective observers that they will discover processes in an external world of their research participants that remains separate from themselves. Grounded theory works are *empirical* studies, whether their data sources are autobiographies, published accounts, public records, novels, intensive interviews, case studies, participant observer field notes, or personal journals. As a result, the empiricism inherent in grounded theory methods makes them less congenial to those postmodernists who advocate abandoning empirical research with thinking, feeling, acting human beings. These postmodernists may, however, be amenable to studying pre-established texts (see Clough 1992; Denzin 1991; 1992).

COLLECTING DATA

Generating Data

Simultaneous involvement in data collection and analysis means that the researcher's emerging analysis shapes his or her data collection procedures. Such simultaneous involvement focuses grounded theory studies and thus not only directs the researcher's efforts but also fosters his or her taking control of the data. The early analytic work leads the researcher subsequently to collect more data around emerging themes and questions. By simultaneously becoming involved in data collection and analysis, you will avoid the pitfall of amassing volumes of general, unfocused data that both overwhelm you and do not lead to anything new. If you already have collected a substantial amount of data, of course begin with it, but expect to collect additional data on your emerging analytic interests and themes. That way, you can follow up on topics that are explicit in one interview or observation and remain implicit or absent in others. For example, when a woman with multiple sclerosis remarked to me about having "bad days," she said, "I deal with time differently [during a bad day when she felt sick] and time has a different meaning to me" (Charmaz 1991a: 52). When we discussed meanings of time, I saw how she connected experiencing time with images of self.

On a bad day, her day shortened because all her daily routines—e.g., bathing, dressing, exercising, resting—lengthened substantially. As her daily routines stretched, her preferred self shrunk. Until I saw how she defined herself in relation to mundane daily routines, I had not asked interview questions that directly addressed this relationship.[1]

The hallmark of grounded theory studies consists of the researcher deriving his or her analytic categories directly from the data, not from preconceived concepts or hypotheses. Thus, grounded theory methods force the researcher to attend closely to what happens in the empirical world he or she studies. From a constructionist, interpretative perspective, the grounded theory researcher must then study the meanings, intentions, and actions of the research participants—whether he or she observes them directly, constructs life histories with them, engages them in intensive interviewing, or uses other materials such as clinical case histories or autobiographies.

From the beginning, the researcher actively constructs the data in concert with his or her participants (cf. Charmaz 1990). The first question the researcher must ask is "What is happening here?" (cf. Glaser 1978; 1992; Glaser and Strauss 1967). Perhaps in their enthusiasm to develop an inductive methodology that tightly linked emergent theory and data, Glaser and Strauss (1967; Glaser 1978) imply in their early works that the categories inhere in the data and may even leap out at him or her. I disagree. Rather, the categories reflect the interaction between the observer and observed. Certainly any observer's world view, disciplinary assumptions, theoretical proclivities, and research interests will influence his or her observations and emerging categories. Grounded theorists attempt to use their background assumptions, proclivities, and interests to sensitize them to look for certain issues and processes in their data. Consistent with Blumer's (1969) depiction of sensitizing concepts, grounded theorists often begin their studies with certain research interests and a set of general concepts.[2] For example, I began my studies of people with chronic illnesses with an interest in how they experienced time and how their experiences of illness affected them. My guiding interests brought concepts such as self-concept, identity, and duration into the study. But that was only the start. I used those concepts as *points of departure* to look at data, to listen to interviewees, and to think analytically about the data. Guiding interests and disciplinary perspectives should provide grounded theorists with such points of departure for developing, rather than limiting, their ideas. Then they develop specific concepts through the research process as they study their data.

What happens if the data do not illuminate the researcher's initial interests? Often, our research topics are sufficiently general that finding interesting data is not a problem, although we may find ourselves pursuing unanticipated leads. Grounded theorists evaluate the fit between their initial research interests and their emerging data. They do not force preconceived ideas and theories directly upon their data. Rather, they follow the leads that they define in the data, or design another way of collecting data to try to follow their initial interests. Thus, I started with research interests in time and self-concept but also pursued other topics that my respondents defined as crucial. To understand their concerns, I felt compelled to explore the problematics of disclosing illness, something I had not anticipated. As a result, I studied how, when, and why ill people talk about their conditions. Still, my interest in time alerted me to see if their modes of informing others about their conditions changed over time.

What kind of data should you gather for grounded theory studies? Rich, detailed data give you explicit materials with which to work. When I ask for rich, detailed data, I ask for full or 'thick' (Geertz 1973) written descriptions of events observed by researchers, extensive accounts of personal experience from respondents, and records that provide narratives of experience (such as transcribed tapes of therapy sessions). Participant observers' field notes, interviewers' transcriptions, patient autobiographies, student journals may all produce rich detailed data. It helps if you elaborate upon even detailed raw data such as the typed transcription of a patient conference. Hence, provide the context by describing the structure of the conference, the events leading up to it, the players in it, and their unstated concerns (if known or implicit). Similarly, it helps to place a personal interview into perspective by adding a description of the situation, the interaction, the person's affect, and your perception of how the interview went. In any case, you need thorough textual renderings of your materials so that you have data that you can study. In short, get as much material down on paper as possible.

Rich data affords views of human experience that etiquette, social conventions, and inaccessibility hide or minimize in ordinary discourse. Hence, rich data reveals thoughts, feelings, and actions as well as context and structure. In my research, I found that respondents' stories about illness often tumbled out non-stop. For example one woman stated:

> If you have lupus, I mean one day it's my liver; one day it's my joints; one day it's my head, and it's like people really think you're a hypochondriac if you keep complaining about different ailments. . . . It's like you don't want to say anything because people are going to start thinking, you know, 'God, don't go near her, all she is—is complaining about this.' And I think that's why I never say anything because I feel like everything I have is related one way or another to the lupus but most of the people don't know I have lupus, and even those that do are not going to believe that ten different ailments are the same thing. And I don't want anybody saying, you know, [that] they don't want to come around me because I complain. (Charmaz 1991a: 114–115)

Rich data afford the researcher a thorough knowledge of the empirical world or problem that he or she studies. By having this kind of data, grounded theorists therefore can more readily discern what participants mean and how they define their experiences. Thus, you begin your interpretations of the data from the respondent's point of view. What you see in the data may not exactly replicate what participants view as going on because you bring different perspectives and concerns to it. (Here I adopt the positivist assumption that it is the researcher's responsibility to find what is "there" and that it is possible to do so because we already share or can learn to share the language and meanings of those we study.) Having rich data means having detailed texts that allow you to trace events, delineate processes, and make comparisons.

The data gathered in grounded theory research becomes increasingly more focused because the researcher engages in data analysis while collecting data. That data analysis drives subsequent data collection. *The grounded theorist's simultaneous involvement in data-gathering and analysis is explicitly aimed toward developing theory.* Thus, an interviewer will adapt his or her initial interview guide to add areas to explore and to delete questions that have not been fruitful. Many qualitative methodologists refine their questions and follow leads (see Atkinson 1990; 1992; Berg 1989; Bogdan and Taylor 1975; Gubrium 1988; Hammersley and Atkinson 1983; Lofland 1976; Lofland and Lofland 1984; Seidman 1991; Smith 1995). But grounded theorists do so to develop their emerging theoretical categories (see Abrahamson and Mizrahi 1994; Biernacki 1986; Charmaz 1990; Glaser 1978; Henwood and Pidgeon 1992; Strauss 1987). Others may do so to gain 'thick description' (Geertz 1973) of concrete behavior without necessarily looking for thick description that fills out, extends, or refines theoretical concepts or enables the researcher to make theoretical connections. In contrast, grounded theorists ask theoretical questions of their thick description. For example, I first became aware of respondents' difficulties about disclosing illness fifteen years ago when I interviewed several young adults who agonized over telling roommates, acquaintances, and dates about their conditions. Rather than only obtaining thick description about these difficulties in disclosing, I began to ask myself analytical questions about disclosing as a process and then gathered data that illuminated that process. Among these questions included:

1. What are the properties of disclosing?
2. Which social psychological conditions foster disclosing? Which inhibit it?
3. How does disclosing compare with other forms of telling?
4. How, if at all, does disclosing change after the person becomes accustomed to his or her diagnosis?
5. What strategies, if any, do people use to disclose? When do they use them?

Despite its analytic thrust, grounded theory researchers can gain both thick description and theoretical development by listening closely to their respondents, attempting to learn the unstated or assumed meanings of their statements, and shaping their emerging research questions to obtain data that illuminates their theoretical categories.

Making Meanings Explicit

Grounded theorists aim to analyze processes in their data and thus, aim to move away from static analyses. Our emphasis on what people are doing also leads to understanding multiple layers of meanings of their actions. These layers could include the person's (1) stated explanation of his or her action, (2) unstated assumptions about it, (3) intentions for engaging in it, (4) effects on others, and (5) consequences for further individual action and inter-personal relations. Throughout the research process, looking at action in relation to meaning helps the researcher to obtain thick description and to develop categories. How does the researcher study meaning?

One view held by some grounded theorists is that meanings can readily be discovered in the research setting. Glaser (1992) states that the significant issues in the field setting and, therefore, the significant data, will be readily apparent to the researcher. He believes that anything other than that preconceives the ensuing research. Unlike Glaser, I assume that the interaction between the researcher and the researched *produces* the data and, therefore, the meanings that the researcher observes and defines. A researcher has topics to pursue and research participants' have goals, thoughts, feelings and actions. Your research questions and mode of inquiry will shape your subsequent data and analysis. That is why you must become self-aware about why and how you gather your data. You can learn to sense when you are gathering rich, useful data that does not undermine or demean your respondent(s). Not surprisingly then, I believe the grounded theory method works best when the grounded theorist engages in the data collection as well as the data analysis phases of research. That way, you can explore nuances of meaning and process that hired hands might easily miss.

Certainly respondents' stories may tumble out or the main process in an observational setting may jump out at you. But sometimes, neither are the stories so forthcoming nor is the main process so obvious. Even if they are, the researcher may need to do more work to discover the subtlety and complexity of respondents' intentions and actions. Closer study and often direct questioning is needed. For example, we do not have a highly developed language with which to talk about time. Thus, many of my research participants' attitudes toward and actions concerning time were unspoken and taken for granted. Yet their stories about illness often were clearly located in conceptions of time and implicitly referred to qualities of experienced time. For example, the woman's statement above referred to the quality and unevenness of her days. If the researcher plans to explore such areas, then he or she often needs to devise ways to make relevant observations or to construct questions that will foster pertinent responses. To illustrate, I asked my respondents questions like "As you look back on your illness, which events stand out in your mind?" "What is a typical weekday like for you?" Glaser (1992) might say I force the data here by asking preconceived questions of it. Instead, I *generate* data by investigating aspects of life that the research participant takes for granted. At whatever level you attend to your participants' meanings, intentions and actions, you can create a coherent analysis by using grounded theory methods. Hence, the method is useful for fact-finding descriptive studies as well as more conceptually developed theoretical statements.

Perhaps the most important basic rule for a grounded theorist is *Study your emerging data* (Charmaz 1983; Glaser 1978). By studying your data you will become much more aware of your respondents' implicit meanings and taken-for-granted concerns. As a novice, you can best study your data from the very start by transcribing your audio-tapes yourself or through writing your own field notes, rather than say, dictating them to someone else. By studying your data, you learn nuances of your research participants' language and meanings. Thus, you learn to define the directions where your data can take you. Studying interview audio-tapes, for example, prompts you to attend closely to your respondents' feelings and views. Charles Horton Cooley (1902) pointed out that we live in the minds of others and they live in ours. Your respondents will live in your mind as you listen carefully over and over to what they say. For example, one student in my class remarked,

> What an impact the words had on me when I sat home alone transcribing the tapes. I was more able to hear and feel what these women were saying to me. I realized how, at times, I was preoccupied with thoughts of what my next question was, how my eye contact was, or hoping we were speaking loud enough for the tape-recorder (Charmaz 1991b: 393).

Paying close attention to respondents' language can help you bridge your research participants' lived experience with your research questions. To do so, you should avoid taking for granted that you share the same meanings as the respondent. For example, my respondents with chronic illnesses often talked about having "good days" and "bad days." Everyone has good days and bad days whether they are talking about work, child care, school, or doing research. As a researcher, however, you cannot assume that your views of good days and bad days mean the same thing as your respondents'. So I probed further and asked more questions around my respondents' taken for granted meanings of good and bad days (cf. Smith 1995). I asked questions such as "What does a good day mean to you?" "Could you describe what a bad day is?" "What kinds of things do you do on a good day?" "How do these activities compare with those on a bad day?" I discovered that good days mean "minimal intrusiveness of illness, maximal control over mind, body, and actions, and greater choice of activities" (Charmaz 1991a: 50). The meaning of good days also extends to increased temporal and spatial horizons, to the quality of the day and to realizing the self one wishes to be. But had I not followed up and asked respondents about the meanings of these terms, their properties would have remained implicit.

Certainly starting the research with strong data gathering skills helps. The skilled interviewer or observer will know when to ask more questions or make more focused observations. Nevertheless, novice researchers can make remarkable gains in skill during a brief time by attending closely to their methods and by studying their data. By gathering rich data and by making meanings explicit, you will have solid material with which to create your analysis.

CODING THE DATA

The first major analytic phase of the research consists of coding the data. In short, coding is the process of defining what the data is all about. Unlike quantitative coding that means applying preconceived codes (all planned before the researcher even collects data) to the data, qualitative grounded theory coding means *creating* the codes as you study your data. The codes emerge as you study your data. By studying your data, you again interact with it and ask questions of it. (Thus, the interactive nature of grounded theory research is not limited to data collection, but also includes the analytic work.) As a result, the coding process may take you into unforeseen areas and research questions.

Coding is the pivotal link between collecting data and developing an emergent theory to explain this data. The crucial phase of coding leads directly to developing theoretical categories, some of which you may define in your initial codes. To begin your grounded theory analysis, start your initial coding by examining each line of data and defining the actions or events that you see as occurring in it or as represented by it. Nonetheless, line-by-line coding means naming each line of data (see esp. Glaser 1978). Hence, line-by-line coding helps you begin to take an analytic stance toward your work. Line-by-line coding keeps you close to your data. You have to study your data to arrive at codes. Through line-by-line coding, you begin to build your analysis from the ground up without taking off on theoretical flights of fancy (Charmaz 1990). Line-by-line coding also helps you to refrain from imputing your motives, fears, or unresolved personal issues to your respondents and to your collected data. Some years ago, a young man in my undergraduate seminar conducted research on adaptation to disability. He had become paraplegic himself when he was hit by a car while bicycling. His ten in-depth interviews were filled with stories of courage, hope, and innovation. His analysis of them was a narrative of grief, anger, and loss. When I noted that his analysis did not reflect his collected material, he began to realize how his feelings colored his perceptions of other people's disabilities. His was an important realization. However, had he assiduously done line-by-line coding he might have arrived at it before he handed in his paper.

From the standpoint of grounded theory, each idea should earn its way into your analysis (Glaser 1978). If you apply concepts from your discipline, you must be self-critical to ensure that these concepts work. Do these concepts help you to understand and to explicate what is happening in this line of data? If they do not, use other terms that do.

Line-by-line coding forces you to think about the material in new ways that may differ from your research participants' interpretations. Thomas (1993) states that the researcher must take the familiar, routine, and mundane and make it unfamiliar and new. Line-by-line coding helps you to see the familiar in new light. It also helps you gain sufficient distance from your and your participants' taken for granted assumptions about the material so that you *can* see it in new light.

If your codes take another view of a process, action or belief than that of your respondent(s), note that. You have to make analytic sense of the material rather than viewing it as say, only a sequence of events or as description. Your respondent may not. How do you make analytic sense of the rich stories and descriptions you are compiling? First, look for and identify what you see happening in the data. Some basic questions may help:

1. What is going on?
2. What are people doing?
3. What is the person saying?
4. What do these actions and statements take for granted?
5. How do structure and context serve to support, maintain, impede or change these actions and statements?

Try to frame your codes in as specific terms as possible. Make your codes active. By being specific and active you will begin to see processes in the data that otherwise likely remain implicit. Glaser and Strauss (1967; Glaser 1978; 1992) assume that any observer will find the most significant processes. Perhaps. But what you define in the data also relies in part upon the perspectives that you bring to it. Rather than seeing your perspectives as truth, try to see them as representing one view among many. That way, you will become more aware of the concepts that you employ. For example, try not to assume that respondents repress or deny significant "facts" about their lives. Instead, look for your respondents' understanding of their situations before you judge their attitudes and actions through the assumptions of your perspective. If afterwards you still invoke previously held perspectives as codes, then you will use them more consciously rather than merely automatically. Of course, observers do vary on the codes that they identify, depending on their training and research interests. In the example of line-by line coding below, my interest in time and self-concept comes through in the first two codes:

Line by Line Coding

shifting symptoms, having	If you have lupus, I mean one day it's my liver;
inconsistent days	one day it's my joints; one day it's my head, and
interpreting images of self	it's like people really think you're a
given by others	hypochondriac if you keep complaining about
avoiding disclosure	different ailments. . . . It's like you don't want to
	say anything because people are going to start
predicting rejection	thinking, you know, "God, don't go near her, all
keeping others unaware	she is—is complaining about this." And I think
seeing symptoms as	that's why I never say anything because I feel
connected	like everything I have is related one way or
having others unaware	another to the lupus but most of the people don't
anticipating disbelief	know I have lupus, and even those that do are not
controlling others' views	going to believe that ten different ailments are the
avoiding stigma	same thing. And I don't want anybody saying,
assessing potential losses	you know, [that] they don't want to come around
and risks of disclosing	me because I complain.

Initial codes often range widely across a variety of topics. Because even a short statement or excerpt may address several points, a researcher could use it to illustrate several different categories. I could use the excerpt above to show how avoiding disclosure serves to control identity. I could also use it to show either how a respondent views his or her illness as inexplicable to others or how each day is unpredictable. When seen from the view of multiple interviews, the excerpt reveals the beginnings of becoming progressively more socially and emotionally isolated. Not telling others about illness leads to withdrawing when ill. Most importantly from a grounded theory perspective, initial codes help you to break the data into categories and begin to see processes. Line-by-line coding frees you from 'going native,' or from becoming so immersed in your respondent's categories or world view that you fail to look at your data critically and analytically. Being critical about your data does not necessarily mean that you are critical of your research participants. Instead, being critical forces you to ask *yourself* questions about your data. Such questions include:

1. What process is at issue here?
2. Under which conditions does this process develop?
3. How does the research participant(s) think, feel, and act while involved in this process?
4. When, why, and how does the process change?
5. What are the consequences of the process?

Line-by-line coding helps you to make decisions about what kinds of data you need to collect next. Thus, you begin to distill the data and frame your inquiry from very early in the data collection. Your line-by-line coding gives you leads to pursue. To illustrate, you may identify an important process in your fifteenth interview. You can go back to your first respondents and see if that process explains events and experiences in their lives or seek new respondents. Hence, your data collection becomes more focused as does your coding.

Focused coding refers to taking earlier codes that continually reappear in your initial coding and using those codes to sift through large amounts of data. Thus, focused coding is less open-ended and more directed than line-by-line coding. It is also considerably more selective and more conceptual (Charmaz 1983; Glaser 1978). Here, you take a limited number of interesting line-by-line codes and you apply them to large amounts of data. By the time you engage in focused coding, you have decided which of your earlier codes make the most analytic sense and categorize your data most accurately and completely. Yet moving to focused coding is not entirely a linear process. As you gather more data, you will find that some respondents or events make explicit what was implicit in earlier respondents' statements or prior events. This kind of 'Aha! Now I understand,' experience prompts you to return to your earlier data and study it with a fresh look. It also may prompt you to return to an earlier respondent to explore an event or issue that you may have glossed over before or that may have been too implicit or unstated to see.

In the example below, I select the codes, 'avoiding disclosure' and "assessing potential losses and risks of disclosing" to capture, synthesize, and understand the main themes in the statement. Again, I try to keep the codes active and close to the data:

Focused Coding

	If you have lupus, I mean one day it's my liver; one day it's my joints; one day it's my head, and it's like people really think you're a hypochondriac if you keep complaining about different ailments. . . . It's like you
avoiding disclosure	don't want to say anything because people are going to start thinking, you know, "God, don't go near her, all she is—is complaining about this." And I think that's why I never say anything because I feel like everything I have is related one way or another to the lupus but most of the people don't know I have lupus, and even those that do are not going to believe that ten different
assessing potential	ailments are the same thing. And I don't want anybody
losses and risks	saying, you know, [that] they don't want to come
of disclosing	around me because I complain.

Focused coding allows you to create and to try out categories for capturing your data. A category is part of your developing analytic framework. By categorizing, you select certain codes as having overriding significance in explicating events or processes in your data. A category may subsume common themes and patterns in several codes. For example, my category of 'keeping illness contained' included 'packaging illness,' i.e., treating it 'as if it is controlled, delimited, and confined to specific realms, such as private life,' and 'passing,' i.e., 'concealing illness, maintaining a conventional self-presentation, and performing like unimpaired peers' (Charmaz 1991a: 66–68). Again, make your categories as conceptual as possible while simultaneously remaining true to and consistent with your data. I try to make my focused codes active (to reflect what people are doing or what is happening) and brief so that I can view them as potential categories. By keeping codes active, you can see processes more readily. By keeping your focused codes as succinct as possible, you have a head start on creating sharp, clear categories. By raising a code to the level of a category, you treat it more conceptually and analytically. Thus, you go beyond using the code as a descriptive tool to view and synthesize data.

The emphasis on process in grounded theory starts with a substantive process that you develop from your codes. 'Keeping illness contained' and 'packaging illness' above are two such processes. As they work with their data, grounded theorists try to aim for defining generic processes. The two processes above are imbedded in more fundamental, generic processes of personal information control about illness and about choices in disclosing that information. For sociologists, generic processes are basic to social life; for psychologists, generic processes are fundamental for psychological existence. A generic process cuts across different empirical settings and problems; it can be applied to varied substantive areas (Bigus, Hadden and Glaser 1994; Prus 1987; Wiseman 1994). Thus, the grounded theorist can elaborate and refine the generic process by gathering more data from the diverse arenas where the process is evident. For example, personal information control and choices in disclosing are often problematic for homosexuals, sexual abuse survivors, drug-users, and ex-convicts as well as for people with chronic conditions. By concentrating on developing the generic process, you will more readily discover its properties, specify the conditions under which it develops, and look for its consequences.

As you raise the code to a category, you begin (1) to explicate its properties, (2) to specify conditions under which it arises, is maintained, and changes, (3) to describe its consequences, and (4) to show how this category relates to other categories (cf. Charmaz 1983; 1990; Glaser 1978; Glaser and Strauss 1967). You do all this work in your written memos that I outline below.

Categories may be *in vivo* codes that you take directly from your respondents' discourse or they may represent your theoretical or substantive definition of what is happening in the data. For example, my terms "good days and bad days" and "living one day at a time" came directly from my respondents' voices. In contrast, my categories "recapturing the past" and "time in immersion and immersion in time" reflect my theoretical definitions of actions and events. Further, categories such as "pulling in," "facing dependency," and "making trade-offs" address my respondents' substantive realities of grappling with a serious illness. I created these codes and used them as categories but they reflect my respondents' concerns and actions. Novice researchers may find that they rely most on *in vivo* and substantive codes. Doing so nets a grounded analysis more than a theory. Nonetheless, studying how these codes fit together in categories can help you treat them more theoretically.

As you engage in focused coding, you attempt to build and to clarify your category by examining all the data it covers and by identifying the variations within it and between other categories. You also will become aware of gaps in your analysis. For example, I developed my category of "existing from day to day" when I realized that living one day at a time did not fully cover impoverished people's level of desperation. The finished narrative reads:

> Existing from day to day occurs when a person plummets into continued crises that rip life apart. It reflects a loss of control of health and the wherewithal to keep life together.
>
> Existing from day to day means constant struggle for daily survival. Poverty and lack of support contribute to and complicate that struggle. Hence, poor and isolated people usually plummet further and faster than

affluent individuals with concerned families. Loss of control extends to being unable to obtain necessities—food, shelter, heat, medical care.

The struggle to exist keeps people in the present, especially if they have continued problems in getting the basic necessities that middle-class adults take for granted. Yet other problems can assume much greater significance for these people than their illness—a violent husband, a runaway child, an alcoholic spouse, the overdue rent.

Living one day at a time differs from existing from day to day. Living one day at a time provides a strategy for controlling emotions, managing life, dimming the future, and getting through a troublesome period. It involves managing stress, illness, or regimen, and dealing with these things each day to control them as best as one can. It means concentrating on the here and now and relinquishing other goals, pursuits, and obligations. (Charmaz 1991a:185)

Note the comparisons between the two categories above. To generate categories through focused coding, you need to make comparisons between data, incidents, contexts, and concepts. It helps to make the following comparisons: (1) comparing different people (such as their beliefs, situations, actions, accounts, or experiences), (2) comparing data from the same individuals with themselves at different points in time, and (3) comparing categories in the data with other categories (cf. Charmaz 1983; Glaser 1978). As I compared different people's experiences, I realized that some people's situations forced them into the present. I then started to look at how my rendering of living one day at a time did not apply to them. I reviewed earlier interviews and began to look for published accounts that might clarify the comparison. As is evident in the distinctions between these two categories above, focused coding prompts you to begin to see the relationships and patterns between categories.

MEMO-WRITING

Memo-writing is the intermediate step between coding and the first draft of your completed analysis. Memo-writing helps you to elaborate processes, assumptions, and actions that are subsumed under your code. When memo-writing, you begin to look at your coding as processes to explore rather than as solely ways to sort data into topics. Making your codes as active as possible from the start enables you to define how various categories are connected in an overall process. Many qualitative researchers who do not write memos become lost in mountains of data and cannot make sense of them.

Grounded theory methods aim toward discovering and defining processes. In that sense, these researchers look for patterns, even when focusing on a single case or individual (see Strauss and Glaser 1970). Because they stress identifying patterns, grounded theorists typically use their respondents' stories to illustrate points—rather than to provide complete portrayals of their lives.[3] Bring your raw data right into your memo so that you preserve the most telling examples of your ideas from the very start of your analytic work. Provide enough verbatim material to ground the abstract analysis fully. By bringing verbatim material from different sources into your memo-writing, you can more readily make precise comparisons. Thus, memo-writing helps you to go beyond individual cases and to define patterns.

Memo-writing consists of taking your categories apart by breaking them into their components. Define your category as carefully as possible. That means you identify its properties or characteristics, look for its underlying assumptions, and show how and when the category develops and changes. To illustrate, I found that people frequently referred to living one day at a time when they suffered a medical crisis or faced continued uncertainty. So I began to ask questions about what living one day at a time was like for them. From their responses as well as from published autobiographical accounts, I began to define the category and its characteristics. The term "living one day at a time" condenses a whole series of implicit meanings and assumptions. It becomes a strategy for handling unruly feelings, for exerting some control over a life now uncontrollable, for facing uncertainty, and for handling a conceivably foreshortened future. Memo-writing spurs you to start digging into implicit, unstated, and condensed meanings.

You probably wonder when should you start writing memos. Begin as soon as you have some interesting ideas and categories that you wish to pursue. If you are at a loss about what to write about, look for the codes that you have used repeatedly in your earlier data collection. Then start elaborating on these codes. Keep collecting data, keep coding, and keep refining your ideas through writing more and further developed memos. Some researchers who use grounded theory methods discover a few interesting findings early in their data collection and then truncate their research. They do not achieve the 'intimate familiarity' that Lofland and Lofland (1984) avow meets the standards for good qualitative research. You need to show that you have covered your topic in depth by having sufficient cases to explore and to elaborate your categories fully.[4]

Memo-writing should free you to explore your ideas about your categories. Treat memos as preliminary, partial, and immanently correctable. Just note where you are on firm ground and where you are making conjectures. Then go back to the field to check your conjectures. Memo-writing is much like free-writing or pre-writing (Elbow 1981; see also Becker 1986). You can do it for your eyes only and use it to help you think about your data. Do not worry about verb tense, overuse of prepositional phrases, or lengthy sentences at this point. Just get your ideas down as quickly and clearly as you can. You are writing to render the data, not to communicate it to an audience. Later, after you turn your memo into a section of a paper, you can start revising the material to make it accessible to a reader. Writing memos quickly without editing them gives you the added bonus of developing and preserving your own voice in your writing. Hence, your writing will read as if a living, thinking, feeling human being wrote it rather than a dead social scientist. From the beginning, you can write memos at different levels of abstraction—from the concrete to the highly theoretical. Some of your memos will find their way directly into your first draft of your analysis. Others you can set aside to develop later into a different focus.

Much of your memo-writing should be directed to making comparisons, what Glaser and Strauss (1967) call 'constant comparative methods.' Hence, you compare one respondent's beliefs, stance, and actions with another respondent's, or one experience with another. If you have longitudinal data, compare a respondent's response, experience, or situation at one point in time with that at another time. Then as you become more analytic, start to make detailed comparisons between categories and then concept with concept. Through memo-writing, you clarify which categories are major and which are more minor. Thus, memo writing helps you to direct the shape and form of your emergent analysis from the very early stages of your research.

At each more analytic and abstract level of memo-writing, bring your data along with you right into your analysis. Build your analysis in the memo upon your data. Bringing your data into successive levels of memo-writing ultimately saves time because then you do not have to dig through stacks of material to illustrate your points. The following excerpt serves as an example of memo-writing taken from my own research:

Example of Memo-Writing

Living one day at a time means dealing with illness on a day-to-day basis, holding future plans and even ordinary activities, in abeyance while the person and, often, others deal with illness. When living one day at a time, the person feels that his or her future remains unsettled, that he or she cannot foresee the future or if there will be a future. Living one day at a time allows the person to focus on illness, treatment and regimen without becoming entirely immobilized by fear or future implications. By concentrating on the present, the person can avoid or minimize thinking about death and the possibility of dying.

Relation to Time Perspective

The felt need to live one day at a time often drastically alters a person's time perspective. Living one day at a time pulls the person into the present and pushes back past futures (the futures the person projected before illness or before this round of illness) so that they recede without mourning [their loss]. These past futures can slip away, perhaps almost unnoticed. [I then compare three respondents' situations, statements, and time perspectives.]

Memo-making leads directly to theoretical sampling, i.e., collecting more data to clarify your ideas and to plan how to fit them together. Here, you go back and sample for the purpose of *developing* your emerging theory, not for increasing the generalizability of your results. When I was trying to figure out how people with chronic illnesses defined the passage of time, I intentionally went back to several people I had interviewed before and asked them more focused questions about how they perceived times of earlier crisis and when time seemed to slow, quicken, drift, or drag. When an experience resonated with an individual, he or she could respond to even esoteric questions. For example, when I studied their stories, I realized that chronically ill adults implicitly located their self-concepts in the past, present, or future. These timeframes reflected the form and content of self and mirrored hopes and dreams for self as well as beliefs and understandings about self. Hence, I made "the self in time" a major category. Thereafter, I explicitly asked more people if they saw themselves in the past, present, or future. An elderly working-class woman said without hesitation:

> I see myself in the future now. If you'd asked where I saw myself eight months ago, I would have said, "the past." I was so angry then because I had been so active. And to go downhill as fast as I did—I felt life had been awfully cruel to me. Now I see myself in the future because there's something the Lord wants me to do. Here I sit all crumpled in this chair not being able to do anything for myself and still there's a purpose for me to be here. [Laughs.] I wonder what it could be. (Charmaz 1991a: 256)

Theoretical sampling helps you to fill out your categories, to discover variation within them, and to define gaps between categories. Theoretical sampling relies on comparative methods. Through using comparative methods, you can define the properties of your categories and specify the conditions under which they are linked to other categories. In this way, you raise your categories to concepts in your emerging theory. By the time you need to conduct theoretical sampling, you will have developed a set of categories that you have already found to be relevant and useful to explain your data. After you decide that these categories best explain what is happening in your study, treat them as concepts. In this sense, these concepts are useful to understand many incidents or issues in your data (cf. Strauss and Corbin 1990). I recommend conducting theoretical sampling later in the research to ensure that you have already defined relevant issues and allowed significant data to emerge. Otherwise, early theoretical sampling may bring premature closure to your analysis.

Through theoretical sampling, you will likely discover variation within the process you are analyzing. When conducting theoretical sampling, you are much more selective than earlier about from whom you obtain data and what you seek from these individuals. You may focus on certain experiences, events, or issues, not on individuals per se, because you want to develop your theoretical categories and need to define how and when they vary. However, observing or talking with individuals likely is the way in which you gain more knowledge about the experiences, events, or issues that you seek to treat theoretically. For example, one of my main categories was 'immersion in illness' (Charmaz 1991a). Major properties of immersion include recasting life around illness, slipping into illness routines, pulling into one's inner circle, facing dependency, and experiencing an altered (slowed) time perspective. However, not everyone's time perspective changed. How could I account for that?

By going back through my data, I gained some leads. Then I talked with more people about specific experiences and events. Theoretical sampling helped me to refine the analysis and make it more complex. I then added a category, 'variations in immersion' that begins as follows and then goes on to detail each remaining point:

> A lengthy immersion in illness shapes daily life and affects how one experiences time. Conversely, ways of experiencing time dialectically affect the qualities of immersion in illness. The picture above of immersion and time has sharp outlines. What sources of variation soften or alter the picture of immersion and time? The picture may vary according to the person's 1) type of illness, 2) kind of medication, 3) earlier time perspective, 4) life situation, and 5) goals.
>
> The type of illness shapes the experience and way of relating to time. Clearly trying to manage diabetes necessitates gaining a heightened awareness of timing the daily routines. But the effects of the illness may remain much more subtle. People with Sjogren's syndrome, for example, may have periods of confusion when they feel wholly out of synchrony with the world around them. For them, things happen too quickly, precisely when their bodies and minds function too slowly. Subsequently, they may retreat into routines to protect themselves. Lupus patients usually must retreat because they cannot tolerate the sun. Sara Shaw covered her windows with black blankets when she was extremely ill. Thus, her sense of chronological time became further distorted as day and night merged together into an endless flow of illness. (Charmaz 1991a: 93)

Theoretical sampling prompts you to collect further data that pinpoints key issues in your research by defining them explicitly and by identifying their properties and parameters. Your subsequent memo-writing becomes more precise, analytic, and incisive. By moving between data collection and analysis in your memo-writing about your theoretical sampling, you will follow leads, check out hunches, and refine your ideas. This way you have solid materials and sound ideas with which to work. Having both will give you a sense of confidence in your perceptions of your data and in your developing ideas about them.

After filling out your theoretical categories, and ordering them through sorting the memos you have written about them, you are ready to start writing the first draft of your paper (see Becker 1986; Richardson 1990; Wolcott 1990). As you write, try to explicate your logic and purpose clearly. That may take a draft or two. Then outline your draft to identify your main points and to organize how they fit together. (But do not write your draft from an outline—use your memos.) Your main argument or thesis may not be clear (to you as well as to others) until you write and rework several drafts. As your argument becomes clearer, keep tightening it by reorganizing the sections of your paper around it.

What place do raw data such as interview excerpts or field notes have in the body of your paper? Grounded theorists generally provide enough verbatim material to demonstrate the connection between the data and the analysis, but give more weight to the concepts derived from the data.[5] Their analytic focus typically leads grounded theorists to concentrate on making their theoretical relationships explicit and on subordinating their verbatim material to it (cf. Glaser 1978; Strauss 1987). Unlike most other grounded theorists, I prefer to present many detailed interview quotes and examples in the body of my work. I do so to keep the human story in the forefront of the reader's mind and to make the conceptual analysis more accessible to a wider audience (see, for example, Charmaz 1991a; 1994a; 1994b).

After you have developed your conceptual analysis of the data, then go to the literature in your field and compare how and where your work fits in with it. At this point, you must cover the literature thoroughly and weave it into your work explicitly. Then revise and rework your draft to make it a solid finished paper. Use the writing process to sharpen, clarify, and integrate your developing analysis. Through writing and rewriting, you can simultaneously make your analysis more abstract and your rendering and grounding of it more concrete. In short, you hone your abstract analysis to define essential properties, assumptions, relationships, and processes while providing sufficient actual data to demonstrate how your analysis is grounded in lived experience.

CONCLUSION

Grounded theory methods contrast with traditional logico-deductive research design. As Glaser and Strauss (1967) noted long ago, grounded theory starts from a different set of assumptions than traditional quantitative research design. The inductive nature of these methods assumes an openness and flexibility of approach. Thus, you follow the leads gained from your view of the data, not from the careful and exhaustive literature review of the traditional research design. A fundamental premise of grounded theory is to let the key issues emerge rather than to force them into preconceived categories. Traditional research design, in contrast, is theory-driven from extant theories in the field. Hence, traditional research design requires the investigator to pre-structure each phase of the research process to verify or to refute these extant theories. In short, each step is necessarily preconceived.

The grounded theorist builds the research as it ensues rather than having it completely planned before beginning the data collection. Similarly, you shape and alter the data collection to pursue the most interesting and relevant material. This approach differs sharply from the traditional research design with its structured instruments that are used in the same way with each research subject.

The purpose of grounded theory is to develop a theoretical analysis of the data that fits the data and has relevance to the area of study. The procedures within the method are then aimed to further theory development. Traditional research design generates data, not theory, to test existing theories by logically deducing hypotheses from them. By offering a set of systematic procedures, grounded theory enables qualitative researchers to generate ideas that may later be verified through traditional logico-deductive methods.

Nonetheless, as Glaser and Strauss originally claimed, grounded theory qualitative works stand on their own because they (1) explicate basic (generic) processes in the data, (2) analyze a substantive field or problem, (3) make sense of human behavior, (4) provide flexible, yet durable, analyses that other researchers can refine or update, and (5) have potential for greater generalizability (for example, when conducted at multiple sites) than other qualitative works. But are most grounded theory works actually theory? No, not at this point. At present, most grounded theory researchers have aimed to develop rich conceptual analyses of lived experience and social worlds instead of intending to create substantive or formal theory. They wish to pursue more basic questions within the empirical world and try to understand the mysteries and puzzles it presents. Thus, these grounded theorists have given greater emphasis to developing analytic categories that synthesize and explicate processes in the worlds they study rather than to constructing tightly framed theories that generate hypotheses and make explicit predictions. Nonetheless, grounded theory methods provide powerful tools for taking conceptual analyses into theory development. For this reason, grounded theory methods offer psychologists exciting possibilities for revisioning psychological theory as well as useful strategies for rethinking psychological research methods.

NOTES

*A version of this paper was presented at the Qualitative Research Conference, Studying Lived Experience: Symbolic Interaction and Ethnographic Research '94,' University of Waterloo, Waterloo, Ontario, 18–21 May 1994. I am indebted to Jennifer Dunn, Sachiko Kuwaura and Jonathan A. Smith for comments on an earlier draft.

1. Her comment provided a valuable source of *comparison*, along with being something to corroborate. For example, this piece of data allowed me to frame new questions: To what extent do people view themselves as separated from or imbedded in their daily routines? Which daily routines? How does sickness affect their view? When do they claim the self that they experience while ill? When do they reject it? For a contrasting view of another person with multiple sclerosis, see Hirsch (1977, pp. 169–170).

2. Grounded theorists assume that professional researchers, unlike student initiates, already have a sound footing in their disciplines. That is why they recommend using disciplinary concepts and perspectives to *sensitize* the researcher to look for certain processes and topics, but not to blind them to other issues. So any well-trained researcher already possesses a set of epistemological assumptions about the world, disciplinary perspectives and often an intimate familiarity with the research topic and the literature about it. The point is for any grounded theory researcher to remain as open as possible in the early stages of the research. The use of sensitizing concepts and perspectives provides a place to *start*, not to *end*. Hence, grounded theorists develop their sensitizing concepts in relation to the processes they define in their data. For example, I took the concept of identity and developed a framework of identity levels in an identity hierarchy (Charmaz 1987). In contrast, the logico-

deductive model of traditional model of research necessitates operationalizing the previously established concept as accurately as possible.

3. Recent critics from narrative analysis and postmodernism argue that the grounded theory emphasis on fracturing the data (i.e., breaking it up to define its analytic properties) does not allow sufficient attention to the individual (see for example Conrad 1990; Riessman 1990). These critics now argue that the task of the social scientist is to reveal the totality of the individual's story. Most individuals I interview do not want their whole stories revealed, or their identities exposed. Nor would they have agreed to participate in the research if telling their stories in entirety had been my intent. To date, grounded theory studies have not focused on individual narratives *per se*. However, that certainly does not mean that grounded theory methods inherently preclude such a focus.

4. Of course, the thoroughness of your work also depends on whether you are doing it for an undergraduate exercise, a graduate thesis, or a professional publication.

5. To date, there is little agreement how much verbatim material is necessary in qualitative research more generally. Some narrative analysts and postmodernists advocate emphasizing the individual's story (see Conrad 1990; Richardson 1992; Riessman 1990) and developing new ways to present it (see, for example, Ellis and Bochner 1992; Richardson 1992). Grounded theory works, in contrast, usually take a more traditional social scientific approach of making arguments, presenting and explicating concepts, and offering evidence for assertions and ideas. But compared to those qualitative studies that primarily synthesize description, grounded theory studies are substantially more analytic and conceptual.

REFERENCES

Abrahamson, J. S. and T. Mizrahi. 1994. Examining social work/physician collaboration: An application of grounded theory methods. In *Qualitative Studies in Social Work*, ed. C.K. Riessman. Newbury Park, CA: Sage.

Athens, L. 1989. *The creation of violent criminals*. New York: Routledge.

Atkinson, P. 1990. *The ethnographic imagination: Textual construction of reality*. London: Routledge.

Atkinson, P. 1992. *Understanding ethnographic texts*. Newbury Park, CA: Sage.

Becker, H S. 1986. *Writing for social scientists*. Chicago: University of Chicago Press.

Becker, P. H. 1993. Common pitfalls in published grounded theory research. *Qualitative Health Research* 3: 254–260.

Berg, B. L. 1989. *Qualitative research methods for the social sciences*. Boston: Allyn and Bacon.

Biernacki, P. L. 1986. *Pathways from heroin addiction: Recovery without treatment*. Philadelphia: Temple University Press.

Bigus, O. 1994. Grounded therapy. In *More Grounded Theory Methodology: A Reader*, ed. B. G. Glaser. Mill Valley, CA: Sociology Press.

Bigus, O. E., S. C. Hadden, and B. G. Glaser. 1994. The study of basic social processes. In *More Grounded Theory Methodology: A Reader*, ed.B. G. Glaser. Mill Valley, CA: Sociology Press.

Blumer, H. 1969. *Symbolic interactionism*. Englewood Cliffs, NJ: Prentice-Hall.

Bogdan, R. and S. J. Taylor, S. J. 1975. *Introduction to qualitative research methods: A phenomenological approach to the social sciences*. New York: Wiley.

Burgess, R. G. 1984. *In the field: An introduction to field research.* London: Allen and Unwin.

Charmaz, K. 1983. The grounded theory method: An explication and interpretation. In *Contemporary Field Research,* ed. R. M. Emerson. Boston: Little, Brown.

Charmaz, K. 1986. Using grounded theory for qualitative analysis, Master Lecture, Sociology Department, York University, Toronto. May 12.

Charmaz, K. 1987. Struggling for a self: Identity levels of the chronically ill. In *Research in the Sociology of Health Care: The Experience and Management of Chronic Illness,* vol. 6, eds. J. A. Roth and P. Conrad. Greenwich, CT: JAI.

Charmaz, K. 1990. "Discovering" chronic illness: Using grounded theory. *Social Science & Medicine* 30: 1161–1172.

Charmaz, K. 1991a. *Good days, bad days: The self in chronic illness and time.* New Brunswick, NJ: Rutgers University Press.

Charmaz, K. 1991b. Translating graduate qualitative methods into undergraduate teaching: Intensive interviewing as a case example. *Teaching Sociology.* 19: 384–395.

Charmaz, K. 1993. Studying lived experience through grounded theory: Realist and constructivist methods. Paper presented at the Symbolic Interaction and Ethnographic Research Conference, University of Waterloo, Waterloo, Ontario, May 19–22.

Charmaz, K. 1994a. Identity dilemmas of chronically ill men. *The Sociological Quarterly* 35: 269–288.

Charmaz, K. 1994b. Discoveries of self in illness. In *Doing Everyday Life: Ethnography as Human Lived Experience,* eds. M. L. Dietz, R. Prus & W. Shaffir. Mississauga, Ontario: Copp Clark Longman.

Charmaz, K. (1994 forthcoming). Between positivism and postmodernism: Implications for methods. In *Studies in Symbolic Interaction,* Vol. 15, ed. N. K. Denzin. Greenwich, CT: JAI Press.

Chenitz, W. C. and J. M. Swanson. 1986. *From practice to grounded theory: Qualitative research in nursing.* Menlo Park, CA: Addison-Wesley.

Clough, P. T. 1991. *The end(s) of ethnography: From realism to social criticism.* Newbury Park, CA: Sage.

Conrad, P. 1990. Qualitative research on chronic illness: A commentary on method and conceptual development. *Social Science & Medicine* 30: 1257–1263.

Cooley, C. H. 1902. *Human nature and the social order.* New York: Scribner's.

Denzin, N. K. 1987a. *The alcoholic self.* Newbury Park, CA: Sage.

Denzin, N. K. 1987b. *The recovering self.* Newbury Park, CA: Sage.

Denzin, N. K. 1989a. *Interpretative biography.* Newbury Park, CA: Sage.

Denzin, N. K. 1989b. *Interpretative interactionism.* Newbury Park, CA: Sage.

Denzin, N. K. 1991. *Images of postmodern society: Social theory and contemporary cinema.* London: Sage.

Denzin, N. K. 1992. *Symbolic interactionism and cultural studies: The politics of interpretation.* Cambridge, MA: Blackwell.

Denzin, N. K. 1995. Symbolic interactionism. In *Rethinking Psychology: Vol. 1. Conceptual Foundations,* eds. J. Smith, R. Harre, & L. Van Langenhove. London: Sage.

Elbow, P. 1981. *Writing with power.* New York: Oxford University Press.

Ellis, C. and A. P. Bochner. 1992. Telling and performing personal stories: The constraints of choice in abortion. In *Investigating Subjectivity: Research on Lived Experience,* eds. C. Ellis & M.G. Flaherty. Newbury Park, CA: Sage.

Fine, G. A. 1986. *With the boys: Little League baseball and preadolescent culture.* Chicago: University of Chicago Press.

Geertz, C. 1973. *The interpretation of cultures.* New York: Basic Books.

Giorgi, A. 1995. Phenomenology. In *Rethinking Psychology: Vol. 1. Conceptual Foundations,* eds. J. Smith, R. Harre, & L. Van Langenhove. London: Sage.

Glaser, B. G. 1978. *Theoretical sensitivity.* Mill Valley, CA: Sociology Press.

Glaser, B. G. 1992. *Emergence vs. forcing: Basics of grounded theory analysis.* Mill Valley, CA: Sociology Press.

Glaser, B. G. and A. L. Strauss. 1965. *Awareness of dying.* Chicago: Aldine.

Glaser, B. G. and A. L. Strauss. 1967. *The discovery of grounded theory.* Chicago: Aldine.

Glaser, B. G. and A. L. Strauss. 1968. *Time for dying.* Chicago: Aldine.

Goffman, E. 1959. *The presentation of self in everyday Life.* Garden City, NY: Doubleday.

Goffman, E. 1961. *Asylums.* Garden City, NY: Doubleday.

Goffman, E. 1963. *Stigma: Notes on the management of spoiled identity.* Englewood Cliffs, NJ: Prentice-Hall.

Guba, E. and Y. S. Lincoln. 1989. *Fourth generation evaluation.* Newbury Park, CA: Sage.

Gubrium, J. A. 1988. *Analyzing field reality.* Newbury Park, CA: Sage.

Hammersley, M. and P. Atkinson. 1983. *Ethnography: Principles in practice.* London: Tavistock.

Henwood, K. L. and N. F. Pidgeon. 1992. Qualitative research and psychological theorizing. *British Journal of Psychology* 83: 97–111.

Hirsch, E. 1977. *Starting over.* Hanover, MA: Christopher.

Hochschild, A. R. 1983. *The managed heart: Commercialization of human feeling.* Berkeley, CA: University of California Press.

Lofland, J. 1966. *Doomsday cult: A study of conversion, proselytization and maintenance of faith.* Englewood Cliffs, NJ: Prentice-Hall.

Lofland, J. 1976. *Doing social life.* New York: Wiley.

Lofland, J. and L. H. Lofland. 1984. *Analyzing social settings.* Belmont, CA: Wadsworth.

Martin, P. Y. and B. A. Turner. 1986. Grounded theory and organizational research. *Journal of applied behavioral science* 22:141–157.

Mead, G. H. 1932. *The philosophy of the present.* Chicago: University of Chicago Press.

Mead, G. H. 1934. *Mind, self and society.* Chicago: University of Chicago Press.

Mead, G. H. 1936. *Movements of thought in the nineteenth century.* Chicago: University of Chicago Press.

Mead, G. H. 1938. *The philosophy of the act.* Chicago: University of Chicago Press.

Park, R. E. 1950. *Race and culture.* Glencoe, IL: Free Press.

Park, R E. and E. W. Burgess, eds. 1921. *The city.* Chicago: University of Chicago Press.

Price, J. L. 1994. Organizational turnover: An illustration of the grounded theory approach to theory construction. In *More Grounded Theory: A Reader,* ed. B. G. Glaser. Mill Valley, CA: Sociology Press.

Prus, R. A. 1987. Generic social processes: Maximizing conceptual development in ethnographic research. *Journal of Contemporary Ethnography* 16: 250–293.

Reinharz, S. 1992. *Feminist methods in social research.* New York: Oxford University Press.

Rennie, D. L., J. R. Phillips, and G. K. Quartaro. 1988. Grounded theory: A promising approach to conceptualization in psychology? *Canadian Psychology* 29: 139–150.

Richardson, L. 1990. *Writing strategies: Reaching diverse audiences.* Newbury Park, CA: Sage.

Richardson, L. 1992. The consequences of poetic representation: Writing the other, rewriting the Self. In *Investigating Subjectivity: Research on Lived Experience,* eds. C. Ellis & M.G. Flaherty. Newbury Park, CA: Sage.

Richardson, L. 1993. Interrupting discursive spaces: Consequences for the sociological self. In *Studies in Symbolic Interaction* 14, ed. N. K. Denzin. Greenwich, CT: JAI Press.

Riessman, C. K. 1990. *Divorce talk.* New Brunswick, NJ: Rutgers University Press.

Rock, P. 1979. *The making of symbolic interactionism.* London: Macmillan.

Seidman, I. E. 1991. *Interviewing as qualitative research: A guide for researchers in education and the social sciences.* New York: Teachers College Press.

Shaw, C. 1930/1966. *The Jack-Roller: A delinquent boy's own story.* Chicago: University of Chicago Press.

Smith, J. 1995. Semi-structured interviews. In *Rethinking Psychology: Vol. 2. Evolving Methods,* eds. J. Smith, R. Harre, & L. Van Langenhove. London: Sage.

Smith, J., R. Harre, and L. Van Langenhove. 1995. Idiography. In *Rethinking Psychology: Vol. 1. Conceptual Foundations.* London: Sage.

Snow, D. A. and L. Anderson. 1993. *Down on their luck: A study of homeless street people.* Berkeley, CA: University of California Press.

Stern, P. N. 1994. The grounded theory method: Its uses and processes. In *More Grounded Theory Methodology: A Reader,* ed. B. G. Glaser. Mill Valley, CA: Sociology Press.

Strauss, A. L. 1987. *Qualitative analysis for social scientists.* New York: Cambridge University Press.

Strauss, A. L. and J. A. Corbin. 1990. *Basics of qualitative research: Grounded theory procedures and techniques.* Newbury Park, CA: Sage.

Strauss, A. L. and J. A. Corbin. 1993. Grounded theory methodology: An overview. In *Handbook of Qualitative Research,* eds. N K. Denzin & Y. S. Lincoln. Newbury Park, CA: Sage.

Strauss, A. L. and B. G. Glaser. 1970. *Anguish.* Mill Valley, CA: The Sociology Press.

Thomas, J. 1993. *Doing critical ethnography.* Newbury Park, CA: Sage.

Thomas, W.I. and F. Znaniecki. 1918. *The Polish peasant in Europe and America.* Chicago: University of Chicago Press.

Turner, B. A. 1981. Some practical aspects of qualitative data analysis: One way of organizing the cognitive processes associated with the generation of grounded theory. *Quality and Quantity* 15: 225–247.

Whyte, W. F. 1943/1955. *Street corner society.* Chicago: University of Chicago Press.

Wiseman, J. P. 1994. The development of generic concepts in qualitative research through cumulative application. In *More Grounded Theory: A Reader,* ed. B. G. Glaser. Mill Valley, CA: Sociology Press.

Wolcott, H. F. 1990. *Writing up qualitative research.* Newbury Park, CA: Sage.

Van Maanen, J. 1988. *Tales of the field.* Chicago: University of Chicago Press.

CHAPTER 24

"That's Not What I Said"

Interpretive Conflict in Oral Narrative Research[*]

KATHERINE BORLAND

In the summer of 1944, my grandmother, Beatrice Hanson, put on a pale, eggshell-colored gabardine dress with big gold buttons down the side, a huge pancake-black hat, and elbow-length gloves—for in *those* days ladies dressed *up* to go to the fair—and off she went with her father to see the sulky (harness) races at the Bangor, Maine, fairgrounds. The events that ensued provided for a lively wrangle between father and daughter as they vied to pick the winner. Forty-two years later Beatrice remembered vividly the events of that afternoon and, in a highly structured and thoroughly entertaining narrative, recounted them to me, her folklorist-granddaughter, who recorded her words on tape for later transcription and analysis. What took place that day, why it proved so memorable, and what happened to the narrative during the process of intergenerational transmission provide a case study in the variability of meaning in personal narrative performances. This story, or, better said, these stories, stimulate reflexivity about our scholarly practice.

Let me begin with the question of meaning and its variability. We can view the performance of a personal narrative as a meaning-constructing activity on two levels simultaneously. It constitutes both a dynamic interaction between the thinking subject and the narrated event (her own life experience) and between the thinking subject and the narrative event (her "assumption of responsibility to an audience for a display of communicative competence"[1]). As performance contexts change, as we discover new audiences, and as we renegotiate our sense of self, our narratives will also change.

What do folklorists do with the narratives performed for/before us? Like other audience members, we enjoy a skillfully told tale. But some of us also collect records of the performance in order to study them. Oral personal narratives occur naturally within a conversational context, in which various people take turns at talk, and thus are rooted most immediately in a web of expressive social activity. *We* identify chunks of artful talk within this flow of conversation, give them physical existence (most often through writing), and embed them in a new context of expressive or at least communicative activity (usually the scholarly article aimed toward an audience of professional peers). Thus, we construct a second-level narrative based upon, but at the same time reshaping, the first.

Like the original narrator, we simultaneously look inward toward our own experience of the performance (our interpretive shaping of it as listeners) and outward to our audience (to whom we must display a degree of scholarly competence). Presumably, the patterns upon which we base our interpretations can be shown to inhere in the "original" narrative, but our aims in pointing out certain features, or in making connections between the narrative and larger cultural formations, may at times differ from the original narrator's intentions. This is where issues of our responsibility to our living sources become most acute.

Years ago, scholars who recorded the traditions, arts, and history of a particular culture group gave little thought to the possibility that their representations might legitimately be challenged by those for and about whom they wrote. After all, they had "been in the field," listening, taking notes, and witnessing the culture firsthand. Educated in the literate, intellectual tradition of the Western academy, these scholars brought with them an objective, scientific perspective that allowed them, they felt, to perceive underlying structures of meaning in their material that the "natives," enmeshed in a smaller, more limited world, could not see. Therefore, it is not surprising that general ethnographic practice excluded the ethnographic subject from the process of post-fieldwork interpretation, nor that folklorists and anthropologists rarely considered their field collaborators to be potential audiences for their publications. More recently, some researchers sensitive to the relationships of power in the fieldwork exchange have questioned this model of the scholar as interpretive authority for the culture groups he/she studies.[2]

For feminists, the issue of interpretive authority is particularly problematic, for our work often involves a contradiction. On the one hand, we seek to empower the women we work with by revaluing their perspectives, their lives, and their art in a world that has systematically ignored or trivialized women's culture.[3] On the other, we hold an explicitly political vision of the structural conditions that lead to particular social behaviors, a vision that our field collaborators, many of whom do not consider themselves feminists, may not recognize as valid. My own work with my grandmother's racetrack narrative provides a vivid example of how conflicts of interpretation may, perhaps inevitably do, arise during the folklore transmission process. What should we do when we women disagree?

To refrain from interpretation by letting the subjects speak for themselves seems to me an unsatisfactory if not illusory solution. For the very fact that we constitute the initial audience for the narratives we collect influences the way in which our collaborators will construct their stories, and our later presentation of these stories—in particular publications under particular titles—will influence the way in which prospective readers will interpret the texts. Moreover, feminist theory provides a powerful critique of our society, and, as feminists, we presumably are dedicated to making that critique as forceful and direct as possible. How, then, might we present our work in a way that grants the speaking woman interpretive respect without relinquishing our responsibility to provide our own interpretation of her experience?

Although I have no easy answer to this question, I believe that by reflecting on our practice we can move toward a more sensitive research methodology. In the spirit of reflexivity I offer here a record of the dispute that arose between my grandmother and myself when I ventured an interpretation of her narrative. First, I will summarize the narrative, since the taped version runs a full twenty-five minutes. Then I will present her framing of the narrative in performance and my reframing during the interpretive process. Finally, I will present her response to my interpretation. While I have already "stacked the deck" in my favor by summarizing the story, reducing it through my subjective lens, my grandmother's comments powerfully challenge my assumption of exegetical authority over the text.[4]

Beatrice began her story with a brief setting of the scene: in the grandstand, she finds herself seated directly behind Hod Buzzel, "who," she states, "had gotten me my divorce and whom I *hated* with a passion." Hod is accompanied by his son, the county attorney (who, Beatrice says, "was just as bad as his father in another way—he was a snob"). Beatrice's father knows them both very well.

Beatrice, the narrator, then explains the established system for selecting a horse. Observers typically purchase a "score card" that lists the past records of horses and drivers, and they evaluate the horses as they pace before the grandstand. Beatrice's personal system for choosing a horse depends most heavily on her judgment of the observable merits of both horse and driver. She explains:

> And if I could find a *horse* that right pleased me, and a driver that pleased me that were together . . . *there* would be my choice, you see? So, this particular afternoon . . . I *found* that. Now that didn't happen all the time, by any means, but I found . . . perfection, as far as I was concerned, and I was absolutely *convinced* that *that* horse was going to win.

Beatrice decides to bet on Lyn Star, an unknown horse driven by a young man. She knows that this young man's father is driving another horse in the race. Her father and the Buzzels select Black Lash, a horse with an established reputation for speed.

The subsequent action exhibits an inherent potential for narrative patterning. Sulky races, in which a driver sits behind the horse in a two-wheeled, single-seat carriage, are presented in a series of three heats. In other words, the same group of horses races against each other three times during the afternoon, alternating with three groups of horses who race against one another in the same fashion. Normally, drivers act on their own, competing individually against their opponents, but the appearance of a father and son in the same race suggests to Bea the possibility that these two may collaborate with one another in some way. Each heat, from the perspective of the audience, involves three stages: selecting a horse and placing a bet, observing the race proper, and collecting on one's winning tickets. With regard to the particular race narrated, an additional structural element is provided by the repetitive strategy employed by the father and son upon whom Bea has placed her hopes.

In each heat, the father quickly takes the lead and sets a fast pace for the other horses while the son lopes along behind. As the horses turn into the second lap and start their drive, the father moves over to let his son through on the rail (the inside lane of the track) thereby forcing Black Lash, the next-to-front runner, to go out and around him. Dramatic tension is produced by the variable way in which this strategy is played out on the course. In the first heat, Lyn Star wins by a nose. In the second, he ties in a photo finish with Black Lash. In the third, the father's horse, worn out by his previous two performances, drops back behind the others, leaving Lyn Star and Black Lash to really race. But because of the way the races have been run, Lyn Star's driver had never really had to push his horse. He does so this time and leaves Black Lash half a length behind.

As a superlative narrator, Beatrice recognizes and exploits the parallels between the observed contest and the contest between observers who have aligned themselves with different horses. She structures her narrative by alternating the focus between a dramatic reenactment of events in the grandstand and a description of the actual race as it unfolds before the observers. Within this structure, the cooperation between the father and son on the racecourse provides a contrast to the conflict between father and daughter in the grandstand.

Before the first heat, Bea's father asks her, "D'you pick a horse?" And she responds that, yes, she has chosen Lyn Star. At this, her father loudly denounces her choice, claiming that the horse will never win, she'll lose her money, and she should not bet. Beatrice puts two dollars on the horse. When Lyn Star wins, Bea turns triumphantly to her father. Undaunted, he insists that the race was a fluke and that Bea's favorite horse will not win again. Nevertheless, Beatrice places six dollars on Lyn Star in the next heat. By now, though, her father is irate and attempts first to trade horses with her so that she won't lose her money, and then, when she declines this offer, he refuses altogether to place her bet. Young Buzzel, who has become an amused audience of one to the father-daughter contest in the grandstand, offers to take her money down to the betting office. Since Bea has never placed her own bets, she accepts.

With the third heat Beatrice's father catapults their private argument into the public arena, as he asks his daughter, "What are you going to do this time?" Beatrice is adamant, "I am *betting on my horse* and I am betting *ten bucks* on that horse. It's gonna win!" At this, Beatrice, the narrator, explains, "Father had a fit. *He* had a fit. And he tells everybody three miles around in the grandstand what a fool I am too. . . . *He* wasn't gonna take my money down!" So Beatrice commandeers young Buzzel to place her bet for her again. When Lyn Star wins by a long shot, Bea's father is effectively silenced:

> And *I* threw my pocketbook in one direction, and I threw my gloves in another direction, and my score book went in another direction, and I jumped up and I hollered, to everyone, "You see what know-it-all said! *That's* my father!" And finally one man said to me . . . no, he said to my father, "You know, she *really* enjoys horse racing, doesn't she?"

To understand how Bea frames her narrative, we must return to a consideration of her initial description of how a horse is chosen. This prefatory material orients the audience to a particular point of view, emphasizing that the race should be understood as an opportunity for racegoers to exercise their evaluative skills in order to predict an eventual outcome. Indeed, the length and detail of this portion of the narrative emphasizes the seriousness, for Beatrice, of this preliminary evaluative activity. This framing of the story gains significance if one considers that Bea's knowledge of horses was unusual for women in her community. Emphasizing the exceptionality of her knowledge, she explained to me that her father owned and raced horses when Bea was a child and "though I could not go *fishing* with my father on Sundays, or *hunting* with him on any day of the week, for some strange reason, he took me with him, mornings" to watch his horses being exercised.[5]

Additionally, in her framing of the narrative, Beatrice identifies the significance of the event narrated, its memorability, as the unique coming together of a perfect horse and driver that produced an absolute conviction on her part as to who would win the contest. Since this conviction was proved correct, the narrative functions to support or illustrate Bea's sense of self as a competent judge of horses within both the narrative and the narrated event. In effect, her narrative constitutes a verbal re-performance of an actual evaluative performance at the track.[6]

What do I as a listener make of this story? A feminist, I am particularly sensitive to identifying gender dynamics in verbal art, and, therefore, what makes the story significant for me is the way in which this self-performance within the narrated event takes on the dimension of a female struggle for autonomy within a hostile male environment. Literally and symbolically, the horse race constitutes a masculine sphere. Consider, racing contestants, owners, and trainers were male (although female *horses* were permitted to compete). Also, while women obviously attended the races, indeed, "ladies dressed up" to go to the races, they were granted only partial participant status. While they were allowed to sit in the grandstand as observers (and, having dressed up, one assumes, as persons to be observed), they were not expected to engage as active evaluators in the essential first stage of the racing event. Notice that even at the very beginning of the story Bea's father did not want her to bet. Betting is inherently a risk-taking activity. Men take risks; women do not. This dimension of meaning is underscored in the second heat when Beatrice, the narrator, ironically recounts that her father was going to be "decent" to her, in other words, was going to behave according to the model of gentlemanly conduct, by offering to bear his daughter's risk and bet on her horse for her.

Significantly, as the verbal contest develops, Beatrice displays greater and greater assertiveness as a gambler. Not only does she refuse to align herself with the men's judgment, she also raises the ante by placing more and more serious bets on her choice. From an insignificant bet in the first heat—and here it bears recalling that in racing parlance a two-dollar bet is still called a "lady's bet"—she proceeds in the second and third heats to bet six and ten dollars, respectively.

In portraying the intensification of the contest, Beatrice, the narrator, endows Beatrice, the gambler, with an increasingly emphatic voice. Her tone in addressing her father moves from one of calm resolution before the first and second heats—"That's the horse I'm betting on," and "No, I'm gonna stay with that horse"—to heated insistence before the third heat—"I am *betting on my horse!*" (each word accentuated in performance by the narrator's pounding her fist on the dining-room table).

Finally, if one looks at Beatrice's post-heat comments, one can detect a move from simple self-vindication in the first heat to a retaliatory calumniation of her father's reputation delivered in a loud disparaging voice—"You see what know-it-all said! *That's* my father!" Thus, at the story's end, Beatrice has moved herself from a peripheral feminine position with respect to the larger male sphere of betting *and* talk, to a central position where her words and deeds proclaim her equal and indeed superior to her male antagonist. Symbolically underscoring this repudiation of a limiting feminine identity, Bea flings away the accessories of her feminine costume—her gloves and her pocketbook.

If on one level the story operates as a presentation of self as a competent judge of horses, on another it functions to assert a sense of female autonomy and equality within a sphere dominated by men. From yet another perspective, the verbal contest between father and daughter results in a realignment of allegiances based on the thematic contrasts between age and youth, reputation and intrinsic merit, observable in the contest between the horses Black Lash and Lyn Star. When her father (tacitly) refuses to place her bet before the second heat, young Buzzel, whom Bea has previously described as an antagonist, and who has been betting with the older men, offers to place her bet for her. In effect, he bets on Beatrice in the contest developing on the sidelines.[7]

Furthermore, with regard to the narrator's life experience, one can view the narrative as a metaphor for a larger contest between Beatrice and her social milieu. For in the early 1930s Beatrice shocked her community by divorcing her first husband. This action and her attempt to become economically independent by getting an education were greeted with a certain amount of social and familial censure. For instance, Beatrice recalls, when her mother entered the date of the divorce in the family bible, she included the note: "Recorded, but not approved." It also forced Beatrice to leave her two young daughters in the care of their paternal grandparents for the five years she attended college, a necessity that still saddens and troubles her today.[8]

My grandparents agree that, in the ideology of marriage at that time, "you weren't supposed to be happy." My grandfather relates that his grandmother suffered severe psychological strain during menopause, was committed to a psychiatric hospital, and, while there, crossed her name off her marriage certificate. In a slightly more active form of resistance, Beatrice's grandmother, after injuring herself while doing heavy farm work, took to her bed for several years. However, as soon as her son married, she got up, moved in with him, and led a normal, active life, becoming the strong maternal figure of Bea's own childhood. Bea's mother separated herself psychologically from both her husband and her family by retreating into a strict, moralistic, and, in Bea's view, hypocritical religiosity. For Bea's predecessors, then, a woman's socially acceptable response to an unhappy marriage was to remove herself from the marriage without actually effecting a formal, public separation. Although Bea's first husband was tacitly recognized by the community as an unfit husband—irresponsible, alcoholic, a spendthrift and a philanderer—Beatrice was expected to bear with the situation in order to protect her own reputation and that of her family.

By divorcing her first husband Beatrice transgressed middle-class social decorum and was branded "disreputable." The appearance in the present narrative of the divorce lawyer and Bea's negative reaction to him leads me to link Beatrice's performance and status at the races to her previous loss of reputation in the larger village society.[9] In both instances Beatrice had to prove in the face of strong opposition the rightness of not playing by the rules, of relying on her own judgment, of acting as an autonomous individual. I would suggest, then, that the latent associations of this narrative to circumstances critical to the narrator's life, even if not consciously highlighted in the narrative, may reinforce its memorability.

What is essential to emphasize, however, is that this is *my* framing of the racetrack narrative informed by contemporary feminist conceptions of patriarchal structures, which my grandmother does not share. Moreover, after reading an initial version of this interpretation, Beatrice expressed strong disagreement with my conclusions. I quote a portion of the fourteen-page letter she wrote to me concerning the story:

> Not being, myself, a feminist, the "female struggle" as such never bothered me in my life. It never occurred to me. I never thought of my *position* at all in this sense. I've always felt that I had a fine childhood. It seems, now, that I must have had a remarkable one. To begin with, I had a very strong father figure. Surrounded by the deep and abiding love of my Grandmother Austin (whom I adored); the clear, unfaltering knowledge of my father's love and his openly expressed pride in me, and the definite disciplines set by my grandmother which provided the staunch and unchallengeable framework in which I moved, I knew absolute security. (The disciplines were unchallengeable because I never had the least desire to challenge them. I would have done anything not to disappoint Grandma or make her feel

bad, and I was so very happy and secure that only an idiot would have tried to upset the situation.)

In consequence of all this, as I grew older, the inner strength which that sense of security had built in me, served always to make me feel equal to anyone, male or female, and very often superior. Feminism, as such, was of no moment to me—none at all. Privately, it has always seemed ridiculous, but that's neither here nor there. It makes no difference to me what anybody else thinks about it.

So your interpretation of the story as a female struggle for autonomy within a hostile male environment is entirely YOUR interpretation. You've read into the story what you wished to—what pleases YOU. That it was never—by any wildest stretch of the imagination—the concern of the originator of the story makes such an interpretation a definite and complete distortion, and in this respect I question its authenticity. The story is no longer MY story at all. The skeleton remains, but it has become your story. Right? How far is it permissible to go, in the name of folklore, and still be honest in respect to the original narrative?

Beatrice brings up a crucial issue in oral narrative scholarship—who controls the text? If I had not sent my grandmother a copy of my work, asking for her response, I could perhaps have avoided the question of my intrusion into the texts I collect. Discussions with our field collaborators about the products of our research are often overlooked or unreported by folklore scholars. Luckily, my grandmother is quite capable of reading, responding to, and resisting my presentation of her narrative. For my own and my grandmother's versions provide a radical example of how each of us has created a story from our own experience. While I agree that the story has indeed become *my* story in the present context, I cannot agree that my reading betrays the original narrative.

Beatrice embraces an idealist model of textual meaning that privileges authorial intentions. It makes sense for my grandmother to read the story in this way. From my own perspective, however, the story does not really become a story until it is actualized in the mind of a receptive listener/reader. As my consciousness has been formed within a different social and historical reality, I cannot restrict my reading to a recuperation of original authorial intentions. I offer instead a different reading, one that values her story as an example to feminists of one woman's strategy for combating a limiting patriarchal ideology. That Bea's performance constitutes a direct opposition to established authorities reveals for me how gender ideologies are not wholly determinative or always determinative of female identity.[10]

Nevertheless, despite my confidence in the validity of my reading as a feminist scholar, personally I continue to be concerned about the potential emotional effect alternative readings of personal narratives may have on our living subjects. The performance of a personal narrative is a fundamental means by which people comprehend their own lives and present a "self" to their audience.[11] Our scholarly representations of those performances, if not sensitively presented, may constitute an attack on our collaborators' carefully constructed sense of self. While Bea and I have discussed our differences at length and come to an amicable agreement about how to present them (i.e., the inclusion of her response to my initial reading in the final text), I might have avoided eliciting such a violent initial response from her if I had proceeded differently from the outset.[12]

I could have tried to elicit my grandmother's comments on the story's meaning before I began the process of interpretation. During the taping session itself, however, this would have proved problematic. As I stated earlier, oral personal narratives occur naturally within a conversational context, and often the performance of one narrative leads to other related performances. These displays of verbal art provide an important context for understanding how the narrative in question is to be viewed, and from my perspective it would not be productive to break the narrative flow in order to move to the very different rhetorical task of interpretation and analysis.

Furthermore, during a narrative performance of this type, both narrator and listener are caught up in the storytelling event. Although associative commentary about the stories is common, at this stage in the fieldwork exchange neither narrator nor listener is prepared to reflect analytically on the material being presented. Indeed, the conscious division of a storytelling session into discreet story units or thematic constellations of stories occurs at the later stage of review and study.

Nevertheless, the narrator's commentary on and interpretation of a story can contribute greatly to the researcher's understanding of it. I now feel I ought to have arranged a second session with my grandmother in which I played her the taped version and asked her for her view of its function and meaning. Time constraints prevented me from doing so. I did solicit an interpretation from Bea with not much success after I had written and she had read my initial version of this article. At that time Beatrice insisted that the story was simply an amusing anecdote with no deep or hidden meanings. Although it may be that some narrators are not prepared to interpret their own stories analytically, Bea's reaction may have been due to her sharply felt loss of authorial control.

With the benefit of hindsight, let me review two points that proved especially sensitive for my grandmother. First, Bea reacted very strongly to the feminist identity my interpretation implied she had. Though some might quibble that this problem is simply a matter of labels, the word "feminist" often has negative, threatening connotations for women who have not participated in the feminist movement. More important, Bea's objection points to an important oversight in my own research process.

When I began the task of interpretation, I assumed a likeness of mind where there was in fact difference: I was confident that my grandmother would accept my view of the story's meaning. After all, she had been very excited about working with me when I told her I wanted to study older women's life experience narratives. She sent me a great deal of material and commentary on the difficult conditions of women's lives in nineteenth- and early twentieth-century Maine, material and commentary that seemed on the surface to convey a feminist perspective. Moreover, she offered her own accounts and stories, some of which dealt with very sensitive matters, assuring me that I should feel perfectly free to use whatever proved helpful to me in my research. How, then, did we, who had a close, confidential, long-standing relationship, manage to misunderstand each other so completely?

The fieldwork exchange fosters a tendency to downplay differences, as both investigator and source seek to establish a footing with one another and find a common ground from which to proceed to the work of collecting and recording oral materials. Additionally, as we are forever constructing our own identities through social interactions, we similarly construct our notion of others. My grandmother has always appeared to me a remarkably strong, independent woman, and thus, even though she had never called herself a feminist, it was an easy step for me to cast her in that role. Although she knew that I considered myself an activist feminist, to her I have always been, first and foremost, a granddaughter. She was, therefore, unprepared for the kind of analysis I performed on her narrative. The feminist movement has been criticized before for overgeneralizing about women's experience in its initial enthusiasm of sisterly identification. Yet it bears repeating that important commonalities among women often mask equally important differences.[13]

For Beatrice, another troubling feature of my interpretation is the portrait it presents of her father. Here the problem arises from our different understandings of what the narrative actually is. I approach the story as a symbolic construction and the people within it are, for me, dramatic characters. Thus, Beatrice's father, the antagonistic figure of the story, becomes a symbol of repressive male authority in my interpretation. For Beatrice, however, the story remains an account of a real experience, embedded in the larger context of her life. She brings to her reading of the "characters" a complex of associations built up over a shared lifetime. From this perspective my interpretation of her father is absolutely false. Whether or not it "works" for the father figure in the story, it does not define the man. In fact, Beatrice's father was one of the few people who encouraged and supported her during the difficult period after her disastrous first marriage. She remembers her father with a great deal of love and admiration and speaks often of the special relationship they had with one another. Indeed, if anyone was the villain of Beatrice's youth, it would have been her mother, a cold, judgmental woman. Nevertheless, in a written account of the racetrack story composed shortly after the event took place, Beatrice herself remarks that at the track, "Father and the Buzzels were acting very male," quarreling over the results of the races.[14]

When I sent Beatrice a copy of my essay in which *her* narrative had suffered a sea change, she naturally felt misrepresented. To complicate matters, my original essay contained a great deal of theory that was unfamiliar and at times incomprehensible to her. Embedded in the context of my own scholarly environment, I had not bothered to provide any accompanying explanation of that theory. Thus, if I had "misread" her text, I also gave her every opportunity to misread mine. I now feel that had I talked to Bea about my ideas *before* I committed them to writing, presented her with drafts, or even arranged to have her read the paper with me so that we might discuss misunderstandings and differences as they arose, her sense of having been robbed of textual authority might not have been as strong as it was.

I am not suggesting that all differences of perspective between folklorist and narrator, feminist scholar and speaking woman, should or can be worked out before the final research product is composed. Nor am I suggesting that our interpretations must be validated by our research collaborators. For when we do interpretations, we bring our own knowledge, experience, and concerns to our material, and the result, we hope, is a richer, more textured understanding of its meaning.

I am suggesting that we might open up the exchange of ideas so that we do not simply gather data on others to fit into our own paradigms once we are safely ensconced in our university libraries ready to do interpretation. By extending the conversation we initiate while collecting oral narratives to the later stage of interpretation, we might more sensitively negotiate issues of interpretive authority in our research.

Quite possibly, this modification of standard practice would reveal new ways of understanding our materials to both research partners. At the very least, it would allow us to discern more clearly when we speak in unison and when we disagree. Finally, it would restructure the traditionally unidirectional flow of information out from source to scholar to academic audience by identifying our field collaborators as an important first audience for our work. Lest we, as feminist scholars, unreflectively appropriate the words of our mothers for our own uses, we must attend to the multiple and sometimes conflicting meanings generated by our framing or contextualizing of their oral narratives in new ways.

POSTSCRIPT

On July 8, 1989, after a ten-month absence, I visited Beatrice and gave her a copy of the present version of this paper for her final comments. She took it to her study, read it, and then the two of us went through it together, paragraph by paragraph. At this juncture she allowed that much of what I had said was "very true," though she had not thought about the events of her life in this way before. After a long and fruitful discussion, we approached the central issue of feminism. She explained, once again, that feminism was not a movement that she had identified with or even heard of in her youth. Nevertheless, she declared that if I meant by feminist a person who believed that a woman has the right to live her life the way she wants to regardless of what society has to say about it, then she guessed she was a feminist.

Thus, the fieldwork exchange had become, in the end, a true exchange. I had learned a great deal from Beatrice, and she had also learned something from me. Yet I would emphasize that Bea's understanding and acceptance of feminism was not something that I could bestow upon her, as I had initially and somewhat naively attempted to do. It was achieved through the process of interpretive conflict and discussion, emerging as each of us granted the other interpretive space and stretched to understand the other's perspective. While Bea's identification with feminism is not crucial to my argument, it stands as a testament to the new possibilities for understanding that arise when we re-envision the fieldwork exchange.

NOTES

*The material upon which this essay is based was originally presented in a paper entitled "Horsing around with the Frame: Narrative, Memory, and Performance," presented at the Fifth Annual Graduate Women's Studies Conference at Rutgers University, New Brunswick, New Jersey, in March 1988.

1. Richard Bauman, *Verbal Art as Performance* (Prospect Heights, IL: Waveland, 1977), p. 11. For a discussion of the differences between narrated and narrative events, see Richard Bauman's introduction in his *Story, Performance, and Event* (New York: Cambridge University Press, 1986).

2. The present "crisis of interpretation" is due to a number of historical factors. Most broadly, the political challenge to Western imperialism has weakened Western claims to authority in many other areas of cultural exchange. Members of groups that have traditionally formed the subject of ethnographic research have recently appeared in university departments and offered penetrating critiques of the biases in previous research. "Native" peoples at home have gained new access to recording equipment and are now constructing self-representations without the intervention of the "foreign" scholar. For a discussion of new experiments in ethnographic texts, see James Clifford and George E. Marcus, eds., *Writing Culture: The Poetics and Politics of Ethnography* (Berkeley, Calif.: University of California Press, 1986), and George E. Marcus and Michael M.J. Fischer, *Anthropology as Cultural Critique: An Experimental Moment in the Human Sciences* (Chicago: University of Chicago Press, 1986).

3. For a discussion of the sexist bias in folklore scholarship generally, see Marta Weigle, "Women as Verbal Artists: Reclaiming the Daughters of Enheduanna," *Frontiers* 3, no. 3 (1978): 1–9.

4. The racetrack narrative I present here forms part of an extended taping session I conducted with my grandmother during a three-day visit to her home in December 1986. A transcription of the full version of Beatrice's narrative appears in my article "Horsing around with the Frame: The Negotiation of Meaning in Women's Verbal Performance," *Praxis* (Spring 1990): 83–107.

5. This remark occurred in a narrative that immediately preceded the racetrack narrative in our taped conversation.

6. In the conversation following the narrative, Bea mentions another race at Topsham that she attended years later where "none of the horses looked like much of anything" to her. Significantly, Topsham does *not* provide the material for a narrative, but is mentioned in passing as a contrast to the race we are considering here.

7. If one considers the conversation surrounding the narrative, it is interesting that this story forms one of a series of humorous anecdotes about Maine characters, mostly older men, known for their intransigence and willful refusal to modify idiosyncratic (my grandparents would add, idiotic) behaviors despite appeals to their reason or better selves by the victimized dependent family or community members.

However, in most of my grandparents' stories of this type, the suffering younger characters must resort to clever subterfuge in order to induce their elders to change. *This* story, in contrast, represents a youthful victory in an open and publicly declared contest, the tactics of subterfuge being relegated to minor characters, helper figures, both on the course and in the stand.

8. This and the following information was related to me during the same three-day period of taping, but it does not form the immediate context of conversation for the racetrack narrative.

9. In her later letter to me, Beatrice explained that Hod Buzzel "didn't represent me as he should have; he didn't do a damn thing for me, except try to sell me out to the Besses." (The Besses were the wealthy farming family of Beatrice's first husband.)

10. One of my original purposes in presenting this narrative was to challenge the notion that women are passive victims of patriarchal oppression. Without denying the constraints of socially reified gender ideologies on women's expressiveness, it seems important to recognize women's active role in constructing their own identities and, in the process, transforming social ideals. Beverly Stoeltje discusses the dialectic between individual behavior, changing environments, and ideals of womanhood in " 'A Helpmate for Man Indeed': The Image of the Frontier Woman," *in Women and Folklore: Images and Genres*, ed. Claire R. Farrer (Prospect Heights, Ill.: Waveland Press, 1975), pp. 25–41.

11. Victor Turner views performances as reflexive occasions set aside for the collective or individual presentation of the self to the self in "Images and Reflections: Ritual Drama, Carnival, Film and Spectacle in Cultural Performance," in his *The Anthropology of Performance* (New York: The Performing Arts Journal Publications, 1987), pp. 121–32. For a discussion of how personal narratives are tools for making sense of our lives, see Barbara Myerhoff, "Life History among the Elderly: Performance, Visibility and Remembering" in *A Crack in the Mirror: Reflexive Perspectives in Anthropology*, ed. Jay Ruby (Philadelphia: University of Pennsylvania Press, 1982), pp. 99–117.

12. In several lengthy postessay discussions, Beatrice, my grandfather Frank, and I discussed both the story and what happened to it during the process of transmission. After hearing the revised version (in which my grandmother's comments were included), Frank stated that he had learned to see features of the society in which he grew up that he had never really been aware of before. Beatrice was less enthusiastic about my alternative reading, but agreed that my perspective was thought-provoking. For her, the more general issue of how stories are transformed with each new telling was the most interesting point of the essay, and she expressed a desire to continue working on projects of the same type.

13. Equally serious is the tendency to discount as vestiges of false consciousness attitudes or behaviors that do not fit into our own vision of feminist practice. In a cogent critique of this tendency in feminist research, Rachelle Saltzman demonstrates how women who use sexist-male jokes within their own gender group see this activity as an expropriation for use rather than an acceptance of a belittled female identity, in "Folklore, Feminism and the Folk: Whose Lore is it?" *Journal of American Folklore* 100 (1987): 548–67.

14. Quotation from a letter written to Beatrice's second husband, Frank Hanson, 6 August 1944.

CHAPTER 25

Unleashing Frankenstein's Monster?

The Use of Computers in Qualitative Research

SHARLENE NAGY HESSE-BIBER

Computer usage within sociology is not a new phenomenon. Sociologists use computer programs for analyzing data. Most computer programs are applied to quantitative methods. Qualitative sociologists have in large part avoided the use of computer programs in the analysis of their data, which primarily consists of the analysis of text (gathered through observations, documents, and interviews) for patterns and meanings. Qualitative sociologists do not usually report the actual techniques they use in their qualitative data analysis. Few have codified their techniques. (There are some exceptions: Glaser and Strauss 1967; Charmaz 1983; Strauss 1987.)

The arrival of lower-priced personal computers and their portability made the computer available to the qualitative researcher in the field and office. At present there is a great demand for software programs for microcomputers. Yet there is a fear as well as promise concerning the use of computerized technology applied to qualitative research, not unlike the fear of Frankenstein's monster.

Mary Shelley's novel, *Frankenstein*, was published in 1818 and reflects the dramatic revolutionary changes in England between 1789 and 1832, during which time the working class was asserting its right to vote and the country as a whole was moving from a preindustrial small-scale agricultural community to a large-scale industrial economy. In many ways, Frankenstein's monster was a symbol of revolutionary change with its accompanying destruction and promise of a new beginning. Those in power feared the working class with its lack of "traditions" would "take over" and become uncontrollable if given the vote, such that chaos and instability would reign over English society (Smith 1992, pp. 317). Victor Frankenstein describes his creation in the following way:

> . . . I suddenly beheld the figure of a man, at some distance, advancing towards me with superhuman speed. He bounded over the crevices in the ice, among which I had walked with caution; his stature, also, as he approached, seemed to exceed that of man. I was troubled: a mist came over my eyes, and I felt a faintness seize me. . . . I perceived, as the shape came

nearer . . . that it was the wretch whom I had created. I trembled with rage and horror . . . (Shelley as quoted in Smith 1992, p. 89).

The fear Victor Frankenstein experiences coming face to face with his monster is often involved in the researcher's relationship to the computer. Just as Frankenstein's monster was held in awe and fear, there is a strong feeling among some qualitative researchers that while computers have the potential to revolutionize the field, there is also the possibility for things to run out of control. A range of fears are expressed as the researcher first begins to consider and proceeds to use computer technology to do qualitative work. This paper outlines five fears critics express concerning the use of computer software programs for qualitative data analysis.

I. ART VERSUS TECHNOLOGY

There exists the fear that machine technology will separate the qualitative researcher from the creative process. For some analysts, the experience of doing qualitative work is more comparable to artistic work. Just as the artist prefers a brush or pencil and paper, so too do some qualitative researchers. Machine technology seems incompatible or inconsistent with art. There is a strong fear that the technology will turn the researcher into an unthinking and unfeeling human being. Some qualitative researchers have commented on how much they like to work with paper or to be able to write in the margins of their interviews (see Richards and Richards 1989). Others describe the process as "mystical," "private," or "idiosyncratic" (Conrad and Reinharz 1984). There is a sense that the machine will turn research into a commodity. With the additional qualitative software features of hypothesis generation and testing of hypotheses which are now available on some computer software programs, there is the additional fear of "data dredging"—and an overreliance on technology to do one's thinking by simply having the software relate code categories automatically, using very little theoretical insight.

II. BLURRING THE LINE BETWEEN QUANTITATIVE AND QUALITATIVE ANALYSIS

Computer software programs automate the organizing, indexing, and retrieving of documents to generate counts of occurrence of codes or concepts on data which can then be input into a statistical software package. Some critics feel that these software features may serve to blur the line between qualitative and quantitative data analysis. For many of the new software programs, there is no limit on the size of the data they can handle or the number of files. The volume of data now collected for some qualitative studies is comparable to quantitative research, and there is the potential fear that qualitative research will be reduced to quantitative research. Qualitative researchers' emphasis on volume is of concern for a variety of reasons.

Fear of Imposing the Logic of Survey
Research onto Qualitative Research

Qualitative researchers may impose the logic of general survey research and increase their sample size in hopes of generalizing their results to some empirical universe. Yet, generalizations made by qualitative researchers derive from a different logic. They are not generalizing about content but are looking to discover underlying patterns or forms within their data that have applicability to a whole range of different contexts. The logic of survey research, on the other hand, often requires that the size of the sample meet certain statistical inference issues such as needing "x" number of cases to ensure that one's results are significant at the $p = 0.05$ or $p = 0.01$ level. These assumptions about numbers are driven by the need to form empirical generalizations. Some qualitative researchers lose sight of this point when they become fixated on volume. Qualitative analysis is driven by a need to make analytical generalizations. Howard Becker (1953) studies marijuana users, not to generalize about marijuana users, but to study a process of getting involved in a deviant subculture. Numbers are important, but they are based on theoretical considerations, such as the level of saturation of code categories. According to Strauss (1987), "theoretical saturation" occurs "when additional analysis no longer contributes to discovering anything new about a category" (p. 21). A researcher needs to study more cases until he or she is not learning anything new.

Sacrificing In-depth Analysis to Meet High Volume Standards

Wanting to become more quantitative by focusing more on volume means that a qualitative researcher may sacrifice in-depth analysis of data in order to pursue high volume analysis. John Seidel describes this development as one symptom of "analytic madness" (1991, p. 107) and suggests that volumes of data "will drive the analysis" and may result in a researcher "missing interesting and important things in the data" (p. 109). Ironically, the very features of computer software programs which help to computerize the process of coding, retrieving, and sorting of data can also serve to limit the type of in-depth data analysis characteristic of qualitative work.

III. DICTATING THE DEFINITION OF A FIELD
AND TYPE OF QUALITATIVE DATA ANALYSIS

Michael Agar (1991) and others (Seidel 1991) caution that computer programs may dictate the very definition of a particular field of study. Agar notes the following concerning the field of ethnography:

> As more and more colleagues acquired computer know how, I heard less about what ethnography was and how to think about it, and more about the newest hardware and software and what it could do, about memory capacity and hard disk access, about the latest laptop and illuminated screen. I worried that the means was beginning to replace the end, that the com-

fortable certainty of bytes and baud might replace the ambiguities of inde-
terminate pattern and emergent research. . . . The computer had shifted, in
my worst-case scenario, from an aid in doing ethnography to a definition
of what ethnography might do (Agar 1991, p. 182).

Computer software program structures often set requirements for how
a research project should proceed. This raises concerns among some critics
that computer software programs will determine the types of questions
asked and the specific data analysis plan:

> Thus, we continually refer to computer-assisted qualitative research to em-
> phasize that the computer should be used to enhance, not control, the work
> of the investigator. While we should take advantage of the computer's abil-
> ities, we should not let our analyses hinge primarily on what a particular
> software program can do. . . . If we compute first and think later we may
> well lose the essence of qualitative sociological work (Conrad and Reinharz
> 1984, p. 10).

Horney and Healey (1991) have also made this point in a paper which
compares two different computer programs for analyzing qualitative data.
They analyzed a single data set using two different computerized software
programs. They conclude:

> Computers change the nature of how data are interpreted and different pro-
> grams provide different points of view. This is at odds with the common
> opinion that efficiency is the primary benefit computers bring to the re-
> search process. . . . An analysis task thus needs to be matched with the re-
> searcher's familiarity with a program and with its metaphors (Horney and
> Healey 1991, p. 12).

IV. MAKING THE RESEARCHER MORE ACCOUNTABLE

Another controversy with the computerization of qualitative data is the issue of validity and reliability of the data gathered. Validity refers to whether
a measure is actually measuring what a researcher thinks it is measuring.
Reliability refers to whether or not the measure produces the same result
each time it is used to measure the same thing. For many qualitative researchers the way one measures validity is often stated somewhat vaguely:
Validity is "how closely one comes to capturing the lives of the people they
study"; others talk about "how well a researcher respects the nature of the
empirical world." Strauss (1987, p. 258) addresses the issue of validity still
another way. In answering a question concerning how much confidence a
researcher should have in an analysis he states:

> Even experienced researchers may not always be certain before they have
> chewed on their suspended pencils long enough to know where precisely
> are the holes—or be certain that, after review, they know there are no im-
> portant holes—in their analyses. Whether experienced or inexperienced, a
> common tactic for reducing uncertainty is "the trial"—try it out on other
> people, individuals, or groups, informally or formally (p. 260).

Little work is published on formal validation or reliability of research works by independent observers within qualitative research. Without a formal language for describing the reasoning chain from the codes to the researcher's conclusion, many possible interpretations can lead to the same conclusions. This makes the process of independent verification even harder.

Computer programs hold out the promise and peril of enabling qualitative researchers to answer the question of how confident they are in their analysis (i.e., Do they really have their core categories right? Are their categories detailed?). Computer programs for analyzing qualitative data require researchers to be more explicit in the procedures and analytical processes they went through to produce their data and their interpretations. The inclusion of artificial intelligence technologies into some qualitative analysis tools will ultimately allow faster, more detailed, and more verifiable coding. Asking qualitative researchers to be more explicit about their method and holding their interpretations accountable to tests of validity and reliability will raise some controversies: Should there be strict tests of validity and reliability for qualitative data? Are we again imposing the logic of quantitative measurement requirements onto qualitative data? What standards for validity and reliability should be used in qualitative research, if any?

Being more explicit about the procedures used to analyze data can make secondary analysis/replication of research studies of qualitative data more possible. At present, it is difficult to follow the exact methodology used in many qualitative studies. If procedures are made more detailed such that secondary analyses are possible, several issues may arise: How do we resolve differences in interpretation of the same data? Whose interpretation is correct? Are several interpretations possible? If so, under what conditions is this true?

The use of artificial intelligence technology will support the researcher in theory generation by allowing many more propositions to be tested in a shorter time period. The ability of some computer software programs to ascertain quickly the number of cases which support a hypothesis or set of hypotheses raises several issues, including: Will some researchers use the hypothesis tester as a data dredger? The hypothesis testing potential of some computer software programs may require qualitative researchers to contend with what up to now has been largely avoided—namely, the establishment of something akin to "significance" levels for qualitative analysis. Most qualitative researchers have been using the terms "some," "many," or "few" to signify when a theme is prevalent or not prevalent in their data. One might now ask: In how many cases did the hypothesis hold up? Should a qualitative researcher apply significance tests to qualitative data? When, if at all, is this appropriate? In asking such questions are we not, again, applying the logic of quantitative research onto qualitative research? Some qualitative researchers would argue that even the single occurrence of a given phenomenon can be theoretically important (see Seidel 1991, p. 113). The fact that this theme is not supported quantitatively by the data is applying the logic of quantitative analysis to qualitative data.

V. LOSS OF CONFIDENTIALITY:
THE USE OF MULTIMEDIA DATA

Some new computer software programs support the analysis of multimedia materials such as audio, video, and graphics. While the inclusion of multimedia, especially the analysis of audio, video, and graphic materials allows for a much more comprehensive analysis of the data, there are important ethical problems involved in working with these data, especially with visual data. Steven Gold (1989) has taken the lead in discussing ethical issues in visual field work, and I would like to present some of the ethical dilemmas he sees as important to consider. Sociologists have used the principle of confidentiality to protect respondents. This is done by ensuring that research results are not associated with any individual, group setting, or organization. Analyzing audio and visual data makes it more difficult for the researcher to ensure the confidentiality of individuals who participate in research gathering. What if someone recognizes a respondent? What if data is lost or stolen? There are also negative unintended consequences of utilizing visual data in qualitative analysis. For example, Gold points out that the circulation of photographs may result in collective harm to a group by promoting negative stereotypes. He notes this problem in a study he conducted:

> I confronted this problem in the course of studying a Vietnamese refugee community. Photographs of refugees' apartments show expensive possessions, such as television sets or stereo and video equipment, which have been collectively purchased in order to consume native-language media. Certain viewers have seen in these images a justification for the claim made by xenophobes that immigrants are "welfare chizzlers" who buy luxury items with government handouts (Gold 1989, p. 101).

The researcher needs to carefully consider the range of confidentiality issues involved when working with multimedia data. The example of the Vietnamese refugee community cited by Gold suggests that the researcher needs to be aware of the unintended interpretation of multimedia data and how easy it is for such data to be misinterpreted.

TO WHAT DEGREE ARE THE FEARS
CONCERNING COMPUTER SOFTWARE PROGRAMS
FOR QUALITATIVE DATA ANALYSIS JUSTIFIED?

As a developer of a new computer software program, HyperRESEARCH™,[1] for analyzing qualitative data analysis, I would like to address some of the fears critics express concerning the use of computers to analyze qualitative data.

Becoming a proactive user is vital in overcoming many of the fears analysts express in utilizing computer software. Each researcher must decide how and under what circumstances this technology will be employed in his or her research project. In the novel, *Frankenstein*, the monster pleads with his master not to detest, fear, and spurn the creature he created:

Remember, thou has made me more powerful than thyself; my height is superior to thine. Oh, Frankenstein be not equitable to every other, and tram-
ple upon me alone, to whom thy justice, and even thy clemency and affec-
tions is most due. Remember, that I am thy creature . . . (Shelley, quoted in
Smith 1992, p. 92).

Lee and Fielding (1991) suggest the problem with computer program technology lies in its misapplication:

Like the monster, the programs are misunderstood. The programs are innocent of guile. It is their misapplication which poses the threat. It was exposure to human depravity which made a threat of Frankenstein's creation.
Equally, the untutored use of analysis programs can certainly produce ba-
nal, unedifying and off-target analysis. But the fault would lie with the user
(1991, p. 8).

The view here is that the researcher becomes entrapped by the machine technology. Pfaffenberger (1988) suggests a simple rule of thumb for assessing
the researcher's degree of involvement with the computer:

When the microcomputer starts to loom larger in significance than the original goals of the research, when it demands less engagement in the research
data and more engagement in the computer, the time has come to reflect
on these goals and to re-establish contact with the values and commitments
that initially motivated your engagement with the human social world (pp.
23–24).

It is also important to understand the limitations of each computer software program so that the program structure does not entirely dictate the
type of analysis planned. Horney and Healey (1991) note that rather than
being a liability, the diversity of program structures can often provide researchers with the opportunity for different perspectives on their data and
will permit "triangulation" of research results. Triangulation is a method
whereby different research methods are used to test the same finding. It is
possible that a given researcher can utilize several different software programs, each of which has its particular strengths and weaknesses. A multiple software design holds the promise of enhancing the validity of research
findings.

Computer software programs also lessen the labor-intensive aspects of
doing qualitative analysis. This is not a trivial issue for the qualitative analyst. Most qualitative researchers still analyze pages of text by cutting, past-
ing, and filing, using scissors and a typewriter or word processor to arrange
the material physically into coded groups on paper. The process of photo-
copying multiple copies of text, cutting them up into coded passages, and
then manually retrieving the coded text takes a great many hours, days, or
even weeks. Software programs for qualitative analysis also speed up the
coding and retrieval process. As an example, in the software program I co-
developed for analyzing qualitative data, HyperRESEARCH™, analyzing
text can be accomplished by typing the original interviews, articles, or other
materials into a favorite word processor, or more sophisticated means can

be used, such as optical character recognition using scanners. Once the material for a subject has been entered into a text file, the researcher can instruct HyperRESEARCH™ to associate that text file with a given "case." The researcher can then display the text file and select portions of text on the computer screen in a manner similar to highlighting a passage of text on paper with a colored highlighter pen. The researcher then assigns a code to the selected (highlighted) text. A code is a name (or label) that points to, or acts as a reference to, the highlighted text. The code is stored on a computerized equivalent of an index card. There is one index card per case. This is analogous to the researcher actually writing a code next to the highlighted paper passage and then recording the code on a 3″ × 5″ index card with reference to where and in what document it appears. The researcher repeats this coding process for each case in the research study. Each case's index card can contain codes from any number of different source files. A researcher may also code her or his own comments and observations about a given case. For example, a given research project may consist of 20 test subjects (cases). For each of these 20 cases, the researcher has a transcribed interview, a self-evaluation, a questionnaire, and the researcher's own "memos" about the subject (the researcher's comments). All these materials can be kept in distinct files and imported into HyperRESEARCH™ and coded in any order.

A useful feature of HyperRESEARCH™ is the Code List, which contains all the codes used so far. This master list of codes may be manipulated in several ways and is ideally suited for more focused coding. Codes may be deleted, copied, or renamed. Any manipulation performed on a master code automatically affects all specific instances of the code on all index cards. Deleting removes the selected code and its "pointer." Copying a code is very useful when combining similar codes and allows researchers to copy the reference associated with one code (e.g., the pointer to the original text) to a new entry on the index card under the new code name.

Automating the time-consuming labor-intensive aspects of doing qualitative work, that is, the time it takes to code, index, retrieve, and store data, allows the researcher to concentrate on the generation and testing of theory. The inclusion of multimedia, especially the analysis of audio, video, and graphic materials in some software programs such as HyperRESEARCH™, allows for a much more comprehensive analysis of qualitative data and provides the researcher with a fuller understanding of social context than only analyzing text would. To code an audio tape or video disc using Hyper-RESEARCH™, a segment of audio or video is viewed or listened to, and the beginning and ending points are "marked" by the researcher. Beginning and ending points can be marked with the press of a button. The marked segment of the audio or video source is assigned a code, just like a segment of a text file. The system adds the new code to the index card list and remembers how to replay the selected audio or video clip. This allows the researcher to directly code original source materials and avoid possible transcription errors. In addition, visual or tonal aspects of an interview such as the mood or posture of the interviewee can now be coded. However, the researcher is not required in any way to use multimedia sources. Each of the coding systems is independent, yet each function interacts with the researcher in the same manner.[2]

Devault (1990) notes how important it is to listen to the language of the interview rather than only analyzing a transcription (text) of that same interview. In a study she conducted on women's experience with housework, she notes that the language women use to convey their experiences often lies in the hesitation with which they state something. She notes that often seemingly trivial passages of transcribed text hide the richness of the data:

> Often, I believe, this halting, hesitant, tentative talk signals the realm of not-quite-articulated experience and finds where standard vocabulary is inadequate, and where a respondent tries to speak from experience and finds language wanting. I tried to listen most carefully to this kind of talk (Devault 1990, p. 103).

Because qualitative research relies so heavily on the analysis of textual material, there may be a tendency for some qualitative researchers to mainly quote respondents who are most articulate in an interview. This may have the unintended consequence of biasing results toward the more articulate group (and that group which the researcher may identify with). The availability of some software programs to easily code, retrieve, and analyze multimedia source material may break down this tendency and increase the representativeness of meaning among a diverse group of respondents if both verbal and non-verbal behaviors are analyzed.

In addition the ability of some software programs to analyze visual material (pictures, photographs, graphics) as well as video will also help to expand the field known as "visual sociology." Visual sociology is defined as "the use of photographs, film, and video to study society and the study of visual artefacts of a society" (Harper 1989, p. 81). Visual sociology can take advantage of the technology we have developed and apply it to visual methods. As Harper notes:

> Computers, which many consider an antagonistic technology to the camera, may make it easier to use visual data in sociological research. Microcomputers can now digitalize images . . . , and they can be stored in conventional electronic files and easily integrated into text, graph, or other files (Harper 1989, p. 94).

At present it is largely underdeveloped and marginal to the sociology discipline. The teaching of visual sociology would be greatly enhanced by the use of multimedia software programs. Some computer software programs also enhance the analyst's ability to generate and test theory. The HyperRESEARCH™ software program, for example, allows a researcher to test propositions by performing Boolean searches on any code or combination of codes via the use of an expert system. The program also allows for hypothesis testing using artificial intelligence. The Expert System software technology developed by HyperRESEARCH™, for example, uses production rules to provide a semiformal mechanism for theory building and description of the inference process used to draw conclusions from the data, which allows for the testing of the reliability and validity of data.

It is also important to recognize that computer-assisted programs begin to question the standard ways of doing qualitative research. This is evident in the controversy surrounding the discussion on issues of quantification, validity, and reliability. Quantifying qualitative data can enhance its validity only if one is careful about how this is carried out. Counting themes or categories in the data always needs to be linked to the respondent's own method of ordering the world (gathered from qualitative analysis). As Silverman (1985) notes:

> The aim is not to count for counting's sake, but in order to establish a thoughtful dialogue with qualitatively-derived insights about the setting and actors' version of the situation at hand (p. 148).

By quantifying, the analyst can assess the representativeness of the data as a whole. Researchers will be able to tighten their analysis and perhaps specify more clearly the application of their research findings to the data (Silverman 1985).

The issue of whether the computer will impose inappropriate validity/reliability standards on the qualitative analyst or if such standards are appropriate still needs to be carefully addressed among qualitative analysts. There also remains the concern as to whether or not some advanced techniques used in quantitative data analysis such as hypothesis testing and more elaborate statistical procedures can be added on to qualitative data analysis without profoundly changing the basic nature of qualitative work.

Computers hold out the promise of revolutionizing the way researchers conduct their analysis, but they also hold out a set of caveats for the qualitative analyst. The researcher who uses these programs should assess their strengths and weaknesses as well as the implications of using computer software programs to analyze qualitative data. It is clear that the interpretation of qualitative data is enriched by the use of computer software programs and that more dialogue is needed on other issues before the fear of Frankenstein's monster is put to rest.

NOTES

1. HyperRESEARCH™ is distributed by Researchware Inc., 20 Soren Street Randolph, MA 02368-1945, USA. Telepone number: (617) 961-3909. Website: www.researchware.com

2. For a more detailed description of all the features of the HyperRESEARCH™ software program please refer to Hesse-Biber, Dupuis, and Kinder (1991), Hesse-Biber and Dupuis (1995), Hesse-Biber, Dupuis and Kinder (1997), Hesse-Biber and Dupuis, 2000.

REFERENCES

Agar, M. 1991. The right brain strikes back. In *Using Computers in Qualitative Research*, eds. N.G. Fielding and R.M. Lee. Newbury Park, CA: Sage Publications.

Becker, H.S. 1953. Becoming a marihuana user. *American Journal of Sociology* 59: 235–242.

Charmaz, K. 1983. The grounded theory method: An explication and interpretation. In *Contemporary Field Research: A Collection of Readings*, ed. R.M. Emerson. Prospect Heights, IL: Waveland Press, Inc.

Conrad, P., and S. Reinharz. 1984. Computers and qualitative data: Editor's introductory essay. *Qualitative Sociology* 7(1–2): 3–15.

Devault, M. 1990. Feminist interviewing and analysis. *Social Problems* 37(1): 96–116.

Glaser, B.G., and A.L. Strauss. 1967. *The discovery of grounded theory: Strategies for qualitative research*. Chicago: Aldine.

Gold, S.J. 1989. Ethical issues in visual field work, pp. 99–109 in *New Technology in Sociology: Practical Applications in Research and Word*, eds. G. Blank, J.L. McCartney, and E. Brent. New Brunswick, NJ: Transaction Publishers.

Harper, D. 1989. Visual sociology: Expanding sociological vision, pp. 81–97 in *New Technology in Sociology: Practical Applications in Research and Works*, eds. G. Blank, J.L. Mc Cartney, and E. Brent. New Brunswick, NJ: Transaction Publishers.

Hesse-Biber, S., P. Dupuis, and T.S. Kinder. 1991. HyperRESEARCH: A computer program for the analysis of qualitative data with an emphasis on hypothesis testing and multimedia analysis. *Qualitative Sociology* 14(4): 289–306.

Hesse-Biber, S., and P. Dupuis. 1995. Hypothesis testing automation for computer-aided qualitative data analysis." In *Computer-Aided Qualitative Data Analysis: Theory, Methods and Practice*, ed. Udo Kelle. London: Sage Publications.

Horney, M.A., and D. Healey. 1991. Hypertext and database tools for qualitative research. Paper presented at the American Education Research Association (AERA), Chicago, IL, April.

Lee, R.M., and N.G. Fielding. 1991. Computing for qualitative research: Options, problems and potential, pp. 1–13 in *Using Computers in Qualitative Research*, eds. N.G. Fielding and R.M. Lee. Newbury, CA: Sage Publications.

Pfaffenberger, B. 1988. *Microcomputer applications in qualitative research*. Newbury Park, CA: Sage Publications.

Richards, L., and T. Richards. 1989. The impact of computer techniques for qualitative analysis. Technical report no. 6189, Department of Computer Science, La Trobe University.

Seidel, J. 1991. Method and madness in the application of computer technology to qualitative data analysis, pp. 107–116 in *Using Computers in Qualitative Research*, eds. N.G. Fielding and R.M. Lee. Newbury Park: CA.: Sage Publications.

Silverman, D. 1985. *Qualitative methodology and sociology*. Hants, England: Gower Publishing Co. Ltd.

Smith, J.M. (Ed). 1992. *Mary Shelley, Frankenstein*. Boston, MA: St. Martin's Press.

Strauss, A.L. 1987. *Qualitative analysis for social scientists*. New York: Cambridge University Press.